Constitutional Democracy in a Multicultural and Globalised World

Thomas Fleiner • Lidija R. Basta Fleiner

Constitutional Democracy in a Multicultural and Globalised World

English translation from the German 3rd revised edition "Allgemeine Staatslehre" by Katy Le Roy

Springer

Professor Dr. Thomas Fleiner
Professor Dr. Lidija R. Basta Fleiner
Route de Beaumont 9
CH-1700 Fribourg
www.thomasfleiner.ch
thomas.fleiner@unifr.ch
lidija.basta@unifr.ch

ISBN 978-3-540-76411-3 e-ISBN 978-3-540-76412-0

DOI 10.1007/978-3-540-76412-0

Library of Congress Control Number: 2008938063

Cover design: WMX Design GmbH, Heidelberg, Germany

Printed on acid-free paper

9 8 7 6 5 4 3 2 1

springer.com

For our children
Claudio, Michael, Andrea, Daniela and Jelena

Preface

After World War II, states transformed into 'collective fortresses' in order to protect competing ideological systems. The debate on post-modern statehood heavily built on ideological disputes between liberalism and communism, over the nature of the economic and social system, and the state and government that could sustain such a system. What is an 'ideologically acceptable' state-concept; which tasks and functions should the state fulfil, and how to legitimate not only democratic, but also authoritarian and even totalitarian regimes? These questions were at the very centre of state theory. However, after the fall of communism in Europe and the former Soviet Union, the discourse of state and government scholarship radically changed. The need for a profound shift in the state paradigm was emerging.

The time after 1989 seemed to proclaim that the nation-state had lost its raison d'être as an island of undisputed and unlimited sovereignty. A globalised world order broke open the 'fortress state' that developed within the tradition of European constitutionalism. Given the simultaneous structural changes to the nation-state's foundations, socio-economic and political reforms going hand in hand with new constitutional designs, the 'state in transition' started paving the way towards a new state paradigm, and not only with regard to the states in the process of democratic transformation from socialist into liberal constitutional democracies. With universally valid fundamental human rights becoming part of the *jus cogens* of international law, the nation-state lost its exclusivity as the basis for the rule of law and the principle of good governance. Does the announced, and subsequently renounced, 'end of history' also lead both to the 'end of nation state' and of the nation-state as basis for human rights and the rule of law? At the same time, theorising on triumphant liberal constitutional democracy as a 'finished concept' faced new critical questions about its fundamental principles. The universality of human rights was contested because of its particular, Western Christian background, which does not embrace the values of other civilisations (e.g., the discussion on Asian values). In addition, the revival of minority rights within an international setting, and their understanding as part of the fundamental human rights, challenged traditional majoritarian democracy's claims of inclusivity and thus its democratic authenticity. Furthermore, the policy concept of good governance most notably launched by the World Bank called for debate on the context related effects of its key postulates. In a nutshell, once seen as self-evident, self-reflected concepts of the modern nation-state, classical democratic constitutionalism – although in the meantime enriched with welfare principles – had to be reconsidered.

Critical universalism as an alternative offered the enforcement of constitutionalism through the adoption of additional fundamental substantive values, notably intercultural peace. More importantly, challenging modern politics in structural terms suddenly became the primary focus of critical discourse on post-modern statehood. Why do we need a nation-state at all, when the globalised market economy already goes against nation state based policies, notwithstanding their different social, cultural and ideological background? The globalisation argument of 'denationalisation of a world of states' even called for the 'privatisation' of the state. This proved wrong, since the nation-state does not lose, but instead transforms its sovereignty. Because its 'external' sovereignty has become weaker, there is a growing need for an ever stronger 'inner' democratic sovereignty. Multiculturality redefined and enriched the paramount questions of procedural democracy and checks and balances with equally important substantive issues on the constitutive foundations for multicultural societies. The answer on the governmental system best guaranteeing human rights, efficiency and effectiveness in policy-making, as well as just distribution of resources, could not be found without at the same time answering another fundamental question: In a fragmented society, to which of the conflicting communities does the state belong? Last but not least is issue of migration. Should new immigrants also matter politically, or only communities with a long-standing presence in the country? Whereas initial nation-state policies on migration and labour recruitment mainly followed economic objectives, major political difficulties have emerged in coming to terms with permanent changes in the ethnic and cultural composition of the population, and the role which political and legal accommodation of such diversity should play in integration politics. As a consequence, ethnic conflicts not only threaten the peace within the state. They also endanger world peace. Multiculturality became an endemic, illiberal challenge to constitutional democracies.

In order to confront ourselves with some of the major transformational problems for the state pulled between internal heterogeneity and unprecedented interdependency at the global level, we have put our analysis into historical and comparative perspectives. We have analysed the nature and causes of ethnic conflicts, and their effect upon the discourse on human rights and the rule of law. We describe the most relevant differences between English speaking countries and continental European countries in terms of their understanding of the state and its administration. The different approaches of lawyers from the common law tradition and those from the civil law tradition concerning the ongoing constitutive dilemmas of European unity are explained. Furthermore, the basic problems of current polities are mapped out within an international comparative context. Finally, the originally Eurocentric French-German tradition of the doc-trine of the state is reconsidered in its new global context. Our key insights, resulting from ten years of common research, could be summarised as follows:

- The theory of liberal democratic constitutionalism falls short of providing immanent answers for the current challenges of multiculturality. The latter challenges the constitutive nature of the modern nation-state in general and its inherently individualist paradigm of human rights in particular.
- In a fragmented society, the state is legitimate not only because it protects individual liberty, but also under the condition that it can democratically guarantee peace among different ethnic, religious or linguistic communities.
- Notwithstanding globalisation tendencies, the nation-state remains the centre of democratic politics. It can decide who will be a member of its democratic polity by deciding on the terms of citizenship. In addition, although

the nation-state shares with the international community the duty to protect human rights, it remains the most important guarantor of their effective implementation.

- Constitution-making has ceased to be an exclusive domain of nation-states. The international community as a constitution making power presents a new phenomenon in epochal terms, since in such cases it is not a constitutional demos which decides on a new constitution.
- Minority problems are not merely those of inadequate or ineffective human rights protection. In all cases of serious and systematic minority rights violations, the issue of the state has been opened in the form of territorial demands and legitimacy denials.
- Not every federal design can in and of itself meet the challenges of multiculturality and minority demands. More than a vertical check-and-balance system, federalism aimed at accommodating multiculturality must *democratically* integrate ethnic, religious and linguistic demands.

This book is the English version of the third edition of the German book with the title *Allgemeine Staatslehre.* Literally translated, this means 'General Theory of the State'. The word *Staat* in German has a different meaning than the English word state. In German the word *Staat* encompasses governmental system, legitimacy, the relationship between 'state' and society, political theory and questions with regard to good governance. In order to meet the expectations of an English speaking audience, the title of the book has been adapted in order to better describe its contents.

The first two editions of the German version have been translated into French and Portuguese. This is the translation of the third German edition, which has been significantly enlarged and completely revised. Here, the centrality of the themes emerging at the beginning of the 1990s, namely: transition, globalisation and multiculturality are taken into account in order to critically reconsider the very concept of the nation-state. This work would not have been possible without the financial support of the Swiss National Science Foundation and of the Swiss Agency for Development and Cooperation of the Swiss Federal Department of Foreign Affairs.

The book is in every sense the result of a common endeavour between its authors, Thomas Fleiner and Lidija Basta Fleiner. Although we grew up in different cultures and political systems, we have always had similar research interests. Our different approaches and in particular the difference in priorities with regard to philosophical and theoretical issues supplemented and influenced almost every chapter. It was possible to build upon our research of the previous 25 years and bring our different views together into a common manuscript. For instance, we believe the book benefits from the integration of aspects of Lidija Basta Fleiner's long term research on democratic transition, constitutionalism and the rule of law in a new chapter on the rule of law.

We have undertaken common research on the problems of multiculturality and federalism over the past ten years within the Institute of Federalism of the University of Fribourg. The outcome is a new chapter on the multicultural state. Our work on constitutionalism and human rights convinced us that a theory of democratic statehood needed first and foremost to examine the relationship bet-ween citizens and their government. But it was also important to understand how governmental processes should be organised, in order to have the rule of law effectively guaranteed in the ever changing context of globalisation and multiculturality. In the first case we wanted to explore what individuals can demand from the state and its officials. In the second case we wanted to know which values should underlie the law that limits state power and controls state governments. Demands towards the state and the legal principles ruling the state are inherently linked to the principles of morality and human rights. For this reason, two chapters, those on human rights and on the rule of law, sometimes overlap. This was unavoidable in order to demonstrate that the related values of liberty and equality have different meanings, depending on whether one adopts the point of view of the individual, or the point of view of the perception of the legal theory and system.

In preparing this book we have been attentive to using readable and readily understandable language. Almost each paragraph is headed with a significant key word. Whenever possible we have written in the first person plural in order to engage the reader in a dialogue.

Several readers of the German version suggested that we translate our book to make it accessible to an English speaking audience. The translation was undertaken, thanks to the financial support of the Swiss Agency for Development and Cooperation of the Swiss Federal Department of Foreign Affairs. In Ms. Katy Le Roy we found an excellent editor for the English version. She reviewed and decisively improved the first version of the translation, which was done by Thomas Fleiner. Her constitutional expertise and excellent knowledge of the German language helped her to find appropriate formulations not only in a linguistic sense, but more importantly also in terms of the differences between common and civil law cultures.

Unlike the German version of this book, the English translation contains an index that was carefully prepared by Ms. Gabriela Mirescu, an assistant at the Institute of Federalism, and supervised by Mr Tobias Kallenbach, teaching assistant to Thomas Fleiner,. This work follows the pattern of previous editions, as it also does not make use of footnotes. When we use quotations or refer to particular arguments of other authors or court decisions and documents, we indicate the relevant source of the literature or the internet material in brackets. The book also contains an index of classical texts of philosophers. Other literature has to be found by means of the classical tools, known and available to scholars. It would be almost impossible to list all the literature in various languages on the broad topics of state theory which has informed our research over many years. Researchers are also welcome to use the library of the Institute of Federalism (www.federalism.ch).

Once again, we would like to express our gratitude to those who helped us in preparing the English translation of our 'Allgemeine Staatslehre'. We would like to thank Ms. Gabriela Mirescu for her careful and committed work on the index. Our special thanks for the final editing of the book go to Ms. Katy Le Roy. She was indeed a most knowledgeable and scrupulous editor. Her remarks and ideas to improve the English version were most helpful and have considerably contributed to the clarity of the text. We owe our sincere appreciation also to Mr. Tobias Kallenbach who prepared the book for the Springer editor. It was his meticulous patience when supervising the index and his extraordinary capacities in electronic formatting that made it possible for this book to go to print in a timely fashion.

With the book 'Constitutional Democracy in a Multicultural and Globalised World', we hope to join the ongoing world-wide debate on how to reflect upon the transformation of the nation state today and the epochal challenges it faces.

Thomas Fleiner
Lidija Basta Fleiner

June 2008

Translator's Note

The translation into English of *Allgemeine Staatslehre: Über die konstitutionelle Demokratie in einer multikulturellen globalisierten Welt* has also involved a process of editing, in collaboration with the authors, to modify the text for the English readership. Thus, whilst most of this book is a direct translation of the original German edition, in some places small sections of text have been omitted or added. In most cases, such omissions and additions have been made for the purpose of modifying the examples that are used to illustrate particular theoretical points, from examples that are specific to Switzerland or to civil law systems, to examples that may be more helpful to an audience beyond Europe or to a reader in the common law world.

In some parts of the text, the translating and editing process has resulted in a change in the formulation of certain words or expressions, so that a reader comparing both editions side-by-side may notice that in some places the translated text does not correspond precisely to the original German text. This is a conscious decision made in collaboration with the authors.

Where secondary sources have been quoted in the German edition of the book, every attempt has been made to use the corresponding published English translation of the same work where such translation exists and has been accessible. In those instances where it has not been possible to access a published English translation of the relevant work, a note has been made in the text that the translation has been done from the German by the translator and/or authors.

The authors have also added small sections of new text and amended details in some parts of the book, to incorporate reference to relevant events that have occurred since the 2003 publication of the German edition of the book.

Translating this work has been a lengthy process. I wish to thank the authors for their constant assistance and remarkable patience, and all those who made this translation possible, especially Flona Ribauw and Rosa Kun.

Katy Le Roy
LLB (Hons), BA (Hons) (Melb)
Assistant Director
Centre for Comparative Constitutional Studies
Law School, University of Melbourne
Nauru, June 2008

Table of Contents

Preface ... vii

Translator's Note ... xiii

Bibliography ... xxiii

1 General Introduction ... 1

1.1 From Local Entities to the Globalised Marginalisation of the Nation-State ... 1
1.1.1 Historical Influences on today's World of States ... 1
1.1.2 Challenges for the States ... 8
1.1.2.1 Globalisation ... 8
1.1.2.2 The Engine of State-Building ... 10
1.2 The Questions of the Theory of State ... 14
1.2.1 Traditional Questions of the Theory of State ... 14
1.2.2 New Questions of the Theory of State ... 15
1.3 What is the General Theory of State and What is its Aim? ... 18
1.3.1 The State: A Different Kind of Society ... 18
1.3.2 The Structure and Concerns of the General Theory of State ... 21

2 From the Tribe to the State in a Globalised Environment ... 31

2.1 The Origin of the State Community ... 31
2.1.1 The Human Need to Build Communities ... 31
2.1.2 The State of the Modern Civil Society – a Supra-Familial State? ... 39
2.1.3 Conclusion ... 43
2.2 Stages of Development of the Community of States ... 44
2.2.1 Introduction ... 44
2.2.2 Human Language as the Precondition for State-Building ... 45
2.2.3 Division of Labour as Condition for Building a State Community ... 47
2.2.4 The Stages of State Development ... 49
2.2.4.1 Influence of the Social Environment ... 49
2.2.4.2 The First Attempts to Build Political Communities at the Time of Hunters and Gatherers ... 50
2.2.4.3 The Planter and the Development of Territorial Communities ... 51
2.2.4.4 The Development of an Economy Based on Division of Labour – Building the Modern Territorial State ... 53

2.2.4.5 The State of the Complex Industrialized Society: Parties and Legislators 58
2.2.4.6 From the Nation-State to a Globalised World 65
2.2.4.7 Universalism and Human Rights 73

3 The View of Man and the State as the Starting Point of State Theories 83

3.1 The Influence of the Idea of the Human Being on State Theories 83
3.1.1 Introduction 83
3.1.2 The View of the Human Nature within Christian Theology: State and State Authority are Ordained by God and thus Indispensable for Human Beings 86
3.1.2.1 AUGUSTINE (354–430): The State as Necessary Evil 87
3.1.2.2 THOMAS AQUINAS (1225–1274): No Humans without State 87
3.1.2.3 Reformation 90
3.1.3 Enlightenment 91
3.1.3.1 War of All against All (THOMAS HOBBES) 92
3.1.3.2 The Significance of HOBBES' State Philosophy for Modern times 95
3.1.3.3 The Reasonable Human Being in Natural Law according to the Enlightment– JOHN LOCKE (1632–1704) and IMMANUEL KANT (1724–1804) 97
3.2 The Image of the State 106
3.2.1 What is the State? 106
3.2.2 The State as a higher being (HEGEL) 110
3.2.3 The State as Representation of the Common Good (Volonté Générale) according to ROUSSEAU 113
3.3 The Justification of State Authority 119
3.3.1 The Problem 119
3.3.2 The State as Part of the Human Condition 120
3.3.3 The Nature of the Human Being 121
3.3.4 Change in the 'View of the State' 122

4 Human Rights 130

4.1 Introduction 130
4.2 The Development of Western Constitutionalism 135
4.2.1 The Development of Legal Protections in England 135
4.2.2 Development of Legal Protection on the European Continent 140
4.2.3 Development of Human Rights in the United States 144
4.3 The Theoretical Development of Human Rights 151
4.3.1 From Stoa to Resistance 152
4.3.2 Renaissance 153
4.3.3 The Age of Liberal Constitutionalism 154

4.3.4 From Liberalism to Social Democracy to Communism 157
4.3.5 Communitarianism 161
4.4 The Types of Fundamental and Human Rights 163
4.4.1 Introduction 163
4.4.2 Procedural Rights 166
4.4.3 Human Rights According to Content 169
4.4.3.1 Human Dignity 169
4.4.3.2 Equality 170
4.4.3.3 Spiritual Liberties 172
4.4.3.4 Guarantee of Property Rights and Economic Liberty ... 177
4.5 Institutional Protection of Human Rights 188
4.5.1 Constitutional Courts 188
4.5.2 Administrative Law Courts 190
4.5.3 Institutions of the Administration 193
4.5.4 International Law 194
4.6 Limits of Human Rights 198
4.6.1 Who Determines the Limits of Fundamental Rights? 201
4.6.2 What are the Acceptable Limits on Fundamental Rights? 202
4.6.2.1 Legal Limits 202
4.6.2.2 Philosophical Limits 204
4.6.2.3 What is Liberty? 204
4.7 Criteria of Justice 209
4.7.1 When does the State need to Intervene? 210
4.7.2 Material Criteria of Justice 212
4.7.3 Formal Criteria of Justice 214
4.7.3.1 The General Will According to ROUSSEAU 214
4.7.3.2 Justice as the Principle of Fairness (RAWLS) 216
4.7.4 Principles of Justice within the Reality of the Modern Liberal State Committed to the Social Market Economy 219

5 Rule of Law 221

5.1 Development of the Rule of Law 221
5.1.1 Introduction 221
5.1.2 The Development of the Rule of Law in the English Common Law Tradition 222
5.1.2.1 Medieval Idea of the Supremacy of Law and its Effects on Modern Liberties 222
5.1.3 Major Constitutional Conflicts of the 17th Century 225
5.1.4 Sovereignty of Parliament and the Fundamental Law 229
5.1.5 Separation of Powers, or Checks and Balances 230
5.1.6 Modern Developments 232
5.1.6.1 The American and French Revolutions: The Rule of Law and/or the Will of the People as (the only) Fundamental Law 232
5.1.6.2 USA 233

5.1.6.3 France ... 234
5.1.6.4 The German Concept of Rechtsstaat (State Rule Through Law) ... 236
5.1.7 Conclusions ... 239
5.2 Development of the Rule of Law in the Different Legal Systems ... 240
5.2.1 Introduction ... 240
5.2.2 What are the Foundations of Law and Justice? ... 241
5.2.3 Common Law – Civil Law ... 243
5.2.3.1 Common Law ... 247
5.2.3.2 Continental European Law ... 247
5.2.4 Principles of Jurisdiction over Administrative Cases ... 249
5.2.4.1 Conception ... 249
5.2.4.2 What are for Comparative Purposes the Distinctive Elements of the European Legal Culture? ... 257
5.2.4.3 Reasons for Differences ... 259
5.2.5 The two Types of Administrative Jurisdiction ... 261
5.2.6 Conclusion ... 263

6 The State as Legal Entity ... 267

6.1 The State as Legal Entity in the Age of Globalisation ... 267
6.1.1 Introduction ... 267
6.1.2 The Changing Shape of Constitutionalism ... 268
6.2 Challenges of Globalisation ... 270
6.2.1 Sovereignty ... 272
6.2.2 Democracy ... 273
6.2.3 Rule of Law and Protection of Human Rights ... 275
6.2.4 Welfare State ... 278
6.3 Elements of the State ... 280
6.3.1 Significance of the Notion of the State ... 280
6.3.1.1 The Development of the Modern Notion of the State ... 280
6.3.1.2 People, Nation and State in the Charter of the United Nations ... 281
6.3.1.3 The Notion of the State in the General Theory of the State ... 282
6.3.2 The People or Nation (Staatsvolk) ... 283
6.3.2.1 The Tension between People and State ... 283
6.3.2.2 The Changing Perception of the Nation throughout History ... 286
6.3.2.3 Solidarity as Prerequisite for the State Community ... 287
6.3.3 Territory ... 294
6.3.3.1 The Development of the Territorial State ... 296
6.3.3.2 The Meaning of the Principle of Territoriality ... 298
6.3.3.3 Limits of the Principle of Territoriality ... 301

6.4 Sovereignty ... 306
6.4.1 The Significance of Sovereignty ... 306
6.4.2 The Dispute between Church and State as Precondition for the Development of the Claim to Sovereignty ... 308
6.4.3 BODIN'S Theory of Sovereignty ... 311
6.4.4 Sovereignty as a Prerequisite for Statehood ... 314
6.4.5 Problems of State Sovereignty ... 316
6.4.6 External Sovereignty ... 319
6.4.6.1 Development and Function of External Sovereignty ... 319
6.4.6.2 The Relationship between International Law and Domestic Law ... 323
6.5 Sovereignty and Might ... 326
6.5.1 Might and Force ... 326
6.5.1.1 Defining the Issues ... 326
6.5.1.2 Identity of Might and Law ... 329
6.5.1.3 Might alone is not enough ... 331
6.5.1.4 The Sociological Relationship between Law and Might ... 332
6.5.2 Sovereignty and Legitimacy of the Law ... 337
6.5.2.1 From Sovereignty of the Monarch to Popular Sovereignty ... 337
6.5.2.2 Sovereign is Whoever can legitimise the Use of Power and Force ... 340
6.5.2.3 The State as Source of the Law ... 343

7 Theoretical Aspects of the Organisation of the Modern State ... 353

7.1 Theory of State Organisation ... 353
7.1.1 Introduction ... 353
7.1.2 Sociological Roots ... 356
7.1.2.1 Historical Influences ... 356
7.1.2.2 Foreign Influences in a Globalised Environment ... 362
7.1.3 The Theory of State Forms ... 367
7.1.4 Criteria of State Organisation ... 370
7.1.5 The Democratic Idea ... 373
7.1.5.1 The Foundations of Democratic Theory ... 373
7.1.5.2 Semi-direct Democracy ... 379
7.1.5.3 Representative Democracy ... 386
7.1.6 Separation of Powers ... 397
7.1.6.1 Development of the Theory of Separation of Powers ... 397
7.1.6.2 Separation of Powers According to LOCKE and MONTESQUIEU ... 399
7.1.6.3 Separation of Powers in a Constitutional Democracy ... 400

7.1.7 Adherence to the Law ... 407
7.1.7.1 Development of the Concept of Legislation ... 407
7.1.7.2 Positivism – Natural Law Theory – Legal Realism ... 408
7.1.7.3 Law and Separation of Powers ... 409
7.1.8 The Organisation of Sovereign Power ... 411
7.2 The Organisation of Modern Democratic States ... 413
7.2.1 Sovereignty Centralised in Parliament ... 413
7.2.1.1 England ... 413
7.2.1.2 Germany ... 423
7.2.1.3 France ... 432
7.2.1.4 Parliamentary Responsible Government in Other States ... 443
7.2.2 States with Divided Sovereignty ... 448
7.2.2.1 The United States of America ... 449
7.2.2.2 The Swiss Confederation (Eidgenossenschaft) ... 456
7.2.3 Sovereignty of Powers Beyond the State ... 474
7.2.3.1 Communist Constitutions ... 475
7.2.3.2 The Sovereignty of the Koran ... 478
7.2.4 The States of Central and Eastern Europe in Transition ... 481
7.2.4.1 The Specific Characteristics of Eastern-European States before the Fall of Communism ... 481
7.2.4.2 Constitutional Aspects of the Process of Disintegration ... 486
7.2.4.3 The Social and Political Environment of Transition and the Problem of Transformability ... 490
7.2.4.4 Major Tendencies of the Post-socialist Constitutions ... 497

8 The Multicultural State: The Challenge of the Future ... 511

8.1 Challenges of the Multicultural State ... 511
8.1.1 Introduction ... 511
8.1.2 Multiculturality and the Modern State Concept ... 512
8.1.3 What are the Causes of Conflicts within Multicultural States? ... 519
8.1.4 What Tools and Procedures are available to States in order to meet the growing Challenges of Multiculturality? ... 521
8.1.4.1 Politics of Tolerance ... 522
8.1.4.2 Politics of Reconciliation ... 523
8.1.4.3 Equality of Peoples and Minorities ... 525
8.1.4.4 Fostering Diversity ... 527
8.1.4.5 Conclusion ... 528
8.2 Towards a Theory of Federalism: Typology of Federations and Models of Decentralisation ... 529
8.2.1 Federalism: Self-Rule and Shared Rule ... 529
8.2.2 Philosophical and Historical Foundations ... 531
8.2.3 Federalism and Decentralisation as a Modern Concept for Democratic Governance ... 533

8.2.4 An answer to the Problems of the Former Communist Countries 534
8.2.5 Peaceful Conflict Resolution 536
8.2.6 Growth of Administrative Efficiency 537
8.3 Federalism and Decentralisation in Comparison 538
8.3.1 What is Federalism? 538
8.3.2 Decision Making Power and Government Authorities 543
8.3.2.1 Constituent Power (pouvoir constituant) and the Constituted Representative Authority (pouvoir constitué) 543
8.3.2.2 Parliaments 546
8.3.2.3 Relationship between Parliament and Executive 548
8.3.2.4 Distinctive Features of Federal States 550
8.3.2.5 Statehood of Federal Units 559
8.3.2.6 Internal Organisation of Federal Units (Autonomous Constitution Making of Federal Units) 564
8.3.2.7 Decentralisation of the Three Arms of Government 569
8.3.3 Shared Rule by the Federal Units at the Federal Level 571
8.3.4 Federal Supervision of the Federal Units 574
8.3.5 Can Fragmented Multicultural Societies be Peacefully Held together by Ethnic Federalism? 576
8.3.5.1 Mapping the Issues 576
8.3.5.2 The Structural Challenges 577
8.3.5.3 Conclusion: Why is ethnic federalism largely dysfunctional? 586
8.3.6 Concluding Theses for a Theory of Federalism 587
8.4 Theory of Swiss Federalism 593
8.4.1 Multiculturality and Swiss Federalism 593
8.4.1.1 Cultural and National Differences in 'Multiethnic' Switzerland 594
8.4.1.2 Swiss Procedures and Institutions for Dealing with Ethnic Conflicts 596
8.4.1.3 'A-national' State 597
8.4.1.4 Legitimacy and Democracy 600
8.4.1.5 Local Autonomy and Decentralisation 607
8.4.2 Minorities and their Legitimisation of the Federation 629
8.4.2.1 What Gives Compromise Legitimacy? 629
8.4.2.2 Core Elements of the Swiss Polity 630
8.4.3 Inherent limits of the Swiss Federal Democracy and its Lessons 644
8.4.4 Conclusion: 14 Constitutional Principles for a Multicultural State 646
8.4.4.1 Legitimacy 646
8.4.4.2 Rule of Law 647
8.4.4.3 Shared Rule 648

8.4.4.4 Self Rule 649
8.4.4.5 Democracy 649

9 Outlook: The Constitutional State at the Threshold of a New Millennium 651

9.1 Introduction 651
9.2 'We are the People' versus 'We are One People' 652
9.3 Inclusive States versus Exclusive Ethnicities 654
9.4 From Real Sovereignty to Symbolic Sovereignty 658
9.5 From Reason to Emotion 659
9.6 Conclusions 662

Index 665

Bibliography

General information mainly about Classical Literature

ALTHUSIUS, JOHANNES. *Politics*. Translated by Frederick S. Carney. Boston: Beacon Press, 1964.

ARISTOTLE. *Politics*. Translated by Ernest Barker. New York: Oxford University Press, 1998.

AUGUSTINE. *The City of God against the Pagans*. Translated and edited by R. W. Dyson. Cambridge: Cambridge University Press, 1998.

AUSTIN, JOHN. *The Province of Jurisprudence Determined*. Edited by Wilfrid E. Rumble. Cambridge: Cambridge University Press, 1995.

BACON, FRANCIS. *The advancement of learning and New Atlantis*. Edited by Arthur Johnston. Oxford: Clarendon Press, 1974.

BENN, STANLEY I., and RICHARD STANLEY PETERS. *Social Principles and the Democratic State*, 6th ed. London: Allen & Unwin, 1968.

BENTHAM, JEREMY. *A Fragment on Government*. Edited by James Henderson Burns and H.L.A. Hart. Cambridge: Cambridge University Press, 1988.

BLACKSTONE, WILLIAM. *Commentaries on the Laws of England*. Edited by Wayne Morrison. London/Sidney: Routledge Cavendish, 2001.

BODIN, JEAN. *Les six livres de la République*. Edited by Christiane Frémont, Marie-Dominique Couzinet, and Henri Rochais. Paris: Fayard, 1986.

BRAUDEL, FERNAND. *Civilization and capitalism, 15th-18th century*. 3 vols. Translated by Siân Reynolds. Berkeley: University of California Press, 1992.

BURDEAU, GEORGES. *Droit constitutionnel et institutions politiques*, 18th ed. Paris: Librairie générale de droit et de jurisprudence, 1977.

CAMPANELLA, TOMMASO. *La città del sole – The City of the Sun*. Translated by Daniel John Donno. Berkeley: University of California Press, 1981.

CICERO, MARCUS TULLIUS. *The Republic and The Laws*. Translated by Niall Rudd, edited by Jonathan Powell. New York: Oxford University Press, 1998.

DAHL, ROBERT ALAN. *Regimes and oppositions*. New Haven, Yale University Press, 1973.

DAHL, ROBERT ALAN. *The Concept of Power*. New York: Bobbs-Merrill, 1957.

DAMASKA, MIRJAN R. *The Faces of Justice and State Authority*. New Haven: Yale University Press, 1986.

DEUTSCH, KARL WOLFGANG. *The Nerves of Government, Models of Political Communication and Control*. 2nd ed. New York: Free Press, 1966.

Federalist. By ALEXANDER HAMILTON, JAMES MADISON, and JOHN JAY. Edited by Terence Ball. Cambridge: Cambridge University Press, 2003.

FRAENKEL, ERNST. „Die repräsentative und die plebiszitäre Komponente im demokratischen Verfassungsstaat (1958)." In *Zur Theorie und Geschichte der Repräsentation und der Repräsentativverfassung*. Edited by Heinz Rausch. Darmstadt: Wissenschaftliche Buchgesellschaft, 1968.

GAIUS. *The Institutes*. Translated by Francis de Zulueta. 2 vols. New York: Clarendon Press, 1946–1953.

GOETHE, JOHANN WOLFGANG VON. „Briefe der Jahre 1814–1832." In vol. 21 of *Werke, Briefe und Gespräche*. Edited by Ernst Beutler. Zurich: Artemis 1951.

GRANET, MARCEL. *Chinese civilization*. Translated by Kathleen E. Innes and Mabel R. Brailsford. New York: Meridian books, 1958.

GROTIUS, HUGO. *The Rights of War and Peace*. Edited by Richard Tuck from the edition by Jean Barbeyrac. 3 vols. Indianapolis: Liberty Fund, 2005.

HABERMAS, JURGEN. *Between Facts and Norms: Contributions to a Discourse Theory of Law and Democracy*. Translated by William Rehg. Cambridge, MA: MIT Press, 1996.

HABERMAS, JURGEN. *The Postnational Constellation: Political Essays*. Translated by Max Pensky. Cambridge, MA: MIT Press, 2001.

HART, H. L. A. *The Concept of Law*. Oxford: Clarendon Press, 1961.

HAYEK, FRIEDRICH A. VON. "The Political Order of a Free People." In vol. 3 of *Law, Legislation and Liberty*. 3 vols. London: Routledge and Kegan Paul, 1982.

HAYEK. FRIEDRICH A. VON. *The Constitution of Liberty*. Chicago: University of Chicago Press, 1960.

HEGEL, GEORG WILHELM FRIEDRICH. *Elements of the Philosophy of Right*. Translated by H.B. Nisbet, edited by Allen W. Wood. Cambridge: Cambridge University Press, 1991.

HELLER, HERMANN. *Staatslehre*. 3rd ed. Leiden: A. W. Sijthoff, 1963.

HIS, EDUARD. *Geschichte des neueren schweizerischen Staatsrechts*, 3 vols. Basel: Helbing & Lichtenhahn, 1920–1938.

HOBBES, THOMAS. *Leviathan*. Edited by Richard Tuck. Cambridge: Cambridge University Press, 1996.

HOEBEL, EDWARD ADAMSON. *The Law of Primitive Man: A Study in Comparative Legal Dynamics*. Cambridge, MA: Harvard University Press, 2006.

HUMBOLDT, WILHELM FREIHER VON. *The Limits of State Action*. Edited by J.W. Burrow. Indianapolis: Liberty Fund, 1993.

HUME, DAVID. *A Treatise of Human Nature*. Edited by David Fate Norton and Mary J. Norton. New York: Oxford University Press, 2007.

HUNTINGTON, SAMUEL P. *Political Order in Changing Societies*. New Haven: Yale University Press, 2006.

JELLINEK, GEORG. *Allgemeine Staatslehre*. 3rd ed. Berlin: Julius Springer, 1914 (reprint 1966).

KANT, IMMANUEL. *The Metaphysics of Morals*. Translated and edited by Mary J. Gregor. Cambridge: Cambridge University Press, 1996.

KANT, IMMANUEL. *Perpetual Peace: A Philosophical Essay*. Translated by M. Campbell Smith. Bristol: Thoemmes Press, 1992.

KELSEN, HANS. *General Theory of Law and State*. Translated by Anders Wedberg. Union, N.J.: Lawbook Exchange, 1999.

KELSEN, HANS. *Demokratie und Sozialismus: Ausgewählte Aufsätze*. Edited by Norbert Leser. Darmstadt: Wissenschaftliche Buchgesellschaft, 1967.

KELSEN, HANS. *Vom Wesen und Wert der Demokratie*. Tübingen: J. C. B. Mohr, 1929.

KHALDÛN, IBN. *The Muqaddimah*. Translated by Franz Rosenthal, 3rd ed. Princeton: Princeton University Press, 1974.

KOLAKOWSKI, LESZEK. *Main Currents of Marxism: The Founders, the Golden Age, the Breakdown*. Translated by P.S. Falla. New York: W.W. Norton & Company, 2005.

KRIELE, MARTIN. *Recht und praktische Vernunft*. Göttingen: Vandenhoeck und Ruprecht 1979.

KRÜGER, HERBERT. *Allgemeine Staatslehre*. 2nd ed. Stuttgart: W. Kohlhammer, 1966.

KUNGFUTSE., *Gespräche*. Translated by Richard Wilhelm. Düsseldorf: Diederichs, 1976.

LABAND, PAUL. *Das Staatsrecht des Deutschen Reiches*. 5th ed. 4 vols. Tübingen: Mohr, 1911–1914 (reprint 1964).

LACTANTIUS FIRMIANUS. *Epitomé des Institutions Divines*. Translated and edited by Michel Perrin. Paris: Editions du Cerf, 1987.

LEIBHOLZ, GERHARD. *Volk, Nation und Staat im 20. Jahrhundert*. Hannover: Niedersächsische Landeszentrale für Heimatdienst, 1958.

LENIN, WLADIMIR I. *Collected Works*. Translated by Joshua Kunitz and Moissaye J. Olgin. New York: International Publishers, 1929.

LOCKE, JOHN. *Two Treatises of Government.* Edited by Peter Laslett. Cambridge: Cambridge University Press, 1988.
LOEWENSTEIN, KARL. *Political Power and the Governmental Process.* 2nd ed. Chicago: University of Chicago Press, 1965.
LUTHER, MARTIN. *Von weltlicher Obrigkeit.* Edited by Wolfgang Metzger. Gütersloh: Güthersloher Verlagshaus Mohn, 1978.
MACCHIAVELLI, NICCOLÒ. *The Prince.* Translated by Peter Constantine. New York: The Modern Library, 2008.
MALBERG, RAYMOND CARRE DE. *Contribution à la théorie générale de l'État, spécialement d'après les données fournies par le droit constitutionnel français.* 2 vols. Paris: Libraire de la Société du Recueil Sirey, 1920–1922.
MARCUSE, HERBERT. *One-dimensional Man: Studies in the Ideology of Advanced Industrial Society.* Boston: Beacon Press, 1991.
MARITAIN, JACQUES. *The Rights of Man and Natural Law.* Translated by Doris C. Anson. New York: Scribner, 1943.
MARSILIUS OF PADUA. *The Defender of the Peace.* Translated by Annabel Brett. Cambridge: Cambridge University Press, 2005.
MARX, KARL. *Capital: A Critique of Political Economy.* Translated by Samuel Moore. New York: The Modern Library, 1906.
MARX, KARL and ENGELS, FRIEDRICH. *The German Ideology.* London: Lawrence & Wishart, 1965.
MARX, KARL. *Manifesto of the Communist Party.* New York: International Publishers, 1983.
MILL, JOHN STUART. *On Social Freedom.* New York: Columbia University Press, 1941.
MILTON, JOHN. *Areopagitica: A Speech of Mr. John Milton for the Liberty of Unlicenced Printing to the Parliament of England.* Clark, N.J.: Lawbook Exchange, 2006.
MOHL, ROBERT VON. „Der Rechtsstaat." In *Encyklopädie der Staatswissenschaften.* 2nd ed. Tübingen: Laupp, 1872.
MOMMSEN, THEODOR. *Abriß des römischen Staatsrechts.* Darmstadt: Wissenschaftliche Buchgesellschaft, 1907 (reprint 1974).
MONTESQUIEU, CHARLES-LOUIS. *The Spirit of the Laws.* Translated and edited by Anne M. Cohler, Basia Carolin Miller, and Harold Samuel Stone. Cambridge: Cambridge University Press, 1989.
MOORE, BARRINGTON. *Social Origins of Dictatorship and Democracy: Lord and Peasant in the Making of the Modern World.* Boston: Beacon Press, 1993.
MORUS, THOMAS. *Utopia.* Edited by George Stade. New York: Barnes & Noble Classics, 2005.
MUTWA, CREDO VUSA'MAZULU. *My People.* 3rd ed. London: Penguin Books, 1977.
NEUMANN, FRANZ. *The Democratic and the Authoritarian State.* New York: The Free Press of Glencoe, 1964.
NIKOLAUS VON CUES. „De concordantia catholica." In *Von der allgemeinen Eintracht.* Edited by Karl Gottfried Hugelmann. Salzburg: Stifterbibliothek, 1966.
NOZICK, ROBERT. *Anarchy, State and Utopia.* Oxford: Blackwell, 1975.
PARETO, VILFREDO. „System der allgemeinen Soziologie." In *„Demokratische" Elitenherrschaft.* Edited by Wilfried Röhrich. Darmstadt: Wissenschaftliche Buchgesellschaft, 1975.
PLATO. *The Republic.* Translated by R.E. Allen. New Haven: Yale University Press, 2006.
POLYBIUS. *The Histories.* Translated by Mortimer Chambers. New York: Twayne Publishers, 1967.
PUFENDORF, SAMUEL VON. *Die Verfassung des Deutschen Reiches.* Translated by Horst Denzer. Stuttgart: Philipp Reclam, 1976.
RAWLS, JOHN. *A Theory of Justice.* 3rd ed. Oxford: Clarendon Press, 1972.

ROUSSEAU, JEAN-JACQUES. *The social contract: or, Principles of political right.* Translated by Charles M. Sherover. New York: New American Library, 1974.

ROUSSEAU, JEAN-JACQUES. *Discourse on Political Economy.* Translated by Christopher Betts. New York: Oxford University Press, 1994.

SCHMITT, CARL. *Constitutional Theory.* Translated by Jeffrey Seitzer. Durham: Duke University Press, 2008.

SCHOPENHAUER, ARTHUR., „Zur Rechtslehre und Politik" (Kap. 9). In vol. 5 of *Sämtliche Werke.* Edited by Wolfgang von Löhneysen. 5 vols. Stuttgart/Frankfurt a. M.: Suhrkamp, 1986.

SENECA. *De clementia.* Translated and edited by Susanna Braund. New York: Oxford University Press, 2008.

SIEYÈS, EMMANUEL JOSEPH. „Qu'est-ce-que le Tiers-Etat?" In vol. 1 of *Œuvres de Sieyès.* Edited by Marcel Dorigny. Paris: Editions d'Histoire Sociale (EDHIS), 1989.

SMITH, ADAM. *An Inquiry into the Nature and Causes of the Wealth of Nations.* Dublin: Whitestone, 1776.

DE SMITH, STANLEY A. *Judicial Review of Administrative Action.* 4th ed. London: Stevens & Sons, 1980.

SPENCER, HERBERT. *The Principles of Ethics.* 2 vols. Indianapolis: Liberty Classics, 1978.

SPINOZA, BENEDICTUS DE. *The collected works of Spinoza.* Translated by Edwin Curley. Princeton: Princeton University Press, 1985.

STAHL, FRIEDRICH JULIUS. *Die Philosophie des Rechts.* Heidelberg: J.C.B. Mohr, 1878.

AQUINAS, THOMAS. *Summa Theologiae: A Concise Translation.* Edited by Timothy McDermott. Westminster, MD: Christian Classics, 1989.

AQUINAS, THOMAS. *On the Government of Rulers: De regimine principum.* Translated by James M. Blythe. Philadelphia: University of Pennsylvania Press, 1997.

TOCQUEVILLE, ALEXIS DE. *Democracy in America.* Edited by Francis Bowen. New York: Modern Library, 1981.

TROTSKY, LEON. *Terrorism and Communism: A Reply to Karl Kautsky.* Westport, CONN: Greenwood Press, 1986.

VATTEL, EMER DE. *The Law of Nations.* New York: AMS Press, 1982.

VERDROSS, ALFRED, and BRUNO SIMMA. *Universelles Völkerrecht.* 3rd ed. Berlin: Duncker & Humblot, 1984.

WATTS, RONALD LAMPMAN. *Comparing Federal Systems.* Montreal & Kingston: McGill-Queen's University Press, 1999.

WEBER, Max. „Die drei reinen Typen der legitimen Herrschaft." In *Gesammelte Aufsätze zur Wissenschaftslehre.* Edited by Johannes Winckelmann. 4th ed. Tübingen: Mohr, 1973.

WU, GENG. *Die Staatslehre des Han Fei.* Vienna/New York: Springer, 1978.

ZIMMER, HEINRICH ROBERT. *Philosophies of India.* Edited by Joseph Campbell. Princeton: Princeton University Press, 1969.

1 General Introduction

1.1 From Local Entities to the Globalised Marginalisation of the Nation-State

1.1.1 Historical Influences on today's World of States

The state a product of the Enlightenment

The nation-state as we know it today is a product of European Modernity. It is a fruit of the European Enlightenment. From the 17th to the 20th Century, the European states spread the concept of the state around the globe through their colonial empires, which were driven by commercial interests and justified by missionary zeal. Within today's globalised world all states regard themselves as equal and sovereign members of the community of states. All have adopted the same fundamental political philosophy from the Enlightenment. The question however which must be asked is: Can the Enlightenment, which centuries ago secularised the state by separating it from the Christian religion, lead us into the future? Is the state of modernity able to solve the current and the future problems of today's globalised world?

Rapid change of the world-map

Taking a look at the world map and surveying the constitutional history of states it is astonishing to find that of the 194 recognized states only 14 can look back upon 200 years of uninterrupted development as nation-states. From the time Japan first became a political entity in 660 BC until the United States Declaration of Independence in 1776, on average a new state was created only once every 175 years. In the 19th Century a new state was born every four years. Whilst in the first half of the 20th Century new states claimed full sovereignty and international recognition every 18 months, in the second half up to 1993 this occurred every five months. Currently we are confronted with numerous conflicts which centre on the creation of new states or the disintegration of old ones, such as in Canada, North Korea, Cyprus, Northern Ireland, the Congo, Indonesia, Georgia (Abkhazia and Ossetia), Russia (Chechnya), China, Somalia, the former Yugoslavia, India and Pakistan (Kashmir), Sri Lanka, Macedonia as well as in Sudan and the Basque Country.

A short overview of the development of the European community of states reveals that there is almost no European state which can look back to an unbroken and uninterrupted history. The Roman Empire, at the time of its greatest expansion in 116 AD, controlled the whole of Mediterranean from Spain to Mauritania,

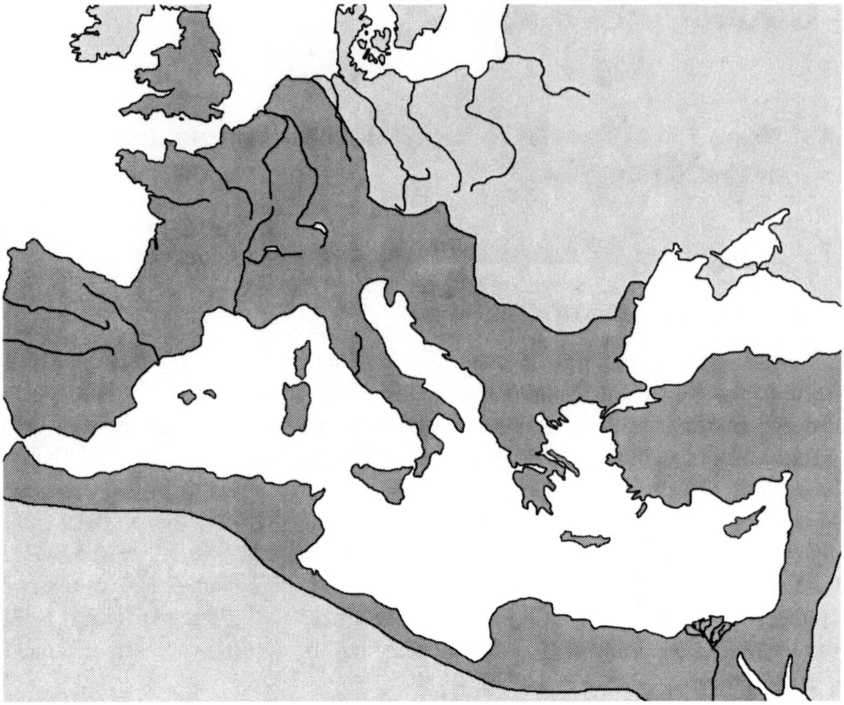

Map. 1. The Roman Empire at 120 AD

North Africa including Egypt and Mesopotamia all the way to the Black Sea. In the north all of England (except Scotland and Ireland), Germany and a part of Poland and of the Ukraine including today's Hungary and Romania were also part of the Roman Empire.

This huge empire disintegrated first into the East-Roman and West-Roman Empires, the dividing line between which ran through what is now the Balkans. The Roman Limes along the Rhine and the Danube which became the shelter for the retreating Roman armies, became over the centuries an important border line along which conflicts ignited but also states and religious communities were born.

The Empire of Charles the Great

The later empire of Charles the Great encompassed today's France, part of Italy, as well as Germany, Austria, Slovenia and Croatia.

Even more important for today's development of the community of states within Europe was the division of the Empire of Charles the Great amongst his three sons. It is evident that the middle part between Germany and France, which was transferred to Lothair, suffered in lengthy wars and was only able to develop

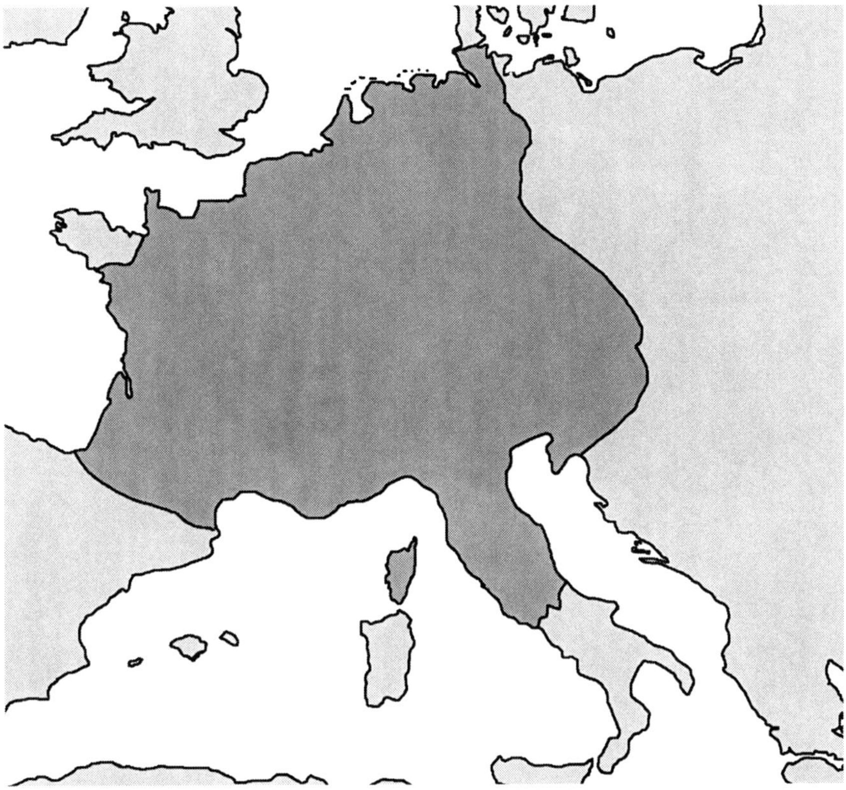

Map. 2. The Empire of Charles the Great

through wars of independence or secession into states such as the Swiss confederation and the Italian city-states. The Alsace, Lorraine, Luxembourg, Belgium and the Netherlands are all regions or independent states which even today do not fit within either the French or the German concept of 'nation'.

The Carolingian Partition

The partition of the empire of Charles the Great to his three sons with equal rights: Charles the bald (West-Empire), Lothair (Middle Empire) and Louis the German (East Empire), left many substantial questions open such as the right of succession as emperor of the entire empire. Moreover the middle empire of Lothair was divided and transferred to his brothers after his death, which exacerbated the instability between France and Germany. This sowed the seeds for the eventual separation of France and Germany, and for centuries of enmity between them.

While the French king made no claim upon the crown of emperor of the entire empire, the German successor demanded, as the only successor of the Emperor, the

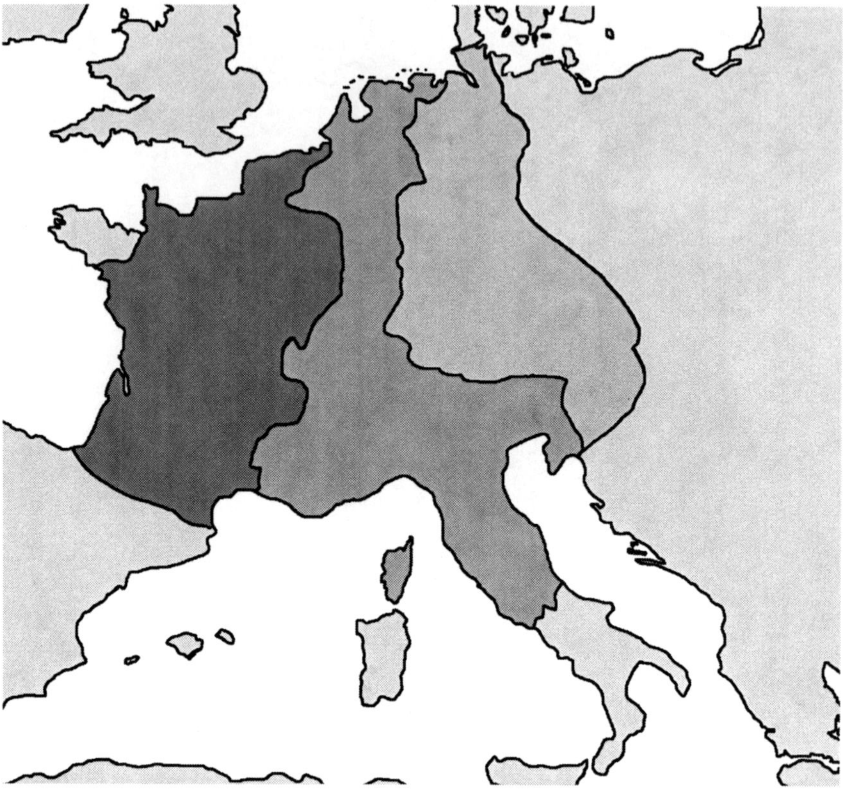

Map. 3. The Carolingian Partition

crown and thus the title to rule over the entire former empire of Charles the Great. Logically he and the following emperors required their subordinate kings to defend their respective territories with their own means and armies. The French king however considered himself to be entitled to defend his territory with his own army. The consequence of this decision of the German 'emperor' was a strong decentralisation and federalisation of Germany, which in 1800 was divided into not less than 1,800 principalities. For this reason Germany in the 19th Century needed first to struggle for its national unity. The development of democracy within the country had to be postponed to the 20th Century.

In France however national unity has never been disputed. The internal conflicts of the 19th Century were not initiated for the sake of national unity but rather to determine the transition from the pre-modern feudal society to the modern bourgeois society ruled by *citoyens*. The legitimacy of the nation was never at stake, but rather the legitimacy of the Monarchy against the later Republic was the issue that fuelled several revolutions and coups d'état. The difference which persists today, between the German concept of the Nation as the basis of the German state, and the French notion of the Constitution giving rise to the state, actually originated back at the Carolingian partition of Europe.

Reformation

The period of greatest significance for the development of the European world of states was the time of the Reformation and the division between the Catholics and the Protestants. The Reformation enabled the protestant states to complete the political separation from the Holy Roman Empire with theological separation from the Pope. This made it possible for those states which had untied themselves from Rome to deal with Pope and Emperor as separate entities with which the state could have different relations. The theological, philosophical and political foundation for absolute indivisible sovereignty was thereby laid. The conflict between religions became a conflict between states which could not be resolved until the peace of Westphalia in 1648.

The Peace of Westphalia: The foundation of modern Europe

With the peace of Westphalia the political guidelines for modern Europe and its state diversity were set. The different religious positions of the various principalities led again to new disputes within the states. The secularisation of the state and the gradual introduction of freedom of religion as a minority right find their modern roots within this period, which also laid the foundation for the understanding of problems faced by minorities.

While the new European peace provided the external conditions for the absolutism of Louis XIV in France, in Germany the basis for decentralisation was created. The princes gained their own sovereignty and the right to enter into treaties whilst the empire gradually diminished in importance.

The peace of Westphalia was also the first occasion on which the principles of state sovereignty and of equality of states were committed to writing. The power-balance among the different European states was determined. Peace between Spain and the Netherlands was established and the foundation for an independent Belgium was laid. For the first time the Swiss confederation received written confirmation of its independence from the empire, which reflected what had been the de facto practice for some time.

England and modern constitutionalism

With the peace of Westphalia came also the foundation stone for the development of modern constitutionalism, for at the same time as state borders were being settled and recognised in continental Europe, in England the first revolution in which Parliament struggled against the crown for sovereign rights was taking place. The *Long Parliament*, which at the end of its anarchic rule removed King Charles I and sentenced him to death, set the scene for the later revolutions in

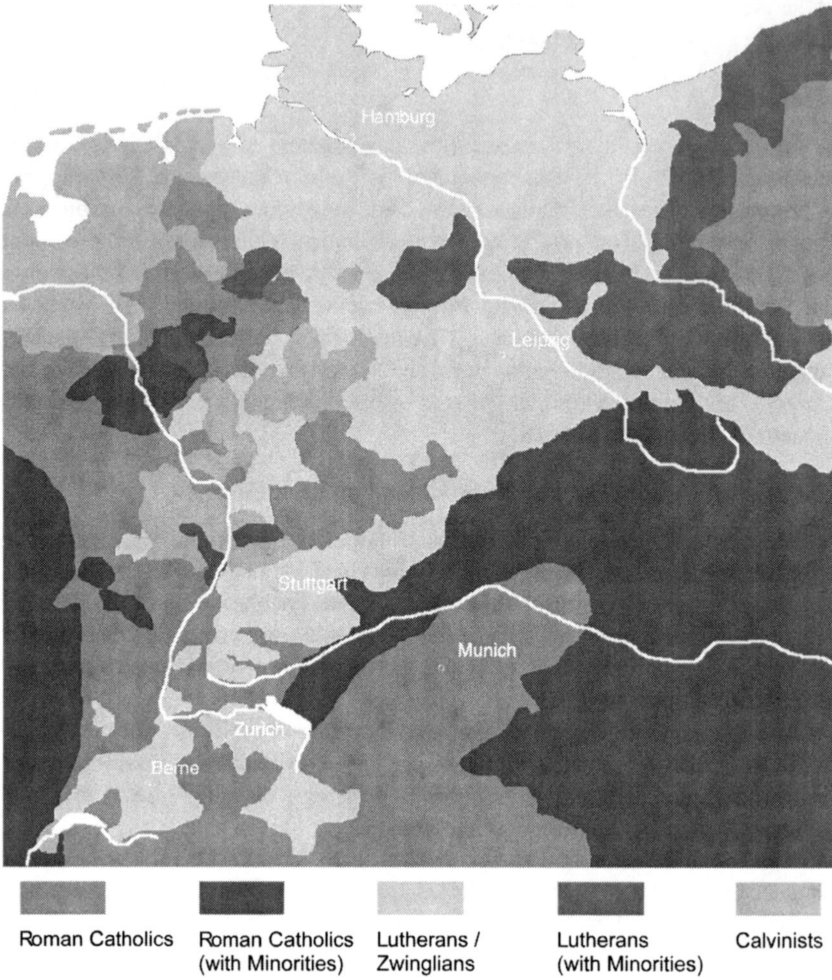

Map. 4. The spread of the different confessions after the peace of Westphalia

England (1688), France (1789) and Russia (1917). It was the first time a Parliament had claimed for itself sovereign rights, and it took 150 years until the French Parliament as *Assemblée Nationale* attempted in similar fashion to achieve a republican triumph over the Monarchy.

The Congresses of Vienna and Berlin

The two next important peace conferences that had a profound impact on the community of European states were the Vienna Congress of 1815 - which first devised the concept of Swiss Neutrality as an important element in the balance of powers among the European states – and the Berlin Congress of 1878. The Congress of Berlin determined a new balance of powers within the Balkans and thereby created the conditions for today's conflicts over state creation, minority rights and the collapse of states.

While within the states of Western Europe the different nations found themselves more or less as homogeneous units within their own territory, the peoples of the Balkan under the rule of the Austro-Hungarian Monarchy on the one hand and of the Ottoman Empire on the other, were mixed together within the same territories, as under the foreign rule the various peoples were unable to establish their own states. However within the frame of the Turkish Millet-system and the Austro-Hungarian autonomy the nations and peoples were entitled to certain collective rights which did grant them some personal autonomy. They could maintain their own language and religion, and had some control over the education of their children. As consequence of this personal autonomy the members of different communities and religions were able to co-exist within the same towns without having to renounce their personal identity. Thus still today in many cities in the Balkan such as Tbilisi and Sarajevo, one can find. Synagogues Mosques, Catholic and Protestant churches side by side.

The Balkans

After the First World War the Austro-Hungarian Empire was dissolved and the territory of Hungary radically reduced, which created significant Hungarian minorities in the Ukraine, Czechoslovakia, Romania and Yugoslavia. At this time the fundamental principle that each nation should be entitled to have its own mother-state was developed – a principle that was decisive for the further development of the Balkans. Accordingly, states were established in order to accommodate the different nations. Only with regard to the multi-nation Yugoslavia was this not possible, as this state covered a territory which had been divided for more than a thousand years by the borderline between East and West Rome, between the East and West Christian church and later between the Ottoman Empire and the European Occident. As a consequence of this divisive history, there is today still no clear territory for Serbs, Croats, Bosnians, Macedonians etc. Thus the victors of World War One decided to establish one state as a motherland for all Slavic peoples living in the South, 'yugo' meaning the South in the Slavic languages: Yugoslavia.

Holocaust and the decline of colonial and communist rule

The 20th Century is marked by the holocaust. Never before in history had a state decided to wipe an entire race of people off the face of the Earth. Notwithstanding the countless atrocities committed prior to the Hitler regime, such a chillingly organised program of genocide had up until Hitler's rule never been carried out in reality. The idea of a super race connected with the claim for the legitimate power of the state to decide who belongs to the super race and which race has to be extinguished leads ultimately, if followed through to its 'logical' conclusion, to a homogeneous state race which is entitled to extinguish any race that threatens the unity and homogeneity of the state.

The other important characteristics of the 20th Century in terms of state development were the liberation of peoples from the external powers of the Ottoman Empire, the colonial regimes and – after the fall of the Berlin wall – the implosion of communism and thus the end of communist rule of the Soviet Union. Such dissolution of foreign rule is, as history since the fall of the Roman Empire has shown, connected with centuries of conflict. This has particular consequences for those peoples formerly ruled by foreign powers: The exercise of political authority by the state is seen as a symbol of force. Within the historical subconscious the state is considered an enemy of the nation. Whoever follows after the colonial rule has to be aware that the state even today is barely able to claim genuine legitimacy amongst the affected peoples. As in many cases the new state authority has been taken over by the majority nation this nation will be identified with the former colonial state and thus bear the brunt of feelings of resentment and rejection formerly reserved for colonial masters. Thus the state has become for many peoples the image of the enemy. For them, only a state that is able to grant the previously oppressed peoples unrestricted identity and thus also an unrestricted feeling of freedom can become an acceptable state.

This has necessarily led to serious conflicts, as new states very rarely cover a territory with an ethnically homogeneous population. Much like in Africa and Asia, ethnic conflicts have therefore also begun to break out in Eastern Europe. Such conflicts involve violent disputes over state identity together with ethnic cleansing.

1.1.2 Challenges for States

1.1.2.1 Globalisation

The fall of the Berlin Wall

An event of great historical significance for the understanding of the concept of the state was the fall of the Berlin wall. With this symbolic fall of the iron curtain in 1989 the concept of the state was decisively altered. For 50 years the world had been economically divided into the industrialised and the non-industrialised world. Of greater political significance, the world had also been divided into a communist and a capitalist sphere of power. States belonged either to the communist or to the western sphere of influence. The two rigid adversary blocks persisted for decades and influenced thinking on the subject of the state substantially. The states were the undisputed fortresses of either the liberal-capitalist or the Marxist-communist ideology. As a major factor of power within the respective alliances, the state and its rule were considered as self-evident necessities. Nobody questioned the legitimacy of the state. The only questions posed were whether the organisation of the state and its governmental system fitted with the major ideology of the respective block and whether the leadership of the state was good or bad. The existence of states, their borders and their significance were not questioned at all.

Sovereignty of the global market

Since the fall of the Berlin wall the theory of state has been presented with the challenge of finding answers to the new existential questions facing states. Now that the animosity between East and West has faded away and that states are gradually forfeiting their sovereignty to the global market, one may even ask why we really need states at all. Sovereign states previously determined their own rules in relation to human rights, which were usually subject to the overriding interests of the state. Today the recognition of human rights has become a universal standard for the assessment of states. The World Bank and International Monetary Fund (IMF) measure compliance with human rights as part of the so-called *good governance* principles, as a precondition for any international financial support. Universal values have marginalised the once important nation-states of Europe to local polities. Are they still needed, considering that their legal orders have largely been integrated and thus marginalised into regional organisations extending to whole continents, such as the European Union?

Localisation?

While consumers seek the global market citizens demand universality of human rights. Within their social and emotional existence however human beings still feel deeply insecure. They seek security and identity within the local province. Globalisation thus is only a trend of the moment. In fact it is tempered and complemented by the need for local security, local values and local autonomy. Instead of speaking of globalisation we should therefore speak of 'glocalisation'. The result of glocalisation is a tendency towards even greater decentralisation. The World Bank and the IMF grant assistance only to states that provide for a realistic program of decentralisation. Many ethnic conflicts of our time are in fact struggles against the power of central government. Decentralisation should grant more rights and autonomy to ethnically distinct peoples. However this leads us to the question: how can states leave some of their responsibilities to the global free market and at the same time devolve many essential tasks to local units without losing their main function as states responsible for the development of the society?

European Union

The European Union finds itself in a special situation. Its roots go back to a treaty aiming to pacify the rift between France and Germany as well as to the later conflict between the west and the east. The new alliance within Western Europe was designed to strengthen the west against the east, and to finally overcome the long-standing enmity between Germany and France. The aim was to forge a community of states based on common economic interests and an integrated European market that could eventually evolve into a politically integrated community. When the European Economic Community was established the economy was still regulated on national bases but the member states were ready to open their markets to the newly formed community of states within the region. At the beginning of this integration process the industries important for the armament of the defence forces had to be tied together within the Community of Steel and Coal. However in the age of globalisation the European economic union has lost much of its significance. The political unity of Europe has therefore become the focus of integration. The uniform currency, the democratisation of institutions, the common foreign policy and the creation of a European 'people' with European citizenship are all major steps towards full integration. The constitution for a European state has suddenly become the central focus of political debate in Europe.

1.1.2.2 The Engine of State-Building

Multiculturality

With these developments state theory has taken on a new dimension. As a result of multicultural polities the federal structure of states gains additional importance. Up to now the main focus of the general theory of state was on the questions of how people should be governed and how the power of the state should be organised and administered to serve the interests of the people. Today however the foremost question is what position and functions the state should have, in view of the world-wide trends of globalisation and localisation. To what extent can states contribute, on top of now universally accepted values, additional liberal or particular national values? How should states deal with the threat of modern terrorism? How is state sovereignty to be distinguished from the sovereignty of the global market? What values bring or hold together the peoples of a state or a nation? In terms of multicultural states the crucial questions are, *which people* should exercise the power of the state, which majority should govern which minority or should be entitled to share in the exercise of government power, and which rights can or should be given to minorities.

The draft for a new treaty on a constitution for Europe, in the version of June 13 and July 10 2003, placed the proposed constitution under the following quote from THUKYDIDES:

"Χρώμεδα γάρ πολιτεία .... καί όνομα μέν διά τό μή ές όλίγους άλλ' ές πλείονας οἰκεῖν δημοκρατία κέκληται". (THUKYDIDES II 37) The English translation of this sentence reads as follows: "Our Constitution ... is called a democracy because power is in the hands not of a minority but of the greatest number". The German version of the official text read as follows: "The constitution which we have ... is named democracy, because the state is not oriented to a few citizens but rather to the majority" ("Die Verfassung, die wir haben ... heißt Demokratie, weil der Staat nicht auf wenige Bürger, sondern auf die Mehrheit ausgerichtet ist"). According to the German version democracy means that the state should operate in the interest of the citizens. According to the English translation democracy is the governmental system which transfers power into the hands of the majority. These two different translations obviously emanate from different understandings of democracy. Either democracy gives power to the majority or it requires the state to orient its policies to the interest of the majority. The central question of who should govern over whom is answered with the English version but left open in the German. In the German version THUKYDIDES answers however the question what should be the standard for good governance. The same quotation within a different translation therefore answers a totally different question. This example reveals that with regard to the most crucial questions of the theory of state there is still a lack of clarity or agreement at the highest European level.

Oppression and exploitation of peoples have also been the cause of conflicts that have led to secession movements, division of states and occupation of foreign territory. The multicultural states of the present day will always be confronted with such challenges as long as they are not able to create an identity for their minorities. The conflict between the Palestinians and the Israelis in the Middle East demonstrates clearly that it is not sufficient merely to grant autonomy to minorities. Either it is possible to build a state within which all peoples can identify with the territory of the state, or it is necessary to accept that this is not possible and to divide the state. The longer this takes, the less the peoples will accept living within a state as a second-class nation. Their drive to defend the interest of their people's community comes from the need for self-determination, the need to find and protect their identity, and to protect their own history. They want to be accorded rights, recognition and treatment on equal footing with the majority of the state, not only as individuals but foremost as a people.

What are the engines which drive human beings to establish new states, to unite or divide states, to centralise or to decentralise? If all human beings as Homo sapiens are the same wherever one goes, why then do states differ so much from each other?

Welfare

Human beings want to design their environment in order to be able to live in peace and welfare with each other according to their needs and interests. They therefore aim to build a political superstructure over their society which is accepted by all or which at least is acceptable to the bulk of the society. With this, the internal aims of the state, which best correspond to people's needs for security, power, wealth, care and recognition, are set.

Religion

The engine which moves society towards the foundation, alteration or transformation of states has always been and is – still partially today – religion. The state has often been used to serve the interests of religion. States were and are charged with implementing and executing the rules of religion through the legal system. On the other hand religion legitimises the source of state power and the power of the rulers. In the Christendom of the Middle Ages, kings ruled the peoples at their whim by divine right. They had absolute power because their rule by the authority of God was not to be questioned.

Preservation of power

One of the engines driving politics and state foundation is also self-interest. The state serves the established structures and their power-holders; it has to preserve through its structures and institutions the recognised political and economic power-positions. The state was in earlier times directed towards protecting the rights of the feudal lords and the aristocracy. The state and its laws had to serve the developed feudal system, the hierarchy of which was protected through the legal order. The feudal system was officially portrayed as the system divined by God, which could not be altered. As religion promised rewards in the afterlife for sacrifice and humility, the worldly inequalities could be justified.

Liberty and equality

Today the engine that drives the alteration of state structures including even state borders is the need of human beings for individual freedom, justice and welfare. The aim of the state is the protection and promotion of individual freedom. If individual freedom is protected within the democratic polity, then – according to the philosophy of liberal constitutionalism – the preconditions for welfare and justice within the society are provided for. Since the French Revolution the political poles have concerned themselves with the often contradictory demands for freedom and for equality. Some are of the view that without equality and in particular equality of opportunities, freedom can never really be achieved. Others claim that too much equality can destroy freedom itself. They argue that equality imposed from above suffocates freedom. Between these two opposing positions societies have been struggling since the French Revolution for the development of the social welfare state. Liberty is always tied up with the common good. Some argue that the interests of the whole or the common good should not be permitted to injure the interests of the individual. Others believe that even the right to liberty must be subject to the common interest.

Property and identity

A further pair of opposing factors which may be connected with personal interests as well as collective interests and which may lead to new state structures are property and identity. The state must above all provide protection of property, as proposed by JOHN LOCKE. However property must also serve the interests of the people, say those defending the identity of the people and the common interests of the nation as a collective unit. When for example in Switzerland the acquisition of real estate for tourism threatened to lead to the selling of most of Switzerland, the legislature limited the freedom of real estate owners so that in future they are only permitted to sell real estate to foreigners to a limited extent.

How should one govern? Who should govern?

The inner engine that drives state building and state development is further defined by the following pair of questions, which can pull in different directions: How should one govern and who should govern? Those who only put the question with regard to good governance overlook the decisive question with regard to the *legitimacy* of the state and of the authority of the state. However if one focuses the question on democracy within a multicultural state, the problem of the "who" comes into focus: Who should or can legitimately rule the state, that is, which people or which peoples, which majorities or minorities should be given the power to rule over which other peoples or minorities?

External defence

The defence of external risks such as forces of nature or hostile tribes or peoples has had a substantial effect on the development of states throughout the centuries. States with extensive and exposed borders (France, China), states with natural borders such as islands (Japan, England), those with aggressive neighbours and states with a territory of strategic importance have developed differently according to their external environment. Dangerous environments have tended to force states to adopt a rigid and often authoritarian and centralised institutional structure. This is also the case for states in which people had to expend considerable energy and time to fulfil their basic needs for survival and therefore had little time to concern themselves with issues of state organisation, culture or democracy. On the other hand, states without external threats and states in which people's basic physical and spiritual needs were readily met, had much greater opportunities to concentrate on their cultural and democratic development.

Economic influence and international markets

The desire for wealth and economic development led many states to seek and obtain material goods in other states and consequently to oppress those states and peoples for their own interests. The economy was often the driving force behind state development, not only internally, but also in terms of foreign policy including decisions on war and peace. The economic interests of colonialism however were often concealed behind religious motives. Christianity's claim to universalism certainly strongly inspired and legitimised colonialism during the 17th and 18th Centuries just as the universalist claim of Islam had done for the rule of the Ottoman Empire from the 13th to the 19th Centuries in the Mediterranean.

Religion and religionist policies

With regard to religions it is important to distinguish religious communities that claim to be universal and believe that mankind can only reach heaven by adopting that religion, from those religious communities whose beliefs are limited to a specific *chosen* people. Those religions restricted to their own people (a people chosen by God), including Judaism, Shintoism and the Singhalese in Sri Lanka, do not usually adopt an aggressive universalist proselytising strategy externally, but do adopt a strict and exclusive approach internally.

The attack on the World Trade Centre in New York of 9/11 demonstrated the fragility of our civilisation which can be threatened not only by enemy states but also by private organisations which serve fundamentalist religious policies. The enemies can no longer be identified by state but rather by non-state terrorist organisations which may be harboured wilfully or against the will of a certain state. States which are suspected of harbouring terrorists and their organisations are now confronted with the fact that other states are willing to wage war against them. As a consequence states need in future not only to seek internal legitimacy but also international legitimacy. States that can claim legitimacy in the eyes of the international community will not have to fear that their internal or external legitimacy will be questioned.

1.2 The Questions of the Theory of State

1.2.1 Traditional Questions of the Theory of State

What is the state?

The theory of state was developed on the European continent. It tried to provide answers to questions related to the development of European states into secularised, democratic republican nation-states. Naturally the theory of state needed to inquire into the purpose, function and the position of states.

The state itself was never called into question. Nobody doubted the necessity of states. The central question therefore was not whether there ought to be states, but rather what the essence of the state actually is. To understand the state, to know its nature and substance and to know how the force of the state is exercised, were earlier the main goals of state theory.

Legitimacy through popular sovereignty

The question of the legitimacy of secular political authority as opposed to the legitimacy of religious authority was as much a concern of the theory of state as the question of good governmental organisation. Popular sovereignty as the basis of legitimate state authority moved to the centre of the academic discourse. Why should the state, which derives its legitimacy from popular sovereignty, be entitled to issue orders to its people or even to require them to sacrifice their lives in case of war? That a ruler who derives his entitlement to rule from the will of God should have such powers would at least not be questioned by members of the relevant religion. But how can a state that derives its legitimacy from the people claim such title of authority?

Good governance

A regime that struggles for legitimation of its political authority will naturally strive to convince the governed of its legitimacy through good governance. The limitation, in the common interest, of state force as well as the functions of the state have thus been the decisive questions which have been addressed by the interdisciplinary science of the theory of state.

1.2.2 New Questions of the Theory of State

Majority principle and the multi-ethnic state

Today the building of the European nation-states is no longer at the forefront of the theory of state. At stake is rather the question whether the state and its form of government have reached their use-by date. The challenge of the multicultural state puts the question of how to govern in the background. Explosive however is the question who should, can and does govern. The state is in principle nothing more than a political authority installed by human *reflection and choice*. Is such political authority really needed in the era of globalisation and privatisation? Should one not just let the sovereignty of the market rule? Can the majority of a people rule over the territory in which minorities are living? For majorities as well as minorities are subject to globalisation. Is the democratic majority principle even applicable to multi-ethnic states?

State structure and the basis of legitimacy

The answer to the question who is entitled to rule the state also has repercussions on the organisation and structure of the state. Federalism for example was long regarded only as an instrument of integration for good governance. When federalism however serves to establish and to legitimise an alliance of states for the creation of a multicultural state, federalism also becomes a useful tool to answer the question who should govern. This however requires a federalism which allows multiple loyalties and diversity created not by assimilation and integration but by fostering differences and specific identities.

The rational human being

The real challenge today is the multicultural state. Until now the theory of state has barely touched upon this basic challenge for modern states. The state of modernity emerged out of liberal thought at the time of the development of constitutionalism during the Enlightenment. Liberal philosophers latched on to the Renaissance idea of the rational individual and based their theories on the image of human beings as Homo sapiens which, independent of culture, religion and tradition are essentially the same and therefore equal. In liberal theories man is variously portrayed as egocentric (HOBBES), the holder of inalienable rights (LOCKE), capable of rational judgements (KANT), part of an exploitative or exploited class (MARX), a reasonable *citoyen* (ROUSSEAU) a 'homo politicus' or as a cost-benefit analysis oriented 'homo oeconomicus'.

As equal and rational creatures, human beings in states all over the world can be viewed as the basis of the legitimate state, as well as being citizens participating in and obeying the rule of the state. Culture is either part of political life only for the purpose of unifying the masses, or it is totally excluded from political life. The idea of a *multi*-cultural state is however foreign to the basic philosophy of the state of modernity.

From the world image of the pyramid to the world image of the network

The world image of the Middle Ages was symbolised by the hierarchy of the pyramid. The world image of the Enlightenment was the mechanised gears of the age of industrialisation. States were part of that machinery. The world image of the current era of globalisation is symbolised by the network. Within a multidimensional network there are almost no clear and transparent structures. To survive in this network of public and private organisations it is necessary to be able to control the important nodal junctions and interfaces of the network. The state has given up its monopoly position to international and local public bodies as well as to private associations and religious communities. The state has become a competitor to the different power-holders within the network. What is or should be its position within this network?

An additional challenge is the universalisation of human rights. While consumers seek the best products and optimal prices on the global market, citizens claim universal human rights, investors profit from the global financial market, employees return to their social homeland and people seek security within their local identity. Globalisation is thus challenged by the trend to localisation.

If states want to take into account the inevitable trend to further globalisation of the world wide information network they will need to significantly alter their self-understanding: They can no longer construct their legitimacy on a one dimensional image of the human being. They need to integrate themselves into the international network and accept that they will not play the central role within it. They represent along with many other institutions only an intermediate stop at which many strands of the network converge.

From national towards global economy

The increasing importance of the global market however is leading not only to a gradual marginalisation of states but also to a diminution of their political influence. States have very little central control over the economic development of their country. The 'national economy' has been replaced by the 'Global economy'. The fate of employees and the fate of human beings generally is determined by foreign investors. Boards of Directors make decisions from afar about the profitability and progress of local enterprises, which can have drastic effects on local communities. But also within states, businesses demand conditions that will enable them to compete in the global market. Wages and welfare, environmental and planning regulation and state taxes are measures of the competitiveness of the state relative to its neighbours.

The space for autonomous political decisions and measures on the part of states is shrinking. Superpowers such as the USA may still be able to steer the global market and to direct their foreign policy in the service of their economic interests. Medium and small states however no longer have such ability. They fall into dependence upon the large states, unless they are able to unite regionally within political associations such as the European Union and thereby gain more political space.

From universalisation to the universaliser

Aside from globalisation, the universalisation of human rights is playing an increasingly important role. States that openly and systematically violate human rights will come under the scrutiny of the international media. As soon as the media – for whatever reason – accuse a state of violating human rights, the state must defend itself before the international community, or risk the intervention of the UN Security Council. The violation of human rights is regarded under the Charter of the United Nations of 1945 as a threat to international peace, and may result in reprimand or punitive action by the international community. With the creation of the International Criminal Court, criminal law has been internationalised. There is no state or government which would be able successfully to rely on the concept of national sovereignty to protect itself from international prosecution. The vehemence with which the United States has fought against this new court shows the extent to which states feel threatened by this universalisation of human rights with regard to their local legitimacy.

States are no longer able to dispose of human rights issues as they please. Constitutional guarantees of human rights and constitutional catalogues of fundamental rights are today part of the minimum standard for a constitution. Recently there have even been constitutions adopted which oblige the courts expressly to have regard the jurisprudence of international courts in relation to the protection of Human Rights (South Africa). As much as this development is to be applauded from the point of view of development of a world ethic and world moral, it must also be called into question. Human rights are indeed universal, but their application is in the hands of the 'universaliser' of the international community. It is the only power that ultimately determines the content of human rights and decrees which states should be declared violators of human rights. The universaliser however lacks worldwide democratic legitimacy. Each member of the international community is accountable only to its own people but not to the alliance of the peoples of the international community. State constitutions have lost their monopoly over codes of ethics and values.

1.3 What is the General Theory of State and what is its Aim?

1.3.1 The State: A Different Kind of Society

Can the phenomena of state be explained?

How often the state is spoken of! At receptions and international conferences, in the fight against terrorism, in the context of tax collection and traffic regulation, in innumerable situations we encounter the state, which has no visible form but a decidedly tangible force. What is this invisible, sometimes anonymous and bureaucratic, at times martialistic, sometimes colourfully flag-bearing construct? How is it that the state can limit our freedom, collect taxes, summon us for military service or even condemn us to death? Why is the state able to dissolve a marriage, declare a contract void, or in case of a controversy with our neighbour to decide on right and wrong?

Worldwide, several different minorities are claiming the right to have their own state. Within their state of origin they feel like second class citizens, exploited or oppressed. From a new and independent state of their own they expect paradise. The demands of minorities, which are ever increasing worldwide and to which mother states sometimes respond with state terror, are often the cause of bitter civil wars and conflicts with international dimensions.

State and state alliance

On the other hand states also join together in the interests of peace or under the pressure of globalisation, to solve the increasingly complex problems of our times. Are these international organisations also states or state like entities? One may reasonably ask the question whether the European Union has already become a state in the traditional sense. If yes, this would be an almost irresolvable problem for Germany, as it would violate article 20 of the Basic Law, which provides that all state power has to derive from the people. If the European Union had the power to exercise state force, it would lack the necessary democratic legitimacy, and therefore all orders made by and all legislation enacted by this union would be unconstitutional. The German Constitutional Court has therefore avoided this question of EU statehood by employing the new label 'alliance of states'.

State and mafia

What differentiates the state from a multinational company such as an oil company? How can the state be distinguished from an international organisation – such as the

United Nations or the European Union? How does the state differ from a football club or even from a criminal organisation such as the mafia or a terror organisation? From where is the power of the state derived, with which the state enforces its interests? Are there inherent limits on state authority? How can the state justify its decisions to individuals or to the entire people? What are the real aims and tasks of the state? How is the state organised? How should it be organised? What are its previous, current or future possible guises? What is the relationship between the state and the economy or specific communities such as cultural, religious or language communities? How and under what conditions can the state make decisions in relation to its citizens, foreign workers, tourists or asylum seekers?

New world order?

With the fall of the Berlin wall the questions of the 'why', the 'how' and the 'what for' of the state have to be put in a totally different way. In the face of the increasingly globalised economy and the international trade organisation WTO, state policies on social security, employment and wages are subject to the growing pressure of international competition. The sovereignty of the state within its own territory is being challenged, as the state has lost the power to deal with domestic issues as it pleases. Policies on environmental protection, communication, energy, crime, health protection and migration can only be determined in common with other states on the basis of international cooperation.

Fading away of the state

LENIN'S prediction of the fading away of the state for the benefit of a new paradise of communist equality, takes on a paradoxical new meaning within a capitalist and globalised world order. What is left of the decision making power of formerly proud democratic republics and nation-states, is more or less confined to matters such as infrastructure, local traffic and local security (police). Defence and foreign policy are either driven by global economic interests or tied to the decisions of the UN Security Council. State economic and financial policies must prioritise the interests of a strong internationally competitive currency over the interests of social equality. The political systems of states are measured by their standards with regard to human rights, democracy, efficiency, flexibility and their capacity for integration.

From homo politicus to homo oeconomicus

Consumers of international products shape the world, while voters and taxpayers serve their interests. Independent political discourse is losing its significance and stands increasingly in the shadow of disputes over the international competitiveness of price indices, finance and employment markets and social policy. The globalised bourgeoisie has relegated the citizen to the local level. The once proud nation-states have effectively become local provinces, struggling jealously for more autonomy within the international community. There is a belief that within a competitive global economy the *invisible hand* will take care of the fair distribution of wealth. Politics as the only real defender of justice has lost much of its credibility. It is no longer taxes but rather prices that are ultimately supposed to ensure a just distribution of wealth. The 'homo oeconomicus' has supplanted the 'homo politicus'.

This however is only one side of today's reality. More than half of the 170 states in existence today were created after the 1980s. In many cases these newly established states are the result of violent disputes or terrorist upheavals. In other words: people were prepared to sacrifice their existence and even give their own lives for the sake of obtaining their own state. For all these peoples the foundation of a new state promised a new paradise of freedom, independence, justice and economic development.

The identity of the political community

In many of these states the 'political' stood and still stands as symbol of national or even nationalistic unity. The political feeling of a 'we' in these new national societies is based on one hand on the rejection of the foreign and alien neighbour-culture, and also on recognition of the value of their own religion, history, culture and or language on the other. The state is celebrated as an indispensable symbol of national freedom, unity and independence in all such nations that have been liberated from the yoke of their former colonial powers and imperialist empires – such as for example the Soviet Union – and established their own independent state. The dissolution of the Ottoman Empire shook the world from the beginning of its collapse in the 19th Century right up to the present day. In the 20th Century the dissolution of the colonial empires and of the Empire of the red Tsar multiplied the tremors.

The state – a completely different community?

The state of modern constitutionalism finds its origin and legitimacy in rational considerations, and the free choice and judgement of the citizens. In this sense it is a completely different society to naturally occurring social units such as the family. The modern state for example possesses the exclusive right (aside from the somewhat limited decision-making power of the UN Security Council) to use force for the execution of the law and to guarantee security and order - the so-called monopoly on the use of force. The state is still the only social construct which – in spite of the globalisation of defence – can require its own citizens to sacrifice their lives.

The state is essentially an artificial construct. As an artificial entity however it is not merely a politically centralised unit comprising atomised individuals of the civil society, because civil society itself is also clustered into families, clubs, sports teams, professional associations and religious and other communities. The state of cultural, economic and social pluralism is a polity that is composed of different collective entities. Those entities themselves have been united by emotions, culture and history and feel themselves at least subjectively as a community bound together by a common destiny. Within the frame of the state, certain entities demand their own collective rights and autonomy, and may go so far – invoking natural law right of self-determination – as to strive for secession. This is the reason why today there is an almost irresolvable tension, with the inherent potential for explosive conflicts, between the state as the rationally chosen and constructed community on the one hand, and other natural communities based on emotional ties on the other.

1.3.2 The Structure and Concerns of the General Theory of State

Is the nation-state outdated?

Do we thus have to ask the basic question, whether the state in its traditional sense – that is, the state of modernity – is still needed? Does not the global, invisible hand care for the stable order of the world economy and thereby provide for a better and more just repartition of goods than could the multicultural state plagued by internal strife? Could not more jurisdiction be granted to the International Court of Justice in order that it could assume general responsibility for law and order and for fighting crime? Is the state a political unit in the process of becoming a political world order, that is, a polity in transition that will eventually develop into a world-state? Or does one have to fragment the proud traditional nation-state into smaller and smaller homogeneous language, religious or cultural communities or ethnicities, and limit the role of the state to caring only for the traditional and cultural development of its natural community?

Do we have to recognise such small entities as 'nation-states' and grant them all traditional sovereign rights? If the state is a unit founded by *reflection and choice*, what then are the criteria according to which the external borders of territorial sovereignty are to be determined? Is it even possible to identify valid and generally applicable criteria for the determination of state borders? Or do borderlines of states not by definition lead to irresolvable conflicts in which millions of innocent victims have to be mourned, because the communities bound by language or religion feel compelled to fight against forced state-unity with the 'hostile neighbour'? Will the world not sooner or later dissolve into anarchy – a world of sovereign islands that either fight against each other or completely isolate themselves from each other through apartheid?

The question of the 'how' and the 'whether' with regard to the state

As an artificial sovereign community founded on rational will, the state is able to make decisions on behalf of its citizens. How far do such powers extend? Where is the line to be drawn on the state's authority to rule? Does the voter who is participating in the political process actually express his democratic will more effectively as a consumer participating in the free market and thereby helping to determine the just distribution of wealth based on competition?

All of these questions go not only to the 'why' and the 'how', but above all to the 'whether' in relation to the state. For the peoples of today they are of crucial importance because they can throw states into existential crises and may lead in many parts of the world to irresolvable dilemmas and conflicts. If those conflicts cannot be resolved there is a danger that thousands more innocent lives will be lost in the coming decades as a result of such intractable questions and problems of identity and statehood.

The uniqueness of the state

Another, no less burning question relates to the uniqueness of the state. Is the state actually still the only legitimate and possible order of political authority? Has the uniqueness of the state not long since been thrown into question by the emergence of international organisations such as the European Union or the United Nations? The call for deregulation and privatisation reveals that this uniqueness is being questioned not only from the outside but also internally. Why must the state assume responsibility for social security? Can private universities not fulfil public education functions within the society just as well as state universities? Is the exercise of executive authority limited only to the state, and if so why? What in fact should we understand the notion of executive authority of the state to mean?

It cannot be the role of this theory of state to deal conclusively with these questions. However it can contribute towards understanding many deeply emotional conflicts from a rational perspective, and can replace many of the existing questions of state with new questions which, hopefully, are less likely to lead to conflicts.

History as a question and response

The states of today have evolved through a drawn out process usually initiated by violent conflicts. It would be arrogant to put this historical process of mankind in question and thus to deny the right of states to exist. What history has produced, and what has been implemented via a free and right-conscious process, corresponds obviously with some fundamental needs and values of human beings. This is one of the principal reasons why in the following chapters we do not look at history merely as matter of stark empirical fact. That is, we do not ask only *how* the state has been created. We also assume that history can provide a normative answer to the question of the justification of the state and thereby reveal to us *why* states have developed. The history of the development of the state therefore serves primarily as a justification of the state because it shows that human beings are not able to survive individually without supra-familial communities. The fact that humans have joined together into polities proves man is a 'homo politicus', who by his nature seeks and requires not only a family unit, but also a political community beyond the family in the form of a rational state, founded by reflection and choice.

Interdisciplinary science

The diverse catalogue of questions about the state proves that it is beyond the scope of a single scientific discipline to provide all the answers. If we want to know how a democratic state is organised, we need to seek answers in political science, sociology and constitutional theory. Hints may also be found within the science of economics, or even psychology. We need to understand human nature and to know how people behave within groups, as well as inquiring into the relationships and mechanisms of various groups of people such as parties, municipalities and ethnic communities. We have to examine whether one can steer these groups rationally, emotionally or only with threats and physical force, as well as how and to what extent a people or peoples can or should participate in the decision making process. Moreover we need to know, what is the substance of power, what are its various manifestations and what institutional and procedural measures can be taken in order to prevent misuse of power.

The phenomenon of the "state"

What then is the subject of a theory of state? A theory of state aims to explain the phenomenon of the state. For this it is indispensable to explore the 'substance' of the state. There are a number of ways to answer the question "what is the state?" One can limit oneself to an empirical examination and only reveal what is common to all the constructs that claim today to be 'states'. Such empirical analyses require however a known set of criteria against which phenomena such as power to govern, constitutional rights, democracy etc. are to be measured and compared. This in turn would demand an analytical and theoretical examination of the state. One will have thus to ask what are the essential criteria by which we can identify a community of people as a state, and which distinguish the state from a football club, a criminal organisation, a multinational company, a municipality or an international organisation.

Do people need the state?

Whoever deals with this question will at the same time have to consider the question of how the state is justified. Do we really need a state? Are human beings in terms of their essential nature suited to the state? Is living within a polity part of what it means to be human? What is meant by the concept of the 'political'? What relationship does the 'political' have with statehood? Why is the monopoly on the use of force held by polities? How can this monopoly of the polity be justified?

Empirical state theory?

Whoever in answering these questions relies on empirical data such as the history of the development of the state, must be aware that fictions, fantasies, ideologies and social facts are closely intertwined, and rarely able to be clearly separated. Social facts however should always be analysed and objectively interpreted. Unfortunately such interpretations are also often influenced by pre-existing expectations in relation to the facts under examination.

The different sciences

An exploration of the question why the state has the authority to rule over human beings necessarily involves several different scientific disciplines. Constitutional theory, jurisprudence, history and even theology and philosophy will all provide discipline-specific but not all-encompassing and conclusive answers to the question how and why the state has come into being. The theory of state is thus an inherently interdisciplinary science that is based on and builds upon the knowledge of various other sciences.

Furthermore, the theory of state can also observe the state as a social construct and examine what special position society gives to the state and public authority compared to other social institutions, and what is the relationship between the state and other social institutions. This is the entry point for sociology.

Normative theory of the state?

Scholars dealing with the theory of state have not been content with a purely empirical examination of the state and its organisation, but have tended to focus on the question *how the state should be*. The theory of state has searched for criteria to identify what is a 'good' and 'just' state. Greek philosophers and theorists of the Middle Ages in particular not only grappled with the phenomenon of the state but also asked how the ideal state should be organised and what its responsibilities should be. How should the decision-making power of the state be exercised in order to serve the common good of the people? Such normative problems were taken up again by IMMANUEL KANT (1724–1804), GEORG WILHELM FRIEDRICH HEGEL (1770–1831), JEAN-JACQUES ROUSSEAU (1712–1778), JOHN LOCKE (1632–1704) and CHARLES LOUIS DE SECONDAT MONTESQUIEU (1689–1755). Today these questions are pursued principally by JOHN RAWLS (1921–2002) and those who debate his theory of justice, as well as by neo-marxists and neo-liberals.

Positivists

The positivist schools take a completely different approach to the theory of state. Some content themselves with an exploration of *the phenomena of power* within the state. They ask how power arises, how one can acquire state power, how it is used and how those who hold power need to behave in order to retain it. Exemplars of this approach include: in ancient China, HAN FEI TZU († 234 before Christ); in the Arabic world of the Middle Ages, IBN KHALDÛN (1332–1406); and in Europe, NICCOLÒ MACHIAVELLI (1469–1527). These 'empiricist' analyses of the political power of the state did not address the question of justification. They asked only how power comes into being, how it can be developed, how one can diminish the power of others, what are the effects of power and how can power be used in such a way as to ensure that it will be sustained and expanded.

Included in the positivist school are also those scholars who view *the state as the sum of its legal norms* but do not pose questions as to what constitutes a good or a just state. For these scholars the state is the sum of such legal norms as a territorial entity must possess in order to be classified as a state. According to HANS KELSEN (1881–1973) the state is essentially nothing more than a system of norms that creates order, and thus legal order (H. KELSEN, p. 16).

The state as an instrument to change society?

Whoever ventures to produce a theory of state needs to be conscious of the fact that the theory of state belongs to those scientific disciplines which have emerged within the *Continental-European* legal system out of the tradition of the growing nation-state of the 19th Century. For Napoleon the state was an instrument with which he could turn the conservative, aristocratic feudal European society into a liberal democracy. For Germany under Bismarck the nation-state was the instrument that brought former empires together as the 'German Nation'. To the *common-law* countries on the other hand, the idea of a collective unit or body equipped with a collectively-based sovereignty is quite foreign. They tend not to ask what attributes an association of people needs in order to achieve sovereignty and to exercise state authority. For countries of this tradition the focus is rather on the separation and limitation of government powers. The question how the state should be constituted, in order to use its power correctly is not put. While American and British constitutional theory is thus aimed at the limitation of state power, in European theory the constitution is seen as an instrument which enables the proper exercise of state power. They ask how the state should be organised in order to give the law the power to steer the governing institutions effectively, and not how the rulers may bend the law to serve their own interests.

Is the state a collective unit?

The focus of common law is rather on government and much less on the state as an abstract and collective unit. The theory of the organisation of state power is in these countries covered under political science or touched upon in constitutional theory. A proper science that is concerned with the state, in the sense of the theory of state, is unknown.

The question whether the state as a collective construct does have a special status could be asked pragmatically in the USA for instance in relation to the basis of the Declaration of Independence from England, or to clarify the relationship between the state and the *Native Americans*.

Self-determination and the European Union

On the other hand many young states have originated out of struggles for the right to self-determination. In these states the focus is not so much on the aims of the state or the governmental system but rather on issues of state sovereignty, state identity and loyalty to the state. In the member states of the European Union attention is focussed on the essence and definition of the state. For these countries it is critical to know whether the singularity of statehood and sovereignty has already been de facto transferred to the European Union. It already appears as though the member states are no longer states in the usual sense, and that they have lost the attribute of absolute state sovereignty by virtue of their membership of the European Union.

State of modernity

The theory of state is also a theory of the state of modernity. The world of states is marked by the Enlightenment idea of the state being democratically legitimised by popular sovereignty and protecting human rights. The people, as individuals enjoying equal rights, legitimise the state of modernity. The modern state is a secularised state that is no longer dependent on the 'grace of God'. However various religious communities are calling the secular nature of the state into question.

Eurocentric state theory?

Often the exposition of the general theory of state and constitutional theory has been limited to a study of the western European states, focusing principally on Germany, France and Italy.

This state theory aims to extend further: it seeks to understand the state as a universal phenomenon of the present time. Within a globalised world order, a theory of state based on Eurocentric cultural thinking is no longer appropriate or useful.

State theory: A child of our times?

General theories of state are – one may claim – more than other scientific disciplines *children of their times*. They are scarcely able to grasp or cover the 'nature' of the state in its full complexity. They try rather to pick up on the problems and questions facing the living generation and current era. In this sense also this state theory will concentrate on issues which concern and move the peoples of our times.

Justification of the state

We will focus first on the question of the *justification of the state*. Do we need the state, or is the state superfluous? Could we simply abandon the state? Then we shall deal with the questions of the *origin* and the *nature* of the state. Which attributes are necessary in order to label a community of humans as a sovereign state? Do the rights of people within a state precede the state, or are they granted by the state? Is state sovereignty the origin and source of all law or is sovereignty itself also constrained by and bound to comply with certain elementary legal principles? Do certain human communities that feel particularly strongly connected as an ethnic people or as a religious community for example, have the right to a special position within the state, or the right to establish their own state? Can the 'political' within the state be decentralised to specific sub-state-units, or are individuals with equal rights the only possible subjects of state sovereignty? Do minorities such as the French-speaking peoples in Canada have a right to a special status or even to unilateral *self-determination* and *secession*? What are the challenges facing those states that, due to immigration or other historical cause, have become multi-cultural states? How are states organised? Are polities without any separation of powers still states in the proper sense? What functions must the state perform? Should the state model itself on socialist China or on the model of the capitalist society? To what extent is the state the origin of the law and the legal order? Is law conceivable without the state?

Humans as subjects and objects of the state

A state is always a *community of men and women*. This human community will be the next subject of our analyses. How and why did it come into being? How has it developed? How can it be explained and justified? What relationship does it have to its individual members? What are its functions and its responsibilities? How can its power be limited? These questions are closely connected to the issue of human rights. Why and how did the idea of human rights develop? Tightly linked to human rights is the rule of law. Its historical development and also the development of the continental European idea of the state under law (*Rechtsstaat*) is subject of the fourth chapter.

State and mafia?

Out of the foregoing catalogue of questions arises another question: What is the *essence and nature* of the state? What conditions must be fulfilled in order to define a community of human beings as a state that can claim to be sovereign and to exert sovereign rights? What distinguishes a state-people from an ethnic people or an autochthonous minority, from aboriginal peoples or from nomads such as the Bedouins, the Tuareg or the Sinti and Roma? Do such minorities have a right of resistance when they are subjugated and systematically oppressed by state terror? How does the state differ from religious communities or international organisations? What are the preconditions and content of state sovereignty? Is sovereignty indivisible? Can political rights be divided and shared by different political communities? What differentiates the State from other groups of people such as the mafia, a terrorist organisation or a football club?

Governmental systems and state organisation

As soon as we know more about the nature of the state, we can begin to deal with its organisation and governmental system. How should democratic state power, which emanates from the people, be organised? How can democracy as majority rule be legitimised? How are modern states organised? How can the different forms of state organisation be distinguished from each other? What types of state organisation are there? According to what criteria are different forms of state organisation to be compared? Does the organisation of the state and the division of state power serve the legitimacy, efficiency or the strengthening of state power or is the goal of state organisation to limit the power of the majority? The seventh chapter deals apart from the established states of western tradition also with the organisation of the state *in transition.* Such states have essentially had to design new states from scratch. Thus in no other state is the close connection between state organisation and the legitimacy of the state so clearly apparent.

The challenge of multiculturality

Created by tradition and history or produced as a result of modern migration, multiculturality is the most difficult and threatening challenge to the state of today. In this sense the eighth chapter deals with the issue of federalism as one of the few state-concepts that has been able to find an answer to the challenge of multicultural diversity. As a case study for structural solutions the second part of this chapter deals with the federal design of Switzerland.

Symptoms and causes of state pathology

States were designed and created by people, and states must also serve the people. The structure and affairs of the state community are configured and handled by humans, with all of their good and bad qualities, their positive and negative behaviours and their human needs and interests. Every scientific examination of state phenomena must therefore proceed from the *specific nature of the human* being. Just as knowledge in relation to people is the concern of numerous scientific disciplines (medicine, psychology, anthropology, history, etc), the cooperation of several disciplines is also necessary to gain a closer understanding of the phenomenon of 'the state'. And just as medicine or psychology have to deal with both healthy and sick people, so the theory of state has to deal with the 'healthy' and 'ailing' state and seek to identify the symptoms and causes of the unhealthy state. This normative approach is, in addition to careful empirical research, an indispensable part of the theory of state.

Law and might

The tense relationship between *Law and Might* is well known. Throughout history it has marked controversies on the state. This theory of state will therefore deal extensively with these counterbalancing forces. Political ethics, concepts of justice, reason and the human capacity for knowledge will also be analysed alongside the examination of power, its origin and its goals, its misuse and limits.

Historical nature of states

All states are *historically* developed constructs. Their organisation and structure can only be understood in the context of their historical development. The observation of a specific historical moment does not suffice to explain and understand the state of today. Every theory, idea, institution and governmental system has its own history. We shall try to include this historical dimension and take it into account as far as possible. However not only history but also the specific character of a people (*Volkscharakter*), religion, geographic position, economic and social development have contributed to shaping individual states. These interactions will also be taken into account.

Questions never have a final answer. They can only be replaced by new questions. Hence this theory of state will not provide exhaustive answers, but rather pose new questions and raise new issues for consideration.

2 From the Tribe to the State in a Globalised Environment

2.1 The Origin of the State Community

2.1.1 The Human Need to Build Communities

Legitimacy with regard to the common people

If one was to ask the so-called 'man in the street', why he pays taxes to the state, one would probably receive the following answers: "Because I have to pay them" – "Because everybody has to pay taxes" – "Because, if I don't pay, the state will force me to pay". If we are not satisfied with these arguments and ask from where does the state acquire the right to demand tax contributions from its citizens, the answer may well be: The Government, the Parliament or the People gave such entitlement to the state, or that the state needs money and it has to get this money from somewhere. If we are still not satisfied and ask how is it that the Government, the Parliament or the majority of the voters (say, 51%) can have the right, against the will of the minority (say, 49%) to decide that taxes will be collected even from those who did not agree with the decision, our interlocutor might feel stumped for answer. Or he might reply that it has simply always been so, or that the constitution gives the Government, Parliament or the majority of the voters the power to compel the minority to pay taxes against their will.

One may ask why the answers of the average 'man in the street' are at all relevant in this context. When we proceed from the starting point that the modern state ultimately requires democratic legitimacy and that every state legal order must have a certain level of acceptance by the population, then of course the opinion of each citizen becomes relevant as the legitimacy of the state legal order derives from the citizens. It is important however to get to the bottom of such answers and to ask which philosophical justification for the state power of compulsion underlies the answers, in order to recognise the fundamental significance that the answers of the average person may have.

Legality – legitimacy

The opinion that the Government has had always this right is certainly inaccurate because 'the Government' has not always existed. It was created at a particular point in time, whether after a revolution, a war or an annexation with the support of foreign power or by a more or less legitimate decision of the people. If one goes back through the succession of different forms of government all the way to the first creation of the state one will always find that the formation of the state, constitution or government has a revolutionary origin, because it could not be formally or legally based on any pre-existing law or constitution. Some such revolutionary transformations may have been legitimate because they were supported by a significant majority of the people. However because of the legal vacuum that preceded them, they are not legal as neither the procedure nor the content of government could be deduced in accordance with existing law.

The Big Bang: Constituent power (pouvoir constituant)

The agent or force that achieves, by revolutionary act, a completely new state constitution that is not derived from an earlier constitution, is known as the *pouvoir constituant*. The *pouvoir constituant* – that is, the constituent power – is considered by many to be the 'Big Bang' of state sovereignty from which all later state decisions are legally derived.

Legitimacy of the Big Bang

But from where does the *pouvoir constituant* derive the power to provide a new constitution for the state and the people? When THOMAS JEFFERSON in June/July 1776 drafted the US Declaration of Independence he certainly was aware of the fact that separation from the English motherland and the foundation of a new state could not be justified only on the grounds that the United Kingdom was exploiting and terrorising the American people. He needed in addition to prove that the people of America had an original pre-existing *right* to create its own government and its own independently constituted state. In this task Jefferson was concerned only with the status of the Colonies relative to the Kingdom, but left open the question of the extent to which the Colonies had the right to make decisions affecting the native Americans.

On what basis can the first establishment of a government or the decision on the procedure for adopting a first constitution be supported? Where for example did the founding fathers of the American Confederation get the authority to legitimise the member states of the confederation by endowing them with their own constitutions? Why was the Diet (parliament) of the Swiss Confederation in 1848 able, in contravention of the treaty of the confederation, to submit to the people and the cantons a new draft constitution? From where can the French-speaking majority of Quebec derive its claim of entitlement, against the majority of the Canadian people or the majority of native Canadians, to unilaterally establish a new sovereign state?

How can the unique constitution-making procedure in South Africa be justified? There, the illegitimate but legal Apartheid Parliament formally initiated the procedure for the creation of a new constitution. The procedure involved a committee comprised of representatives from key political groups (without direct democratic legitimacy). This committee proposed a two-stage procedure: First the committee had to agree on the key principles to be included in the new constitution, and an interim constitution containing these principles had to be enacted. Second, based on this interim constitution, a new constitution-making assembly was elected to establish a new constitution. The Constitutional Court was required to certify that the new constitution was consistent with the key principles agreed to at the beginning of the process.

From where do constitution-makers derive their legitimacy for the drafting of a new constitution? This fundamental question has many different answers. Some claim that the requirement for legitimacy is satisfied by the fact that the supporters of the new government are stronger than their adversaries. They already had de facto power and based on this power the new government had the title to enact new laws. In other words: power legitimises the law. Others in turn may be of the opinion that the people, based on the natural law right of all peoples to self-determination, has the right to give itself a new constitution and thus a new governmental system, if approved by the majority of the people, and that the majority thereby always has the right to impose its will on the minority. This is a corollary of the democratic principle. Others however would object that even the majority is subject to the rule of law and must comply with basic legal principles and therefore cannot interfere with the inalienable rights of minorities. The first revolutionary state act therefore does *not* constitute a Big Bang from which all laws are derived. Even the *pouvoir constituant* is bound by fundamental legal principles. All revolutionary movements would – as THOMAS JEFFERSON noted – claim to derive their legitimacy from the injustice they have suffered and thereby claim the authority to establish and enact a new constitution. Thus when revolutions base their legitimacy on overarching legal principles, they cannot themselves violate those principles.

Legitimacy superior to the law

Within the monarchies of the Middle Ages however the answer would have been different: The monarch has the power to govern by virtue of the grace of God. As the monarch according to this understanding of the pre-modern state stands above the law, he or she can change the law and the constitution at any time, without a revolutionary act. A similar argument for the legitimacy of absolute power can also be found in states in which either one party, one nationalist ideology or a single religion declares itself to be superior to the law and the constitution.

Legitimacy of the state entity

Some peoples seek to derive their legitimacy as a people or as a state unit from the claim that they are God's chosen people and thus have the title to build their own state. The Jewish people considers itself to be chosen, as does the Singhalese people in Sri Lanka and the Japanese people which is held together by Teno the son of God.

A small minority of those questioned will however deny any right of existence to the state at all. Their arguments will be as follows: given that state power is bad in itself, and as the democratic majority does not have the right to enforce decisions on the minority, and given that in the free market system the 'invisible hand' is best able to ensure equity and justice, the state should be abolished or at least reduced to the absolute minimum and mankind liberated as much as possible from the authoritarian rule of the state.

Thus we can see that state authority can be justified by theology (from the grace of God), by anthropological-philosophical arguments (man has inalienable rights), by legal philosophy (man should not be ruled by man but by law, in the sense of the rule of law), by sociology (power justifies law) and by anthropology (man is political by nature). Those who explore the different theories which regard the state as necessary and which therefore also justify its authority, will find that such theories almost always fall back on the real or imagined history of mankind. For these theories the evidence that state authority is indispensable is to be found in the fact that throughout the history of mankind all societies have developed supra-familial political communities with the power to rule over members of the community. History is therefore the proof that states as supra-familial communities are necessary.

Does history create legitimacy?

In some theories on state authority, it can be difficult to separate fiction from historical fact. Some exponents of contract theories such as THOMAS HOBBES and ROUSSEAU do not assert that the people of the original society literally concluded a social contract with each other by which they transferred certain governing powers to the monarch. For these scholars the social contract is rather a theoretical fiction, a legal precondition or as HANS KELSEN puts it a 'basic norm' (*Grundnorm*) from which additional rules of state authority can be deduced. This fictitious presupposition of free contractual agreement for the building of a polity and for the transfer of power to rule thus provides the justification or legitimacy for state authority. Other exponents of contract theory on the other hand, such as JOHN LOCKE, are of the opinion that people in primitive times literally concluded a first contract in order to set up a polity, and with a second contract transferred limited authority to the rulers. As one can see, it can be difficult to separate historical facts and fiction. Those who see the state as an essential and immanent institution and corollary of human nature will try to prove that the state has always been a historically significant institution.

Myth as history

Almost all cultures have derived from old legends or other traditions a more or less set idea of the way in which the state community was formed. These legends and customs are remarkably similar across different cultures and continents. Thus instead of going down the usual track to ancient Greek history or the ancient times of the German tribes we will turn to the ancient Chinese state theory in order to demonstrate that the same basic questions with regard to state development were asked in earlier times and in other cultures, and that they were answered in a very similar fashion.

The original society in the Chinese tradition

With regard to the starting point of the development of the state, or the 'original condition' of human society, there are two entirely opposite theories. One theory purports that the original condition was chaos and that indiscriminate conflict threatened the survival of mankind (HOBBES; SHANG KUN SHU, cf. GENG WU, p. 49). The other theory claims that in the original state of nature mankind lived in peace and harmony, (ROUSSEAU, LOCKE, LAO TSE, MARSILIUS V. PADUA, KARL MARX) and that people should be able to return to this state of nature (MARX, LAO TSE).

Han Fei

The Chinese philosopher HAN FEI, who has often been called the MACHIAVELLI of ancient Chinese philosophy, gives us the following description of conditions in the primitive society: "In ancient times men did not need to cultivate the fields. They had enough fruit and seeds to eat. The women did not need to weave, as there were enough animal furs for clothing. Nobody had to make an effort to gather food, because the number of people was small and food was available in abundance. There was no conflict among the peoples, and measures such as punishments and rewards were not yet known. Peace and order reigned everywhere" (GENG WU, p. 50). The original state of nature was according to this description a peaceful anarchy. How could political state authority develop out of this chaotic natural state? According to many old legends of the ancient civilisations of Greece, Babylon and also of China, human beings started to feel insecure and threatened by their environment. Finally a '*gifted one*' came and showed people for example how they could protect themselves against wild animals. "Then however a great and holy man appeared and plaited branches of trees to make a nest in which he was able to escape many dangers. The people was so happy with him that it made him a king" (HAN FEI, Chap. 49 (WU TU), quoted from: W. EICHHORN, *Kulturgeschichte Chinas*, Stuttgart 1964, p. 11, translated from German by the authors). The bases of authority according to HAN FEI are thus the talent, the capacity and the quality of the ruler. The charisma of the good leader is the origin of state power.

Kuan Tze

A contrasting account can be found in the Chinese 'legalist' text of KUAN TZE. According to this author, the original state of society is war: "Then the wise man appeared and, supported by masses of the people, issued orders to prevent brutal battles, so that the perpetrators of violence had to go into hiding. The wise man was committed to acting for the advantage of the people. He taught the people virtues and was accepted by the people as their ruler. Virtue and ethical norms were created by the wise man. Because virtue and ethics were based on reason the people adopted and followed them voluntarily. The wise man decided upon right and wrong. He applied punishments and rewards. He appointed people to different levels of seniority, and the people arranged themselves in accordance with this hierarchy. Thus the state was founded" (KUAN TZE, Chapter II, para 37, quoted in: GENG WU, p. 52, translated from German by the authors).

The state: A bulwark against external dangers

According to the theories of the ancient school of the Chinese legalists, the state – that is in this context, the power of the king – developed only gradually. As long as each person could fend for and feed himself, a state polity was not necessary. However the protection against external dangers such as those posed by war, wild animals or natural disaster, forced people to undertake collective measures. The people transferred power to the most intelligent, strongest, most capable and chose them to be Kings. Authority emerged out of the needs of the society whose existence was threatened. Monarchy was not a divine institution. The monarch was empowered by the people. People did nevertheless believe that the king was superior to everyone else based on his supernatural abilities, which is why he had the capacity and also the legitimacy to lead the people. It was probably not until later that the authority of the ruler acquired a patriarchal note. "Under this sky there is nothing that does not belong to the King. Nobody who lives on this earth is not a subject of our King" (saying at the time of the Chou Dynasty (GENG WU, p. 53)).

Difference with regard to European constitutionalism

In both cases it is noteworthy that even the ancient Chinese theory of state obviously proceeded from a fiction or speculation about the state of society within even earlier times, in order to draw lessons and conclusions for the modern theory of state. In doing so, the Chinese theory of state – just like the much later European Enlightenment theory of state – had as a starting point one of two opposing images of the original state of nature: either the period of *paradise* or the the period of *conflict and anarchy*. However the conclusions which HAN FEI and other philosophers drew from these speculated states of society differ considerably from the conclusions drawn by the philosophers of European constitutionalism from the same historical scenarios. For the Chinese philosophers the state of nature served to prove that the good, wise and capable ruler is needed. The philosophers of the Enlightenment used the fictive state of nature in order to rationalise the secularisation of state authority, and then to answer the question whether the authority of the state is unlimited or has to be limited. However they did not touch upon the issue of who should be the ruler. The answer to this question was left to Marxist theory. The secularisation of state authority was not an issue for Chinese state theory. In China the authority of the ruler was based on a philosophical world view, but not on a religion, and did not rely for legitimacy upon the 'grace of God'.

The need for an order superior to the family

The need for an esteemed and capable King for the protection of the tribe was apparently also in other societies one of the main reasons for the establishment of the first communities with centralised political power. The great Arabic statesman and thinker IBN KHALDÛN (1332–1406) saw this as the origin of state building. "When men achieve a certain level of organisation in their society .... they need somebody who can hold them back, dampen their desire to fight and protect them from each other; because aggression and injustice are part of human nature" (IBN KHALDÛN, p. 47). However for IBN KHALDÛN, it was not external threats but rather the internal conflicts in societies that had descended into anarchy which drove people to build supra-familial political state structures. Because, similarly to HOBBES, he saw human beings as aggressive and prone to conflict, he believed they needed strong leadership to maintain order in society.

Undoubtedly, state institutions within the different archaic societies developed differently (E. A. HOEBBEL, p. 289). Nevertheless it is possible to detect some common basic tendencies in the early development of these institutions: State-like constructs with independent institutions and centralised power, with their own jurisdiction and generally applicable norms, only arise in complex and developed societies marked by a *division of labour*. At the level of the hunter-gatherer society, which is marked by the strong economic and social autonomy of the family unit, such institutions are not needed. It is only upon the development towards the extended family, the kinship group and the tribe that the need for authoritative and long lasting leadership becomes apparent. At the former level the problems of living together were primarily resolved within the family, either by the father in a patriarchy or the mother in a matriarchal society (the people of the Tuareg), or sometimes by a council of elders. Supra-familial structures first became necessary when there was greater contact and division of labour between families and tribes (cf. MARSILIUS OF PADUA, part 1, chapter III).

Shelter from external threats

Supra-familial institutions develop primarily when a society due to its economic development has achieved a certain level of division of labour, when a society needs to protect itself against external threats, and when the traditional customary law is no longer sufficient to guarantee internal security and order. An additional condition, which was highlighted by IBN KHALDÛN, is a strong *feeling of togetherness* amongst the group. Without a basic preparedness for solidarity, there will be no foundation upon which to build political institutions.

Centralised institutions initially are almost always created through democratic or at least some form of oligarchic self-determination. The appropriate representatives of the tribe or the group democratically elect the ruler whom they feel should be recognised and followed. Very often the ruler – particularly in African tribes – is surrounded by a council of elders (oligarchic), which advises him and should also prevent the misuse of power (R. SCHOTT, 'Das Recht gegen das Gesetz' in *Recht und Gesellschaft*, Festschrift Schelsky, Berlin 1978, p. 605 ff).

Master of the tribe

The group expects the head of the tribe, the king or prince to exercise leadership in the common interest of the entire tribe or community. He should govern justly and strive to ensure that the cohesiveness and sense of belonging in the community is sustained and strengthened. It is however for the ruler alone to decide what is in the interest of the tribe, which decisions are just and what he can do to contribute to the welfare of the tribe. Thus the person who will be chosen as leader is the one who can demonstrate particular skilfulness, dedication, wisdom and/or strength. If the leader however succeeds in establishing an obedient army for campaigns and conquests, he can also use this army to enforce his orders and strengthen his internal power and to demand absolute loyalty from his subjects by force.

Feudalism

With such an army the conditions are set for a feudalistic and patriarchal system of leadership. The feudal master tries to support his authority by divine law, for example by claiming that God gave him the power to rule, and that he exercises the power in the name of God. He attempts thereby to become untouchable, that is - to be above the laws which he creates, and to be able to change such laws at whim with regard to his subjects. In addition he tries to extend his privileges to his family – by introducing hereditary succession – and to his court. The maintenance of the army is guaranteed by taxes. He distributes estates to his favourites who help him to control the people and to collect taxes. The more serious the inequality and the misuse of power, the more quickly he and his inner circle will be removed from power by other tribes or groups.

Zoon Politikon

There is another aspect of human nature that effects the creation of state institutions: Whoever reads ancient history will recognise the profound truth in the statement of ARISTOTLE (384–322 B.C.) that the human being is by nature a *Σοοη Πολίτίκοη* - that is, a creature which is made for supra-familial, political communities. According to ARISTOTLE human beings are not isolated individual creatures. They exist rather - whether it be as children, fathers, mothers, slaves etc - as part of a given social structure. *Man therefore cannot survive as an individual alone*, but only as part of a community within which he/she has certain tasks to fulfil (ARISTOTLE, book I, 1253a and book III). IBN KHALDÛN and the ancient Chinese theory of state also point out the need of human beings to live within a community. Human beings are threatened by the dangers of nature. They cannot feed themselves all the way into old age, nor perform all tasks themselves, whether it be hunting or collecting plants, making tools or developing all the necessary skills for such tasks. Human beings are dependent upon a community structured by the division of labour. Man's sexual drive leads to the creation of communities with people of the opposite sex, which he needs to find outside of the family or even the tribe, because of the taboo against incest. People also develop supra-familial connections through commerce and trade. In addition, the need for security from hostile tribes and threats of nature, as well as the need for social interaction and common festivities such as religious celebrations, contribute to the development early communities.

Worship of ancestors

In almost all archaic societies the worship of ancestors contributes decisively to the creation of new institutions of political authority. For example in ancient China, ancient Rome and in African tribes ancestor-worship is closely connected to the standing of a family within the social hierarchy. The authority to enforce customary law is also strongly anchored in the ritual of ancestor-worship. If a member of the group fails to comply with the laws of the tribe, they will be punished by the ancestors. Witchcraft, sorcery and religion also have their roots in the worship of ancestors. Common to all these phenomena is that they serve to enable the ruler to reinforce his authority and to guard against internal unrest.

2.1.2 The State of the Modern Civil Society – a Supra-Familial State?

The political community

The modern rational state is – in contrast to the family established by nature – an artificial polity created by political will. It is the only social entity with a legitimate claim to unlimited authority over its own people including the *monopoly on the use of force*. Unlike the natural community of the family, the ideology of authority of the modern state is not based on nature and the social tradition of a predetermined community but on rational *reflection and choice*.

The modern polity shaped by rationalism and individualism developed slowly over a long period. This development occurred through the gradual transition from the extended family to the larger clan, then on to the construction of new supra-familial polities composed of individual citizens, for example as political members of the French nation in the sense portrayed by ROUSSEAU or SIÉYÈS.

From the kin-group to the small family

The function of the family as an economic, productive and existential unit has changed over the course of history, and the development of the welfare-state has seen the state assigned with many new functions which were originally within the responsibility of the family. The self-sufficient extended family was not only an emotional but also an economic and productive community. It was to a large extent economically self-sufficient, and therefore had considerable autonomy. The comprehensive functions of the extended family or clan, which was responsible for the existence, survival and welfare of its members, have been radically reduced over time, primarily as a result of the growing interdependence of society in the industrial and technological age.

Today the small nuclear family is primarily an emotional unit and continues to some extent to fulfil an educative function. However the family's role as a productive and economic unit has been taken over by the state and its social agencies. The economic activity of family members takes place outside the family, whilst state institutions provide for social welfare and for the education of children.

The association of citizens ('citoyens')

The political association of citizens was originally made up of autonomous male property owners. 'Autonomy' was therefore primarily the right to use, acquire and alienate property. Property rights were seen as the starting point which entitled a citizen to all other liberties, whereas today the basis for all rights and freedoms is human dignity which should be granted to every human being regardless of wealth or social position. The modern industrial society however made every individual independent. The state extended the concept of citizenship, which was originally confined to male property owners, to all members of the national community living within the territory of the state. The single individual replaced the family collective that had been represented by the male property owner, and the individual became the counterbalancing pole to the state polity. The civil society of free individuals, which did not recognise collective rights, replaced the structured feudal hierarchy of the Middle Ages. The original unity and self-sufficiency of the family as an economic and productive unit was subsumed by the state and its society.

Community of competitors and community of taxpayers

Consequently, wealth is no longer distributed according to the function and position of families. The just distribution of wealth is supposed to be ensured either by free market competition or by the state taxation system. The free market should guarantee a just distribution of wealth, if one assumes that the *invisible hand* distributes wealth on the basis of performance, that the state will prevent the degeneration of free competition into anarchy or monopolies, and that everyone has the equal opportunity to participate. The state has to provide for law and order so as to protect the free market from abuse and criminality, and enable the market to develop. The democratically legitimated welfare of the people however should be guaranteed by the just distribution of those benefits that are excluded from the free market such as public education, health care, etc. It is up to the state and in particular the state taxation system to ensure this democratic distribution.

Integration of the modern citizen within a complex network

The modern human being is tied emotionally to the family (understood in the broadest sense as a place of emotional security). Aside from this he/she is also a consumer, tenant, employee, member of a social security system and a citizen. He/she participates in the state as a taxpayer, voter and contributor to social security or superannuation, but also as a pupil, student, pensioner and in some instances as a soldier or as a taxpayer for defence. Moreover, as a consumer, tenant, employee, road-user, and as a user of energy and the environment, he/she is also integrated within the society.

Interdependence of society

The need of human beings as *zoon politikon* for social integration and mobility has led to the ever-increasing interdependence of society. This interdependence requires a rational political administration which is either steered by the democratic majority in accordance with acceptable and legitimate criteria of justice or is provided by the cost-benefit driven free market society, in which order is determined by the 'invisible hand' of the free market.

Reason and emotion

Reality shows however that people's emotional ties and needs are not confined only to the family. The human self cannot be divided into three separate dimensions: the rational citizen of the state, the cost-benefit driven consumer of the competitive market-based society, and the emotional family member. The complex nature of the human being causes it to search beyond the family for emotional ties and loyalty. The need of human beings for absolute and unquestionable values underlies the development of emotional, fundamentalist nationalisms, sects and religious communities. Such groups may seek to defend their values by enlisting or commandeering the modern rational state for their own purposes or by fighting against the state which rejects their claims.

Is the state a rational but also partially natural community that is tied together by birth, tradition and beliefs? Or does the state have to separate itself from naturally occurring communities to become a strictly rational political community with a universal claim (e.g. France) to which each individual can choose to subscribe based on his/her *reflection and choice*?

Absolute loyalty

Ethnic communities require undivided loyalty from their members. They claim to enjoy a 'natural right' to self-determination and to their own statehood and at the same time refuse to recognise the legitimacy and authority of the existing state. Ethnic minorities disclaim state decisions and withhold their loyalty and participation. The existing nation-state on the other hand serves its majority ethnicity, legitimises the ethnic homogenisation of the territory and oppresses minorities with state terror, violation of human rights, racist nationalistic discrimination as well as expulsion. Through such measures ethnic states manage to rule the emotions of the majority.

These new supra-familial artificially constructed communities which require total loyalty result, when they represent the majority, in a charismatic totalitarian state. When such a community is in the minority, it fights for its own state within the state. In both cases the rational legitimacy of the constitutional state is replaced by the charismatic emotional ties which require total identification with and loyalty to the religious, language or cultural community.

The original family requires total loyalty from its members. 'Dissidents' may be disowned or banished. Family feuds, intra-tribal punishments and extra-tribal revenge, and total dependence on the family are known forms of such absolutism which have come to be regulated by the state though family law, and laws on inheritance, guardianship and social security. Can the state now as a rational over-arching community require the same unconditional loyalty of the citizens that have entrusted their fate to the state?

Multiculturality

One must in the end also ask the question whether the state really is just a community of citizens founded on reason. Multicultural states such as the 'melting pot' of the United States, the diverse federation of Switzerland, or the kemalist ideology of Ataturk-based republican Turkey, have created strongly emotionalised myths from their original state rationale, which serve to reinforce the composition of the community and help to hold the multicultural society together.

Legitimacy over human beings and over territories

Who belongs to the society of citizens? Does the human individual really become part of the modern polity by reflection and choice? Or do myths, symbols, religious beliefs or charismatic tradition in fact take the place of rationality in many communities? The external geographic and territorial conditions of many Western European states have been shaped by violent conflicts, wars, coups and revolutions as well as by totalitarian rulers or monarchs. Even after the revolutions that gave birth to popular sovereignty, some western democracies of Europe maintained the original borders of their former monarchies. Overseas however these same states, committed to their missionary ideas of cultural, intellectual and religious superiority, extended their colonial territories and shifted borders according to their needs and interests without questioning the legitimacy of their claim to power with regard to the indigenous populations living in these territories.

Peoples without a territory

Ultimately unsolved are the traditional state rules for communities of peoples which do not have their own territory or do not wish to be confined to a specific territory, such as the Sinti and Roma, the Tuareg or the Bedouins. Such peoples have scant opportunity to find their place in the modern jacobinist social and state order, although it seems there is no alternative but for them to attempt to find a way to integrate themselves within this order. On the other hand there are peoples such as the Aborigines in Australia whose legal culture is not at all influenced by the legal culture of Roman law which declares that people and states can exercise dominion over territory. According to their understanding, territory does not belong to people, but rather people belong to territory. The peoples are the property of the soil in which they have their roots. Their land is part of their human existence. If it is 'violated', for instance for the exploitation of mineral resources, the people feels that it's very right to existence has been threatened.

States are not islands of sovereignty

In reality the state can only be a rational community established by reflection and choice when it possesses a limited claim to power and authority. Only the concept of a sovereignty limited by inalienable rights can be the legitimate basis of the rational state. This means in other words that neither a majority nor a minority can legitimately claim a sovereign entitlement to enforce their ethnic interests to the detriment of the inalienable rights of the other. States are not impermeable islands of sovereignty, just as families cannot be isolated units within the society. States are part of the community of peoples that are jointly responsible for the survival of mankind. They bear responsibility for the environment of the next generation. Within this world community, states can only carry a limited mandate and must also carry the obligation to care for the wellbeing of all people within their territory, whether they be citizens, visitors, foreign workers, asylum seekers or refugees.

A new concept of the state with limited sovereignty

As long as states are able to claim total legitimacy and a monopoly on the use of force, all communities which feel threatened by their minorities or which as minorities want their claims to be recognised, will use their statehood or their demand for statehood to pursue their own ends. Only a state concept with a limited understanding of sovereignty which also places tight limits on the monopoly on the use of force will be able to avoid a situation whereby ethnic majorities or minorities will regard exclusive statehood for their ethnic group (at any cost) as their only option.

2.1.3 Conclusion

Dilemma of the state of modernity

The state has thus developed as a rational association of people that sits above the family. History proves however that the family cannot be understood only as a community held together by emotions, and nor can the state be reduced to a supra-familial construct based purely on reason. Social reality reveals that the family is certainly not the only human community that is bound together by emotions. Emotion also plays a role in religious communities, language groups and cultural associations. So too the state is very rarely a political community founded on reason alone. This complexity of today's reality has not been taken fully into account by the modern theory of state. For this reason we are today confronted with the unrealistic idea of the purely rational force-monopolising state in which sovereignty and 'the political' must be centralised. This perspective strips all other groups and communities such as language or religious communities but also federal units of their part in 'the political' and the rational. The state is not the only political entity which is composed of a group of individuals that share equal rights and, with regard to the constitution, common ideas and understandings.

The quest for a new understanding of the state

For this reason the state needs to grant political rights to other communities. It has to accept that it does not have a monopoly on sovereignty or 'the political'. In other words the post-modern state will have to surrender the notion of sovereignty as a quality vested only in the state. It has to find ways to enable other reason- and/or emotion-based communities to fulfil political tasks in areas such as culture, education and information or even in fields like health, policing and social affairs.

This however posits a new and different understanding of the state. Sovereignty can no longer be seen as absolute and indivisible. Sovereignty is rather to be understood as a limited and thereby also divisible value. Accordingly, the state no longer has unrestricted authority over the lives of its subjects. It is embedded within a globalised whole and confronted with the multiple loyalties of its citizens. Within this framework the state has certain functions to perform with regard to security, police, maintenance of order, infrastructure and social services – but can also delegate some of these tasks to other national or international groups.

2.2 Stages of Development of the Community of States

2.2.1 Introduction

We have seen that the state is an artificial community built by human reflection and choice. This raises three questions which are of crucial importance for the understanding of the state and which require closer examination:

- Why were human beings, in contrast to animals, able to create and live within artificial communities?

- What were the reasons and motives that led human beings, beyond their natural family unit, to create particular supra-familial communities and to move away from other particular forms of community?
- What were the reasons for which human beings were prepared to renounce part of their independence and individuality – even to sacrifice their lives – in order to join such communities?

These three questions will be discussed in the following sections and analysed from the perspectives of various theories.

2.2.2 Human Language as the Precondition for State-Building

Robinson Crusoe

We shall in the following sections of this theory of state often refer to DANIEL DEFOE (1659–1731) and his story of Robinson Crusoe and Friday. This story was written during the Enlightenment period. It is an impressive depiction of the self-assuredness with which the European colonial powers considered all members of their culture and of the Christian religion as superior beings called upon to colonise the world. The example of Robinson on his lonely island makes clear the way people at the time of the Enlightenment felt within a – albeit artificial – primitive society and to the extent to which they were dependent on abstract rules in order to survive as a community.

When Robinson found shelter on his lonesome island this could of course not be called a state. Initially he felt completely lost and alone, and had no contact with the natives, whom he discovered much later. With the animals that he domesticated he could not build a state, as a state requires a community of reasonable beings that depend on each other and feel a sense of belonging to a community. Such sentiments, judgments and assessments which form the bases of an artificially constructed society are only possible when the living beings involved in the community can communicate with abstract norms such as "We need to cooperate in order to survive", "You have to obey me", "I can command you", or "You have to inform me". Such abstract notions however can only be transmitted by language. Language is thus the most essential condition for the creation of artificial communities.

Human capacity for language and communication

Without language a state, that is – a supra-familial community that is committed to common values – is unthinkable. Language enables people to understand and deliberate on abstract norms, and to grapple with and seek to reach agreement on common values such as the value of national unity and the value of liberty and democracy. Only through language can the foundations of a polity based on the solidarity of its members be formulated and arranged. With the help of language, conflicts between people can be rationally discussed and settled. Only language enables the formulation of abstract rules such as we find in constitutions and laws.

Values formulated by language

Even the most basic ideas on values and prohibitions such as the prohibition of incest are only conceivable when somebody can understand concepts such as mother, daughter, husband, wife, sister, brother, uncle, aunt, and in addition has the capacity to apply such abstract notions to concrete situations. The worship of ancestors that was so important for the development of the Chinese social structure, and the obligations that a man and woman and their relatives take on through marriage, are further examples of values that are premised upon the ability to communicate thoughts by language, to think abstractly, to make judgments and to make decisions and take action accordingly.

Only Homo sapiens can establish a polity

Only through language is it possible to establish and foster the common interest within a society, and only through language can the members of a society be persuaded to subordinate their interests to the common good. "And it is a characteristic of man that he alone has any sense of good and evil, of just and unjust, and the like, and the association of living beings who have this sense makes a family and a state" (ARISTOTLE, Book I, 1253 a). And the tool at man's disposal that enables him to do this is language.

Animals therefore cannot build a 'State'. One sometimes hears the expression a 'colony of termites' or 'society of termites'. But this is by no means a reference to an artificially constructed community such as a reflection and choice-based state with its own decision-making institutions. Termites are programmed to form a society, but they cannot alter its structure or design, nor can they decide on its geographical boundaries or even decide whether or not they wish to belong to the society.

Thus, the state is an order constructed by human beings and focussed on human beings. It is premised upon the capacity to communicate through language and the ability to make decisions.

Plurality of human beings who are able to communicate

Robinson thus could not found a state community on his island, neither with the animals nor with the natives of whose existence he was unaware. His isolation made any attempt to build a state impossible.

This situation changed decisively from the moment Friday appeared on the island. The two men had to develop and agree upon certain basic ground rules in order to live together. Either on the basis of an equal partnership or a hierarchical arrangement, they would find a way to cope with their fate and survive together.

2.2.3 *Division of Labour as Condition for Building a State Community*

Need for protection

However, in order for human beings to join together to establish a supra-familial community they need not only the capacity but also the preparedness to accept and obey the rules of this new community. They will only be ready to take this step when they are convinced that as single individuals or families they cannot survive without an artificially created supra-familial polity. Human beings must therefore have an innate existential need to create supra-familial political communities. As we have already seen, according to many philosophers of ancient China as well as the European Enlightenment, humans are by nature dependent on the state as the instrument of order, because they need an authority over and above the family or the tribe that can safeguard them from external and internal dangers. This protection however only first becomes necessary when human beings live together in close proximity within a particular territory.

If we want to know why human beings need the state as an order of authority it is just as important to explore why humans join together in ever-larger communities. Why are humans not content to live isolated within the natural community of the family? Why do they choose to form and live within larger communities beyond the family? As we will see in the following sections, human beings by nature have the need for an ever-increasing division of labour. According to ARISTOTLE humans are community driven creatures because they cannot survive simply as isolated individuals or families.

This is demonstrated on Robinson's lonely island. As soon as Friday arrives on the scene, the need arises for the two strangers either to fight against each other or to try to work together on a strategy for survival. Finding themselves in peril, both men together try to meet the challenge of their fate. It is this *existential emergency – of having to try to survive on the island – which forces them to build a community*. The first step in order to survive on the island is to overcome the basic problems of communication by trying to find a common language. Their common fate requires solidarity, mutual trust and the readiness to accept certain common goals in the overriding interest of survival.

Division of labour

Very soon Robinson and Friday agree upon a *certain division of labour*: One goes hunting while the other keeps a lookout; one cultivates the soil, the other builds the hut; one looks after the fire, the other prepares the meals. Each man works at the same time for himself and for the other. Such a society based on division of labour however requires that each member can rely on the other. This is only possible on the basis of mutual trust. Had they not been able to trust each other, each of them would have had to guard, hunt, cultivate and prepare the dinner for himself. Division of labour reduces the burden of both men, and gives each of them the chance to focus on the tasks to which his abilities are best suited, thereby serving the common interest of both. In this way they both have a better chance of warding off potential dangers.

Diversity in aptitude and inclination

Thus it is their different abilities and interests, their need for community and their common fate that bring these two men together. The first human communities probably developed in a very similar way. However we must not overlook the fact that DANIEL DEFOE'S 17th Century novel, written in the spirit of the Enlightenment, tells the story of a *purely male society*, when in reality, the *relationship of the two genders to each other* was of great significance for the development of the first political communities. This relationship however is based less on a rational and consciously experienced common fate and more on the natural drive for reproduction and self-preservation as well as on the emotional bond between the sexes. In this respect the prohibition of incest helped to lead to the creation of communities, as relationships had to develop between different families.

Certainly the *extended family* can almost everywhere be identified as the origin of the communal life of human beings, from which supra-familial and thus political organisation gradually developed – usually by the force of the strongest tribe. This is true not only of Japan, China and the African continent but also for Europe, Australia and South America (e.g. the empire of the Incas). The model for the design of the first concept of authority to rule was the authority of the mother or father or of the eldest in the extended family. They had legitimate authority because they were the closest to the ancestors. As within the family, the aim of members of the larger community was also to protect themselves from external dangers through cooperation and division of labour.

Worship of ancestors

From its earliest development, political authority was closely connected to religion, ancestor worship, magic and sorcery. The special bond between the eldest and the ancestors gave them wisdom, persuasiveness and legitimacy to impose rules on their 'subjects' and to decide on their conflicts. Rulers who cannot legitimise their authority by the natural hierarchy of age and ancestry need to try to establish their superiority and legitimacy on some other basis. It is a small step from the worship of ancestors to religion and from religion to the idea that rulers are the earthly representatives of God and therefore have the legitimate authority to rule over other people. Thus for centuries kings governed their kingdoms based on their entitlement either as representatives anointed by the grace of God or as direct descendants of God (such as Teno in Japan).

2.2.4 *The Stages of State Development*

2.2.4.1 Influence of the Social Environment

Economy and geography

If the fundamental thesis is correct that the division of labour facilitated the establishment of and influenced the structure of political communities, then the development of states must have occurred in various phases according to the intensity of the division of labour. As we have seen, the division of labour is a reflection of the level of economic development of a society. We can therefore observe different stages of political development according to the different stages of economic development.

Fernand Braudel

The stage of the economy had a decisive influence on the division of labour and on the political development of state institutions. As the French historian FERNAND BRAUDEL observes, the most important question in this regard was how much labour was required of human beings in order to ensure there was enough food for the survival of the society. If the work of a relatively small number of people could produce food for many, then other people could apply themselves to the institutional and cultural development of the community. Where the production of food required central coordination, such as irrigation for growing rice plantations, this led very early to the development of centralised forms of organisation. In places where people practiced agriculture such as in the middle of Europe, they needed to be able to grind the grain in mills close enough to be reached within a day. This led to the development of the small decentralised municipal structure in this area. Where people cultivated the soil by hand, their labour produced only enough to feed themselves, and perhaps some additional relatives. In these areas nobody had the time get involved in participatory and democratic institutions, let alone the time to conceive of and to establish such institutions. When people developed new techniques e.g. to cultivate soil using horses, the economic conditions for a new social order were fulfilled. This was the foundation for the later development of equal rights and prepared the groundwork for the further technical advancement of civilisation.

These rudimentary observations reveal the strong influence of geographic and economic conditions on the development of political and social institutions. They also demonstrate that modern information and communication technology such as the internet and electronic media are likely to have a profound influence on state and society in the future, although it is too early to know the nature and extent of that influence. The technical conditions now exist for universal engagement in direct participatory democracy, and thus for the limitation of the principle of representation by the parliament. Where will this lead us?

Open questions

Many questions however remain unanswered. Why did people in early Middle Ages decide to replace cheap slave labour with horses, which were considerably more expensive? Why did nations that had long been content to confine their travel only to their immediate coastlines, suddenly decide to travel across vast oceans to discover and colonise foreign lands? Does Christianity and its claim of universality provide a complete and satisfying answer to both questions? Certainly religions have influenced the political development of states just as economic, geographic and climactic factors have done. A clear answer to these questions could give us some hints as to what influence current social and technical developments may have on the future direction of politics and the state.

2.2.4.2 The First Attempts to Build Political Communities at the Time of Hunters and Gatherers

Council of elders

Even at the first stage of economic development, that is, at the level of the hunter-gatherer society, we can detect the earliest forms of supra-familial communities. Several families join together in groups and form a local village community or a group of nomads. Such groups are ruled by a master whose authority is recognised on the basis of his abilities. Often we can also find early forms of councils. As the eldest serve as the heads of their families and are released from daily work in the hut or fields, they are able consult with each other and advise on the affairs of the supra-familial community. This leads to the first development of democratic assemblies. The leaders or the council of elders must primarily provide for defence against external threats, resolve internal conflicts and punish members of the group who violate (unwritten) customary rules. From religious or moral convictions, ethical norms are gradually developed, from which in turn the first unwritten legal rules are devised. However in all other respects such groups have little in the way of formal structure. If the leader loses the acceptance of the community, another member of the group will assume his place.

Division of labour and defence

The size of a particular village community depends on the available food resources. If ample food is available, larger communities will develop. If food is scarce, extended families or clans will split up and settle either in the nearby area or further afield. Thus there is a gradual dispersal over a vast area of related members of a tribe with common customs and affinities.

A decisive factor for the establishment of the first large supra-familial groups was probably the need and desire of individuals and families to live in a community in which labour was divided, in order to protect themselves against external dangers and to facilitate the resolution of inter-family conflicts. These supra-familial groups did not initially have any concrete political institutions, but were largely anarchic.

2.2.4.3 The Planter and the Development of Territorial Communities

Land ownership and exchange of goods – foundation of the modern state

At the second stage of societal development peoples start to become settled and to regularly cultivate the land as planters. As they can produce enough food and have tools and instruments for cultivation at their disposal, the first territorial borders emerge. The regular cultivation of the same area leads to the first ideas of property (Dominion). The need to guard against foreign dangers creates the first ruling authority (Imperium). The first stable political structures arise.

The growing complexity of social relationships characterised by land ownership, division of labour and exchange of goods results in a greater feeling of dependence and need for protection and security of families. These factors were key to the development of political structures. This second stage of societal development can rightly be seen as the starting point of the development of the modern state.

Territorial authorities

In Christian Europe, the first concepts of state authority developed on the basis of such territorial ideas. Some measure of territorial separation of church and state authority developed through the claim of immunity of the church with regard to particular protected church territories. Borderlines were also drawn around small territorial and administrative units under royal authority. Interestingly, even at this early stage of societal development, a diverse range of political structures developed. While in some instances the seeds of absolutist despotism were sown, in other cases we can find the first signs of democratic development.

He who has gained power is never prepared to hand it back voluntarily

Once man has achieved power he strives to retain and expand his authority, and to pass it on to his descendants. Power should entail unlimited legitimacy, and should no longer be subject to the measure of quality, performance or justice. Rulers no longer want to be held to account, or to have their qualities and abilities subject to regular scrutiny. On the contrary, they require absolute obedience. Religion, magic and ancestor worship are the means by which they seek to legitimise their rule on the path to dictatorship.

Master of the family

As soon as the leadership of the ruler is assured, all manifestations of democracy – such as the council of elders – are eliminated and the *foundation for an increasingly centralised feudal authority is laid.* We can find such developments for example in ancient China, Egypt, India and Japan.

The institutions of political authority were initially limited to the roles of conflict mediation among family members and, in so far as there was no institutionalised system of revenge, also between the clans; administering customary law; and to protecting the tribe from external threats. However, the autonomy of the clans and families was still so considerable that they were often able to escape the influence of the ruler. It was the *head of the extended family that had total power over his relatives*. He could execute sanctions, including in some cases the death penalty, a power that was recognised in Roman law. The different family structures appear to have had a marked influence on the form and structure of supra-familial authority. ARISTOTLE for example compares the King with the good husband and father: " ... The rule of a father over his children is royal, for he rules by virtue both of love and of the respect due to age, exercising a kind of royal power. And therefore Homer has appropriately called Zeus 'father of Gods and men,' because he is the king of them all. For a king is the natural superior of his subjects, but he should be of the same kin or kind with them, and such is the relation of elder and younger, of father and son.." (ARISTOTLE, book I, 1259 a-b).

The development of ancient empires

When small tribes needed better protection against a strong enemy they sought shelter within a larger alliance or association of tribes. The structure of this bigger association could be very loose (e.g. the German empire in the Middle Ages). In many cases the princes of smaller communities were also able to attain power over the entire alliance and disempower the leaders of other tribes within the group (e.g. France and China). The displaced tribal masters were then often downgraded to servants of the crown. They lived in the court and supported the ruler when they had his favour and thus could profit from privileges granted by the ruler. Such favours and privileges could however only be granted when the ruler could collect enough tithes. In order to exact such contributions from the population he needed a loyal court to which he could delegate the tasks of collecting dues from the subjects. Court and king thus became interdependent, and for this farmers had to pay the price.

Economy of slavery

In other cases the stronger tribes tried to conquer new territories and subjugate other tribes. By this means, the feudal authority in some regions took on the form of slave master. The population of the conquered enemy were given or sold as slaves to the subjects in order to help them perform their duties. Within the tribe the master usually tried to single out his own family members and distinguish them from the rest of the subjects by bestowing honours upon them. These family members supported the leader and helped back up his authority. They usually received particular areas to manage from which they could enrich themselves by collecting tithes from farmers.

When the dependence of the followers on their leader was substantial, he often tried to increase this dependence, e.g. with higher taxes, in order to further consolidate his authority. A typical example of this strategy even in the 20th Century was Ethiopia under the emperor HAILE SELASSIE. When the farmers were not able to pay the 70 to 80 per cent tax from their meagre income their property was expropriated and they became employees or even slaves of the feudal master.

Imperium – dominium

Subjects who lived within the territory of their master were under his protection but had in turn to be loyal to him. The original power of the head of the family, his 'dominium', expanded into political authority, or 'imperium', over the bigger association. From this, feudal law was developed, for example in Germany, which established a hierarchy with the king as the highest feudal lord.

2.2.4.4 The Development of an Economy Based on Division of Labour – Building the Modern Territorial State

Development of towns

The later development of the state was increasingly marked by the foundation of towns. Towns appeared along well-travelled routes of commerce. Princes and kings also founded towns to protect their borders, to protect the roads of the armies, or as places for court sessions. Within these towns there developed territorially-based political authority. Towns became the domicile and shelter for peoples of different tribes, including peoples with different religions and different legal traditions (for example, the towns of the Ottoman Empire), who lived together under the same rules and authority. This authority was usually therefore no longer based on the religion of a particular tribe. The various religions were to be treated equally. In ancient Rome the Gods of all people were depicted and worshipped in the same temple in order to accord equal respect to all religious beliefs.

Jewish ghettos

During the Middle Ages, towns of Christian Europe were however also much influenced by the Crusades against Islam. The minority Jewish population had to live in ghettos, in constant fear of pogroms. Within the ghettos a new Jewish law developed strongly influenced by the Tora. These rules were however not only based on religion but were also of democratic-oligarchic origin. This led for the first time to the establishment within towns of some small autonomous districts that had their own state-like political authority.

Individualism

Naturally the economic and social autonomy of the families within these towns was reduced. They depended as individuals predominantly on the community and what it was able to produce or procure, whereas in the countryside people lived embedded within the autarky of the extended family. In the towns, extended families diminished in importance. Instead, life was increasingly centred on the single individual.

Christianity: The sinful individual

This position of the individual was reinforced by Christianity's individualistic view of humanity. According to Christian teachings, every human being stands before and is answerable to God as an individual who is responsible for his own conduct. Thus the individual can also be the bearer of rights and duties. Man is not embedded within the family as in Japanese Shintoism, he is not a negligible part of a professional or social group as Confucianism teaches, and he does not seek happiness by living an ascetic life and renouncing his individuality as required by Buddhism. Indeed there is no religion that places as much emphasis on the independent, responsible individual as does Christianity. Only within Christianity does every person stand before God as an individual with equal rights and direct responsibility to God for his/her actions. Only Christianity knows the idea of the sinful human being who is banished from paradise because of personal guilt for his behaviour. This relationship between the human in paradise and the sinful human was to have a decisive impact on the theories of state.

Towns and the common good

Law and authority were decreasingly linked to tribes and instead were based much more on the *territory* of the town. While the individual's bonds with the extended family were loosened, his dependence on the larger community of the town increased, due in large part to the growing complexity of the division of labour within the town walls.

The town had not only to offer protection, it was also expected to provide certain services for the community: roads, town walls, water supply, common baths and hospitals and even currency. In short, the bearer of political authority assumed responsibility over and above basic protection, for more and more services in the interests of the community.

Public service and bureaucracy

The interest of the community, that is, the common good or the public interest, increased in importance. The dependence of the polity upon common services was usually linked to an expansion of the bureaucracy. The first forms of a new civil service law were developed for public employees of the towns who were engaged to provide services for the community. While within the area of tribal control, family members of the ruling tribe could manage some territories autonomously, the increasing division of labour within the town required a certain degree of specialisation. Tasks and positions of employees, or the first 'civil servants', were no longer allocated on the basis of family connections, but rather according to merit and ability. This led to the development of a professional public service - one of the defining characteristics of the modern state. Closely connected to the development of the public service was the development of a standing army, with which princes could protect their territory and conquer other lands. This army was no longer composed of a random group of volunteers as it had been in tribal times, but rather consisted of paid mercenaries and later of trained professional soldiers.

Sense of community

The growth of public services, of a state bureaucracy, of professional civil servants and soldiers as well as the emergence of a sense of *community consciousness* are the main indicators of this third phase of the development of the state. Where the relevant social conditions were present, we can these developments in similar form almost everywhere, including in Rome at the time of Cicero, in 16th Century France, 15th Century England and in the Ottoman Empire as well as in the Middle Empire (China).

Centralising power

This new consciousness was accompanied by a substantial increase in the internal and external power of the ruler. French absolutism, the Ottoman Empire, England under Queen Elizabeth I and the Middle Empire under the Ming Dynasty attest to this. The increase in power corresponds to the growing dependency of the people upon the polity, as dependence generates power. Consequently, in this phase of state development we can observe an unprecedented struggle for power.

While European leaders attempted to consolidate their external power through their battle against the church and to shore up their internal power against the strengthened aristocracy, rulers of other states brought the Church, priests and religion into the service of their central power (for example in China, the late Roman Empire, the Catholic Church under Constantine, etc). The expansion of power enabled the ruler to intervene directly in the authority of the head of the family or tribal leader and to place the individual members of families under the direct control of state authority. The polity as a supra-familial community thus gradually became a state comprised not of families but of individuals as subjects.

Legislation

At this time we can observe the first attempts to develop legislation and legal systems. Notwithstanding the general principle of Islam that the law is to be found within the Koran as the only valid legislation for Muslims, the rulers of the Ottoman Empire found it necessary to enact general rules regulating the behaviour of their subjects. The laws of the Middle Empire applied only to the common people but not to the aristocracy, which was bound only by rites. Nevertheless these norms are the precursors of modern legal acts because they were valid for all common people according to the principle of equality. Laws in this sense can also be found in the European states towards the end of the Middle Ages and during the Renaissance. Rules of town guilds or regulations on duties and rights of soldiers, rules of court procedure and regulations prescribing dress codes for citizens were enacted.

These regulations reflect the development of a more complex social order. Up to this point, law had developed mainly as customary law based on religious beliefs. From this juncture, the state – and in particular the ruler – was not only able to decide upon and apply the law in particular cases, he could also enact prospective laws of general application. With this power the state starts to steer and design the order of society. The ruler goes from being the highest judge to the highest legislator.

Aristocracy

In this phase of state development society begins to stratify into a hierarchy based on social status. In China those families that were bound only by 'rites' but not by ordinary laws were at the top of the hierarchy. In early Europe the aristocracy and the church were above the third estate. Within the old Roman Empire, the aristocracy (patricians), the nobles and the senators had priority over the disenfranchised plebs. The nobility was always strongly bound to the monarchy and the crown and also enjoyed special privileges. While the Muslims – as IBN KHALDÛN (p. 191) describes – in earliest times did not have a system of social stratification of families. But later as kings expanded their power, privileges were granted to the families closest to them, which were given special mandates. This lead to an aristocracy of public offices.

The nobles served the interests of power and administered crown offices. On the other hand they were determined to *retain and expand their privileges*. If the king was strong, such as the Russian Tsar, the nobles would seek shelter in his court to protect them against the claims of the people. If the king was weak, as in the Britain, the aristocracy would attempt to expand their own power and restrict that of the king.

Development of different legal cultures

The different principles and traditions of the common law and the civil law systems have their origins within the different developments in legal cultures during the Middle Ages. While the countries of the civil law system are influenced by an 'activist' concept of state, based on the idea that it is the role of the state to change the society, countries of the common law tradition see the role of the state as being limited to the task of acting as a moderator or independent umpire to maintain the balance between different social forces.

Different understanding of the state

These concepts can be traced back to different understandings of justice that have developed over centuries. The common law systems consider the judge to be an independent umpire whose task is to solve conflicts among the parties and to find the just balance. The civil law systems consider the judge to be an extension of the law itself. As a representative of the state, the judge must be blind to the hierarchical position of the parties, but must search for and see the facts and the applicable law, and make a decision according to the demands of law and justice. He/she has to implement legislation. Whilst under the common law whoever wins the case is right, within the civil law system the party that is legally in the right should win the case – and it is the job of the judge to find out which party that is.

Civil law system

One can trace this different function of the judge back to the fact that on the European continent of the 12th Century the canon law taught at the universities began to play an increasingly important role. The law was not the law of the people but the law of a scientific elite, hierarchically separated from the people. The judges representing the hierarchy had to use scientific and dogmatic analyses to find and apply the law for the parties seeking justice. The application of the law and the role of the judge thus could no longer be performed by laymen but only by experts trained in the science of law. This hierarchical thinking corresponded to the new idea of the chain of authority. The more important the expert – in other words the closer he was to the king by the grace of God – the more just and true was the decision. The hierarchy determined truth and justice.

The judgment was not the result of an argument about the facts carried out before a (democratic) jury of the people, but a scientific application of the law to a concrete case. The law had a concrete existence independent from the facts. The judges needed not only to find the law that had to be applied to the facts, they also determined what the true facts of the case were via the inquisitorial procedure.

Accordingly on the European continent quite a different understanding of the state developed to that in the Anglo-Saxon world. In place of the king who rules by the grace of God being the fountain from which all law sprung, was the concept of the secular state based on popular sovereignty as the source of the entire legal order from the constitution right down to the lowest local regulations.

Common law

In contrast to Continental law, the English law administered by the Norman kings remained strongly connected to the jurors chosen from the common people. The jurors with the assistance of the judge had to determine the facts from the material put to them by the parties and to decide the case based on criteria developed through the wisdom of generations of judges. The facts had to be determined through an adversarial procedure and just criteria for the resolution of the conflict had to be found. Law and fact were much more closely intertwined than in the European legal method where the relevant law had to be found by the judge, who then applied the law to the facts.

2.2.4.5 The State of the Complex Industrialized Society: Parties and Legislators

i. From Subject to Citizen

He who has the capacity for reason can say "No"

The territorial state emerged, in accordance with economic and social developments, in different periods (cf. the Roman Empire and the European states). The modern rational state of political parties and the legislature however developed only in response to the industrialisation of Europe. In this period, economically and philosophically as well as legally, the transition to the state of modernity – that is, to the nation-state of European tradition – was prepared.

The modern industrialised state is the result of the economic, cultural and above all the ideological development of Europe. During the Renaissance and later the Enlightenment period people recognised their capacity to say "no". He who can say no is able to question state authority. The king who rules by the grace of God cannot hide behind the argument that divine legitimacy can never be questioned, once people have recognised that their ability to reason enables them to question any authority.

Only a person who is convinced that he/she has the ability and judgment to assess state authority is able to say "no". He who can recognise in himself the capacity to judge, accepts the 'sovereignty' of the reason of the Homo sapiens. The recognition of the 'sovereignty' of individual reason must therefore bind the state to the people and thus lead to the requirement for the state to possess democratic legitimacy.

He who is able through reason to distinguish truth from untruth, right from wrong, will also claim to be able to separate the just from the unjust. This opens the door to the modern state ruled by legislation. The laws enacted by the legislature are no longer based on inherited wisdoms. Laws and norms are the result of a rational discourse of the people that claim to be better able than any lone ruler to judge what is just and unjust.

Homo sapiens

If human beings are the only life form that is able based on reason and language to make independent decisions, then all members of the species *Homo sapiens* must be fundamentally *the same* and therefore have equal rights. The appreciation of individual reason is the entry point to centuries of discourse on liberty, equality and equal rights. Persons with the power of judgment do not need a state authority that tells them how to live their lives. Thus the ideological condition for the acknowledgement of basic human rights was present. Property rights, economic freedom, and freedom of thought and expression became the fundamental concerns of peoples oppressed by state authority. Human beings as beings with reason and the will and intelligence to make their own plans and decisions concerning their lives cannot be treated as subservient subjects.

With the era of industrialisation the modern state developed into the state of a nation, with its own legal order, its own economic system and with the recognition of property rights. In the revolution of July 1830 the French King Louis Philippe declared himself to be no longer the King of France but the King of the French people. This new legitimacy of the monarchy led to a new self-understanding of peoples and of their states. Former subjects became rights-bearing citizens and democratic decision-makers on state authority.

ii. From Serfs to Employees

The misery of early industrialisation

The early industrialisation of England in the 18th and 19th Centuries expanded the economic division of labour and at the same time diminished the autonomy of the family. People became more dependent upon the formal labour market and in particular upon the factory owners and businessmen. Because of their existential dependence, the labour force of women, children, the elderly and also fit male employees was exploited. Their incomes were usually below the necessary minimum for survival. Even if they worked ten to twelve hours a day, workers' pay was barely enough to feed their families.

During this time the economic autonomy of families in the countryside was also drastically reduced. Farmers with meagre incomes who were dependent on their patrons or on the extended family felt drawn to the town and its freedom. However, within the town they had to live crammed together in miserable apartments and struggled to earn enough for their families. As soon as children reached adolescence they had to leave the family and search for means to earn their own income.

State welfare

The state now assumed responsibility for tasks that had earlier been the preserve of the extended family. It not only offered protection from external and internal dangers and sustained the free market system through division of labour and basic legal principles. It also had to assume responsibility for educating children, and as the low-income family was no longer able to care for the ill, elderly and handicapped members of the family, the state had to adopt this role and provide the necessary support. This development dates back to the end of the 19th Century when social security systems started to develop. The state also had to ensure that this system of interdependence could not be abused and that workers were not exploited. It was during this period that the first legal guarantees for the protection of workers' rights were enacted. Furthermore the state was compelled in the interest of welfare to intervene in the economy in order to prevent sudden unemployment and to protect threatened branches of the economy, to counteract inflation and to secure adequate supply of basic staples and necessities for the polity. The welfare of the people imposed important new responsibilities on the state in addition to the basic protection originally afforded by the minimalist state.

Social opponents – social partners

Whilst the social hierarchy predetermined the relationship of dependency between serfs and lords in the feudal state, the relationship between employees and employers is determined in the industrial age by negotiations and battles between labour unions and employer organisations. The state is charged with acting as the moderator between these opposing interest groups, and at the same time the interests of these groups have a direct influence on important state activities. The 'sovereign' state no longer serves the social hierarchy. From this time forth it has to prove itself as a servant of the community and the people as well as an arbiter of the conflicts within the community. The *increasing existential dependency* of the individual upon the state and upon employers also leads to the *heightened need of the people for greater liberty and democracy.*

Centralising state power

The expansion of industrialisation undoubtedly sowed the seed for the progression to the *total state.* At the centre of dispute was no longer the preservation and expansion of the power of certain families. The public interest was not confined exclusively to physical protection and the provision of particular state services. The central issue became fair pay and the just distribution of wealth. The discussion of these controversies shifted from the salons of intellectuals into the halls of parliament and the media.

Closely connected to industrialisation is the *centralisation of power.* The small agrarian states and principalities of the 17th and 18th Centuries were not able to cope with these new tasks. They had to give in to the need for the foundation of bigger industrial nation-states. The merger of the small Germanic kingdoms into a customs union and then into the German Empire, the foundation of the Italian state and also the foundation of the United States one hundred years earlier were the consequences of this development.

Increasing democratisation: Representation of the people

The expansion of state power, which was further enhanced by the tools of mass communication, triggered the call for democracy. *Separation of powers, democratisation and socialisation* became the slogans of the time. Because people were no longer prepared to entrust all powers to a single monarch, the power of the state was increasingly transferred to a parliament composed of elected representatives of the citizens. The communist and socialist parties however wanted to go further and democratise not only state power but also economic power. For this reason they sought complete state control of the economy and at the same time the subordination of the state to will of the working class.

With increasing democratisation and the need to continuously adapt state measures to changing economic conditions, the state functions of legislation and planning became ever more important. The state and the people were to be steered by legislation. This strengthened the influence of democratic institutions such as parliaments. However in many instances such institutions were too cumbersome and ponderous to be able to handle day-to-day decisions. They could only steer the activity of the state through general norms and legislation. The implementation of the laws and daily decision-making power had to be transferred to the ever-expanding anonymous bureaucracy of government.

Protection and realisation of liberty

The diverse dependencies in which people are entwined in modern society necessitate the enactment of innumerable laws that regulate the increasing network of constraints upon liberty and aim to provide at least some *free space* for the citizens.

The mandate of the state is no longer restricted to the protection of *law and liberty* it must also provide the *conditions necessary* to make use of liberty. While the state had earlier had to ensure law and order, it later acquired the responsibility to care for the welfare of the community in order to make sure that people could enjoy liberty and exercise freedom within the society.

Urbanisation

An important social problem with considerable effects on the development of the state is the growth of urbanisation. In cities, the overcrowded areas and in particular the slums are afflicted by poverty, despair, and social exclusion. Life is marred by traffic chaos, collapse of water and electricity supply, deficient sanitation, and strikes. Some cities can barely be governed; people's economic autonomy is lower than ever; people barely interact with each other, even though they are living crammed together. Society loses its bearing.

Bureaucracy

States can only keep such developments under control by attempting to provide services and by intervening in and governing all aspects of society for the protection and order of society. This provides the bureaucratic administration with the impetus to inflate into a new *unaccountable state within the state*. Public servants often can no longer be controlled. They establish their own realms of power within public offices and often seek to supplement their income through corruption. The citizens on the other hand feel powerless, finding themselves at the mercy of an anonymous bureaucracy. In order to prevent misuse of the power of the administration and to prevent corruption the state has to improve and again expand its institutions, for example by introducing administrative law and informal control mechanisms such as the Ombudsman.

Mass media

In addition to the power of the bureaucratic administration, the power of intermediary forces is also growing. The influence of the *mass media,* which can instantly reach millions of people around the world, has increased considerably in the last twenty years. In contrast to politics in earlier eras, politicians who lack a charismatic media persona now have very little chance of being elected. The media decide the fate of heads of state and prime ministers. Democracy is played out via the media. Those who control the media control the state.

The *concentration of wealth* has led to the growth of huge multinational corporations that compete at the international level, independent of the nation-state and its territorial boundaries but able, due to their economic power and importance, to influence the policy of many nation-states. The aim of these corporations is to dismantle direct and indirect trade barriers, to harmonise state economic regulation (or to deregulate) and to strengthen the international protection of the global free market in the interests of unfettered competition. As a consequence they use every means at their disposal to ensure that in the states that are important for them, their interests are reflected in state policy, notwithstanding that such interests may be diametrically opposed to the interests of the majority of the population.

iii. Four Revolutions!

Goals of the revolutions

The era of industrialisation is dominated by four revolutions: in the 'Glorious Revolution' of 1688 the English aristocracy seized power from the Crown. The Glorious Revolution would not have been possible without the *Long Parliament* and the condemnation of Charles I to the death penalty four decades earlier. In 1767 the American colonies seceded from the English Crown and in 1787 established a democratic republic that stood against all absolutist monarchies of Europe. Like the British in the Glorious Revolution, the American revolutionaries were not driven by the will to radically change society but rather to change the power structure of government and thereby to guarantee the liberty of the citizens. In 1789 finally the French farmers and workers carried out the *bourgeois* revolution in order to set up a state of equal citizens (*citoyens*) and property owners. Their goal was not only to change the power structure of the state but also to change the society by destroying the feudal system and recognising equality. In

1917 the Russian serfs laid the power of the state in the hands of the proletariat, which was to make collective decisions on the state and its authority (although the power of 'the proletariat' meant in practice that the Communist Party had absolute power). The Russian revolution changed society by expropriating all private property and vesting it in the state in order to control the economy, as well as by introducing a new political system. In England the aristocratic lords, in America the colonial people, in France the farmers and in Russia the serfs – invariably guided by an intellectual elite – ignited and carried out their revolutions.

Glorious Revolution: The revolution of the aristocracy

The Lords in England were able to keep and even expand their original power regardless of the fate of the crown because – unlike the French nobility – they were not in a relationship of total dependence upon an absolutist king. The English aristocrats lived off the processing and sale of wool, and their interests lay in ensuring their products could be profitably sold on the market. They did not live off taxes or tithes that had to be squeezed out of the farmers. They relied therefore on the competition of the free market and on their independence from the Crown. With their power gained by the revolution however they did not seek to change the society nor did they intend to change the basic state institutions. Revolution meant for them only independence of the aristocracy with regard to the Crown.

American Independence: The revolution of a colony

So too the fathers of the American Revolution did not intend to change the society with their new Constitution, but rather to cast off the colonial power. The state and the government that were installed under the Constitution of 1789 did not need to be totally re-designed and nor did society need to be radically readjusted. The state was rather in the service of the pioneers of American independence. The American Revolution was not directed against their own state and its structures but against a foreign state. The new Constitution was therefore not aimed at changing the American society but rather at justifying the democratic status of the society before the monarchic European world.

The French Revolution: A revolution of the bourgeoisie

In France however the revolution *was* directed towards fundamentally changing the state, its governmental system, and society. The feudal social order needed to be transformed: the aristocracy had to be integrated into civil society, and a state comprising equal citizens and a new democratic legitimacy had to be created. This goal could only be achieved on the basis of a new concept of the state. Thus, the power of the state could not be employed merely to mediate between the interests of the aristocracy and the bourgeoisie. The state had to become an instrument to change the social structure and social order, for example through laws designed to achieve equality. With these expectations the law took on a whole new purpose. It was no longer simply a written confirmation of generally accepted wisdom. It had to become an efficient implement with which to remodel the society. Legislation, as the expression of the so-called general will in the sense of ROUSSEAU (*volonté générale*), thus became the 'source' of justice. The touchstone of law and justice was not the jurisdiction of the courts and their precedents but rather the legislature which enacted laws to effect change in the system of government and the structure of society.

New understanding of state and law

The French Revolution led to a new understanding of the state and the law. The state was no longer employed to preserve the traditional social order. Justice was no longer the concern only of the courts, but rather justice had to be delivered by the parliament as lawmaker. Moreover, from now on the courts were to lose their jurisdiction over the administration. Interpretation and implementation of the laws was not to be entrusted to conservative judges. In order to achieve this goal NAPOLEON created a new field of 'public law', which he withheld from the jurisdiction of the traditional courts that could deal only with matters of private law. The executive was thereby able to issue ordinances, decrees and administrative acts without being subject to judicial scrutiny or control. Democracy entailed a representative system of law making. But the implementation of the law made by the elected legislature was the responsibility of the unaccountable executive and its administration. With this development the foundation for the new continental European legal culture was laid. A permanent gulf opened between the common law and the civil law tradition.

The Russian Revolution: The revolution of the proletariat

The French Revolution in the 19th Century constructed the 'nation' of equal citizens (*citoyens*). In 1917 the Russian Revolution had much grander aims. It wanted to influence the world beyond the Russian nation. Indeed the Russian Revolution was supposed to trigger a worldwide Revolution. Its ultimate goal was to abolish the state, which was seen as the cause of all injustice. According to communist theory, the state had a transitory character and existed only to enable society to prepare for an international society without states. Once the state came under the control of the proletariat, the proletariat would lead the way to an international social order in which every person would be equal and no one would be exploited.

The state was seen not only as an instrument for internal change of the national society, it was also an instrument for the battle to achieve the world revolution. In place of the legislator the hierarchical party was installed. The party utilised the state and the constitution in the interest of the revolution, and could change or abolish the constitution and the law at whim.

Consequently, the world was divided in two blocks. One block of states wanted to bring about the world revolution. The opposing block wanted to defend the national interests of a free economy within a free bourgeois democracy. The

Western states were thus mobilised for the defence of their values. States became ideological fortresses. Disputes and discussions on the sense, the limits, the value and the function of states were frozen. The entire community of states stiffened in the shadow of the cold war power balance and the atomic threat.

2.2.4.6 From the Nation-State to a Globalised World

i. The Challenge of the Nation-State

What is the Earth's carrying capacity?

One of the major problems facing our world order is undoubtedly the *explosion of the world population and the shortage of water and other raw material.* In early 2007 the world population exceeded 6.6 billion people. This is two billion more than at the time the first edition of this book in German was published 1980. By 2020 the world population is expected to reach eight billion people. Will it be possible to prevent worldwide conflicts over water supply and raw material? Can the earth provide enough food in order to feed all human beings? Will such exponential population growth devastate the environment and ultimately our planet? Protection of the environment and the use of raw material and water are no longer matters that states can deal with in isolation.

Equality of distribution?

Today 20 per cent of humans dispose of 80 per cent of the available capital, goods and resources. The same disproportionate relationship applies to science and research capacities. Since the mid-1970s more than a third of mankind has been living in cities. In 1995, 43 per cent of the world population was living in urban areas, and this figure has now reached half of the world population. Since 1955 half the world population has been literate, and in future education will be able to reach every human being, even in the most remote places on earth. Nevertheless whilst the proportion is decreasing, the actual number of illiterate people is growing.

Global need for knowledge

In future humans will have to solve much more important and complex problems than did their ancestors. The human being who submitted to nature needed to know a great deal about the diverse range of plants, trees and animals in his environment. The anthropologist Jack Roberts found that the Nawajo-Indians needed to know some 12,000 things in order to be able to survive within their environment. The human being who seeks to control nature – like man in the era of industrialisation – needs to know much more. He must not only know what exists in nature but also what one can do with nature and how it can be changed. Humans who want to cooperate with nature need to know still more. They must possess all the knowledge of those who submit to nature and those who control it, as well as an understanding of the complex mutual interactions of elements of nature, the real effect of the human footprint on earth, and how to live in a way that is environmentally sustainable. (K. DEUTSCH)

Global information

Computer technology and the internet have introduced a new technological revolution. The knowledge of mankind is now stored worldwide and available to anyone who has access to the necessary infrastructure and has the skills to find information and to utilise and exploit it. Information, including false information, can be quickly and easily distributed all over the world. Information is no longer contained within state borders. A state which, for example, prohibits the publication of public polls immediately before an election in the interests of a fair democratic process must reckon with the fact that such information can be published on the internet and made accessible to the voters within the relevant country in spite of any prohibition. High costs and the limited availability of frequencies limit the possibilities for broadcasting information via radio and television. However today every individual who can afford a PC and an internet connection is able at very little expense to spread news, but also hatred and incitement to violence, all around the world.

Mobility

International communication and the worldwide mobility of people, products and services leads not only to global competition in science and information. It leads also to labour market and production competition, as companies search the world for locations in which the costs of production and labour are lowest. The consumers of services and products no longer depend on local or national providers. They have access to a huge range of products and services from all over the world, much of which can be obtained via the internet. Even employees on low salaries can be transported (and exploited) worldwide: for example, on ships in international waters goods can be produced without being subject to any taxes or state regulation in relation to product standards or workers' entitlements. The markets for products and services as well as the financial market have become globalised. Even so, notwithstanding some exceptions and abuses, the labour market is still to a large extent locally structured.

Economic waste and shortsightedness

The states themselves produce deficits of billions of dollars, which are either passed on to the next generation or marginalised by inflation and thus indirectly paid by those living from their pension (who earned their pension before inflation and thus have less buying power). Publicly listed companies feel obliged to produce the highest possible profits for the interest of their shareholders. Employees' salaries have to give way to the interest of the shareholder. Short-term gains take priority over long-term interests. Even some of the biggest companies do not hesitate to falsify accounting records to protect their share value. If the peace and stability of a society is disturbed or threatened on a long-term basis, companies may look worldwide for other places more secure for their production. Multinational companies but also criminal organisations deal with turnovers that far exceed the budget of many states. The financial market of the small state of Switzerland has a daily turnover of 80 billion Swiss Francs!

American values

The globalised economy is increasingly driven by American values based on the Calvinist theology of success. Whoever is successful in the economy, politics, culture, science, entertainment or even in the courtroom or on the battlefield has, according to this belief-system, secured their place in heaven. Only the capable and successful person is also a good person. The just distribution of wealth is taken care of by the 'invisible hand'. The minimal state (NOZICK) must only provide for peace, order, security of the competitive market and protection of property. Every person should if possible be afforded the same opportunities – but it is not for the state to assess performance – rather it is the 'invisible hand' that ultimately determines success or failure.

Social peace

Democracy and the ballot paper are supposed to take account of long-term interests such as the environment, but such interests are often deliberately overlooked. The negative experiences of Manchester liberalism are forgotten. The desire for economic profit raises the motivation and performance of people and companies. However, those who cannot make a profit without additional performance and output do not shrink back from corruption, exploitation and abuse. The growing indebtedness of the South and the East are examples of such developments. To whom are multinational corporations and their shareholders are accountable? 'Incentive' and 'accountability' are the key words of a free market economy. However, accountability in terms of long-term interests and therefore accountability towards the next generation is not guaranteed.

ii. Challenges of the International Community

Political world order?

The globalised economy is embedded within a political world order which is effectively controlled exclusively by the United States. The American President as well as the Congressmen and Senators are however accountable only to their voters. There is no system of checks and balances in relation to the impact America has on the rest of the world. Thus in instances of failures in international politics and in terms of the forceful pursuit of goals that serve the interest of the American economy, the US government is only accountable to the American constituency, but not to the other peoples and states affected by their actions. Nor is there any accountability on the part of American voters towards peoples and states that feel the effects of their choices. In spite of this the American President has the capacity to effect 'regime change' beyond his own borders if foreign governments are seen to threaten American interests, often based on information that cannot be verified. Such intervention on the part of the United States purports to be designed to establish democratic governments, although the very principles of legitimacy and democracy in the affected states are trampled on in the process.

Local stability

Even a globalised economy can develop only within stable political conditions of local democracies. Political stability however can only be realised in the long term by states and governments that have legitimacy and credibility in the eyes of their people. In a modern democracy, this legitimacy cannot be achieved without some degree of genuine solidarity among the different social strata on one side and across ethnic divides on the other.

International interventions

A consequence of globalisation is the political, economic, cultural and even sporting interconnectedness of states and peoples around the world and within regions. Throughout the world, the World Trade Organisation (WTO) binds states to the principles of global economic competition. At the political level, it is the United Nations, which on the basis of its post-World War II mandate has global responsibility for peace. The United Nations however can only make legally binding decisions through its Security Council. Thus, those states that possess a veto power on the UN Security Council decide alone on peace keeping and peacemaking measures on behalf of the international community. They determine which aggression is a threat to peace according to chapter VII of the UN Charter, and thereby decide which internal conflicts justify international intervention. Taking into account their almost unlimited military and economic power, the US effectively has a more or less unfettered leadership position within the Security Council. Thus the US can also decide which states they want to combat (and how and when) on the basis of their right of self-defence against terrorism.

European Union

At a regional level, some states in Europe set themselves the goal after World War II of securing lasting peace in Europe by strengthening economic ties within the region and establishing an economic community. The economic interweaving of the region was intended to serve the interests of political peace. Out of this economic community has now emerged a political alliance of states that wields the greatest economic power in the world, and that is therefore also increasingly able to assert and enforce the political and strategic interests of its member states at the global level. Today the political and economic incentives of the community are so strong that practically no European state can escape its grasp.

This community however also presents the theory of state with a totally new challenge. A large part (over 40 per cent) of the internal domestic law of the member states is founded today on the legal provisions of the European Union. The member states nevertheless insist on maintaining their traditional state sovereignty and refuse to contemplate an official transfer of sovereignty to the Union. It is still the internal politics of member states that dominates political discourse. At the European Union level the public has not yet really been engaged in or committed to political issues concerning the Union. Legally all decisions of the EU are still considered to be part international law. Laws of the European Union can only be given effect by incorporation into the domestic law of each of the member states. The European Court of Justice has become the legal engine of the Union, its decisions leading the way for the integration of European citizens.

Whatever position one may have with regard to this new legal construct, one can hardly regard it as a pure international association of states. In fact the Union has absorbed part of the state sovereignty of the member states. The law and its implementation are structured according to the state principles of a federation. Legislation however is still made on a confederal basis. The economic Union has become a 'quasi-state' or, as described by the German constitutional court (Bundesverfassungsgericht), a *sui generis* composite of states. Thus this new construct, the European Union, has subverted the classical distinction between international law and domestic law as separate legal orders.

Sovereignty of the global market and local common interest

In a world of increasing intra-state and international dependence, global interconnectedness, uncontrolled expansion of the power of global companies and the threatening power of international criminality – degeneration into anarchy can only be prevented if the public interest can be defined through a rational and democratic debate in which every person can participate equally. International institutions need to submit to democratic control and become accountable in order to counter effectively egoistic private interests. At the same time states need to have the political room to move and the economic means to be able to provide security for the people in terms of their livelihood, health, opportunities and pensions.

It seems however that this is no longer the decisive question for state legitimacy. Decisive is rather the question whether the small nation-states are still able, in the face of global problems, to perform their primary 'political' functions effectively. In other words: Is it meaningful to guarantee democracy for the small nation-state and to establish a welfare state at the national level, when the free political space available to states and therefore also the space for democratic decisions at the national level has been (and will continue to be) radically diminished by international politics and globalisation?

There is another consideration that stands diametrically against this question. International politics is today still largely dependent upon the might of the most powerful. States with economic or military power or strategic importance dominate international decision-making mechanisms in one-sided pursuit of their own national interests. If states were to surrender what is left of their autonomy, they would be exposing their citizens to a completely one-sided economic world order that has no democratic legitimacy.

Reason and emotion

In the era of globalisation, the 'political' still retains a local component, and will retain this in future. Law and order, culture and education, health and environmental protection, housing and transport as well as social security cannot be dealt with exclusively by international rules and regulations. They require the involvement and cooperation of all levels: local, national and international, for sensible regulation.

Two contradictory developments oppose each other: The nationalistic need for local identity and the global necessity for rational cooperation. Humans are emotionally attached to their local environment. History, tradition, identity and a sense of 'home' are values that can only be instilled locally. Rationally however, we have to acknowledge that in spite of their local attachment, people may lose their 'home' in the long run if they are not prepared at the same time to seek cooperation and participation at the regional and international level. Citizens have to be prepared to relinquish some political independence in order to gain regional and international justice. Emotionally people identify with the state as an island of sovereignty within the sea of international relationships. Rationally however, one has to accept that this symbol of political independence is a thing of the past.

Leviathan state

On the one hand states face claims for greater local autonomy, which are primarily based on emotion and sometimes on nationalism. On the other hand states have to integrate into an international political network that significantly restricts their political autonomy. The question we therefore have to ask today is: has the state exhausted its usefulness as the original source of law and justice? If the answer is yes, what then is the legitimate position and function of the traditional nation-state within a globalised and localised world?

The state (with the exception of the USA) has, both in theory and in political reality, reached the end of its days as absolute sovereign Leviathan. International law and the legal orders of most states are still based on the constitutional fiction of the idea of sovereignty as the basis for legitimacy of state decisions. The reality of international interdependence reveals however that the legal order is based upon a fiction that is no longer tenable. The state is embedded within an international political order. The only question is only what are the consequences for the traditional state faced with this reality? Will the state be completely marginalised or will it retain an important role as the bridge between domestic law and international law, which is still determined by states as the main actors at the international level?

Internal and international legitimacy

'The political' requires democratic legitimacy. National justice and the national legal order depend upon this democratic legitimacy and acceptance. The state will continue to be the political unit that has the legitimacy to maintain the intrastate balance, to determine local autonomy and to represent the political community of the state at the international level. The state will not be entirely pushed aside by the international legal order, because it will continue to be necessary to have a 'local' authority which can assume responsibility for social peace, multiculturality, intrastate decentralisation, protection of fundamental rights and implementation of international law. These tasks still fall within the responsibility of the traditional state. However, the state will no longer be able to claim absolute and indivisible sovereignty. The state is bound by a supranational legal order at the international level and in some cases at the regional level. If a state wants to access loans or aid from international institutions such as the World Bank, it must show evidence of good governance and demonstrate transparency, democratic acceptance, political accountability and decentralisation of state power.

The world order does not replace legitimacy

States will continue to support their legitimacy through common value systems that include the tradition, history and culture that hold the community together. Only on this basis can social solidarity be fostered, and without solidarity within state borders the peaceful coexistence of states at the international level would be unfeasible. Up to now the main task of the international legal order has been to restore and maintain peace among peoples and states. States have been mandated to keep order among individual citizens. In future, fragmented and multicultural states will be faced with the task of keeping peace not only among individuals but also between the different ethnic communities within the state.

Who controls the international division of labour?

The increasing division of labour between humans at the local level led to the establishment of the first supra-familial political communities. Today the increase-ing complexity of the international network that expands the division of labour at the international level has created new dependencies, and this necessitates new enforceable mechanisms of decision making which limit the autonomy of the single states. International organisations such as the United Nations Security Council, the International Labour Organisation and the World Trade Organisation are responsible for making decisions regarding war, labour and trade that would previously have been made on a unilateral or bilateral basis by sovereign nation-states. Such organisations wield enormous power, but are not subject to any of the accountability mechanisms that apply to the internal decisions of individual sovereign states. Ironically, the same international institutions that demand transparency, democratic acceptance and political accountability from member states do not themselves adhere to such principles or standards.

Holocaust: The most brutal absurdity of absolute sovereignty

Undoubtedly the most fateful development for Europe was the Holocaust, which aimed to completely eradicate the Jewish race. Legitimised by absolute popular sovereignty, the Führer of the German nation decided that the Jewish race must be exterminated, not only in the interest of the German people but in the interest of mankind, and that the superiority of the Aryan race must be recognised. The ideologically-based nation wanted to prevent its racial purity from being threatened. Germany portrayed itself as the leading Nation of humanity, threatened in its existence and therefore entitled to exterminate the race declared by the Führer to be sub-human. The people agreed that other races either had to be exterminated or expelled in order to make room for the Aryan super race.

This dehumanisation was only possible because the claim to total sovereignty was transferred to the people, and the people became hostage to their own sovereignty. The Holocaust reveals the danger of absolute and unaccountable popular sovereignty in the sense of HOBBES: *auctoritas not veritas facit legem* (power, not truth, makes the law).

The Holocaust moreover demonstrates where a purely ethnic understanding of the nation can lead. The Holocaust must therefore be seen as the historical turning point in the development of the democratic idea of popular sovereignty, and as an historical event that is never to be forgotten and never to be repeated. No history of ideas should ever hide or suppress the facts of this event. It is part of the reality and of the danger of any concept of an absolute people's sovereignty.

The fall of the Berlin Wall

After World War II the world was divided into two ideologically opposing camps and into three main (and very different) economic regions. As long as the states were integrated in the ideological blocks, their statehood, legitimacy and authority remained incontestable. The states were independently able to save their people from the ideological enemy.

This changed radically with the fall of the Berlin wall in 1989. This fall symbolises the implosion of the reign of the communist party within the Eastern European States. It left behind not only a vacuum of power but also a state vacuum. The states of the communist world had been regarded as opponents of the West but still also recognised as states with full sovereignty and membership of the United Nations. In fact they were not real states in the sense of western constitutionalism. The state was a mere façade and alibi for the hierarchical rule of the communist party. The party controlled the apparatus of power without any constitutional limits. The state was under the rule of the party, and the constitution was merely an instrument used to conceal this reality and to feign democratic constitutionalism. Once the power of the party had disintegrated the former communist societies had to establish new states and a new concept of the state.

2.2.4.7 Universalism and Human Rights

The concept of the state of modernity is based on the idea that the state exists to serve man. Individual human beings are the origin of the state. The state has to be in their service. Authority is based in part on consensus and acceptance, and in part on equal rights and the rule of law. The claim in ancient times was the other way round: The individual was the subject of the state and in the service of the state. How should the relation between state and man be conceptualised today in the era of globalisation?

Simultaneously with the globalisation of the market came the universalisation of reason and ethics, and thus the internationalisation of human rights. The internationalisation of human rights restricts considerably the independence and absolute sovereignty of states. Within the recently ignited international discourse on human rights the principal focus is on individual rights. Group and collective rights may also be recognised and are often at the core of claims for autonomy, self-determination or even the secession of particular minorities.

Universal values?

Today, if human rights are flagrantly violated, states cannot defend themselves before the international community by relying on their local *raison d'état* and sovereignty. States cannot justify human rights abuses with their national, traditional or religious convictions nor validly claim that they are embedded in particular values such as for example, 'Asian values'. Under the guidance of the United States the international community decides which values are the subject of the internationally recognised idea of human rights.

Individual rights

This new development of the idea of human rights is primarily influenced by the concept of the individualistic state that can be traced back to JOHN LOCKE. The social contract is subject to individual rights, and the state does not have the authority to interfere with man's inalienable rights. For JOHN LOCKE the exclusive function of the constitution is to limit state power and not, as per HOBBES, first to enable state power. Powerful states within the international community now feel themselves empowered, in the name of defending human rights, to intervene militarily or with economic sanctions in other states, notwithstanding the principle of state sovereignty.

Credibility of human rights

This leads to the politicisation of human rights generally, as all states that publicly defend the unrestricted fulfilment of human rights will always also take their economic, strategic and political interests into account. States will therefore defend human rights when this also serves their geo-strategic and economic interests. With regard to states that are of no economic or political significance to the states that publicly champion human rights, the extent of international intervention is likely to be limited to some half-hearted rhetoric about the defence of human rights. States which are in their direct economic interest but which are powerful and not willing to tolerate criticism will also not become direct targets of a human rights policy. Selective human rights politics and selective justice therefore undermine the essential idea of universal human rights.

In this sense with regard to human rights we can categorise states into the following four classes:

- States which are so powerful that they consider themselves entitled to prescribe to other states how they should protect human rights (USA, EU);
- States whose human rights record becomes the target of powerful states because the powerful states want to use human rights politics to conceal their pursuit of other strategic and economic interests within the region (Iraq);
- Marginal states that have no bearing on powerful interests and are therefore able to violate the human rights of their citizens without being scrutinised or penalised by the international political community (many African states);
- States that are so important economically that out of self-interest nobody dares to seriously question their human rights record (Russia, China).

Unity of the state?

Modern constitutionalism secularised the legitimacy of the state and via the 'social contract' placed it in the hands of the people. However, precisely who constitutes 'the people' is a question for which constitutionalism has no answer. Today the historically developed state claims to be based upon popular sovereignty. This sovereignty however is often contested by the minority nations that live within, but are not recognised by, the state. Those minority nations claim autonomy or even unilateral secession, based on the right to self-determination. With this request the unity of the state is fundamentally questioned and undermined. The indivisibility of the multicultural state is denied.

The theoretical concept of constitutions, which builds upon the concept of civic individualism and human equality on the one hand and upon the notion of a state entity on the other, denies that individuals who are basically equal can be divided according to ethnicity. The internal peace of the state would be threatened. The state has to reconcile conflicts between individuals through the rational legal order. Conflicts between cultural, religious or linguistic communities that occur within the unity of the state are constitutionally ignored.

The state of post-modernity however will have to face this new challenge. It will have to reconcile conflicts not only among individuals but also between different peoples. The postmodern state will not only require legitimacy in the eyes of the majority of its citizens, but also vis-à-vis the various minority groups within the state.

Nationalism and minority problems

Just as the four major revolutions did not lead to 'the end of history' or to the end of conflicts, nor did the fall of the Berlin Wall have this effect as FRANCIS FUKUYAMA (*The End of History*, Bloomington 2000) had supposed it would. However this event did have the effect of marginalising the nation-state as well as the state of citizens (*citoyens*). At the same time conflicts have increasingly become intra-state in nature. Under the leadership of the United States the international community intervenes in these conflicts and has assumed the function of a world-wide police power, without world-wide legitimacy.

With the dissolution of the communist parties the state-façade of the communist states was also eroded. In those homogenous states where the authority of the party imploded without affecting the legitimacy of the territorial borders, the constitutional façade of the communist period could generally be converted into a functioning constitutional system. For multicultural states in which the legitimacy of the state and its territory imploded along with the party however, the affected peoples suddenly found themselves in a stateless void. Such peoples had to try to build a new nation-state with legitimate authority, and sought to rely on their original right to self-determination. However, as these nations were often dispersed and as other nations lived within their territory they were again confronted with the claim to self-determination of those new minorities. Historically the nations in South Eastern Europe were under the domination of the Ottoman Empire or the Austro-Hungarian Empire. In both empires the peoples had some original autonomy that enabled them to disperse notwithstanding the territory and therefore peoples were not confined to specific territories or ethnically homogeneous states. In the wake of communism the affected states were all confronted with new minorities challenging the legitimacy of the territorial boundaries of the state.

The state as colony with a new constitutional façade

This sharpening of ethnic conflicts between the 'stateless peoples' of Eastern Europe also extended to the former colonies of the western states. The constitutions and states that have replaced the former colonial authorities and territories are today seen by many minorities as merely new manifestations of colonial rule by the majority. In some of these cases minority or majority nations demand that in place of the vacuum left by the departure of the colonial regime, a new state be established that has legitimacy with respect to all nations living within its borders, not just the majority.

The international community

At the global level, in the wake of the Cold War between the eastern and western blocks, the international community has taken on a leading role in the promotion of western 'universal' values throughout the world. This international community is a relatively loose association of those states that have taken it upon themselves, under the leadership of the United States, to achieve the worldwide realisation of universal values. Those states that were not under the rule of communism, and who in part attributed the implosion of communism to the success of their own politics, assumed the lead in the worldwide achievement of their own interests. These interests are often veiled in the legitimacy of 'universal values', however there is no legitimate process to determine a worldwide general will.

Rule of Law

The rule of law and human rights have been universalised through the International Covenant on Civil and Political Rights and the International Covenant on Economic, Social and Cultural Rights of 1966 as well as with the recently established International Criminal Court and the new UN Human Rights Council established in 2006. While it is undisputed that all states are obliged to comply with human rights and the rule of law, the concrete application and content of human rights has remained controversial. The questions of whether social and economic rights are to be considered as much a part of human rights as civil and political rights, and what the position of collective rights with regard to minorities should be, have remained core questions of the international debate and discourse on human rights. But even with regard to the right to life there are major differences. The USA for example, which has still not abolished capital punishment, guarantees the right to life subject to the existence of the death penalty. In Europe however, Protocol 6 to the European Convention on Human Rights clearly prohibits capital punishment in times of peace. It even regards the permanent insecurity of those who have been sentenced to death and subjected to a long wait in prison as constituting torture and thus violating article 3 of the Convention.

Universality and universaliser

Even more problematic is the universalisation of human rights from the point of view of their content: Who is competent to define the content of those rights? Few people question the universality of human rights, but as long as there is no legitimate body that can define the content of universal human rights the universality lacks basic legitimacy. In many recent conflicts the international community has justified its military intervention on the grounds of protection of human rights and restoration of the rule of law. International law however is not prepared for such universalisation or the consequences of intervention such as the establishment of de facto protectorates of the United Nations (Somalia, Bosnia and Herzegovina, Kosovo, East Timor). International organisations that are responsible for security in these situations are lacking in legitimacy and cannot guarantee the rule of law. Such organisations are not accountable to any court and have no system of separation of powers. The state apparatus that can provide the basis for law and order still bases its legitimacy on popular sovereignty! International interventions are not a substitute for popular sovereignty. The international community restricts its focus to the protection of human rights. The preconditions for the establishment of a just political order must in accordance with the traditional theory of state emanate from the *pouvoir constituant* that derives its legitimacy from the sovereignty of the people.

International Criminal Court

With the establishment of the International Criminal Court, which has jurisdiction to try international war crimes and crimes against humanity committed by even the highest representatives of a state, the international community took an important step towards the universalisation of human rights. The United States however still refuses to submit to this international criminal jurisdiction, as it wishes to maintain its world-wide policing role to protect its own interests, and fears the politicisation of the ICC jurisdiction to the detriment of the US. The main problem however is not politics. The judiciary as the third branch of government is inevitably politicised. The main problem is legitimacy. Though the United States considers itself legitimately empowered to intervene in other states on behalf of the international community, it denies the legitimate authority of the International Criminal Court to adjudicate on crimes that American soldiers may have committed in the course of such interventions. In 2002 a federal law was passed in the United States which requires the executive to intervene – militarily if necessary – for the protection of American soldiers in the event that they are brought before the International Criminal Court.

Selective justice through the media

Reports of human rights violations committed in even the most remote corners of the world can today be disseminated via internet and television almost instantaneously all around the world. Internationally renowned media outlets financed by private advertising are however also able to be selective in their reports of human rights violations, and thereby to influence public opinion and the foreign policy of particular governments. Some idealistic international non-governmental organisations (NGOs) aim to inform the international public and governments about human rights abuses in order to mobilise political leaders in the interest of a universal human rights policy. Thus, human rights are no longer a matter for the internal decision-making of isolated sovereign states. The field of human rights is entrusted to a diffuse and complex, often opaque, international network that may ultimately undermine its own credibility.

Double standards in human rights policies

Grave breaches of human and minority rights committed by a state can – as we have seen – be condemned by the UN Security Council and fought with international economic sanctions or even military intervention. Human rights and minority rights are thus tied up with international politics. Those suffering oppression at the hands of the state may hope for the support of the international community, which if necessary, will be prepared to intervene under the leadership of the US. But ultimately even human rights are subject to the political and strategic interests of the United States and the global economy.

Iraq

The American/British intervention with the 'coalition of the willing' in Iraq demonstrated that the US superpower is able, even in the absence of a UN Security Council resolution, to intervene militarily and to occupy foreign territory based on arguments of human rights violations, the fight against terrorism and protection from 'weapons of mass destruction'. This preventative war was not expressly authorised by the Security Council, but nor was it condemned. Although the Charter of the UN provides that military intervention can only be justified in response to an act of aggression, it is now apparent that without changing the Charter it has become acceptable for those who breach the Charter to justify their action on the basis of the alleged defence of human rights, even as preventative protection against a potential aggressor. The recent intervention of Israel in Lebanon provides another example of such 'preventative' action.

Regional protection of human rights

Human rights are the subject of legally enforceable international conventions, both at the global and regional levels. Within Europe the European Court of Human Rights plays a leading role. This court can make legally binding decisions on human rights violations, as the court of final instance. Thus member states have empowered the European Court of Human Rights to have the final say in relation to human rights, surpassing the jurisdiction of national courts including constitutional courts. The ECHR can review national legislation that is alleged to breach human rights and may declare such legislation invalid (even in relation to legislatures of member states that do not have judicial review in their domestic law). Human rights are thus withdrawn not only from the purview of the legislature, but also from that of the *pouvoir constituant*.

Good governance

In relation to countries which depend on international credit from the World Bank or the International Monetary Fund, these credit providers have developed criteria of 'good governance' that have to be fulfilled. Aside from the rule of law and the observance of human rights, criteria for 'good governance' include: transparency of government activities, public accountability of the government and its members, and the transparent conduct of open and periodic elections and/or referenda. Public institutions need to reflect the needs of the people. Authorities have to justify their decisions and they must be able to implement those decisions effectively. All people living in the country must be able to benefit from economic development. Every citizen must have access to information, and freedom of thought and freedom of expression must be guaranteed. Recently the World Bank has even required public functions to be decentralised.

With these standards the question of legitimacy arises again. From where does an international institution, financed with the tax revenue of member states, derive its legitimacy to determine what constitutes 'good governance' and to dictate how countries should be governed? The legal and political responsibility for the catastrophic consequences of a wrong decision will not be borne by the international credit institution nor by its employees, as the example of Argentina at the beginning of the new century demonstrates.

Environmental protection

The protection of the environment and sustainable use of resources are of critical importance for the long-term survival of mankind. The environment is not bound by state borders – the oceans, the air and the ozone layer belong to all human beings. And yet, local actions can have an enormous effect on the entire planet. In daily activities (traffic and energy consumption), as well as with high-risk investments (nuclear power plants) or high-risk research projects (gene technology), there may be unthinkable repercussions on the global or regional environment. Those who act locally often carry at the same time a global responsibility. However international law does little to hold anyone accountable for the environmental consequences of their actions. The first international attempts to limit the global strain on the environment have been consistently rejected by the world's greatest consumer of energy: the United States. The protection of the global environment also is embedded within the international network of economic interest!

Terrorists against states

Up to now a distinction has been made between international law as the basis for international peace, and domestic law as an order that regulates human beings within a particular state territory. Recently the dividing line between these two legal orders has become blurred. Since 9/11 with regard to terrorism there has not been any law that has been recognised as being clearly applicable to conflicts. Thus, the USA has refused to comply with international humanitarian law and the Geneva Conventions with respect to prisoners of the 'war against terror' because it classifies them as 'unlawful combatants' rather than prisoners of war. This is in spite of the fact that these people were captured in the course of a war waged by the American military in Afghanistan. It now appears that any foreign national who is arrested by the American army in a foreign land can, under American military law, have judgment passed on them by a decree of the American President rather than by an impartial court after a fair trial.

In addition to the fall of the Berlin Wall, the terrorist attacks of 9/11 in New York and Washington have also had a significant impact on the development of the understanding of the state and its function. For the first time in history a private terrorist organisation declared and waged war against a superpower. The more powerful a state the more asymmetric and uncontrollable warfare becomes. In future, war will be waged not only between states but also between the state and private organisations that are dispersed and difficult to locate. As a means of self-defence in response to the 9/11 attacks, the US could not directly attack the private organisation, but instead attacked the territory of the state in which the US believed members of the terrorist organisation were being granted shelter. Thus the right to self-defence can now be claimed against states and peoples that are at the mercy of terrorist organisations. States and peoples can therefore be dragged into a war against their will if they arouse the suspicion that they may harbour terrorist organisations – as seen in the recent case of Lebanon. A clear distinction between the state and private persons no longer exists. States and their populations are being held responsible for the actions of private organisations within their territory, whether it be actual terrorist attacks or simply terrorist activity on the internet.

Fading state borders

Globalisation has led to the erosion of borderlines between nations and peoples. Up to now the state and democracy have been constituted within clearly defined territorial borders. In future, territory will gradually lose its constitutive force for the state. Sovereignty – the symbol of the independence of the nation-state – is fading. The increasing internationalisation of politics and globalisation of the economy have resulted in many state functions being transferred to the international community. International organisations at a regional and global level, as well as ad hoc groups such as the 'coalition of the willing', are taking on policing functions that were previously the responsibility of the nation-state. States have to vouch for their citizens. They bear the responsibility if in the view of the international community they have not taken adequate measures to guard against 'terrorism' as defined by the international community.

The once sovereign nation-states now have to fulfil the expectations of the international community. Even the global market places expectations upon nation-states. States are supposed to be capable of providing for internal stability and ensuring peace among various multicultural communities. The goal of securing peace, which was formerly an international function within the responsibility of the United Nations, has now in part been transferred into the sphere of domestic responsibility of states.

The international community now determines many of the matters that formerly fell within the domestic decision-making capacity of states. Nation-states and especially the weaker states have to submit to the community of states.

Local responsibilities

This does not mean that the nation-state has exhausted its function. On the contrary: As a state and member of the international community it is still responsible for domestic stability, harmony and internal security. Social responsibilities, and implementation and application of the Rule of Law remain almost exclusively within the domain of nation-states. Only the nation-state possesses democratic legitimacy. Although the nation-state has lost the fiction of absolute sovereignty, it remains in reality a political entity that is responsible both internally and externally for its people and its territory. The nation-state can only deal with this development however, when it pushes at the global level for more legitimacy, responsibility and observance of the rule of law on the part of those institutions (and states) wielding international power.

Challenges of the 21st Century

This new environment has unforeseen consequences for nation-states, for the community of states and in general on the understanding of the state:

1. States can no longer make unilateral decisions on the granting of human rights. Since they depend on international cooperation they have to demonstrate that they guarantee the universally valid core of those rights. In relation to human rights the sovereignty of states is in any case no longer the ultimate source of law and society.
2. With the internationalisation of human rights states forfeit their previous claim that the granting of human rights is derived from their sovereign authority. Decisions on human rights no longer find their legitimacy from within the constitution of the nation-state. However, human rights only enjoy supra-state legitimacy to the extent that they are based on a general consensus and connected with certainty of law and equal rights. And this consideration leads to the still open question of whether and to what extent human rights have achieved a universal character and thus have to be included in every state constitution.
3. The states of our time can no longer make their own independent decisions in relation to the economy and finances. The tax rates of industrial states have to be internationally competitive. In this competitive global environment, the developments in social services established over the course of the 20th Century are under increasing pressure. No major political party can afford to accept or promote lower competitiveness for the sake of higher social expenditures and salaries. The space for political decision making has therefore radically diminished with regard to domestic issues such as welfare and social services, economic and financial matters, the environment, science, education, health, food and drug administration, transport and labour.
4. The strengthening of nationalism will also lead to new internal structures within states. Claims of minorities for greater autonomy, and efforts to achieve peace through federalisation in order to accommodate the interests of different ethnicities will only be possible by accepting a fundamentally new conception of the

state. The nation-state of the 19th Century was a democratic unitary state in the French or British sense. Federalism was considered simply as an additional tool for better separation of powers in order to limit state power more effectively for the sake of individual freedom. A state composed of different cultures, religions and ethnicities will discover that decentralisation and federalism can serve an important function in terms of identity, which can provide the state with a new chance to achieve legitimacy not only with regard to its minorities but also in respect of its majority.

5. The interconnectedness of the global economy will continue to affect not only states but also their regions, districts and cities. In addition to traditional treaties and trade agreements between states, regions and cities will begin to enter into international agreements beyond their state borders. Nation-states will therefore have to surrender some of their foreign policy functions not only to international organisations, but also to their own local subunits and local authorities.
6. The international interconnection of economics and politics is attributable to the basic human need to achieve greater freedom through mobility and the division of labour. However the division of labour creates dependencies. The existence of dependencies gives rise to new power. This power in turn must be limited, controlled and exercised in the general interest. For these reasons it is necessary even in the age of globalisation to have political institutions that do what they can to ensure that the power created by the increasing interconnection of the international community remains connected to and constrained by the politics of the state.

3 The View of Man and the State as the Starting Point of State Theories

3.1 The Influence of the Idea of the Human Being on State Theories

3.1.1 Introduction

Human nature?

The question of the relationship between the state as an abstract construct founded by a collective of human beings and wielding authority on the one hand, and human beings on the other hand, is ultimately of a philosophical nature. The question is:

What are the essentials of human nature that are important for the understanding of the state and its authority?

In other words: Why does the human being, in contrast to animals, need a state? And if humans are unable to survive without the state, what should the state look like? How is the state to be structured and designed?

The answer can depart from to extremes:

a) Humans are by nature good beings, all humans are angels: In this case the state would have to be seen as a negative and unnecessary construct because angels do not need a state.
b) Humans are by nature evil beings: All humans are devils and cannot be forced by any state authority to obey orders or live peacefully.

There is no state philosopher who proceeds from the idea that humans are purely good or purely evil. Their understanding of human nature is always more complex and subtly differentiated than these black and white alternatives. For some, humans tend to be generally good, and therefore the state in accordance with this understanding should be circumscribed in its functions and power. For others however, humans are generally malicious creatures but are capable of learning and thus can be brought to order by reason and force.

When we come together with other people, we have our own particular idea of how they will or should behave according to our understanding of human nature. We have expectations with regard to those with whom we interact. Humans are proud, sensitive, ambitious, full of hope, loving, malicious, egocentric, loyal, understanding, communicative, depressive, antisocial, helpful and generous. We thus assume that humans based on their nature behave differently to animals. If the behaviour of a person however does not correspond to our expectations of human nature we will consider it abnormal: bestial, wicked or angelic or even holy.

Humans are capable of learning

Let us imagine that the human is a being that can neither learn nor understand, and that is incapable of communicating. Such a being would not be able to build a state. The establishment of a state presupposes beings that can learn, and that can receive, process and forward information. State regulation of human behaviour through laws is only meaningful when the rules can be understood and obeyed by the people living within the state. Man must not only understand the laws but must also be able to comply with them – in other words, he must be capable, on the basis of his own reason, of following the rules. Without this ability to comprehend and to judge the correctness of a legal order, and without freedom of will, laws could not be enacted by parliament nor followed by citizens. So too there could be no judgments of criminal conviction, as criminal law presupposes the liberty of humans to reflect and to choose and therefore makes them responsible for their behaviour. As mentioned above, if all human beings were purely good or purely wicked, states in the modern sense would be nonsensical.

Can one distinguish between superior and inferior human beings? Humans as Homo sapiens, independent of race or gender, belong to the genus of the most highly developed living beings. There have however always been movements that have sought to distinguish and categorise human beings according to their race, gender or religion. Such attitudes have been used to justify discrimination against certain races, nations and the female gender as a whole and have legitimised oppression and human rights abuses (segregation, apartheid), the exploitation of people as slaves, and even the attempt at extermination of an entire race (Holocaust).

Humans can say "No"

In Europe until the 15th Century, it was generally believed that humans were naturally assigned to a particular fixed position with the feudal hierarchy of society. According to this understanding, each man and woman had his or her allocated place within the universe, and performed the role assigned to them by fate, which corresponded to their nature and status.

The European Renaissance marked the beginning of a radical shift in the view of the nature of human beings. In this period the humanists recognised that humans can be distinguished from other living beings principally by the fact that as beings endowed with reason they are fundamentally equal and therefore need not accept that their fate is predetermined nor that they have been assigned an unalterable position within the social hierarchy. To some extent humans can determine their 'nature' through their own capacity and will. Humans can enlarge their knowledge independently, and based on their knowledge and reasoning capacity can form judgments and make decisions. In short: they have the consciousness and the volition to say "no" or "yes". His capacity for reason makes man the only being in the world that is not merely an object but also a subject that can consciously and deliberately shape his environment.

The state as a coercive order

The foundation was thereby laid for the later secularisation of the state and for the transfer of state authority from the 'grace of God' to the people. However, the important question of whether the human being is actually dependent upon a political community – in the sense of the state as a rational artificial construct established by reflection and choice – remained open. A state can, if necessary, enforce legal obligations by means of coercion and force. Some states confer upon themselves the power to impose the death penalty on criminals as revenge or deterrence. In cases of legitimate defence states are still able, for the protection of their state integrity, to require their citizens to make the ultimate sacrifice: to give their own life.

In earlier times the king based his legitimacy on religion: God gave him the divine right to rule as king. Today, states can derive their legitimacy only through democracy, that is, from popular sovereignty. But from where does the majority within a democracy derive the authority to rule over the minority? Ultimately such power can only be philosophically explained by reference to the nature of the human being. Only if we can clearly demonstrate that minorities also need a state, albeit with limited authority, are majorities able to justify their decisions with regard to minorities. Thus, one has to try to explain that a supra-familial artificial polity corresponds to a necessary and immanent need of human nature. If humans were angels they could live without any authority. They would, based on their insight and nature, always make good and correct decisions and would without laws and without force always treat others kindly. Angels don't need a government. Those who share this optimism will argue that state is a negative and unnecessary construct and should be abolished for the benefit of mankind.

Malevolent humans

At the opposite end of the spectrum we can find theories of state according to which human beings are by nature evil and malicious beings that would live in a perpetual state of war, were it not for the force and authority of the state that keeps them in check. Thus it is the state that enables people to live in peace. If humans were all fiends the state would be as pointless as it would if humans were all saints. States which guide humans with laws are thus only meaningful when human beings need binding obligations as guidelines for doing the right thing, and at the same time are capable of learning and conforming to the will of the legislature and the state authority. Thus, the state theories of the Enlightenment that initiated the secularisation of the state were characterised by a view of human nature that was somewhere in between the extreme views of man as angelic or demonic in nature.

Rational egoists

Some theorists see man as an egoistic creature that strives to pursue its own selfish interests, but is also able through reason – within limited parameters – to act sensibly without coercion and to stand up for the common good. For the advocates of this view, man cannot live without the state and state authority, but the force and authority of the state should be confined only to areas where the state is absolutely necessary, and people should otherwise be left free to act according to their reason. In this moderate group the spectrum of different and nuanced views is very wide: it ranges from those who emphasise the reason of man (I. KANT) right through to exponents of the view that man is a profit-seeking creature, and that therefore the *invisible hand* will ensure the just distribution of wealth (ADAM SMITH).

Others however see man as inherently conflict-prone, argumentative and violent. According to this perspective, humans can only survive if they form an artificial association which is able to hold them peacefully together through authority, force and coercion.

In the following pages we will explore the connection between the conception of man and the theory of state, based on select examples of the most prominent exponents of these different tendencies. These examples will reveal that the Enlightenment views of human nature, which led to a new understanding of the modern state, were decisively influenced by the view of human nature found in Christian philosophy.

3.1.2 The View of Human Nature within Christian Theology: State and State Authority are Ordained by God and thus Indispensable for Human Beings

The search for the human of paradise

The modern European philosophy of state is indelibly marked by Christian thought. At first, modern thought justified the power of the ruler with religious and moral arguments, as all ethical questions were regarded as being inherently religious questions. *Not until the development of the modern concept of natural law connected to human reason was it possible to separate ethical issues from religion.*

In early Christianity, thinking on the state was oriented more towards the world hereafter than it was focused on the political reality of this world.

The significant influence of the biblical view of human nature and the atomised individual upon theories of state in modern constitutionalism was demonstrated by GEORG JELLINEK (1851–1911) in his essay on 'Adam in the theory of state'. Those theories influenced by Christianity are primarily concerned to explore the human condition before and after the state of paradise. In paradise, would humans still need a state? In such conditions would state force be necessary to enforce laws? Would human beings not naturally want what is good and thus serve the common interest, without any directives or orders? Is the state therefore only a consequence of original sin, a construct that has thus become a necessary evil? Must human beings accept the power of the state in all its manifestations as the unfortunate but necessary consequence of the original sin?

3.1.2.1 AUGUSTINE (354–430): The State as Necessary Evil

The original sin and the fall of man

The fall of man is, either expressly or as a theoretical precondition, the starting point of considerations on the theory of state for those theorists directly influenced by Christian theology. For AUGUSTINE (354–430), the state has its origin in the nature of man based on Adam. The initially harmonious relationship of Adam and Eve with their Master in paradise is a demonstration or preview of the City of God. The goal of mankind is to attain the City of God, however the realisation of this state (*de civitate dei contra paganso*, the city of God against the pagans) will only occur at the end of time. In contrast, Adam the sinner and his successor Cain created the city of men or the earthly city (*civitas terrena*), which is essentially marked with the irreversible curse of the original sin.

If man was angelic, without guilt or sin, there would only be the City of God in which eternal peace prevails. Because humans are sinful they have to submit to earthly authority, even when it is exercised by scoundrels. "The earthly city, which does not live by faith, seeks an earthly peace, and the end it proposes, in the well-ordered concord of civic obedience and rule, is the combination of men's wills to attain the things which are helpful to this life... And each victory even though it goes to the bad is a punishment of God in order to humiliate the losers and to purify them from their sins be it to punish them for their sins" (St AUGUSTINE *City of God*, Book XIX, Chapter 17).

Original sin and power

The earthly city according to AUGUSTINE is marked by war, misery and need. For this reason the first goal of each human community must be to establish peace. This peace however will always be merely an earthly peace. Permanent and eternal peace will only come when the Son of God returns to Earth and establishes the City of God.

The theme of the heavenly city and the earthly city is essentially the story of two opposing views of man, determined by religion. The guilt caused by the original sin dominates as the basis of authority. In other words: the question of the justification of power is simply not put, because it is a political question. For AUGUSTINE there is no political 'state power', because the state is merely a consequence and an expression of the religious views of humans.

3.1.2.2 THOMAS AQUINAS (1225–1274): No Humans without State

Zoon politikon

THOMAS AQUINAS takes a different view of the relationship of human beings to the state. Influenced by the philosophy of ARISTOTLE, according to which man is by nature dependent upon community, he concludes that it is not the guilt of humans but rather their sociability which results in the establishment of authority structures within supra-familial communities. Furthermore, a household or a village cannot be self-sufficient in the way that a city, province or state can: "[self-sufficiency] exists in a city, which is a perfect community with regard to all the necessities of life; but still more in a province because of the need of fighting together and of mutual help against enemies" (THOMAS AQUINAS, *De regimine principum on Kingship*, Book I, chapter 1).

Authority and paradise

In contrast to AUGUSTINE and later LUTHER, for whom the state is a consequence of the Fall of Man, THOMAS AQUINAS sees the state independently of the original sin as something that corresponds to the natural need of human beings. In paradise as well as post-paradise humans by nature are unable to exist without the state. But how does THOMAS AQUINAS explain the need for coercive power or at least authority even within the state of paradise? He asserts that just as there is a state in paradise as well as in the aftermath of the original sin, authority is also suitable in both situations, as it is part of human nature. However he distinguishes the two types of authority: in one sense, authority can be understood as the opposite of enslavement. The person who has subjugated another person as slave wields authority as the master. In another very general sense authority can also be understood as that which exists in the relationship between a human being and a master to which he/she is somehow subordinate. 'Master' from this point of view is the one who is in a position or an office with the responsibility to guide free peoples. Whilst authority in the first sense is incompatible with the innocent state of nature, authority in the second sense is entirely consistent with the original state of nature. To exert authority in the second sense means that the power over other free human beings is aimed at the fulfilment of the welfare and the common good of those subjects. Such authority over human beings existed in the original state of nature. The state as a supra-familial form of community is needed because human beings are by nature sociable beings. And AQUINAS writes that a social life cannot exist amongst human beings without some leadership or authority. A leader should possess great knowledge and virtue, and use those gifts for the benefit of all, in the sense intended by Peter: "Each one should use whatever gift he has received to serve others…" (1 Peter 4:10) (THOMAS AQUINAS, *Summa Theologica*, Question 96, Art. 4).

Common good as the goal of authority

In the condition of paradise, authority is directed towards the common good, which everyone tries to achieve. Because human beings are burdened by the original sin they need however also to tolerate authority that they do not accept, in certain cases even slavery.

But who gives the ruler the right to rule others? "Therefore God so governs things that He makes some of them to be causes of others in government; as a master, who not only imparts knowledge to his pupils, but gives also the faculty of teaching others" (THOMAS AQUINAS, *Summa Theologica*, book I, Question 103, Art. 6).

Authority by the grace of God

The highest authority in world is God (Jesus Christ) the *kyros*. It is from God that states and their rulers derive their authority to govern. This is a view was often repeated and confirmed by the later catholic teaching. "Hence, it is divinely ordained that he should lead his life—be it family, or civil—with his fellow men, amongst whom alone his several wants can be adequately supplied. But, as no society can hold together unless some one be over all, directing all to strive earnestly for the common good, every body politic must have a ruling authority, and this authority, no less than society itself, has its source in nature, and has, consequently, God for its Author. Hence, it follows that all public power must proceed from God. For God alone is the true and supreme Lord of the world. Everything, without exception, must be subject to Him, and must serve him, so that whosoever holds the right to govern holds it from one sole and single source, namely, God, the sovereign Ruler of all. There is no power but from God." (*Encyclical On the Christian Constitution of States*, Pope Leo XIII, 1885).

Whatever the view of human nature, the state in the Christian world was a consequence of the rule of God over mankind. State power to use coercive force was legitimised by divine authority. Man was created by God, and it was God's will to submit man to state authority. The rulers, who were responsible for realising the common good (*bonum commune*), fulfilled the will of God on this earth and were legitimised by the Pope as kings with divine authority. State authority was ultimately authority ordered by God. The law too had its origin in divine wisdom and God's will. Law and legislation were ordained and prescribed by God.

Sources of liberalism?

However, with secularisation, state and law were stripped of their divine origin. How was this possible? The Christianity of the Middle Ages had itself, principally through the influence of THOMAS AQUINAS, begun to pave the way for later secularisation. The idea that humans stand as subjects in relation to the state was in essence already to be found in scholarly works, above all in the writings of THOMAS AQUINAS. He required from the body politic that it give to each individual what is his, that is, that its decisions should enable each individual to achieve his goals. Thus AQUINAS departs from the basic idea that humans are merely objects of the will of God or of a political authority. Rather, they are to be respected as subjects with individual will.

Nine principles of THOMAS AQUINAS' theory of state

The key elements in the theory of THOMAS AQUINAS are:

1. Man is a rational animal created by God;
2. Man carries personal goals within himself;
3. Man is a being with his own worth and dignity;
4. Man is by nature free, and survives as a result of his own will;
5. Man is a subject and can as such not be reduced to a generality;

6. Man is not only an individual and a subject but is also by nature a social being (*zoon politikon* for ARISTOTLE);
7. Because man is by nature sociable he is also by nature a political animal;
8. The aim of politics and of the state is to enable each individual to achieve his own goals;
9. The state is founded by the nature of man, whilst man finds his origin and his goal in God.

3.1.2.3 Reformation

i. MARTIN LUTHER (1483–1546)

Two kingdoms

The view of AUGUSTINE was developed and extended by MARTIN LUTHER in his essay 'On Secular Authority'. He divides the world into kingdoms, the kingdom of God and the kingdom of the world:

"Here we must divide Adam's children, all mankind, into two parts: the first belong to the kingdom of God, the second to the kingdom of the world. All those who truly believe in Christ belong to God's kingdom, for Christ is king and lord in God's kingdom, as the second Psalm [v. 6] and the whole of Scripture proclaims…Now: these people need neither secular Sword nor law. And if all the world were true Christians, that is, if everyone truly believed, there would be neither need nor use for princes, kings, lords, the Sword or law. …. All those who are not Christians [in the above sense] belong to the kingdom of the world or [in other words] are under the law. There are few who believe, and even fewer who behave like Christians and refrain from doing evil [themselves], let alone not resisting evil [done to them]. And for the rest God has established another government, outside the Christian estate and the kingdom of God, and has cast them into subjection to the Sword. So that, however much they would like to do evil, they are unable to act in accordance with their inclinations, or, if they do, they cannot do so without fear, or enjoy peace and good fortune. In the same way, a wicked, fierce animal is chained and bound so that it cannot bite or tear, as its nature would prompt it to do, however much it wants to; whereas a tame, gentle animal needs nothing like chains or bonds and is harmless even without them. If there were [no law and government], then seeing that all the world is evil and that scarcely one human being in a thousand is a true Christian, people would devour each other and no one would be able to support his wife and children, feed himself and serve God. The world would become a desert. And so God has ordained the two governments, the spiritual [government] which fashions true Christians and just persons through the Holy Spirit under Christ, and the secular government which holds the Unchristian and wicked in check and forces them to keep the peace outwardly and be still, like it or not" (MARTIN LUTHER, *On Secular Authority: To What Extent it Should be Obeyed*, No. 3 and 4 (1523)).

Civitas terrena

According to LUTHER, Christians do not need laws. As Christian believers they behave themselves properly even without laws. On the other hand, it is necessary to enact laws for non-Christians in order to maintain peace and keep them under control: "Therefore care must be taken to keep these two governments distinct, and both must be allowed to continue [their work], the one to make [people] just, the other to create outward peace and prevent evildoing… It [the Sword] is not a terror to good works, but to the wicked" (M. LUTHER, On Secular Authority). But, because few believers behave as real Christians and therefore there cannot be a Kingdom of Christians, worldly authority – or in the words of AUGUSTINE, the *civitas terrena* – has to be established all over the world.

ii.HULDRYCH ZWINGLI (1484–1531) and JEAN CALVIN (1509–1564)

The Parliament of Zurich and the theology of alliance

With the Reformation, the first important turn towards the development of people's sovereignty was initiated. Relying on LUTHER'S theory of the two kingdoms and on the biblical story of the ancient people of Israel and their covenant with God, the reformers ZWINGLI and CALVIN replaced the concept of king and pope being empowered by the grace of God with the concept of God's will being vested in the people of the believers. Worldly and spiritual authority found their bases, justification and origin in the alliance between the believers and God. The ruler no longer derived his title directly from God, but rather from the people, whose sovereignty over right and wrong stemmed from their alliance with God. Institutionally, these ideas were first realised by ZWINGLI in the Parliament of Zurich. The philosopher JOHANNES ALTHUSIUS transformed this view of theology into a theory of state.

3.1.3 Enlightenment

From Christianity to 'modernity'

With these new ideas the power of state authority was bound to the alliance of the people with its God. Accordingly, it was no longer to God directly, but rather to the people, that rulers were accountable for the exercise of their authority. Rulers were no longer able to avoid responsibility toward the people by arguing that they are responsible only to God and that subjects are therefore not entitled to question their authority.

Secularisation of the state and state authority

The next step was the total separation of the legitimacy of authority and legal rights and obligations from the Almighty or any transcendental might. This move to a legitimacy fully detached from God was only possible through the general secularisation of state and law. In a secular legal system, law and justice should be based on some foundation other than theology and religious ethics.

From the sovereignty of God to sovereignty of the people

But how can one justify the entitlement of the people, even without the alliance with God, to become the origin, basis and starting point for the legal order? How is 'the people' able to justify itself as the 'Big Bang' from which all authority and sovereignty is derived? Surely the majority of a people cannot claim to have the right to make valid and binding decisions for the minority. The German reunification for example was legitimised by a decision of the majority of the voters. But was this majority legitimately able to decide for the minority? The minority can only be bound by the decision of the majority, if the following is undisputed:

1. that the German people is a single entity that can make decisions by majority; and
2. that this entity has the legitimate legal authority to enable the majority to enact a constitution and to enact binding legislation.

The first question will be dealt with in Chapter eight. This question has become especially topical and controversial in the era of postmodernism. The second question however was mainly an issue of the Enlightenment, which led to the foundation of modern constitutionalism. This question will be treated within the following pages by exploring various philosophical theories of the Enlightenment period, which largely based their understandings of legitimacy on their particular conceptions of the human being.

3.1.3.1 War of All against All (THOMAS HOBBES)

Cromwell, the Leviathan?

The real founder of modern constitutionalism is THOMAS HOBBES (1588–1679). HOBBES developed the theoretical foundation for the justification of the state and political authority that was logical and coherent, and which took God out of the equation as far as law, state and politics were concerned. Perhaps as a result of witnessing the existential fear and insecurity of the people during the English civil war, the need of human beings for security and survival was for him the highest possible value. Within this turbulent milieu, after the abolition of the monarchy and the execution of Charles I in 1649 by the Long Parliament and before the instalment of Lord Cromwell as Lord Protector and Head of State (1599–1658) by the Rump Parliament in 1653, HOBBES' main oeuvre *Leviathan* was completed and published in 1651. In this important philosophical work he legitimises the right of subjects to change their ruler in the event that the ruler is no longer able to protect his subjects.

The 'egocentric' human being

"So that in the nature of man, we find three principal causes of quarrel. First, competition; secondly, diffidence; thirdly, glory. The first maketh men invade for gain; the second, for safety; and the third, for reputation. The first use violence, to make themselves masters of other men's persons, wives, children, and cattle; the second, to defend them; the third, for trifles, as a word, a smile, a different opinion, and any other sign of undervalue, either direct in their persons or by reflection in their kindred, their friends, their nation, their profession, or their name. Hereby it is manifest that during the time men live without a common power to keep them all in awe, they are in that condition which is called war; and such a war as is of every man against every man" (THOMAS HOBBES, *Leviathan* Part 1 chapter 13).

Social contract in order to pacify the War of All against All

This war of all against all can only be subdued by a strict coercive order that mediates the quarrels of human beings. As human beings' greatest fear is a violent death, they are content to live under such an order on the grounds of self-preservation. Such peaceful order cannot however be established with laws alone, "... and covenants, without the sword, are but words and of no strength to secure a man at all. Therefore, notwithstanding the laws of nature (which every one hath then kept, when he has the will to keep them, when he can do it safely), if there be no power erected, or not great enough for our security, every man will and may lawfully rely on his own strength and art for caution against all other men" (THOMAS HOBBES, *Leviathan* Part 2 Chapter 17).

For this reason laws need to be enforced with coercive power, if necessary by use of force. Peace can only be achieved if each individual transfers all his power or authority to one or more others to exercise on his behalf.

"The only way to erect such a common power, as may be able to defend them from the invasion of foreigners, and the injuries of one another, and thereby to secure them in such sort as that by their own industry and by the fruits of the earth they may nourish themselves and live contentedly, is to confer all their power and strength upon one man, or upon one assembly of men, that may reduce all their wills, by plurality of voices, unto one will: which is as much as to say, to appoint one man, or assembly of men, to bear their person; and every one to own and acknowledge himself to be author of whatsoever he that so beareth their person shall act, or cause to be acted, in those things which concern the common peace and safety; and therein to submit their wills, every one to his will, and their judgements to his judgement" (THOMAS HOBBES, *Leviathan* Part 2 Chapter 17).

This is only possible by a contract under which all people submit themselves to authority:

"This is more than consent, or concord; it is a real unity of them all in one and the same person, made by covenant of every man with every man, in such manner as if every man should say to every man: I authorise and give up my right of governing myself to this man, or to this assembly of men, on this condition; that thou give up, thy right to him, and authorise all his actions in like manner. This done, the multitude so united in one person is called a COMMONWEALTH; in

Latin, CIVITAS. This is the generation of that great LEVIATHAN, or rather, to speak more reverently, of that mortal god to which we owe, under the immortal God, our peace and defence" (THOMAS HOBBES, *Leviathan* Part 2 Chapter 17).

Leviathan: The Commonwealth

"From this institution of a Commonwealthare derived all the rights and faculties of him, or them, on whom the sovereign power is conferred by the consent of the people assembled" (THOMAS HOBBES, *Leviathan* Part 2 Chapter 18).

The representative of this state thus has all powers. Although HOBBES does not rule out systems of government other than monarchical government, he still clearly gives priority to the monarchy. These rulers are entitled to sovereign legal authority because all legal authority emerges out of the covenant by which the state and state authority were created.

"It is true that they that have sovereign power may commit iniquity, but not injustice or injury in the proper signification. ...and consequently to that which was said last, no man that hath sovereign power can justly be put to death, or otherwise in any manner by his subjects punished. For seeing every subject is author of the actions of his sovereign, he punisheth another for the actions committed by himself" (THOMAS HOBBES, *Leviathan* Part 2 Chapter 18).

Prometheus

With the construction of the social contract HOBBES managed, like Prometheus in the Greek legend, to steal the 'fire of sovereignty' from the gods. In the case of Prometheus, the consequence was that human beings became more independent from nature. With the theory of the social contract, HOBBES transferred sovereignty and the ultimate basis for the validity of state and law to mankind and thus to the peoples of a secular world. He released the state and political authority from any legal (not moral) responsibility towards God. Rulers have a moral obligation to God to be just and righteous, but this does not change the fact that subjects must submit to the legal orders of the ruler even though the ruler's acts may be immoral.

Under the social contract, human beings that exert state authority acquire the legitimacy to make decisions affecting the fate of the polity and all of the people entrusted to the polity. The social contract became the fictitious big bang from which the state, political authority, justice and law were said to have originated.

The social contract is limited to the protection of the people and the maintenance of internal peace. The state authority however is entirely free to assess and determine what must be done to achieve these ends. The people are indeed protected by the Leviathan, but who protects the people *from* the Leviathan? HOBBES concedes that those who exert state sovereignty may exhibit the negative aspects of human nature and be egoistic, deceitful and brutal, but he accepts this as a lesser evil (and the price to be paid for the greater good: Leviathan affords protection and thus survival). Would he have made the same judgment if he had known of the brutalities of the Nazi regime?

The 'Big Bang'

The view of the power-hungry human being that cannot be restrained merely with laws but only by force leads not only to the secular justification of the state, but also to the justification of the unlimited and absolute might of the state. Although the state is bound by morality, the state is also the single source and origin of all laws.

The unique achievement of HOBBES stems from the fact that his theory of the social contract is based upon a view of the human being that sees man as possessing the reason and will to make decisions concerning his own fate, and therefore also capable on the basis of *reflection and choice* of creating an artificial supra-familial body politic. It is self evident that all those who belong to the polity are equal citizens able to make rational decisions, who have entered into the social contract based on their understanding of the necessity of the social contract for their own protection.

It is important however to bear in mind that HOBBES, unlike LOCKE, does not take as his starting point the idea that in primeval times men did in fact literally conclude a social contract. For HOBBES, the social contract is a fictitious precondition of the state, without which the state and political authority are unthinkable. Mankind could not survive without the state and political authority, which are an inherent consequence of the nature of man.

3.1.3.2 The Significance of HOBBES' State Philosophy for Modern Times

HOBBES and the later legal positivism

The idea of the social contract brought about a fundamental change in the theory and practice of state and law. From this point on, positivist theory relied on the concepts of the social contract and the Leviathan, as evidenced in the important positivist works of JOHN AUSTIN (1790–1859), HERBERT HART (1907–1992) and HANS KELSEN (1881–1973). Now the secularised state, law and justice are at the mercy of the rulers' discretion. State and law can be shaped and altered according to the visions of the Leviathan. The status and the position of the individual within the hierarchy are no longer dependent on the verdict of God. With the fire of Prometheus man became independent from nature; with the 'fire' of HOBBES on the other hand, society was secularised and man achieved independence from the Almighty.

State absolutism of the European continent

HOBBES' theory of the absolutist Leviathan had its greatest influence on the European continent. The European nation-states that emerged after the French Revolution were marked with the idea that human rights do not precede the state but rather are derived from the state. The state must first be created in order that the state can grant rights under its constitution. The state according to this understanding, is the only source and basis of law and the constitution. In contrast to this perspective, the Anglo-Saxon and American understanding of the state was primarily influenced by the ideas of JOHN LOCKE born half a century later.

States as islands of sovereignty

Modern philosophy led to a new interpretation of the relationship between state and man. There were two key starting points:

- The science of the anthropology became part of (and a prerequisite for) the philosophy of state.
- The state was regarded as having an indispensable function in securing the life of the human being.

HOBBES, whom one can without doubt regard as the true founder of modernity, constructed the state as the only corrective to the war-riddled state of nature. He thereby reduced the 'political' to only one possible polity, which has a monopoly on the use of force and the securing of peace, both internally and externally. The theoretical preparation was thereby in place for an anarchic world community comprising centralised states that conduct themselves as isolated islands of sovereignty.

Healing the shortcomings of man through the state

The analysis of human nature is for HOBBES an indispensable prerequisite for the explanation and justification of the state. Out of the nature of the human being he deduces the need for a state, since without the state mankind could not survive. The state thus becomes the remedy for the deficiencies of the state of nature. According to HOBBES, man is characterised by a double-nature:

a) Humans are natural beings; and also
b) Reasonable beings.

The human being by its nature will pursue the drive to expand at the cost of other human beings (*bellum omnium contra omnes*), and it is the state alone that can curb this urge for power.

Nature and significance of the social contract

As a reflexive and reasonable being, man is capable of banding together with his own kind to form a state. The foundation of the polity is based on a social contract, which constitutes an act of submission by the people to be bound by the polity. The key features of this act are:

a) Reason reveals the path to peace, through natural law.
b) The social contract is empty a far as freedom and liberty are concerned; it contains only two articles (articles of peace):
   ba) peace should be sought,
   bb) peace can be achieved and imposed by state force.
c) The state is thus the indispensable consequence of the necessity to establish peace within the society.

d) The laws of the state must be enforceable, by use of force if necessary.
e) Peace can only be established when each individual transfers all his power and authority to one or more others (Leviathan).
f) This can only be achieved by a contract under which all are prepared to submit to the one single institution with the power to command. The contract is limited only to the protection of peoples and to the maintenance of internal peace.
g) Bearer of this authority is the representative of the state, a *Leviathan*, that is – an artificial body politic. The sovereign (Leviathan) represents the will of those who installed it via the social contract.
h) With the conclusion of the social contract people become citizens: they emerge out of the state of nature (*status naturalis*) and enter into the civil state (*status civilis*).
i) The sovereign is the bearer of supreme and unlimited power. Why? Because the law is derived only out of the social contract (positivism) and therefore legally the sovereign can do no wrong.

Positivism, decisionism and moralism are the main characteristics of HOBBES' philosophy of state. He achieved the conclusive secularisation of sovereign political authority. Because the sovereign bears absolute power and because sovereign authority is indivisible, the separation of powers is neither possible nor necessary.

3.1.3.3 The Reasonable Human Being in Natural Law according to the Enlightment– JOHN LOCKE (1632–1704) and IMMANUEL KANT (1724–1804)

i. JOHN LOCKE

Social Contract for the Protection of Inalienable Rights

State of nature

JOHN LOCKE also constructs his ideas on the basis of an assumed state of nature of the human being. "To understand political power right, and derive it from its original, we must consider, what state all men are naturally in, and that is, a state of perfect freedom to order their actions, and dispose of their possessions and persons, as they think fit..." (JOHN LOCKE, *Second Treatise on Government*, Chapter II Section 4 (1690)). Such liberty can only be given up by a social contract:

"Men being, as has been said, by nature, all free, equal, and independent, no one can be put out of this estate, and subjected to the political power of another, without his own consent. The only way whereby any one divests himself of his natural liberty, and puts on the bonds of civil society, is by agreeing with other men to join and unite into a community for their comfortable, safe, and peaceable living one amongst another, in a secure enjoyment of their properties, and a greater security against any, that are not of it." (J. LOCKE, *Second Treatise on Government*, Chapter VIII Section 95).

According to LOCKE (and in contrast to HOBBES), the social contract does not entail the transfer of all rights and powers to one institution or ruler, but rather to the majority that makes decisions on behalf of the community. However, not all rights and powers are ceded to the community, but rather only such powers as are necessary for the realisation of the common good of the community.

"But though men, when they enter into society, give up the equality, liberty, and executive power they had in the state of nature, into the hands of the society, to be so far disposed of by the legislative, as the good of the society shall require; yet it being only with an intention in every one the better to preserve himself, his liberty and property; (for no rational creature can be supposed to change his condition with an intention to be worse) the power of the society, or legislative constituted by them, can never be supposed to extend farther, than the common good; but is obliged to secure every one's property, by providing against those three defects above mentioned, that made the state of nature so unsafe and uneasy. And so whoever has the legislative or supreme power of any commonwealth, is bound to govern by established standing laws, promulgated and known to the people, and not by extemporary decrees; by indifferent and upright judges, who are to decide controversies by those laws; and to employ the force of the community at home, only in the execution of such laws, or abroad to prevent or redress foreign injuries, and secure the community from inroads and invasion. And all this to be directed to no other end, but the peace, safety, and public good of the people" (J. LOCKE, *Second Treatise on Government*, Chapter IX Section 131).

Necessity for general laws

Contrary to HOBBES, the state of nature for LOCKE is not a state of war. However there are neither laws nor judges that can legitimately determine the settlement of disputes. Natural law might be apt to the task of regulating right and wrong, but people are moved by their own interests and are not familiar with natural law. It is therefore necessary to devise clear and transparent positive legal rules of general application (J. LOCKE, *Second Treatise on Government*, Chapter IX Section 124).

The content of these laws however should correspond to the natural law. Moreover, the state should not interfere with the inalienable rights and freedoms of man (which precede the state), and in particular it should not interfere with private property (understood as the fundamental right from which other rights and liberties flow).

The state of nature that is characterised by the freedom of the individual is regulated only by natural law. However, in order to be able to better protect the people and in order to punish those who violate natural laws, a body politic is necessary. This body politic is established by a social contract on the basis of a common consensus, and transfers limited executive authority to the ruling institution. This differs from the unlimited power of HOBBES' Leviathan.

Special features of the social contract according to JOHN LOCKE

The content of LOCKE'S social contract is quite distinct from that of the social contract of HOBBES:

a) Not all powers and rights are transferred to the state but only such executive authority as is absolutely necessary in order to protect and preserve man's inalienable rights.
b) The goal of state power is limited to the maintenance and protection of *property*. *Property* according to LOCKE encompasses all those rights that are central to the existence of human beings, namely: life, liberty and real property or estate.
c) The state can only exist on the basis of the consensus of its citizens (*Government by consent*);
d) In addition to the positive law there exists a fundamental law to which even the sovereign is subject (*Government by law, Rule of Law*). Thus, sovereignty is not absolute but rather, is limited and divisible.

With JOHN LOCKE, the Enlightenment view of the law of nature begins its ascendancy. From now on the liberty of human beings is regarded as an inalienable right, and the positive laws should be made in the image of the natural laws that have been discerned by reason. The state now has as its primary aim the protection of the life, liberty and property rights of individuals.

Main differences between HOBBES and LOCKE

Principal issues

The crucial question for THOMAS HOBBES was:

How can peoples be protected from the spectre of civil war (in other words from themselves)?

JOHN LOCKE reformulated this question as follows:
How can peoples be protected from their protector?

State authority according to LOCKE is limited authority. The main goal of the constitution is thus to limit state powers. For HOBBES on the other hand, the authority of the state is unlimited. Accordingly, the primary goal of the constitution must be to empower the state and vest it with authority, in order that the state is able to fulfil its function of protecting human beings from each other.

Right to resistance

When the aim of the foundation of the state (protection of the rights granted by natural law) is not respected by the ruler, the peoples whose rights have been violated have the inherent right to resistance. The positive laws of the state should accord with the natural laws, and the scope of state authority is thereby restricted. Accordingly, the state cannot infringe the inalienable rights and freedoms of man. With this philosophical theory JOHN LOCKE developed the foundations for a constitution that has as its principal aim the limitation of the powers of government.

Secularisation of the state

LOCKE took the secularisation of state power even further than HOBBES: There should a strict separation of church and state, and the government should not regulate religion. Principles of liberty require the state to be tolerant of all religions. In this sense LOCKE represents the early Enlightenment.

For HOBBES, the sovereign is the bearer of the highest authority and as such is also competent to regulate spiritual affairs. The Leviathan does not however have the power to dictate or interfere with individual religious beliefs, as this is an aspect of the individual's inner personality and such private matters are segregated from politics and regarded as inviolable.

Reality and fiction

Whilst for HOBBES, the social contract is a purely fictitious philosophical device, LOCKE is of the view that people actually did consent to enter into such a contract. We can speculate whether he was influenced by knowledge of the tangible contract that the first settlers of the American colonies signed in 1620 on board the Mayflower. Under this contract the settlers committed themselves to establish a government supported by all and to create the first colony of the United Kingdom in Plymouth, New England.

ii. IMMANUEL KANT

Submission to the law

KANT declines to explore whether humans in the state of nature were permanently at war with each other. For him, the crucial fact is that the competing interests of different individuals can and do lead to disputes. According to KANT, there is thus a permanent threat of conflict.

> "It is not experience from which we learn of human beings' maxim of violence and their malevolent tendency to attack one another before external legislation endowed with power appears. It is therefore not some fact that makes coercion through public law necessary. On the contrary, however well disposed and law-abiding men might be, it still lies a priori in the rational idea of such a condition (one that is not rightful) that before a public lawful condition is established individual human beings, peoples and states can never be secure against violence from one another, since each has its own right to do *what seems right and good to it* and not to be dependent upon another's opinion about this. So, unless it wants to renounce any concepts of right, the first thing it has to resolve upon is the principle that it must leave the state of nature, in which each follows its own judgment, unite itself with all others (with which it cannot avoid interacting), subject itself to a public lawful external coercion, and so enter into a condition in which what is to be

> recognised as belonging to it is determined *by law* and is allotted to it by adequate *power* (not its own but an external power); that is, it ought above all else to enter a civil condition" (I. KANT, *The Metaphysics of Morals*, Part II § 44).

However in practice it is hardly possible to explore the real origin of the highest power.

> *A people should not* inquire *with any practical aim in view into the origin of the supreme authority to which it is subject, that is, a subject* ought not to reason subtly *for the sake of action about the origin of this authority, as a right that can still be called into question (*ius controversum*) with regard to the obedience he owes it. For, since a people must be regarded as already united under a general legislative will in order to judge with rightful force about the supreme authority (*summum imperium*), it cannot and may not judge otherwise than as the present head of state (*summus imperans*) wills it to. – Whether a state began with an actual contract of submission (*pacta subiectionis civilis*) as a fact, or whether power came first and law arrived only afterwards, or even whether they should have followed in this order: for a people already subject to civil law these reasonings are altogether pointless and, moreover, threaten a state with danger" (I. KANT,* Metaphysics, *§ 49).*

Although KANT concedes that there may be flawed state constitutions, it remains the task of the sovereign, not of the people, to correct the problem. KANT rejects the idea of a right to resistance. The positive laws alone are not sufficient to distinguish between right and wrong. This question can only be deduced by the application of practical reason, which also provides maxims for just and righteous behaviour.

> *"A state's well-being consists in their being united (*salus rei publicae suprema lex est*); by the well-being of a state must not be understood the* welfare *of its citizens and their* happiness; *for happiness can perhaps come to them more easily as they would like it to in a state of nature (as Rousseau asserts) or even under a despotic government. By the well-being of a state is understood, instead, that condition in which its constitution conforms most fully to principles of right; it is that condition which reason,* by a categorical imperative, *makes it obligatory for us to strive after" (I KANT,* The Metaphysics of Morals, *§ 49).*

Categorical imperative

> *"The categorical imperative, which as such only affirms what obligation is, is: act upon a maxim that can also hold as a universal law. – You must therefore first consider your actions in terms of their subjective principles; but you can know whether this principle also holds objectively only in this way: that when your reason subjects it to the test of conceiving yourself as also giving universal law through it, it qualifies for such a giving of universal law" (KANT,* The Metaphysics of Morals, *p17).*

And in his essay 'Perpetual Peace' KANT writes:

> *"Having set aside everything empirical in the concept of civil or international law (such as the wickedness in human nature which necessitates coercion), we can call the following proposition the transcendental formula of public law: All actions relating to the right of other men are unjust if their maxim is not consistent with publicity" (KANT,* Perpetual Peace, Appendix II*).*

Thus only that which is of general application, and published and knowable, can constitute law. With this KANT laid the foundation for a formal theory of justice, which was substantially developed at the end of the last century by JOHN RAWLS.

We are the people – we are ONE people

The state philosophy of the Enlightenment created the basis for popular sovereignty. The key phrase of the Enlightenment was "*We* are the people". When the subjects of the East German Republic protested against their regime in 1989, they used this slogan in their fight for the achievement of civil rights. However, as soon as they were freed from their yoke they were faced with a new slogan – "We are *one* people" – and were integrated within the German Federation of the west. The question of who actually constitutes the people that are bound together under the social contract, or *should* be united by the consensus of the social contract, was not answered during the Enlightenment period. However, today it has become the key issue which breathes life into the nationalism of post-modernity.

iii. Exploitation and emancipation (KARL MARX, 1818–1883)

Who is the bearer of authority?

For liberal state theory only the 'negative state' is a real and legitimate state. Accordingly, the state is only legitimate insofar as it guarantees individual freedom. For this reason state power needs to be limited. The issue of who is the actual bearer of state power is of no consequence for the scholar of the Enlightenment. Essential however, is that the bearer of the authority of the state has *limited* powers. The bearer of state authority can – in fact should – regularly be replaced. Thus, the question with regard to the *bearer* of state authority was simply never raised or problematised by Enlightenment liberalism.

For MARX and his successors (Marxists) however, the question of who bears state authority has always been at the very centre of state theory. The bearer of political authority is according to Marxist theory always part of the ruling social class. This class dominates the state and uses the power of the state to exclude the other classes. The dominating class employs the state as an instrument of oppression and discrimination against the lower classes. Thus for Marxism, the central focus is on the question *who* is the ruler and not *how* does the ruler govern.

Emancipation of human beings

MARX himself was committed to the universal emancipation of the human being, that is for the emancipation of humans *as humans*. For him it was the working class that could initiate and achieve this emancipation by taking over the reins of state authority. This was the only antidote to the entrenched class interests inherent in organised political power by which the bourgeoisie misuses state authority to oppress the proletariat.

Transitional character of the state

It would however be an oversimplification to reduce the entire Marxist theory of state to this single point. These theories were published for the first time within a political program, which was written by MARX with his friend and closest collaborator FRIEDRICH ENGELS (1820–1888) for the Communist League in 1848. In the first years of his work MARX was principally concerned with the analysis of state and law. Within these analyses he began from the proposition that state and law are in an epochal sense in a state of transition. Based on this position, MARX launched his critique of the law as well as the state. In order to remain true to his principal objective, that is the universal (not bound to state borders) liberation of the human being, MARX did not develop a theory for the justification of the state.

Nevertheless, in his works on the Jewish question and in his critique of the state philosophy of HEGEL, the young MARX pointed out that the state and the law will play a decisive role in the emancipation of the human being. He saw in the liberal constitutional state of modern times the highest level of human emancipation, at least with regard to the then existing world order. In other words, MARX did recognise that the modern liberal constitutional state had an epochal relevance, but he also considered that the significance of the state was bound to the historical period of that time and thus was merely transitory in character. Accordingly, MARX recognises democracy as a 'material principle of the constitution' and understands the constitution as an expression of 'the sovereignty of the people'.

The economic foundations of the state

For MARX, the developed liberal states correspond to a political design or an external expression of the constitution that is in clear contradiction of their own social and economic foundations. That is, the structure and purported ideals of democratic liberal states actually conflict with and are contradicted by the conditions that such states produce, namely, the class differences and alienation of labour produced by the capitalist market economy. It is in these economic foundations of the market economy that the real structural problems in the basis of the modern class-divided society lie. These economic bases were thoroughly examined by MARX in his later phase as he worked on his Theory of Capital.

The original sin of the economy

In order to prove that the economic foundations which led to irresolvable differences between the classes were the result of the current conception of man, Marx secularised the theme of the original sin and applied it to economic relations. Whilst HOBBES takes as his starting point the sinful human being, MARX reaches back for his theory to a state of paradise before the 'original sin'.

> "The legend of theological original sin tells us certainly how man came to be condemned to eat his bread in the sweat of his brow; but the history of economic original sin reveals to us that there are people to

whom this is by no means essential. Never mind! Thus it came to pass that the former sort accumulated wealth, and the latter sort finally had nothing to sell except their own skins. And from this original sin dates the poverty of the great majority who, despite all their labour, have up to now nothing to sell but themselves, and the wealth of the few that increases constantly, although they have long ceased to work" (K. MARX, *Capital Vol I*, Chapter 26, p. 873).

Original accumulation of wealth

This original accumulation of wealth was only possible because the worker was separated from ownership and control of his conditions of labour. "So-called primitive accumulation, therefore, is nothing else than the historical process of divorcing the producer from the means of production" (K. MARX, Capital Vol I, Ch 26, p. 874–5). Originally, the hunters and gatherers could live from their own labour and were able to cover their immediate needs. The agricultural worker, who cultivated the soil owned by the lord and received a wage for his work, did not work in order to cover his own needs but rather to cover the needs of his master and employer, and he did not receive the wage that corresponded to his needs but rather which corresponded to the market value of his labour.

Alienation between the value of commodities and the value of labour

According to MARX, this development became even more pronounced during the period of industrialisation. The starting point of his thinking is the fact that the laws of supply and demand on the free market determine the price of the goods required to cover one's needs. The wage of the employee however is not determined according to the value of the commodities produced but only on the basis of the cost of production. Thus a gulf develops between the price of commodities and the cost of the labour required to produce the commodities. Ultimately it is not the worker who profits from the surplus value but rather the employer – in other words, the capitalist. By appropriating this added value the capitalist, in the view of MARX, is exploiting the worker.

The class state

Such a process is not without social consequences. Because the capitalists try to maximise their profits, whilst the workers on the other hand have an interest in increasing their wages and thus diminishing the profit of the capitalist, there will be ongoing disputes and incessant class conflicts. The rich will do everything in order to preserve their position of dominance.

"All the preceding classes that got the upper hand sought to fortify their already acquired status by subjecting society at large to their conditions of appropriation" (K. MARX and F. ENGELS, *The Communist Manifesto*). The ruling classes thus also made use of the state for their own interests, so that the state as a consequence became a state for the dominant capitalist class.

Class state and nation state

This principle of the class-based state which subjugates the entire society to the objectives of the dominating class is connected to the processes of centralisation and nation building.

"The Bourgeoisie keeps more and more doing away with the scattered state of the population, of the means of production, and of property... The necessary consequence of this was political centralisation. Independent, or but loosely connected provinces, with separate interests, laws, governments and systems of taxation, became lumped together into one nation, with one government, one code of laws, one national class-interest, one frontier, and one customs-tariff" (K. MARX and F. ENGELS, *The Communist Manifesto*).

The transition to the association of free human beings

As already mentioned, the historical philosophy of MARX assumes that the modern state is not the final stage of social development and that a return to the social state free of classes can and will be brought about. In this final condition, political power in the true sense will no longer exist. "In place of the old bourgeois society, with its classes and class antagonisms, we shall have an association, in which the free development of each is the condition of the free development of all" (MARX and ENGELS, The *Communist Manifesto*).

Starting from such critical understanding of state and law, social democracy at the end of the 19th and the beginning of the 20th century made its mark as a non-orthodox wing of Marxism, and contributed to liberalism and Marxism being brought closer together by the concept of human rights.

The early writings of MARX

The wing of the orthodox/communist Marxists on the other hand prefer to overlook the earlier writings of Marx. What the orthodox wing needed was to establish an ideology that was capable of justifying absolute communist rule without any regard to liberty. Thus the constitutional state based on democracy was a fiction for the communist Marxists. The guarantees of liberty and equality by the state are merely a pretence. In reality, the state's only role and function is to provide a cover for the exploitation of the working class for the profit of the bourgeoisie. For the leader of the October Revolution and the founder of the first socialist state, the Bolshevik VLADIMIR ILJITSCH LENIN (1870–1924), the state was a "product of society at a certain stage of development; ... the admission that this society has split into irreconcilable antagonisms which it is powerless to dispel" (LENIN, *The State and Revolution* (1917, published 1999 Resistance Books), p 16). As such, it had to be eliminated with terror and violence.

Socialism (ROSA LUXEMBOURG and KARL KAUTZKY)

The first sharp critique of such a revision of Marxist thinking emerged from within Marxism, being raised by the social democratic wing lead by ROSA LUXEMBOURG (1871–1919) and KARL KAUTZKY (1854–1938). Both were fully conscious (as was MARX) of the emancipatory potential of the modern state. Thus they insisted that the proletariat should not fight for its interests by means of revolutionary destruction, but rather should accomplish its objectives democratically through the parliamentary institutions within the existing constitutional state.

Communism and authority of the party

As soon as communists attained power, they distorted and misused the basic thesis of MARX with regard to the exclusionary class character of the liberal state as the basis of justification for their own totalitarian regime. Whether the accumulation of power and force was legitimate depended, according to the communist ruler, exclusively on whether the ruler was committed to the universal liberation of the exploited and alienated classes. If power and violence are in the hands of the bourgeoisie then they are simply bad per se. If on the other hand power and violence are in the service of the communist party, and the party thereby controls the state, then one can without any hesitation entrust it with unlimited power because such power will only be used for the benefit of the universal interests of the working class.

The brutal history of oppression and the terror of the communist regimes from the October Revolution until 1989, and the political and social 'desert' in those states in transition, are sufficient proof of where this 'liberation' of human beings may lead us.

3.2 The Image of the State

3.2.1 What is the State?

The collective of the political community

Are states above the law, or is there a special legal order that applies to the conduct of states? Is the so-called *raison d'état* a basic value that stands above all law and morality? Can the right to self-determination of peoples be regarded as the unlimited right of each nation to demand their own sovereign state? Can minorities, based on their right to self-determination, unilaterally establish their own sovereign state and thus rule over all other ethnic groups living within their sovereign territory? Ethnic and nationalist conflicts reveal where such a conception of the state can lead us. The USA, Canada, New Zealand and Australia claimed the collective right of their settlers to political authority over the territory, and asserted this authority over the native inhabitants. On the other side, the native inhabitants demand their collective rights over the territory that has been inhabited by them for hundreds or thousands of years. A collective right however assumes that the community is of a higher value than just the sum of all its individuals. ROUSSEAU mentions in this context the inalienable right of states to sovereignty.

Collective rights

In this context the core questions which have to be put can be formulated as follows: Do human beings exist because of the state or does the state exist to serve human beings? Can the state require from its citizens the ultimate sacrifice, namely their life, if this is necessary for the survival of the community? Is the abstract state as a political body of citizens also the bearer of fundamental rights in the same sense as rights-bearing individuals? If the state as a collective entity can be the bearer of fundamental rights how can it deny such collective rights to any minority within its territory that considers itself also to be a collective unit? Should such collective rights be on an equal footing with individual human rights?

If there were clear and obvious answers to these questions the world could be spared from many bloody conflicts!

Is the state a collective human being?

The anthropomorphisation or personification of the state, which for example sometimes finds its expression in identification with a hero of liberty, is a well-known phenomenon. The personification of the state enables people to better identify with the state. The statue of liberty of the United States, Joan of Arc in France and Wilhelm Tell in Switzerland are but a few examples of such personifications of the identity of the state. Very often such emotional connection to the state goes much deeper. For the majority it becomes part of their own personal identity and existence, whilst for the minority it has the opposite effect and becomes instead a symbol that justifies violence against the oppressive majority.

The preamble of the constitution of Croatia for example starts with a declareation of the "millennial national identity of the Croatian nation and the continuity of its statehood". This shows the significance that can be attributed to the state as a political unit and a foundation for national development. Of course, this applies only to ethnically homogeneous states, which have to an extent become hostage to their unitary ethnic nation. In this case the state plays a part in the individual existence of its member citizens. The citizens recognise within the state their language, history and existence. They are connected to the state and unable to break free of this emotional attachment.

Exclusive and inclusive state

Many also recognise themselves within their state as being 'special' in comparison to people of other states, particularly people of neighbouring states. They regard and define themselves as 'We' against the 'Others' who are different, strangers, adversaries or even enemies. The state degenerates to an instrument of resolute and even inhuman segregation. The 'We' serves also to distinguish oneself from the 'Other' foreigners or established minorities living within the same state. Out of the 'We' and the 'Other' there develops a notion of friend and foe, or 'us' versus 'them', which is easily inflamed and readily exploited (for example through the media).

Those who do not fit within the national identity and who have to live as an excluded minority within such a state will regard the state, with its discriminating concept of citizenship and its tyranny of the majority, as the cause of their exploitation and dehumanisation and will fight against the state. Because such minorities cannot identify with the state of the 'others' nor with the political and legal system, they lack the sense of security and identity necessary for their existence. They do not feel as though they are equal human beings with rights because they do not have equal opportunity to participate in the 'political'. The friend-foe notion as the basis of nationalistic and chauvinistic convictions is transferred to the intra-state opponents of the majority nation.

Human beings need identity

The human being has the obvious need to identify not only with his family but also with the more abstract state polity. How else can one explain the joy of a nation when its team wins a world championship or an Olympic title? Thus, the state is something more than a mere system of abstract norms. It embodies the emotional collective consciousness of the members of the majority nation.

On the other hand, the state bears the brunt of constant criticism and must suffer for any misfortune that befalls its members. "The state wastes tax money"; "it is corrupt"; "it only protects the interests of the wealthy establishment, it is too bureaucratic and centralised". These and many other accusations are directed at the state. At the same time, people are proud of the achievements of 'their' state. If a state is criticised by foreign media or foreign politicians, the entire people feels accused. Even accusations against an obvious tyrant in foreign courts will be regarded by the nation formerly maltreated by this tyrant as a humiliation.

Symbol of the crown

Within the former absolutist monarchies in which the prerogatives of the crown have been reduced to the merely symbolic representation of the state, the monarchy has remained a potent symbol of the unity of the state. The crown radiates an almost sacred force. In multicultural states such as Spain or Belgium, the symbol of the crown also has a certain integrative influence that may, even today, provide a vital connection between diverse groups.

Exclusive and inclusive political values

If there is neither a national nor a monarchic unifying force then states need to base their unity on other values which can enable the members of different cultures to identify with the unity of the state. States that have grown largely through immigration from Europe have for example found such values within the 'American way of life' or in Catholicism (Latin America). Switzerland finds its national unity within political values such as federalism and democracy, and at the same time aims to strengthen national unity by fostering diversity. In its constitution South Africa declares its commitment to unity in diversity, similarly to Nepal.

The Unitary Function of Idealistic and Universal Values

France on the other hand, proclaims a constitution with universal values. The values of the French Revolution are universal and are valid for every human being. Whoever identifies with these values and at the same time lives within the French territory, belongs to *us*, the French. In fact however, the French nation symbolised by the national character of the French and their French language still has exclusive effects and not an overall inclusive function. Some decades ago the ethical values proclaimed by the French Revolution and the French language still had a universal character. Today this universality is questioned. The French state can no longer lay claim to the universality which had distinguished it from all other states in the 19th Century. Whilst the draft of the constitution of 1791 provided that foreigners who had resided in France for more than one year were entitled to French nationality and citizenship, today France cannot maintain this openness. The steadily growing nationalistic tendencies reveal that even in France 'universality' has its limits. Even the French constitution could not maintain the concept of the equal *citoyen* in all territories covered by the constitution. How could one otherwise justify the clear reference to the *peuples d'outre mer* (peoples of the overseas territories) in the preamble to the French Constitution? "the Republic offers to the overseas territories that express the will to adhere to them new institutions founded on the common ideal of liberty, equality and fraternity and conceived with a view to their democratic development" (Preamble, Constitution of France 4 October 1958).

Antiquity

The state constitutes a whole that is more than just the sum of its atomised parts. This phenomenon of a whole that exceeds the sum of its components has led several philosophers to deduce that the state does not emanate from a group of individual persons, but rather is something which is greater than the sum of its individuals; it is an independent unit with an added value which has its cause in itself and can thus only be explained as an entity in itself.

"[I]t is evident that a city is a natural production, and that man is naturally a political animal… [T]he notion of a city naturally precedes that of a family or an individual, for the whole must necessarily be prior to the parts, for if you take away the whole man, you cannot say a foot or a hand remains… That a city then precedes an individual is plain, for if an individual is not in himself sufficient to compose a perfect government, he is to a city as other parts are to a whole; but he that is incapable of society, or so complete in himself as not to want it, makes no part of a city, as a beast or a god. There is then in all persons a natural impetus to associate with each other in this manner, and he who first founded civil society was the cause of the greatest good; for as by the completion of it man is the most excellent of all living beings, so without law and justice he would be the worst of all, for nothing is so difficult to subdue as injustice in arms" (ARISTOTLE, Politics, Book I, 1253a).

Individualism of the Enlightenment

Contrary to the individualistic theories of state of the 17th and 18th Centuries, which justified the state on the basis of the individuals comprising or authorising the state (for example popular sovereignty and social contract theory), for most thinkers of antiquity the state is a predetermined and pre-existing reality which is superior to the individual person. "Every state is a community of some kind, and every community is established with a view to some good; for mankind always act in order to obtain that which they think good. But, if all communities aim at some good, the state or political community, which is the highest of all, and which embraces all the rest, aims at good in a greater degree than any other, and at the highest good" (ARISTOTLE, *Politics*, Book I, 1252a). So too for PLATO (428–348 BC), the state is a predefined necessity (PLATO, book 11 369 b--e). CICERO (106–43 BC) and POLYBIOS (ca. 200–ca. 117 BC) attribute the state to the social nature of human beings (See CICERO, book 1, 25; POLYBIOS, book VI, 5).

The contrast between the understanding of the state in the antiquity and in the period of the Enlightenment is thus unmistakable: "One has tried to explain the contrast between the understanding of the state in the antiquity and in modern times with the following sharp antithesis: in the period of antiquity man existed for the sake of the state, whilst in modern times the state exists for the sake of man" (G. JELLINEK, p 35).

The multicultural challenge of post-modernity

The notion of the state as a cohesive unit, a single unified entity, poses for young and multicultural states a decisive challenge. If a young democracy does not succeed in integrating the multiple identities within its polity into a common '*We*' it will not be able to survive. The issue of the state as a unitary whole has become one of the crucial issues of our times.

3.2.2 The State as a higher being (HEGEL)

During the Enlightenment period we can find in some writings on the theory of state, in particular those of HEGEL and ROUSSEAU, the foundations for a state theory that considers the state to be an independent unit from the sum of the individuals living in it. HEGEL sees the state as something absolute and as a higher being in relation to mankind; for ROUSSEAU the state embodies the common good, the so-called general will (*volonté générale*), as an absolute and unquestionable value.

Is the state more than the sum of its components?

Does the state stand above the human being, does it somehow represent a higher being? Or is the state only a motley collection of people which has no higher value than the sum of the individual persons living within its territory? If the whole – that is, the state – is no more than the sum of its components, then it cannot be entitled to claim any special rights in relation to its component parts. The state has in relation to its citizens no basis upon which to justify its authority. But if the state is, so to speak, a 'higher being' (H. KRÜGER, p. 818 ff) then its subjects are obliged to obey its authority. In this case the state would not need to base its authority to enact binding laws on any kind of partnership or original social contract, but rather it could justify this authority on the basis that it embodies a 'higher being' than individual men.

The state as the peak of development of world history

This theory of the state as a higher being was developed by HEGEL. HEGEL sees world history as the development of the world spirit towards an ever-greater spirituality, morality, liberty, and rationality. At the pinnacle of this development is the state, which is the motor of history leading mankind to an ever-higher existence. The state represents the highest spirituality and rationality, because within the polity the community of men and women is united under the authority of reason. The destiny of the body politic is not delivered to blind fate but entrusted to the combined reason of all its members. Out of the originally brutal and despotic state there developed in turn the Greek Polis, the Roman state, the monarchy of the Middle Ages and the modern rational and limited constitutional monarchy.

The constitutional liberal state is the highest accomplishment of the world spirit

The development of the state thus is the development towards ever-increasing liberty. This view of HEGEL however is at risk of an over-estimation of modern statehood.

"The state is the realised ethical idea or ethical spirit. It is the will which manifests itself, makes itself clear and visible, substantiates itself. It is the will which thinks and knows itself, and carries out what it knows, and in so far as it knows. The state finds in ethical custom its direct and unreflected existence, and its indirect and reflected existence in the self-consciousness of the individual and in his knowledge and activity. Self-consciousness in the form of social disposition has its substantive freedom in the state, as the essence, purpose, and product of its activity." (G.W.F. HEGEL, *Philosophy of Right*, § 257 translated by S.W. Dyde).

The state represents highest reason and morality

Through the state, the history of world achieves its ultimate and divine perfection. "This substantiality, when thoroughly permeated by education, is the spirit which knows and wills itself. Hence, what the state wills it knows, and knows it in its universality as that which is thought out. The state works and acts in obedience to conscious ends, known principles and laws, which are not merely implied, but expressly before its consciousness. So, too, it works with a definite knowledge of all the actual circumstances and relations, to which the acts refer."

"...It must further be understood that all the worth which the human being possesses – all spiritual reality, he possesses only through the State. For his spiritual reality consists in this, that his own essence – Reason – is objectively present to him, that it possesses objective immediate existence for him." (G.W.F. HEGEL, *Philosophy of History* § 41).

The state is also the realisation of reason. "The laws of morality are not accidental, but are the essentially Rational. It is the very object of the State that what is essential in the practical activity of men, and in their dispositions, should be duly recognised; that it should have a manifest existence, and maintain its position.... The State is the Divine Idea as it exists on Earth." (G.W.F. HEGEL, *Philosophy of History*, § 40). The Constitution represents the attainment and application of rationality.

'Supra state' constitution?

In contrast to HOBBES and LOCKE, HEGEL does not question the source of state authority to enact the constitution or to prescribe rights and obligations for its citizens. The question of who should determine the constitutional ground rules is for HEGEL the wrong question. This question presupposes that only one particular atomised group of people can establish the basic constitutional legal order. However this atomised community of individuals does not of itself create a state entity, which itself is a prerequisite for a constitution. "But it is strictly essential that the constitution, though it is begotten in time, should not be contemplated as made. It is rather to be thought of as above and beyond what is made, as self begotten and self-centred, as divine and perpetual." (G.W.F. HEGEL, *Philosophy of Right*, § 273).

He who internalises the spiritual laws is free

As the state embodies the objectivity of the divine spirit, the human being as subject is obliged to obey the laws of the state. HEGEL has his own corresponding understanding of freedom: he rejects LOCKE'S view of freedom that entails entitlement to do whatever one pleases. For him, the progression of world history leads to ever-greater freedom. In the ancient oriental despotic empires, subjects were not free and had to obey the arbitrary authority of the despots. Not until the development of the Greek city-state was there limited freedom for the male head of the family. Real freedom and equality for everyone was, according to HEGEL, first possible in Christendom. In this sense the Reformation was a major step in the advancement of freedom.

So what is HEGEL'S conception of freedom? Man is, according to his view, free when he obeys the will of the laws.

"The universal and subjective Will; and the Universal is to be found in the State, in its laws, its universal and rational arrangements. ...We have in it, therefore, the object of History in a more definite shape than before; that in which Freedom obtains objectivity, and lives in the enjoyment of this objectivity. For Law is the objectivity of Spirit; volition in its true form. Only that will which obeys law, is free; for it obeys itself – it is independent and so free. When the State or our country constitutes a community of existence; when the subjective will of man submits to laws, – the contradiction between Liberty and Necessity vanishes" (G.W.F. HEGEL, *Philosophy of History*, § 41).

BLUNTSCHLI The state as a collective human being

Another proponent of the view that the state is a higher being is the Swiss philosopher JOHANN KASPAR BLUNTSCHLI (1808–1881). He belongs to the school of the so-called organic theory of state. According to his theory the state is an independent being similar to man, with a head (government), body, arms and legs (J.K. BLUNTSCHLI, p. 14).

Can Legal Obligations be derived only from the Higher Being of the State?

Undoubtedly people often identify with their state and come to regard it not just as a legal entity but also as a natural person able to act on its own account. However it would be wrong to deduce from this small grain of truth that the state is therefore a special being independent from its citizens, in order to sanction the subjugation of man to the state. On the other hand, it cannot be denied that in certain cases the private interests of particular persons must take a back seat to the interests of the state as a whole. If the state is to run public schools, citizens must pay taxes to make this possible. In the interest of the defence of the country citizens can be compelled to undertake military service. Some mountain municipalities in Switzerland still impose obligations for compulsory labour (originally conceived in the Middle Ages) according to which citizens are obliged in cases of catastrophes, such as avalanches or floods, to assist by providing their labour to the municipality. The private interest of each person will thus in certain cases be overridden for the sake of justice, to give priority to the interest of the community and the common good.

3.2.3 The State as Representation of the Common Good according to ROUSSEAU

Common good and individual good

The common good is in general given priority over the private good or personal well-being of a single individual. How can this position be justified? We have established that the state has the function of providing security and guiding the community for the common good of its interdependent citizens. The state thus administers the common good: The protection and the promotion of human freedom, and the guarantee of the existential and general needs in a social order determined by the division of labour. Individuals cannot accomplish these tasks on their own. People surrender part of their autonomy as a result of the development of society and the economy, and their individual autonomy can only be exerted to a limited extent by participating within the local community or the state.

Robinson and Friday can achieve more when they divide their labour and each does what best corresponds to his abilities. In common they also dispose of greater knowledge than would each of them on his own. In this respect the knowledge of each single individual is not added but increases exponentially when brought together, because each profits from the knowledge of the other and thus can make new discoveries and gain further insights. Therefore, the community can know more than the sum of its components. This however does not mean that Robinson and Friday should become slaves to a higher authority. The mutual dependence of common knowledge and of the division of labour should serve to maximise the personal development of each. The 'common' cannot be detached and made independent from individual interests. The dependence of human beings upon society must ultimately be managed by the state in the interest of each individual as well as in the common interest.

How does the 'common' emerge?

The 'common', which is created as a result of different people living together within a state, takes priority over individual interests only to the extent that this serves the common good. If individual interests were always given precedence, the result would ultimately be the exploitation of the community by some of its members. If a private land owner was able to successfully resist the expropriation of his/her land by the state for the construction of a road because he/she wanted to construct a private villa, then the common interest of having the optimum transport connection between two villages would have to give way to the individual interest of the private owner. The dependence of those who rely on transport connections would accordingly be abused. The inhabitants would have to pay for an expensive road around the villa and drivers would have to pay the price for the higher risk of accidents and chaotic traffic conditions.

The common becomes independent

ROUSSEAU'S theory of the general will or *volonté générale* attributes considerable independence to the so-called 'common'. Rousseau distinguishes between the will of all (*volonté de tous*), which corresponds only to the sum of all single interests, and the general will in which all interests of the society converge.

> *"THE first and most important deduction from the principles we have so far laid down is that the general will alone can direct the State according to the object for which it was instituted, i.e., the common good: for if the clashing of particular interests made the establishment of societies necessary, the agreement of these very interests made it possible. The common element in these different interests is what forms the social tie; and, were there no point of agreement between them all, no society could exist. It is solely on the basis of this common interest that every society should be governed" (J.-J. ROUSSEAU, II Book 1 Chapter 1)*

Like HOBBES und LOCKE, ROUSSEAU also starts from an assumed state of nature of the human being. The oldest form of all natural society is the family. As soon as the children of the family have grown up they become independent (J.-J. ROUSSEAU, Book I Chapter 2). One of the main reasons that this state of nature cannot be maintained is the steady increase of the population. As the population grows, people need to join together to form new communities. For HOBBES it is the vicious character of man, and for LOCKE the need for security, which leads people to make the transition from the natural state and to conclude a social contract in order to enter the *status civilis*.

> *"But, as the force and liberty of each man are the chief instruments of his self-preservation, how can he pledge them without harming his own interests, and neglecting the care he owes to himself? This difficulty, in its bearing on my present subject, may be stated in the following terms: "The problem is to find a form of association which will defend and protect with the whole common force the person and goods of each associate, and in which each, while uniting himself with all, may still obey himself alone, and remain as free as before." This is the fundamental problem of which the Social Contract provides the solution" (J.-J. ROUSSEAU, Book I chapter 6).*

The social contract produces the citizen (citoyen)

With this social contract a new political body is created, the members of which become citizens, or *citoyens*. This new artificially constructed unit embodies a common 'self' that leads its own life and is given a particular will. The social contract thus creates a new and higher unit. By virtue of the fact that the people participate as *citoyens* in the state that is created by the social contract, they become partners in the new higher being, partners in the state authority, and thus national citizens. The people of the state of nature are transformed into a new kind of being: into the political *citoyen*.

> *"THE passage from the state of nature to the civil state produces a very remarkable change in man, by substituting justice for instinct in his conduct, and giving his actions the morality they had formerly lacked.... Let us draw up the whole account in terms easily commensurable. What man loses by the social contract is his natural liberty and an unlimited right to everything he tries to get and succeeds in getting; what he gains is civil liberty and the proprietorship of all he possesses.... We might, over and above all this, add, to what man acquires in the civil state, moral liberty, which alone makes him truly master of himself; for the mere impulse of appetite is slavery, while obedience to a law which we prescribe to ourselves is liberty" (J.-J. ROUSSEAU, Book I chapter 8).*

The law is the expression of the general will (volonté générale)

Why, according to ROUSSEAU, do the citizens need to obey the order of the state? The will of the state expresses itself in the form of the general will the *volonté générale*. Because "the general will is always right and tends to the public advantage", one must adhere to the general will and comply with the laws it produces (J.-J. ROUSSEAU, Book II, chapter 7).

This general will is to be distinguished from the sum of the individual wills (*volonté de tous*). The sum of the single particular wills and interests does not serve the common good but only the private interests of all or at least of those who represent the majority, that is, the sum of those who have agreed to the decision. How can one prevent the situation in which the laws are a manifestation of the *volonté de tous* and not, as they should be, of the general will? When parties influence the decision, for example in a referendum, then the decision loses its universal character. For this reason it is only possible to capture the general will when the highest possible number of opinions can be reconciled to a common denominator. This common denominator corresponds to the general will; it is not the sum of all wills but rather the exponential cumulative value of all interests.

"It is therefore essential, if the general will is to be able to express itself, that there should be no partial society within the State, and that each citizen should think only his own thoughts" (J.-J. ROUSSEAU, The Social Contract, *Book II Chapter 3).*
"Every law the people has not ratified in person is null and void – is, in fact, not a law" (J.-J. ROUSSEAU, The Social Contract, *Book III Chapter 15).*

ROUSSEAU and democracy

However, ROUSSEAU recognises that there are and have to be different types of government. For him, the old constitutions of the small Greek city-states and of the Roman Empire, where laws were approved in the open peoples' assemblies, are ideal. However he is of the view that this is only possible within very small republics, and that in any case executive power cannot be exercised directly by the people. In this sense there has never in any place been a full and genuine democracy, and nor can there be.

"Were there a people of gods, their government would be democratic. So perfect a government is not for men" (J.-J. ROUSSEAU, Book III, chapter 4).

The tyranny of the general will

Just as for HEGEL the law is an absolute in the sense of the highest realisation of the moral idea, so too for ROUSSEAU the general will of the citizens associated by the social contract is an absolute. The general will is for ROUSSEAU akin to a higher being to which all are submitted. This absolute *volonté generale* later became the foundation for the absolute and totalitarian regimes of the communist parties. In many states with strong presidential powers, the president appears to be the incarnation of the *volonté générale,* which cannot be called into question. However, ROUSSEAU at least requires that this general will is bound to the decision of the people and requires the legitimation of the democratic majority.

Today's reality of the commons

The commons was not created by the social contract or by the constitution of the state, but rather precedes these constructs. There always exist some pre-state commonalities based on common language, history, culture or religion. If within a multicultural state common political values can be found, they may develop gradually (as for example the republic against the monarchy) to become an effective connection that can hold a multicultural society together (cf France, the USA, the Confederation of Switzerland). Common identities provide the basis for the commons. Today however, social and economic relations can also lead to the development of commonalities and aspects of shared identity. The wide broadcast of radio and television, the internet, the common dependency on raw material and sources of energy, as well as increasing mobility are all factors that create commonalities between human beings. Economy, technology and communication result in the fading of borders, and although borders remain, they gradually lose their significance.

Globalisation of the commons?

Such commonalities no longer stop at the state border. The internet creates new transnational commonalities, and CNN and BBC have constructed a world of news and information that also produces global commonalities. It is up to the state to ensure that the interdependencies that result from commonalities are not exploited, and that globalised commonalities do not completely displace the 'political', that is, democracy within the national sphere.

Where is the international general will (volonté générale)?

As long as families and in particular extended families were autonomous they were able to care for the elderly and infirm members of the family. With increasing industrialisation however, the dependency of individual family members on society also increased. As a consequence, the state was required to expand its social services in order to meet the challenge of these new dependencies. Today it is expected to preserve the social security system from the threat of being undermined by new economic and global dependencies. What use are the best social security laws when the international labour- and financial-markets make the financing of the social security system by the taxpayer unsustainable? States and peoples today need a new *international* 'general will' (*volonté générale*) which, like the national general will, is based upon democratic legitimacy.

The general will does not belong to the discretionary power of the nation-state

The general will or the common good can thus not be made and unmade at the whim of the state. It is rather a concrete determination of the general interest that has evolved on the basis of national and international relations. States have to take into account and to foster this general common interest. While states in earlier times were able to influence social development and different interdependencies with political power, today their hands are often tied by the globalised market economy. States must therefore try to create a new international decision-making process and new space for international cooperation in the interests of an international 'general will' or 'common interest'. At the intra-state level, they have to be content to implement the limited domestic *volonté générale* to the extent that they are able.

The added value of the nation-state

The state community is not a pure addition of its members, but rather represents a value which is more than the sum of its components. However, this higher value is limited to the factual social commonalities and dependencies and does not entitle the state to completely separate itself from its citizens and to treat them as mere subjects. Rather, the state should direct its activities to the service of the community and should ensure that its actions are consistent with liberty and justice, otherwise its decisions and activities will not be justified – that is, they will be illegitimate. The 'general' however, is no longer confined within the territory of the state. It must become part of an international community of interest, as state politics today can no longer be legitimised on a national basis alone.

The citizen (citoyen) of ROUSSEAU: a challenge for today and tomorrow

ROUSSEAU'S theory of state has influenced the modern state with far reaching consequences for democracy, for totalitarianism legitimised through the *volonté générale,* as well as for the republican nation-state of citizens (*Citoyens*). His theory of the transition of man from the state of nature to rational *citoyen* for example, became the foundation of constitutionalism in France as well as in Turkey. When man in the state of nature acquires his higher being as a human as political citizen (*citoyen*) and becomes a partner in the political authority, he thereby becomes a political animal that henceforth will take part in the general will on the basis of its reason and rationality. The citizen is interested in political justice, which is achieved through the decisions of the democratic majority in which he takes part. Within the political community he puts aside his 'nature' and pre-state values such as culture, language, tradition, religion etc. The state as the incarnation of reason, rationality and the political is, according to this theory, comprised only of political beings, *citoyens*, but not of members of any other collective such as a religious or ethnic community.

Reason as the only legitimate basis of state unity

ROUSSEAU thereby laid the foundation for the republic which is legitimised by a political nation (such as France, Turkey). Anyone can become a citizen, if he is willing to adopt the Turkish or French constitutional values. The fact that a person may regard himself as Kurdish or Corsican is not only politically irrelevant, but also undermines the ideological legitimation of the state itself. The political is reduced to what is reasonable and just for the community, in other words, to the general will, freedom and the rational obedience of the law. This reduction of the 'political' to economic well-being, social justice and the protection of individual freedom however, contradicts the reality of many minorities who seek their own political autonomy to be able to foster their culture, language and religion within the political community. The 'political' cannot be exhaustively defined. It is determined by the tasks and responsibilities assigned to the state through the democratic process. What is political is ultimately determined through the general democratic discourse. Tasks that in one state are political, public and determined democratically may in another state be confined to the private sphere.

Can man be reduced to the rational citizen?

On the other hand, it cannot be denied that even those states that profess to be 'citoyen-states' always (clandestinely) promote culture – even if it is only the language interests of the majority. In the multi-cultural USA for example, the emotional debate surrounding the 'English–Only' movement and the laws in many states that prescribe English as the official language, demonstrate that even in a land that is open to immigration the state is employed in the protection of the majority culture and the promotion of assimilation of minorities into that culture. This is also evident in France, in the state promotion of Francophone interests and protection of the French language (Académie Française). And a similar phenomenon is apparent in Turkey's inclusion in its foreign policy of the protection of members of the Turkish nation (without citizenship) outside the borders of the Turkish state (for example in Cypress). Such examples cast some doubt on whether the true 'citizen-state' is a reality.

3.3 The Justification of State Authority

3.3.1 The Problem

Justification – sovereignty – legitimacy

The question of how the state can be justified is a question of legitimacy. Without sovereignty there is no legitimate state. The question of legitimacy contains within it the question of sovereignty. Sovereignty is the foundation of the right and power of the state to make and enforce state decisions. But this power is only legitimate if it can be justified. The object of justification is *imperium*, that is, the enforceability of state power.

One who poses the question of the justification of the state does not expect simply an explanation of the purpose of function of the state. The question of the purpose and therefore of the necessity of the state, that is, of how and why the state came into being, must be separated from the question of the value of the state. The question therefore is not "why *should* state force be tolerated?" but rather, "why does man choose to tolerate state force? Why does man want to obey the laws of the state?" One who questions the justification of the state expects to receive an answer that explains what value the state has for individual that would justify their acceptance of state force and authority.

The question of the validity of the law

If one seeks to justify state force one needs to be able to prove that the power of the state to require its citizens to make the ultimate sacrifice can be morally justified. Therefore it is not possible to justify the state without making a distinction between right and wrong, what is just and unjust. This question of the moral justification of the state relates specifically to the state's coercive force. Wherein lies the validity and enforceability of the laws of the state? The state is legitimate, if people are convinced that they are obliged to obey the rules of the state.

There are different views on the question of where the basis of validity of the state monopoly on the use of force, and the obligation to obey the state, really lies. Prior to the 19th Century however, state philosophers did not make a distinction between the question of the purpose of the state (its creation) and the question of the value of the state (its justification).

3.3.2 The Sate as Part of the Human Condition

What is the basis for the binding force of state rules?

On what basis are people able as a democratic majority to impose their will on a minority? How are governments able through their Parliaments to make binding rules and to accord rights to or impose obligations on individuals? How is it that some are empowered to rule over others? How can some people in the exercise of their state functions enact binding laws for other people? From where does the judge derive the right to convict and sentence the accused?

Political decisions of the state are legal orders that are binding, and that can be enforced through the coercive power of the state. Those who break the law are to be punished. Within the purview of the state fall all those decisions, procedures, institutions, regulations and measures which can, if necessary, be enforced with the coercive power of the state and which must therefore rely upon popular sovereignty for their legitimacy. The social sphere and the private sphere encompass decision-making mechanisms and measures that lead to contractual or statutory agreements that can be enforced by social sanction or by an order of the court (and so with the help of the state). The legitimacy of such agreements is based on the consent and agreement of those involved as contractual parties or members of an association (such as members of a club, shareholders in a company, etc).

The state as precondition for a human order of peace

If society does not wish to operate under the 'law of the jungle' whereby the might of the strongest always prevails, but wishes rather to have a peaceful order, society must manage the mutual dependence and cooperation of its members through decision-making processes that are legitimised by contract or by majority decision. The outcomes that result from these decision-making processes must also be capable of enforcement, either directly or through the judgment of a court with the help of the legitimate political power of the state to use coercive force. Even the most liberal legal order can only function effectively if its citizens can be assured that the rights and obligations acquired through agreement can if necessary be enforced. The trust that is essential in order for people to live together within a society depends in part upon people's integrity, but also requires that people can be reassured by the knowledge that in the case of a breach of trust, the law can be enforced. Only a coercive legal order can achieve trust in justice among freely associating citizens.

3.3.3 The Nature of the Human Being

The division of labour presupposes an order of peace

The state is not simply a result of the aggressive and hostile nature of man, as suggested by HOBBES. Certainly there is the danger that without leadership or authority, a complex and interconnected human community would fall apart because conflicts would become unmanageable. But even if this was not the case, it would still be necessary to have a superior authority through which relations between individuals can be regulated and which can provide for the division of labour, security and essential needs. The state is not a consequence of the *homo homini lupus ('man is a wolf to man')*, but rather the result of the social interdependence of man, which itself results from the increasing division of labour, the growth in population, the improved organisational and technical ability of man and the sociability of man.

One dimensional views of man

One-sided and one-dimensional views of man can thus lead to false conclusions with far-reaching consequences. Whoever observes man in his present state, must acknowledge that aggressiveness is only one side of human nature. There are also altruistic, helpful, hard-working and conscientious people. The reality of human society is very diverse and can hardly be reduced to a one-dimensional view of the human being. Beside the mother who can no longer feed her starving children one may find a soldier who despairs at his inability to help those hungry children. Or one may see a police officer who takes his frustrations out on his helpless prisoners. Beside the stressed manager of a company one may encounter a secretary who fulfils her duties conscientiously but also has her mind on the party that awaits at the end of the working day. One person may strive to earn a lot of money and attain a position of power, whilst another may be content to feed his family and make his children happy. In view of this complex reality it would be a serious error to base a theory of state on a one-dimensional view of human nature.

The state as the result of history

State authority cannot be traced back to a fictitious or factual original social contract from which all later titles to state authority can be deduced once and for all. As such a contract presupposes an existing legal order with the basic principle that contracts must be honoured (*pacta sunt servanda*), it cannot be relied upon as a prerequisite for the establishment of a state legal order. The state in fact developed and adapted gradually with the history of mankind. It is bound to the nature of human beings, which cannot exist without social interaction and community. However, state authority can only be justified if it is exercised in the interests of the well-being and free development of the people.

The sociable human being depends on a political community

Man is, as a social being, dependent on the community. The community is first experienced within the family. Increasing population density, the economic interest in a greater division of labour and man's social nature then lead to the development of supra-familial political communities. These associations must assign to the political authority certain functions originally fulfilled by the family, in order to be able within the framework of the division of labour to ensure freedom, to protect the community from external threats and to regulate internal conflicts. This administration is political if it reaches decisions through rational and recognised decision-making mechanisms, if its decisions can be enforced through coercive force, and if it governs in the general interest of the community.

Supra-familial authority can only be justified if it is exercised for the common good and rationally administered. However, we can only speak of a state in the sense it is understood today, if the supra-familial communities have joined together to form a larger political association and the authority within this association is exercised justly. Supra-familial authority is not justified in itself, but rather only when it serves the interests of the community and when the decision-makers are accountable to the community.

3.3.4 Change in the 'View of the State'

As such political associations are a result of the development of the division of labour, they must always be seen in their historical context. The state was not formed through a one-off act (such as a social contract). The state in fact emerged gradually and has developed and changed constantly throughout the course of history.

Human beings become interdependent because of external circumstances

The gradual development of the state has shown us the following: forms of authority and power relations are created, because people become dependent upon each other as a result of external circumstances beyond their control. Parents can make decisions concerning their child because the child is dependent upon them and because this generally serves the long-term interests of the child. They care for the child, protect it and know its capacities and interests. People are therefore thoroughly familiar with forms of authority within the family. When the family loses some of its autonomy as a result of increasing social interconnection and division of labour, it must hand over some authority rights to the community. The community however, only has the right to exercise authority in so far as is necessary by virtue of the actual dependency of people upon the community. Politics must ensure that the authority produced by dependence is exercised in a manner that is just and reasonable, that is, in the interests of freedom and internal peace.

Diverse conceptions of the state

If the authority of the state is derived from the concrete social situation of a society, then it must be moulded according to social development. A state that limits itself to protecting the community against external dangers and solving internal conflicts will be organised differently to the state in a developed complex industrial society that has to ensure economic survival and greatest possible autonomy for the polity within a globalised economic order.

The structure and justification of state authority are closely connected to the particular conditions in the relevant states that are determined by level of development, education, historical tradition, national character, size and geography. Nobody would contend that the Republic of China should be organised and led by the same principles as the tiny states of Andorra or Liechtenstein.

State against misuse of power

Undoubtedly, power and authority have been and are repeatedly abused. Just as there are bad parents that maltreat their children, so there are state regimes that take advantage of people's dependence, and exploit and abuse their people.

Abuse of authority, mismanagement, exploitation and disregard of fundamental human rights are attributable to vesting too much power in the hands of too few individuals. Constitutional lawyers, politicians, political scientists and state philosophers should heed above all else the famous saying of LORD ACTON: "*Power corrupts and absolute power corrupts absolutely*."

The faulty Leviathan?

HOBBES wanted to put an end to the permanent abuse of power by laying absolute power in the hands of a monarch. But how can the abuse of power and arbitrary rule by a monarchy, Leviathan or a dictator be prevented? If one is to base a theory of state on the fact that man is tainted with vices and defects, one must ensure that the state, which is steered by man and which seeks its legitimacy through this theory, comprises organs of government that minimise the scope for human error and abuse. This however, is only possible if rulers can be held responsible for their activities within government and if they are required regularly to account for their actions. Only controlled and accountable power is power in the political sense. Uncontrolled power degenerates, is susceptible to corruption and is undemocratic. It is directed against the interests of the democratic polity. Only through the institutionalised, permanent accountability of the ruling power can human error and vice on the part of the rulers be minimised.

Constitution as the instrument for the limitation of powers

The 20th Century gave us a brutal demonstration of what people are capable of, if they can exercise unlimited power for which they are not accountable. Unfortunately, the start of the 21st Century gives us little cause for hope that we will be freed forever from state brutality and totalitarianism and that democratic states will endeavour to better embody their moral justification. Mistakes and insights from the past should however not lead us to the opposite extreme and to propose anarchy as the vision of the future, as this model would deprive the state and the 'political' itself of any legitimacy. Rather, it is essential to ensure that the constitutionally created institutions of the state organise and distribute power in such a way that the authorities and persons that exercise that power do so for the benefit and well-being of the people, that they check and counter-balance each other, and that the extent of their power is limited.

For the state in a complex industrialised society it is important that people be able to develop freely within a peaceful environment. The promotion of peace and freedom does not however lead ultimately to the withering away of the state and to an association of free people (as posited by young MARX), as the state is the product of the interconnectedness of people and the division of labour. The freedoms that are secured by law should mitigate and ease the dependencies that result from this interconnectedness. When, in the age of migration, the law vests in a state authority the power to decide over domicile, and therefore over existence of people within the state, there must be procedures and institutions that ensure that such power is not exercised arbitrarily or abused. If the social security system offers a basic living allowance for disabled persons, the employees of the state should not be able to abuse the dependency of the disabled. If the constitution protects the rights of minorities, the legislature should not be able through the 'tyranny of the majority' to repeal or breach the constitution with impunity. These functions can only be properly fulfilled by a state with a broadly supported legitimacy. A gradually withering state would open the doors wide open to corruption and anarchy. Only a legitimate state can ensure that the existing power is exercised rationally, in accordance with standards of justice recognised through public and political discourse. The state must rationalise power and be able to account to its citizens for the exercise of power.

Legitimacy

How can we determine whether state authority is being exercised justly? If the state authority is supported by the broad acceptance of the people, one can assume that at least the basic conditions for just procedures, institutions and solutions are present. One can only regard a state as lawful and legitimate if the political authority of the state is recognised by the people. This is of course only possible if the people regards itself as a community that can be governed by common rules (consider for example IBN KHALDÛN'S feeling of togetherness). If there are people who feel as though they are second-class citizens and who therefore cannot identify with the state because they belong to a minority suffering discrimination, the state will lack the necessary legitimacy. Minorities too must be convinced that authority will be exercised in their best interests and without discrimination.

This acceptance however does not take place by virtue of a permanent fictive original contractual consent. It stems rather from the fact that the people obey the rules of the legal order, and do so not only from fear of the sanctions and punishments that may be imposed, but above all because they recognise the penalties as just and lawful and feel themselves obliged to follow lawful rules.

Legitimacy according to MAX WEBER

According to MAX WEBER (1864–1920), the legitimacy of authority can have different bases. He describes legitimacy as *legal* when it is founded on a rational charter and exercised accordingly; as *traditional* if it is based on the belief in the holiness or divinity of the existing order and powers of the ruler (patriarchal authority); and as *charismatic* when it is based on emotional and affective devotion to the ruler because of his magical powers, his heroism or his special abilities. The best basis for legitimacy and the most enduring is the just exertion of legal authority that is based on the rule of law. If the greatest possible number of people is convinced of the reason and the justice of the ruling authority and the law, the authority has attained the highest level of legitimacy (M. WEBER, p. 475).

When existing social power is entrusted to the state it should always be exercised in the common interest of the entire population. All powers must be exercised in accordance with the purpose of the state, that is – for the well-being of the community, including minorities – and must be seen to be so exercised. "Then all human institutions develop powers. But without assessment of the function which is specific for state power it can neither be distinguished from the power of a band of robbers, from a coal cartel nor from a bowling club" (H. HELLER, p. 203).

Who watches the watchers?

Closely connected to the issue of the just exercise of power is the question, 'who should be entitled to control the rulers?' There has never been a tyrant who has not claimed that he exercises power in the best interests of his people. However, authoritarian and totalitarian rulers always insist that they can decide autocratically what is in the public interest. Only they can decide what is in the interest of the common good, not the uneducated people. Thus James I of England declared in his famous speech on 21 March 1610 to his Parliament:

"I conclude then this point touching the power of kings with this axiom of divinity, That as to dispute what God may do is blasphemy... so is it sedition in subjects to dispute what a king may do in the height of his power. But just kings will ever be willing to declare what they will do, if they will not incur the curse of God. I will not be content that my power be disputed upon; but I shall ever be willing to make the reason appear of all my doings, and rule my actions according to my laws...."

However, even though the ruler may be controlled by Parliament and the courts, the question remains who watches over the watchers, because also the courts or the Parliament can fail in their duties. The only way to avoid such developments is to institute a carefully designed system of checks and balances in which all powers can mutually control each other and their activities are open to public scrutiny.

Condemnation of the tyrant after his death?

Nevertheless, throughout history there have always been means to provide for at least some limitations on the powers of an absolute monarch. HUGO GROTIUS (1583–1645) reports on the old custom in Egypt where kings could be accused of violation of major governmental principles. If they were declared guilty, the judge denied them an official funereal ceremony (H. GROTIUS, Book I, Chapter 3, XVI).

In SOPHOCLES' famous drama *Antigone*, the new King of Thebes denies Antigone the right to bury the former king (her brother) because he was a tyrant. Antigone however has her divine family obligations to provide a fitting burial for her brother, and she is therefore confronted with the dilemma of how to resolve the conflict between two legal orders. H. GROTIUS tells us the story of ancient kings who were entrusted with unlimited powers, but if they misused the Royal prerogatives they could be stoned to death.

Rule of law and 'Rechtsstaat'

Whether authority is vested in a king or in the democratic majority of the people, the question always arises whether the 'sovereign' is superior to the law or whether it is also bound by the law. Certainly one cannot regard the sovereign as an organ that exists merely to execute the predetermined laws. On the other hand, the sovereign has no right to commit brutal injustice. Law, justice and injustice are not – as HOBBES contends – first created by the state. *There are elementary basic legal principles that are recognised by all peoples and that cannot be violated by the state and the sovereign.* The elementary principle of the rule of law is founded on the conviction that man should not be ruled by man but by law.

The word 'law' has a meaning that goes beyond the positive law. An action or decision is considered right or wrong not only because it is legal or illegal, but also because it is either in harmony with or in violation of basic legal principles.

The Sovereign is within the law

Accordingly, the sovereign does not stand above the law but within the law. Although the sovereign is largely responsible for creating and shaping the legal system, in doing so it has no power to violate the generally recognised basic legal principles. These basic principles correspond to the fundamental, rationally-based values shared by the vast majority of the population with regard to the dignity of human beings and the credibility of procedures by which an independent judge ultimately decides on right and wrong. However, even the formal majority of the citizens of a state can sometimes be misled to accept measures that violate fundamental human rights. In particular, minorities or members of other races cannot be protected by majoritarian democracy alone. The persecution of the Jews in the Third Reich, apartheid and racial discrimination in the old South Africa, and other instances of ethnic cleansing in the 20th Century provide dreadful examples of the extremes to which the tyranny of the majority can degenerate. JOHN STUART MILL (1806–1873) was aware of this danger:

"Like other tyrannies, the tyranny of the majority was at first, and is still vulgarly, held in dread, chiefly as operating through the acts of the public authorities. But reflecting persons perceived that when society is itself the tyrant — society collectively over the separate individuals who compose it — its means of tyrannising are not restricted to the acts which it may do by the hands of its political functionaries. Society can and does execute its own mandates; and if it issues wrong mandates instead of right, or any mandates at all in things with which it ought not to meddle, it practices a social tyranny more formidable than many kinds of political oppression, since, though not usually upheld by such extreme penalties, it leaves fewer means of escape, penetrating much more deeply into the details of life, and enslaving the soul itself. Protection, therefore, against the tyranny of the magistrate is not enough; there needs protection also against the tyranny of the prevailing opinion and feeling, against the tendency of society to impose, by other means than civil penalties, its own ideas and practices as rules of conduct on those who dissent from them; to fetter the development and, if possible, prevent the formation of any individuality not in harmony with its ways, and compel all characters to fashion themselves upon the model of its own. There is a limit to the legitimate interference of collective opinion with individual independence; and to find that limit, and maintain it against encroachment, is as indispensable to a good condition of human affairs as protection against political despotism" (J.S. Mill, On Liberty, *Introduction).*

For this reason it is not sufficient that the decisions of the sovereign take into account the basic legal principles generally recognised by the people – the sovereign needs moreover to respect reasonable, justifiable and universally valid fundamental legal principles. Sovereignty is not the 'big bang' from which the whole legal order is derived in the sense proposed by HOBBES. Sovereignty is the competence but also the responsibility of the state to provide a basic order for the well-being of the population within its territorial borders.

Rationality of the rulers

The state of modernity is based on the conviction that since the Renaissance human beings have had the ability to say "no". He who has the capacity to say "no", because he is able through reasoning to assess the exercise of power, must also be capable of giving institutional and procedural effect to this "no". If, however, the state authority succeeds in convincing the people of its validity through reason, the "no" will be reduced to a tiny minority. Thus it is *reason* that must be authoritative. When the sovereign misuses its powers and breaches the elementary principles of justice and reason, it loses its legitimacy. Without legitimacy there is no sovereignty. Based on the right to resistance, human beings can thus establish a new state order, provided they set themselves the goal of establishing a state with a new legitimacy. Man remains, even when entrusted with power, a reasonable being capable of learning and self-improvement, if he is under control. For this reason the limitation of powers within the state will lead to a better, more legitimate and more just system of government.

The common good as essential element of the state

The state can be distinguished from a band of robbers because it is required to use and administer the power entrusted to the polity for the interest of the people living in the polity. It must take care of the common good of all peoples and has no power to privilege the special interests of certain persons or power-holders (J. RAWLS, p 253). Whenever a state or ruler has misused power over a long period of time, they have always had to surrender authority sooner or later. Even in the 14th Century the statesman of the Ottoman Empire IBN KHALDÛN was of the opinion that any ruler who lives only for his personal luxury and does not care for the common interest of his tribe will lose his authority. "When the natural tendencies of royal authority to claim all glory for itself and to acquire luxury and tranquillity have been firmly established the dynasty approaches senility and is approaching its downfall" (IBN KHALDÛN, *The Muquaddimah: an Introduction to History*, Chapter III, Section 11).

4 Human Rights

4.1 Introduction

Universal cultural heritage?

The basic ethical and moral principle that human beings have rights and obligations towards each other can be found in every culture. The 'golden rule' of ethical reciprocity finds expression in almost all cultures and religions, such as the Jewish and Christian rule "love your neighbour as yourself" (Moses and Jesus); "do unto others as you would have them do unto you"; "treat others as you wish to be treated", and other similar formulations. In relation to rights we need to ask not only whether human beings can claim human rights, but who can determine the content of these rights and who has the authority to enforce these rights. Those who rule the state cannot arbitrarily determine the content of rights and how they can be implemented or upheld, or which rights are valued and in which circumstances. Rather, the peoples living within the state must be able to demand their inalienable rights against the state, through independent courts.

Justice must be seen to be done

Representatives of foreign governments put pressure on China to improve its human rights record. The demand of Albanians in Kosovo for an end to abuse of their human rights led to the first military intervention by NATO in the name of human rights. The US invasion of Iraq was also said to be aimed at the protection of human rights. South Africa has a new constitution which guarantees the human rights and equality of all people in South Africa regardless of race, religion or language. In several other African states human rights are being grossly abused through ethnic conflict, military regimes, dictatorships and police terror. In France, citizens of North African origin complain of systematic discrimination, and in Switzerland asylum seekers and refugees are faced with hostility towards foreigners.

Human rights have thus become part of the game of politics. The Council of Europe has condemned Turkey for its treatment of the Kurdish minority. Turkey, for its part, accuses Western European states of misusing human rights politics in order to weaken the Turkish state, and even of undermining the Turkish state through support of the Kurds.

Islamic fundamentalists contest the universality of human rights, which they see as a product of the Enlightenment and Christian philosophy. They claim that human rights have no place in a state that is obliged to pursue religious goals. The sacred mandate of the state is to fulfil God's will, and to pursue anyone who disregards this precept. Whoever violates the laws of God cannot claim the protection of any human rights. A right to religious freedom is foreign to this concept of the Islamic state.

International protection by organisations and courts

International conferences are held regularly in an attempt to strengthen the protection of human rights. The Organisation for Security and Cooperation in Europe (OSCE) holds a conference of member governments every year to look at how rights can be better protected in the member states. The United Nations requires its member states to produce yearly reports on the human rights situation within their territory. In March 2006 the UN General Assembly replaced the Human Rights Committee with the Human Rights Council in an attempt to improve the effectiveness of the UN in human rights protection. And, over half a century ago, the members of the Council of Europe created their own human rights instrument, the European Convention on Human Rights. Under this convention, citizens of member states can bring actions against their state before the European Court of Human Rights.

Double standards

States however have an ambivalent attitude towards human rights. While the US government accuses other states of human rights violations, dozens of prisoners convicted of murder wait on death row for the execution of their death sentence. These years of fear and uncertainty for prisoners awaiting execution constitute severe torture, according to a judgment of the European Court of Human Rights.

Often states accuse other states of human rights violations but overlook violations committed by their own legislature and administration, that is, their main interest seems not to be to improve human rights for each person but to internationally discredit other states. Human rights issues are often also used to stir up ethnic conflicts in neighbour states. Hungary enacted legislation that enabled Hungarians living in neighbour-states to ask the Hungarian Government for international intervention in order to protect their human rights in the neighbour-state, rather than encouraging these people to use the proper legal remedies available within the respective state. Members of a discriminated ethnic minority may even oppose any international measure to improve their human rights situation because they *want* the majority government to seriously violate human rights in order to use the human rights violation as political argument for secession and international intervention.

The Chinese government long opposed the concept of human rights as individual rights, which they saw as an instrument of western ideology designed to undermine communist authority.

Human rights: Hope and disappointment

The history of mankind includes a history of brutalities, slavery and the violation of the basic dignity of human beings. As is true today, there have always been rulers who have abused their power and brutally mistreated their subjects. The secret police is not an invention of our times, but existed in ancient China, and in other old societies.

But no matter how cruelly human dignity has been abused through torture and slavery, the hope and struggle of some people for a just and humane social order which guarantees the free development of the individual have never been extinguished. The longing for an independent life within the family, tribe or community, the pursuit of happiness in this world or the hereafter, has always been widespread, just as there have always been attempts to abuse power and to destroy such liberties.

Human rights are now firmly in the consciousness of today's society. For many scholars, they have even become part of the international *jus cogens* and are thus directly binding on the domestic law of each sovereign state. Human rights have become an important political instrument, which can be used to protect citizens as well as to condemn states and governments before the world public. Human rights take a central position in the media, which alerts the public to gross human rights violations.

The virtuous human

Courage, intelligence, religiousness, stamina, humility, love, honour and loyalty are virtues valued not only by ancient Greek philosophers, but also recognised for several thousand years by tribes of Africa (C. MUTWA, p. 141) and found in ancient Chinese philosophy (CONFUCIUS, 551–479 BC).

Ideas about the good, just and careful ruler can be found not only in the teachings of PLATO and ARISTOTLE, but also in India (H. ZIMMER, p. 104ff) and in China, where the following quote is attributed to EMPEROR WEN (162 BC): "I get up in the early morning twilight. I don't go to sleep until late at night. All my energies are dedicated to the Empire. I care for the entire people and suffer for them" (M GRANET, p. 257, translated from German by the authors).

Inscribed in the Soul of the People

However widespread the basic concepts of just authority serving the common good were, the notion of human rights as rights that can be enforced by an independent court even against the might of the state has its roots in the history of European political thought. We have already established that originally almost every ruler based their authority on supernatural forces or 'God's law'. Even the laws of the state were originally based on religion – the law was decreed by God (or according to the Chinese belief, by Heaven) and therefore irrevocable and also binding on the ruler. The law was inscribed in the soul of the people. If it was misused or bent by the ruler, his authority or that of his descendants would be doomed to ruin. All law was thus considered human law because it was directed towards the good of every human being; one could even say all law was an expression of human rights. The idea that individuals might possess special rights in relation to their rulers that would limit the power of the rulers was within this context superfluous.

The rational person can say "No"

European 'modernity' begins with the ability, the insight and the readiness of human beings to say "no". People who can say "no" must be able for example to evaluate the merits of the government and its laws, and to decide based on this assessment whether they want to continue to support the government. To be able to assess the merits of the ruling authority a person must know what information is necessary in order to make a judgment, must be capable of understanding and evaluating this information, and must have the capacity to consider possible alternatives. People who say "no" must be able to decide which values are relevant in making such assessment and why those values are decisive.

Only people with the same capacity for reason and judgment as those ruling over them can say "no". The conception of man that recognises the reasoning ability of every individual must acknowledge that every member of the species 'Homo sapiens' is essentially equal and that therefore nobody can claim to be entitled by the grace of God to rule over other people. Only those who have been chosen by the people can achieve legitimacy for their authority.

Human capacity for judgment

The Renaissance secularised the human capacity for reason and replaced religion with rationality. In the following period, liberal modernity replaced sovereignty by the grace of God with popular sovereignty. Without the conception of people as equal and rational beings this secularisation would not have occurred. The idea that the individual has human dignity and the capacity for rational and independent judgement was a precondition for secularisation.

Human rights limit the power of the state

With the gradual secularisation of authority from the late Middle Ages the concept of human rights began to emerge. When God legitimised authority, it had been constrained and limited by the supernatural law determined by God. But now that the secularised ruler was able to set his own law, it became necessary to lay down special rules and establish safeguards to prevent the ruler from abusing his power or from using his authority for his personal interests. A state with a constitutionally guaranteed separation of powers must ensure that its institutions respect pre-constitutional rights, which are based on reason. Those who are convinced that human rights precede state sovereignty and that those rights are inalienable can only recognise the legitimacy of a state constitution if its primary aim is to limit the power of the state. Constitutions thus should not only enable and legitimise state power, but above all should fulfil the task of *limiting* state power.

With the secularisation of worldly authority, reason became the key determinant of justice and ethics. Reason recognises natural law, and the theory of natural law formed the basis of modern 'human rights'.

Homo sapiens

Secularisation also resulted in a shift in the values underpinning society. In place of religious values, which had often been misused by monarchs as a pretext for the absolutism of authority, secular values were adopted. These secular values had to be broadly acceptable to all people regardless of their religious affiliation or beliefs. Thus the system of religious values was replaced with the rationally based idea of human rights, and this new secular value system became the foundation of the constitutional state. Human rights became the yardstick of a rational value system. Human rights now serve as an ostensibly universal and secular code of ethics based on reason. Many states accordingly claim that human rights are universally valid and applicable, because they are derived from the reason of the universally equal Homo sapiens. On the basis of this justification they claim that the international community has the right to intervene economically or militarily in the affairs of sovereign states that commit gross violations of human rights.

From the right to resistance to popular sovereignty

Secularised ethics that were separate from religion developed into a generally applicable, universal ethical code. Rights founded on natural law are inalienable. The original equality before God becomes equality before the law. Out of the natural law that precedes the state, man becomes the creator of the state. In short: from the right to resistance (the capacity to say "no") develops popular sovereignty.

Secularisation of the idea of the state

Opponents of the secular, rationally deduced and universal natural law emphasise that the idea of human rights is of western origin, having its roots in the philosophy of the Enlightenment and in the individualistic tradition of Christian scholarship. Human rights therefore can at best only have a particular, rather than a general, claim to validity. They may not be valid or relevant for example in the context of Chinese philosophy, which is based on the idea of harmony and which accords less significance to the individual than does Christian tradition, which is based on the responsibility of the individual before God.

Human rights and minority rights

Human rights today are also supposed to protect minorities. It is only via the international condemnation of the violation of human rights that minorities subject to discrimination by the tyranny of the majority are able to internationalise their plight. Historical experience reveals however that human rights are often used only as a pretext to defend the interests of minorities. As soon as these minorities gain power based on secession or the grant of greater autonomy, they pay little regard to respect for the human rights of newly created minorities within their territory.

Undoubtedly the need for better protection of minorities has led to a further universalisation of human rights discourse. Western states for example, which have their origins in modern constitutionalism, make the claim that the human rights enumerated in their own constitutions are universally applicable and are therefore binding on every state in the world.

Asian values?

States with Asian cultural traditions on the other hand, have their roots within Confucianism or Hinduism, the value systems of which focus much more on the collective and the family than on the individual. Thus, their priorities differ substantially from the human rights catalogue of western states. Islamic sates and the indigenous peoples of North America and Australia also refer to values from their own culture and tradition (for example, corporal punishment) that often contradict the classical 'human rights' of the west.

Implementation of human rights by the Bretton Woods institutions

In the era of globalisation of the economy the idea of universally valid and binding human rights has been given a new impulse by the World Bank and the IMF. These institutions prescribe principles of 'good governance' to which they expect those states that rely on their loans to conform. This vague notion of good governance includes amongst other things, democratic legitimacy, accountability, transparency, decentralisation and above all the rule of law and human rights – as part of the principle of the rule of law. This close connection between the idea of human rights and the principle of the rule of law (that men are governed by law, not by men) links the concept of human rights with the modern institutions of the state, for example: the separation of powers, the right to due process, access to a fair and impartial court, and the precondition of democratic control for the legitimacy of government. From the idea that people need to protect themselves against the abuse of government power there developed a universal governance program that is now used by creditor countries to impose universal constitutional and governance principles on debtor countries as a condition of international loans and aid. These countries are expected to adapt their systems to conform to the universal standards of the international community. The main justification for these conditions is the conviction of many politicians that poverty is mainly a result of bad governance and that poverty can only be effectively overcome in countries with a system of good governance that is also attractive for foreign investors. However, it must also be acknowledged that many of the causes of governance problems in debtor countries have been inherited from colonial times.

Human rights as part of the theory of state

The following questions have now to be addressed:

1. To what extent can human rights be traced back to the ideological tradition of the Christian Enlightenment?

2. How did institutions for the protection of human rights develop?
3. What is the content of the various distinct fundamental rights?
4. What is the status and significance of human rights in relation to traditional state sovereignty?
5. What interconnection is there between the idea of human rights and modern concepts of justice?

We consider 'human rights' primarily to be supra-state rights that are derived from a generally accepted ethical philosophy and which contain moral obligations to protect people from any misuse of force or authority. They limit sovereignty and thereby limit the power of the state. If on the other hand we use the term 'fundamental rights' we are referring primarily to the intra-state and constitutional formulation of human rights.

In view of recent developments, we must question whether the modern state, developed out of French and British constitutionalism of the 17th and 18th Centuries, will in future have the same meaning and relevance as it did at the time of the foundation of the nation-states of Europe. Human rights were a catalyst for the creation of the modern nation-state. Will human rights still have a decisive impact on the internationalisation of states? Are states that continue to base their unity on nationalistic ideology still states in the sense of modern constitutionalism? In the face of a globalised economy is the concept of a 'world-state' the model that will transform or replace today's nation-states?

4.2 The Development of Western Constitutionalism

4.2.1 The Development of Legal Protections in England

Magna Carta

The most impressive and significant historical document in relation to the early development of human rights is the English Magna Carta of 1215. This charter, which is still valid in the United Kingdom, enshrined the principle of the liberty of the church but also the liberty of the free citizens: "It is accordingly our wish and command that the English Church shall be free, and that men in our kingdom shall have and keep all these liberties, rights and concessions, well and peaceably in their fullness and entirety for them and their heirs, of us and our heirs, in all things and all places forever".

By signing the Magna Carta the King confirmed the rights of free men or citizens, and confirmed the duty of the Crown to protect and defend those rights. The Magna Carta guaranteed not only substantive rights but also procedural rights and in particular the rights of accused persons to a fair trial. The King did not restrict himself to a ceremonial declaration that he would respect people's rights, he also set down the institutions and procedures that were responsible – independently of him – for determining questions in relation to the protected rights. The rights therefore contained more than just their moral content. In future the Crown could not simply disregard those rights nor determine unilaterally without any council or court the content of those rights. Rights had been recognised, and at the same time it had been determined who would be responsible for protecting them.

Besides the Magna Carta, there were a number of similar charters during the same period, which provided for the rights of free citizens. The Golden Bull of Hungary from 1222 for example provided similar rights for the gentry and for free men. In Sweden, such rights were protected under the Codex of 1350. The Swiss Declaration of Independence also enshrined rights that subjects could enforce against their rulers. Unlike most of the charters of other European states, the Magna Carta has retained its full validity. It has influenced the decisions of United Kingdom courts up until today, and still applies as part of the customary, unwritten constitution of Britain.

Petition of Rights

The next major step in the development of the protection of human rights was the Petition of Rights, which was sent by Parliament to the Crown in 1628. In addition to guaranteeing the principle of no taxation without representation by providing that taxes cannot be levied except with the approval of Parliament, the petition also expressly guaranteed the right of subjects not to be imprisoned except pursuant to the judgment of a court. It provided that the King could only exercise emergency powers in case of war. Twelve years later the Long Parliament commenced, which ended with the unseating and execution of Charles I after Oliver Cromwell was installed as Chief Protector.

Habeas corpus

The Act of Habeas Corpus 1679 solemnly entrenched the right not to be imprisoned except by order of a court – a right that had earlier been granted under the Magna Carta. Ten years later, the Bill of Rights that came out of the Glorious Revolution confirmed these rights. The Habeas Corpus Act guaranteed the right of subjects to bring an action before the courts against the servants of the Crown, for violation of rights. The judges appointed by the Crown had in some cases the right to decide on disputes between officers of the Crown and subjects and, if the servants of the Crown were found to have broken the law and exceeded the limits of their authority (acting *ultra vires*), the courts were empowered to protect the complainant against the illegitimate action of the state. The Lord Chancellor had the authority to entertain certain writs and thereby could extend the jurisdiction of the courts over servants of the Crown.

Habeas Corpus became in the common law world *the* key human right, which – much like the right to human dignity on the European continent – became the basis for the entire Anglo-Saxon understanding of human rights.

What is the fundamental right of Habeas Corpus?

Habeas Corpus affords every person who has been detained or imprisoned the right to challenge his or her detention. Persons detained for questioning, those awaiting trial, those sentenced to death or people involuntarily admitted to a psychiatric clinic for example, can via a writ of habeas corpus without any special formalities demand to be brought personally before a judge to obtain an independent judgment as to whether the deprivation of liberty is lawful. Whilst in earlier times such writ was submitted to the Lord Chancellor and it lay at his discretion whether he would grant the court jurisdiction to hear each particular case, habeas corpus actions can now be brought as of right and are not subject to any limitations or discretion.

The judge deciding on the writ of habeas corpus has the power to order the civil servant who has the detainee in custody, for example the director of the prison, to bring the detainee before the court. If the civil servant disobeys the order of the court, he may be guilty of contempt of court.

In European continental law the right and procedure of habeas corpus were long unknown. Even today in an administrative action it is usually only possible to seek to have an act quashed or declared invalid, but not to have an administrative act amended. In continental law, the concept of an action against particular civil servants with the corresponding power of a judge to make orders directed at particular civil servants is still an alien concept.

Further to the Act of Habeas Corpus, during the 17th Century the courts also made some significant constitutional decisions that were important for the development of the common law legal consciousness, and that clearly declared that the law is superior to the Crown and that even the Crown is subject to and bound by the law.

Enforcement of human rights by the courts

Human rights bind the state and limit state power. But if the courts do not have jurisdiction over state institutions, human rights are effectively worthless. The early development of English constitutionalism reveals impressively that those who sought to defend the rights of subjects were clearly aware that without a document that expressly enshrines and confirms human rights, and without the clear vesting of appropriate jurisdiction in the courts, human rights are without real value.

The Revolutionary 17th Century

In England, the 17th Century was also of great significance for the development of democracy and the secularisation of the state. From 1640–1649 the English Parliament sat as the Long Parliament and assumed executive power. It ultimately deposed King Charles I and condemned him to death for high treason. Oliver Cromwell then took over the government of the state as Lord Protector. This was the first time in European history that the subjects had taken over the sovereign power of the state. It set an example that was followed 150 years later in the French Revolution.

The philosophical justification for this revolution was provided by HOBBES. He lived in London during the anarchic times of the Long Parliament, and then in *Leviathan* described the behaviour he had observed as a 'war of all against all'. Finding himself in this society without law and order it became clear to him that men cannot survive if they are left to their own devices. In the war of all against all nobody can survive. One must therefore assume that in order to survive people are prepared via a social contract to submit themselves to the secular authority of a state. It is then the task of the state through its legal system to *end* the war of all against all.

The English Revolution marked the first time that subjects had said "no" to the state authority. They assumed for themselves the right to change the state order based on their pre-state right to exercise resistance. The political foundation for the secular state legitimised by popular sovereignty was thereby laid.

Charles I had good reason to summon the Parliament in 1640: in order to raise taxes to finance the war against Scotland to strengthen the Anglican Church against the Scottish Presbyterians, he required parliamentary approval. As another rebellion broke out in Ireland during the Long Parliament, the leading parliamentarians at Westminster began to fear that the army financed with their taxes could in the end be used against them. The cause that led to the establishment of secular state authority was thus a religious and cultural conflict.

JOHN LOCKE

At the end of the 17th Century the liberal Whigs prevailed over the conservative Stuart monarchy that had been installed after the reign of Cromwell. This 'Glorious Revolution' produced the Bill of Rights of 1689. In addition to confirming earlier human rights guarantees, the Bill of Rights contained a general right to free elections. This right was designed to protect the members of Parliament against the influence and encroachment of the Crown on Parliament. A general and free right to vote however did not emerge until the 19th Century.

The Bill of Rights also expressly obliged the Crown to obey the laws enacted by Parliament. When one considers that on the European continent it was not until the 19th Century that such obligations could be enforced, and only against heavy resistance by the respective monarchs, it is astonishing that in England general rights and freedoms were established so much earlier.

If THOMAS HOBBES was the court philosopher of Lord Protector Oliver Cromwell, then JOHN LOCKE was the philosopher of the Bill of Rights. His convictions that human rights preceded the state and are therefore inalienable, and that rights also bind the state sovereign, lie at the very heart of the Bill of Rights.

Free men

This development however, has to be assessed within the social context of the time. Only free men enjoyed rights – that is – those with property. Women, children and unpropertied workers were largely bereft of rights in relation to the state. Even the expression 'free elections' did not have the meaning that it does today. The Bill of Rights served Parliament as an instrument of protection against the King. With the demand for free elections Parliament wanted to ensure that the King did not misuse his influence in elections. However the Bill of Rights did not serve to protect citizens against the possibility that Members of Parliament might abuse their position in relation to the voters. These 'free elections' were thus not yet an expression of the general will of the people.

Development of legal protections within the common law

In England, the development of the idea of human rights as pre-state rights ran parallel to the development of legal protections for subjects against the misuse of state power by servants of the Crown. In order to enforce a right in the common law system, one must be able to identify a recognised cause of action that can be expressed in a valid writ. The writ forms the basis of the claim for enforcement of the right and the basis of the court's jurisdiction and procedure. When a claim cannot be expressed in a writ there is no avenue to bring the matter before a court for consideration.

Contempt of court

Within the frame of their jurisdiction however, the common law courts possess far-reaching powers, which can be exercised even in respect of the administration of the Crown. Under threat of contempt of court for example, courts can compel any party – including representatives of the state – to appear before the court and to comply with court orders, and criminal penalties can be imposed for failure to comply. In proceedings concerning the extent of state authority, the state is not an abstract institution, but is represented by a civil servant who must be responsible for the action on behalf of the Crown. An abstract entity cannot be brought to justice before a court, because it is anonymous, and also therefore cannot be subject to criminal penalties. Individual civil servants or representatives of the Crown on the other hand, must answer personally for the institution they represent and must bear responsibility for fulfilling the orders of the court.

This is one of the main differences between common law and civil law. In civil law systems of continental Europe, courts have no power to enforce their orders or decisions in respect of the state administration. In court proceedings the state is always an intangible, abstract entity with no criminal responsibility. Civil servants are immune from criminal prosecution in respect of their actions on behalf of the state (unless their immunity is lifted). So it is that the common law courts are more readily able to enforce human rights claims than are the civil law courts.

Public law – private law

Unlike the European civil law, the English law has never made the doctrinal distinction between private law and public law. If writs against the state administration were admissible, those courts with jurisdiction to entertain the relevant writs could assess the legality of the actions of the administration and determine the case. Provided there was a valid writ for a recognised cause of action, it was irrelevant to the court whether the parties to the proceeding were private individuals or representatives of the state.

Lord Chancellor

The original common law however contained amongst the traditional writs only very few that could be used to bring an action against servants of the Crown. In order to supplement this shortfall, and above all to improve the legal protection of individuals against servants of the Crown, the Lord Chancellor over time introduced special new actions and remedies including prerogative writs such as the writ of mandamus under which a civil servant could be ordered to perform certain actions. The development of legal protections against the might of the state was thus in the hands of the Lord Chancellor. He alone was able to improve the legal protection of subjects by introducing new writs for new causes of action.

Ultra vires

The court, which assesses the legality of an action, omission or decision of a servant of the crown, considers whether the servant of the Crown has acted within the law. If they have, then they can in no way be penalised or directed by the court. However to the extent that their action has no legal basis or they have acted outside or in breach of the law, they cannot rely for protection upon their position as servants of the Crown. If civil servants act beyond the limits of their authority (*ultra vires*), the courts are empowered to review their actions. The Crown and its servants are subject to the law just as all subjects are. Nobody can rely on their special position as servant of the Crown if they have acted beyond the law that the Crown is obliged to observe.

4.2.2 Development of Legal Protection on the European Continent

Monopoly of the legislature in continental European law

The concept of the state and the rule of law developed quite differently on the European continent. The starting point was the French Revolution. According to Article 3 of the Declaration of the Rights of Man, the bearer of sovereignty is the nation. Apart from the nation there is no authority or entity entitled to assume or exercise sovereign powers or functions. Only those who derive their authority from the sovereign nation can legitimately exercise state power. Law and justice can be derived only from the nation.

New law replaces old law

The symbol, expression and representation of the nation and its sovereignty is the national parliament, the *Assemblée National*. The parliament enacts legislation and thereby produces new laws. The just state is the state in which laws are respected and complied with. The laws are the expression of justice (état légal). Only those legal claims that are based on a law passed by the National Assembly are valid legal rights and part of the recognised law. Those laws that prior to the revolution had been determined by the precedents set by court decisions, were extinguished. Old wisdoms, which had guided the courts in their decisions, lost their validity. From this point on, the law was comprised only of laws that had been created or confirmed by Parliament since the Revolution. The Revolution thereby severed the law from the historical legal tradition, and established a new revolutionary source from which all post-revolutionary law must spring.

Stare decisis within Anglo-Saxon jurisprudence

Thus we can clearly see a fundamental conceptual difference between the legal understanding of the European continent and that of the Anglo-Saxon law. In common law systems the law has diverse roots, even today. It is the law developed gradually over centuries by the decisions of the English courts. It is however also the law produced by the legislation of the sovereign Westminster Parliament. In Anglo-Saxon law there has been no revolutionary break with the past, and no overthrow of legal tradition as occurred in France. The common law is a legal system that has developed out of the practice and decisions of the various courts. In England, every court makes decisions based on relevant precedents, thereby contributing to the development of the law with new precedents. The development of the law has been entrusted to the jurisdiction of the courts, which make decisions based on the principle of *stare decisis*, applying legal principles developed through the precedents of the respective courts.

Law-making monopoly

By vesting sovereignty in the National Assembly (as representative of the sovereign nation) the French Revolution put the law exclusively in the hands of Parliament and gave Parliament a monopoly on law making. Thus the law became a unitary and indivisible body of norms, which emerged from and could always be traced back to the sovereignty of the National Assembly. Court decisions lost their significance for the development of the legal system, and the role of the courts was reduced to deduction and interpretation of the laws passed by the sovereign. The role of the courts in making or developing the law was restricted to the room that was left within the frame of interpretation.

Impact on human rights

The French Revolution and in particular Napoleon, who spread French legal thinking throughout the European continent, set the course of the development of human rights. Napoleon set himself the goal of transforming the feudal social order into a bourgeois society according to the liberal ideas of the French Revolution. He believed however that this goal could only be attained if he liberated the executive and the administration from dependence on the courts and vested them with far-reaching powers and freedoms so that they could pursue their goals without unnecessary hindrance. The traditional courts and their conservative judges were for Napoleon an obstacle to the realisation of his revolutionary goals.

The creation of the new public law

How could the administration be freed from the bonds of the conservative judges? In order to 'immunise' the administration from the jurisdiction of the traditional courts, Napoleon decided to create a separate 'public law' for the administration which would enable the administrative and executive actions of the state to be removed from the jurisdiction and control of the traditional courts. The courts retained their jurisdiction over private law. From this point on it was no longer within the purview of the judges of private law to ensure the legal protection of citizens from the administration and to protect citizens' human rights against infringement by the state.

Conseil d'Etat as administrative court

In order that citizens still had some avenue for complaints about the misuse of state power, Napoleon established the Council of State (*Conseil d'Etat*). This Council of State was responsible, amongst other things, for receiving and hearing citizens' complaints against the government and the administration. However the Council of State could not make final and binding decisions in relation to such complaints. As an organ with advisory capacity, the Council of State could recommend to the government that it alter certain decisions or remedy its actions.

In the course of its service as an advisory body the *Conseil d'Etat* earned recognition and respect through its creative and instructive interpretation of the law, such that by 1874 it was able to declare itself to be an administrative court with decision-making power. Contrary to the theory that law-making power lay exclusively in the hands of the legislature, the *Conseil d'Etat* developed a system of precedent in the field of public law that was influential not only for France but for the whole field of continental European administrative law. Even today, the most important principles of administrative law can be traced back to the decisions and jurisprudence of the *Conseil d'Etat* in the 19th Century.

The German theory of government responsibility (Fiskustheorie)

This is essentially true also for Germany, although in Germany limited legal protections against the state developed first through the expansion of private legal rights. Before administrative courts could protect subjects against the misuse of state powers, the traditional private courts extended their jurisdiction over certain private legal relations between the prince and his subjects. If the prince or his servants breached the private law, the affected subjects could seek compensation through the private law courts pursuant to the theory of government responsibility (*Fiskustheorie*). However it was not until the German Basic Law (Constitution, or *Grundgesetz* of 1948) that a real and comprehensive system of legal protection against the misuse of power by the state was established. Article 19 of the Basic Law guarantees access to justice and a right to sue the administration. Prior to this development citizens were effectively at the mercy of the authorities, without any effective protection by independent courts.

No independent protection against human rights violations

For the protection of human rights on the European continent it is significant that, in contrast to the common law, there was for a long time no independent avenue for complaints against the executive. The protection of human rights was under the direct or indirect influence of those authorities that were supposed to be held to account for the misuse of power.

Independent administrative courts were later established. However, in comparison to the powers of the traditional private law courts, the powers of the new administrative courts were markedly limited. Their authority was confined to quashing administrative acts. They were not however able to order civil servants to perform or refrain from performing certain actions, nor could they order that court orders be followed under threat of punishment. The common law offence of contempt of court is unknown in continental European law. Employees of the administration are answerable to their superiors, and can be disciplined by them. In relation to independent judges however they enjoy immunity, which can only be lifted by a special decision of the administration.

The legal remedies available to those complaining about the actions or omissions of the administration are very limited. Administrative law jurisdiction covers only what are formally classified as 'administrative acts', and the main remedy available is an order to quash an administrative act. Even today there is almost no possibility to require or compel the administration to take positive action or to fulfil obligations. A new Swiss law has expanded the scope of administrative law by introducing a new remedy: to require the administration to make an administrative decision on the question of its obligation to act.

Article 6 of the European Convention on Human Rights

Human rights and the rule of law on the European continent were considerably improved in 1950 by Article 6 of the European Convention on Human Rights.

Article 6 guarantees access to an independent and unbiased court for determination of the legality of limitations upon civil rights. The European Court of Human Rights has given Article 6 a wide and generous interpretation, probably in reliance on the Anglo-Saxon understanding of property rights. This means that today Article 6 can be relied upon for independent judicial protection against all infringements of the rights relating to the personal existence of the individual.

4.2.3 Development of Human Rights in the United States

Mayflower

The development of the idea of human rights in the USA is of special significance. This development began in 1620, when on the Mayflower the first settlers signed a document that read in part as follows: "And by Virtue hereof [we] do enact, constitute, and frame, such just and equal Laws, Ordinances, Acts, Constitutions, and Officers, from time to time, as shall be thought most meet and convenient for the general Good of the Colony; unto which we promise all due Submission and Obedience" (*Mayflower Compact*, Agreement Between the Settlers of New Plymouth, 1620).

This agreement was similar to the social contract that lay at the centre of HOBBES' and LOCKE'S theories of the state (developed later in the same century), and that led to the secularisation of law and the secularisation of the legitimacy of state sovereignty. What is significant is that these early settlers obligated themselves to enact laws and constitutions that recognised equal rights, and to adopt those laws through a democratic procedure. With this commitment to equality and legality the settlers of the Mayflower laid the foundation for the development of human rights in the United States. Consequently, 150 years later substantive catalogues of human rights guarantees were included by the founding fathers in the first written constitutions of the member states of the United States, such as for example in the constitution of Virginia.

The first contradictions of multiculturality

The development of human rights in the USA has been and remains highly contradictory. It demonstrates that even in a society that bases its culture on individual rights, the protection of human rights cannot always be safeguarded. Even a country with an established culture of constitutionalism is not immune from lynch-mob justice, ethnic cleansing of the native people, racial discrimination, class polarisation and prejudice. Settlers trampled on the rights of the indigenous peoples. This discrimination was justified by the liberal Chief Justice Marshall, with the argument that the native Americans were not members of civilized nations, but rather wild savages (see *Johnson and Graham's Lessee v William McIntosh* US 1823 523 ff).

Sub-humans

Since Marshall's statement, discrimination, decimation and expulsion of other human beings has been justified in America and elsewhere with the argument that the affected people are not 'normal' people that deserve to be treated humanely but rather that they are underdeveloped and somehow inferior. These people are less intelligent (slaves, apartheid), belong to an inferior and sub-human race (Holocaust), or they are people who by nature are particularly dangerous, such as terrorists, communists, Muslims, etc. This is clearly contrary to the idea of human rights, which is based upon the basic principle of equality of all Homo sapiens, and the belief that man – regardless of race, culture, religion and language – is a reasonable being capable of rational judgement and responsible action.

Declaration of Independence: Right to resist

With the American Declaration of Independence, the idea of human rights was elevated to a whole new level of rights development. As it became clear that the American colonies wanted to unilaterally secede from England, Thomas Jefferson was commissioned to draft a declaration of independence. In order to provide to the monarchical world of Europe convincing justification for this radical step, he set out two principal arguments. First, he claimed that peoples have an inherent and inalienable right to resistance, which in particular cases entails a right to determine their own system of government and, based on their inalienable right to self-determination, to separate themselves from a tyrannical government. To demonstrate that in the concrete case at hand the American settlers had the right to secede from the colonial power of England he relied on his second argument, that the English government had violated the inalienable rights of the people of the confederated states.

Inalienable rights

Without the recognition of the inalienable rights of all people, the American Declaration of Independence could not have been written. The idea that people have rights that precede the state and that the state is responsible for the protection of these rights was the philosophical foundation of the Declaration of Independence. If these pre-state rights are violated, people have an original right to resistance against the state authority that has committed or allowed this violation, as well as the right to establish their own new state which in turn will be obliged to protect the pre-state and inalienable rights of its citizens.

Rights of slaves

Jefferson's original draft of the Declaration of Independence also included slaves as bearers of human rights. Jefferson, however, was required to delete this part of the draft, as nobody at that time was prepared to bear the consequences of a state order involving equal rights for all persons including slaves. With this double standard the contradictory nature of American human rights policy finds its official beginning.

Constitutional jurisdiction of the Supreme Court

The next major but logical step in the protection of human rights was the famous Supreme Court decision of *Marbury v Madison*, led by Chief Justice Marshall, in which the highest court declared a law passed by Congress to be invalid because it contravened the Constitution. American constitutional law thereby laid the groundwork in 1803 for the development of constitutional jurisdiction and judicial review of legislation. In Europe such jurisdiction was recognised much later, developing gradually from the Norwegian constitution at the end of the 19th Century, and the Austrian Constitution drafted by Hans Kelsen which provided for constitutional review of legislation. This development finally reached Germany, France and Italy in their post-World War II constitutions and the establishment of their constitutional courts.

The basis for examining the constitutionality of a law was the historical common law belief with regard to the basic rule of law, 'that men must be governed by law and not by men'. According to this principle, even the law-maker (legislature) is subject to the law and must respect the universal rights derived through reason from the nature of man. The guardian of these rights is the court. In recalling this enlightened and pioneering decision of John Marshall we should not however ignore the fact that the decision also reflects certain concrete political interests. Marshall's preferred party had lost the recent Presidential election. But with the introduction of constitutional jurisdiction for judicial review, the court could at least exercise some limited control over the government majority in Congress. In any case, the fact that the argument of the Court in *Marbury v Madison* has not been overruled but rather has become the basis of expansive constitutional jurisdiction and powers of judicial review, clearly demonstrates that the decision was ultimately based upon a generally accepted legal culture. The decision strengthened the enforceability of human rights, not only against the executive but also against the tyranny of the majoritarian legislature.

Segregation until the Warren Court

Even the highest courts cannot completely ignore the social environment and the political climate in which they operate. As part of their environment, their capacity to independently forge a geographically and historically universal notion of justice based on rational considerations of ethics is limited. This of course is one of the reasons why the Supreme Court for more than a century permitted racial discrimination within American society and upheld the laws of segregation and apartheid, under the principle of 'separate but equal'. It was not until 1954 that the Afro-American minority succeeded in convincing the Court that separate schools for coloured children and white children did not accord with the principle of equality, but rather constituted unlawful discrimination against the coloured race. In *Brown v. Board of Education* the Supreme Court, led by Chief Justice Warren, held that segregated education was a breach of the equal protection clause of the US Constitution because such apartheid deeply humiliates the discriminated minority and thereby puts them at great social disadvantage. Therefore, in accordance with the principle of equality of opportunity and equal protection of the law, white and coloured children must be educated together in common schools. This decision resulted in a new policy of active mixing of races within schools, which in turn led to serious unrest in many American states as some sections of white society resisted the change.

A speciality of the common law

In this example we can observe an important strength of the common law system. The subject matter of the claim, or the cause of action in *Brown v. Board of Education*, could not even have been entertained under continental European administrative law. The subject matter of the action was not an administrative act or an administrative decision that could have been annulled by a court. Rather, the plaintiffs sought from the court an order to compel the administration to admit coloured children to schools that had been reserved for white children (writ of mandamus or mandatory injunction). A continental European court would not have had the power to order the administration to take certain measures or to refrain from certain action, nor to enforce such order.

The revolution of the Warren decision in *Brown v. Board of Education*

Following the decision in *Brown v. Board of Education*, the Supreme Court made other important decisions in relation to strengthening the rights of Afro-Americans. Private racial discrimination, such as the exclusion of particular minorities from restaurants or private parklands, was met with the argument that the state should not be misused to enforce such discriminatory measures with police power. The Court held that the state is not permitted to assist in measures of social discrimination. The judiciary was thereby able to make an important contribution to the eradication of social discrimination – a fundamental problem for human rights and minority rights in multicultural societies.

Affirmative action

Decisions in relation to affirmative action are of even greater significance for the eradication of discrimination. According to the theory of affirmative action, legal discrimination is permissible if it is designed to redress the negative discrimination and disadvantage suffered by particular minorities, for example by providing employment quotas for minorities to compensate for their chronic under representation in the workforce. If the opportunities of minorities are limited because of their general social disadvantage, the state needs to introduce measures to improve their opportunities, for example through a bonus-system for particular minorities. Today the Supreme Court has restricted the scope of affirmative action and has largely returned to the principle of 'colour-blindness'.

Rights of the accused (Miranda rule)

American constitutional law is also significant with regard to other human rights questions. Whilst in Europe, the law of criminal procedure has always been regarded as a set of legal norms designed to serve the substantive criminal law, the common law has since Magna Carta accorded separate and central recognition (and constitutional status) to the procedural rights of the accused to fair treatment. The American Constitution and later the Supreme Court strengthened these procedural rights and developed further the concept of habeas corpus. Priority has been given to the right to silence, that is, the freedom of the accused against self-incrimination and the right not to be compelled to be a witness or to give evidence against him/herself. In the famous decision of *Miranda v the State of Arizona* (1966), the Court decided that from the moment of arrest the accused must be informed of his/her right to remain silent (Miranda rule).

The importance of juries

The close connection between human rights and the criminal process is also evident in the particular court process of Anglo-Saxon criminal law. In contrast to the European concept whereby the state lawyer is simultaneously responsible for protecting the interests both of the public/the state and the accused, in the common law a criminal proceeding is an adversarial process between two parties. The parties to the process have the task of seeking to convince the jurors, who have been randomly selected from the public by ballot, of the guilt or innocence of the accused. The jurors are 'blind' and are expected to know only the facts that have been presented and proven during the proceeding. It is possible for the parties to negotiate in relation to the process, so that for example the prosecutor might conclude an agreement with the accused that he will only be charged with one particular crime rather than all the crimes he is accused of having committed, if he pleads guilty and agrees to act as a witness against another accused ('plea bargaining').

Representatives of the people

Given that juries are comprised of randomly selected citizens, they constitute a random sample of different sections of society and are thus said to be representative of the people. Whilst in a democratic election it is possible to manipulate voters with election promises or demagogic assertions, such manipulation of jurors in a court proceeding jealously controlled by the parties is much less likely – provided that the parties can afford good lawyers. The conduct of the criminal trial before a randomly selected jury of peers is regarded as an important pillar of democracy in the Anglo-Saxon system. This is why, according to the Anglo-Saxon understanding, trial by jury is acknowledged as a democratic right, and is expressly guaranteed in the VIIth Amendment to the US Bill of Rights.

Tension between the people's representatives

In this context it is interesting to observe the relationship between electoral democracy and democratic juries in the field of labour law in the 19th Century. During this period the democratically elected Congress passed business-friendly legislation under the influence of economic interests, whilst the courts led by democratic juries often took pity on the hopeless situations of employees and decided in favour of workers. Labour law courts often applied or interpreted the labour laws in ways that the legislators had not expected. There developed a conflict between the representatives of the people in Congress and the representatives of the people in the courts. And, as the courts had the power to enforce their decisions with contempt of court, even elected magistrates that were under the influence of economic interests had to submit to the will of the juries.

In spite of everything, human rights protection is inadequate

In spite of these encouraging developments we repeatedly find that in history as in the present, there are some barely comprehensible contradictions in the US approach to human rights. On the one hand, the courts have done much to strengthen the protection of human rights and the rights of minorities against the misuse of state power. On the other hand, the US still refuses to adopt international human rights standards that today have almost become a common universal good of the international community. The most obvious and incomprehensible contradiction still remains the application of capital punishment in many states, as well as at the federal level. The poor treatment of prisoners is also contrary to the principle of human dignity. Discrimination against foreigners, the denial of habeas corpus for illegal immigrants, discrimination against women as well as the refusal to accept the jurisdiction of the new International Criminal Court and the contravention of the Geneva Convention for the prisoners in Guantanamo are further examples of unjustifiable contradictions of the universal application of human rights. From these reflections we can draw the following conclusions:

Human rights are always threatened

1. The development and improvement of human rights protections is never complete. Even when the protection of human rights is at its highest level, serious regressions can never be ruled out.
2. Knowledge about human rights should not be confined only to legal education. Human rights need to find a broader base amongst the people and to become embedded in the cultural heritage of the nation. Particularly in the USA, discussion of human rights largely remains legalistic and academic.
3. Human rights cannot be separated from their social and economic context.
4. The death penalty in the USA has its roots in an obsolete conception of the criminal law. In earlier times, the function of criminal penalties was akin to

revenge. However, if today one sees the role of criminal law as being educative, and having the ultimate objective of enabling offenders to resume their place in society, then the death penalty can no longer be justified.

5. Ultimately it must be borne in mind that the obligation to respect human dignity is marked by the idea that throughout his life man must have the ability to change his beliefs and behaviour. This chance is denied to a person who is executed. From the European perspective, which regards human dignity as the starting point of all human rights, capital punishment undermines the very idea of human rights. In Anglo-Saxon thinking on the other hand, in which due process and habeas corpus form the foundation of human rights, a person who has been afforded a fair trial has exercised his/her human rights, and the verdict must be accepted. However the many known false convictions and miscarriages of justice in the USA reveal, as does the disadvantage of the poor and racial minorities through bad and uninterested defence lawyers, that the court process is no guarantee of a just verdict.
6. Whoever takes – as many Americans do – the Calvinistic view that whoever has success in this world belongs to the righteous people, and will also have success in the world beyond, will accordingly take the view that whoever loses a case is not righteous and must receive and accept the verdict they deserve.
7. The human rights idea as a basic protection against misuse of state power presupposes the secularisation of the legitimacy of the state. Human rights developed on the basis of a state secularised through a social contract based on popular sovereignty. The state is bound by human rights and the power of the state is thereby limited. Religion on the other hand prepares people for the life hereafter. To this end the guardians of religion were allowed, even obliged, to punish those who did not fulfil their religious obligations. The guardians of religion in their exercise of state power are accountable only to their God, but not to the people. They do not have any secular responsibility. The idea of human rights however assumes that those who exercise the power of the state are responsible to the secular authority of the courts for their actions and for the respect of inalienable rights.

Judicial protection is central

To this day there is no nation in which the great majority is prepared to afford unconditional and integral respect for human rights to all people including foreigners. No nation is willing to forego short-term advantages (for example by granting equal opportunity to foreigners) or to accept disadvantages (for example a diminished feeling of security in relation to suspected terrorists as a result of the unrestricted application of the principles of the rule of law and due process in criminal proceedings) in the interests of human rights. The developed states of the west are struggling with foreign immigration, the tensions of multiculturality and the fear of terrorism. Most African and Asian states are still in the process of transition from and feeling the effects of colonisation (such as lack of legitimacy of state borders and authority). Executive governments and parliaments that are interested in re-election will not fight for political goals that do not attract votes. Human rights don't win elections. It must therefore be anticipated that human rights will often be sacrificed to populist fears and emotions.

Ultimately human rights can only be realised when judges possess the requisite constitutional jurisdiction as well as genuine independence and authority. If the professionalism and credibility of the judiciary is beyond dispute, the judiciary will be able to make independent and authoritative decisions consistent with the rule of law, and immune from political and social pressure.

4.3 The Theoretical Development of Human Rights

The idea of equality

The concept of human rights has various roots. Human rights as pre-state rights are rights that correspond to the nature of human beings. According to liberal constitutionalism such rights precede the constitution and the state. Human rights are however in our view also rights that can be enforced against the state authority. States and their constitutions must acknowledge and respect human rights. When rulers disregard human rights, when they misuse their power, people have the right to resist state authority. Closely tied to the idea of a right to resistance is LOCKE'S claim that human rights are inalienable and irrevocable. No person can renounce or divest himself of the rights that have been granted to him by nature. From today's perspective, it is astonishing that from the time of the Stoa philosophy of ancient Greece it took thousands of years until the notion of the equality of all people came to be generally accepted. The equality of men and women and the equality of races only became generally accepted principles long after the French Revolution.

From the demand for justice to the right of resistance

Within European history, political ideas have progressed through various stages to bring us to the modern understanding of human rights. The Stoa philosophy of ancient Greece required that the law-maker enact just laws. In the Christian Middle Ages the prevailing view was that man is made in the image of God, and the individual is therefore the bearer of rights given by God (including for example the right to resist tyranny). The philosophy of the Renaissance centred around the reason of the individual and recognised the right of the sovereign individual to determine the scope of his rights.

4.3.1 From Stoa to Resistance

The idea of justice

The history of the concept of human rights finds its roots in the idea of justice. The Greek and Roman philosophers of the Stoa postulated that rulers were obliged to observe the principles of justice. He who rules justly, is complying with the laws of nature. They did not differentiate between the laws of nature, which cannot be violated, and the laws regulating the behaviour of men. For them justice was therefore in harmony with the laws of nature. The idea that all men are fundamentally equal and therefore that justice and laws should proceed from this starting point was, in this context of a society and economy built on slave-labour, still barely conceived. However, the Roman philosopher SENECA put forward amongst the first ideas in relation to the fundamental equality of men as Homo sapiens. He claimed that slaves ought to be treated humanely. Yet it took almost another two thousand years until the equality of all people, regardless of sex or race, was generally acknowledged.

Women are inferior to men

In a certain sense one can credit Christianity and the Christian scholastic philosophy with having laid the anthropological foundation for the general principle of equality. The Christian religion assumes that man was made in the image of God. It follows therefore that *every* person must have the claim to be made in God's image. But in fact even the religious scholars were not consistent in their adherence to this principle, particularly when it came to equality of the sexes. THOMAS AQUINAS for example famously stated that women are inferior to men and can be treated differently, because they are 'unfinished' men. Whilst this view might sound outrageous today, still today people resort back to such arguments to justify grave discrimination. Whenever discrimination against women or particular races or ideological or cultural groups needs to be justified, the justification is always based on the assertion that those people are essentially inferior in character or intelligence to other human beings.

Man as the image of God

The idea of the Christian scholars of man as the image of God also had further, very significant consequences for the development of human rights. If man is the image of God, he must also be able to make decisions about himself and his future. Men, who are the image of God, must as individuals be capable of responsibility, and must be bearers of rights and obligations. Thus, the foundation for the further development of individual rights was laid. From this point on human rights were not understood merely as commands upon the ruler to enact just laws. Rather, every individual became the bearer of human rights and was entitled to pursue and enforce those rights against the rulers. Although the Popes later condemned the individualism of liberal philosophy, the historical philosophical basis of liberalism is found in Christian scholarship.

Reason defines human rights

In examining human rights one must look not only at the content of those rights and the bearers of rights. One must also be able to determine *who* it is that determines the content of rights. Whoever is able – with a claim to universality – to determine what human rights are, who bears human rights and the manner in which those rights can be claimed before a court, ultimately determines the fate of human rights. In a certain sense the Christian scholarship of the Middle Ages has already answered the question. Human rights are natural laws given by God. The human being is able through reason to recognise and deduce the content of these natural law rights. Christian scholarship thereby laid the foundation for the triumph of reason and rationality that occurred in the Renaissance and continued later in the age of liberalism.

Loyalty of rulers and vassals

The political ideas of the Middle Ages have their roots not only in the Christian religion and within Roman law, they were also inspired by cultural values of the old Germanic tradition. The idea of the obligation of the ruler to take care of his vassals, and the concept of the vassals' loyalty to their ruler is derived from German thinking. The idea that the subjects are entitled to resist their ruler if he fails to protect them or abuses his power can also be found in old German thought.

4.3.2 Renaissance

Reason as the instrument of secularisation

Two central preconditions for the development of human rights developed during the Renaissance period: the secularisation of the state and the sovereignty of the reason of the individual. In the Middle Ages, politics served the church. The Pope had the mantle to rule over spiritual and religious matters, and he vested the emperor with the temporal mantle to rule in the name of God over the subjects entrusted to him. This presupposed the separation of spiritual-theological and political authority. In the age of the Renaissance, which culminated in the Reformation, this separation between church and state, between religion and politics, was more thoroughly and consistently executed. State political authority was secularised. Religious authority legitimised itself through the uncontested authority of God. Worldly authority on the other hand had from now on to find its legitimacy in the secular world. Authority had to be legitimised by the people who were subject to that authority. This laid the foundation for the later democratic revolutions.

Rulers who can no longer rely for their authority on a god-given right must follow the laws that correspond to human nature. They cannot rule against the nature of men; the inalienable rights that are given to man by nature cannot be taken away from him by an authority legitimised by secular reason.

Universality

The European development of the idea of human rights is closely linked to the Judeo-Christian tradition. Without this tradition the concept of human rights would probably not have developed as it did. If however the idea of human rights is so closely intertwined with Christian religion, how can the notion that such rights are universal be justified? The idea of the sovereignty of reason as well as the notion that political authority is of a secular nature, stem ultimately from the Christian tradition. And indeed one of the major challenges to the 'universality' of human rights is the charge that this concept is really an instrument of the Christian colonisation of other cultures in disguise.

The golden rule of ethics

On the other hand, one can find ideas about the value and dignity of human beings, about just political order and about the abuse of authority in almost every culture. The golden rule of ethics or religion appears in similar form in almost every culture: "do unto others, as you would have them do unto you". This golden rule of ethics is ultimately also the basis upon which human rights can be justified and defined. In so far as human rights correspond to this golden rule and can be deduced from it, they should be able to make a claim to universal validity.

Who is the universaliser?

It is then crucial not only to know how the content of human rights is determined, but above all *who* ultimately determines this content. It may well be that human rights have universal validity. But the 'universaliser', that is, the power that determines within a globalised world the validity and enforcement of human rights and that can decide who has infringed human rights, can hardly claim to have general or universal legitimacy.

4.3.3 The Age of Liberal Constitutionalism

Constituent power

Secular authority can only be justified if it is constituted by the people that will be ruled by that authority. Political authority is the governing power that is established, determined and ultimately also constituted by the people. The idea of the state as an artificial construct established by men through reflection and choice, in which political authority is exercised within a defined territory, emerged in the era of liberal constitutionalism. Whoever wants to exercise constituent power, to claim the right to create authority by constituting it, to be the source of the law and the state, must not only ensure a basis for the legitimacy of such authority, they must also confront the question of whether such constituent power can be exercised without any limits or restrictions, or whether pre-state rights of man impose limits on the constituent power.

Nature of human beings

The state can only be justified if human beings have a natural and pre-constitutional disposition to depend on an artificial political order beyond the family. Two different accounts of the pre-state nature of human beings made their mark on English constitutionalism.

The egocentric man: HOBBES

THOMAS HOBBES was firmly of the view that man is by nature an egocentric being, which would descend into anarchy and chaos if not integrated within a strict order. Men submit to the authority of the Leviathan by their own free will in the interests of peace, because they cannot survive in a state of anarchy. The pre-state nature of man is thus inclined towards a form of authority that aims to guarantee peace between men. For this reason men must accept the absolute order of the Leviathan. They no longer have any choice, but must submit to the order and accept every decision as lawful. 'Auctoritas not veritas facit legem' – authority, not truth, makes law. Liberty is not entirely or fundamentally excluded by this order. However, it is the prerogative of the Leviathan to provide as much freedom as peace will permit. The primary function of the constitution is to empower and legitimise the Leviathan. The constitution maker decides how much freedom will be permitted. Liberty does not precede the state, but rather is created and granted by the state and its laws.

Pre-state rights of man: JOHN LOCKE

JOHN LOCKE takes a different view of pre-state order. For LOCKE, man in the state of nature is the bearer of inalienable rights. However, in the state of nature man's liberty and the property he has acquired through work are endangered. What precedes the state is therefore not the egocentric nature of man, but rather man's fundamental rights such as those to liberty and property. It follows that the aim of state order must be to protect liberty and property. This protection is however only possible if the power of the state is limited. The objective of a constitution must therefore be to limit state power in the interests of the rights of man. State power must be constrained by the rights that precede the state, and state goals must serve the protection of these rights within the state order. Thus, of critical importance is not how man can protect himself against civil war (HOBBES), but rather how man can protect himself from the protector.

Is the law created by the state or the state created by the law?

Should the goal of the state be liberty or peace? Should state power be limited for the sake of individual liberty? Is the basis of the law to be found in the state or in the pre-state nature of man? Are human rights first created and granted by the constitution or do they precede and constrain the state? With his theory of the Leviathan, HOBBES laid the foundation for the later positivist conception of the state as the single and absolute source of law. The state and sovereignty became the 'big-bang' source of law and justice. LOCKE on the other hand laid the foundation for the natural law and human rights-based approach to liberalism. Law that is based on the nature of human beings must be universal. He thereby provided the basis for justification of the American Declaration of Independence almost 100 years later, as well as the theoretical foundation for the rule of law and constitutional jurisdiction in the USA: 'That men must be governed by law and not by men'.

Those who follow LOCKE will be committed to the constitutional and judicial protection of human rights. Those who follow HOBBES will subordinate the protection of rights to the primary goals of peace and security.

Liberty and equality

Liberty and equality were fundamental for both founders of the new era of constitutionalism. Liberty is the ultimate goal of the state, and became the guiding principle of liberalism. Both HOBBES and LOCKE defend universal liberty and the equality that results from it, based on a constitutional state the values of which accord with the nature of man. The two theorists differ only in whether they accord priority to liberty or peace, and in their characterisation of human rights as natural rights or as positive state laws. LOCKE defends liberty beyond the state; HOBBES defends liberty within and subject to the peaceful order of the state.

Separation of state and society

How can liberty be realised within the state? For LOCKE, as we have seen, the state is not entitled to interfere with the liberty of the individual. Consequently, there must be a clear separation between the public and private spheres. State and society are to be separated from each other: the state is bound by the liberty of society. For HOBBES on the other hand, liberty is based on the peace achieved by the state. Only in times of peace can liberty be enjoyed.

Whilst for LOCKE, authority is legitimate if it is limited and observes respect for human rights, for HOBBES authority is legitimate only on the basis of the capacity of the Leviathan to secure peace.

Only the people can protect human rights

For ROUSSEAU these are inadequate grounds for the legitimacy of authority. For him the question of legitimacy hinges not on 'how' but on 'who'. With regard to this question there are two alternatives: either the ruled are ruled by rulers, or the ruled rule over themselves. For the first time ROUSSEAU puts human rights in close connection with democracy. ROUSSEAU does not content himself with the concept of liberty 'before' or 'beyond' the state. Rather, he insists on liberty 'within' the state. The realisation of this liberty depends on three preconditions:

- The state must guarantee and protect the equality of human beings.
- The state must be ruled by the ruled. Only when the ruled are able to guide the state will they ultimately find liberty.
- The state must pursue and achieve the common good. The common good is not to be reduced to the welfare of a local community. The common good in the sense of ROUSSEAU is the *volonté générale*; there is only one universal common good and only one universal justice.

The simultaneous realisation of equality and liberty through direct democracy leads to peace within the state and is ultimately identical to the universal common good, that is, the *volonté générale*.

4.3.4 From Liberalism to Social Democracy to Communism

Visions of liberalism

Liberalism places the right of every individual to self-determination at the centre of justice (JOHN MILTON). The keywords of JOHN LOCKE were property, life, liberty and estate. The aim of authority was to achieve government by consent. For SPINOZA, the vision is expressed in the battle-cry of Parliament that without the approval of the representatives, no tax can be raised: 'no taxation without representation'. Government by law however could only be developed on the basis of the separation of powers (J. LOCKE). According to KANT, the freedom of every individual meant also the freedom of all equals, and for JOHANN GOTTLIEB FICHTE (1762–1814) liberty was not a status but a goal.

The following reflection of ROUSSEAU is worthy of note:

> "It is therefore one of the most important functions of government to prevent extreme inequality of fortunes; not by taking away wealth from its possessors, but by depriving all men of means to accumulate it; not by building hospitals for the poor, but by securing the citizens from becoming poor" (J.J. ROUSSEAU, A Discourse on Political Economy (1755)).

The aim of state authority

From this point on the philosophical discourse in relation to the state focuses on the question: What should be the ultimate and principal goals of political or state authority? Liberty, equality, internal peace and the universal common good were all undisputed goals of the state. But what was in dispute was the relative priority that should be accorded to these goals, and real content or meaning of each of them.

Equality and freedom

In particular, the meaning or content of 'equality' was disputed. In Article one of the French Declaration of the Rights of Man of August 26, 1789, the right to equality was clearly expressed as follows:

> "Men are born and remain free and equal in rights. Social distinctions may be based only on considerations of the common good."

Liberals and socialists were fighting a common battle side by side. It was only towards the end of the 19th Century that they finally separated and followed different paths. The starting point of this separation was the Marxist view that, whilst freedom and equality should be aims of politics, individuals within the existing society are not free but exploited. Man, who has been chased out of paradise, is not a free individual but an exploited human being. Liberty thus is only possible if man returns to the state of paradise and thus to freedom. The goal of every political order therefore has to be to guide human beings to liberty and to emancipate the exploited individual. With this new perception the first major controversy between the traditional liberal conception on one side and the emancipatory socialist view on the other side appears. Should the state recognise the status quo of liberty and only aim to strengthen the protection of liberty, or does the state have an emancipatory mandate to liberate men from exploitation and to create the conditions for greater liberty?

Contrary to the Marxist view, which regards the fulfilment of the emancipatory role of the state as being possible only through one party, the social democratic parties accepted the basic idea of a pluralistic democracy in which they aim to convince the majority of the people to transfer this emancipatory task to the state.

Minimal state

By way of contrast, according to the neo-liberal view the goal of political authority should be to secure a minimal state with minimal authority. The only task of the state should be to provide the conditions for fair competition in an open market in which everyone has the opportunity to freely participate. If the state steers the market with political power and if it interferes with competition by means of political majorities, the harmony of the invisible hand will be disturbed. If the state is not content simply to guarantee equal opportunities, but goes so far as to interfere with the results of the free market, politics will produce injustice and inequality. The losers should not be allowed to enrich themselves at the expense of the winners. The only acceptable justice is the distribution of wealth as it results out of the fair competition of the free market.

Status activus?

Rights and freedoms, according to strict liberal doctrine, are only negative rights. They require the state to refrain from interfering with the individual and they protect the individual against unlawful encroachment upon liberty by the state. For this reason persons whose rights are infringed must be granted access to justice in order to defend their rights against illegal state intervention. Such institutional legal protection however is much more difficult to realise when the court is not only asked to protect the individual against state intervention but to actively promote and support discriminated communities of persons. The classical liberal school of thought therefore fundamentally rejects this status activus of fundamental rights.

Separation of powers

As negative rights, freedoms or liberties in the sense of LOCKE should also limit state power. The real goal of the rule of law and of government by law and not by men can only be achieved if state power is limited. And the most important constitutional principle that limits state power is the separation of powers. The separation of powers and with it the checks and balances between the branches of government are indispensable conditions for the effective implementation of human rights within the state.

Equal opportunities as compromise

Between these two contrasting political views there also emerged compromises that served in part to expand the content of human rights quite substantially. In order to improve the ‘equal opportunities’ of that part of the population which through no fault of its own suffers from discrimination and/or conditions of disadvantage that hinder its capacity to participate, the concept of social and economic rights emerged to level the playing field. Through social and economic rights such as the right to education, employment, housing, a healthy environment and health services, the legislature has been charged with the task of creating the economic and social conditions that will ensure the greatest possible number of people genuinely have the opportunity to exercise their freedoms and to participate in the market and in society.

Social rights

Unlike the classical rights and freedoms that serve as negative rights that prohibit certain state action or intervention, social and economic rights generally require positive action by the state. Social rights effectively mandate the law-maker and the executive to achieve certain goals. It is therefore difficult for the court to directly implement or enforce social and economic rights on its own. Whilst the classical rights and liberties bind the three branches of government: the judiciary, the legislature and the executive, it is generally only the legislature and the executive that are bound by social and economic rights.

Affirmative action

Within the Anglo-Saxon states the institution of *affirmative action* has developed. Based on this principle, members of a group or race which has long been disadvantaged can be supported by positive state measures in order to overcome discrimination and enable them to 'catch up'. Such positive discrimination in favour of minorities necessarily has the consequence that members of the majority will be somewhat disadvantaged, for example in their educational or employment opportunities. In so far as such positive discrimination is aimed at restoring justice for long-suffered injustices, the majority may be willing to accept the discriminatory consequences on its part. Thus discrimination against the majority will in certain circumstances be permissible, based on the principle of affirmative action.

State action and effect of fundamental rights on third parties

In addition to the legislature, constitutional courts also have tried to ameliorate disadvantage in situations where private persons seek to misuse their liberty and their superior social status to discriminate against other private persons of a weaker or underprivileged group. The principal example of this development is the 'state action doctrine' devised by the United States Supreme Court.

According to this principle, the state cannot be used by private persons in order to protect and implement their private claims if this would involve the use of state force to effect racial discrimination or other forms of discrimination against disadvantaged minorities, such as excluding African-Americans from restaurants reserved for white people.

Some states on the European continent with civil law systems want to achieve similar aims via the doctrine of '*Drittwirkung*'. This theory assumes that rights not only bind the state but that they also have horizontal effect and application between private individuals, and therefore that private individuals should not be permitted to act in a discriminatory manner. The basis of this doctrine is however hotly contested.

HABERMAS: The ethics of communication and discourse

The theory of JÜRGEN HABERMAS (1929) is based in part both on liberalism and socialism. For HABERMAS, the foundation for the legitimacy of the state is not the social contract, but is rather the continuous discourse of citizens. Based on mutual dialogue, common values emerge which become the basis of the authority of the law. People's sovereignty thereby becomes a real pre-state human right which enables constant discourse and thus provides legitimacy for state authority. Citizens become the participants in discourse through which they create law and follow the law. With this theory HABERMAS was able to overcome the separation, necessary in liberal theory, between the state as protector of liberty and the society as the basis for individual free development. The state is replaced with the public of the political discourse. The public of course has to respect privacy of the individual.

4.3.5 Communitarianism

Values of the community

The new communitarianism sought to separate itself from traditional liberalism. It refers to the values of the community, and prioritises the value of common welfare over the value of individual liberty and individualistic capitalism. From this approach there emerge new human rights, which are rooted within the principle of self-determination of peoples and within collective rights of minorities and the general protection of minorities. Liberties are interpreted from the point of view of the community. Harmony of the community and not individual liberty becomes the main goal of the state. The controversy over 'Asian values' relative to human rights has also to be seen within this context.

Collective rights

The claim for collective rights has arisen as a consequence of the idea of the social contract, which legitimised state authority through the people and popular sovereignty. Cultural, linguistic and religious minorities that will never achieve a majority position within their state demand the introduction of collective minority rights including the right to autonomy, which will enable them to protect and promote their identity. Until recently, these minority- and autonomy rights were expressly granted only in the constitutions of Latin American states, particularly with regard to their native populations. On the European continent the Minorities Charter of the Council of Europe (*Framework Convention for the Protection of National Minorities* of 1 February 1995) constitutes the first step towards constitutional protection of the collective rights of national minorities. Although the Framework Convention does not provide any individual legal guarantees as the Human Rights Convention does, it is nevertheless an important step forward with regard to the acceptance of collective rights of minorities. Elsewhere too, it has proven difficult to protect and enforce collective rights in the same manner as the traditional rights and freedoms of the individual. In those Latin American constitutions that provide some protection of the collective rights of indigenous peoples, the acknowledgement of these rights is essentially declamatory and rhetorical.

Human rights within a globalised market

The new development of globalisation however has altered the situation drastically. Human rights have acquired almost universal recognition, but at the same time states have forfeited much of their scope for action. Thus, states are now more limited in the extent to which they can fulfil the emancipatory function of providing material equality or equality of opportunities. The sovereignty of the global market has substantially limited the sovereignty of the nation-state. The state can ultimately only legitimise its authority with regard to its citizens by respecting the universality of human rights and by seeking to create the optimal conditions that will enable its citizens (and its economy) to participate and succeed in global competition.

Legitimacy of the universaliser?

Nation-states legitimise themselves by respecting universal human rights and by maintaining their capacity to participate successfully within the competitive global market. The main question however is: On what basis is the sovereignty of the global market legitimate and how do those who control the global market and ultimately also determine the content of universal human rights legitimise themselves? From where do the superpowers derive their legitimacy when they decide that it is legitimate to violate human rights in the course of the 'war against terrorism'?

Harmony as a human right

In spite of the end of the Cold War and the rise of globalisation, the fact remains that the world is still split in two different camps: The socialist camp led by China, and the liberal camp led by the US superpower. Unlike the former Soviet Union, China is attempting to liberalise its economy, however it maintains steadfast resistance against a comprehensive guarantee of liberal human rights in the western sense. The main argument put forward by China to justify this resistance is based on the idea of social equality and solidarity. A country with 1.4 billion people must strive first and foremost for harmony. This harmony can only be achieved through economic justice and strict implementation and execution of the laws. The right to social security and existence, it is objected, must take precedence over other liberties. A state which in the interests of a liberal social order is prepared to accept that poverty and a great inequality between rich and poor are the price to be paid for liberal freedoms would, according to the Chinese way of thinking, violate human rights much more drastically than a state which for the sake of social justice and social peace limits individual liberties.

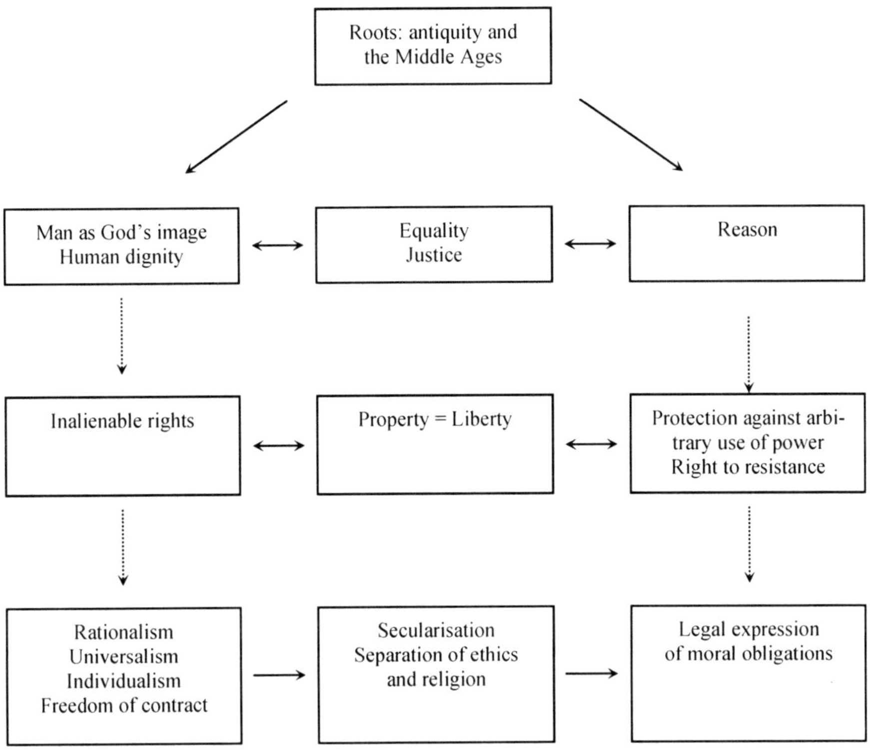

4.4 The Types of Fundamental and Human Rights

4.4.1 Introduction

Criteria of distinction

Human rights can be categorised and analysed in a number of ways. In order to be at all effective they require efficient procedures for effective implementation. Human rights however have a different history and different consequences according to the particular content of the right. If human rights build upon the nature of man they cannot simply be reduced to negative rights against possible state intervention. In order to be able to make an assessment of political decisions, a person must also have the possibility to participate in the political decision making process and thus to participate in the exercise of the authority of the state. Human rights therefore are also *political rights*, which guarantee the participation of citizens within their polity. Taking into account the different criteria and types of human rights we shall first deal with procedural human rights, then analyse the content of human rights as negative rights, and finally examine political rights.

Protection against predominance

The institutional development of fundamental rights reveals that the legal recognition of fundamental rights emerged out of an intra-state power struggle between the different branches of government and between the citizens and their government. In the foreground of this struggle was the attempt to limit the executive power of the monarch. In the course of the ongoing expansion and establishment of democratic forms of government minorities now seek to expand fundamental rights so as to protect minorities against the tyranny of the democratic majority.

Protection of liberty – guarantee of emancipation

Today in almost all democratic constitutions we can find more or less comprehensive catalogues providing guarantees of fundamental rights and liberties. The differences are mainly to be found in the formulation and interpretation of these rights. While for some states, fundamental and human rights are the bases and the instrument for the struggle to establish a specific system such as for example the dictatorship of the proletariat, other states see these rights as a way to limit the power of the state. Some proclaim and celebrate fundamental and human rights as the means to 'liberate' the people through a collectivist order, although the path to creating such order ultimately destroys individual liberty, because during the never-ending transition period the state authorities require unlimited powers to enable them to achieve their goals. Whilst for others, fundamental rights are part of a system of the rule of law which promotes the personal development of the individual within society. Some think that the concrete guarantee of liberties leads to anarchy and destroys national aims because people always try to misuse their freedoms in order to exploit the disadvantaged. For others collectivist systems are *per se* enemies of fundamental rights because they deny liberty to the individual person.

Constituted rights?

While some states are content to formulate fundamental rights as goals of their constitution, some do not expressly enumerate such rights within their constitution at all but prefer instead to establish institutional guarantees to provide for effective protection of rights within their state system. For some, fundamental rights are wonderful promises of a future paradise; others measure them against existing realities.

Fundamental and human rights have undoubtedly become the primary starting point for intra-state and international political controversies. Whilst in the last century the organisation of state power was in dispute, and during the 19th and early 20th Century the issue of sovereignty was at the centre of state politics, today it is fundamental and human rights that are the focus of any important political debate.

States are no longer evaluated principally in terms of the extent to which they are democratic, but rather according to their attitude towards and effective and efficient protection of human and fundamental rights.

In the following sections we shall look primarily at the content and the significance of the different fundamental rights. First however, we have to analyse the different interpretations of fundamental rights.

Dignity and liberty

Whoever regards human beings as rational beings, as did the Enlightenment philosophers, would grant to such beings the legitimate claim to self-realisation and to free development of the self. The human being is the only creature with the intellect to distinguish right from wrong, and with the rationality to decide what it wants to do and to be the cause of its own actions (in the sense of KANT). Man must therefore also have the liberty to plan his life and to realise his plans accordingly. This Enlightenment view of the human being led to a comprehensive justification of fundamental rights and freedoms. In the foreground of the European philosophy of liberty has therefore been the development of the individual personality in the sense of human dignity.

China

In the philosophy of the Far East we find very different ideas about the development of the individual personality. The society reflects the hierarchical order within which everyone has their designated place, and within which man will find personal happiness only by accepting the hierarchical order of things and his place within it. Prince Ging from Tsi asked master Kung about the Government. Master Kung answered: "The prince shall be prince; the servant shall be servant; the father shall be father; the son shall be son." The prince answered "Indeed so! If the prince is not prince and the servant not servant, the father not father and the son not son: Although I have my income, can I then still enjoy it?" (CONFUCIUS p. 125).

Such reflections seem to be quite strange from the perspective of a meritocracy guided by the principle of equal opportunities, in which liberty must also include the possibility to break through the predetermined social order and to advance up the social hierarchy. But according to the Far Eastern perception, such ambitions would disturb a person's inner peace and calmness.

India

Even more radical in this regard is the old Indian philosophy, according to which the person is a mask (in accordance with Greek and Latin origin of the word 'persona') from which human beings have to detach themselves. Those who want to develop must find their way to the inner self. This is only possible by detaching oneself from one's needs and interests, by living an ascetic life and thus becoming independent from one's own person or mask. The real inner self can only be found if one is able to detach from the external world and to focus entirely on one's internal being.

Christianity

These brief highlights demonstrate how the understanding of freedom and liberty is influenced by and depends upon philosophical and cultural background. A European person, influenced by the occidental Christian tradition ("Be fruitful and increase in number; fill the earth and subdue it. Rule over the fish in the sea and the birds in the sky and over every living creature that moves on the ground." (Genesis 1:22)) may have different views on individual liberty and freedom than a person from China, India, Africa, Japan or Latin America.

Raison d'Etat and individual rights

But even within cultures and nations one can still find substantial diversity. The Swiss understanding of freedom is traditionally strongly linked to the collective and co-operative society of the municipality. This leads to an understanding of liberty which is much more connected to the common democratic decision of the community than the individualistic Anglo-Saxon perception of liberty, and the effects of this difference can be seen in the approach to concrete issues. In the English tradition, for the sake of freedom of the press it is permissible to question the state or the government, and even in times of great danger press censorship is not permitted (for example in England during the Second World War). Within Germany, Switzerland or France on the other hand, limits would be placed on this freedom in such circumstances, for the sake of the public interest and the *raison d'etat*.

Core content

All of these reflections do not mean that fundamental rights are completely relative. There exists a core of elementary humanity which – independent of the philosophical, cultural, historical, religious and economic context – must have universal validity. The maintenance of human dignity and respect for the fundamental equality of all human beings should, independent of context and location, always be observed.

4.4.2 Procedural Rights

Independent and impartial courts

Procedural rights belong to what are known as the *first generation* rights. Procedural rights guarantee fairness for all parties in a court proceeding, and a hearing before an independent and impartial court. The verdict of the court must not only be just it must also be credible. *Justice must not only be done but also be seen to be done!* This includes the right of all persons who believe their rights to have been breached, to have access to an independent court. Procedural rights also require that in all instances which lead to restrictions on human rights only the court can decide, or at least that the final decision on such restriction belongs to an independent court. The court must have no prejudice or bias, either politically or with regard to the parties. The court must be independent in the sense that judges do not depend on political guidelines from other branches of government, judges cannot be removed from office because of their decisions, and in particular that they are not dependent on a political party. A political body may be empowered to elect the members of the court, such as the Parliament in Switzerland or the President in the US with the approval of the Senate. However, once elected the members of the court should become entirely independent from the legislature and the executive. In the US the members of the Supreme Court are elected for life. In addition, the Constitution guarantees that their salary should not be diminished during their term of office.

Independence also means authority. A court is only independent when it has full jurisdiction to hear and determine the merits of the case with regard to the facts and the legal issues, and when it is made up of suitably qualified and competent judges. Competence includes the ability to direct the parties in often very complex proceedings, and mastery of the rules of procedure and the law in order to reach decisions that properly accord with them. There is also an obligation on the state to provide judges with a salary that compensates them appropriately for their work. If one wishes to avoid corruption, it must be wiped out at the roots!

Audiatur et altera pars

In order to assess the relevant legal issues the court needs to decide on the facts, and to draw the correct legal conclusions based on those facts. The old principle *audiatur et altera pars* (which literally means ‘hear the other side’) guarantees that parties must be heard by the court and must have procedural rights in order to present their view of the facts and to question the view of the opposite party. In other words, a person should be given the opportunity to respond to charges or claims made against them, and should be given a fair hearing. Equality of arms within the judicial procedure requires that the parties are able to adduce evidence and that they can express their view on the evidence of the other side. Equality of arms not only guarantees fairness and credibility, it is also an essential condition for the optimal determination of the facts. Experience teaches us that people are often, based on prejudice or laziness, too readily satisfied with a version of the facts that may be far from the truth. Only when all parties are able to participate on equal footing in the fact-finding process can there be a distinct chance that the facts determined by the court will not be too far from the actual truth.

Competence to determine the facts

The question of who has the power and the responsibility to determine the facts is also significant. In the procedure that applies in matters of Swiss federal administrative law, the administration has the power and the responsibility to determine the facts through an inquisitorial procedure. According to this procedure there is no rule distributing the burden of proof as there is for example in the procedure applicable to civil law cases. Accordingly the administration decides what evidence is sufficient in order to determine the truth. Under this procedure the concerned parties have only limited possibilities to influence the fact finding by the administrative authority. In the face of a politically influenced administration or against preconceived opinions of civil servants the parties are practically powerless. Even extensive procedural rights cannot restore equality of arms within the proceedings. For this reason, with regard to proceedings in which the rights of the parties can easily be restricted, only an independent court (not the public administration itself) can make the final determination.

In continental European criminal procedure the facts must also be determined by the judge and not by a jury. However this procedure at least provides for a clear rule with regard to the burden of proof in favour of the defendant. If the prosecution cannot produce sufficient evidence of guilt, the defendant must be acquitted for lack of evidence.

Relevant facts and the law

When the court has come to a credible and independent determination of the facts, it must make a legal judgment accordingly. The legal basis for the court's conclusions must be transparent and comprehensible. Only then will the affected parties have the opportunity to have the relevant legal questions reviewed by a court of a second instance.

Equality of the parties however is only guaranteed if the parties have access to a suitably qualified, competent and motivated legal representative. In many states that grant accused persons the right to free legal representation, the lawyer that is provided to the accused is often either incompetent or, because of the meagre compensation, completely unmotivated. The more the proceedings are dependent on the parties, such as in the *adversary system,* the greater the danger that one party will unfairly dominate proceedings and that the court will accept the propositions of the stronger party. In such cases the final verdict may not have credibility because of the unequal arms of the parties: unequal representation may result in injustice.

Jury trial: adversary system

According to the Anglo-Saxon tradition, the most effective way to ensure the independence and impartiality of the court is to have the facts determined by a randomly selected jury of common people, rather than by the judge. A panel of jurors chosen by ballot and agreed upon by the parties is seen to be the best guarantee of independence and neutrality (Vth Amendment of the American Constitution). The right to trial by jury is regarded as a democratic fundamental right in the Anglo-Saxon common law tradition.

The role of the jury is to determine the relevant facts based on the evidence adduced by the parties. With regard to the rules of evidence the common law requires different burdens and standards of proof depending upon the nature of the proceeding. In criminal matters, the burden of proof is on the prosecution, which must prove its case beyond reasonable doubt. In civil matters, the burden rests on the plaintiff to produce sufficient evidence to prove its case but the standard of proof is lower, that is, on the balance of probabilities.

Habeas Corpus

Access to an independent court includes also the right of all those whose liberty of movement is restricted because of arrest or any other form of involuntary detention by the state, to be brought as soon as possible (at least within 24 hours) before an independent judge who can decide on the legality of detention (habeas corpus). Experience has shown that detained persons are at greatest risk of being tortured within the first 14 days of their detention. Whoever is under the unaccountable control of another person is completely defenceless, and is likely to be subject to exploitation, torture or other humiliation. History teaches us that when people exercise uncontrolled and unlimited power over other human beings they almost always give in to the temptation to misuse this power.

4.4.3 Human Rights According to Content

4.4.3.1 Human Dignity

Homo sapiens

In terms of their content the various human rights can ultimately all be traced back to the basic right of human dignity. The human being has the intellectual capacity to plan its life, to make decisions about ethical values, religion and politics and to obtain the necessary knowledge upon which to base such decisions. But the human being also requires certain preconditions in order to be properly able to exercise these substantial capacities. Human beings, which are capable of learning and adapting, need to have the freedom to inform themselves and to exchange their opinions as well as to publicly express their views.

Personal freedom and human dignity

Humans as creatures that can independently decide on their own spiritual and temporal identity need to be protected with regard to their full spiritual and bodily integrity. This dignity is irrevocable. Any restriction of this integrity is a serious violation of the fundamental right to human dignity. Every person must have the opportunity and the right to say 'yes' or 'no' according to his own free will. To say 'yes' or 'no' is however only possible if one is free to form opinions and make judgments and if one is able without fear to freely and expressly communicate one's decisions and the reasons for them.

Right to life

Corporal or bodily integrity includes the right to life, to live with human dignity and freedom and the right to be free from torture or other forms of inhuman or degrading treatment. For a long time capital punishment was not considered to be contrary to human dignity. Today however many states consider capital punishment a substantial violation of human rights, for two main reasons. First, there is no procedure that can completely protect people from the possibility of a miscarriage of justice. How then can the death sentence be justified if there remains the slightest doubt about the correctness of the verdict?

Second, each person should be granted the possibility through his own reason and judgment to change and to better him/herself. Every person who is executed is deprived of this basic opportunity.

Privacy of personal information

In the era of unlimited global communication that aspect of personal freedom involving protection of personal data becomes increasingly significant. Human dignity entails in part that every person must be able to protect his private and personal life from any illegitimate interference either from other private persons or from public institutions or representatives. Personal data to which authorities have access for example through records of social security, education, tax collection or even divorce proceedings, cannot be provided to third parties without the consent of the affected person. Wire-tapping of telephone or emails should only be allowed under very limited circumstances and provided the authorities authorised to tap are always strictly and independently controlled. When personal data is transferred to third persons or institutions or otherwise stored, the affected persons must be properly informed in order that they have the possibility to correct inaccurate data if necessary.

According to their content human rights can be further categorised into to rights guaranteeing equality, rights that protect intellectual and spiritual liberty, and those which are oriented to property and economic freedom.

4.4.3.2 Equality

Treat equals equally

The principle of legal equality has long posed a number of challenging problems in terms of its content and interpretation. Equals should be treated equally, unequals unequally. This raises the difficult question of what should be the relevant criteria upon which to distinguish between equals and unequals. For a long time it was widely believed that denying women the right to vote was entirely consistent with the right to equality, because women – unlike men – were not capable of participating in the political affairs of the state, because of their role within the family and within society. This argument seems absurd today, but nevertheless it was long successfully employed against the claim for women's right to vote. Meanwhile it is undisputed that the physiological differences between the genders cannot be a valid basis for unequal treatment legally, politically or socially.

Public interest

The basic principle of equality is based on the belief that all people, as members of the human species, are fundamentally equal. They have the ability to absorb information, to learn, to make rational judgements and decisions, and to communicate. All people must therefore be treated equally. Unequal treatment is only acceptable when it is in the public interest of everybody. This is the reason for which it is acceptable for example to provide protection for women during pregnancy.

Equal opportunities – equal results

Of great significance is the question of what form or aspect of equality requires protection by the state. Should the primary focus be on equality of opportunity, or should the state also concern itself with equality or inequality of results - for example seeking to balance unequal fortunes through social security or redistribution of wealth? This challenge for the principle of equality also arises in relation to the tax system. According to the principles of liberalism the state should only guarantee equality of opportunities. The social welfare-state however, pays regard not only to opportunity but also to results in order to guarantee for each individual at least a decent minimum standard of living.

Discrimination of minorities

In international charters the guarantee of equality is essentially limited to the prohibition of discrimination. People should not be subject to discrimination or treated unequally because of their inherent characteristics such as gender, race, language, or religion. The prohibition of discrimination against women, of racial discrimination and also discrimination of religious communities belongs to this category of basic human rights. However, with regard to these forms of discrimination against minorities the focus of the rights-guarantee is on the individual as the bearer of rights. For example if an individual has a different mother tongue to the majority, he should not be subject to discrimination. However, whether the language community as a collective has a group right that can be enforced against the majority has, until relatively recently, barely been taken into consideration.

The right to equality is particularly directed at prohibiting discrimination on the basis of immutable characteristics that people have by virtue of their birth or their identity. Gender and race are inborn, religion and cultural heritage are part of the human identity, and physical and intellectual disability cannot be changed through personal will.

Equality however means not only the right to equality as an individual, but also the right to equality of the collective. For example, in Switzerland the members of the Romansh-speaking minority should feel that they as a cultural group have the same rights as the members of the German-speaking majority.

4.4.3.3 Spiritual Liberties

i. Freedom of Religion

Religious freedom a minority right since ancient times

The intellectual freedoms have their historical roots within traditional religious liberties. Of course, a comprehensive concept of the freedom of conscience and expression has only been developed in modern times. In the late antiquity FIRMIANUS LACTANTIUS (260–340 AD) more commonly known as 'the Christian Cicero' declared: "And still it is the religion, in which liberty primarily has taken its seat. Religion after all is prior to all other issues something voluntarily chosen. Thus, nobody can or should be forced to worship something he does not want." (F. LACTANTIUS, *The Epitome of the Divine Institutes*, Chapter LIV). Freedom of religion was understood as a minority right of the persecuted Christians. However, as soon as the Pope and Christianity had attained the upper hand, AUGUSTINE authorised the Church to be able to force people to enter into the church (*compelle entrare*). THOMAS AQUINAS later distinguished between former believers who had deserted the Church, and those who were simply non-believers. Apostates could be forced to re-enter the Church (THOMAS AQUINAS, book II, part II, question 39, art. 4). AQUINAS left open the question of whether or to what extent non-believers could be forced to enter the Church for the first time. However he was clear to condemn the worship of false idols as a sin (THOMAS AQUINAS, book II, part II, question 94, art. 2).

Principle of territoriality: The right to emigrate

After the Protestant Reformation the political powers in Western Europe followed the religious split with a strict territorial separation between Catholic and Protestant principalities. Accordingly each prince prescribed the belief of his subjects (*Confessio Augustana, 1555*). In France, the first references to freedom of conscience appeared in the commentary of the Edict of January 1562 and later in the Edict of Amboise in 1563. These proclamations mentioned the guarantee of the private cult as a right granted to the gentry. This liberty was later limited to particular territories through the Edict of Nantes (1598), but within those territories the liberty was strengthened. Later another step towards a broad freedom of conscience and belief was the right to emigrate (*ius emigrationis*).

Principle of tolerance

In England however the concept of religious tolerance developed rather differently. The right to emigration could not be realised in the British Isles in the way it had been in the small European principalities. In the 16th Century Henry VIII established the Anglican Church and unified political and spiritual power. The rights afforded to Catholics were restricted relative to Protestants (for example, they were denied the right to bear arms, which was granted to Protestants under Article 7 of the Bill of Rights), however they were not banned or exiled for their religious beliefs, as occurred in some continental principalities. Having long been tolerated but subject to discrimination, in 1829 the Catholics were finally integrated and granted political rights through the *Catholic Emancipation Act.*

Freedom of establishment

The Baptists claimed an unlimited freedom of conscience and of belief. According to their belief, the revelation is to be deduced by the individual conscience. For this reason they demanded a clear and strict separation between Church and state. The Baptists achieved their greatest influence in the American states. In the *Agreement of the People* (1647) for instance it was proclaimed that the political community has no authority to influence the beliefs and conscience of individuals. This famous agreement that later influenced the freedom of establishment clause of the American Bill of Rights was drafted by the Levellers. This fundamental right is now explicitly granted in the First Amendment of the American Constitution: "Congress shall make no law respecting an establishment of religion, or prohibiting the free exercise thereof". Probably as a reaction to the strong linkage between state and Church in the British Kingdom, the founding fathers of the American Constitution followed those principles already established by the Levellers and provided through the First Amendment in 1791 for the complete separation of church and state and thereby for the integral freedom of conscience and belief. A special provision prohibiting the state from giving preference to one religion ("Congress shall make no law establishing one religious sect or society in preference to others") was clearly rejected. This rejected proposal reveals however the problem that faced the settlers. Should peace be guaranteed among the different religious communities by promoting each of the religions equally and therefore by prohibiting the state from privileging one or more religions over others, or should the state be generally prohibited from any official involvement in religion?

This 'Freedom of Establishment Clause' was created in the interests of friendly cooperation between members of different religions that had immigrated to

America, and unlike the defrocking of the state in the French Revolution, was not intended to be hostile to the churches or religions. Thus, the separation between church and state has always to be assessed differently according to whether it is based on the American or on the French tradition.

Liberty of cult and worship

On the European continent important philosophers in different centuries such as SPINOZA, KANT, HEGEL, PESTALOZZI and FICHTE made strong appeals for freedom of religion. The principal concern of FICHTE was a comprehensive freedom of worship and cult. Every religion should be entitled to carry out rituals and worship in accordance with their own beliefs. Out of this right to worship within private houses there later developed the general freedom of religion.

However in many countries freedom of religion was initially restricted to the Christian religion. Thus, for example Article 44 of the first Swiss Constitution of 1848 guaranteed freedom of worship only to the various Christian religions. In 1866 non-Christians were granted freedom of movement and settlement and it was not until 1874 that the general freedom of religion was granted to everyone including members of the Jewish religion.

ii. Freedom of Opinion

Freedom of thought and freedom of expression

Today the freedom of conscience and belief within the pluralistic state is understood as a fundamental right that guarantees not only religious freedom but also freedom of thought and expression more broadly. Every person is free to think and believe what he/she pleases, and should also be free to express, communicate and publish these thoughts and opinions. Freedom of opinion was a logical consequence or extension of the freedom of religion and conscience. However, although this right is based on the liberty and development of the individual, historically it is more closely connected to political rights such as freedom of the press and parliamentary privilege, rather than to freedom of conscience and belief.

Milton

The undisputed father of freedom of the press is JOHN MILTON (1608–1674), the secretary of OLIVER CROMWELL. In his famous speech in 1644 MILTON defended this freedom: "Truth and understanding are not such wares as to be monopolised and traded in by tickets and statutes and standards. We must not think to make a staple commodity of all the knowledge in the land, to mark and licence it like our broadcloth and our woolpacks... Truth is compared in Scripture to a streaming fountain; if her waters flow not in a perpetual progression, they sicken into a muddy pool of conformity and tradition. A man may be a heretic in the truth; and if he believe things only because his pastor says so, or the Assembly so determines, without knowing other reason, though his belief be true, yet the very truth he holds becomes his heresy" (J. MILTON, A speech for the liberty of unlicensed printing to the Parliament of England, 1644). With this famous speech MILTON created the basis for the realisation of the comprehensive freedom of the press within the Anglo Saxon state. This freedom has never been so fully and unconditionally realised on the European continent as it is in Anglo-Saxon states. European courts have for example never protected so-called 'hate speech' as being part of freedom of press and opinion, whereas American courts have even allowed the Ku-Klux-Klan to conduct protest marches in the middle of traditional Jewish quarters.

Freedom of opinion as an expression of personal freedom

The intellectual freedoms are so integrally connected to the nature of man that their illegitimate restriction would be an infringement of human dignity. They guarantee that people are not reduced to objects or puppets of others, but that they should have the possibility as conscious and independent subjects to determine their own actions. The intellectual freedoms should grant every person the right to form their own opinions and to plan their life according to their personal conviction.

As MILTON pointed out, the independent development of the human mind and also of the knowledge of mankind is not possible without freedom of opinion. Only when people are able to freely express their thoughts can they exchange, test, criticise, modify and extend their views and their knowledge. This is the basic precondition for democratic discourse, which is the foundation of modern democracy. A society that does not provide freedom of opinion destroys its historical, cultural, spiritual and intellectual roots. Truth according to our understanding is not something that can be dictated; rather it must be capable of independent and objective verification, and must be recognised by others as being true. Such knowledge however can only be acquired in a society in which theories and ideas can be freely discussed and critically examined.

Democracy and freedom of opinion

The historical development of freedom of opinion is closely connected to the expansion of democratic political rights. It is a precondition for democratic control and the democratic decision-making process. Free and informed democratic decisions that serve the common interest are only possible if the decision making process takes place in the context of an open discussion and critical assessment of all possible alternatives, in which everyone has a fair opportunity to express their views. This is true for example of electing people to public office, as it is for direct democratic decisions in a referendum.

Of course freedom of opinion alone is not sufficient to guarantee a legitimate democratic decision. Emotions, demagoguery, prejudice, corruption and favouritism may still distort democratic decisions. However, a comprehensive guarantee of freedom of opinion and the free publication of views in the press can limit such distortion, provided the media is not under state control. Freedom of opinion can curb the formation of extreme positions, and gives hope to those whose views are not reflected in majority decisions that, through contributing to public debate, they may at a later date sway the majority with their arguments. Freedom of opinion is the basis for the trust of all those who feel that they are unjustly treated by the state, that they might through free expression be able to convince the majority to recognise and redress such injustices. The democratic majority should not oppress the minority, otherwise democracy may become a form of tyranny. And precisely such tyranny is possible in a state divided by different ethnicities (see JOHN STUART MILL (1806–1873) and ALEXIS DE TOCQUEVILLE (1805–1859)).

Participation of the people

Freedom of opinion in this sense also helps to guarantee the achievement and maintenance of a stable social order that can adapt without violent revolution to gradual social and economical changes. Thanks to freedom of opinion and expression those who have complaints against the state can be heard without delay, and the particulars of abuses and errors can be promptly communicated to the competent authorities. Freedom of opinion enables discourse between the government and governed. It strengthens the capacity of both sides to learn and to respond quickly to new developments. Authorities that do not know or do not have to know what the people thinks will sooner or later become isolated and detached, creating a gulf between the authorities and the people.

Freedom of information

Freedom of opinion is however meaningless without access to comprehensive information on government, the administration and the economy. Freedom of information is therefore the corresponding counterpart to freedom of opinion, and requires full realisation. The extent to which state authorities or other leading social forces are prepared to provide access to information is often a clear barometer of the extent to which freedom of press and freedom of opinion are actually guaranteed in reality within the relevant state.

As part of personal liberty, individuals must have the right to obtain the information they need in order to be able to form opinions and make decisions. People must also be able to distribute and publish information and opinions, and to do so in their own mother tongue in which they can understand and express the finest nuances of meaning. Freedom of information, freedom of the press and freedom of language are important elements of freedom of opinion and expression. Moreover, freedom of artistic expression, of research, teaching and learning as well as communication with modern media are all part of the fundamental rights relating to intellectual freedom.

4.4.3.4 Guarantee of Property Rights and Economic Liberty

Globalisation

Guarantee of property and economic freedom are elementary conditions for a global free market system. In the Middle Ages it was not human dignity but rather the protection of property rights that was regarded as the essential starting point for all other rights and freedoms. Whoever owned real property was also entitled to other legal rights. Property rights included dominium as well as imperium. Owners had the right to use their property for their own benefit, to alienate or sell their property, and also authority over the subjects living on their property. Those who were without property were essentially devoid of legal rights. Until well into the 19th Century, property was a condition of entitlement to participate in the political life of the state. The right to vote was limited to the propertied class.

i. Guarantee of Property

Core right in the Middle Ages

At the centre of all fundamental economic rights and freedoms is the guarantee of property. In the Middle Ages this was more than just an economic right; the guarantee of property was the starting point for many other freedoms. The guarantee of property once had the same significance as the core right of human dignity has today. It included at that time much more than the mere ownership of land: it provided for work, autonomy and authority.

JOHN LOCKE

The view of private property in Western countries has been decisively influenced by the ideas of JOHN LOCKE, who based his entire theory of the social contract on the theory of property. As we have seen, LOCKE takes an optimistic view of the original state of man in nature, imagining humans as rational and free. The state therefore should not be permitted to limit freedom. According to LOCKE, in the original state of nature all people are free and equal. How then was LOCKE, in spite of this egalitarian view of man, able to justify inequality with regard to property and fortune in 17th Century England?

Property and labour

According to LOCKE, humans in their original state did not have personal property. The hunters and gatherers owned the whole Earth collectively. Everything was common property. Each had the right to acquire and use what was necessary for his existence. This appropriation was not occupation by force and violence (as with GROTIUS), but rather acquisition based on human labour (J. LOCKE, *Second Treatise on Government*, Chapter V). It was through labour and in particular through the cultivation of land that man acquired real estate, just as in earlier times humans acquired necessities by hunting for meat and gathering fruit. However, nobody should acquire more than they need for survival. One should not be allowed to collect fruit and then let it go to waste.

Money: The nuts in the cellar

This limitation however ended with the invention and introduction of money (J. LOCKE, *Second Treatise*, chapter 36). Money does not perish as fruit does. Money enables people to accumulate the 'fruits of labour' without risk that they will spoil, just as nuts can be kept for a much longer time than fruit.

"And thus came in the use of money, some lasting thing that men might keep without spoiling, and that by mutual consent men would take in exchange for the truly useful, but perishable supports of life. And as different degrees of industry were apt to give men possessions in different proportions, so this invention of money gave them the opportunity to continue and enlarge them" (Sec 47–48).

Natural law

According to LOCKE, the fact that possession acquired by labour is recognised in the state of nature is evidence of a pre-state right to property, which the state cannot infringe. The right to property precedes the state and the state therefore should not be able to interfere with this right. The state has the task of guaranteeing protection of property, but it cannot infringe into matters relating to ownership.

Contrary to LOCKE, HOBBES saw property rights as falling within the scope of absolute state authority. According to HOBBES, private property could be interfered with by the state. As the guarantee of private property rights was created by the state, such guarantee could also be withdrawn or denied by the state.

Protection of owners

Indisputably, the opinions of LOCKE have still today an extraordinary influence on the perception of the concept of property rights in Western states.

"Property, whose original is from the right a man has to use any of the inferior creatures, for the subsistence and comfort of his life, is for the benefit and sole advantage of the proprietor, so that he may even destroy the thing, that he has property in by his use of it, where need requires: but government being for the preservation of every man's right and property, by preserving him from the violence or injury of others, is for the good of the governed. For the magistrate's sword being for a *terror to evil doers,* and by that terror to inforce men to observe the positive laws of the society, made conformable to the laws of nature, for the public good, *i.e.* the good of every particular member of that society, as far as by common rules it can be provided for; the sword is not given the magistrate for his own good alone" (J. LOCKE, *First Treatise*, Chapter VIII Section 92).

Property and State Power

Use of territory

The development of the first ideas of property is closely connected to the gradual settlement of the original nomads. As soon as tribes started to become settled, they needed to cultivate the soil and make it fertile. The land had to be cleared of trees, the soil had to be tilled and houses and castles needed to be protected from enemies with embankments and ditches. Real estate was initially in the possession of the tribe that was to defend it against enemies. The tribe controlled and ruled over this territory. Each family was allocated a certain area for working. They were accountable to the ruler of the tribe for their use of the soil. They had no right to dispose of the land or to sell their real estate. In certain places, such as Ethiopia, such ownership concepts existed until the end of the 20th Century (See J. MARKAKIS, p. 118 ff).

Fiefdom

Eventually, families that belonged to the lower classes of society and could only cultivate small areas of land came under the control of larger land owners and entered into bondage. The vassals however, who have been given land by the king as a fief were required to pay certain taxes to the king and had to serve in the military. The use of land and cultivation of the soil were thus tied up with personal obligations to the king. These fief relationships were extensively elaborated in the fief-rights of the European Middle Ages. The authority of the king and the ownership of land, that is - empire and dominion, were united. Land was not at people's free disposal. Its use was connected to the fulfilment of specific obligations such as military service of the vassals or the services of people towards their master, and even the particular use of the soil was prescribed (for example in the three-field system).

Taxes and democracy

The first major disputes between the king and his vassals in relation to land ownership focussed on the obligation to pay taxes. The vassals wanted to participate in decisions concerning the level of the taxes: '*No taxation without representation*'. In addition to having a say in relation to taxation levels, the vassals also achieved – particularly in England but also on the continent – the gradual separation of political authority (*imperium*) and property rights (*dominium*). The rights of property owners were thus demarcated from the authority of the king, the dictates on the use of property were removed and the right of property owners to freely dispose of their property was expanded. These developments led ultimately to a field of civil law specifically concerned with property that provided for the individual owner full discretion over the use and disposal of property. The state could only interfere with property rights in order to levy taxes or to expropriate land in cases of overwhelming public interest.

Market and property

The emergence of this view of property was strongly influenced by the developing market- and money-economy. Labour was no longer rewarded with goods or with welfare provided for by the fief ruler, but rather with money. Those who had been serfs became farm workers in receipt of a meagre salary. With this development the last direct connection between work and property ownership was dissolved. Labour could now be transformed into capital and therefore be seen as property or as a commodity in itself.

Property and state

The separation of property from the power of the state was also one of the causes for the separation in continental Europe between civil or private law and public law. Property was a matter for the civil and private law that afforded the owner unlimited rights to use and dispose of property. Aside from the imposition of tax, the state could not interfere with property rights. The state could expropriate privately owned property under limited circumstances but only according to law and with payment of adequate compensation to the private owners (See SAMUEL VON PUFENDORF).

Collectivisation of property

The development of property rights within the market economy and welfare state was characterised by the increasing depersonalisation and collectivisation of property within shareholder companies, the provision of social security by the state, and the emergence of the banking and credit business. The new institutions of shareholder companies and trusteeships enabled a legal and de facto independence of capital to which owners were connected only through privately owned shares. In such institutions the owners of capital no longer made direct decisions as to how the capital was to be used, but rather the controlling board of directors or trustees would perform this role. The banking and credit business enabled an incredible growth of capital. And the newly expanded state service infrastructure (schools, transport, hospitals, etc) and social security system required citizens to pay a considerable portion of their income in taxes or premiums. The citizen thus had a stake in the welfare state.

Property and society

Besides the collectivisation of property in private companies, the significance of the social impact of the use of property also gained greater recognition. Laws relating to town planning and environmental protection imposed new limitations on the use of private property. But also original restrictions, such as limitations on the free use and disposal of agricultural land and forest, were expanded. In addition, the increasing number of waged employees who participated in the economy through their labour but did not own property led to an expansion of democratic institutions within the state including the removal of property qualifications on the right to vote. With the support of trade unions, employees also gained greater involvement in management decisions.

Participation rights

Man is no longer a subject in need of protection by the state, but rather has become an active participant and partner in the state and society. The personal welfare of the individual in terms of life, liberty and protection is no longer linked to land and soil, but to opportunities for employment, education, housing and to certain services of the state. This has inevitably led to the dissolution of the old *paterfamilias* liberalism and to the development of basic social rights. The life, freedom, independence, income and security of the *paterfamilias* were formerly guaranteed by the protection of property rights. Now however, in order to afford the same protection to the atomised mass of citizens, the state must offer protection of intellectual freedoms and social rights including access to housing, employment, education and social security as well as protecting individuals against certain risks such as accident, illness and unemployment.

Social bonds

Today, fortune and property are detached from political rights, and every individual is supposed to enjoy the equal opportunity to acquire property. However, it would be an illusion to believe that property rights are fully detached from common social ties. Property ownership is tied to the possibilities for the use and disposal of property, which are determined by state legislation including planning rules and regulation of foreign ownership. The value of assets depends on economic trends and is exposed to the risk of inflation. On the other hand people have through their social security systems agreed to some redistribution of property according to need and to some degree of intergenerational obligation in relation to property.

Freedom of Economy

Invisible hand

Following economic liberalism (ADAM SMITH, 1723–1790), social Darwinism (HERBERT SPENCER, 1820–1903) successfully asserted the existence of a new liberty, namely: the right to free economic development. This freedom was primarily directed against state protectionism and corporatism. The theoretical basis for such liberty had been set out by ADAM SMITH. He was of the opinion that general economic welfare could best be realised if everyone was free to pursue his own interests. In this case everyone would act as *homo oeconomicus* that is, according to his own assessment of costs and benefits. Accordingly, every individual would buy and sell goods, offer and accept employment, and make investments that would bring the optimal benefit at the lowest cost. Costs and benefits should be seen not only in monetary terms, but can also be individually subjective. The individual will be best motivated to work and to take initiative if he is able through his economic activities to pursue his own interests. If every person enjoys this freedom, the goal of optimal general welfare will be realised. Even the capitalist who is only interested in his own personal welfare will be guided towards this end by the so-called 'invisible hand'. According to this theory, it is the invisible hand that guides the free market system and ultimately results in a just distribution of goods and capital within the society.

Social Darwinism

The theory of social Darwinism also contributed to economic liberalism and provided additional support to the principle of free market competition. CHARLES DARWIN'S (1809–1882) theory of evolution was based on the recognition that the evolution of flora and fauna can be traced back to the process of selection of the fittest, which dictates that in any given environment it will always be the strongest and most adaptable creature that survives. This concept of the selection of the fittest was adapted by WILLIAM G. SUMNER (1840–1910) and SPENCER and applied to human society. For SUMNER, the social order is the result of a battle, in which every person pursues his own interests at the expense of the other. The best, strongest, fittest and the most ingenious fighters will come out on top, and this is just and correct because it is the result of natural selection. Accordingly, the free market economy will automatically lead to a just and correct distribution of wealth.

Homo oeconomicus

Influenced by VILFRED PARETO (1848–1923), the advocates of economic liberalism supported the idea that all scientific, economic and state activity should be analysed from the perspective of costs and benefits. The aim of all such activity should always be to optimise benefits or profits. However, as state activity is often more costly than private economic activity because of the expense of state administrative apparatus and because the state does not provide private economic incentives, state activity must be limited and as much activity as possible should be conducted through the private economy (including for example telephone, radio, television etc.).

The most extreme advocates of this liberal economic theory can be reproached on a similar basis to that on which the extreme Marxist ideologies can be criticised. Based on theoretical hypotheses that radically oversimplify the nature of man (here the *homo oeconomicus*), they draw political conclusions in relation to the goals a polity should seek achieve. In addition, the liberals presuppose that everyone has an equal opportunity to participate in economic competition, that nobody can establish a monopoly and that each individual is able to correctly identify his own interests and to bargain accordingly. This however remains an unrealistic fiction.

Free market

Moreover, the state is not merely a political community that exists for the satisfaction of individual interests. The state is also a community held together by a certain degree of social solidarity, and can only survive if the community is also prepared to protect it weakest and most vulnerable members. People are not interested purely in optimising gains and minimising costs. Their actions are also motivated by other factors such as cultural or spiritual values that do not involve the making of cost-benefit analyses.

Economic freedom has in some states become a constitutionally entrenched right, as for example in Switzerland with the development of the constitutional protection of 'freedom of trade and industry'. Based on this fundamental right, the legislature and the courts ensure that state and private activity are carefully separated and that the free market system is protected as a fundamental individual right.

Right to choose an occupation

The constitution of Germany, known as the Basic Law, protects economic freedom in the personal sense by protecting the right to choose one's own occupation or profession (Article 12). The state must be prohibited from dictating the professional path of the individual citizen. Instead, each person should be able to plan and decide on their career according to their abilities, personal preferences, and opportunities.

Economic liberty within a global environment

The constitutions of most states do not expressly guarantee economic freedom. However, many states do afford constitutional or legal protection of rights and freedoms that are closely connected to economic freedom such as the personal right to choose and practice a profession, freedom of contract, freedom of association (labour unions) and property rights.

Today, property rights and economic freedom are in effect universally guaranteed as a result of globalisation of the free market and also indirectly through the WTO treaty. According to this treaty, states are only allowed to intervene in the free global market in the interest of protecting the life and health of consumers.

ii. Fundamental Social Rights

Before man is able to make use of his freedoms certain basic conditions must be satisfied. If an individual has to expend all his energy simply in order to survive, rights and freedoms will be of little use to him. What good does freedom of the press serve if the bulk of the population can neither read nor write? Without social welfare there is no real liberty. Individual liberty may however also be stifled by social solidarity. Indeed, fundamental social rights can be neither completely denied nor treated equally to the classical negative freedoms.

Mandate of the state

In contrast to the economic liberties and other *negative* rights that prohibit certain action by the state, social rights require *positive* action by the state for the benefit of those who are in need of social assistance. Social rights include for example the right to shelter and to a decent standard of living, the right to work, and the right to education, which should guarantee that all children have equal opportunities in the field of education.

The content and status of social rights have always been and are still widely contested. Some protest that social rights stand in conflict with traditional rights and freedoms and lead to the infringement of property rights and interference with economic freedom. The right to labour for example can only be implemented if the state intervenes in the economy and compels businesses to retain or hire workers even though it may be inefficient or unprofitable to do so.

Right or legislative mandate?

Another criticism that is made of social rights is that they cannot be directly implemented or enforced by a court in the way that classical negative rights can. A court would be overstretched if for example it was faced with a group of unemployed people seeking to enforce their right to work or a group of homeless people seeking to enforce their right to shelter, because the court does not have the financial resources nor the administrative capacity to enforce these rights, and for reasons of separation of powers it cannot compel the executive or the legislature to do so. It is for this reason that in most states social rights are not constitutionally guaranteed and are not justiciable before the courts. It is argued that to guarantee social rights would only create false expectations amongst the citizens, which the state would not be able to fulfil.

For this reason social rights need to be given a different legal and constitutional status to the classical rights and freedoms. They should be seen as mandates or instructions to the legislature. The legislature and the government are responsible for fulfilling the social function of the state and implementing a social system that takes into account the relevant financial and economic constraints and possibilities of the state.

Taken in this way, there is no real contradiction between fundamental social rights and traditional freedoms. Social rights oblige the executive and the legislature, whilst respecting the traditional rights and freedoms, to provide the social conditions that enable citizens to enjoy their freedom and to make use of their liberties. In this sense social rights do not conflict with classical rights and freedoms, but rather complement them.

iii. Political Rights

Democracy and human rights

Democracy is the twin sister of human rights. Without democracy there can be no real human rights. The basic idea of human rights is premised upon the view that all human beings have the capacity to make decisions and to plan their future. Every individual should in his/her private sphere have as much freedom as possible and every human being also needs the possibility to influence decisions of the community and polity in which he/she lives. The right of political participation in the decision making process is the indispensable counterpart to individual liberty. If a person is able to make decisions concerning his/her own life, he/she must also be capable of joining with others to help determine the direction of the political society. Shared rule for decisions of the polity is thus the counterpart to the individual self-rule of any single citizen.

We must however also be mindful that the democratic majority principle is always exposed to the tension between human rights and democracy. Majorities should never misuse their democratic rights in order to oppress minorities. Democracy must be constrained by respect for human rights and minority rights.

Internet

The right to vote in elections and the right to stand as a candidate for election are at the core of the political rights. In those states that have semi-direct democracy, political rights also include the right to initiate a referendum, to propose new legislation and to vote in referenda or on initiatives. In the age of the new electronic media, sooner or later this right will be expanded to include the right to participate in electronically conducted referenda and plebiscites. The new media and in particular the possibilities that have been opened by internet communication, will lead to a reshaping of democracy. It may well be that in future parliamentary representation will not necessarily be required, if citizens are able via the internet to participate regularly in votes on important issues; or perhaps that representatives in parliament will need to seek the direct input of the citizens via internet votes with regard to politically significant and contested issues.

Equality of arms

Besides the right to vote, the requirement for a fair democratic procedure with corresponding equal opportunities is a component of political rights. The right to information and the access of all interested parties to the media are fundamental aspects of these rights. Only if the people can build a clear opinion on the issues at stake, when each voter knows what consequences his or her vote might have, and if citizens are not deceived with false or distorted information, will the democratic vote have legitimacy and credibility. If there is no equality of arms it can hardly be said that the result of the vote is a true reflection of the will of the people.

Procedural democracy – substantive democracy

When in this context the term democracy is used, it refers to procedural democracy and not to substantive democracy. The procedure determines the rules of the game. The main idea is that nobody can know in advance what the outcome of the democratic procedure will be. This however is only possible when the rules of the game provide for a fair procedure and all participants comply with those rules. If the rules are violated, political rights are infringed.

If equality of arms is guaranteed, the democratic procedure can make sure that as much knowledge and information as possible is disseminated and digested. Moreover, a fair procedure will ensure that the concerned parties will accept the result because everyone submitted to the agreed rules of the game and the rules of the game were properly followed.

iv. Rights of National Minorities

Concept of minorities

A national minority is a group of individuals which has its own identity based on ethnic, linguistic, religious or cultural communality and which is numerically smaller than the majority population, and therefore not in a ruling or dominant position within the state. Its identity is different from the rest of the population. Based on this identity and common heritage the group has its own feeling of community and a desire to foster its tradition, culture and language within that community.

The concept thus contains the following elements: *national minority, number, nationality or citizenship, a subjective element of choice and objective characteristics such as ethnicity, religion, language and tradition.*

The discourse on the question of defining the concept of a minority has always been linked with the question of whether minorities should have collective group rights. In contrast to individual rights, collective rights are rights that are held by and can be claimed by a group as a collective unit.

Minority rights in international law

The real problem of the definition of minorities is aimed at identifying the *legal basis for minority protection.* Under which laws and by which rights should minorities be protected?

The generally accepted principles of minority protection according to international standards are as follows (according to the Framework Convention on the Protection of National Minorities of the Council of Europe of 1995):

1. The prohibition of any discrimination, that is, the general application of human rights without any discrimination;
2. The right of minorities to use their mother tongue in public and in private;

3. The right of minorities to establish and manage their own educational, cultural and religious institutions and associations;
4. The right of minorities to establish and maintain contacts within their country and with their kin in other countries;
5. The right of minorities to have access to information in their mother tongue, and to publish, distribute and exchange such information.

Right to a special status?

The principle of a special status (positive discrimination) for minorities including the special rights listed above is intended to bring about the conditions whereby minorities feel that they are on an equal footing with the majority.

With regard to national and ethnic minorities, minority issues often turn into questions that the state itself has to address. These issues become critical when they are manifested through ethno-nationalism and secessionist demands, which are examined in the next section.

v. Human Rights – Human Obligations

Article 53 of the current Chinese Constitution provides that inhabitants of the People's Republic are obliged to obey the Constitution and the laws, to keep state secrets, to protect public property, to work with discipline, to protect the public order and to respect the ethics of society. Such constitutional rules have until recently been frowned upon in the liberal western tradition. But now there are also new proposals from high-ranking liberal experts for the introduction of charters of obligations to counterbalance charters of human rights. Such proposals are based on the argument that there can be no rights without corresponding obligations.

General Declaration of Human Responsibilities

In 1997 a group of private individuals calling themselves the Interaction Council drafted the Declaration of Human Responsibilities (www.interactioncouncil.org) as a proposed counterpart to the Universal Declaration of Human Rights. Article 3 of this charter provides for example: "No person, no group or organisation, no state, no army or police stands above good and evil; all are subject to ethical standards. Everyone has a responsibility to promote good and to avoid evil in all things".

Do there really exist with regard to human *rights* also corresponding human *responsibilities*? Human rights are claims that individual persons can enforce against the state order. The state legitimises its political order on the basis of the social contract. It exerts secular authority over human beings, and this authority needs to be limited. The aim of human rights is to place such appropriate limits on state power and state authority. A corresponding catalogue of human responsibilities would not limit state authority but rather would considerably expand it.

4.5 Institutional Protection of Human Rights

4.5.1 Constitutional Courts

The pre-constitutional validity of human rights

When we look back to the institutional development of human rights in England we will recall that it was the ordinary courts which were entrusted with the protection of human rights, in particular through the principle of habeas corpus. Indeed, within the Anglo-Saxon states it has always been the ordinary courts that have guaranteed compliance with constitutional rights. The US Supreme Court, which in the famous case *Marbury v. Madison* (1803) laid the foundation for the constitutional review of legislation, is the highest court in the United States and has both ordinary and constitutional jurisdiction. Since *Marbury*, constitutional review has been part of the jurisdiction of all ordinary federal courts in the US.

Jurisdiction over constitutional matters developed very differently on the European continent. Legal thinking on the continent is less influenced by the philosophy of LOCKE than by the philosophical principles of HOBBES. Accordingly, the perception that fundamental liberties have no pre-constitutional standing but have only been created by the constitution is predominant. Moreover, the courts only have such jurisdiction as has been expressly granted to them by the constitution. For this reason constitutional jurisdiction with regard to the protection of human rights could only develop after such jurisdiction had been legally granted to the courts. Those courts were usually not ordinary courts but special administrative courts with jurisdiction to review administrative decisions, and special constitutional courts with jurisdiction to review legislation. In this regard one can distinguish three different institutional developments. Within Europe there developed three different institutional forms of constitutional jurisdiction.

The Swiss solution

One of the oldest institutions in Europe that has jurisdiction with regard to constitutional review is the Swiss Federal Court. Since 1874 this court has had jurisdiction to review cantonal decisions, including legislation, in terms of their compliance with the Federal Constitution. The Federal Constitution did not create a special constitutional court for this purpose, but gave this task to the ordinary Federal Court. The basic principle that federal law is superior to cantonal law (and cantonal law that is inconsistent with federal law is void to the extent of the inconsistency) has to be applied by all courts, which effectively means that all courts in Switzerland including cantonal courts are able to look into constitutional issues. Moreover the legislature has introduced a special procedure called state recourse (*staatsrechtliche – since 2007 öffentlichrechtliche - Beschwerde*) by which citizens can bring complaints of cantonal breaches of the Constitution before the Federal Court. However the courts only have jurisdiction to test the constitutionality of cantonal laws. Federal law is not subject to this procedure. The legal unity of the federal state takes precedence over the cantonal democracies. And at the federal level, the political majority has always consistently rejected proposals to extend the constitutional jurisdiction of the Federal Court to cover federal legislation, especially legislation that has been sanctioned through referendum.

The Norwegian-Austrian solution

At the end of the 19th Century Norway created a specific Constitutional Court that was the only organ empowered with exclusive jurisdiction to deal with alleged infringements of the Constitution. This court and its specific and limited jurisdiction provided inspiration for the legal philosopher HANS KELSEN as he drafted a new Austrian Constitution after World War I. Thus a similar institution with similar jurisdiction was created for the new Austrian democracy. The most famous constitutional court in Europe, that of the Federal Republic of Germany, was also modelled on KELSEN'S Austrian Constitutional Court. This type of specific constitutional court later influenced the design of the Spanish Constitutional Court and many other new constitutions of Eastern-European states after the fall of the Berlin Wall. Within the system of checks and balances among the different branches of government it is the only body that is authorised to decide on questions concerning the application and interpretation of the constitution. If a constitutional question arises in proceedings before an ordinary court, the constitutional question must be referred to the constitutional court for final determination.

Constitutional Court and general will

A completely different system was developed in France. When Napoleon established the French Council of State (*Conseil d'Etat*) it was conceived as a body that would hear all complaints from citizens concerning the administration, and then advise the executive and the administration on how best to respond to those complaints. Thus the Council of State was initially a quasi-court with an advisory function. Only later did it develop into a real administrative court with decision-making power.

The French Constitution of 1958 established another advisory body, the Constitutional Council (*Conseil Constitutionnel*), to assess and advise on constitutional questions. This Constitutional Council very quickly evolved into a real decision-making constitutional court. However unlike in Germany, the Constitutional Council had no power to review a law already in force, but rather only before it took legal effect. France sought carefully to avoid interference by the third branch of government (the judiciary) with the legislative power of the parliament. Therefore the Constitutional Council only had jurisdiction to decide on the constitutionality of a proposed law *before* it had officially come into force.

With the constitutional amendment of July 2008 however, the Constitutional Council has acquired *a posteriori* jurisdiction to review legislation. Under new Article 61-1 of the Constitution, the *Conseil d'Etat* or the *Cours de Cassation* can refer questions to the Constitutional Council on whether a statute infringes constitutionally protected rights and liberties. This will tell to what extent this amendment will effectively change the basic concepts and practice of constitutional review in France.

Unified European approach

The impact of the resistance of some European states to judicial review, and of the different approaches to constitutional jurisdiction, has been significantly reduced as a result of the establishment of the European Court of Human Rights. The Court, situated in Strasbourg, has jurisdiction over all European member states in relation to their compliance with the human rights provisions contained in the European Convention on Human Rights. A general review of the decisions or actions of any member state with regard to violation of this Convention is now possible at the European level.

4.5.2 Administrative Law Courts

Status and jurisdiction of administrative courts

It is often overlooked that the protection of human rights cannot be achieved only through constitutional courts, and that in fact administrative law courts also play a crucial role. It is most often the organs of the administration and administrative actions and measures that affect the rights of individuals in everyday life. If people are to be protected from state encroachment upon their rights they need to be able to seek help and protection from the administrative law courts. Constitutional courts protect individuals from violations by the legislature; administrative law courts offer protection against violations committed by the administration and the executive.

Administrative courts and separation of powers

For a long time states resisted the introduction of the administrative law courts. They argued that the doctrine of separation of powers prevents the judiciary from intervening in the decisions of the executive. This argument ignores the fact that the theory of separation of powers guarantees not only the separation and independence of the three branches of government, but importantly also mutual checks and balances by and between the three powers. The idea of MONTESQUIEU that power must constrain power can only be realised if the three branches of government are not hermetically sealed off from each other, but rather serve to mutually control and constrain each other in the American sense of checks and balances.

German and French solution

This dogmatic and political reluctance to limit the power of the executive branch was the main reason why in Europe, in spite of the example set by the French Council of State at the end of the 19th Century, it was not until after the Second World War that judicial review of administrative decisions really began to develop. It was in particular Article 19 of the Basic Law of Germany which brought about a real breakthrough in administrative law jurisdiction in Germany and in those countries influenced by German administrative law. This Article essentially provides for a general right of access to the courts in all instances of alleged rights violations, including violations committed by administrative authorities.

In France as we have seen, administrative jurisdiction has much older roots. As early as 1874 the Council of State issued of its own accord a binding administrative law judgment, without submitting it to the government for final decision. The Council of State thereby effectively issued a declaration of independence with regard to the executive branch and elevated itself from advisory body to the status of administrative court.

In addition, the *Conseil d'Etat* played another very important role in the development of European administrative law. Whereas in the German Empire of the 19th Century administrative law developed with great difficulty in the face of an almost omnipotent administration that ruled 'by the grace of God', the Council of State in France was able over several decades to develop a body of important administrative law principles as guidelines for administrative decisions. These principles imposed clear limitations on the power of the administration. And these principles of administrative law were to have an important influence on German administrative law and thereby on the administrative law of all states with a civil law legal system.

Access to relief

In addition to the status of the administrative courts, their independence and jurisdiction, it is also necessary to examine the extent to which citizens have access to relief before one can determine the real extent of the protection against violation of human rights by the administration. If access to the courts is limited by strict rules of standing and/or narrow causes of action, or if the remedies available to citizens for redress of breaches of administrative law are inadequate, the effective protection of human rights will be compromised.

The Anglo-Saxon writs

In the Anglo-Saxon legal system there has not developed a specialised administrative law judiciary as there has on the continent. Nor does Anglo-Saxon law recognise a strict separation between public and private law. Legal protection against the administration and the servants of the Crown has gradually developed since the Middle Ages, primarily through the development of new legal remedies under special writs. Today there is no measure or action of the administration that could not be challenged according to the Anglo-Saxon law before an ordinary court. The law provides the means to challenge the actions, omissions, errors, plans and regulations of the administration. The complainant must be in a position to claim that specific legal rights have been violated and must formulate the claim under the appropriate writ.

Contempt of court

If an ordinary common law court comes to the conclusion that a person's right has been infringed by the administration, it can compel the person against whom it has made the ruling to execute the order of the court and may prescribe concrete measures for the implementation of the orders of the court. If court orders are not followed, the responsible administrative official, not the administrative institution as a collective, may be charged with contempt of court. Courts may also take other measures to execute a judgment directly, as in one extreme example where an American court ordered a school to provide equal treatment of both genders and threatened that if the school did not follow the judgment, the court would take over the management from the school board and run the school itself (OWEN FISS, 'Two Models of Adjudication' in Robert Goldwin and William Schambra (eds), *How Does the Constitution Secure Rights?* Washington 1985, p. 36 ff).

Administrative act

On the European continent the courts have much less scope to make prescriptive orders against the administration. Access to the courts in administrative matters is also somewhat more restricted. European administrative law centres around the 'administrative act', which is a concrete decision of the administration affecting the rights and obligations of private individuals. For an administrative law complaint to be brought before a court it must relate to a specific administrative act. The possibilities for challenging other administrative actions or omissions or internal planning are therefore considerably restricted. If one wanted to enhance the institutional aspect of the legal protection of human rights within the continental legal system one would need to focus on expanding access to the administrative courts and the available legal remedies.

The acciòn de tutela in Columbia

An interesting institution in this context is the *acciòn de tutela,* which has developed in Columbia, and to a certain extent also the *amparo* developed in some other Latin American states. The *acciòn de tutela* is a legal remedy by which a person may seek to have any act or omission of the administration reviewed by the court for possible breach of human rights. The complaint need not be in any prescribed form and may be submitted by any person. The court is obliged to examine the complaint on the merits and to assess whether the complaint is justified. The Columbian courts can also enforce decisions with contempt of court and thus enforce orders that compel or prohibit certain decisions or acts by the administration.

Inherent limits of the power of constitutional and administrative courts

Constitutions may provide extensive powers to their constitutional courts, as for example in the recent Constitution of Hungary. However, the recent experience of constitutional or administrative courts that have been given extensive powers and far-reaching jurisdiction has shown that the courts are not really in a position to substantially alter the politics of their country. Courts can only advance in small steps. If they possess too much power they will tend to become caught up in political dependence, which in turn will considerably reduce their room to move. The grey area between legal jurisdiction and political decisions in constitutional affairs requires careful drafting in relation to the functions and the powers of the constitutional court. For this reason the recent Ethiopian Constitution has given the power to interpret the Constitution, in particular with regard to the division of powers between the states and the federation, to the second chamber, which has thus become a semi-political and semi-judicial branch of government.

4.5.3 Institutions of the Administration

The protection of human rights cannot be left entirely to the courts alone. Courts can only act on a writ or a complaint. Through their judgments they can only resolve individual matters and may to a limited extent indirectly influence the future conduct of the administration through precedents. For this reason, a state that takes the fulfilment of human rights seriously will also have to provide for additional institutions to strengthen the protection of human rights. High standards of professional training for the judiciary, the administration and the police force are necessary components of a state policy guided by concern for human rights.

Ombudsman

The old and well-known institution of the ombudsman is becoming increasingly widespread. The institution of the ombudsman is as old as the concept of constitutional review, having first been introduced in Sweden at the beginning of the 19th Century.

The ombudsman is an administrative position, often provided for and defined in the constitution, and usually appointed by parliament or government. The main function of this institution is to investigate and report on complaints made by members of the public in relation to the administration. In response to complaints or sometimes on his/her own initiative, the ombudsman gathers relevant information and reports on problems in the conduct of the administration. The administration is obliged to provide the ombudsman with all necessary information and documents. Based on this fact-finding, the ombudsman can recommend that the administration revoke or alter decisions, that it amend its procedures or that it undertake measures to build up the trust and confidence of the people.

However, the ombudsman does not have the power to issue binding decisions or orders, and it has no power to enforce its recommendations. Yet through reporting on its investigations and making recommendations, the ombudsman can contribute to the credibility of the administration and may be effective in persuading the administration to improve its performance and therefore its relationship with the public.

The ombudsman can also bring pressure to bear on the administration by reporting its findings in its reports to parliament, and by generally making its findings public. Parliament and/or the media might then call on the administration to account for its errors and shortcomings. In some states the ombudsman is also authorised to initiate criminal complaints against the administration. The efficacy of the ombudsman thus depends to a great extent on its power to undertake investigations on its own initiative, on whether it has unlimited access to all relevant information, and on whether it is entitled in extreme cases to initiate criminal proceedings.

Police

In many states the police is regarded as the long arm of the law. It is the task of the police to enforce the laws of the state, and to serve and protect the state. The position of the police therefore reflects the nature of the state. If the state is principally regarded as an instrument to mould society in accordance with a particular ideology, the police will be used as an instrument that helps the state to achieve its goals. If however the state is seen as an institution to provide and guarantee a peaceful order for the people, then police will serve the people and afford them the required protection. In this case the police will serve the interests of the harmonious development of the polity. If this aim is achieved the police can contribute substantially to building a relationship of trust between state and citizen. When the police force is constructively involved in the community, able to skilfully deal with social problems and to integrate those who are socially excluded, and above all to protect those who are in danger, it can create a positive climate for the respect of human rights.

4.5.4 International Law

Selective 'justice'

The idea of the universality of human rights led in the 20th Century to a significant expansion of human rights guarantees at the level of international law. Indeed, today states can no longer hide behind their *raison d'etat* or sovereignty when they are accused of serious human rights violations. The internationalisation of human rights however also led to the politicisation of human rights.

Minorities that want to break away from the state often turn to the international community for help. They accuse their state of human rights violations in order to internationalise the conflict. Whilst governments often suppress any opposition movements with state terror, minorities also resort to terrorism and human rights violations in order to provoke their governments into state terror and intimidation. This scenario of internal conflict within a state has in recent years often led to international intervention.

This raises the question of how the international community can legitimately justify such military intervention. Who or what gives the international community authority to expose the lives of innocent people to the risk of so-called 'collateral damage'? Once the territory has been occupied by military forces, international bodies are established and mandated to secure a new military and political order within the 'liberated' or occupied territory. On what basis are these largely unaccountable international bodies authorised, without any effective judicial control, to enact or decree new laws, to exercise political authority and police powers and even to undertake judicial functions without any proper separation of powers? International law has not been able to provide answers to these questions. As long as interventions for the protection of human rights are not clearly regulated and defined, and as long as the international administration of a country which has violated human rights is not transparently accountable, these international interventions will remain disputed. Since the criteria for the intervention are vague and unclear, such intervention will remain selective. Selective justice however, leads to an undesirable politicisation of human rights and of course to considerable injustice.

International human rights instruments

There are a number of multilateral treaties of international law that declare the existence of human rights and require states to protect these values. At the global level these include the UN Universal Declaration of Human Rights of 1948, the International Covenant on Economic, Social and Cultural Rights of 1966 which entered into force in 1977 and the International Covenant on Civil and Political Rights also adopted in 1966 which entered into force in 1976.

There exist also regional bodies and agreements, including the Organisation for Security and Cooperation in Europe (OSCE) and the European Convention on Human Rights of 1950. The various conventions for the protection of refugees also serve to protect human rights, in particular the Convention relating to the Status of Refugees of 1951. Article 33 of this Convention expressly prohibits "the expulsion or return ('refouler') of a refugee in any manner whatsoever to the frontiers of territories where his life or freedom would be threatened on account of his race, religion, nationality, membership of a particular social group or political opinion" (Principle of Non-Refoulement).

Bilateral enforcement

The international enforcement of human rights however remains unsatisfactory. One of the ways in which compliance with human rights may be enforced or encouraged, is through the classic art of bilateral diplomacy and the use of diplomatic sanctions. However, to date very few states have been prepared to jeopardise their bilateral relationships with other states for the sake of the idealistic protection of human rights. State interests are unfortunately always put before human rights interests. Often however, states use intervention for human rights protection as a pretext to conceal other strategic or economic interests. Accusations of the violation of human rights are intended to not only to improve the human rights situation, but also primarily to compel a state to submit to the imposition of foreign interests in other areas.

Multilateral accusations

The second possibility for international human rights enforcement is the multilateral charge against a state for its human rights violations. Resolutions of the United Nations, international committees or commissions (such as the UN Human Rights Council or the OSCE) may make a real contribution to the better protection of human rights. However states will always use all available diplomatic means to avoid such international condemnations. And, as these resolutions are ultimately unenforceable and the credibility of the international community can always be effectively undermined by political arguments, even these resolutions may have only limited effect.

International monitoring

There are other measures that may be taken to protect human rights, such as international monitoring operations, but these will often require the willingness of the relevant state to cooperate with the international community. The OSCE and the European Union for example undertook such missions in the former Yugoslavia in order to monitor and improve the human rights situation. These missions entailed conflict-monitoring operations, and an ombudsman for the protection of minorities. As these were short-term missions, it is difficult to build a conclusive picture of their impact and efficacy. However it is important to note that whenever such missions occur they require highly trained monitors with extensive experience and skills. Such experts are often not available for these short missions in difficult environments.

Human rights court

The most effective means for the international protection of human rights would be the establishment of an international court of human rights, with jurisdiction based on international law to hear and determine individual complaints of human rights violations against state authorities. This would enable victims of human rights abuse to bring complaints against their state before an international tribunal. However, whilst the International Covenant on Civil and Political Rights and related human rights instruments envisage the possibility for individuals to directly enforce their rights, they do not vest such jurisdiction in any competent international court. The only supra-national court that has the jurisdiction to make final and binding judgments against a state for violating human rights is the European Court of Human Rights. However, international law does not provide any instruments that enable the enforcement of compliance with such court orders within the state in respect of which they have been made. Thus, it still remains within the sovereign power of a member state to decide whether it provides the necessary means for the domestic execution of such judgments.

International Criminal Court

It may well be that the recent establishment of the International Criminal Court will have a positive effect on human rights and compliance with international humanitarian law, and may help to prevent the commission of serious crimes against humanity for example in wars or states of emergency. The knowledge of heads of state, soldiers and civil servants that they cannot hide behind state sovereignty but may instead in fact be charged and tried for such crimes may have a positive effect on the way in which citizens are treated by the state.

Domestic enforcement of internationally guaranteed human rights

Ultimately however, it is through the domestic law and the procedures and institutions that domestic law provides within a state, that human rights can be most efficiently and effectively protected. In terms of content, states can increasingly and successfully rely on international law to support domestic constitutional and legislative actions to improve human rights protection within their state. In this context, the issue of the *monistic* or *dualistic* application of international law becomes most important. In states with a monistic system, international law is self-executing and the domestic courts are therefore obliged to directly apply international human rights guarantees and other conventions to which the state is party. The courts do not need to wait for the legislature to incorporate human rights conventions within domestic legislation. Most common law countries take the dualistic approach to international law. In a dualistic system the courts cannot apply international law, including international treaties that impose binding international obligations on the state, unless and until such international law has been incorporated within the domestic legal system by legislation. Thus for example the British courts were for a long time unable to apply the European Human Rights Convention. Only after the British Parliament enacted the *Human Rights Act 1998* to give effect to the Convention were the courts able to directly apply the European Convention in the domestic context.

International institutions for the protection of human rights

The international community has created a variety of institutions for the protection of human rights. Some, such as the Universal Declaration of Human Rights, have a merely declaratory function. Others, such as the regional OSCE, encourage multilateral diplomacy as a means of human rights protection within the member states. The International Covenants on civil and political rights, and on economic, social and cultural rights are not purely declaratory but are legally binding on the state parties to the Conventions, and envisage the provision of domestic institutions to give effect to their provisions.

On 13 September 2007 the United Nations General Assembly adopted the Declaration on the Rights of Indigenous Peoples, with an overwhelming majority of 143 votes in favour and only four votes against (Canada, Australia, New Zealand, United States). This significant development is based upon 20 years of negotiation, and contains a general right of indigenous peoples to self-determination and self-government, collective and individual rights, rights to participate in decisions in matters which would affect their rights, and the right to autonomy. The Declaration requires states to protect the cultural identity of indigenous peoples and includes the obligation to protect their land.

At the regional level for Europe the focus is on the institutions of the Council of Europe. The European Convention on Human Rights is of central importance, as the access of individual complainants to the independent European Court of Human Rights has facilitated the concrete protection of individual human rights in member states. Also of significance are other charters which do not provide for individual complaints to the European Court of Human Rights but which have gained considerable political importance and provide other mechanisms for implementation. For example, the Framework Convention on National Minorities (1994) provides for an independent expert committee which regularly visits member states in order to monitor minority protection within those countries, and which reports to the Council of Ministers. Similar provisions and mechanisms have been introduced within the European Charter for Regional and Minority Languages (1992) and the European Charter for Local Self-Government (1995).

In addition to the Council of Europe, the European Union has since December 2001 had its own Charter of Fundamental Rights, with a most impressive preamble:

> "...it is necessary to strengthen the protection of fundamental rights in the light of changes in society, social progress and scientific and technological developments by making those rights more visible in a Charter.
> This Charter reaffirms, with due regard for the powers and tasks of the Community and the Union and the principle of subsidiarity, the rights as they result, in particular, from the constitutional traditions and international obligations common to the Member States, the Treaty on European Union, the Community Treaties, the European Convention for the Protection of Human Rights and Fundamental Freedoms, the Social Charters adopted by the Community and by the Council of Europe and the case-law of the Court of Justice of the European Communities and of the European Court of Human Rights.
> Enjoyment of these rights entails responsibilities and duties with regard to other persons, to the human community and to future generations."

4.6 Limits of Human Rights

Are there limits to human rights?

Can members of religious sects insist that their children should not be operated upon even in case of emergency because it is against their religious beliefs? Can religious communities provide for corporal punishment or capital punishment based on religious beliefs, and for the execution of such punishments? Does freedom of the press entitle the press to publicly defame people? Can a company that has established a monopoly boycott companies that intend to enter into the competition? Can violence at a mass-demonstration be condoned and protected under freedom of speech?

Everyone would have to concede that in these examples the relevant rights and liberties cannot be applied without limits. Even the exercise of human rights is subject to certain limits. But how far should those limits go? Can the state conceal information of corruption that might uncover a scandal? Can a peaceful demonstration in support of a cause that is unpopular with the government be suppressed? Can the slaughter of animals without anaesthetisation be prohibited on the grounds of animal protection in a country that allows hunting? These examples demonstrate the need for criteria and procedures in order to make credible and justifiable decisions in such borderline cases.

Who defines the limits?

Can media organisations publish falsehoods or even obscenities in the name of freedom of the press? Does freedom of religion entitle people to perform exorcism? Can the state limit freedom of expression or the right to strike with regard to its own civil servants? Does freedom of conscience entitle a person to refuse to undertake compulsory military service? Is the state empowered to prohibit certain political parties if they are deemed to be a danger to public order and security? Can the state deny human rights and due process to persons suspected of terrorism-related crimes?

These current and burning questions highlight the issue of the limits of fundamental rights. Fundamental rights do not have unlimited validity. All rights and freedoms must be balanced against the rights and freedoms of others. Fundamental rights do not entitle people to threaten the public order or to violate public morality. But who has the right to determine where liberty starts and where it ends?

Public order and the legislature

Article 11 of the European Human Rights Convention makes the following provision in relation to freedom of assembly:

> "No restrictions shall be placed on the exercise of these rights other than such as are prescribed by law and are necessary in a democratic society in the interests of national security or public safety, for the prevention of disorder or crime, for the protection of health or morals or for the protection of the rights and freedoms of others. This Article shall not prevent the imposition of lawful restrictions on the exercise of these rights by members of the armed forces, of the police or of the administration of the State."

Many states have similar provisions in their national constitutions with regard to the permissible limitations of fundamental rights.

Human rights are binding on the legislature

Limits on fundamental rights may be permissible if they are prescribed in a law enacted by the legislature. The legislature however, does not have unlimited scope to determine the extent of the limits on rights. It can only impose limits on rights and freedoms if such limits are justified in the public interest such as for instance the security of public order or the prevention and punishment of crime, the protection of health or for the protection of rights and freedoms of other persons. Any limitation that is not justified in the public interest or which goes further than required to achieve the desired aim would not be reasonable or proportional, and would therefore not be permissible. The limits placed on rights and freedoms must therefore be based on the overwhelming public interest, or on human dignity – that is – on the rights and freedoms of others.

States of emergency

A particularly tricky question is whether the state is entitled to go beyond these limits in situations of emergency or in cases of self-defence.

The European Convention on Human Rights offers no answer to this question. Accordingly, the member states may impose further limitations on rights and freedoms in order to defend themselves in a situation of emergency. There remains however a core bundle of human rights from which there can be no derogation even in times of war. This core includes the right to life, the prohibition of torture, the prohibition of slavery and the rights of accused persons to secure protection of the law (see Article 15 of the EHRC).

Even though it is undisputed that in emergency situations human rights may have to be limited, the following important questions must be addressed:

1. Who has the power to declare an emergency situation?
2. What limits have to be observed by the government even in an emergency situation?
3. What are the criteria by which the existence of an emergency situation can be determined?

Does the 'War on Terror' constitute an emergency?

Many constitutions vest the power to declare an emergency in the head of state. However, the accountability of the head of the state for such decision and the criteria for determining an emergency are usually left undefined or only scantily addressed. After the attacks on New York and Washington of September 11, 2001, America established an alliance against terrorism. Can we regard this 'war' against private terrorist organisations as an emergency situation, as is often claimed? If so, there would no longer be any clear basis on which to distinguish between an emergency and the normal situation. Sovereignty would be exercised only by the state institution which is empowered to declare an emergency, and that institution would effectively have the power to completely undermine democracy and human rights (cf. the decision of the US Supreme Court in *Hamden v. Rumsfeld* on June 29, 2006).

4.6.1 Who Determines the Limits of Fundamental Rights?

Function of the constitution

The question of the limits to be imposed on fundamental rights and freedoms is often considered and addressed by constitution makers when a constitution is being drafted. The limits of fundamental rights are therefore often determined on the basis of express constitutional provisions. Article 36 of the Swiss Constitution for example provides:

> "1. Any limitation of a fundamental liberty requires a legal basis. Grave limitations must be expressly prescribed by law. Exempt are cases of clear and present danger.
> 2. Any limitation of fundamental liberty must be justified by public interest or by the need to protect the fundamental liberties of others.
> 3. Limitations of fundamental liberties must be proportionate to the goal pursued.
> 4. The core of fundamental liberties is inviolable."

Article 19 of the German Basic Law also makes a provision for limitations of fundamental rights. According to this provision, fundamental rights can only be limited by legislation but in no case can 'the essence of a basic right' be infringed.

Pre-state validity and the essence of rights

Is the constitution maker entitled to limit the scope and application of fundamental rights? This issue is closely intertwined with the question of the pre-state validity of fundamental rights. According to LOCKE for example, fundamental rights are derived from nature and precede the state, therefore they can neither be limited by the whim of the constitution maker nor by the state established under such constitution. Article 19 of the German Basic Law arguably also reflects this view, by prohibiting any infringement of the essence of a basic right. This guarantee of the essence of a basic right provides unqualified protection of the substance of fundamental rights. There are however a wide variety of contrasting opinions on how the 'essence' of a right is to be identified and thus on the real extent and significance of the prohibition contained in this provision.

If we accept that one of the tasks of the state is to promote and protect human dignity, then the constitution maker will have to respect this essential principle when it seeks to define what limits can be placed on fundamental rights. Fundamental human dignity will always have to be respected.

The constitution maker will often determine the core or the 'essence' of fundamental rights and also determine who is entitled to decide on limitations of fundamental rights. The constitution maker may provide general rules for such limitations (as in Article 36 of the Swiss Constitution) or may prescribe specific limitations that are permissible for each different fundamental right (as in the European Human Rights Convention and constitutions that have based their Bill of Rights on the Convention

Majority principle and minority protection

Who – besides the constitution maker – has the authority to determine the limits of fundamental rights? One of the most celebrated achievements of the liberal state was to take away from the monarch the prerogative to interfere with the liberty of citizens, and to oblige the monarch to comply with decisions of the *legislature*. Fundamental rights were thus in the 19th Century largely within the power of the legislature. The administration could only interfere with the rights of an individual on the basis of express legislative authority. The Anglo-Saxon principle '*no taxation without representation*' was effectively applied to all liberties of the citizens: rights and freedoms can only be restricted if the people's representatives in the legislature have passed a law that expressly makes such provision.

Self-restraint of the legislature

But even the legislature can violate fundamental rights, if for example it privileges the majority at the expense of minorities. Fundamental rights not only afford protection to individuals and society against state intervention, they also protect minorities against encroachment of the majority. However, the legislature is ill-equipped to ensure that minority rights are adequately protected, since it makes it decisions purely on the basis of the majority principle. For this reason, there is a growing acceptance that in addition to the legislature, constitutional courts have a very important role to play in the protection of minority rights. A weak constitutional court will however hardly be in a position to change national trends in relation to minorities. In a country that has to overcome minority discrimination, a strong court with comprehensive jurisdiction for constitutional review is of utmost importance. It is also imperative that the democratic legislature imposes some limits upon itself and grants its minorities rights which will not be infringed even by the majority of the legislature. Without such *self-restraint of the legislature* the protection of minority rights will ultimately be weak and ineffective.

4.6.2 What are the Acceptable Limits on Fundamental Rights?

4.6.2.1 Legal Limits

Question upon question

Can a country which is threatened by a neighbouring state prohibit a media publication which openly supports the hostile policy of this neighbour state? Demonstrators claim the right not only to take to the streets with protest banners, but also to block the streets with a sit-in protest. Can they rely on the freedom of expression in this case? A large publishing company achieves a monopoly and displaces all other publishers within the region. Is such company entitled to refuse to publish opinions of which the head of the company does not approve? Or, can this company openly endorse only one political party? Can Mormons or Muslims claim for themselves the right to have several wives, based on freedom of religion? Is the state entitled to impose censorship on films and literature for the protection of public morality? Does a political party that promotes the suppression of freedom of thought and expression thereby forfeit its own freedom of opinion? Can the state impose prohibitive taxes on brothels? Can a chemical factory be prohibited from producing products that damage the environment? Can the state, on the grounds of the 'war on terror', infringe the fundamental rights of defendants to a fair trial? To answer these and similar questions, we ultimately have to determine what are the limits of fundamental rights.

Limits of the courts

In courts with constitutional jurisdiction in various states, judges have over time developed principles to deal with these questions. The Federal Court of Switzerland for example, has over the last 100 years developed the principle that fundamental rights may be limited in cases where the security of the state and/or the constitutional order is at stake. Freedom of opinion for example, cannot be invoked in order to promote a violent revolutionary overthrow of the governmental system. Thus one is not allowed to incite somebody to commit an offence against the state (e.g. propaganda for terrorist activities). This limit is determined by the constitutional order. An open constitution, to which unlimited amendments can be made by democratic means, will also have to allow party policies that propose a revolutionary alteration of the system such as the realisation of a communist constitution, if such goals are pursued by democratic means. If however, the Constitution includes limits on revision, as several constitutions do (see for example the Germany Basic Law Art. 20), and provides that certain elements of the constitution cannot be altered, freedom of opinion is also limited accordingly. Freedom of expression will not extend to protection of the promotion of policies that contradict entrenched and unchangeable provisions of the constitution.

Tolerant society?

Rights may also be restricted in the interests of public order and the security of individuals. A religious community that requires of its members attitudes and behaviour that might endanger the security of others, cannot reply upon freedom of religion to protect its position. If demonstrating hooligans threaten important values such as life and property, such demonstrations may be prohibited. It is clear that, even with regard to these cases, the scope of fundamental rights and the extent to which they are limited will depend on the concrete political climate and situation within the relevant country. Within a volatile political climate in which the slightest spark may ignite a dangerous conflict, freedom of opinion may need to be more restricted than it is within an open and tolerant society.

Public interest

The most disputed restriction on fundamental rights is the criterion of public interest. As a general rule, constitutional courts take the view that the legislature is entitled to limit the fundamental liberties of the individual when the general public interest of the society is at stake. In each concrete case the courts will weigh the public interest against the interest of guaranteeing individual liberty. If they come to the conclusion that, with regard to the principle of proportionality, the scale is clearly tipped in favour the public interest, they will place the general interest ahead of the enforcement of private liberty.

Principle of legality and of proportionality

These reflections are valid for limitations of fundamental rights that are of a general nature and thus may be given effect through laws of general application. If fundamental rights are to be limited in a particular case, such limitation must be based on an explicit legislative act and the limitation of the right must be proportional. That is, the means by which the right is limited must be proportionate to the ends being served by the limitation, and should not go further than necessary to achieve the relevant objective. For example, it may be permissible for the state to prohibit members of the Mormon faith from entering into more than one marriage at the same time, but it would be going too far for the state to ban the Mormon religion simply because it supports polygamy.

4.6.2.2 Philosophical Limits

The philosophical basis for limits on rights and freedoms is disputed and cannot easily be applied in practice. The starting point is the general notion of freedom (or liberty), which of course is used in a number of different ways. When the term is used in the context of the freedom or liberation of the Palestinian people, it refers primarily to the right to self-determination of the Palestinian people. When we speak of freedom of trade and commerce, we think of liberty from state interference. In the context of the term *free elections*, we are referring to the freedom to choose between different alternatives.

4.6.2.3 What is Liberty?

Liberty as freedom of choice

In order to analyse the limitations on freedom one must know what the concept of freedom or liberty entails. Liberty can be understood as the possibility or the chance that puts someone in a position to choose between different alternatives. This is the positivist understanding of liberty as freedom of choice. He who is able to choose between different alternatives possesses some degree of freedom.

Liberty as conformity with the law

Liberty can however also be understood quite differently. HEGEL for example sees liberty as the possibility for human beings to be in harmony with the world spirit and the laws of nature. Thus, he who has the ability to know what is right and to act accordingly is free. For ROUSSEAU, freedom entails being able to submit oneself to the general will, or *volonté générale.* The realisation of the *volonté générale* is liberty in its proper sense. If one understands liberty in the sense of HEGEL or ROUSSEAU, the question of the limits that may be placed upon rights and freedoms is irrelevant. In this case it is the state that decides the content of liberty through law or in accordance with the *volonté générale.* He who does not submit to the *volonté générale* can make no claims about legitimate or illegitimate restrictions on liberty.

STUART MILL

The debate on the limits that can be placed on liberty can only take place if liberty is understood in the positivist sense of JOHN STUART MILL as freedom of choice. The individual must be free to choose among different possibilities without having to decide which alternative is generally good or bad, better or worse. Liberty is not to be restricted to the right to choose what is good; liberty also entails the right to make bad decisions and poor choices.

Autonomy and chance

How is this freedom of choice to be understood? Liberty can only exist with regard to a relationship between two or more people. When students decide to leave their lecture in order to go and have coffee together, they are exercising a certain degree of autonomy. This autonomy may be limited by their fear of being criticised by their peers or fear of failing their exams if they miss too much of the course. The greater their inner independence, the greater will be their autonomy and chance to choose freely among their alternatives.

Authority and might

Whoever seeks to influence the students and impede them from their coffee break is exerting power. If this power is considered legitimate, it is labelled authority. And this is where the question of the justification of limits on rights and freedoms is raised. Up to this point we have dealt with freedom in the sense of social freedom, which involves the opportunity within a particular social environment to make decisions, take action or refrain from action. This kind of social freedom can only exist if the social conditions are present that allow people the space to make free subjective decisions. The extent to which these conditions will be present depends on the concrete social situation and on the capacity of the individual to decide independently of social criticism.

One very important aspect of the social environment is the political environment. The state can impose certain absolute limits on freedom by attaching penalties or criminal sanctions to certain actions or omissions. In times when military service has been compulsory and refusal to serve has been prohibited, those who refused on the basis of their religious beliefs had to face prison sentences. The state, in contrast to society, has the ultimate means to enforce its will: the monopoly on the use of coercive force.

Political freedom

When we speak of freedom within the state, we are referring to political freedom. From the point of view of the state people may be free to choose their religion, but this choice will be influenced by family, tradition, language and culture. Those influences however, are not relevant to the discussion of political freedom. In terms of political freedom, we are concerned only with the question: to what extent can the state limit freedom of choice when it comes to religion and the free practice of religion?

Under what circumstances can the state limit the political freedom of choice? The state can establish dependencies (whereby a person loses some aspect of his/ her liberty and freedom of choice and becomes the object of external social or political forces) only when it has the authority to do so. Authority however, requires legitimate justification of the limitations imposed by the state. In most cases, such as the obligation to pay taxes, formal legislative authority is sufficient in order to limit the liberty of the individual. But if the liberty is part of a human right such as freedom of religion or freedom of expression, a simple formal legislative act will not be sufficient in order to limit freedom. As a matter of fundamental principle, human rights can only be limited in cases where such restrictions serve an even higher good, e.g. the prohibition of circumcision for girls for the protection of their life. This ultimately means that liberty can only be restricted in the interest of liberty. The state can require that certain freedoms be restricted if this is necessary to maintain the state order, which itself aims only to guarantee freedom.

Liberty within a network of relationships

Political and social liberties exist only within a network of relationships among different people. If a person is free, one cannot predict his behaviour in advance. The cause of his actions is not determined by external factors but rather by his own subjectivity (See BENN, p. 1 and R. S. PETERS, p. 199). In this sense each individual is largely in control of his own liberty. An individual who has a weak character will be more dependent on external circumstances and thus less free than an individual who is prepared to take great risks and accept the consequences of his decisions.

If somebody has the 'freedom' to influence the behaviour of others, this will be regarded as power if it is evaluated neutrally, and will be regarded as authority if it is evaluated in a positive sense and considered as justified and legitimate.

The opposite of liberty is dependency. If man becomes the object of external circumstances, he loses his subjectivity and becomes dependent on external social or political powers.

Free from coercion

The freedom of an individual is always determined in relation to society. However, this does not mean that the society or the polity alone can determine the content and scope of freedom. Not only those who behave in conformity with the law (G.W.F. HEGEL) or with the '*volonté générale*' (J.-J. ROUSSEAU) are free. In the political community, he who is able to make independent decisions without legal, bureaucratic or social constraints is truly free. Freedom is thus something intrinsically relative, something that by its very nature is limited by the given society. Individual freedom is also determined by the degree of real freedom within the polity and its society. A people which has to struggle against famine is as restricted in its real freedom as its single individuals. On the other hand, a wealthy and internationally independent state is able to grant its people much more real freedom than can a state in which the population is barely able to survive.

Formal and real freedom

When we refer in the following to freedom or liberty, we are referring to political freedom. Political freedom is formal freedom within the state or polity, which is both limited and guaranteed by the law of the state. This political freedom reflects the social freedom. Even if a state guarantees freedom of conscience and religion in its constitution, this freedom may be denied in social practice if for example the majority living in a small town discriminate against and socially exclude a minority because of their beliefs, to the point where the minority is effectively forced either leave town or to change their beliefs. Those who cannot find a job, who fear being evicted from their apartment or whose children are mistreated in school are just as restricted in their liberty as those who may be compelled by the force of the state to accept a new religion.

An intolerant society can tyrannise the minority even though the political state may provide comprehensive formal guarantees of rights and freedoms. A tolerant and, in the sense of KARL POPPER, open society can provide within a liberal climate a lot of space for liberty and free coexistence, even if there are less formal guarantees of political liberty (See also J. S. MILL; BENN, p. 1 and R. S. PETERS, p. 220).

Liberty as absence of coercion

Political and legal or formal liberty in the sense of LOCKE, exists when each person is entitled to do whatever is allowed within the law, or what is not expressly forbidden by law (J. LOCKE, *Second Treatise*, chapter VI, p. 57). Liberty thus presupposes in the negative sense the absence of external coercion exerted by the discretionary power of the state. From the positive point of view, it provides the possibility to choose among different alternatives of behaviour. Liberty thus has both a positive and a negative aspect. It is of little use for the state to give everyone the freedom to choose their own path of higher education or vocational training, if people have no means to actually make different choices (for example if they do not have the financial means to choose any form of tertiary education).

Freedom and equality

Of fundamental importance is that political or formal liberty is accorded to all people on an equal basis (J. RAWLS). Legal rights and freedoms cannot be limited only to a small minority or given only to men, or to members of a particular race or religion. The fundamental principle of equality requires equal rights and freedoms for everyone. If the state is to impose limits on political freedom, such limits must therefore be applied in relation to all people equally.

Freedom of the other

What conditions must exist in order for the state to be able to limit freedom? "...all restraint, *quâ* restraint, is an evil... Such questions involve considerations of liberty, only in so far as leaving people to themselves is always better, *cæteris paribus,* than controlling them..." (J.S. MILL, Ch. V, p. 239). Restrictions thus are always only permissible when they can be justified. According to BENN and PETERS, this is a formal principle that obliges the state to justify each limitation of freedom because each limitation of freedom is inherently bad. So what are the valid or legitimate justifications for the limitation of freedoms? The only legitimate justification for MILL is the self-preservation of the other or of the community (J.S. MILL, Ch. V, p. 240 ff). Restrictions of freedom thus are justified if they are aimed at avoiding harm or damage to other persons. In other words: The liberty of each person is limited by the liberty of the other.

Liberty and state solidarity

So far, so good. The practice of liberal states however recognises other justifications for the restriction of freedom. Not only the rights of others and the protection of the social order can provide a legitimate basis for the limitation of freedom, but also overwhelming public interest. The state compels parents to send their children to school and requires taxpayers to pay for public education. Both are limitations on the liberty of the individual. Are the justified?

If the state in the sense of LOCKE is responsible only for protecting the property and liberty of individuals, then such limitations cannot be justified. However, the state is in our view also a community based on solidarity which should strive to ensure that, even within an increasingly interdependent society, the individual still has some space for free development. Caring for the free development of the individual includes ensuring that everyone receives a good education. Limitations on the liberty of all individuals (such as the obligation to go to school) are thus justified when they ultimately enhance the space for liberty of choice. Indeed, they may even be necessary, provided that liberty overall will not be even more restricted. If for example the state uses tax revenue to provide support to elderly persons, but excessive state control means that the elderly lose all their liberty and freedom of choice, such an intervention cannot be justified. A general system of compulsory retirement insurance or superannuation on the one hand limits the freedom of each individual and on the other hand expands the liberty of elderly and retired people because they feel socially and financially secure. Such liberal system must be preferred over excessive state intervention.

Restrictions on liberty as a means to enhance freedom

Freedom can ultimately only be limited in the interest of freedom. Freedom is however not only an individual good but also a communal good. What is the use for example of a comprehensive state guarantee of economic freedom, if the whole economy of the state gradually becomes dependent on other states or foreign companies? Of what use is a comprehensive guarantee of freedom of the press if the majority of the population cannot read or write? Since liberty is always related to the community, it should never be misused for antisocial behaviour. Liberty must be exercised by each individual in a manner consistent with the individual's responsibility to the community. Such responsible exercise of freedom cannot be controlled nor prescribed by the state, but rather must be entrusted to each citizen. Without this foundation of trust liberty cannot be realised. If liberty however is generally and regularly misused, it will be necessary for the state to impose restrictions on freedom.

Limits on freedom and the view of human nature

The system of limits on freedom is thus extremely complex. Whether particular restrictions are justified cannot usually be determined in the abstract, but only in relation to concrete circumstances. Such decision will also be influenced by the decision makers' view of human nature. Those who trust the good sense of the individual and who believe in a minimal liberal state, will impose stricter limits on the power of the state and less limitations on freedom than those who take a more negative view of human nature and believe that people always tend to misuse their liberties.

4.7 Criteria of Justice

Jacob Good owns a large garden, which needs regular care. Young Martin from the neighbourhood usually helps on Saturday afternoon to mow the lawn. Martin has a friend living in poor conditions whose mother is severely ill. At Martin's request Jacob Good employs Peter Poor, the friend of Martin. He promises to pay him a small salary as compensation for the work. He asks himself what are the criteria according to which he should determine the level of the salary to be paid to Peter Poor. Shall he pay him according to the achievement principle and thus pay him less than he pays Martin because he has only just begun work? Should he take Peter's special needs into account and pay him more than he pays Martin? Should he first stick to the contract and promises given to Martin and decide freely on the compensation for Peter? In short, Jacob Good needs to decide what are the just criteria by which to make his decision.

The complex and multifaceted human being

Human beings have diverse needs: religious development, social prestige, economic and/or political power, commitment to ideals, creativity and innovation, as well as security and protection. These needs are satisfied through different communities such as church, state, family and economy. The relation of people to these communities has many different effects. It would thus be wrong to create out of this diversity a homogeneous and all-encompassing state. The state as a coercive community cannot meet all the different needs of the community-oriented human being, but rather is only one part of the various communities in which people participate. On the other hand, the state that cares for the social welfare of its population cannot without any reflection be accused of robbing the taxpayer. People who live within a state are dependent on the solidarity of the polity. Both rich and poor profit from the solidarity of the polity, which can only survive if it takes care of all sections of the population.

Justice within the welfare state

While the advocates of liberal state solutions had to decide what the state needed to provide for the protection of human beings, today's generation has to decide what is *just* within a welfare state. If the distribution of goods between Robinson and Friday is unjust, the state needs to intervene. If the state is to provide for another system of distribution according to what is 'just', one has to ask what are the principles by which the state should be guided. Justice thus determines on one side the limits of free economic activity and on the other side the *direction* of intervention by the state.

4.7.1 *When does the State need to Intervene?*

In seeking to answer the question of which decisions of the state are just, we begin with the assumption that the tasks of the state are principally determined by the dependency of human beings, and that such dependency is caused by the growing interdependence of the social and political society.

Obligation for social care

Let us return to the example of Robinson and Friday and imagine that Friday, the older partner of Robinson, grows old and that he is no longer able to do enough work to take care of his own needs. Within a social order in which the care for elder members of the family is the responsibility of the extended family or the tribe, Friday would be able to enjoy his old age without having to worry about hunting for his own food. It is also conceivable that Friday may throughout his working life have put some of his earnings aside and managed to save enough in order to face his old age without worry. In both examples, the state need not be under any special obligation to provide social care. In many states however, such forms of care for the elderly no longer exist, or exist only for a small and wealthy minority. Within industrialised countries, previous family and kinship structures have been dissolved, in part by social developments and in part by legal changes. Personal savings are also less likely to be able to support people in their old age, sometimes because by the time a person reaches old age their savings may have been so devalued by inflation that there is not enough to live on. For Friday, it is not possible to make private provision for his care in retirement, either through extended family or savings. He will therefore have to depend on the society. In the face of this dependency it would be most unjust if the state, for the maintenance of which citizens contribute taxes throughout their working lives, did not offer any form of care or assistance to its elderly people.

This example reveals only one aspect of justice: In the event that dependencies lead to consequences that are inhumane, state intervention is needed. At what point and with what measures the state has to intervene, will be determined by the fundamental values of the social and political order, such as for example the protection of human dignity. Justice in this case is no more than a guaranteed minimum standard. This applies for all dependencies such as those of the tenant upon the landlord, the consumer upon a company misusing its monopoly, and that of the employee upon the employer.

Minimum requirements

Are there positive criteria that the state must apply to reach a just decision? What measures does the state need to take to make adequate provision for Friday? Does the state have to provide him with a pension that is just enough for him to live on, or should it finance a higher standard of living for his old age? Should his pension be calculated solely according to Friday's previous insurance or superannuation contributions, or should it be based on Friday's actual needs?

These questions ultimately turn on the old postulate, well known since ARISTOTLE: "to each his own". This is however an empty formula if we do not know the criteria for just distribution. Throughout history the question of what should be given to each human being has had many different answers. While some advocate that each should be granted his vested entitlements, others interpret this principle to mean that each should be paid according to his performance. Still others believe that justice can only be realised if each can live according to his needs.

Formal justice

The difficulty of answering this question led many philosophers to attempt to define justice not according to material criteria, but rather according to formal criteria. KANT'S *categorical imperative* provides one example of such formal criteria. According to this principle, actions and decisions are just when they can be generalised. If we turn this principle around, then it follows that whatever is general and acceptable to everyone must also be just. A creative extension of this criterion of justice can be found in the writings of RAWLS. For him, actions and decisions are just when they can be accepted by everybody under certain conditions. ROUSSEAU also provides a standalone answer to the question of justice. Justice for him is found in the general will (*volonté générale*), which has to be distinguished from the sum of all individual wills (*volonté de tous*).

In the following section we will further analyse these different criteria of justice and explore their significance for political decisions.

4.7.2 Material Criteria of Justice

For each the protection of his rights (HUME)

For DAVID HUME (1711–1776), justice means respect and recognition of the rights of the other, especially property rights (cf. D. MILLER, p. 157 ff). HUME does not inquire whether the distribution of property has been made according to just criteria or how property should be justly distributed in future. For him, what is important is that everyone should respect the rights that men have acquired through ownership, inheritance or work. He admits that some may not use their rights for the common good, but this is not relevant. What is relevant is that each respects the rights of the other, and that by observing this principle the general peace is guaranteed. This concept of justice corresponds to the traditional feudal society. The function of the state is to protect existing rights and to ensure that nobody can illegitimately acquire somebody else's property or transfer it to a third party.

To each according to his performance (SPENCER)

This traditional theory of justice however could not meet the requirements of the new social order in which everything, including the distribution of wealth, was being redrawn. What could now be considered as just? SPENCER (1820–1903) offered an answer. For him the principle 'each according to his own' is fulfilled when all activities are rewarded according to individual performance. "Each individual ought to receive the benefits and the evils of his own nature and consequent of conduct" (H. SPENCER, Vol 2, p. 17). The behaviour of human beings is not to be judged subjectively according to their effort or commitment but according to their success or performance, which can be objectively verified. How does this guarantee a just distribution of wealth? According to SPENCER, this will be just because it accords with the law of nature, which dictates that the stronger will receive more and the weaker will receive less. He thus applies DARWIN's biological theory of survival of the fittest, in the context of social and economic life (H. SPENCER, Vol 2, p. 17). He who is best able to adapt to his environment and therefore best able to survive, should also receive the largest share of the wealth.

According to which criteria should one measure the performance of the individual? SPENCER rejects the idea of objective criteria, which would be determined according to fundamental values by political decision. Instead, he advocates criteria that can withstand free competition. Performance should not be measured by the state, but rather by the free market (H. SPENCER, Vol 2, p. 472). Accordingly, a state that desires the just distribution of wealth should guarantee to each individual equal opportunities and ensure the conditions of free competition. In particular, the state should not be allowed to assess the performance of individual persons. People should prove themselves within the free economic battle of all against all. Any objective assessment of performance would, according to SPENCER, have socialist or totalitarian consequences.

To each according to his needs (KROPOTKIN)

Life within the slums of large industrial cities was sufficient to demonstrate in the last century that the pure principle of 'each according to his performance' cannot lead to solutions that meet the human requirement for justice. Hard labour of women and children, misery and hunger have no place within a just society. So it was that the first socialists led by SAINT-SIMON (1760–1825) argued for a just distribution of wealth according to an objective evaluation of the performance or output achieved by each member for the benefit of society. Workers' wages should be calculated according to the abilities and responsibilities of the worker, but not according to the market price of the work. Other socialists such as PIERRE-JOSEPH PROUDHON (1808–1865) demanded the same wage for each hour of work regardless of the type of work or the output.

For PETER A. KROPOTKIN (1842–1921) those demands were not radical enough. They corresponded too closely to capitalist ideas about the sale of labour. He rejected the idea of the distribution of wealth based on performance, and instead proposed that wealth be distributed according to the needs of each member of the society. Such distribution should however not be organised by the state. As an anarchist, KROPOTKIN was of the opinion that in small autonomous communes each could work according to his abilities and the needs of the collective to produce collective goods. Each member of the collective would share in all goods and should therefore receive the share that he needs. These autonomous communes would be connected to each other through a federal system, which however would not exercise any political force in relation to the communes (cf D. MILLER, p. 209 ff).

4.7.3 *Formal Criteria of Justice*

4.7.3.1 The General Will According to ROUSSEAU

General will as absolute justice

For ROUSSEAU, the general will (volonté générale) of the people corresponds to and is the expression of justice. This general will contains a formal element: authority based on general laws. 'General' however, does not mean an addition of the needs, interests or desires of every individual, but refers rather to an integral common denominator to which each individual can consent. The laws should therefore, in order to correspond to the general will, also be enacted by a procedure that enables the people to participate and to express its consent.

> "There is often a great deal of difference between the will of all and the general will; the latter considers only the common interest, while the former takes private interest into account, and is no more than a sum of particular wills: but take away from these same wills the pluses and minuses that cancel one another, and the general will remains as the sum of the differences.
> If, when the people, being furnished with adequate information, held its deliberations, the citizens had no communication one with another, the grand total of the small differences would always give the general will, and the decision would always be good. But when factions arise, and partial associations are formed at the expense of the great association, the will of each of these associations becomes general in relation to its members, while it remains particular in relation to the State: it may then be said that there are no longer as many votes as there are men, but only as many as there are associations. The differences become less numerous and give a less general result. Lastly, when one of these associations is so great as to prevail over all the rest, the result is no longer a sum of small differences, but a single difference; in this case there is no longer a general will, and the opinion which prevails is purely particular.
> It is therefore essential, if the general will is to be able to express itself, that there should be no partial society within the State, and that each citizen should think only his own thoughts: which was indeed the sublime and unique system established by the great Lycurgus. But if there are partial societies, it is best to have as many as possible and to prevent them from being unequal, as was done by Solon, Numa and Servius. These precautions are the only ones that can guarantee that the general will shall be always enlightened, and that the people shall in no way deceive itself" (J.-J. ROUSSEAU, Social Contract, 2nd Book, Chapter 3).

Totalitarian general will?

Critics have always decried ROUSSEAU on the basis that his idea of the general will contains a totalitarian and collectivist element. But this does not correspond to ROUSSEAU'S own understanding. In *Political Economy*, he explains the content to which the general will has to correspond: "Look into the motives which have induced men, once united by their common needs in a general society, to unite themselves still more intimately by means of civil societies: you will find no other motive than that of assuring the property, life and liberty of each member by the protection of all" (ROUSSEAU, *Political Economy*). MARSILIUS OF PADUA had earlier expressed similar ideas: "Just as the law is one eye out of many different eyes which means it is an observation which has been assessed by many observers, so it is safer in order to avoid judicial error to ensure that judgments are made according to the general law made by many rather than according to the discretion of the judge... For this reason we allow men to rule only in conformity with reason, that is, with the law" (M. VON PADUA, *Defender of Peace*, Part I, chapter XI, § 3–4).

The most noble obligation of the legislature according to ROUSSEAU, is to align the laws to the general will. The general will accords with justice: "so that man need only be just, in order to comply with the general will" (J.-J. ROUSSEAU, *Political Economy*, p. 47). "The body politic, therefore, is also a moral being possessed of a will; and this general will, which tends always to the preservation and welfare of the whole and of every part, and is the source of the laws, constitutes for all the members of the State, in their relations to one another and to it, the rule of what is just or unjust.." (J.-J. ROUSSEAU, *Political Economy*, p. 31). The first commandment of justice is to rule the people according to the law. But what should be the content of the laws? Laws need to awaken the love of each citizen for the fatherland.

"The security of individuals is so intimately connected with the public confederation that, apart from the regard that must be paid to human weakness, that convention would in point of right be dissolved, if in the State a single citizen who might have been relieved were allowed to perish, or if one were wrongfully confined in prison, or if in one case an obviously unjust sentence were given" (J.-J. ROUSSEAU, *Political Economy*, p. 59).

Welfare state and general will

However, it is not sufficient for the state to care only for the protection of the rights of single individuals. "In fact, does not the undertaking entered into by the whole body of the nation bind it to provide for the security of the least of its members with as much care as for that of all the rest? Is the welfare of a single citizen any less the common cause than that of the whole State?" (J.-J. ROUSSEAU, *Political Economy*, p. 9).

"Let our country then show itself the common mother of her citizens; let the advantages they enjoy in their country endear it to them; let the government leave them enough share in the public administration to make them feel that they are at home; and let the laws be in their eyes only the guarantees of the common liberty" (J.-J. ROUSSEAU, *Political Economy*, p. 63).

Prevention of poverty rather than redistribution

How should the state deal with existing economic inequalities? Should it make the rich poor and the poor rich? "It is therefore one of the most important functions of government to prevent extreme inequality of fortunes; not by taking away wealth from its possessors, but by depriving all men of means to accumulate it; not by building hospitals for the poor, but by securing the citizens from becoming poor" (J.-J. ROUSSEAU, *Political Economy*, p. 65).

This task can only be realised by the state on the basis of the consensus of the voters. "That taxes cannot be legitimately established except by the consent of the people or its representatives, is a truth generally admitted by all philosophers and jurists of any repute on questions of public right, not even excepting Bodin" (J.-J. ROUSSEAU, *Political Economy*, p. 93).

According to ROUSSEAU, the state is primarily required to protect property and freedom. "It should be remembered that the foundation of the social compact is property; and its first condition, that every one should be maintained in the peaceful possession of what belongs to him" (J.-J. ROUSSEAU, *Political Economy*, p. 91). "There can be no patriotism without liberty, no liberty without virtue, no virtue without citizens" (J.-J. ROUSSEAU, *Political Economy*, p. 67).

Solidarity and order of peace

For ROUSSEAU, the state is an association that is there to protect its citizens. This protection can only be realised within a just and peaceful order, which itself can only exist if the state enacts just laws. Those laws need to be based on the common understanding that the state is also a community of solidarity that serves the welfare of all citizens. This community can only be sustained if all are prepared to contribute their part to solidarity. It then becomes possible to protect property and to achieve freedom without totalitarian violence.

4.7.3.2 Justice as the Principle of Fairness (RAWLS)

Veil of ignorance

For RAWLS, justice is not found in a democratically institutionalised *volonté générale* but rather, in a decision that is acceptable to rational people because it can be generalised. All those decisions which can find a consensus amongst all free and rational human beings who seek to protect their own interests, must accord with justice. RAWLS assumes however, that these free and rational people are making such decisions in some kind of original or natural state. In this state they have no knowledge of their own abilities, preferences, ideas of good and bad, their own position and rank within the society or the level of development of the society (cf. criticism of H.L.A. HART, p. 132).

RAWLS is however not content with a formal or procedural basis for the development of principles of justice. He attempts to define some substantive content of justice based on the principles of equality, inequality and openness (J. RAWLS, p. 19).

Where and when is the principle of equality authoritative?

The state must respect the principle of unconditional equality with regard to fundamental liberties and fundamental rights. The rights and freedoms of every person must be protected in the same way and to the same extent. Discrimination on the basis of race, gender or nationality is impermissible.

Freedom should however not only be protected against organs of the state. The state needs also to ensure that there is the space to exercise freedom within society. Each member of the society must have equal opportunities to make use of his/her liberty. If restrictions are to be placed on the free development of the individual citizen, for instance with regard to the use of his land, such restrictions should be balanced by a corresponding right to participate in the collective decision (for example, political rights in the local council decisions on zoning, right to appeal against zoning plans etc).

Freedom finds its limits within the liberty of the other and in the need to protect the integrity of the state. Freedom of conscience and religion is limited by the religious freedom of the other. The state cannot for example allow the establishment of a religion that is intent on actively destroying all other religions. Freedom of the press cannot be allowed to produce a situation in which a handful of media outlets prevent the publication of other sources of media and thereby monopolise the political and social opinion of the population. If the state requires compulsory military service for young men, it should respect the right to refuse military service on religious grounds as long as such refusal does not impede the ability of the state to fulfil its defence responsibilities.

When can inequality be justified?

There is no state and no area in which the principle of equality can be fully and unconditionally implemented. In particular, it will never be possible to guarantee an absolutely equal distribution of wealth. To what extent can inequalities within the state be justified? Surely they can only be justified as long as the poor can also profit from the advantages of the rich. The higher salary of the manager of a company should ensure that the position of manager attracts the best person for the job, that the company is therefore under the best possible management and the interests of the workers are secure (J. RAWLS, p. 258 ff).

Feudalism, hereditary aristocracy and closed financial oligarchy cannot be justified within an industrial state, taking into account the dependency of the individual upon society. The individual will not profit from such inequality. However, we must also take into account that the state will increasingly be faced with shortages of resources and supplies. In managing such shortages, the state will have to ensure a fair reduction of supply and a just distribution of what is available. If electricity has to be rationed, one cannot reduce supply based on previous consumption. Such policy would reward the wasteful and punish the frugal. When however companies have to choose between making some employees redundant or retaining all employees on a part-time basis, the part-time work may be more just than the dismissal of employees, as those who would otherwise have been dismissed would not have benefited in any way from the advantage of those who were retained.

This observation has the following significance for a state with a free market economy: The state should guarantee the economic freedom of the market and thus the free distribution of wealth, as long as everyone can ultimately profit from such freedom. However, as soon as only some profit to the disadvantage of others (such as the sick, the elderly, etc), the state must intervene.

Principle of openness

The principle of inequality needs to be complemented by the *principle of openness*. A rigid and unequal social order can never be legitimate. Privileges must be open and accessible to everybody. In particular, it must be ensured that there are equal educational opportunities for all members of society. The underprivileged must be given the opportunity to get an education and to improve their social position. Rigid financial oligarchies need to be broken up.

Openness does not only entail social mobility. It also involves an ability to constantly adapt to the changing conditions of the social and political environment. The state has to remain flexible. State institutions should be capable of learning and adapting, and be able to alter their policies and attitudes accordingly. They should not be closed to new ideas, new needs and new constraints. The greater the flexibility of the state and the more open it is, the more likely it is that the state will find just solutions.

Responsibility and solidarity

The principles of equality, inequality and openness of RAWLS are simply empty phrases unless they are augmented by the principle of responsibility and solidarity. Every state order presupposes a minimum level of solidarity and responsibility. Those who see the state only as an institution to serve their individual needs and interests, and as an instrument to facilitate the unrestrained individual pursuit of profit, contribute to the subversion of the state and ultimately to its destruction.

Responsibility and solidarity also require the authorities of the state to act in accord with these principles. Civil servants should not misuse the power with which they have been entrusted. Their own career interests should not override their responsibility to promote and serve the legitimate interests of the public. As the achievement principle is only of limited application within the state administration (performance cannot be measured by profit), value should be placed upon creativity and innovation in the public service, and civil servants should have a heightened sense of solidarity in order to achieve these aims. Responsibility and solidarity should also contribute to enhancing the eagerness to learn amongst the civil service. If the authorities are not prepared to learn and have no desire to inform themselves or the public, the necessary partnership between the state and society will never be realised.

4.7.4 *Principles of Justice within the Reality of the Modern Liberal State Committed to the Social Market Economy*

The reality of the modern state committed to liberty and welfare reveals that the principles of justice developed in the various theories are somehow all taken into account within the reality of modern politics. The main difference between the modern liberal states is that they accord different priorities to the different principles of justice.

Protection of rights

The idea of HUME that the primary function of the state is to protect rights, finds its expression in the guarantees of property and liberty. In addition, contract law, probate law and property law are committed to this principle. The achievement principle of SPENCER finds its political expression in the guarantee of free competition. In situations where performance cannot be assessed by the free market, such as salaries for civil servants or public grants for agriculture, political authorities have to establish general and rational criteria in order to evaluate performance objectively.

To each according to his needs

But the modern state also takes account of other human needs. The basic principle of social welfare, that everybody is entitled to security of his or her existence, attempts to satisfy at least the minimum standard of living for every person within the state. This principle is also taken into account in the context of bankruptcy laws, which provide that creditors cannot recover those goods that are absolutely necessary for survival. The guarantee of minimum wages and other minimum working conditions as well as the right to a free public education are also influenced by this principle of meeting basic needs.

Fair procedures

The procedural guarantees developed by ROUSSEAU or RAWLS can be found within the principle of legality. The liberal constitutional state can only be ruled on the basis of law. Laws need to have the general consent of the citizens or of their representatives and must be enacted via a fair and rational procedure that is transparent to the public.

However, modern states today are required to apply principles of justice to solve problems that did not arise to the same extent in earlier times. The increasing scarcity of resources and water, major ecological catastrophes and the challenge of migration provide just a few examples. Raw materials are only available to a limited extent. This fact will in future compel the state to take even greater account of the needs of the citizens, for example when fixing quotas or systems for rationing resources. In the interest of both current and future generations, liberty may have to be restricted. Justice needs not only to take into account the needs of the living, but also the needs of future generations.

5 Rule of Law

5.1 Development of the Rule of Law

5.1.1 Introduction

Rule of law – rules of law

When we use the term 'rule of law' we are referring to the rule of law in the English or common law sense, which is somewhat different to the French term '*Etat de Droit*' and to the German notion of the '*Rechtsstaat*'. The obligation of states to follow the rule of law could be understood in a number of different ways:

- Does it refer to the rule of laws, that is, to the subordination of state institutions to particular 'ideologies' or natural laws understood as binding prestate principles to which positive law must adhere (notion of the French *état de droit*)?
- Does it refer to the rules of law, that is, to the obligation of state institutions to obey the positive laws enacted by the legislature (*état légal* in French or *Rechtsstaat* in German)?
- Does it refer to the rules of the laws, that is, to the subordination of state institutions to the positive laws, which in turn follow and are based upon particular pre-state ideologies?
- Or does it refer to the rule of law, that is, to the claim that there are universally valid pre-state legal principles, deduced by reason, to which all states and sovereigns including constitution-makers are subject? In this case one would have to ask the question 'who is the universaliser'? That is, who has the authority to make binding determinations as to what the rule of law means and requires?

In the following pages we shall use the term 'rule of law' principally in the sense of the general idea of a universally valid, rationally deduced law.

Rule of law and "Rechtsstaat"

The idea that the positive embodiment of the state legal order must always adhere to the fundamental principles of law and justice was developed primarily within the Anglo-Saxon legal tradition. The German notion of the *Rechtsstaat* is an expression of the requirement that all authorities and institutions created under the constitution of the state must comply with the positive law. The Anglo-Saxon notion of *the Rule of Law* on the other hand encapsulates the basic and fundamental principle according to which political might and power is always limited and controlled by the law in the sense of pre-state and pre-positive law.

That men should not be ruled by men but by law was first expressed as the principle of the 'Rule of Law' in 17th Century England, by republican James Harrington in his famous work *The Commonwealth of Oceana* (1656). The idea itself is however much older. Early Greek political philosophers argued for the supremacy of law as protection against the arbitrary rule of tyrants (ARISTOTLE, *Politics*, Book III, 15 ff). But it is principally the Western European medieval idea of a higher law that limits even the power of the King, which has shaped the modern concept of the rule of law. Within Western Europe the jurisprudence developed through the common law courts in England strengthened this legal principle. Through their case law the common law courts of England ultimately had a major influence on modern legal philosophy throughout Europe and the West.

Preparedness of the common law for the development of the rule of law

The common law system, which was continuously developed based on rational arguments before the courts and was able to adapt to social developments, proved itself to be much more receptive to the idea of the rule of law than were the continental European legal systems in which the law was fixed by the sovereign lawmaker. In addition to the practice of the common law courts, political philosophy also contributed significantly to the development of the idea of the rule of law. JOHN LOCKE'S theory on the legitimacy of government was particularly influential. His claim that governments must achieve legitimacy by acceptance and consensus (*government by consent*) and that the authority of the power-holders can only be legitimate if it is based on the continuing support of the subjects, is ultimately derived from the principle of the rule of law.

In order to follow the emergence of the rule of law one must examine the historical development of the idea of the *authority of the law* within the English legal tradition. One can then take the further step of tracing the development of this principle in Germany and in France, which differed considerably from the way in which the principle developed in the United Kingdom.

5.1.2 The Development of the Rule of Law in the English Common Law Tradition

5.1.2.1 Medieval Idea of the Supremacy of Law and its Effects on Modern Liberties

Magna Carta

The modern concept of individual liberty would not have been possible if the idea of establishing legal limits on the arbitrary acts of the Crown had not already gained acceptance in the age of European feudalism. In the early Middle Ages in

Western Europe this idea found expression in various charters, which guaranteed property rights of the King's vassals and thus obliged the King to respect the private rights of his subjects.

As already mentioned in the context of the development of the principles of human rights, the *Magna Carta Libertatum* (The Great Charter of Liberties) of 1215 is a milestone in the legal history of the human struggle for personal liberty and the development of the rule of law. In contrast to the other charters drafted in the Middle Ages, the Magna Carta is still valid today. It was drafted under pressure from the peers of King John and aimed to impose limits on the arbitrary power of the King. The King was effectively forced to proclaim the charter in 1215. The Magna Carta can undoubtedly be seen as the document that laid the foundation for the later development of the rule of law.

In spite of the Magna Carta the English king remained an absolute monarch, but he could no longer make arbitrary decisions. *A constitutional monarchy* was thereby created. This meant that in England from that time on the King's acts of executive power were legitimate as long as they were in accord with the established legal framework. The old Anglo-Saxon idea of the *free man* who is born with certain inalienable rights (privileges) against the Crown found its first legal expression in the Magna Carta. Thus the medieval principle of the supremacy of law became a constituent element of the common law.

The supremacy of law as a basic principle was deeply rooted in the nature of the medieval feudal polity, as it was based on a certain pluralism of power that was divided and balanced between various mutually limiting power centres. One could even say that to some extent this pluralism of feudal authority paved the way for the theory of separation of powers in the sense of mutual checks and balances between state powers and institutions. The concept of the rule of law as a product of the separation of powers however came about much later.

Much of the veneration of Magna Carta as one of the earliest constitutional documents in history is focussed on the famous provision in Article 39:

> "No free man shall be seized, or imprisoned, or dispossessed, or outlawed, or in any way destroyed; nor will we condemn him, nor will we commit him to prison, excepting by the legal judgement of his peers, or by the laws of the land."

Mother of the modern state

To this day scholars remain divided on the issue of the legal nature of the Magna Carta. Some argue that, like all other charters of that time, it merely confirmed existing customary law. Others contend that the Magna Carta was a fundamental constitutional law in the proper sense of the term, which made a revolutionary break with earlier feudal tradition and established new rights and freedoms. What is uncontested however is that the broad terms in Article 39 of the Charter, such as "no free man" and "by the laws of the land", enabled interpretations which over the course of history saw the transformation of the Magna Carta from a charter of medieval feudal society into a modern document that has become an important foundation of modern law. The open and sometimes quite imprecise formulations in the charter lend themselves to considerable expansion and adaptation to the social and legal context of the modern welfare state. In this sense, one can indeed rightly regard the *Magna Carta* as the 'mother' of modern liberty and constitutional government.

There are two main reasons for this assessment of the effect of the Magna Carta:

1. First, the formulation "no free man" is based upon the equality principle, and as such was able over centuries to be re-interpreted so that it no longer referred to the status of free aristocratic peers, but to all citizens.
2. Second, since the common law entails the ongoing development of legal rules on the basis of precedents and the logic of induction, it is much more flexible than the continental legal system of statutes and other fixed rules and regulations. The common law is therefore better able to take account of the requirements of modern society, by refining and developing the law on a case-by-case basis.

Petition of Rights

The *Petition of Rights* of 1628, a statement of the objectives of the English legal reform movement that led to the Civil War and ultimately to the execution of King Charles I in 1649, was also based on the traditional 'liberties' of England. The petition strengthened the claim that private property and personal liberty represented fundamental human rights, inherent in the common law and based on fundamental principles that were derived from nature and binding on the sovereign. The classical Habeas Corpus right of protection from arbitrary imprisonment was worded as follows:

> "No man, of what estate or condition that he be, should be put out of his land or tenements, nor taken, nor imprisoned, nor disinherited nor put to death without being brought to answer by due process of law" (Petition of Rights, Section IV).

Habeas Corpus

The *Habeas Corpus Act* of 1679 supplemented the Petition of Rights with a procedural guarantee under which every person has the right in the event of imprisonment to be brought promptly and directly before a court on a writ of habeas corpus to defend their freedom. This right was expanded by the *Habeas Corpus Act* of 1816, which extended the prohibition of arbitrary imprisonment in criminal cases to all cases of arbitrary and indefinite detention.

(More on these basic documents in L. Basta, *Politika u granicama prava*, Belgrade 1984, p. 20–40).

From the Magna Carta to Habeas Corpus

In Article 39 of the Magna Carta we can see the origins of the right to due process of the law, and thus the seed of the procedural and substantive rights guarantees later contained in the Vth (1791) and XIVth Amendments (part of the Civil War

Amendments of 1869) of the American Constitution as interpreted and applied by the Supreme Court.

Taking into account the political context of the charter and the potential for extensive interpretation of its major provisions, the Magna Carta was celebrated by HENRY DE BRACTON in the 13th Century as the constitution of liberty (*constitutio libertatis*). Inspired by the underlying philosophy of this document, the famous judge and priest of the Cathedral in Exeter formulated the maxim which still figures as the most accurate formulation of the medieval supremacy of law doctrine: *Rex non debet esse sub homine, sed sub Deo et lege* (The king ought not to be under man, but under God and the law).

5.1.3 Major Constitutional Conflicts of the 17th Century

The institution of the British Parliament

Of major significance for the political and institutional development of the rule of law in medieval England was the appointment of the English Parliament as a permanent institution of the Crown in 1265, which continued to grow in its political influence. The fundamental principle for the authority of the English Parliament, *no taxation without representation,* had already been secured half a century earlier in the Magna Carta which provided in Article 12 that "no scutage nor aid shall be imposed in our kingdom, *unless by the common council of our kingdom*". Nonetheless, it was only with the firm establishment of the Parliament that this principle gained full validity and recognition. The historical foundation for the later development of representative democracy was thereby laid. Furthermore, the road was paved for a revolutionary breakthrough to take place in the 17th Century: Parliament established legal limits on the power of the King, and the authority of Parliament was considerably enlarged.

Representation

The history of the English Parliament has no parallel on the European continent. In the period between the 14th and 16th Centuries it developed into a representative body, although it was not yet a democratic institution. Whilst Parliament was initially formed to consolidate and even to expand the political power base of the King, over time it became the most powerful competitor and opponent of the King's authority. Thus the stage was set for the greatest constitutional conflict in English history, which led to a civil war from 1642–1649 and was brought to a close by the Glorious Revolution of 1688–1689 and the enactment of the Bill of Rights. The Parliament came out victorious and contributed a new milestone to the development of the rule of law: constitutional monarchy. The earlier balance between the Crown and Parliament was to be superseded by the sovereignty of Parliament.

No separation of powers

In order to understand properly the critical issues dominating the great constitutional conflicts of the time, one must bear in mind that at the beginning of the 17th Century there was no clear organisational or functional separation between the three powers (legislative, executive and judicial). The King-in-Parliament had the power to make laws, and at the same time sat as the highest judge in the highest court of Parliament. As the conflict between the King and Parliament reached its peak, it had to be decided which institution would ultimately have the upper hand. A political confrontation over the powers was unavoidable once the question emerged as to which bearer of power will prevail in the case of a conflict: the King, the Parliament or the courts of common law.

Crown prerogatives

In constitutional terms the conflict centred on the question of the royal prerogatives, i.e. those powers of the crown that were established by the common law. The first of the two Kings of the Stuart dynasty, James I (1603–1625), and his Chancellor, the famous philosopher Francis Bacon (1561–1626), exercised absolute monarchical power and were of the view that the King in the exercise of his prerogatives stood above the positive law of England, i.e. above both statutory law (the acts of Parliament) and the common law. The King thus had the power for example to amend laws passed by Parliament and to intervene in the practice of the courts to 'correct' common law precedents.

This view was firmly opposed by Sir Edward Coke (1552–1634), Chief Justice, first at the Court of Common Pleas and then at the Court of the King's Bench. In a number of well-known cases Chief Justice Coke developed powerful arguments to support the supremacy of the common law not only over the royal prerogatives, but also over acts of Parliament. "In many cases the common law will controul acts of Parliament and sometimes adjudge them to be utterly void: for when an Act of Parliament is against common right or reason, or repugnant, or impossible to be performed, the common law will controul it and adjudge such Act to be void" (COKE CJ, *Dr Bonham's Case* (1610) 8 Co. Rep. 107a, 118a, 77 Eng. Rep. 638, 652).

The constitutional conflict over royal prerogatives was in essence a conflict between natural law, and the positive common law. It was also a conflict between two competing political and legal traditions, at the time equally dominant in Europe: the European continental tradition, and that of common law England. James I wanted to follow the continental European doctrine (which also applied in Scotland) of royal absolutism. According to this doctrine, the King was not subject to any parliamentary or judicial control, but stood above the law. The King not only enjoyed royal prerogatives, but as sovereign also enjoyed a higher authority than the legislature and the judiciary. This doctrine accorded with the classical, pre-modern natural law theory, such as that developed by BODIN. The King according to this theory has divine royal rights vested in him by the grace of God, and is the highest law-making authority and the highest judge. He is the absolute sovereign, subject not even to his own laws. BODIN'S theory laid the ideological foundation for the absolutism of the French monarchy, and reflected the major contemporary political trends on the continent. It also gave James I the theoretical basis on which he could seek a constitutional justification for his absolutism.

Collective wisdom constrains tyranny

However, England had long since rejected the concepts of divine right and absolute monarchy. Legal theory and the practice of the courts in England were heading towards the modern age. At the same time major changes to the constitutional foundations of England were introduced in a manner typical of the English common law tradition: through a conservative form of an appeal to 'common reason' and the 'collective wisdom of the generations'.

James I vehemently defended his 'divine right' to absolute and unlimited decision-making power under the royal prerogatives in an attempt to preserve the right of the King to exercise unconstrained authority. It was precisely this claim to absolute power that Parliament so steadfastly opposed. So it was that for the first time a fundamental power struggle between the King and Parliament arose. It is interesting to observe that the *political* power battle was fought using *constitutional* (*legal*) arguments.

EDWARD COKE and his supporters were fully aware of the magnitude of the challenge they faced: How to revise the constitutional framework to fashion a new relationship between the executive power on one side, and legislative and judicial, power on the other, and at the same time maintain the fiction that in constitutional terms everything remained fundamentally the same? Those who read the debates that took place in the English Parliament at that time will be impressed by the sharp contrast between the explosive, revolutionary political and constitutional positions being taken, and the cooperative and at times timid tone of the discourse by which these issues were resolved.

Inviolability of rights is immanent to the common law

It is only by bearing this historical context in mind that one can grasp the far-reaching impact of some of the early decisions of the common law courts. In the judgments of Chief Justice EDWARD COKE we can discern certain key elements of the rule of law as understood within the Anglo-American common law tradition (the most important of which are the *Case of Prohibition* (1608), the *Case of Proclamation* (1610) and *Bonham's Case* (1610), see O. Hood-Phillips, *Leading Cases in Constitutional and Administrative Law* (3rd ed. 1967) London):

- That, unlike the continental law, the common law only recognises the validity of general rules if they have already been applied and developed in concrete cases. Only in cases of concrete application can it be determined

whether general rules have the capacity to regulate the situations of everyday life.
- That decisions and acts of the executive are legitimate only if they are formally proclaimed as legal acts.
- That the guarantee of the inviolability of individual rights is inherent in the common law and this guarantee stands above the positive law.

From this we can derive two postulates that are significant for the further development of the rule of law:

1. That the positive law should be controlled by fundamental legal principles and by reason. This idea dominated the constitutional debates of 17th and 18th Century England for only a few decades. The question of the sovereignty of Parliament was a more direct focus of these debates, including the notion that the sovereign is not subject to any pre-positive legal rules. And this debate in turn laid the foundation for the modern concept of a constitution as a written document that limits and controls the powers of the legislature.
2. That positive law, including the constitution, is neither the basis for nor the source of human rights, but rather the positive expression of the pre-existing obligation of the sovereign to observe human rights. This highlights another fundamental difference between the common law and the continental law. Constitutional jurists of the continent took the view that the constitution created human rights, and was not there merely to guarantee the protection of already existing rights.

These different standpoints led to fundamentally different understandings of the nature of the state in the two legal traditions. Whilst according to the Anglo-Saxon view the state is primarily a 'moderator' between different social forces, the state is seen in continental Europe as an instrument with which the ruling parties (the majority) can change society. During the two major modern revolutions in France and America, this difference became even more apparent and led to very different conceptions of the rule of law.

Institutions to limit the power of the rulers

The major constitutional conflicts in England all ultimately had a common goal: they were aimed at the establishment of appropriate legal institutions to limit the power of state authorities, in order to protect the rights of individuals against the abuse of power. This is why the two great themes which dominated political and constitutional theory of the 17th and 18th Century England, namely whether the sovereign parliament is bound by fundamental law, and the issue of the mutual control and limitation of the three powers, had a decisive influence on the modern understanding of the rule of law. Both themes – from different points of view – addressed the very *leitmotiv* of the rule of law: How to constitute 'the empire of laws and not of men'.

5.1.4 Sovereignty of Parliament and the Fundamental Law

How can fundamental rights limit the sovereignty of parliament?

Almost every relevant writer in political philosophy in England at the time was engaged in the debate on the relationship between the sovereignty of Parliament and fundamental human rights. Over the span of two centuries two great names stand out in this context: JOHN LOCKE (1632–1704) and WILLIAM BLACKSTONE (1723–1780) argued that the claim of the lawmaker for limits on the extent of sovereign power (parliamentary sovereignty) on the one hand, and the claim for the universal validity of fundamental norms and values that protect and guarantee the rights of individuals on the other hand, are in their relation to each other complementary. It is only by combining these elements that limited government, i.e. government by law, can be guaranteed. However, there was also an influential minority of political philosophers which rejected any inherent relationship between the sovereignty of Parliament and fundamental law: THOMAS HOBBES (1588–1679) and JEREMY BENTHAM (1748–1832) both argued for the legally unlimited sovereignty of the state, and both influenced the analytical and positivist legal theory of the 19th and 20th Centuries.

The debate was conducted primarily in the light of the modern, rational philosophy of natural rights and social contract theory. The inalienable natural rights were translated into positive law in order to set legitimate limits on political power, and to charge government with the responsibility for protecting the rights of individuals.

The central issue of sovereign power

The reason why this debate is so important for the modern development of the rule of law lies in the fact that it tackled two propositions that until then had not been adequately addressed within the discourse on limited government:

- That the question of the nature of the sovereign power of the state implies in itself the question of the limits of sovereign power.
- That the rule of law can be interpreted as a legal principle that requires that state authority is bound by positive law, and not by fundamental pre-positive law in the classical sense of the rule of law.

While the latter positivist understanding of the rule of law became a key issue during the 19th and 20th Centuries, the nature of sovereign powers and their interrelationship was the focal point in the 17th and 18th Centuries. With the exception of HOBBES and BENTHAM, who defended the extreme variant of the unlimited sovereignty of Parliament, the answer to this problem was at the same time relatively clear but also in itself contradictory: In order to prevent the violation of human rights caused by the arbitrary exercise of power, political power must have clearly set limits. But what remains unclear is the nature or source of these limits: Are these limits based on positive law, on natural law, or moral principle? Most proponents of the natural law doctrine held the view that natural law, positive law and morals were one unified entity. This was certainly the position of JOHN LOCKE. His philosophy of natural rights and theory of limited government as government by consent mark the highpoint of classical liberal constitutionalism in England, which was later to be influential on the founding fathers of the United States.

Mixed government and separation of powers

At the centre of the debate over the protection of fundamental rights was the question of how the system of different powers could be combined with fundamental rights as a means of limiting the power of the sovereign. The classical theory of the common law posited the idea of a corporate sovereignty, in order to maintain the notion of a sovereign Parliament and at the same time recognise limits on Parliament imposed by fundamental rights. It is the King-in-Parliament who is the supreme legislator. This entails a functional symbiosis between the legislature and the executive (mixed government). The Parliament is the supreme bearer of legislative, law-making powers, and *not* of political power as such (*sovereign power*). Parliamentary sovereignty meant only that Parliament had absolute liberty in exercising *legally defined* legislative powers. During the American and the French revolutions a further distinction was made between law-making power and constitution-making power. This led naturally to the democratic principle that it is the people as the ultimate sovereign that possesses constituent power.

5.1.5 Separation of Powers, or Checks and Balances

Separation of powers as precondition for the rule of law

Why is the separation of powers necessarily linked to the idea of the rule of law? Because the political philosophy that underpins the separation of powers seeks to transform the political relationship between the different arms of government into a legal relationship. The doctrine of the separation of powers seeks primarily to realise a liberal goal: *political* freedom can only be achieved if it is also *legally* protected. In other words: one can interpret the separation of powers as the realisation of the rule of law, because it creates the institutional preconditions for government according to law.

What then have been the different emphases of this theory throughout history?

– Originally separation of powers was seen as a static concept of mixed government.

  a) In so far as the two branches of government are independent from each other they automatically also limit each other. It would be premature in this context to regard this as mutual control of powers.
  b) Only those activities of the Crown that fall within the powers and prerogatives of the Crown (intra vires) are a valid exercise of the power

of the Crown. Acts that go beyond the scope of such valid authority (ultra vires) however are illegitimate and thus illegal.

- The victory of Parliament in the constitutional conflict with the Crown over the scope of its powers meant that the legislature gained control over the Crown and its prerogatives. This opened the way for a shift from a static to a dynamic concept of mixed government. From this point onward, the focus was on the balance of the relationships between the different branches of government.
- Once the ability to control the other branches had become recognised as a major feature of the system of separation of powers it became clear that the theory of the separation of powers could no longer be limited only to the separation and division between the legislative and the executive branches and their functions (the judicial independence had already been guaranteed in the *Act of Settlement*). A real balance among the different branches of government can of course only be guaranteed when the powers are not completely, but rather only partially separated and thus able to mutually control each other (checks and balances).

It is probably for this reason that the real 'founders' of the of the theory of separation of powers, JOHN LOCKE and CHARLES-LOUIS DE SECONDAT MONTESQUIEU (1689–1755), referred in their writings primarily to the mutual control and balance of powers and less to the separation of those powers. In any case the theory of the separation of powers including the checks and balances inherent therein has since this time been regarded as a basic element of the rule of law.

In his *Second Treatise of Civil Government* (1690) LOCKE begins with the clear message that there would be no individual or social freedom if the same authority that enacts legislation also had the power to decide on the application and interpretation of that legislation (Chapter XII, §143). It is difficult to imagine a better formulation of the essence of this doctrine. LOCKE combines the traditional concept of sovereignty of the parliament with the idea of an autonomous executive to emphasise the dynamic balance of the two branches, which are only partially separated from each other. His model of the relationship between legislature and executive undoubtedly inspired the founding fathers of the American Constitution when they designed the relationship between the legislature and the President as *Chief Executive*.

Power should be a check to power

MONTESQUIEU described the English constitution as an ideal form of separation of powers, although his description did not correspond to the reality of the way in which the British monarchical system functioned at that time. In any case his analysis did lead him to make a clear argument for the principle of separation of powers. In order to prevent the misuse of political power, it is necessary to establish a system of separation of powers under which the powers exercise mutual control over each other. "*Il faut que le pouvoir arrête le pouvoir*" (*power should be a check to power*) (MONTESQUIEU, Esprit des Lois L. XI).

5.1.6 Modern Developments

5.1.6.1 The American and French Revolutions: The Rule of Law and/or the Will of the People as (the only) Fundamental Law

Whatever is not prohibited is permissible

The first modern constitutions brought the inalienable natural rights of life, liberty and property into direct relation to the state and its authority. These rights became protections against interference by the state, thereby making them rights of *freedom from* public authority: everything is legally permissible if not explicitly forbidden. With the first constitutions that were based on the entirely new concept of the social contract as the basis of modern polity, the individual ceased to be a mere object of domination. For the first time it was acknowledged that the individual as part of the sovereign people can participate in creating the rules and institutions by which he is to be governed. Accordingly, all individuals are to be seen as equal and autonomous rational human beings vested with rights and duties. The principle of formal equality thereby ultimately reduces justice to the equal distribution of rights.

Human rights and government by consent

In the American *Declaration of Independence* (1776) and in the first Bill of Rights (the first ten amendments to the American Constitution, which are known as 'the Bill of Rights'), as well as in the French *Declaration of the Rights of Man and Citizen* (1789), the expression of universal natural rights as negative liberties and political freedoms was the means by which the idea of popular sovereignty was related to natural rights and the consent of the governed.

The American and French revolutions thus essentially had an identical revolutionary goal: to turn natural rights into positive legal rights and to establish democratic government. In both cases the constitution was the functional document that was supposed to realise this revolutionary goal. A written constitution was regarded as an act by means of which procedural prerequisites for arriving at a rational, democratically grounded consensus on political authority could be expressly laid down and given the force of positive law.

State as moderator – state as engine

It is here that the common features of the two great modern revolutions basically end. The differences, attributable to the very different historical backgrounds of the respective revolutions – to which we have already referred – revolve primarily around fundamentally different understandings of the nature and the role of the state and its relation to civil society. According to the American understanding the role of the state is limited to finding a balance between the various forces within society. The state is ultimately a moderator between the existing social powers. According to the French view on the other hand, the state serves the function of changing society, that is, of transforming the old feudal society into a modern civilian society. From these different points of view there derive two different concepts in relation to:

1. The underlying principles of democracy through which popular sovereignty is to be realised and the form of government legitimised; and
2. The nature of constitutionally entrenched fundamental rights and the function of the constitution in relation to these fundamental rights.

Consequently there developed different conceptions of the relationship between the constitution and democratically based sovereignty.

5.1.6.2 USA

Fundamental rights versus colonial authority

The 'revolutionary act' of the American colonies was aimed at removing obstacles (British colonial rule) to the realisation of pre-existing basic human rights and providing the basis and conditions for the settlers to constitute their own independent state. In other words, the revolutionary conditions in America meant that America was predestined to conceive of and define sovereignty as a limited form of authority.

This implied that from the very beginning democracy was seen as an instrument to achieve the realisation of the liberal concept of human rights. The principle of popular sovereignty was practised through constitutional conventions and constituent assemblies.

The goal of the constitution was to guarantee and to realise existing pre-state and pre-constitutional human rights. The existence and content of these inalienable rights should be exempt from the democratic decision-making process. Here, the direct connection to the English common law tradition is unmistakeable. One of the leading political minds of the time, THOMAS PAINE, spoke of state authority as "government *out of society*" (PAINE, p. 65–67). In other words, the society *produces* the state. A logical consequence of this idea is that the power of the state must be limited, and must be subject to the consent of the people. The sovereign constituent power of the people remains nonetheless limited by the principles of fundamental and inalienable human rights.

Private and public spheres

The separation between human rights and democracy according to American constitutionalism goes back to the clear separation between the private and public spheres, that is, between the state and (civil) society. Individual liberties are considered by LOCKE to be inalienable rights which limit the power of the state to interfere with private rights and which also act as a constraint upon the tyranny of the majority. It is only logical that liberalism sees human rights as nothing more than constitutionally negative rights with primarily negative content.

On the other hand democracy is also seen as a result and consequence of the existing constitutional rights and freedoms. The primary function of democracy from this point of view is to protect the other more fundamental rights. If one follows this line of reasoning to its logical conclusion, one has to perceive human rights as rights that legitimise the democratic authority of the state. Democracy is legitimate in so far as it protects rights by its limitation of the tyranny of the majority and in so far as it puts those rights into effect by providing the right to participate in legislative decisions that limit individual freedom.

Such theories however are only plausible if one dispenses with the notion of the sovereign as the highest authority and the supreme and sole source of law. This in turn is only conceivable if the law and supreme political authority do not share the same source of validity. This intellectual approach was and remains to this day one of the most significant differences between the Anglo-American and continental legal philosophies and conceptions of the rule of law.

5.1.6.3 France

Human rights and the transformation of society

In contrast to the American Revolution, the French Revolution had first to *produce* the conditions for the protection of human rights and for the constitution of democratic government, and therefore to abolish the arbitrary rule of absolute monarchy. Natural rights, in consequence, could be given the force of positive law only as *rights of the citizen.* An individual can be free only as a member of political community; in other words: *within the state and not against the state.* This particular historical background to the French Revolution and its influence on fundamental political and legal principles left a decisive mark on the continental European concept of the state. Within the European constitutional tradition, the state and its constitution not only guarantee rights, but also establish and create rights.

Of course the actors and philosophers of the French Revolution were also motivated by democratic constitutional ideas and theories. These ideas corresponded to their own understanding of the *État de droit* as a parallel to the rule of law.

Sovereignty of the nation

Article 16 of the *Declaration of the Rights of Man and Citizen* of 1789 contained the noteworthy normative judgement that "any society in which the guarantee of rights is not secured or separation of powers not determined has no constitution at all". Article 8 of the Constitution of 1791 provided that a revision of the Constitution would only be legitimate and legal if it was done in the manner and form prescribed by the Constitution itself. In this context it must be borne in mind that the French idea of the supremacy of the Constitution was directly related to the idea that the Constitution was an expression of the unlimited sovereignty of the people.

The French understanding of the 'nation' as the bearer of the sovereign constitution-making power was developed in order to provide a legitimate basis on which the people could be the ultimate source of both constitution-making and law-making power. EMMANUEL SIEYÈS (1748–1836) made a distinction between constituent power (*pouvoir constituant*) and constituted power (*pouvoir constitué*) and effectively secularised the divine right to create a new constitution from nothing, transferring this power from God to the people. His further (ultimately unrealised) stipulation was that there should be provision for a 'constitutional jury' to examine complaints brought by citizens in relation to laws or actions that allegedly violated the Constitution. Here SIEYÉS evinced the common, deeply rooted, mistrust of the traditional judicial power. The revolution mistrusted the royal courts that had been established prior to the Revolution, and this remains a significant feature of the French concept of the rule of law.

One of the primary functions of the constitution is to provide the force of positive law to the people's absolute sovereign constitution-making power. The sovereign will of the people cannot be lawfully limited, but rather is the source and basis of all constitutional law. The constitution gives positive legal form to the sovereign will but cannot influence its content, since there is no fundamental law higher than the will of the people.

The absolute and unlimited people's sovereignty can be exercised only by the people and is non-transferable. This means that a system of separation of powers that entailed a division of sovereignty would be neither conceivable nor permissible.

The notion that the law flows from the people as the highest source of legal authority is clearly expressed in the idea of the French nation: "What is a Nation? A body of associates, living under a common law, and represented by the same legislature" (SIEYÈS, *What is the Third Estate?*, 1789). This is consistent with ROUSSEAU'S well-known radical democratic idea of the general will (*volonté générale*) as the ultimate source of law and justice.

Rule of law(s)

Given the historical background and theoretical foundations, it is easy to understand why the rule of law doctrine in France was oriented more towards a strict principle of legality than was the corresponding English doctrine. The rule of law was in France originally understood as the *rule of the laws passed by the sovereign Assemblée Nationale.* The concept of *État de droit* did not arise until after the First World War. The progression to the notion of pre- or supra-state limits on the law and law-making authority first came about under the influence of more recent political and constitutional theories, which grapple with the questions of the extent to which there exist general international values and standards and the extent to which human rights are supranational rights which stand above the state and to which all states are subject.

Rule of law versus volonté générale

The various understandings of the rule of law all underscore the necessity of a common concept of constitutional democracy as the basis of the legitimacy of constitutional justice. Judges must have the authority to hold public authorities, including elected representatives, to account for unconstitutional actions and to compel them to uphold fundamental rights and freedoms. This hardly accords with the idea of democracy as developed by Jean-Jacques ROUSSEAU. But nor does the idea of constitutional jurisdiction and judicial review expressly contradict ROUSSEAU'S concept. The renewed form of democracy requires the constitutionality of legislation, because according to today's understanding it is only then that democracy can be truly legitimate.

5.1.6.4 The German Concept of Rechtsstaat (State Rule Through Law)

The idea of a minimal state

Although Germany shares with France the same continental law tradition, and in spite of the fact that 19th Century liberal theorists were very strongly influenced by the ideas of the French Revolution, the concept of the *Rechtsstaat* remained a key concept of German constitutional theory and one that reflected the traditional German understanding of the state. At any rate, especially in its initial phases, the concept was significantly inspired also by the English rule of law. Common to all three (English, French, German) concepts is that the rule of law as a liberal idea envisages a minimal state.

Law and state are not autonomous

The German word '*Rechtsstaat*' reveals in itself the far-reaching differences and the critical point of departure between the doctrinal foundations of the rule of law and the *Rechtsstaat*. The term '*Rechtsstaat*' combines the words '*Recht*' (law) and '*Staat*' (state) into one entity; the two inherently belong together and are inextricably linked. In contrast, the Anglo-American tradition of the rule of law is a concept autonomously developed through the common law system, and does not postulate and inherent connection between the state and the law, but is as a concept separable from and independent of the state.

Prussia: the King as representative of the state

The term '*Rechtsstaat*' and the ideas it encapsulated were first developed in the political theory of the first half of the 19th Century. This era in Germany was very different indeed to that in England, which had already had a constitutional monarchy for more than a century – a form of authority limited by the rule of law. The constitutional and parliamentary debates in England were by this stage focussed on electoral reforms to enlarge the democratic franchise. On the European continent on the other hand, the 'enlightened absolutism' of the Prussian monarchy was at its peak. It was uncontested that the King as sovereign represented the state *vis á vis* the subjects (not citizens). Neither the political fact of the absolute power of the state nor its legality were questioned.

'Rechtsstaats' principle as a principle of legality

In the early phase of modern German constitutional history, the concept of the *Rechtsstaat* was exclusively focused on the exercise of legal control over the administration. The *Rechtsstaats* concept was tied to legal and state positivism, which entailed a strict separation between the political and the legal. It therefore emphasised formal legality, and was normatively neutral in relation to any particular form of government. The idea of connecting the concept of the *Rechtsstaat* with popular sovereignty and the democratic form of government was not yet established.

Accordingly, even the liberal political thinkers of the time adopted this formalistic and positivist concept of the *Rechtsstaat*. The philosophical contribution of IMMANUEL KANT (1724–1804), which proposed a substantive and material concept of Rechtsstaat as a precondition for the very existence of the state, did not have a major influence on German political and constitutional thinking. As a convinced liberal (although with certain conservative views), KANT demanded that the strict separation between the public and private spheres be legally guaranteed, and emphasised the importance of mixed government as a means of ensuring checks and balances.

Robert von Mohl

We must also not overlook the fact that initially the *Rechtsstaat* concept was more akin to the Anglo-American idea of the rule of law than it was at the end of the 19th Century, when the formal positivist concept of the *Rechtsstaat* reached its climax. The theory of the *Rechtsstaat* emerged in Hannover, which, as a result of its royal connections with England after the Glorious Revolution of 1689, was influenced by English political and legal tradition more so than the rest of Germany. One of the founders of the *Rechtsstaat* concept, ROBERT VON MOHL (1799–1875), had studied the American constitutional system and was influenced by Anglo-American constitutionalism. MOHL placed the substantive principle of individual liberty at the centre of the concept of the *Rechtsstaat*. Nonetheless, MOHL accepted that liberty could be limited by special rights of state authorities and was strongly opposed to any form of the separation of powers.

Positivism

Largely as a result of the failure of the revolution of 1848, in Germany the substantive content of the *Rechtsstaat* principle was gradually lost (see FRANZ NEUMANN). The main liberal values and in particular human rights and their constitutional protection were sacrificed to the principle of legality. Infringements of human rights were permissible provided that they were set in accordance with the positive law and thus complied with the principle of legality. Individual freedoms were essentially at the mercy of the executive, which was controlled by the parliament only to a limited extent.

At the end of the 19th Century FRANZ JULIUS STAHL provided what remains the best-known definition of the *Rechtsstaat* as a negative, purely formal concept that strictly separates the legal structure of the state from its political structure. According to this definition, the concept of the *Rechtsstaat* is limited to legal form and has no bearing on the content or aims of the state. The *Rechtsstaat* merely addresses the legal form needed to enact a given content and a given state objective, whatever they may be. The protection of human rights has no place as part of the concept of *Rechtsstaat* so defined.

Weimar: economic and social goals

The Weimar Republic of 1919 led to a renaissance of the concept of the *Rechtsstaat*, and to the development of a substantive normative content to the concept. The Social-democratic constitutional doctrine during the Weimar era introduced a new constitutional concept, that of *institutional guarantees.* In contrast to the subjective rights of the individual, institutional guarantees were supposed to provide a constitutional means to achieve particular social goals. The entailed a new role for the modern state: the constitution should identify particular fields of action that are to be promoted and legally protected by the state and in which the state will work towards the achievement of specific social goals. (ULRICH K. PREUSS, *Constitutional Aspects of the Making of Democracy in the Post Communist societies of East Europe*, Zentrum für Europäische Rechtspolitik, Bremen 1993, p. 15).

Thus the door to a new constitutional paradigm was opened. The idea that the state should set and pursue particular social and economic goals threw two of the major pillars of the liberal *Rechtsstaats* concept into question: the first is the notion that social harmony results from the unimpeded function of the free market and that human rights place negative limits on public power; and the other relates to the separation/opposition of state and society (society understood as the simple aggregation of separate individuals) based on the understanding that the principal threat to individual autonomy is the state.

Rechtsstaat with normative content

Herman Heller (1891–1933) re-enforced the normative constitutional concept of the Rechtsstaat by arguing that freedom is only possible when the social conditions for liberty, equality, and the secure protection of the law have been secured by the state. In 1930, Heller wrote that the *Rechtsstaat* cannot exist without a consensus of all its citizens, and such a consensus can be reached only by means of social democracy, which must be the basis of the "*sozialer Rechtsstaat*" (welfare state rule through law) (H. Heller, p. 443 ff).

After World War II the substantive concept of the *Rechtsstaat* was further developed by the Federal Constitutional Court of Germany. In some of its early decisions the Court invoked natural law as a 'supra-constitutional' principle to which positive law must be subject. Undoubtedly these decisions were also influenced by the German Basic Law, which expressly provides that the core of fundamental rights cannot be infringed by the constitution and that if the state should seek to disturb or overturn the basic democratic order, resistance against the state is constitutionally permissible.

5.1.7 Conclusions

Democracy and rule of law

The origins, trends and limits of liberalism and its relation to democracy have been central to the development of the rule of law. The far-reaching impact that the understanding of the nature and the role of state and law has for the relationship between democracy and the rule of law is clear. This impact can be summarised in the following question: Does the basic value of the inviolability of human rights which underlies the modern constitution, also limit and control the democratic sovereign? Or is it the other way around – that the democratic state determines the content of human rights? To put the question more provocatively: Who is to resolve a conflict between the legal and the political sovereign?

The formal versus the substantive 'Rechtsstaat'

The key issue at stake here relates to the very nature of a given form of government and its basic political underpinnings. In other words: Is the rule of law limited to the formal requirement that political decisions be made and publicised in a prescribed legal form, or does the rule of law or '*Rechtsstaat*' also necessitate effective limits and controls on the holders of political power?

What in the field of human rights can be universalised?

Each of these open issues could effectively be grouped under the umbrella of human rights. The idea that human rights are inalienable and that they are immanent to the concept of the rule of law itself leaves open a number of fundamental questions that still need to be addressed at the level of international law and the international community. One such example is the key question, who has the legitimacy to decide over the content and abrogation of 'universal' human rights? The answer to this question is not merely of theoretical relevance, but rather in view of the place of the contemporary nation-state and the ongoing supra-national processes of globalisation it is of significant practical importance.

What is the content and meaning of the 'universal' values of life, liberty and dignity? Can universal rights be derived from these values that must therefore be observed by all states and all cultures, across all generations past, present and future? The problem of global actors also requires explanation: who has the right and the legitimacy to define what is universal and to determine who and which generation is in particular cases the legitimate 'universaliser'? On what basis can unilateral or multilateral 'humanitarian interventions' be justified?

How is the basic liberal underpinning of the rule of law to be interpreted within a multicultural context? Which fundamental rights remains 'universal' in a multicultural society, and how should such society address demands that cultural diversity be accommodated? These questions can become explosive if diversity and fragmentation cannot be peacefully addressed through the political process. The democratic integration of the multicultural society as a new type of incorporative society and as a structural pre-condition for the viability of human rights policy, is yet to be achieved.

5.2 Development of the Rule of Law in the Different Legal Systems

5.2.1 Introduction

Growth in the scope of administrative powers

The powers of the state and administration have greatly expanded in the 20th Century in all states. This expansion of powers is particularly evident the increasing and ever more complex activity of the administration. The power of the state is today largely manifested as the power of the administration. In their daily lives, people are increasingly dependent upon and affected by the decisions of an anonymous bureaucracy. The administration guides, both directly and indirectly, the daily life of the citizens. Thus, if one wishes today to inquire into the rule of law and the *Rechtsstaat*, one needs to know how the power of the administration and its servants is or can be limited.

In order to limit the powers of the administration various states have developed different mechanisms designed to strengthen the rule of law, for example by improving access to justice, enhancing judicial independence and expanding the jurisdiction of the courts. Such mechanisms aim at strengthening the protection of citizens against misuse of powers by the administration.

What questions have to be asked?

If one wants to know how the principle of the rule of law is concretely exhibited within administrative law, one must find answers to the following questions:

1. What are the basic fundaments of law and justice?
2. What kind of courts protect citizens against arbitrary acts or decisions by the executive?
3. What causes of action are available to individuals in order access the courts in matters of unlawful or erroneous exercise of administrative powers?
4. What jurisdiction do the courts have to protect individuals against misuse of powers by the administration and what remedies can they grant?
5. What are the criteria or standards on which the courts base their decisions?
6. What are the rights and obligations of the parties within the judicial process?

5.2.2 *What are the Foundations of Law and Justice?*

Christian individualistic conception of man

The European legal systems are marked by the Christian-individualistic conception of man. According to the Christian doctrine man is as an individual answerable to God, and must therefore also be an individual bearer of rights and obligations. Man is not embedded within the family or the tribe as for example in Japanese Shintoism. He is not a negligible part of the professional or social estate as in Confucianism, and he is not expected to find happiness within asceticism and in renunciation of his individualism as for example in Buddhism. Indeed, there is no other religion that places so much emphasis on the importance of the individual as does Christianity. Only within Christianity does man stand as an equal and individual person before God, and have to account to God for his individual actions.

Notwithstanding this common thread in all European legal cultures, the European legal systems have split – at least since the French Revolution – into two very different legal systems.

Hierarchy and authority – collegiality and reason

The legal system on the European continent was strongly influenced by the hierarchical thinking of canonical law. According to the basic idea of the Christian Church the higher up in the hierarchy someone is, the closer they are to God and thus to truth and justice. In the Middle Ages this reasoning resulted in the administration (as servant of the King) being accorded a privileged and authoritarian rank in the social and legal hierarchy, above the common people. After the French Revolution the divine authority of the King was replaced by the popular authority of the head of state, or by the '*volonté générale*', and thus the elevated status of the administration remained. Accordingly the jurisdiction of courts over the administration must be limited and it must respect the status and authority of civil servants. Courts are asked only to apply the law as determined by the absolute authority of the legislature, not to develop their own law.

Common law: citizens as partners of the administration

On the other hand the common law system finds its original roots in medieval England and in particular in the 17th Century marked by the Glorious Revolution and JOHN LOCKE. The Aristocracy was able to establish itself, after the Long Parliament and the Glorious Revolution, as a partner to the King. The Commons and the Lords were essentially a club of major landowners who administered their estates in common. In addition to Parliament which enacted the statutes, the courts retained their case-by-case law-making role. The land-owning majority of the members sitting in Parliament could not simply disregard the legitimate interests of individual members of the minority. The significant role of the courts in protecting legal rights and developing the common law and equity meant that the legislature's expression of the public interest could not be elevated as it was in France to the status of a sacred *volonté générale* that was inherently true, just and unaccountable.

The judge as moderator

In the development of the common law system, the judge had no hierarchical position over the parties. He was rather a 'moderator' who stood between the parties and reached a decision based on relevant precedents. The judge had to ensure a fair trial, equal treatment of the parties before the law and equality of arms. According to the common law system, a just decision depends upon a fair procedure, rather than necessarily upon a good law.

Whoever is right, wins – versus – whoever wins is right

According to the continental European understanding of the law those who are legally 'in the right' should win the case. According to the common law understanding those who win the case are in the right. In the latter case, fair procedural rules that ensure the equality of arms between the parties are of particularly great importance.

In the common law world, the importance of the adversary procedure, the position of the parties (who determine the relevant facts and legal arguments that are to be presented) and the weak authority of the judge with regard to substance reflect a system based on a realistic image of the human being. The system recognises that no judge, civil servant or party is infallible, and that notwithstanding this fallibility the law must seek to ensure that the best possible result is reached.

Hierarchy of the world order

The countries of the European continent with civil law systems adapted the concept of hierarchical authority developed during monarchical absolutism, placing the state governed by the majority of the people at the top of the hierarchy (rather than the crown). ROUSSEAU'S *volonté générale* and HEGEL'S theory of the state as the peak of human development served as the philosophical underpinning. This artificial elevation of the state over the individual, so foreign to the common law way of thinking, had a decisive influence on the administrative law of civil law countries.

Institutions must be designed for fallible humans, not angels

The foundations of public law in common law countries are quite different. The common law does not accord a privileged or superior status to the state nor to the public interest. It is rather based on the idea that all humans including leaders and judges are fallible, and that good institutions must therefore be capable of functioning effectively and fairly with this reality in mind. If one proceeds from this supposition, then the rules of procedure and procedural rights assume considerable importance. Furthermore, the laws enacted by the majority of the democratically elected parliament are not the sole source of development of the law. The cumulative wisdom of generations reflected in the precedents of the common law has an important place alongside enacted legislation. Public office and the civil servants who are applying the laws and making administrative decisions on behalf of the executive therefore do not have the same status and prestige in the common law system as they do within the civil law system.

5.2.3 Common Law – Civil Law

Pro-active state concept

Civil law legal systems are marked by a pro-active concept of the state. According to this concept, state authorities and institutions have a legitimate social engineering function: they are responsible for setting and achieving certain political and social goals within the society. Countries of the common law tradition on the other hand are content to consider their government as a mere arbiter between various competing social interests. It is the task of government and the administration to maintain the balance among the different social forces, to prevent conflicts, and to provide for a just resolution of conflicts when they arise.

Different concepts of judiciary

These different understandings of the state can be explained in part by the different development of the legal and judicial systems over a period of centuries. Exponents of the common law system see the judge primarily as an independent arbitrator, who has to solve conflicts and to find the just settlement between the parties. For those within the civil law system however, the judge is an extension of the law itself, that is, a representative of the state embedded within the hierarchy of the legal system. The task of the judge within the state hierarchy is to find justice and to impose the law as it applies to the parties before the court.

Thus, the judge has to play a much more active part in court proceedings of all kinds in the civil law system, than does his/her common law counterpart who is simply an impartial arbiter. In continental European legal systems, the parties are subordinate to the judge. The judge in criminal and administrative matters must determine the facts of the case, using the inquisitorial procedure whereby the judge or civil servant can make their own inquiries into the facts. In common law systems on the other hand, the judge merely assumes a coordinating function between the disputing parties. The law determines which party will bear the burden of proof, and what the standard of proof required will be. The questions then arise of who will bear the risk of insufficient evidence and whether a certain evidentiary test must be satisfied, such the 'arbitrary and capricious test' or the 'substantial evidence test'.

In common law systems the judge has less power with regard to the fact-finding of the parties. However, compared to a continental judge, the common law judge has greater authority as an impartial arbiter and greater power to ensure procedural fairness and equality between the parties.

Influence of canonical law

These differences in the judicial function can be traced back to the fact that on the European continent in the 12th Century, the canonical law taught at the universities began to assume increasing importance. The law was no longer the law of the people, but rather the law of a scholarly elite hierarchically separated from the people. The judges representing the crown and the feudal hierarchy had to employ dogmatic, scientific analyses to find and apply the law for the parties seeking justice in their courts. Jurisprudence, interpretation of law and in particular the practice of the judiciary could therefore no longer be carried out by laymen but only by professionals and experts in the field of legal science.

Legal science and jurisprudence had to perform a number of functions. They had to systematise the law, summarise and analyse it, identify the relevant law applicable to a particular case, and then ultimately enable the determination of the relevant facts and the making of a decision based on the law.

Hierarchy of instances

The new development of a hierarchy of several instances in which lower instance decisions could be reviewed corresponded to this new hierarchical thinking. The more important – that is, the higher and closer to the crown - the experts and tribunals were, the more authoritative was their decision. The verdict or decision was not the result of a dispute argued before a jury but a scientific application of the law to a concrete case. The law existed independently of the facts.

Authority of the facts

Civil law judges had not only to find the law that was to be applied to the facts, they had also to find the facts via an inquisitorial procedure. By way of contrast, in England the law remained to a great extent linked to the jurors chosen from the common people. Jurors, with the help of the judge, had to decide on the facts presented by the parties through an adversarial procedure, and the court then had to find just and relevant criteria according to which the case could be determined. Law and facts were much more closely interconnected than in the European legal thinking, where law was given and the facts had to be found by the judge.

Ideal procedure

This in turn led in the common law countries to the procedure for establishing the facts being given much more weight and value than the procedural rules on the European continent. For this reason in most common law proceedings the adversary system is used, whereby the parties are responsible for presenting (contradictory versions of) the facts. The rationale behind the adversary system is that a process whereby the parties seek to prove their contested versions of the facts provides the optimal likelihood of arriving at the truth. Within the civil law inquisitorial system, the judge and the administration are entrusted with the power and obligation to search for and establish the facts.

The lengthy and often costly adversarial procedure for the establishment of facts has led to the removal of the fact-finding function from the courts in many administrative matters. Typically for administrative law matters in common law jurisdictions, the facts of a dispute are determined by administrative tribunals, which are required to follow rules of procedural fairness and evidentiary rules relating to the burden and standard of proof. The common law courts generally consider only questions of law in such matters, the facts having been argued and settled at the tribunal stage.

The right to be 'heard'

It is revealing that with regard to the basic entitlement to a fair 'hearing', in civil law countries the principle is reduced to the right of the parties to submit written statements. In contrast, in the common law countries the principle of natural justice or due process is only satisfied if parties are heard in an oral procedure before an independent judge. In the USA administrative decisions (adjudicatory acts) with similar status to court judgments can be made in a trial procedure in which the facts are established according to the same adversary system practised in the courts.

Administrative law: Execution of legislation

Administrative law in civil law countries serves primarily to implement the public interest of the society determined by the legislature (MIRJIAN R. DAMASKA). The judicial review of administrative actions fulfils two different functions in these countries: On one side it has to ensure that the public interest and the will of the democratic legislature are properly realised; On the other hand it must, as in the courts of common law countries, protect the rights and interests of individuals against the state and the administration.

Lack of distinct administrative law branch of common law

Administrative law as a special and distinct branch of the law is practically non-existent in common law countries (although in some common law countries in recent decades there has been a growth in legislation dealing specifically with administrative law). The state apparatus of those countries does not enjoy privileged status over individuals as does the administration of civil law countries. The administration is charged with running the bureaucratic apparatus and securing public order. It derives its powers and duties from legislation. If a civil servant acts beyond his/her legal authority he/she can be held legally accountable just as any other private person acting illegally. The court which has to decide on the legality of administrative acts or omissions has to determine whether the administration acted outside or in breach of its legislative powers and responsibilities.

Status of legislation

However legislation has a different meaning for the judge in common law tradition than it does for judges in civil law systems. As for the American courts the constitution is part of the highest applicable law of the land, American judges have much greater scope when reviewing administrative activities to take into account basic constitutional principles of fairness and justice. Of course, they must also consider and apply relevant legislation in order to reach a decision. But written legislation does not have the same value as on the continent, where the role of the continental European judge is limited to determining whether the administrative act was legislatively authorised. In common law jurisdictions, in addition to legislation, the recognised principles and rules of the 'rule of law' which limit the discretion of the administration have to be taken into account.

Access to justice

For citizens who wish to bring an action against the administration, access to the court and the availability of legal remedies are essential starting points. Recognition of this fact has led over the course of history in common law countries to great importance being placed on the development of formal writs and remedies. Causes of action and corresponding legal remedies have been given almost the same importance in the common law tradition as the continental legal systems have given to fundamental rights. Thus, it may be understandable that scholars of common law countries see the '*Rechtsstaat*' principle of civil law countries that do not have prerogative writs as having major drawbacks. On the other hand civil law scholars regard a state without a written constitution such as New Zealand as fundamentally suspect.

5.2.3.1 Common Law

Ruled by law not by men

As already mentioned the common law builds upon the basic principle that men should not be ruled by men but by law. Law is not reduced merely to the positive legal rules enacted by the legislature. All values that are authoritative for the realisation of justice through legal institutions, including the precedents and principles that judges are to follow in reaching decisions, also form part of the legal system.

Private law – public law

Furthermore, contrary to the continental European law, there is no clear separation between private and public law, as the ordinary common law courts have jurisdiction to hear disputes between private persons as well as complaints of private individuals against the public administration.

5.2.3.2 Continental European Law

French Revolution

Legal systems of the countries on the continent have their philosophical roots in the French Revolution. According to the theories of the French Revolution, the national Parliament (*Assemblée Nationale*) is the bearer of absolute sovereignty, including law-making and constitution-making power. The law-maker is sovereign and is therefore the original and exclusive source of law and justice. It determines and defines the *volonté générale*. The French Revolution not only centralised the French territory, but also the entire legal system. From the time of the Revolution onwards, the only law was that which was enacted by the National Assembly. The task of the judge was to apply the positive law made by the legislature, and to use the abstract legislative norms to deduce a conclusion in each concrete case. The '*Rechtsstaat*' according to this understanding, is realised to the extent that all positive rules enacted by the legislature are correctly applied in each concrete case.

The State as an institution for social engineering

Napoleon regarded the state as an instrument with which to change the hierarchical feudal society into a modern society of individual citizens enjoying equal rights. In order to achieve this goal he needed a strong and independent executive that was able to implement the will of the legislature in society. He was of the opinion that this difficult task could only be achieved if the administration became independent from the traditional jurisdiction of the ordinary courts. The conservative judges had to be prevented from interfering with or exercising control over administrative acts and decisions. Thus, Napoleon decided to create a new field of law that was exclusively applicable to the administration and excluded from the jurisdiction and control of the ordinary courts. The immunity of the executive and its administration from the traditional court jurisdiction was the principal justification for the newly created public law. From this point on in France, it was the public law which regulated all legal relations between the state and private persons.

Ideological separation between public and private law

The result of this separation was that all matters relating to the administration were regulated and controlled only by the public law. The traditional courts with private law jurisdiction no longer had the authority to deal with legal issues in which the public administration was involved. The public law was withdrawn from their jurisdiction. Disputes between private individuals and the administration were controlled exclusively by the public law. Neither the executive nor the administration had any legal responsibility in terms of the jurisdiction of the classical traditional courts. In order to give individuals some legal protection against misuse of public power by the administration, the public law had to provide for certain instruments and remedies with which private individuals could seek to hold the administration legally accountable.

Since the French Revolution, there has been a continuous battle between democracy and the state administration with regard to the strengthening and expansion of the jurisdiction of the administrative courts. While in common law countries the traditional courts were able to expand their jurisdiction with regard to the administration through the development of case law and through the creation of new writs by the Lord Chancellor, on the continent only the legislature had the authority to expand the jurisdiction of the administrative courts by new or amended statutory law. The 19th and 20th Centuries were marked by this permanent struggle for better legal protection of private individuals against the administration on one hand, and the need of the administration to have the necessary powers to fulfil its legal functions on the other hand. The outcome in civil law countries was that the administrative courts that were created by the continental legislatures were vested with fairly limited jurisdiction only to quash administrative decisions, but had no power to enforce decisions by holding servants of the administration in contempt of court.

5.2.4 *Principles of Jurisdiction over Administrative Cases*

5.2.4.1 Conception

Administrative courts with jurisdiction over public law statutes

Administrative courts have special jurisdiction to hear complaints brought by private individuals against the administration. In a special legal procedure, the court can review the legality of the actions of the administration based on the rules of public law.

This kind of jurisdiction first developed on the European continent towards the end of the 19th Century, but became more significant and established in the 20th Century after World War II. Such administrative law jurisdiction is only possible if the following conditions are fulfilled:

1. There is a special public law that regulates decisions and actions of the executive and the administration.
2. This public law empowers the administration to unilaterally establish legal rights and obligations for individuals, and thereby submits citizens to the authority of the state and to the public interest enforceable by the state.
3. It is recognised that although the executive and the administration enjoy certain privileges of office, they can make mistakes and therefore their decisions must be capable of review by other institutions.
4. The rights of private individuals, which must be protected against the administration and the executive, are recognised.
5. There is a conviction that a judicial procedure involving two more or less equal parties provides the optimal conditions for accurate fact-finding and a just decision.

'Immunity' of the administration

With the establishment of public law, separate and independent from the private law, a new and autonomous legal system was created. With this new law, the administration could grant rights to or impose obligations on individuals by way of 'administrative acts'. The decisions of the administration became enforceable in a manner analogous to judicial verdicts issued by a court. The administrative institutions such as police were required to enforce the decisions.

The new public law laid the foundation for the legitimacy of the modern authoritarian state. The authorities, that is, the executive and the administration, embodied the public interest or general will in the sense of ROUSSEAU'S *volonté générale*. As the *volonté générale* could not be questioned or reviewed, there could be no legal proceeding that questioned the authority of the executive. The public law relieved the executive and the administration of accountability to the ordinary courts.

Fallible administration?

It was only gradually recognised that the executive branch including the administration can make mistakes, and that it is therefore in the interests of the legislature to submit the application of and compliance with its statutes by the administration to the jurisdiction of the courts. This insight enabled the gradual development of the jurisdiction and powers of administrative courts. However, the jurisdiction and powers of administrative courts are still considerably limited even today. They can only review administrative acts, and those acts can only be quashed in respect of the future, not with retrospective effect (*ex nunc* and not *ex tunc*). Moreover, erroneous administrative acts that are not challenged within the prescribed deadline will be deemed to be healed of their faults, because upon the expiry of the deadline the acts become final and valid administrative acts that are not open to question. Thus, the institutions required to enforce administrative acts must enforce even erroneous acts if they have become valid through the passage of time.

Immunity of the state?

Public law assumes that the administration and the executive are superior to individuals and citizens, and that those who work for the state as the holders of public office require special protection in relation to the carrying out of their public functions.

More pragmatic is the Anglo Saxon concept. Of course in England, the Crown also enjoys immunity from legal suit. However, the Crown is neither above the law nor is it subject to a specific public law excluded from traditional court jurisdiction. It is because the judge is a servant of the Crown and makes decisions in the name of the Crown that the Crown cannot be party to a civil dispute. As long as servants of the Crown act within their lawful authority, they cannot be called to account for their actions before a court. Only when they act beyond their powers (*ultra vires*) are they subject to the ordinary jurisdiction of the courts. The assessment of whether civil servants have acted within their powers (*intra vires*) or beyond their powers (*ultra vires*) is part of the traditional jurisdiction of the courts. Actions that are found to be *ultra vires* cannot be remedied nor can they be quashed in respect of future application (ex nunc). As they were always beyond the law, they are deemed never to have had any legal validity.

In the *Crown Proceedings Act* of 1947, the British Parliament decided that in tort cases where parties require financial compensation for damages caused by the administration, a writ against the state may be permitted and thus the courts can require the state to pay damages for unlawful damage or injury caused by its servants.

Principle of legality

The tremendous expansion of the administration over the last century has many different reasons and causes: The separation of government from the royal prerogatives empowered the legislature, but also expanded the power of the administration; the welfare state necessitated the creation of new agencies with vague and discretionary powers; and people's need for security within a society threatened by new and unforeseen dangers empowered the state with additional means to control the individual. As a result of this increasing responsibility of state administration it became necessary to significantly extend the scope of court jurisdiction over administrative actions. However, this development progressed rather differently in England than it did on the European continent.

Development of the continental European administrative law

According to the British tradition, a minister, even in his capacity as a member of government, was subject to the common law and could therefore be brought before a court. However, the continental European legislatures accorded ministers and civil servants a privileged status over ordinary people under the public law, which provided them with general immunity. This immunity protected ministers and civil servants from criminal charges and from civil suit in most circumstances. With regard to their public activities they have no personal responsibility for their measures and decisions; if they violate the law legal action can be brought against the office but not the office holder.

It was not until the end of the 19th Century that administrative law jurisdiction began to develop, led by the French Conseil d'Etat. This was a significant development for public law and included remedies for complaints against the administration for action beyond discretionary power.

Control of administration

There are many different ways in which control over the administration can be designed and many different manners in which such control can be carried out. However, in order to limit administrative power effectively, some form of judicial control is essential. The extent of the jurisdiction of an independent judiciary over the administration reveals the degree of tension between a state based on partnership on one side and the authoritarian state on the other, thereby making clear that the legal conceptions of civil law and common law are ultimately based on different understandings of human nature. In the civil law system, civil servants appointed by and working on behalf of the state have a higher status and legitimacy than ordinary citizens, because they are believed to act in the interest of the public or in the interest of the *volonté générale*. However, as the two systems have begun to merge, these fundamental differences are gradually diminishing.

Privilege of the executive

States that have a separate and independent administrative court system responsible for applying the public law assume that the state and the executive must be equipped with their own public law in order to implement their legislative tasks and goals. This law privileges the executive, as it empowers the executive and its administration to enact decisions that have similar force to a judicial decision. States that do not have a separate field of public law, such as common law states, do not enjoy special privileges *vis á vis* the courts – besides the immunity of the Crown. These states are 'partners' of the citizens, and citizens can challenge the validity of acts and omissions of the state administration before the ordinary courts.

Democracy

The concept of democracy is based on an individualistic view of man (*one man, one vote, one value*). Accordingly, the individual as a member of the nation shares in sovereignty and can, as part of the majority, create new law, modify it, abolish it and change it. The French Revolution transferred to the legislature (as the body representing the nation, giving expression to the *volonté générale*) the exclusive power to create new law. The second and the third branches of government were charged with enforcing and implementing the law enacted by the legislature. Courts were no longer able find their own law based on reason and traditional, historical and collective wisdom. The French Revolution was a significant turning point for the development of continental European administrative law.

Legal protection of the individual and the will of the legislature

Within this system, the courts and their jurisdiction do not play a role in controlling the administration. A limited form of control of the administration developed in France through the Conseil d'Etat, but only as a quasi-executive (non-judicial) body and only gradually.

In cases of complaints by citizens against the administration and the executive, the Conseil d'Etat primarily looked into the question of whether the government and the administration had correctly implemented the will of the legislature. It was only very slowly that administrative law jurisdiction became an element of the legal protection of individual rights. The need for proper legal protection of the individual with regard to administrative misuses of power was only addressed as part of the control of the public interest and the correctness of the implementation of the law. This was particularly true for French and Swiss administrative law, less so for the development of German administrative law.

The principle of legality and the idea that the administration can only impose obligations on the individual based on a clear statute, serve primarily a democratic function. The administrative judge must ensure that the administration complies with the laws and that it only interferes with the rights of citizens when it has been so empowered by the majority – that is, by the legislature.

Protection of pre-constitutional rights in the common law tradition

Contrary to the continental law, the legislature in the common law world never completely displaced the judge as a law maker. The Parliament, at least in the UK, enjoys absolute sovereignty. However, for matters in relation to which no statute has been enacted, it is the role of the judge to apply and develop the common law. The court is not responsible for examining whether the administration or the executive has generally implemented the statute correctly according to the public interest. It has only to assess the plaintiff's writ and examine whether the administration has acted *ultra vires* and thereby violated the rights of the individual. The individual is a bearer of pre-constitutional rights which can only be limited or reduced by the Parliament and therefore have to be protected by the courts against the executive and its administration. Under the American Constitution, which largely adopted JOHN LOCKE's philosophy of inalienable rights, the judge has to protect individual rights not only against misuse of administrative power, but moreover against infringement by the majority of the legislature. The individual is, independent from the will of the majority, the bearer of pre-constitutional rights. The fundamental rights and freedoms of the American people are not granted by the grace of the legislature or the constitution maker, but rather precede the Constitution.

Administrative courts and 'état légal'

The specialised administrative judiciary finds itself in a conflicting relationship with the principle of democracy. On one hand, the jurisdiction of the administrative courts facilitates the proper implementation of democratically adopted legislation and thus the realisation of the democratic 'will' of the legislature. On the other hand, it limits the space or freedom of the executive and the administration to realise the political will of the majority (*volonté générale*) and to carry out this task with the minimum necessary control mechanisms. In this sense, the administrative judiciary fulfils a similar function to judicial review of legislation by a constitutional court. The judicial control of the constitution protects the minority against the power of the majority-controlled legislature. Judicial control of the administration protects citizens against the misuse of powers by the all-powerful administration. Ultimately the administrative courts ensure, via the principle of legality, that the rights of citizens can be limited and legal obligations imposed only where expressly and validly provided for by law.

Different understandings of the separation of powers

The idea of MONTESQUIEU, that freedom can only be guaranteed if the different powers or branches of the state are separated and able to hold each other in check, has led to two different concepts of the separation of powers. In the American Constitution the focus is on the functional separation of the different arms of government. For example, judicial power can be exercised only by the courts, which means that the courts cannot be restricted in the exercise of their judicial function either by the legislature or the executive. It also means that all legal disputes between the administration and citizens will ultimately have to be decided by a court. And this view of separation of powers finally leads to the consequence that adjudicative functions which are carried out by the administration can only be credibly exerted if the administration observes a procedure which is similar to a court procedure.

Thus, only courts have the right to make a final determination in legal disputes, including disputes involving the administration. Within the framework of checks and balances the judge has the right, as the only legitimate authority that can mediate and decide a legal controversy, to intervene in legislative and executive power to the extent that this is necessary for the resolution of the legal dispute.

A completely different understanding of the concept of separation of powers is found in the French legal tradition. The French concept focuses on the independence of the different branches of government from each other, regardless of their function. In other words, the focus is not on mutual checks and balances but on *separation* of powers. The functions of the three separate branches may be overlapping. Therefore the executive may exercise judicial functions and decide complaints against the administration (*ministre juge*), and in doing so its independence from the judiciary must be guaranteed. Thus, it is not the function that is independent, but the institution or the authority. For this reason the judicial branch has no authority to intervene in the executive branch or to adjudicate on the actions or decisions of the administration. Even if the administration exercises judicial power, it still belongs to the second branch of government (executive) and is there-fore not subject to the jurisdiction and control of the ordinary courts.

But in France, even within the framework of the executive branch, the independence of the administrative court (*Conseil d'Etat*) and its jurisdiction to hear complaints about the administration developed only gradually. The Conseil d'Etat has to decide on legal disputes between the administration and private individuals, and so performs a judicial function. At the same time, its decisions ensure the correct enforcement of the law and in this sense it serves the executive branch.

Even magistrates make mistakes

The different understandings of the separation of powers can be traced back to different conceptions of the human being. Those who believe that human beings are fallible even if they are selected to serve as magistrates, will have to create institutions that remain effective even with flawed human beings. For this reason, the founding fathers of the American Constitution stressed the limits of powers and the mutual checks and balances between the different branches of government. Those who believe, however, that each citizen is committed to the *volonté générale*, will place greater trust and authority in an elected magistrate and thereby ensure that the Magistrate is able to carry out his/her functions efficiently without the burden of restrictions and controls. According to a German saying, those who are given an office by God are also given the necessary intellect to carry through their responsibility ("Wem Gott ein Amt gibt, gibt er auch Verstand").

The effective protection of liberty and property according to the common law tradition is only possible by limiting the power of all institutions through a system of checks and balances among the branches of government and by guaranteeing procedural fairness, not by the written guarantee of rights.

Human rights

There are two important differences that should be highlighted between countries with common law tradition, and countries with civil law tradition in relation to human rights and the related demand for legal protection against the misuse of power. Within the civil law countries, fundamental rights are rights granted to the individual by the state and in particular by the constitution, and are generally negative freedoms to protect the individual from certain types of interference by the state. Constitutional and administrative courts will step in to protect individual rights in cases where plaintiffs can show that their subjective rights have been violated. For an Anglo-Saxon judge however, such rights are pre-constitutional. Administrative authorities can only interfere with individual freedom and property when they are expressly legislatively authorised to do so.

The second important difference is closely connected to the first: civil law countries generally focus on the guarantee of substantive rights and freedoms such as freedom of expression, association and movement. Common law countries on the other hand, focus primarily on procedural rights: they guarantee a fair hearing before an independent judge in order to protect unlawful interference with property rights or constitutional liberties. The *procedure* is considered to provide for even more effective protection of property rights and other freedoms than does the substantive constitutional law. This approach reflects a view of human nature that credits the judge with the ability to find justice after according the parties a fair hearing in a fair adversarial procedure, without having to rely on constitutional rights, whereas in civil law countries the judge is bound to the will of the constitution maker and has much less freedom in applying constitutional provisions to a concrete case.

Secularisation of the state

The Christian conception of the world, marked by the idea that human beings have to serve two masters – namely, God and the Emperor – laid the foundation for the separation of spiritual and secular authority. Only based on this idea was it possible to transform the godly Kings who ruled by divine right into Kings who ruled by the grace of the people, and thereby to secularise state authority. And of course, a state administration dependent on secular legitimacy can more readily be subject to judicial control than a state authority legitimated by the grace of God that protects the common interest of its people in God's name.

While on the continent this secularisation is tied up with positivism and the vesting of law-making authority exclusively in the legislature, in the UK, the judge retained the role of finding and utilising the rational legal wisdom that preceded the state.

Minimalising human error

A further important element of European legal tradition that is much more pronounced in the Anglo-Saxon sphere is the insight into the fundamental fallibility of human beings. Whether as a citizen, judge, king or a member of parliament, man is fallible. Whilst this fallibility may be mitigated or minimised through education and experience, a risk of error or misconduct always remains. Even if judges and civil servants receive the best professional education and training, they will always be tempted to misuse their power. It is for this reason that the value of state institutions has to be assessed on the basis of their capacity to minimise human error, or to limit the impact of such errors.

It would therefore be a mistake for the constitution or the state to vest government or civil servants with uncontrollable power or a monopoly on the use of force. As civil servants acting in the name of the state are just as prone to error as private individuals, they should not be granted any special powers or privileges. Only the common law systems take this wisdom to its logical conclusion and implement it. In continental Europe on the other hand, the administrative law makes a legal distinction between the office and the office-holder. In other words, authorities are not acting as private persons, even when they act beyond their authority or in breach of the law. This means that any representative of a public office functions in an abstract official capacity, detached from their concrete personality, and thereby can exercise through the fiction of the public office almost the same authority as a judge. As administrative acts and decisions are made not by civil servants but by the office, such decisions are final and enforceable in a manner similar to a decision of the court.

Adversary system

The recognition of the fallibility of man has not only influenced the different concepts of separation of powers, but also court procedures. The adversary system is based on the idea that the truth as to the legally relevant facts can best be established in a procedure in which both parties pit their accounts against each other and contest the facts, with equal arms and on equal footing. The parties are expected to fight for the truth by presenting evidence and argument before the 'blind' jury or the 'blind' judge. Anything that could unfairly influence this fact-finding (prejudicial media reports, inadmissible evidence, etc.) has to be prevented in order to exclude any possible prejudice of the judge or jury.

The adversary system was displaced in the continental European legal system with regard to criminal and administrative procedures by the inquisitorial system. The inquisitorial procedure required the procurator representing the state in the procedure to actively search for and determine the facts. His office had the obligation to examine all facts and to provide conclusive answers to the court. The court was only required to verify this truth. Thus, the procedural rights of the defendant were limited to questioning the facts produced by the procurator, but he was not entitled to present his view of the facts with equal arms and equal opportunity. These two very different approaches led to the development of quite different procedural systems, including different functions of the judges and the jury in civil law and common law countries.

5.2.4.2 What are for Comparative Purposes the Distinctive Elements of the European Legal Culture?

Essential elements of the European culture of administrative law are undoubtedly the separation of powers, the allocation of jurisdiction between the different courts, divergent procedural rules, different remedies and different concepts with regard to the sources of law, as well as a quite different function of the judiciary in terms of jurisdiction to control the administration.

Similarity between the continental European and the Anglo-Saxon concept of judicial control of the administration can be found in the design of the independent judicial or quasi-judicial instance (Conseil d'Etat), which can review decisions of the administration based on complaints from affected persons. However, we should not overlook that with regard to the question of how independent an instance must be in order to recognised as a judicial instance, there exist significant differences of opinion between continental and Anglo-Saxon lawyers.

Different rules have however been developed in relation to the subject matter for review, the independence of the court, the possibilities for appeal and the fact-finding procedure.

Subject matter of the dispute

What can be the subject of a legal dispute with the administration? According to the French and Swiss legal systems, only formal administrative decisions (called administrative acts) can be subject to review by the court, whilst in the German system any legal controversy can be brought to the administrative court if it concerns the alleged infringement of basic subjective constitutional rights by any action of the administration. In Switzerland under a recent constitutional amendment, access to justice against administrative measures has been considerably enlarged. In 2007 the legislature passed enabling legislation to give effect to the constitutional amendment concerning the right of access to justice, however there is still no constitutional review of federal legislation and the new constitutional provision in principle excludes decisions of the parliament and of the federal executive council from judicial review (Art 189 para 4).

In the UK, the subject of the dispute is not a pertinent issue. The common law, developed on the basis of different types of legal action, is more concerned with whether there is an applicable writ available with which to bring an action. The writs determine the goal of the action and the jurisdiction of the court, including the remedies that can be issued and enforced by the court.

Independence of the judiciary

The common law tradition is based on the principle that men are governed by law and not by men. Men are vested with inalienable rights that cannot be changed or modified by the constitution or the sovereign. Thus, the courts are the trustees which guarantee those inalienable rights.

According to the continental system the sovereign is the fountain of justice, and produces, according to ROUSSEAU, the *volonté générale* or the general will. The courts have to apply the general will of the sovereign, and thus they have to be accountable to the public.

How independent are the courts or the administrative tribunals? In the Anglo-Saxon British or American legal system, most legal disputes with the administration are decided before the ordinary courts. In Germany and in part in Switzerland, special administrative courts have jurisdiction over legal disputes with the administration, or, as in Switzerland, special chambers or divisions of the ordinary courts. In France, at the lower level administrative tribunals are vested with jurisdiction over public law, and in the final instance such matters are heard before the Conseil d'Etat. As an administrative court the Conseil d'Etat has developed de facto independence from the executive, although it is not independent in the same sense as the *Juges ordinaires*.

Ministre juge

Another significant feature of civil law systems is the fact that a legal dispute may in the first instance not be brought before a court, but rather determined by an administrative body that is competent to supervise and review decisions of its subordinate administrative agencies. This concept, known in the French system '*ministre juge*', is foreign to the common law tradition, since the administration has no power to exercise judicial or quasi-judicial functions (functional separation of powers). However, in many common law countries one can find administrative tribunals that can determine administrative matters at first instance, although they do not formally exercise judicial power nor have the status of a court.

Fact finding

An important difference is also to be found with regard to procedure. The procedure for establishing the facts before a court in the common law system is essentially an adversarial contest between the parties. On the other hand, civil law countries in matters of public law follow the inquisitorial principle. Accordingly, it is the task of the administration and ultimately the administrative court to find and declare the facts of the case. As the administration bears responsibility for fact-finding, there is no provision for distribution of the burden of proof as with civil law matters.

The administration is of course obliged to find and produce the *true* facts relevant to the case at hand. In continental administrative law this has become established as a legal obligation to investigate and determine the facts, and at the same time, the necessary procedural rights and obligations for fact-finding have been transferred to the administration to enable this role to be fulfilled. This has led to the administrative acts that result from this fact-finding procedure being accorded the same status and validity as a decision of the court, even though the facts are not determined within a procedure providing equal arms and chances to the parties concerned.

The English administration is of course also obliged to objectively present the relevant facts, even without express legal obligation. In an administrative law dispute the court will examine the facts presented by the administration for '*error on face of the record*,' but it does not certify the objectivity and truth of the facts presented by the administration. In common law jurisdictions, it is ultimately an adversarial contest between the parties that is seen to provide the fairest means of arriving at the facts.

Contempt of court

Whilst common law courts can enforce their decisions by means of *contempt of court*, that is, by threat of criminal sanction, administrative courts of civil law countries have no equivalent or corresponding method of enforcement. Civil law administrative courts can quash a decision of the administration, but they cannot enforce their decision via contempt of court, nor can they compel a civil servant to perform or refrain from specified actions. This leads to the result that, even in countries in which administrative courts are empowered to order the performance of certain tasks by the administration, the courts cannot enforce their orders. If the administration is not willing to obey the court, the court has no appropriate charge or penalty at its disposal for the purposes of enforcement.

5.2.4.3 Reasons for Differences

The special status of the administrative act or decision

With the separation of public law from private law, Napoleon not only separated the jurisdiction of the courts and laid the basis for two separate court systems, he also handed the administration an important instrument for the execution of administrative decisions: the administrative act ('*acte administratif*'). Though this instrument was developed prior to the Revolution, it was after the creation of Napoleonic 'public law' that it became the central and decisive instrument for administrative law on the whole continent. The French *acte administratif* became, through the scholarship of OTTO MAYR, the crux of German administrative law doctrine until the enactment of the new statute on administrative procedures after the Second World War. It also had a decisive influence on Swiss administrative law with the reception of the German administrative law by FRITZ FLEINER and its later development by MAX IMBODEN.

Function of the administrative act

The administrative act fulfils many different functions at the same time: It is the binding order of a competent administrative authority with an effect similar to a judicial ruling. It also ensures that a particular administrative procedure is followed.

In addition, the administrative act creates trust and provides legal security, as it can only be revoked in accordance with specific rules. The administrative act is enforceable and enjoys the privilege of the assumption of its validity, as long as it is not challenged. If the act is not challenged before the court or a higher administrative instance within the legal deadline, any flaw in the act is healed. Thus, it has to be executed by the relevant enforcement authority even though it was originally faulty.

Similarity to judicial ruling

With the institution of the administrative act, the administrations of the continental European countries were able, unlike their common law counterparts, to enact decisions that were directly enforceable with regard to the persons affected. The idea that was developed in the Middle Ages of a centralised, hierarchically structured and rationally based legal system was thus strengthened with the Napoleonic concept of an executive and administration additionally empowered with competences similar to judicial jurisdiction.

The adjudicative power of the administration

The overemphasis on executive and administrative power can also be seen in the doctrine of the formal and substantive legal validity of administrative acts, which is a status otherwise reserved for and only justified in relation to decisions of independent courts reached after a fair judicial process. The very fact that administrative acts are automatically legally valid and enforceable, and that they are assumed to be correct and only reviewed in case of a complaint, reveals the fundamental importance of this institution for the continental European legal thinking and legal system.

Volonté générale

As long as the citizens (or subjects) do not contest administrative acts, they have to tolerate their enforcement. Ultimately, administrative acts are to be seen as a means to implement and enforce legislation, in respect of which the administration has a privileged position relative to the subjects. The administration can implement legislation via the administrative act on its own initiative and can also determine the relevant facts in concrete cases. It can make enforceable decisions, which if necessary can be executed by the police force or other administrative means available. Thus, the doctrine of the administrative act is closely connected to the dependence of the citizens on *volonté générale*, which is given expression in legislation enacted by the legislature, and whereby the common or general interest will always be privileged over any private interest.

Administration subject to law

Administrative power and jurisdiction over the administration developed very differently in England. Like the courts in other monarchies, the courts of the UK were also courts of the Crown that determined legal disputes in the name of the

Crown. In contrast to other monarchies however, the principle '*The king can do no wrong*' had a purely procedural meaning. The king and the courts acting in his name were not above the law, and were not at liberty to distort or bend the law in favour of the Crown. For this reason, the common law courts could always apply the law to servants and offices of the Crown and could thereby determine whether the administration had acted within the limits of its legal powers (*intra vires*), or whether it had exceeded its legal powers and acted beyond the law (*ultra vires*).

Although servants of the Crown have to act and decide on behalf of the Crown for the benefit of the common interest, their decisions are not akin to a court ruling and are not automatically enforceable. If an administrative decision has to be enforced against the will of the person concerned, a separate order of the court is required. Thus, public obligations with regard to the administration are treated similarly to private obligations. The administrative law of the common law countries functions effectively without the weighty construct of the 'administrative act'.

The king can do no wrong

If one wants to bring an action against a servant of the Crown, the king or queen has to waive their immunity from suit. English kings have made provision for such waiver for centuries, which enabled the early development of the prerogative writs (complaints against the servants of the Crown) including *habeas corpus* and the writs of *certiorari* and *mandamus*. In all such cases the king or the Lord Chancellor gave the courts the power to require the administration to justify imprisonment or other restriction of personal liberty (*habeas corpus*), to order the administration to make a decision (*certiorari*) or to compel or prohibit an activity or measure of the administration (*mandamus, prohibition, injunction*).

5.2.5 The two Types of Administrative Jurisdiction

Consequently, the continental civil law and the common law have developed two different types of administrative law and administrative jurisdiction. Within the common law system, disputes between private individuals as well as those between private individuals and the administration or between different administrative authorities are all heard and decided by the ordinary courts within the framework of their existing powers and prerogatives. In countries with a continental legal system, specific administrative courts (Germany and Switzerland) or the Conseil d'Etat and administrative tribunals (France) have been established and are responsible for all disputes involving the administration.

Criteria for assessment

The common law courts assess the activities of the administration essentially according to the same sources of law and basic legal norms that apply to actions of private individuals. This means that an action or decision of the administration will be contrary to the law if it cannot be justified on the basis of the common law, parliamentary statute, royal prerogative or by natural justice. If the power to take such action cannot be supported by any of these sources of law, the administration has acted *ultra vires*. In making this assessment however, the court does not interfere within the discretion of the administration. If the administration acts within its legal powers, the decision or measure is considered to be lawful because it is *intra vires*. As far as the court observes the statutes enacted by the parliament, the criteria for assessment correspond to a large extent to those which in civil law countries are known as principle of legality (Gesetzesvorbehalt).

Common law remedies

In common law systems, citizens do not have to wait until the administration formally issues a decision in order to have recourse to the courts. Rather, using the appropriate writ, a person may bring an action before the court seeking an order to compel the administration to perform a certain action or an order to prevent it from a certain planned activity.

With the remedy of habeas corpus, those who have been deprived of their liberty through imprisonment, involuntary admission to a psychiatric clinic, imposed tutelage or deportation order can demand to be brought before an independent judge within twenty-four hours. The judge then has to assess the lawfulness of the restriction of liberty. Habeas corpus is one of the oldest prerogative writs, dating back to the Middle Ages.

Other prerogative writs include certiorari, mandamus and prohibition. The writ of certiorari enables a person who is affected by an administrative decision to have that decision quashed by the court. The writ of mandamus is a remedy that orders the administration to take a certain positive action, for example, an order that mandates the construction of a road. With the remedy of the writ of prohibition or prohibitory injunction, the court can prohibit the administration from carrying out certain activity (such as the construction of a proposed public building).

Today, the various prerogative writs have largely been consolidated under the traditional injunction (a court order to compel or prohibit an action).

Recours pour excès de pouvoir

In civil law countries, the French principle is generally observed whereby a complaint can only be made against an administrative act that has already been made, and in all other cases the only possible recourse is a claim for compensation against the administration if damages have been suffered. The *recours pour excès de pouvoir* is the most important and traditional remedy of the French administrative law (complaint for acting beyond discretionary power, akin to the common law concept of *ultra vires*).

In Germany, the formal administrative act was once a prerequisite for invoking the jurisdiction of the administrative courts and making a complaint, however it is now possible to bring any legal dispute against the administration before the administrative courts, provided the complainant can show that the matter raises a question of substantive rights (based on the guarantee to access to justice under Article 19 of the *Grundgesetz* or Basic Law).

Standing

Standing to bring a claim against the administration before a court has been expanded in many countries in recent decades in order to open access to justice against the administration. In earlier times, only those who could claim the violation of subjective rights (Germany), legal rights (England) or property rights (USA) could have access to the court. Today however, in most countries access to justice is generally available if the citizen can show that his/her interests are affected.

Function

Whilst in the UK and in Germany the function of administrative justice is mainly to protect individual interests against illegal actions or decisions of the administration, in France and Switzerland it serves the additional function of safeguarding the public interest. For this reason standing is sometimes expanded in order to provide scope for court review in cases where the public interest might be harmed. One important example is the right of NGOs in the field of environmental protection to complain against administrative decisions that purportedly violate general environmental interests. This in turn transfers to the court greater responsibility for control of the administration and the legislature, which they are not always well placed to fulfil.

5.2.6 Conclusion

Partnership v hierarchy

The two different concepts of judicial control of the administration can be traced back to the different conceptions of the state and of human nature that underpin the respective views. The strong position of the courts in the common law system must be understood in the context of the strong position of the parties and the restriction of the judge to the decision-making function. In contrast, we have seen that the continental European system places the judge in a hierarchically superior position to the parties, accords fewer procedural rights to the parties and is thereby a more hierarchically structured and authoritarian system than the partnership-like common law system.

Dominance of the volonté générale

Justice in the continental European sense is to be found in the hierarchy of the legal order through the *volonté générale* determined by and expressed through the democratic law-making procedure, whilst in Anglo-Saxon law, justice can only be found through an adversarial procedure between parties on an equal footing. According to the common law view, the correct or just law can only be found in a legal battle before an impartial arbiter, whilst on the continent the correct or just law is that which is created through the democratic legislative process.

The administrative law of civil law countries therefore gives expression to the view that citizens are no longer the subjects of an absolute ruler, but rather subjects of the *volonté générale* of the democratic legislature. Government and administration are executing and administrative organs of the *volonté générale* and must therefore have the appropriate authority to implement the will of the majority. This inviolable position is in England enjoyed only by the Crown. However, as the law has increasingly separated government and the administration from the privileges of the Crown, administrative authorities can no longer claim a special status relative to citizens. In contrast to the German 'Fiskustheorie', which distinguishes between the private legal actions and public legal actions of the executive, in England the government and the administration were increasingly subject to the general jurisdiction of the courts.

In common law countries, the administration did not retain the patriarchal character that it assumed in civil law countries. The superior, super-human character of magistrates, civil servants and administrative authorities in civil law countries, which finds expression for example in the rights of immunity outlined above, is based solely on the fact that the administration is responsible for realising the will of the majority (the *volonté générale*).

European Human Rights Convention

The forces of globalisation compel both systems to move closer together. In this process, each system can learn from the other. The civil law system should accord much greater value to the procedural rights of parties, especially in relation to fact-finding. The common law countries must acknowledge that process alone is not sufficient to effectively guarantee justice. The substantive law and substantive constitutional rights, such as the right to life for example, are at least as important as procedural rights.

In Europe, the European Human Rights Convention and the broad jurisdiction of the European Court of Human Rights are contributing to the gradual but discernible merging of the two systems.

New Public Management

Finally, mention should be made of the recent developments that can be grouped together under the term 'New Public Management' (NPM). These developments include the privatisation of certain public utilities and services, which in some cases has been required of member states of the European Union. This new development applies a private sector management approach to the public sector, and includes principles of private competition within the administration. NPM requires authorities to address citizens as customers or clients rather than subjects.

NPM aims to make government more cost-efficient, and assumes that the administration should be steered by clear function-oriented goals. Within the framework of these goals, the administration should decide which measures it will undertake to achieve the optimal realisation of its goals. The allocation of revenue is determined on the basis of the goals to be achieved, and expenditure is measured against the performance of goals.

If one assumes that this new approach to administrative activity is primarily designed to handle citizens as clients or customers rather than as legal subjects, then NPM should be conducive to the legitimacy of the modern administration. With regard to the rule of law and to fundamental rights, the basic idea of the NPM development is that greater competition and market-orientation in the public sector will also result in the better protection of human rights. This might be the case in certain areas. However, in areas where the public interest requires the public monopolisation of a certain function or service, legislative protection of the public interest and access to administrative justice are indispensable.

6 The State as Legal Entity

6.1 The State as Legal Entity in the Age of Globalisation

6.1.1 Introduction

Has 'homo oeconomicus' replaced the 'homo politicus'?

The conception of the universal, modern nation-state is something that has long demanded fundamental reconsideration. Today this concept is confronted with the post-modern challenge of globalisation. This in turn results in a shift in the institutional character of modern constitutional democracy and its purely internally focussed legitimacy. Replacing the democratic legitimacy of the people, external factors assume an increasingly important role in shaping the internal identity of the democratic constitution of the state. The growing importance of the global market not only throws traditional nation-state oriented politics into question, it also requires scholars and practitioners to consider the possibility of the privatisation of the state. The global '*homo oeconomicus*' is now faced with the critical responsibility of making decisions on political, social and economic questions. Based on the generally recognised identity of the global consumer, the *homo oeconomicus* as an actor in the global market will have to assume the role of the global '*citoyen*'.

Collective identity?

However, it must at the same time be acknowledged that human rights, which identify the global and universal *citoyen,* belong to the fundamental values that ultimately also legitimise the local nation-state. Human rights successfully limit the power of the nation-state. These universal rights are now, in the age of globalisation, part of the supranational world. The global *homo oeconomicus* and the local *homo politicus* now compete with each other. The first embodies the 'sovereignty' of the global market, and the latter finds its roots in the nation-state. However, in the last ten or fifteen years, the *homo politicus* has begun to question the individualistic liberal foundations of the nation-state. It should now be conceded that, taking multiculturality into account, collective identities such as those of different cultural and religious communities should be recognised as having a political and collective value.

Undoubtedly, globalisation and multiculturality have become the real structural challenges of politics in the modern age. From different perspectives, both globalisation and multiculturality put the traditional liberal nation-state in question, and thereby also question constitutional democracy as the proper institutional foundation of legitimacy.

6.1.2 *The Changing Shape of Constitutionalism*

Fundamental values of constitutionalism

Modern constitutionalism is rooted in the basic values of liberty, which prescribe limits on the power of the state via a constitution. The primary goal of a constitution is to limit government power. The constitution as the basic law of the state must be a constitution of liberty (*Constitutio libertatis*). The aim of the liberal state is individual liberty, and such liberty can only be protected within a political system in which there are limits on governmental authority. Whilst the state of modernity may well have changed considerably over time in terms of values and ideology, we can identify the original values of the modern state as follows: A liberal society is a society in which every individual enjoys a recognised and protected sphere of free space for individual movement and development. This free space has clearly to be distinguished from the public sphere in which individuals have to obey only such rules as apply generally to all individuals in the same way (see HAYEK, *Constitution of Liberty*, London 1960, p. 207 ff).

Normative liberalism seeks to limit and regulate power, and to protect liberty through law. These goals should be united within a legal framework that establishes an efficient and protective state authority (separation of powers, checks and balances and protection of fundamental rights). The legal order should transform the political into the legal and legitimacy into legality. Constitutionalism is thus the means by which liberalism can be given tangible legal form.

Constitution as process

Constitutionalism determines the relationship between the government and the governed within the framework of the rule of law. In this sense, the principles of due process, equal rights and general validity of the law are essential to a constitution and to constitutionalism. Thus, the constitution of a particular state can be seen as the fundamental public act that gives positive legal expression to the procedural preconditions that enable the political community to reach a democratic and rational consensus. A constitutional ideology that is rooted in a process-oriented perception of justice is not however value-neutral. These constitutional principles are tied to the fundamental values of human rights, universalism, liberalism, rationalism and contractual liberty, and therefore cannot be regarded as neutral and positivist principles. On the contrary: all these values contain a substantive content, that is, they aim at the liberal goal of individual freedom. They are the product of a particular political and ideological perspective, which is incompatible with authoritarian and discriminatory ideologies of government.

Democracy and human rights

From a subtly differentiated point of view, also the democratic majority principle can be understood as a tool that limits the might of the state. It can however also be misused as a means to constitute the tyranny of the majority. Constitutionalism sets itself the goal of preventing majoritarian democracy from running amok. Whilst it is the people within a constitutional democracy that possesses sovereign constitution making power (*pouvoir constituant*), this power and the authority it establishes can only serve liberal goals if they are bound to observe fundamental rights. Constitutionalism establishes constitutional democracy not as a pure expression of the power of the majority, which can create law, but rather as a democracy that is bound by constitutional rights. The primary task of democracy must therefore be the protection of fundamental rights. Democracy is justified in so far as it is better able than any other process to protect human rights. If one takes this consideration, to its logical conclusion, one will see human rights as a basis for the legitimacy of a democratic system. Democracy as a system of popular sovereignty thus is only legitimate to the extent that it realises human rights.

Democracy, seen from the perspective of ROUSSEAU and according also to the Swiss perception, can on the other hand also be seen as a tool that guarantees freedom. Through the democratic adoption of laws the people can democratically decide to what extent the law will limit individual freedom. Democracy is understood as a means to provide as much self-determination of the individual as possible. Each individual can determine by the democratic process to what extent it will accept new legislative obligations or restrictions. Within a small community at the local level individuals will have greater democratic input in such decisions than they will at the central national level. Seen from this point of view, democracy aims not at achieving a small majority, but much more at a comprehensive consensus of the people, in order to legitimise additional limitations of freedom. Such view is of course in contradiction to the LOCKEAN concept of human rights as inalienable rights that are to be protected by the courts and by the democratic decisions of the people's representatives in Parliament.

End of History

Towards the end of the 20th Century, with the well-known and provocative argument that the fall of communism marked the 'End of History', a new era of constitutionalism began. The simplistic and unhistorical proposition of the end of history was applied to constitutionalism in order to argue that Western liberal democracy (as the optimal form of government) had reached the peak of its development and there would therefore be no need for any further changes or developments. Constitutional democracy as the final answer was supposed to have clearly and irreversibly conquered its opponent, namely, arbitrary or despotic forms of authority. Constitutionalism was thus to be regarded as a common good, that should no longer be questioned or analysed. Therefore, only the tension between norm and reality, that is, the practical implementation and interpretation of certain notions, can be the subject of post-modern scientific discourse.

European Union

However, the theory of the end of history ignored the structural challenges that lie at the heart of constitutionalism and the nation-state, such as the legitimacy of the state itself and the constitutionality and design of new forms of political cooperation between states within the European Union. Today, in the face of globalisation, it is with precisely these questions that constitutionalism must grapple.

From procedure to substance

If one wishes to strengthen the constitutional and philosophical foundations of the modern state, one has to critically examine the reduction of earlier constitutionalism to procedural principles and negative rights. Modern constitutionalism should, in addition to procedural principles, place more emphasis on substantive values. It should also pay less heed to the apparent contradiction between state and society and the tension between individual and collective rights, and rather should pay closer attention to the legitimacy of positive rights. In this context peace and human dignity could be regarded as universal values.

The problems of constitutionalism

The problems of modern and post-modern constitutionalism can be divided into the following themes:

- The relationship between rule of law and the welfare state;
- The challenge of multiculturality as opposed to the a cultural 'citoyen';
- The emergence of a supranational constitutionalism without a demos and the function of national constitutions with regard to regionalism;
- The structural obstacles and contradictions in the consolidation of democratic constitutions in post-communist states;
- The internationalisation of national constitution making through the international community;
- The concept of good governance as a precondition for loans and financial support by the Bretton Wood institutions.

6.2 Challenges of Globalisation

The effects of globalisation can be seen in the internationally regulated economy, communication and the ever-increasing power of global institutions and regulations, including the global network of non-governmental organisations. Thus, one should not simply reduce the process of globalisation only to the economy. And even with regard to the economy, one must bear in mind the fact that the labour market is still local and not global.

The process of globalisation must be assessed from two different perspectives:

The End of History or the change of the nation-state?

1. *Globalisation of the economy* is according to the 'end-of-history' view not only the end point of the economy but also of the political community as such. Seen from this perspective, the neo-liberal ideas on globalisation of the economy contradict to a certain extent the original concepts of political liberalism. Traditional constitutional liberalism is inherently linked to and centred around the idea of the nation-state. Therein lies the fundamental contradiction between the neo-liberal process of globalisation and the classical liberal concept of the traditional nation-state.
2. *Globalisation as a new form of internationalisation* entails a gradual increase in the supranationalisation of state structures. Accordingly, national as well as inter-state and supra-state structures such as the European Union as a federal-like association of states will only be able to survive within a global environment.

Opportunity for the nation-state

In a similar sense, globalisation can be seen as an opportunity to redefine the nature of 'the political' and to come up with a structurally new definition of the nation-state. These concepts could thereby be incorporated in the new and complex environment of transnationalism, internationalism and supra-nationalism. Undoubtedly globalisation will diminish the autonomy of the nation-state in terms of political decision-making. However, in place of this loss the nation-state will to some extent gain a new and different form of sovereignty, as the sole bearer of international responsibility to implement international law within its national borders. It is precisely for this reason that the nation-state will retain an important role in the development of international authority. In particular, the nation-state will remain the primary source of valid and binding law.

Back to the personal law of the Middle Ages?

Whichever way one understands globalisation and whatever one expects of it, the phenomenon of the increasing dissolution of territory, combined with a return to the personalisation of laws in a manner reminiscent of the Middle Ages, cannot be ignored. Examples such as absentee participation in elections by citizens who no longer reside in their home state, and the indictment of Pinochet by the UK House of Lords, demonstrate the reversion to the personalisation of law. Territory however will always remain a constitutive principle of the modern nation-state. Even ROUSSEAU, who demystified the close connection between territory and human rights, acknowledged that universal rights are connected to territory in the sense that they are implemented within the territory of the state, e.g. the French the nation-state. The monopoly of politics based on territory and the alignment of the political community solely to the nation-state will however be irretrievably relegated to the past. The external frame of the nation-state and its identity will thus be called into question. At the same time, the territorial state will gain greater internal legitimacy and a more complex identity, through greater internal decentralisation and regionalisation and the fostering of local identities. Globalisation and regionalisation seem thereby to drift apart. It will remain the task of the nation-state to re-balance those drifting forces and to maintain a common identity, in order to be able to operate flexibly and effectively within the international community.

Relevance of the territorial frontier

It should not be forgotten that the very emergence of the sovereign territorial state at the time of the Peace of Westphalia was the result of a common decision of the international community, and that the territorial borders of the affected states were secured through international treaties. Although culture and space are no longer inextricably interwoven, and although human rights are universally protected, territorial borderlines are still controlled by the nation-state. The nation-state controls which persons and which products are allowed to enter the state. The nation-state can also expel people from its territory. It is also the nation-state that determines who is entitled to nationality and citizenship, who can reside within its territory and who can access the social benefits of the welfare state. Even the cosmopolitan 'citizen of the world' is tied to a particular nation-state by the coincidence of his birth.

Foundations of constitutional democracy

Globalisation has undoubtedly created a new dialectic in relation territoriality, which originally belonged only to the nation-state. As globalisation poses a challenge to the traditional territoriality of the nation-state, the foundations of constitutional democracy such as sovereignty, human rights and the social welfare state – which are ultimately determined through territoriality – will also have to be reconsidered.

6.2.1 Sovereignty

Common sovereignty

Today the nation-state in common with international and supranational bodies carries out the classical state functions of legislation and the protection and implementation of human rights. Both functions were earlier closely connected to the sovereignty of the nation-state. And whilst the nation-state may gradually lose its monopoly over some of these traditional functions, this will not necessarily lead to the total dissolution of the nation-state. Although nation-states may no longer claim the right to make unilateral decisions on war and intervention as a basic element of their sovereignty, they still make important decisions in relation to nationality, citizenship and entry to their territory.

Sovereignty cannot be reduced merely to external sovereignty. Sovereignty has also to be perceived as internal sovereignty of the state in the sense of the state's claim to authority and its legitimacy. Internal state sovereignty is reflected in the democratic sovereignty of the nation and in the authority of the state to enact and implement laws.

Transnational networking

It seems clear that globalisation as a worldwide process of transition and transformation will lead to new international and transnational networks of the nation-state. This will substantially change the character and functions of the nation-state, and thereby also change people's perception of what can be understood as politics and political effectiveness, what should belong to democracy and what can legitimise the democratic system of the nation-state.

Can the political be global?

If one however wishes to arrive at a new understanding of the 'political', one will necessarily have to ask the question: is the global society as a political community at all thinkable? And, if the answer to this is 'yes', the next question that follows is: to what kind of democratic participation will this lead in a world in which the states are internally regionalised and externally globalised? In the past, the nation-state was automatically particular in a universal world because of its sovereignty; today its particularity is closely tied to universality, because the nation-state uses its sovereignty to implement universal values within its domestic system.

6.2.2 Democracy

Demos as source of the nation

In the age of globalisation, democracy faces new challenges for two reasons: On one side one has to reconsider the notion of the legitimacy of the nation in the sense of the demos as source of sovereignty. Moreover, the governmental system and its decision making process as well as the democratic responsibility with regard to the people within a globalised world have to establish themselves on a new footing and a broader scale. These considerations raise another question: can democracy in fact be de-nationalised? Can democracy effectively be separated from its origin, namely the nation?

Democracy and the rule of law

The advocates of an economically ruled globalisation would of course affirm this question. In doing so however, they ignore the two essential bases of modernity: modernity itself emerged out of the principle of the nation and, based on this, out of an inner homogeneity of its members and participants. By definition the nation-state of modernity is based on the constitutional interdependence between democracy and the rule of law, the combination of which is seen as the only means to prevent despotism and tyranny. This mutual dependence of democracy and the rule of law can only be guaranteed through the procedures of the territorial nation-state.

A global democracy would not be viable

Structurally, a globalised constitutional democracy cannot be viable. Why? The procedural conditions necessary to give effect to constitutional liberty cannot be implemented globally. They are linked to the nation, as ultimately it is only the nation that can legitimise constitutional democracy. If one takes the heterogeneity and the deep diversity of the global world society seriously, a new world war would necessarily be the consequence of any attempt to establish a world state.

Globalisation without legitimacy

Globalisation transfers the political decision making process to new structures that lack democratic legitimacy and which are unable to establish any robust basis for legitimacy. The political decision making process cannot be separated from democratic legitimacy. The field of current international '*Realpolitik*' however has drifted towards non-transparent unclear political structures, which by today's standards have no claim to political legitimacy. Traditional politics is gradually disappearing and is being replaced with a form of 'un-politics' – in other words – the politics that directly touches and moves people within a particular nation-state, and which is directly connected to the political and democratic office-holders within the nation-state, is gradually being lost.

Quasi-government without a constitution

The international quasi-government (institutions such as the UN Security Council and the WTO) rules without a constitution, as there cannot be a viably constituted world government. On the other hand, all those with an interest in the global market have also a strong interest in the legitimate governance of the world economy. It may be that the world economy can be governed, but only the nation-state can effectively participate in such international governmental activity.

Democracy without demos?

Without a demos there is no democracy. The demos however, can only emerge out of a people that is formed by the nation-state and not simply from mankind at large. The transnational activism of particular individuals is not the same as democratic civic engagement. A global and at the same time critical public cannot emerge from humanitarian activism. Undoubtedly, globalisation has to some extent led to the development of a new international civil society, but this new worldwide civil society does not extend so far as to give rise to a new form of global citizenship.

Cosmopolitan democracy?

The most interesting arguments in favour of a de-nationalised democracy are at the same time rooted in a rather dangerous ambivalence. The first tempting argument postulates a cosmopolitan democracy (DAVID HELD, *Democracy and the Global Order: From the Modern State to Cosmopolitan Governance*, Polity Press Cambridge 1995). It is certainly correct that political democracy has to be re-evaluated. It is also correct that the real problem lies in the nature of representation and in the people to be represented, as well as in the extent of citizens' rights of participation. By simply identifying the problem however, one cannot automatically conclude that the only reasonable solution is to be found in a globalised democracy. Although the political community appears to be changing, it is not necessarily transforming itself into a global political world community, but rather in reality the political community is becoming increasingly trans-nationally interconnected through internationalisation.

Open versus closed democracy

Even the argument of ANTHONY GIDDENS on the 'democratisation of democracy' is ultimately unconvincing (*Beyond Left and Right: the Future of Radical Politics*, Polity Press, Cambridge 1994). He detects the same basic political problems; his thoughts are based on the same modern political paradigm, namely that democracy should result in autonomy and that this aim can no longer be achieved with the traditional democracy of today. The idea of a world constitution, as well as the promotion of an open democracy as opposed to a closed democracy, assigns the notion of the 'democratisation of the democracy' to the purely formal constitutional level, without explaining how this democratisation of democracy can be achieved.

6.2.3 Rule of Law and Protection of Human Rights

The 'citoyen' as a symbol of universal values

Through their constitutions the modern Western nation-states have endorsed the importance of human rights, and have given positive legal expression to fundamental and political rights. These states have thereby assigned sovereignty to the people and thus established states ruled by democratic legitimacy. The state society exists through its members, the citizens, which have become the symbol of the universal value of human rights and of the democratic political community. On the other hand, the citizen also symbolises the particular context of a certain nation-state. Nobody demands that the borderlines of the nation-state should be removed or universalised. Nor does anybody expect or require the political community to be or become universal. In this context rather, the differences such as diversity and particularity are to be highlighted. The promotion of citizenship rights is determined by and constrained within the borders of the nation-state.

No monopoly on the implementation of human rights

Today however, the same nation-states that once proclaimed the universal validity of human rights are no longer able to fully guarantee all those rights within their own state borders. International law has in the meantime assumed responsibility for human rights, and affords human rights protection through international procedures that enable citizens to bring actions against their state in an international forum. This apparent 'globalisation' of constitutional law is however in reality nothing more than a 'transnationalisation' of constitutional law which manifests itself in particular in the area of human rights. It should also be acknowledged that international bodies often require the cooperation of nation-states for the implementation of their decisions.

Nation-states adopt international human rights standards

National constitutions are increasingly adopting international standards of human rights guarantees, with the result that within particular nation-states, internationally guaranteed human rights receive directly enforceable constitutional protection. In some states, constitutionally guaranteed human rights are interpreted in agreement with the practice of international courts, and in certain states the courts are constitutionally obliged to take into account the decisions of international forums and courts. The horizontal comparative approach is also acquiring greater importance as a method for the reception of foreign decisions within the domestic law of nation-states. This method is also used as an incentive for the further creative development of the national law.

Global transformation of human rights

In the era of globalisation the question arises: can human and civil rights, which have developed within the territory of a nation-state, still autonomously and effectively be guaranteed by the nation-state? And can those rights effectively be transformed into global human rights? Globalisation has led nation-states to accept that certain political rights of citizens are to be protected within the framework of a global or at least regional international law, such as for example the law of the European Union.

Universal credibility – universal protection

The basic questions of globalisation with regard to human rights can be put as follows:

- To what extent will the globalisation of human rights, as manifested in the positivist embodiment in international conventions, also be accompanied by the effective and efficient international protection of such rights (and therefore be credible)?
- As already mentioned, the value of human rights is universal. Their embodiment and protection however, is particular. Can human rights still

be effectively protected at the global level even in the face of the expanding gulf between world cultures?

Economic sanctions of the United Nations

From the point of view of human rights we are faced with a further fundamental challenge, which reveals itself in the contradiction between national constitutionalism and globalisation: that is, the function and the position of the United Nations and its claim as the only world government to have the monopoly on the use of force, even in relation to the protection of human rights. Here, the democratic deficit of the United Nations becomes starkly manifest. Indeed, within the Security Council a handful of states can make decisions of the greatest existential consequence, without democratic legitimacy. This can lead to problems of fundamental constitutional significance, for instance when economic sanctions are imposed that have a direct impact on innocent people and may ultimately even violate their human rights. Does one not have to recognise the reality that through internationalisation the internal constitutional protection of human rights can be substantively diminished?

No legal remedy with regard to international actors

Moreover, the new developments of the international guarantee of peace and peace-enforcement reveal that peace-enforcement can only be carried out by very few nations. These nations assume a dominant role as international actors with regard to all other nations, and usurp the monopoly of force of the United Nations. Indeed, they have become the real holders of international peace making and peacekeeping power, without being accountable for their actions and decisions. The International Criminal Court provides some scope for imposing criminal responsibility and punishment on peacekeeping forces and other actors in cases of gross violations of basic human rights and commission of crimes against humanity. But the court itself has no real accountability. Accused persons tried by the court have no remedy against unlawful indictment or violation of due process. With regard to international protectorates such as the United Nations Mission in Kosovo (UNMIK), there is still no means for individuals to bring any kind of action in relation to unlawful restriction of their human rights or to defend these rights if they are violated by an international actor. To the extent that we are not able to impose legal accountability on international actors, the international rule of law and with it the legitimacy of the international community will remain in jeopardy.

International Monetary Fund and World Bank

The problem becomes even more serious when the international actors are not states, but financial institutions that assess the human rights situation within specific states. In these cases there is a lack not only of democratic decision making procedures, but also of remedies for protection against such international actors or any means to hold such actors accountable before an independent judiciary. These global actors operate outside the framework of international human rights protection and beyond the reach of judicial control that could hold them accountable for their actions and decisions. Thus, globalisation is already failing to keep up with the new challenges that have arisen in terms of affording effective legal protections against international actors and institutions.

Do the ends justify the means?

In this context, how credible is the notion of the universal rule of law, based on universal reason and universal justice? The example of the wars in Afghanistan and Iraq show the contradiction of the phenomenon of transnational intervention, as well as the classical dilemma of constitutional law in a completely new light: Is it acceptable to violate positive international law in order to pursue and obtain morally undisputed justice deduced from reason? Moreover, one has always also to ask the question whether the reason for intervention is not so much to combat 'evil' and to restore universal justice as it is rather to protect the national interests of the intervener. In the case of the invasion of Iraq, the national interests of the United States and other participating forces, as well as the moral indignation of the American citizens, appear to have been major motivating factors behind the international intervention and its failed claim to bring 'reason' and 'justice' to victory.

6.2.4 Welfare State

Integrative concept of human rights

With the demand for social and economic rights, the two pillars of the liberal state have been called into question. Can the inner peace and harmony of a society only be maintained and secured in a free market system based on the negative function of liberties? Is it really possible, on the ideological basis of separation between the state and a society of autonomous individuals, to build a political community that can legitimise liberal state authority? Today it is assumed that in addition to the second generation of human rights, a third generation of rights is also necessary in order to legitimise the first generation and its limits. Both at the domestic level and at international law we are confronted with demands which aim at the integration of all these different human rights concepts into a comprehensive concept that encompasses all aspects of human life and dignity. The move to functionalise social and economic rights means that the constitutional policy of the welfare state can no longer understand human rights merely as negative rights. Human rights must today be regarded as having both positive and negative status, which will lead ultimately to an integrated concept of human rights.

Emancipation in the competitive society

These new developments in the relationship of human beings to the state, marked by the increasing influence of the welfare state, are blurring the traditional distinction between social rights and political freedoms, and leading to stronger claims for emancipation of the individual. At the same time, new dependencies between the institutions of the state and its individuals are developing, as individuals come to be seen as 'clients' of the state administration. Citizens are now confronted with two contradictory possibilities for emancipation: On the one hand they are freed from the classical control mechanisms and thus have greater opportunities for individual development and autonomy within society; on the other hand, the autonomy that the citizen acquires through welfare results in a more integrated society and thus ultimately in a reduction in autonomy.

Freedom and social security

JÜRGEN HABERMAS rightly warns against seeking to halt the effects of the globalised and internationally regulated economy through the compromise of the welfare state. And indeed the structural changes in the economy will put into question the highly regulated nature of the welfare state that was built upon a successful combination of the principles of the nation-state and the values of the welfare state (HABERMAS, *Jenseits des Nationalstaates*, Munich 1998, p. 73). This highly efficient combination of social security and individual liberty can no longer be guaranteed by the nation-state, as states no longer have sufficiently autonomous economic or social power to guarantee social justice or to realise social rights. Supranational organisations and globalisation have radically reduced the autonomy of nation-states in the field of economic policy.

Nation-state as partner of social policy

However, the nation-state still retains responsibility for the realisation of social policy. As already mentioned, the labour market has thus far hardly been globalised, but rather is still strongly linked to the nation-state. Ultimately the people will always hold the government of the nation-state accountable for any economic deficiencies.

This highlights the paradox of globalisation for the welfare state: On the one hand, economic and social policy are embedded in the nation-state and legitimised by the affected citizens within a state. On the other hand, the nation-state can no longer fulfil the expectations of its sovereign people nor realise the social policies demanded by its demos. This has led to the emergence of tense debates over the reconstruction of the welfare state under the pressure of globalisation, which may lay the basis for the deconstruction of the welfare state.

Social rights

Based on the need for social harmony, social and economic rights have led irrevocably to greater provision for welfare in the classical liberal state. At the same time, globalisation has brought a new dimension to the structural dilemma of a purely negative interpretation of human rights: it is increasingly accepted that negative freedoms can only be enjoyed if certain basic social and economic conditions are met, but global economic competition threatens the welfare state and puts states that protect social rights at a competitive disadvantage. However, there is today a mainstream view that poverty and inadequate health care constitute violations of human rights. These rights have to be raised and called for at the level of the international community. In this sense, the draft for a charter of the European Union with its commitment to solidarity contains an impressive catalogue of social and economic rights, including the right to human dignity (Art. 1), the right of the family to social protection (Art. 13 para 2), the right to education (Art. 16), the rights of children (Art. 23), social rights (Art. 31), the right to holidays (Art. 35), and the right to health protection (Art. 42). In a similar sense also the draft for a constitution of the European Union contains social rights (Art. II 6ff). Although these documents have not received the approval of all member states and have therefore not come into force, one can safely assume that any deepening of the political structures of the European Union will involve some protection of social and economic rights.

6.3 Elements of the State

6.3.1 Significance of the Notion of the State

6.3.1.1 The Development of the Modern Notion of the State

From hierarchical feudalism to popular sovereignty

Within the feudal structure of the Middle Ages, power and authority were to a great extent still ‘privatised”, and involved personal dependence upon a landowner or master. The landowners and masters were in turn dependent upon their count or prince, to whom they owned duties of loyalty and by whom they could be asked to serve as soldiers in the military. In return for these obligations the ruler compensated them by protecting their property and their authority. The masters of handcraft apprentices in the towns were connected through their guilds, which administered the monopoly of handcraft and distributed to each guild a particular contingent of production. The totality of the guilds administered the town, which usually stood under the special protection of the prince or of the empire.

The centralisation of the ruling power in the hands of the prince led to a break-up of these highly structured and hierarchical dependencies. The numerous personal dependencies of the subjects were gradually transformed into a direct and undivided underling relationship of the subject to the prince or the king. The might of the king no longer depended upon personal dependencies and obligations, which for example could arise through property, marriage, birth or trade, but rather on his military powers. Later, the ruler ceased to represent only the next tier in the hierarchy such as princes and counts but came instead to represent the interests of the entire people subject to his authority.

From the 'stato' of MACHIAVELLI to the sovereign state

For each such unit of people ruled over by a king, a name had to be given (e.g. Venice or France). But how were these units of people dependent upon their prince or king by virtue of his military authority (but not necessarily linked by family, property or tradition) to be labelled or described? MACHIAVELLI coined in this context the term 'lo stato', by which he was making reference the Greek city-states and to the '*status rei publicae romanae*' of the Roman Empire. While the label and with it the notion of the state began to take hold in relation to the new undivided relationship between the king and the people, from the 15th Century onwards the functions connected with the state came to be described as 'politics' (based on the Greek word 'polis').

People, sovereignty, territory

As the new relationship between the king and his people could be legitimised neither by religion nor by tradition, a new secular basis for the legitimacy of the power of the Crown had to be sought. Some identified this legitimacy in the fiction of the 'social contract' or in the notion 'sovereignty'. A state was considered to be sovereign, when the domestic unity between the king and his people was generally supported, and if this unit was externally independent and thus able to conclude international treaties and otherwise exercise its legal personality under international law.

In this we can already detect the constitutive elements of the state of modernity: The modern state is the unit, which is determined domestically by the people and the territory within which it can exercise territorially centralised rational political power as sovereign, and which can independently exert this power externally with regard to other states as subjects of international law. The question however as to how the various elements of modern statehood are to be defined and valued has become the cause of much political debate and conflict.

6.3.1.2 People, Nation and State in the Charter of the United Nations

State – nation – people

Within the preamble of the Charter of the United Nations, the 'peoples' of the United Nations undertake to maintain peace and to prevent war. However, we find that in Article 3 and the following regulations of the Charter only *states*, but not *peoples* or *nations*, can be or become members of the United Nations. These terms are used without defining what specific meaning or significance particular terminology may or should have. In the solemn declaration of the preamble however one does not find the abstract notion of the '*state*', but rather it is *peoples* that solemnly swear to "unite [their] strength to maintain international peace and security". On the other hand we do not use the expression 'United Peoples' nor 'United States' but only *United Nations,* by which is meant the member states as well as the peoples and individuals living within those states.

The uncertainty centres around the questions: in respect of which territory and which peoples is statehood to be recognised, and when are state and people one and the same (and when are they not)? Who for example can claim the right of self-determination? Is it the member states of the United Nations, or the peoples living within those member states? There are many ethnic minorities which claim statehood for themselves and which, based on this claim, demand a unilateral right of secession. Every dissolution of an empire such as the Ottoman Empire, the Austro-Hungarian Empire, the European colonies or the USSR results in the drawing of new borderlines. And the collapse of these multi-ethnic empires has always involved appeals for the right to statehood and self-determination, whether on the basis of common tradition, culture, language or religion.

6.3.1.3 The Notion of the State in the General Theory of the State

Is the state a predetermined entity?

The term 'state' and the concept it denotes are often seen as a pre-existing reality, and it is therefore seldom that the actual origins of the state are explored. The legal order and the constitution derive the legitimacy to create the law from the sovereignty of the state; Sovereignty and state are so to speak seen as the 'Big Bang' of the law enacted by the state, its justice, its monopoly on coercive force and even the very existence of the nation. International law is understood to be the law made *by* the subjects of the international law (states), *for* the subjects of international law (states) to regulate inter-state relationships. The presupposition of the state as a predetermined and fixed entity is at any rate not peculiar to the legal discipline. Political philosophy, sociology, economics and political science all presuppose a certain notion and a certain perception of the state.

Significance of the notion of the state

The general theory of the state has to provide a notion of the state that is practical for today's world. This task is not however a purely academic undertaking. Rather, such analysis of the constitutive elements of the state has concrete practical consequences for people and the state, even for the existence of states and the relationship of human beings to the state. Whether a particular people or territory will be granted the right to proclaim itself as a state is a question of critical existential importance for fate of the particular people/territory and its neighbours. The question for example whether the entire Island of Cyprus is one state, which has part of its territory illegally occupied, or whether the island is legitimately divided into two states is not merely an academic question. Why did the international community celebrate the reunification of the two German peoples when the Berlin Wall fell, whereas 70 years earlier, the same international community explicitly prohibited the unification of Germany and Austria in the Peace Treaty of St-Germain-en-Laye? What is the effect of British laws including British citizenship in Northern Ireland, when the Constitution of the Irish Republic claims the whole island is under the rule of the Republic? These questions are, as many examples demonstrate, of a highly explosive nature. We do not propose to offer definitive solutions in the following pages, but rather to ascertain the fundamental issues and causes of these conflicts from the point of view of the philosophy of the state.

The three elements of the state

Since the emergence of the liberal nation-state in the 19th Century, theories of state have tended to regard the following three elements as essential for a state: people or 'nation', territory, and sovereignty. A state without people is unthinkable. However, who belongs to 'the people' or 'the nation' of the state (*Staatsvolk*) and whether a state can encompass a number of peoples are highly controversial issues of definition. The modern state also needs a territory in which its own laws are exclusively applied. In addition, the state needs domestically and internationally to be recognised as a sovereign entity. In other words, it must have the capacity and power to enforce its laws within its own territory. If it is no longer able to exercise coercive force to execute laws or can no longer justify its authority, the existence of the state will be called into question (the term 'failed state' is sometimes used in this context, for example in relation to Somalia at the beginning of the 21st Century). The revocation of statehood however should not be made arbitrarily. The Badinter Arbitration Committee, composed of the presidents of the constitutional courts of the member states of the European Union, has decided that a federation in which the constituent units are in permanent conflict and stalemate, and which is therefore unable to make decisions, is in the process of dissolution. In such situations the constituent units within the federation have the right to self-determination, which is not to be understood as a right to secession but rather as the right to lift themselves out of the legal vacuum created by the dissolution of the federal state, and to build their own state. This decision has effectively relegated federal states to second-class status. As a consequence, it seems that today states are reluctant to consider federal solutions in order to keep their conflicting multi-ethnic societies together or to solve problems with minorities, because federalism is seen as the first step towards dissolution of the state.

6.3.2 The People or Nation (Staatsvolk)

6.3.2.1 The Tension between People and State

Can there be a state without a people?

It is obvious that there can be no state without human beings. But there can also be no state without a 'people' (*Staatsvolk*). Whilst there are many peoples that are unable to build their own state (for example Tibetans, Tamils, Armenians, Kurds, Palestinians) and some that are only partially united in one state (including for example Germany, Hungary and Albania) there are also immigration countries, which are made up of immigrants from a variety of peoples. In relation to such heterogeneous states we must not forget however that the territory once belonged to the indigenous inhabitants, which today are at best recognised as minorities within their own territory and at worst confined to reservations. Finally there are states such as France or Turkey, which first created their 'people' or 'nation' through the constitution. In these cases the nation follows the state (civic principle) and not the state the people (ethnic principle). In such states the 'nation' is (in theory) comprised of every person living within the relevant territory who accepts the universal values of the republican constitution.

Citizens and foreigners

In addition, states make a distinction with regard to nationality between citizens who enjoy full rights within the state, and foreigners who may be afforded only limited rights (for example, they usually have fewer political rights than citizens). If one examines the different laws relating to citizenship, one will find significant differences in the way that different states regard their people or nation and the concept of citizenship. Some states for example allow dual or even multiple citizenship. Some prohibit dual nationality on the basis that a person can only be loyal towards one state. Some states tie citizenship to belonging to a certain ethnicity or culture. Germans without German nationality who have lived in Romania since the 12th Century are considered as part of the German people and are given preference if they seek German residence or citizenship (Basic Law of Germany, Art 116). On the other hand, Turks who have lived in Germany for decades as foreign workers and taxpayers have considerable difficulty acquiring citizenship and assimilating into the German people. States whose borders do not correlate to the geographical spread of their 'people' or nation often regard themselves as representatives of their people even beyond their borders. Such states may even take legal and diplomatic action to defend the interests of 'their' minority living within the territory of a neighbouring state. Hungary for example recently enacted legislation vesting legal rights in Hungarian minorities living in neighbour states, which rights the Hungarian government is obliged to defend against the governments of neighbour states. This was a controversial move, and Hungary was forced to soften its policy in order to avoid confrontation with its neighbour states and with the European Union.

The chosen people

There are however peoples which perceive themselves as chosen by God. The Jewish nation, the people of Japan and the Sinhalese from Sri Lanka for example hold such beliefs. This particularity of course also has an influence on the relationship of those peoples with the state. The state of Israel was founded on the basis of Zionist ideology. Zionists were influenced by HERZL'S ideas on the nation-state and wanted to establish a state for the Jewish people. Orthodox Jews however reject Zionism as an idea, because only the anticipated Messiah has the prerogative to establish a state for the chosen Jewish people. This is one of the reasons that the state of Israel does not have a formal written constitution (although the Knesset has passed several laws that in fact have constitutional status).

French nation and German people

What is the relationship between the people and its state? According to the French perception, the people — that is, the 'nation' — is created by the state. The state has given itself a revolutionary democratic constitution and the people living within the state and loyal to those universal values are considered part of the French nation. In contrast, Germany regards the German people a pre-constitutional entity and believes that this people created the German state. German self-identity is therefore not necessarily tied to nationality – for a long time the German people had no nation-state of their own – rather, it is based on a sense of belonging to a people that preceded (and later created) the German state.

In immigrant countries, the people is made up of those who have chosen by immigration to belong to the territory of the respective state and who can identify with its constitutional goals. The preamble of the American Constitution for example implies that everybody living in the territory belongs to 'We the people of the United States'. Excluded however were the original inhabitants, who did not immigrate to the territory but had lived there since time immemorial.

Perception of the state and the people in the Balkans

Upon independence, the peoples formerly ruled by the Austro-Hungarian Empire and the Ottoman Empire in South-Eastern Europe developed their own understanding of 'people' and state that was largely characterised by the idea of the pre-constitutional unity of the people. This ethno-nationalism was built up in opposition to the multi-ethnic states, which were often perceived or experienced as 'multi-ethnic prisons'. According to this perception of the state and the nation, in principle each ethnic nation has the right to establish its own state, but not to establish multiple states. Persons belonging to an ethnic nation who live in a state other than the one their ethnic nation has established are to be considered as a special minority, that is, as a nationality but not a nation. Thus, the Kosovo Albanians in the former Yugoslavia would not be able to create a new state for themselves, because the Albanian nation-state has already been established. In the former Yugoslavia the different ethnic nations were so widely mixed throughout the territory that it was decided after World War I to set up one common state for all of the different southern Slavic nations. With the break up of communism in former Yugoslavia however, almost all of these ethnic nations claimed the right to establish their own state. This necessarily led to deep conflicts, as the changing borders caused by secession and the establishment of new states resulted in the creation of new minorities. Those who had previously belonged to the inclusive mother nation suddenly became members of an ethnic minority within a new state, that is, second-class citizens.

6.3.2.2 The Changing Perception of the Nation throughout History

MANZINI: "Now we must make Italians!"

In the era of globalisation, worldwide migration and increasing violence and conflict within multi-ethnic states, one can no longer seriously speak of sociological or historical factors that lead to nation building or which legitimise secession or self-determination. At the end of the 19th Century however, revolutionary founders of states were still convinced that with a revolutionary state one can also create a revolutionary nation. From the time immediately after the struggle for the unification of Italy comes the famous statement of MANZINI: "We have made Italy, now we must make Italians!" In other words: Each state has to find solutions that make it possible for all people living within the state to identify with the state. This can no longer be done by creating a new ideological nation as proposed by MANZINI, but only by concepts which take multi-ethnicity seriously. The ethnicity-focused perception of 'the people', which is still the cause of many conflicts today, excludes minorities and hampers harmonious integration. In the era of globalisation the challenge for a theory of the state is to seek a new understanding of the nation, which is accessible to all people living together within a particular territory.

i. Exclusive Concept of the Nation

Historical community of tribes

Supra-familial authority structures originated in the dependence of the tribal or kinship community. Originally the members of tribal communities also considered themselves as belonging together because of their kinship and common origin. All members of the same tribe stemmed from one common original ancestor, or at least believed that they did. Thus for example the Zulus in South Africa are still today convinced that they all originate from the same common tribal ancestor. Such common descent was the precondition for the establishment of authority structures over a larger community. The communal spirit attributable to blood relations as well as a common historical fate promoted a feeling of community in such overarching social groups.

Community united by war

A real and lasting feeling of belonging together can be developed negatively by the permanent exclusion of 'others'. It is well known for example that in 1870 the German Chancellor Bismarck initiated the German-French War in order to bind the German nation together. In order to achieve German national unity he had to create a negative image of, and wage war against, the French. This 'them' against 'us' construct was and remains an effective but highly problematic political tool to unify a people in the name of defence.

Linguistic and cultural community

In addition to common descent, having the same language and the same culture were and remain today significant connecting links among different members of the same tribe. Common culture, language and descent together provide the conditions for a feeling of community, which is an important precondition for the development of the state.

Common destiny

However, such a feeling of community is not necessarily confined only to the tribal or kinship group. Common historical experience or common suffering in the past (community of fate or destiny), common political beliefs, common 'way of life' or common religion can also lead to community formation and solidarity, just as common descent can. Whatever the cause, our primary interest in the present context is the question, what is the significance of the feeling of group togetherness for the development of state authority?

ii. Inclusive Concept of the Nation

Community of values

A nation which is open to and composed of different peoples and cultures can only be built upon the basis of common values with which the majority of the population can identify and which they are prepared to commit to and defend. The founding basis of the French nation was the declaration of human rights as universal values, with which all persons living in France could agree. Consequently, the Constitution of 1791 enshrined the principle that every person who had been living in France for a year or more should automatically receive French citizenship.

Today, the declaration of universal values does not suffice in order to hold or bring multicultural states together. Rather, states are faced with the difficult challenge of pursuing values which are good for all *individuals* living in their territory and which at the same time are appropriate for all *peoples* living within the state with their linguistic, cultural and religious particularities. The treaties of the European Union for example oblige the Union to foster the different cultures of Europe, to ensure mutual respect for cultural diversity and to support the protection of common cultural heritage.

6.3.2.3 Solidarity as Prerequisite for the State Community

No state without legitimacy

A state can ultimately only exist when people are prepared to sacrifice some of their interests and forego certain advantages for the benefit of the state and its community. Thus, every state community depends upon the willingness of its members to accept and exhibit community solidarity. In the modern state for example, citizens contribute between 20 and 70 per cent of their income in taxes and social security contributions. This is evidence of a certain level of solidarity, without which such a system would be unthinkable. The state community also requires other sacrifices from its members such as military service for example, which may in some cases require soldiers to risk their lives for the sake of defending the state. People however only agree to such solidarity and sacrifice when in return they are part of a state community with which they can identify, of which they can be proud, and in which they feel secure and content. States that are not built upon the basis of a united people that precedes the state must therefore establish values that can evoke this indispensable preparedness for communal solidarity.

People who are not or cannot be integrated will not demonstrate solidarity and cannot be compelled to solidarity even by force. The history of the last 200 years provides a very clear demonstration of the explosive energies that may reside within a people which has long been denied autonomy and which has persistently suffered serious discrimination (See for example the Kurds).

Solidarity and nationalism

The recognition of the significance of the feeling of togetherness for state solidarity should however not be confused with ethno-nationalism. Ethno-nationalism identifies the state in a one-sided fashion with the pre-sate 'nation', and assumes that only a homogeneous nation which excludes or even removes all 'others' can build a state. A community based on solidarity on the other hand, which is composed of different nations that share common experiences or a common way of life, rejects ethno-nationalism as a nation building factor.

Community and security

As was accurately observed by ARISTOTLE, man is essentially a social being which is dependent on community. Humans obviously seek security and comfort within the community. If they do not find this security and comfort, they will not be prepared to integrate into the society. But it is not only the individual that needs security; peoples and minorities also need autonomy in order to be able to provide their members with security with regard to their cultural expression and development, and in order to be able to shape their own destiny. If one denies cultural communities the opportunity to follow their own path, they will pit themselves against the state ruled by the majority nation, and regard the state as their enemy and the cause of all suffering and exploitation.

Indeed, the traditional theory of state has often not properly acknowledged the necessity of a feeling of national unity for state building. The texts on the theory of state have paid close attention to the differences between the notions of people, nation and race. However, they have paid scant attention to the concept of solidarity or togetherness, which, as IBN KHALDÛN emphasised, is essential for the formation of a state. The state is not only a community based on rational will, it is also the product of historical development and is a unit connected by common destiny. The state community creates a space in which individuals and the groups of which they are part feel at home and secure in their development, thereby providing a foundation for common solidarity.

i. Nation and Social Contract

Who belongs to the state?

Social contract theories have assumed and continue to assume that the unity of the people which establishes public authority or enters into the social contract is not determined by the contract itself. Such theories tend to leave open the question of whether the unity between those entering the contract is pre-existing, that is, whether there is some historically developed unity or unity grounded on some other basis (for example through war). As islanders, for the English 'the people' or nation was (with the exception of the Scottish and the Welsh) a predetermined and uncontested entity. Thus the questions of who enters the contract or who belongs to the state were not significant for British social contract theorists (HOBBES und LOCKE). On the British Island it was somehow evident who belonged to the people. In contrast, borders and peoples were not so clearly geographically pre-determined in other parts of Europe.

Based on what unity (territory, culture or language) could what kind of community thus conclude a social contract for the establishment of public authority and thus establish a state? As this question was not solved by social contract theories, many scholars of state theory believed that a state could be founded by any arbitrarily chosen community, provided that the question of territory was clear. The borderlines were to be determined by territory and not by culture. This was of course a fatal mistake. It led many western statesmen in relation to the colonial empires and in the wake of the Great Wars, to divide, dissolve or create states and peoples simply by the stroke of a pen on a map.

Autonomy of peoples

The positivism and absolutism of HOBBES contributed significantly to an overestimation of the state and its possibilities. Certainly it is possible under certain circumstances for communities of different peoples to be integrated and to live harmoniously together. Switzerland provides a good example. This however, is only possible if the different communities are granted adequate autonomy and if a common fundament is found – for example, common political values such as federalism, direct democracy, and neutrality – which can hold those different communities together and make it possible to develop the necessary sense of solidarity.

ii. The Status of Foreigners

Discrimination

The modern constitutional law of almost all states is absolutely valid for everybody, except that it places foreigners on a different footing from native citizens. Foreigners or transnational citizens are limited in the extent to which they bear and can exercise fundamental rights, especially in relation to political and economic rights. Some fundamental rights are only applicable to them for the duration of their visa or residence permit. As soon as they seek to extend this permission however, they cannot necessarily count on respect for the rule of law in terms of the procedure for renewal. It is often part of the discretionary power of the administration to decide whether it will expel a transnational citizen, or extend or renew a permit to stay. Such decisions obviously have drastic life-changing effects on the persons concerned.

As soon as citizens of a certain state feel threatened by the presence of 'too many' foreigners on 'their' territory they will try to protect their interests by political means, which may have strong discriminatory effects on foreigners. The social discrimination of foreign workers in Western states is an eloquent example.

From the foreign national to the transnational citizen

In the era of globalisation and the universal validity of human rights, such discrimination can no longer be justified. When it comes to legal protection and the rule of law, administrative bodies should not be equipped with unaccountable decision making powers. The principle of responsive, accountable government that can be called to account before independent courts and by Parliament, must also be observed in relation to foreigners. Globalisation should not be limited to the internationalisation of the market. Civil rights and other rights of citizens within the state must also become international or transnational if people are not to be discriminated against in terms of products and services. Human dignity requires respect for the rights of all people regardless of their nationality.

Whoever recognises the universal application of human rights will regard the strict distinction between 'citizens' and 'foreigners' as outdated. Although foreigners are not national citizens of the respective state, they are transnational '*citoyens*' and have the inherent right in all states to dignity, equal treatment and respect for their human rights. The social contract that establishes ongoing public authority is not limited only to nationals as partners of the contract, but extends to all authorities which share responsibility for the well-being of all people living in the respective state. Transnational citizens belong to 'the people' that is the bearer of popular sovereignty. This is the sense in which the European Union rule is to be understood, which requires member states to introduce and establish Union citizenship at the local level.

iii. The Status of Ethnic or Racial Minorities

Self-determination and minorities

States cannot be constantly and arbitrarily divided and re-established. They need – if they want to achieve sustainability – to be built on the basis of historically developed nations and ethnic communities, and should not destroy or displace these nations or communities. Members of minorities need to have opportunities for autonomous development, and should not be excluded or treated as second-class citizens by the majority. If minorities demand secession based on the right of self-determination, the fulfilment of their 'right' to statehood can almost never provide a definitive solution to the minority problem. Following secession there is unlikely to be ethnic homogeneity in the new state. In most cases the existing minorities will be supplemented by new minorities, made up of people who formerly belonged to the majority nation but now live outside their 'mother state'. These new minorities can hardly be expected to be loyal to the new state. They too are likely to demand a right to self-determination and secession, and the pattern would likely be replicated in an ever-descending spiral. If a universal right of secession for minorities was to be recognised, what legitimate legal argument could be employed in order to limit the right of secession based on geographic size or the population size of a (would-be) state? The principalities of Liechtenstein and Andorra have less than 100,000 people. Any internationally recognised right of secession would create a permanent legitimacy crisis in zones of widespread multi-ethnicity.

This incessant questioning of the state and its borders offers the ideal breeding ground for the development of new secessionist movements. The violent dissolution of former Yugoslavia is a striking example of this fatal dynamic. The right to self-determination should not be simplistically reduced to the right to a new state with new borders. If we are to specify the content of the 'right to secession' it must take the social, economic and cultural needs of members of minorities into account. But if the right to self-determination is seen as a means to serve the welfare of minorities, then instead of focusing on secession, more sophisticated solutions to minority grievances must be found, such as greater autonomy and participation in the decision making process of the majority, by which the legitimate claims of minorities can be satisfied.

The right of self-determination in international law

Even if the notion of the *members of a people* is not identical with the *nationals of the member-states* of the United Nations, under international law one cannot deny the right of the member-states to govern, including governing for and over their minorities. The right to self-determination enshrined in the charter of the United Nations does not equate to a right to secession and revolution by which state sovereignty can be dissolved.

The Charter of the United Nations makes clear the way in which states can establish a solid foundation, based on the self-determination of their peoples. If states do not recognise the rights of their minorities nor undertake any action to gradually integrate their minorities within the power structures of the state, they will sooner or later be confronted with a violent outbreak of minority conflict. The principle of self-determination must in particular be observed when new states are to be founded. If the United Nations is to contribute to the establishment of new states, it must be led by the principle of self-determination and seek to ensure that each people within the respective territory is recognised as a constitutive element of the new state.

Requirement for state legitimacy

States have to provide the conditions for the integration of minorities in order to avoid a break up of the state community. In this context legitimacy is the key. A state which is supported only by its majority and which ignores, oppresses or attempts to assimilate its minorities will in the long run be faced with serious internal conflict. The state must therefore direct its policies in such a way as to achieve legitimacy also in the eyes of minorities. The rule of the democratic majority will only be legitimate in relation to minorities if these minorities are not merely tolerated within the state and afforded human rights protection, but if they are also recognised as an essential political force which has to be integrated into the political decision making process. Only with common institutions that are also accountable to minorities will a permanent peaceful conflict management be possible.

iv. State – People – Nation

The democratic nation constituted by the state (demos)

What is the relationship between people, nation and state? If one understands the people as a pre-state entity, which is first brought together as a concrete unit by the state (France and Turkey), the common identity between state and nation or people is permanently guaranteed. In this case the people is the legal notion, denoting all persons united within the territory of and under the authority of the state.

The classical theory of state developed in the French Revolution assumes this unity of state and nation. The fathers of the French revolutionary constitutions wanted thereby to demonstrate that the new bourgeois state was the result of the revolutionary consciousness of the nation. Thus they were much less concerned to distinguish between the sociological concept of the nation and the philosophical or legal notion of the state. Their main concern was to unite the people in its combat against the feudal authority of the French aristocracy (see C. DE MALBERG, p. 13).

The pre-state people (ethnos)

The famous German author JELLINEK espouses a different view. He is of the opinion that the nation is a given sociological unit that *precedes* the state, but which of course is also influenced by the state (G. JELLINEK, p. 116 ff). Whoever sees the nation as a sociological unit, will have to conclude that there are states which comprise several nations (Great Britain) and at the same time that there are nations which are spread across several states (Arabic states).

Whoever analyses the problems of minorities and the causes of intra-state and international conflicts will establish that the concepts of 'people' and 'nation' cannot be reduced to the sovereignty and the territorial boundaries of existing states.

However, this immediately raises the question of how the people or the nation can be adequately identified and defined, if not as a unit determined by the state. JELLINEK correctly points out that it is not possible to determine the nation on the basis of one common element alone, such as language. According to his understanding the nation is rather a historical social unit (G. JELLINEK, p. 117). This unit is determined by several elements such as history, language, culture and/or religion. In addition to these elements, a common identity, a sense of solidarity and the will to form a political unit are also essential.

If we conceive of the nation or the people as a unit independent from the state, we have to address the question of whether and to what extent these units have their own rights in relation to sovereign states, such as for example the right to self-determination.

Geneva Conventions

The claim for self-determination is also recognised in the Geneva Conventions that set out the humanitarian laws to be observed in conflict situations. Article 1 of the First Additional Protocol to the 1949 Geneva Conventions (1977) provides that an intra-state conflict has to observe the rules of international conflicts if it is a conflict in which one part of the population invokes its right to self-determination to fight against a racist regime, foreign occupier or colonial authority. In these cases civil war is to be treated as an international war. This limitation of the right of self-determination to particular circumstances and struggles against certain forms of authority (such as colonial powers) reveals that even those states that have over the last 30 years helped to achieve the acceptance of the right to self-determination, do not want to see it fully realised. Based on this distinction between the fight for independence against a colonial power and other forms of minority conflict, the African states have agreed among themselves to reject any attempt by tribal conflicts to undermine the territorial integrity of the artificially created sovereign African states (Organisation of African Unity (OAU) Charter of 1967).

The dilemma is thus apparent: one who regards the people or the nation as a sociological unit and who acknowledges the right of peoples to self-determination under international law, undermines the existing sovereignty of the states. One who rejects this notion leaves the states with the freedom to oppress their minorities. How can this dilemma be resolved?

The United States War of Independence (secession from England)

In the Declaration of Independence of 4 July 1776, the American settlers justified the exercise of their right to self-determination and independence on the grounds that the British colonial government no longer served the freedom and welfare of the colonies and could therefore no longer be recognised as the legitimate government. The settlers opted to take the path of self-determination because they were willing and able to establish an independent state that would better serve the welfare of the people.

Secession of the Southern States?

One should however not forget that eighty years later the southern states wanted to separate from the north and also claimed a right to self-determination and secession. However, this battle for secession was fought under the same flag of inalienable rights, which according to THOMAS JEFFERSON justified the independence of the United States from Britain (and which meant that the southern states did not have a legitimate claim to secession, as their rights were already guaranteed by the legitimate government).

Does JEFFERSON'S justification for the separation of the United States from England still hold some validity today? It is the task of every government to recognise and integrate minorities. The rights of these minorities with regard to language, culture and religion must not be ignored or destroyed by assimilation. Rather, these rights must be protected by giving minorities sufficient autonomy to practice their culture and to maintain their identity. If minorities are oppressed, the sovereign state will lose its legitimacy with regard to those minorities. If the situation should escalate to war, the relationship of the conflicting parties is ruled by the international law of conflicts, that is, Additional Protocol II to the Geneva Conventions.

6.3.3 Territory

Globalisation and territory

Territorial boundaries are another essential characteristic of the modern state. Without territory, there is no state. For this reason states, peoples and minorities fight most bitterly over territory. After the fall of the Berlin Wall as the territorial border of the former DDR and symbol of the divide between the capitalist and communist worlds, not only was the DDR dissolved, but so too was the power of the communist parties in almost all former communist states. This suggests that in spite of globalisation, territorial borders have maintained their symbolic value.

On the other hand, we can point to examples that demonstrate the reverse: that in the age globalisation territory is losing its significance. With increasing mobility, the internationalisation of the finance, commodity and service markets, with internet communication and satellite television, territory is gradually decreasing in importance and relevance. In the United States for example, courts are dealing with claims against banks in Switzerland. Under American law, an American court has jurisdiction in a case, if a party to the case has a strong connection to the American territory, even if the subject matter of the case and its consequences mainly concern events and parties outside the United States. Indeed the common law, which has a much older tradition than the continental European law, has a much less territorial understanding of the jurisdiction of the court than its continental counterpart, as the case of Chilean dictator Pinochet being tried before the highest British court demonstrates. Recently, Belgium enacted a new law that gives the courts jurisdiction over all war crimes regardless of where they may have been committed (universal jurisdiction).

Limitations on freedom of the press and freedom of expression can on longer be imposed as effectively as they could in earlier times. Racist incitements to violence from the USA, where hate speech is constitutionally protected, can readily be published on the internet and thus accessed all over the world, including in countries in which such hate speech is legally proscribed. If a state wants to limit freedom of expression it would have to block all telephone lines in order to prevent the transmission of forbidden information via the internet. China for example imposes restrictions on internet access, which it is only able to do because relevant American service providers and search engines agree to abide by China's rules in order to have access to the Chinese market.

Territory as symbol of sovereignty

On the other hand, territory can be of existential significance for states and human beings. For many people mobility is still not a reality. Many people must stand in the queues of foreign consulates for hours, in the hope of securing a visa – that is, permission – to visit relatives, or to obtain a work permit that may be desperately needed. Without the visa or permit their liberty is heavily restricted. States today still exclude many people from their territory. And territory remains the symbol of state sovereignty. Whoever has followed the bloody conflict over the 'indivisible' symbolic sovereignty of Jerusalem knows of the terrible human fate that can attach to territorial conflict.

Territory and constitution

The territory determines the legal order and the constitution by which people are ruled. Territory can also determine what food, medicine and other products are available to the consumer. And territory can have important effects on the status of individuals: when Croatia became independent from former Yugoslavia, overnight the Serbs living in Croatia with Yugoslavian passports became foreigners and foreign workers. Yugoslav soldiers in military barracks in Croatia became enemy soldiers overnight. Territory still determines the fate of many people.

Accordingly, we have to examine the following questions:

- Why and to what extent is territory decisive for state-building?
- What legal consequences does territory have for state sovereignty?

6.3.3.1 The Development of the Territorial State

The need for territorial borders developed only in the latter stages of the gradual settlement of tribes in the Middle Ages. The development of agriculture, clearing and maintenance of pastures, building of city walls and castle moats and the establishment of regions of jurisdiction all contributed to the development of a territorial relationship between land – which had previously been collectively owned – and public authority.

Authority attached to people rather than territory

Originally, the authority within kinship groups and tribes was connected to particular persons and not related to territory. The kinship group was a unit held together by personal ties, connections, and dependencies. It is true though that already in the early Middle Ages some territorial concepts of authority were emerging. The existence of the Roman limes for example reveals clearly that the Roman Empire was already a geographical state in which power, authority and jurisdiction were connected to territory and also exercised over a specific territory. In any case, in the period of the European Middle Ages the Romans had already been settled in these areas for centuries. During this period the Germanic tribes on the other hand were not territorially settled, but rather were still migrating. Thus, personal ties and interpendence were rather based on blood relationships, which was also the tie connecting Arabian nomadic tribes together (IBN KHALDÛN, p. 98 ff).

In the European Middle Ages national borderlines were practically unknown. The '*Sacrum Imperium Romanum*', the Holy Roman Empire, regarded itself as an Empire that ruled over the entire world, in which the Pope was the spiritual ruler and the Emperor the worldly leader. Because the division of the Empire into three independent parts as envisaged by Charles the Great (803) was at least partially revoked upon the coronation of his successor (813), the tension between the power of the Emperor and his kings remained hidden. It was not until some time later that the Kings of France and England demanded of the Emperor that within their own Kingdoms they be accorded equal rights and recognition as the Emperor. It was in this sense that GILES OF ROME (1247–1316), the educator of Philip the Fair, argued in his famous work *De Regimine Principum* that the Empire was no longer the final imperium but rather the 'regnum' was the final political entity.

Later, in 1302, John of Paris wrote of the European Occident in his publication *Tractatus de regia potestate et papali* as a continent divided into several nation-states. Whilst in terms of religion and the church there was still one spiritual world order under God, the same was not true at the worldly level (see C. F. MENGER, p. 11 and H. MITTEIS, p. 208 ff).

Separation of 'imperium' and 'dominium'

When tribes and kinship groups first began to settle, the soil was initially commonly held and cultivated. The land belonged to the tribe, while the usufruct for production and housing was divided among the various families. As families depended on the usufruct of the land but the power to decide on allocation of property and usufruct still remained with the tribe or kinship group, families remained dependent on their tribe.

The gradual separation of authority to rule and power to control and allocate property was decisive for the further development of the European territorial state. It gradually became accepted that those who were cultivating the land should also control the land and have the right to dispose of it. This shift in property rights was strengthened by widespread clearing of land, as those who devoted the effort to clearing land and preparing the soil for agricultural production expected also to acquire ownership of that land.

With this development, there came about a change in the dependence of the kinship group. The kinship group assumed responsibility for protecting its members – it acquired the function of 'patron-protector'. In return, the members of the group were required to provide services for military defence, to perform other voluntary community service, and to pay an annual tithe.

Over time, the authority over the tribe or kinship group was transferred to a king or duke. These rulers gradually acquired more sovereign rights and royal prerogatives over their subjects. In the late Middle Ages these royal rights, such as jurisdiction over petty matters, could even be purchased.

Centralism and decentralism as a consequence of the development of the territorial state

This gradual development towards the territorial state had as already mentioned, a decisive influence on state development. The network of personal dependencies diminished as an instrument to hold different families and individuals together. Instead, the factual and legal position of the prince over the people and the territory became increasingly important. Power and might could be much more readily and efficiently exercised over a fixed and determined territory and the people living within that territory than over a more or less loose association held together by personal relationships.

With the emerging territorial perception of public authority and jurisdiction came also a tension between forces of centralisation and decentralisation. France and England broke away from the originally united Holy Roman Empire to become independent states. After Maximilian I renounced the coronation as Emperor by the Pope, the legal authority of the Empire with regard to France and England was formally lost. In 1486, an imperial law referred for the first time to the Holy Roman Empire of the *German Nation*. In 1499, the Swiss confederation formally separated itself from the Empire in the Peace of Basel. Finally, in the peace of Westphalia of 1648, the territorial division of Western Europe was legally sealed by international law.

Authority of the kings ruling by divine right

The German Empire had been divided into many small and a few large principalities. The princes of these territories exercised almost absolute power and derived their authority from 'the grace of God'. The need to put an end to the permanent battles between the territories led finally to a mutual recognition of the territory and assets of the various princes. The feudal rulers were able to make the bundle of different private and feudal rights that they had inherited, acquired or won, appear as rights vested in them by the grace of God, and thereby legitimise their authority by the grace of God.

In England, the Lords were not able to exercise absolute authority over their boroughs and thus gain total independence from the Crown. However, as the power of the king was also limited by the Lords and later the Commons, in England (in contrast to the continent) it was also not possible for the Crown to achieve absolute centralisation of power. In France on the other hand, the king successfully exerted his absolute authority even over the original feudal rulers. Unlike the English Lords, who could live from their own income derived from the products of the their estates and from early industrial activity — especially the processing of wool, the French feudal rulers had to depend for their income on taxes, which they exacted from farmers with the support of the king. The king was thereby able to expand his power and to draw the feudal aristocracy into a situation of dependence upon the Royal Court at Versailles. Thus the necessary conditions for centralised French absolutism were realised.

The dispute between church and state

Besides the struggle over the centralised unitary state, the development of the territorial state in Europe can also be traced back to the profound dispute between the power of the church and the power of the state. This conflict was played out primarily in the battle for sovereignty between the Emperor and the Pope. But even at the lower level of district courts, the princes tried to impose the unity of the law within their territorial jurisdiction, notwithstanding traditional church jurisdiction over some matters. Inevitably, this led to a major dispute between church and state. The state imposed taxes on inalienable church property, asserted a right to participate in the election or nomination of church dignitaries such as Bishops, and assumed the right to visit and inspect convents and monasteries.

6.3.3.2 The Meaning of the Principle of Territoriality

Uniform application of the law within the territory

The development of the territorial state enabled the uniform application and implementation of the law within a particular territorial jurisdiction. Prior the establishment of territorial authority, the members of tribes were subject to their own tribal or customary laws, regardless of where they happened to be living. With the development over time of territorial authority, people became subject to the law that applied within the relevant territory, regardless of the tribe or clan from which they originated. The law was no longer connected to the person, but to the territory. Consequently, the judiciary was structured on the basis of territorial divisions – hence municipal, district, county and town courts.

This division of course led to the development of different laws and legal systems in different territories. However, as people could not be confined to remain permanently in the same territory, it became necessary to consider whether and to what extent the legal rights and obligations applicable in one territory should be recognised in another. The answer to this difficult question is today found in international private law. If for example a couple marries legally in Canada and then settles in the United States, the couple does not need to marry again in their new jurisdiction, as the Canadian marriage will be legally recognised in the United States. However, states retain the right to make some reservations with regard to such recognition, based on the principle of the '*ordre public*' according to which a state does not have to recognise foreign legal decisions that are clearly against the basic legal standards and values of the state of domicile. Thus in Switzerland for example, the marriages of a Sheikh to several women, which have been concluded legally in an Arabic state may be recognised; but it would violate the principle of *ordre public* if the Sheikh sought to conclude an additional marriage in Switzerland. Switzerland can refuse to permit this additional marriage even though the Swiss rules of international private law would in principle require that Arabian law be respected in such case. A medical doctor educated in Tunisia cannot practice her profession in Switzerland without first meeting the requirements imposed by Swiss law. The ability of states to impose territorial restrictions on the free movement of people, goods and services is however being increasingly limited by the free trade and commerce rules of the European Union and the World Trade Organisation (WTO). This provides another example of the principle of territoriality losing its significance.

Developments beyond Europe

One has to be aware however that these territorial developments are essentially confined to Europe and European legal orders. On other continents, power, might, and jurisdiction of the state have developed according to different principles. For this reason, modern territorial concepts cannot be applied without reservations to other legal systems such as those that emerged out of the legal history of the Ottoman Empire.

International law as law between states

The uniform application of the law within the territory of the state also led in the late Middle Ages to the development of a new type of law that applied to and between territorial sovereign states: international law. In the Middle Ages, disputes between peoples or territories were generally settled according to the legal norms of the canon law. However, as soon as states became independent from the church this law could no longer serve as the instrument of conflict resolution between states. For this reason it was necessary to establish a new legal system applicable to sovereign territorial states. The Peace of Westphalia which ended the religious wars in 1648, entailed an agreement that was based on the sovereignty of the states and the new concept of international public law – which applied to and between the states as subjects and which gave the states new legal rights and obligations in respect of their relations with each other.

Domestic law and international law

This newly established international public law applied in principle only to states. Based on the principles of sovereignty and territoriality, each state had the prerogative to decide the extent to which international legal obligations would be applied or implemented within the domestic law of the state. This sharp distinction between international and domestic law leads today to serious problems, as in many cases international legal norms and obligations need to be consistently and directly applied domestically in order to have any positive effect – for example in the case of international laws for environmental protection or international crime. In addition, international law is often binding not only on states but also on constituent units (such as provinces) within federal states. These constituent units are then responsible for implementing or adhering to international law, but as they are not recognised as sovereign subjects of international law they can neither sue other states or federal units for breach of this law nor can they be brought directly before an international court by other states or international organisations. Only the sovereign federal state as a whole, that bears responsibility for all territory within its borders, can be held legally accountable under international law.

Validity of the principle of personal application

Today, legal systems generally recognise the principle of territoriality as opposed to the principle of personal application. Based on the principle of territoriality, the state is the only competent authority to regulate legal relationships and determine legal norms with regard to people within its territory. The principle of personal application of legal norms is now only of very limited scope. Thus, states can for example regulate the citizenship rights of their nationals living in other states, and oblige such nationals to serve in the military or to pay fees or taxes. States may also invite their nationals living abroad to participate in elections and other polls or referendums.

One has however to be aware that legal obligations of nationals living abroad cannot usually be directly enforced by the state, as the state cannot exercise sovereign authority to execute legal orders within the territory of another state in which such authority is not recognised. In such cases, states depend on the support of the state having jurisdiction over the respective territory.

As a direct consequence of the principle of territoriality, states need to conclude international treaties on legal assistance. Such treaties enable states to obtain the support of partner states to forcibly execute criminal sanctions or to extradite persons to their state of nationality. Such treaties might also provide for cross-border cooperation in the investigation of crime, including interrogation of witnesses in a foreign jurisdiction.

6.3.3.3 Limits of the Principle of Territoriality

European Union

In the course of globalisation, the principle of territoriality is being increasingly eroded, particularly in relation to the member states of the European Union. About two thirds of the current legislation valid in theses states is based directly or indirectly on the directives and ordinances of the European Union. The member states of the European Union are still responsible for converting European Union law into domestic law and for executing those laws within their territory. The territory of the EU however has for some purposes replaced the territory of the individual member states, for example in relation to the regulation of foreigners crossing EU borders (under the Schengen Agreement).

World Trade Organisation (WTO)

Of even greater significance are the determinations of the World Trade Organisation (WTO). The fundamental philosophy of the WTO is based on the idea of a global free market system. Accordingly, member states are prohibited from taking measures to protect their domestic industries or national economy. Member states are permitted to impose regulations on trade and production for the purposes of public health and consumer protection, but they may not restrict the import of products and services for the purpose of protecting their own companies from foreign competition. Even public authorities in member states must comply with WTO rules of free market competition when contracting with private companies. This means that there must be a transparent tendering process that is also open to foreign bidders, provided that foreign bidders don't offer the lowest price based on exploitative labour practices (Anti-Dumping Agreement).

Power, politics and WTO

The prescriptions of the WTO however do not take into account the specific historical, social and economic characteristics of the member states. Historically rooted structures with regard to agriculture for example have a connection to the culture, landscape and to the society of a country. If the same rules applied to agricultural products the world over, this could lead to serious social problems in some countries. In free competition on the open market the strongest participant will win. When the strongest competitor misuses its power and monopolises control of the market, and when in addition it can influence the policy of the most powerful state in the world, other national economies do not stand a chance. The preconditions for genuine free competition are not fulfilled. Major companies that control the worldwide production of goods are profit-oriented and only politically dependent on the country in which they are officially based. From these headquarters decisions are made about the expansion or closure of businesses in foreign countries. Such decisions may have far-reaching social effects at the local level. However, for the company located far away, the risk of social conflicts in the affected country or countries is of little concern or consequence.

Social peace is local and not in the short-term interest of global shareholders

For the economic development of any country social peace is indispensable and is therefore also in the long-range interest of the national economy. However, the extent to which social peace is in the interests of development of the worldwide economy may be more limited. Of course, the world economy has an interest in social peace and political stability in all countries. But the executive body of a corporation is responsible for optimising the short-term profit of its investors. Shareholders are not usually prepared to finance long-term investments for the benefit of social peace. This again poses a serious challenge to the government of a territorially limited nation-state accountable not to shareholders but to its citizens, since it is not able to influence the strategy of the corporate management that is located beyond the territorial borders of the state, far away from the negative effects of its economic decisions.

Think globally, act locally

Global thinking and local action are, for example in the field of environmental protection, indispensable. The environmental policy of every state has direct or indirect effects on the territory and the people of neighbour states (for instance, atomic power-plants), on the geographic region (pollution of major rivers and lakes), and even on the climate of the whole planet (energy consumption and CO_2 emissions, US refusal to ratify the Kyoto Protocol). Environmental protection but also the increasing threat of international criminality and terrorism are potent examples of the effect that domestic policies and actions can have at the inter-state and international level, and they highlight the need for states to be held internationally accountable for their actions. These challenges require a new vision of the state constitution and in particular of the domestic and international accountability of states for their foreign policy. Whilst the European states are dealing with the increasing interdependence of states through strengthened international cooperation and international law, the USA on the other hand increasingly attempts as the 'World-Leviathan' to impose its own interests on the rest of the world.

THOMAS HOBBES' view of society, which he based on his observation of anarchy in London in the 1640s, has shifted to the international community. Whilst in the 18th and 19th Centuries the European continent was led by the HOBBESIAN worldview whereby the Leviathan had absolute power, the USA tended to follow LOCKE'S view of limited government. Since this time the balance of power and therefore ideology between Europe and the USA have diametrically changed. The now dominant USA is mainly led in its foreign policy by the view of HOBBES, while Europeans are now much more inclined towards the philosophy of JOHN LOCKE and IMMANUEL KANT.

Development of the law regulating the relationship of neighbours

Even the rigorous application of the principle of territoriality cannot avoid all legal conflicts over jurisdiction. Where for instance should a businessman pay taxes if he runs a business in Germany but lives in Switzerland? Such issues between neighbouring countries are mostly regulated in treaties on double taxation, which clearly determine the law to be applied. But how are states to respond if their citizens' health is endangered by the import from a neighbouring state of contaminated livestock or food? Such threats cannot be dealt with exclusively through bilateral agreements. New regional organisations are required which can give effect to appropriate regulations not only in the interest of one state, but of an entire community of states. Regionalisation and globalisation are leading to the creation of a new regional and/or global public interest, which however, because of the democratic deficit of international politics, remains hostage to political power games between states. To respond to these new challenges, a transnational shift in the perception of law and state is required. The territory of individual nation-states cannot be legally or politically isolated. Only if states are prepared to open their territory to the international legal network and cooperate with regional and international rules for the realisation of the regional and international public interest, will states be effectively able to meet the threats and challenges of globalisation.

International waters

One area which has never been fully subject to the principle of territoriality is the control of international waters. The rules regulating the traffic of ships on international rivers such as the Rhine or the Danube, the cooperation of riparian states on inland waters such as Lake Constance, or the rules on the rights of access, navigation and the use of the sea are all the subject of disputes which cannot be solved simply on the basis of the principle of territoriality. With regard to lakes shared by several riparian states, some assert that the borderline is to be drawn in the middle of the lake, whilst others are of the opinion that the entire body of water is the common property of all riparian states. Such a dispute exists between Germany, Austria, and Switzerland with regard to the borderlines on Lake Constance. And an examination of the regulation of fishing rights on the Doubs River that runs along the French-Swiss border, reveals that the strict application of the principle of territoriality can have absurd consequences. The border between France and Switzerland runs in some parts down the middle of the river and in other sections along the Swiss or along the French shore. The fish and fishing rights however, do not belong to the neighbour states according to the line of the state borders and nor does the responsibility for fishing regulation and control.

The sea

The disputes over the extent of coastal states' geographic range of control and authority over the sea are well known. Mining rights, fishing rights, customs and police control are the most important sovereign rights that have to be regulated in relation to seas and coastal waters, and are often the subject of international disputes. It is the task of international law, of the United Nations and in particular of the International Court in the Hague to develop principles which produce acceptable regulatory solutions for all nations. These principles have to take account of the fact that the high seas are international waters that belong to everybody ('*res communis omnium*', H. GROTIUS, *Vom Recht des Krieges und des Friedens*, Book II, Chapter 3, IX). As a consequence, everyone must have access to international waters. This principle, developed by FRANCISCO DE VITTORIA (ca. 1490–1546), GABRIEL VASQUEZ (1549–1604) and GROTIUS (*Mare liberum*, 1608) is to be implemented at a time in which the high seas are simultaneously being exploited for their treasures (oil, plankton etc) and being misused as a garbage dump for the world. It should also be noted that coastal states are not allowed to prevent landlocked states such as Switzerland from accessing and using the sea.

Coast and high seas

One has to distinguish between the high seas which belong to all (*communis omnium*) and which have to be accessible for navigation by all states, and the exploitation of mineral resources under the sea. The mineral resources are the common heritage of mankind. It must therefore be guaranteed that the exploitation of this heritage is for the common benefit of all peoples. Such goal can however only be achieved if the United Nations transfers and allocates usage rights (with concessions and conditions) according to a just formula or criteria of distribution. This authority of the United Nations over the ocean floor begins 200 nautical miles from the coast. Up to this distance, the right to exploit minerals under the ocean floor belongs to the respective coastal state.

In earlier times, the limits of coastal sates and the borderline of the high seas was determined by the extent of the coastal state's capacity to exercise military control over its coastal waters (*Imperium terrae finitor obi finitor armorum potestas*, H. GROTIUS, *Vom Recht des Krieges und des Friedens*, Book II, Chapter 3, XIII). This led to different interpretations of the extent of coastal zones on the basis of different arms capabilities (three mile zones, 12 mile zones, etc). In the age of rocket technology, coastal states can no longer measure their sovereign limits on the basis of the range of their weapons. What is important is that sovereign authority extends to a distance that is mutually recognised by the coastal states.

Air space and outer space

Had it been foreseen at the time of the development of the territorial state that mankind would eventually not only control the oceans but also the space above the earth, principles to regulate sovereignty over and navigation of air space would also have been developed. However it was not until the 20th Century that regulation of the air space over territory became necessary. In relation to air space it is generally accepted that states will mutually recognise a state's sovereignty over air space up to the height at which such sovereignty can sensibly be exercised and enforced. The space that extends beyond the earth's atmosphere however (outer space) belongs in common to mankind, just as the high seas are commonly owned. Thus, neither states nor private enterprises have the right for example to assert sovereignty over the moon or a part of the moon. The rights of states in relation to outer space are regulated in international treaties.

The international borders of a state can thus not be represented as a simple line, nor can the state be seen as a flat surface area. Rather, the state and its borderlines are three dimensional, with the third dimension extending from the line of the border above the surface of the soil up to the enforceable limits of air space, as well as below the surface.

Occupation and annexation

Can states acquire and exert sovereignty over new territory? In this context a distinction is made between areas that are not already part of an existing state, and territory that is already under the control and authority of a state. During the colonial era, the theory prevailed that land that is unoccupied (or inhabited 'only' by non-European native inhabitants) can be lawfully acquired by settlement, that is, by ongoing physical occupation and control. Based on this theoretical right, the Europeans settled or conquered the colonies and displaced the indigenous inhabitants.

UN Charter and Geneva Conventions

What is the legal situation in relation to the occupation of territories that are already under the sovereign authority of an existing territorial state? As the Charter of the United Nations expressly prohibits acts of aggression against states, any military acquisition of territory of a sovereign member state of the UN is illegal under international law. The acquisition of territory may be legally permissible by means of contractual agreement (such as a peace treaty). Areas that have been occupied by military forces in the course of a war or other military intervention are covered by the IVth Geneva Convention of 1949 on the right of civilians in occupied territories. This Convention determines the obligations and the legal powers of the occupying forces with regard to the civil population. The fact however that Israel formally refutes the application of the IVth Geneva Convention within the territories occupied after the six-day war, on the basis that these territories have never been under the sovereign authority of a state party to the

Geneva Convention, reveals that even the application of international humanitarian law can be controversial in practice.

In any case the IVth Geneva Convention gives factual circumstances and relations a particular legal significance. According to Article 6 of the Geneva Convention, only a limited number of the prescriptions of the Convention are applicable if the occupying forces control a territory for more than one year after the cessation of hostilities. If a territory is acquired by the unilateral act of the victorious state, it is an annexation. Although annexation is impermissible under the Charter of the United Nations, various wars of the recent past reveal that such belligerent acts still occur.

Treaties on state borders

The precise course of effective state borders is, where possible, set out in international and bilateral treaties. If such treaties do not exist, the states have to rely on customary law. However, customary law is vague and open to different and controversial interpretations. Varying interpretations of customary law often lead to territorial disputes between neighbour states such as Russia and China, India and China or Chile and Argentina.

6.4 Sovereignty

6.4.1 The Significance of Sovereignty

From the state of nature to the society of the sovereign state

The development of the notion of the state and the theory of sovereignty within the history of European thought on legal and state philosophy can undoubtedly be regarded as a particular and unique product of European culture. Even though one may rightly criticise this tradition as problematic, it will continue for a long time to have important effects on the development of states. In terms of the development of human autonomy, we can distinguish between three distinct phases:

In the first phase, humans were completely dependent upon nature; they were objects of nature. Nature was more or less considered to be their deity.

In the second phase, individuals became increasingly independent from nature through the discovery of fire. With this development people achieved some degree of 'individual sovereignty'. The myth of the eternal punishment of Prometheus for having stolen fire from the Gods and giving it to people tells us of the magnitude of this development at the time.

In a certain sense, one can describe as the third phase the phase of sovereignty. With the notion of sovereignty, human beings 'stole' the fire of law and justice and established secular authority in place of the gods. With the advent of secular sovereignty it was no longer religion that determined right and wrong, but rather the state. The state became the source of law and justice. The almighty secular Leviathan was born out of this sovereignty.

Robinson and Friday

Let us briefly recall the story of Robinson and Friday. Both are living on an isolated island in the middle of the ocean. They come from different countries, cultures and religions. They each have a different perception of law and justice and each feels loyalty to their homeland. Robinson follows the laws of his home country. What he has since childhood known as right and wrong, he also considers on the island to be right and wrong. The same is the case for Friday. He also distinguishes between right and wrong, just and unjust, in the manner he has learned from his family and his tribe.

According to the old public international law of Europe, Robinson is entitled, provided he occupies the island by military force as a representative of his home state, to overpower Friday and compel him to obey the laws of Robinson's people. If he does not kill him, he has the right to use him as a slave. Friday is entitled to do the same, if he is the stronger one. The theory of sovereignty and the state developed since Middle Ages provides them with another possibility. They can for instance agree, either in common or under the authority of either Robinson or Friday, to take control of the island and its inhabitants and to determine henceforth what rules shall be applicable on the island. They can agree to enact, either alongside or in place of the old traditional laws, new rules and regulations. In this case they are not only taking their own fate in their hands, but also determining for all people inhabiting or visiting the island the rules relating to what is right and wrong, just and unjust.

Based on this development of their consciousness, a communal order can be developed which is more independent and self-sufficient because it is not based on a backward-looking, traditional value-system but on values established by the 'founding fathers'. This marks the emergence of the rational state, in which laws are no longer based on a more or less opaque prehistory but on rational decisions of the legislature.

Demos

The theory of sovereignty however is much more far-reaching. Robinson and Friday, who belong to completely different cultural groups, are able to reach a common rational decision to establish a new community. This community does not depend on language, religion or tribal history. They call this new community the 'state'. Their state is not one that has gradually emerged over the course of history, rather, it is a deliberately and consciously constructed community. If their relatives should land on the island they would initially have to be regarded in this community as foreigners, but could later be 'naturalised' or acquire citizenship. It is the law that determines who belongs to the community, and not blood or origin or language. The state is in other words a community order rationally and wilfully created on the basis of the demos (the people) it comprises.

But from where do Robinson and Friday derive the right to create new laws for the island, and to replace the original legal system with a new legal order that they have agreed upon? From where do they derive the right to establish a new state-community that is equal in rights to other states? Why do their decisions and their will suddenly have greater validity than the traditional law?

The magic word: Sovereignty

The key to answering all of these questions is 'sovereignty'. Sovereignty is essentially the 'big-bang' or the original source from which the state, law and secular justice have emerged. It is from sovereignty that the state derives its right to organise itself as a state and to set the valid law for its population. As soon as Robinson and Friday become a sovereign community, they can govern over the island; sovereignty entitles them to do so.

Absolute – limited sovereignty

What we see in the story of Robinson and Friday in terms of illustrating the notion of sovereignty is certainly a somewhat oversimplified portrayal. In historical reality, state communities are not formed suddenly, and do not have an instant self-awareness of statehood. Since the beginning of the development of the theory of sovereignty, there have been substantial legal and philosophical objections to absolute sovereignty, which effectively limit the autonomy of the state in relation to law making. Proponents of natural law theory, following the concepts of LOCKE's inalienable rights, are amongst the principal exponents of limited sovereignty. According to this theory, the powers of state and the scope of state sovereignty are bound and limited by inalienable rights. The contrary view, derived primarily from the theory of HOBBES, is that by means of the social contract the state acquires unlimited rights and unlimited sovereignty. The social contract is the original and ultimate source of all law, by virtue of which all law can be derived only from the state.

Notwithstanding some reservations, it can justifiably be argued that the theory of sovereignty has been decisive for the development of state and political communities, because it has given these communities a sense of self-awareness and thereby enabled rational government and the development of autonomous organisations.

6.4.2 The Dispute between Church and State as Precondition for the Development of the Claim to Sovereignty

How did the theory of sovereignty develop? Why did it first emerge on the European continent? Undoubtedly the dispute between church and state in the Middle Ages, as well as the disputes between the French King and English King, and between the Emperor of the Holy Roman Empire and the Pope respectively, were decisive for the development of the theory of sovereignty.

Unity of religion, morality, law and state authority

We have seen that almost all authority relationships have a religious origin or background. Once they had acquired power, rulers sought to entrench and legitimise their power with the aid of religion or magic, and to base their authority on divine right. But not only the rights of the ruling authority, rather all rights and laws were attributed to a sacred origin. For this reason, laws could not easily be altered by a political ruler. Political authority, law and religion were united. In the Roman Empire for instance the priests served the state. As MOMMSEN has pointed out, even at the personal level, priesthood and political leadership coincided and the career paths ran parallel. The double-aristocracy of the Middle Ages that developed out of the conflict between church and state was in ancient times completely unknown. In ancient times, the gods were always a necessary part of the state (T. MOMMSEN, p. 70).

A similarly close connection between religion and state can be found in the Jewish and Islamic state. The Caliph is at the same time the head of the church as well as the head of the political union (IBN KHALDÛN, p. 160 ff). The concept of the Israelites being the chosen people has a religious origin. Also within African cultures (C. MUTWA, p. 102) and Japanese Shinto tradition we find that political authority has religious origins.

Give to Caesar the things that are Caesar's

The relationship between Christianity and the state developed very differently. Christianity began during and within the Roman state, which based its authority on different religions and numerous gods. However, as Christianity did not recognise several gods, the Romans saw the Christian religion as a threat to their state authority. Thus from its very inception the Christian religion was forced to develop a self-understanding, which granted to it the right to existence within the framework of the existing state authority of the Roman Emperor. With statements such as 'give to Caesar the things that are Caesar's, and to God the things that are God's', this tension between state authority and the transcendental authority of God was supposed to be resolved. The conflict however, remained. Should people be more obedient to God or to the Emperor? Which authority prevails in case of inconsistency: that of God or that of the Emperor?

The theory of the two swords

In this sense, the dispute between church and state had already begun at the time of the foundation of Christianity. Unlike other religions, which served to establish and legitimise political authority, Christianity has since its foundation questioned political authority and the role of political authority in religion. This conflict was essentially suppressed during the Roman Empire, as for opportunistic reasons Christianity became the official state religion. However, this did not completely eliminate the seed for disputes and conflicts that were to arise later between political and religious authority. This tension began to show during the Middle Ages. The theory of the two swords provided at least a temporary solution to this tense relationship. According to this theory, the Emperor holds the worldly sword and is the highest political authority, whilst the pope holds the spiritual sword and has supreme authority in relation to church and religious matters (since approximately 1050). Pope Gregory VII was of the view that the Pope as God's representative on Earth holds both swords, and that through coronation of the Emperor he lends the worldly sword and political authority to the Emperor.

Gradual independence of political authority

In the history of the Christian states, the consolidation of the position of the Pope and the centralisation of the church are significant. At the beginning of its comprehensive authority in Western Europe, the church was able to exert a decisive political influence over the Emperor. The Archbishops participated in the selection of the Emperor, and the Pope anointed the Emperor. Nevertheless, the seed for the separation of church and state was already sown. The two powers stood in direct competition with each other.

Ultimately, this competition necessarily led to a conflict between the church and the political powers. The state resisted any political interference by the church, and at the same time sought to exert some influence over the religious authorities. Granting church institutions immunity from the secular political jurisdiction was the first step towards the separation of church authority from the state authority. In the so-called Investiture Conflict, church and state contested the power to appoint Bishops and the submission of Bishops to the authority of the Emperor. In the early Middle Ages, many communities successfully resisted extensive interference of the church. In 1112, the citizens of Cologne submitted a report directed against the Archbishop for the securing of city liberties. This is just one of the many examples which demonstrate that the political power of the state was able gradually to assert its independence from the church.

Absolutism

The feudal structure relied on a traditional hierarchical order, which distributed limited fief-rights to different holders of fiefs. Feudal masters did not have unlimited rights with regard to their subjects, but rather only such powers as were necessary to fulfil their protective responsibilities. The most powerful princes and dukes however, tried continuously to remove any limitations on their power and to extend the scope of their authority over their subjects. They wanted to exert their independence externally in relation to the Pope, and also to assert independence and sovereignty internally with regard to their subjects.

The French King succeeded in establishing such sovereignty without restriction. He was able to establish himself as an absolute monarch. In England however, the King was bound by the Magna Carta and by the decisions of Parliament. The sovereign, subject to the rule of law, was the 'King in Parliament' – that is, the King together with the Parliament. The German Emperor also failed, in contrast to the French King, to impose absolute power over his dukes and princes. Thus it was not possible to centralise sovereign power under one centralised imperial administration, and Germany remained an area of small competing principalities.

The way in which the sovereign power of the state developed in Europe differed from state to state. It depended on the different course of disputes between the dukes, the empire, and the estates on one hand, and on the controversy between worldly or secular authority and the Pope as the spiritual ruler of Europe on the other.

6.4.3 BODIN'S Theory of Sovereignty

Sovereignty is the absolute and continuous power to command of the state

The French philosopher JEAN BODIN helped to legitimise the independence of political authority from church authority with his theory of sovereignty: "a commonwealth is the rightly ordered government of a number of families and of those matters which are their common concern, by a sovereign power" (J. BODIN, book I, chapter 1). According to BODIN, only institutions which can exercise the highest authority of command on a permanent and uncontested basis can properly be regarded as sovereign: "sovereignty is that absolute and perpetual power vested in a commonwealth which in Latin is termed majestas ..." (J. BODIN, book I, chapter 1).

This highest authority of command is, according to BODIN, realised in the hereditary monarchy or when a monarch is elected or appointed for life. In both cases, the ruler of the state is not answerable to any other secular authority. If the ruler is elected only for a certain limited period then he is not sovereign – he is merely an office bearer. In this case the real holder of sovereignty is the aristocracy or the people, depending on who is empowered to elect and unseat the ruler.

No right to resistance against the king who rules by divine right

According to BODIN, the sovereign is not accountable for his actions and decisions to any human institution, but is at least answerable to God. No secular institution however is authorised to pass judgment on the king. Accordingly, BODIN denies the people the right to resistance or the right to tyrannicide.

Whilst not expressly articulated, BODIN'S theory of sovereignty was impliedly directed against the power of the church and the Pope, in that the sovereign was not responsible to the church nor to the Pope. BODIN did not consider the monarch as the holder of the sword to rule the secular world. His concept of sovereignty viewed the sovereign monarch as God's direct representative and governor on earth who is directly accountable to God. With this concept the theory of the king ruling by the grace of God, or by divine right, was born.

Discretionary power of the Royal Legislature

"If we insist however that absolute power means exemption from all law whatsoever, there is no prince in the world who can be regarded as sovereign, since all the princes of the earth are subject to the laws of God and of nature, and even to certain human laws common to all nations" (J. BODIN, book I, chapter 8). BODIN thus does not advocate absolute political power unfettered by any superior law. On the other hand, the sovereign is in BODIN'S view not even bound by the laws that he himself has enacted. He can sign his laws with the formula '*car tel est notre plaisir*' (if such is our good pleasure), a formula which was used by the absolutist French Kings.

BODIN'S perception of the law led to a clear break with the traditional legal order of the Middle Ages. From this point on even 'unjust' laws had to be obeyed, because they sprang from the sovereignty of the crown. The sovereign had absolute power to change and create law, provided such law did not plainly contradict divine and natural law.

According to the legal tradition of the Middle Ages, the source of all law was not the state but rather God as the creator of the Earth. For this reason, courts and judges followed in this period a principle that today seems counterintuitive: *older law overrides younger law*. BODIN'S theory of sovereignty was the starting point for a 'revolutionary' new conception of the law: That law is only valid by virtue of the sovereignty of the state and not because it corresponds to the traditional custom handed down over the ages. The law had no longer necessarily to reflect the cumulative wisdom of history.

Preparation of the final secularisation of state authority

Based on BODIN'S theory of sovereignty, the state acquired the competence and authority to enact new law, which breached old law and thus was stronger than custom and tradition. The foundation for positivist theories of law and state was thereby laid. However, BODIN himself must still be counted as a natural law theorist, since he did not take the second important step towards the total secularisation of state authority, namely attributing the source of state legitimacy to the people rather than to God. "Because there are none on earth, after God, greater than sovereign princes, whom God establishes as His lieutenants to command the rest of mankind, we must enquire carefully into their estate, that we may respect and revere their majesty in all due obedience, speak and think of them with all due honour. He who contemns his sovereign prince, contemns God whose image he is [made] ..." (J. BODIN, book I, chapter 10). The complete separation of state power from the authority of God was not proposed or effected until more than a century later, by the philosophers of the social contract theory and in particular HOBBES. BODIN left the Promethean fire, or at least the smouldering ashes of sovereignty, with the Gods. But his theory of sovereignty paved the way for the total secularisation of sovereignty and the emergence of social contract theory, which accorded popular sovereignty the status of being the original source of authority for state, law, and justice.

Although BODIN always attempted to rely on God as the basis of supreme political authority, we can also find in his writings some attempts to recognise sovereignty as the formal source of ultimate authority: "If a sovereign magistrate is given office for one year, or for any other predetermined period, and continues to exercise the authority bestowed on him after the conclusion of his term, he does so either by consent or by force and violence. If he does so by force, it is manifest tyranny. The tyrant is a true sovereign for all that. The robber's possession by violence is true and natural possession although contrary to the law, for those who were formerly in possession have been disseized" (Chapter 8).

Sovereignty of the organs of the state

A further point of incoherence within BODIN'S theory of sovereignty is the unclear distinction between the sovereignty of the state and sovereignty of the office holders or the organs of the state. The sovereignty of state organs refers to the question of which organ or institution within the state community has sovereignty with regard to other organs or institutions. On the other hand, the sovereignty of the state itself refers to whether the state unit as such is internally and externally recognised as sovereign.

BODIN is primarily concerned with the sovereignty of the organs of the state, that is, the sovereignty of the king and the sovereign power of the prince or duke in relation to his subjects and the estates. Of course, BODIN is fully aware that the king does not hold unlimited power and that he has in certain cases to consult the parliament. Thus he cannot impose unlimited taxes on the people. It is significant however, that in case of an emergency he does not depend on the approval of his estates. "But if any necessity should arise of imposing or withdrawing a tax, it can only be done by him who has sovereign authority ..." (Chapter 10). For BODIN, the sovereignty of the prince or the king presupposes the sovereignty of the state.

Law and might

In the writings of BODIN the relationship between law and might remains unclear. Is the sovereign whoever has the might to enforce his orders within a state community? Or does might also require a certain legitimacy? Although BODIN'S remarks on the sovereignty of the tyrant could lead us to the conclusion that for him the power to enact laws is the product of absolute might and does not require any further legitimacy, he also emphasises that this right should not be misused. Nevertheless, he denies that anyone has a legitimate claim to pass judgment on the actions or decisions of the sovereign king.

Consequently, BODIN rejects the possibility that sovereignty may be divisible into different parts. The prince can not share his sovereignty with a second prince. "If the prince can only make law with the consent of a superior he is a subject; if of an equal he shares his sovereignty; if of an inferior, whether it be a council of magnates or the people, it is not he who is sovereign" (J. BODIN, book I, chapter 10).

Content of sovereignty

In his treatment of the attributes of sovereignty, BODIN shows almost statesman-like vision and foresight. What competences and powers must a state or a king possess in order to be described as sovereign? The first aspect of sovereignty is the right to enact laws that are binding on every individual. This power includes the competence to abolish existing customary law and to provide for new privileges. "All the other attributes and rights of sovereignty are included in this power of making and unmaking law, so that strictly speaking this is the unique attribute of sovereign power" (J. BODIN, book I, chapter 10). Additional attributes of sovereignty include the right to declare war and make peace, to appoint holders of high office, to determine disputes and declare the law, to receive oaths, to grant pardon and otherwise exercise the prerogative of mercy, to determine the rules of weights and measures, to coin money and to raise taxes.

6.4.4 Sovereignty as a Prerequisite for Statehood

The state as an order for peace and unity

According to BODIN, the state is an indivisible, externally independent entity which cannot enact valid law for any external power. It is the state that determines which organ of the state has the authority to enact legal norms that are valid for everybody within the state. For BODIN, this ultimate power to determine the internal organisation of the state belongs to the prince or king. In contrast, the theory of the social contract which developed later did not place sovereignty in the hands of the prince who is accountable only to God, but in the hands of the people, thereby taking the final step in the secularisation of the state.

The function of the state as an order for peace and unity is the foundation and the justification for the domestic validity of the law. It has not only empirical but also normative significance. The prince must acquire independence both internally and externally, that is, independence from the church and from other states. Other power-centres for their part must recognise and respect this independence and may not interfere in the internal affairs of the respective state.

Sovereignty and statehood

The normative significance of the theory of sovereignty however, is not limited merely to the recognition of sovereignty. A state is only a state if it has sovereignty. Sovereignty therefore is not a consequence of statehood, but rather a prerequisite for statehood. Only territorially defined communities that are internally and externally recognised as sovereign can properly be regarded as states. This of course means that statehood is negotiable, that is, it can be gained, changed or revoked through conquest, annexation or occupation. When a unit achieves sovereignty over a particular territory it becomes sovereign. Thus, states can be dissolved, changed or newly founded. This forms the theoretical basis for the justification of European colonialism. But also the annexation of enemy territories by military occupation is possible and, if based on a 'just' war, permissible. Statehood is given to those who are in the position to exert sovereignty over a certain territory.

Monopoly of force

According to the theory of sovereignty the state is also the unit with the authority to control law and order, and to use force for the enforcement of the law. Only the sovereign ruler has the power and the responsibility to mediate and resolve disputes. Private feuds, tribal revenge, and lynch-justice are therefore unlawful. Only the state has the power and the right to use force, that is, to wage wars or punish criminals.

Law follows might

The absolute and uncontested authority of the prince or king relies on the condition that he has achieved sovereignty over a certain territory and that he can rule the peoples in this territory independently of any foreign power. In other words, his factual and political power also gives him legal legitimacy.

BODIN'S successors took these reflections further, in that they expressly recognised effective power as the only basis of the law. Therefore, those who are the effective power-holders are also entitled to enact legislation. Power alone determines the law. This means that not only the state but also the prince is replaceable. If the prince is removed from his throne and a new tyrant manages to gain sovereign power, the tyrant will be recognised as sovereign and will have the power to make and unmake laws.

Sovereignty understood in this way permits even further-reaching actions: whoever can enact law is also entitled to declare former unlawfulness as legal and vice-versa. The justification and the preconditions for a state that can effect revolutionary changes in society are thereby created.

Prince, feudal hierarchy and people

By legitimising the prince as the sovereign by the grace of God, the prince is separated from the Pope and authority is thereby somewhat secularised. But this authority still remains supernatural and transcendental with regard to its subjects. The peoples are obliged to obey the authority of the prince not only because he exercises enforceable power but also because he represents God's kingdom on earth.

The sovereignty of the prince is reflected in the duty of the people to obey his direct authority, and not the authority of the master of the clan or the vassal. However, as we have seen, the hierarchically structured feudal order of the society of the Middle Ages is in contrast to this concept of direct authority over all citizens. Only the idea that the prince must represent the interests not only of his vassals but also of his entire people enabled the later centralisation and rationalisation of state power.

People's sovereignty

With the theory of the social contract, the idea of a secularised popular sovereignty was finally able to replace the concept of sovereignty of the prince by the grace of God, and the process of gradual secularisation of the state was complete. The legitimacy of state power was seen henceforth as stemming from the people, not from God. In this context it is ultimately insignificant, whether the people transfers all its rights to the monarch through the social contract (as proposed by HOBBES), or whether the people concludes a social contract and then only in a second contract, a contract of authority, empowers the sovereign ruler to rule over the people (as proposed by PUFENDORF).

Reason replaces God

Through the social contract, sovereignty loses its transcendental connection and is instead placed in the hands of the nation. Secularised authority is justified by the people, not by God, and sovereignty is now tied to reason or the '*ratio*'. It is therefore no accident that with the triumph of reason – which is the basis for the sovereignty of the individual – the theory of sovereignty was opened up to new developments.

While the laws of the king who ruled by the grace of God were legally binding and legitimate because of divine authority, such laws were also expected to serve the common interest of the people. With the shift of state authority from God to the people, new concepts surrounding the notion of the general interest also emerged. From the idea of the *bonum commune* to ROUSSEAU'S *volonté générale* (general will), the idea of the public interest – the secularised understanding of the general welfare of the people – arose.

Limited popular sovereignty

Of course, not all scholars advocating the theory of popular sovereignty saw it as justification for absolute and centralised state authority. According to LOCKE for example, there exist pre-state rights, which are inalienable and cannot be renounced by the people in a social contract.

6.4.5 *Problems of State Sovereignty*

Legal fundament of sovereignty

A state that has plenary and unrestricted power over its territory and its people is considered sovereign. Thus it is clear that state, law and power are connected, but what is the nature of their relationship to each other? Is power subject to law?

Does the validity of law depend on its enforceability? Or can a law exist which is binding and obligatory but not enforceable? Is the factual exercise of power always also lawful or can it be unlawful? In the next section, these difficult problems of the state and legal philosophy will be further examined and illuminated.

Whoever claims to be entitled to make law presupposes that there exists a law which vests the lawmaker with such entitlement. If sovereignty is a legal notion, it logically entails the presupposition of a pre-existing and superior law.

To date, the theory of state has not been able to overcome this dilemma of the preconditions to sovereignty. HEGEL recognised that the theory of the social contract presupposes a legal system that recognises contracts. The contract is a creature of the legal order and can only be imagined as a legal document in the context of an already existing legal order. Thus the theory of sovereignty gives rise to the fundamental dispute between those who acknowledge a legal order which is superior to state sovereignty (natural law) and those who claim that the law is derived only from sovereignty itself (THOMAS HOBBES, JOHN AUSTIN (1790–1859) and HANS KELSEN).

Different notions of sovereignty

Different authors use the term sovereignty in a number of different senses. Some regard sovereignty only as a political notion, whilst others see it as a legal concept. Some refer to sovereignty only in an absolute and unrestricted sense, whereas some assume that sovereignty is inherently relative and limited, even divisible. We will now take a closer look at these different concepts, in order to enable a closer examination of the fundamental issues of sovereignty.

The discussion of BODIN'S theory of sovereignty has already revealed that sovereignty has to be examined from a number of different perspectives. For example, a distinction must be made between sovereignty as ultimate responsibility or competence, and sovereignty in the sense of absolute might. Whilst sovereignty as responsibility or competence is a *legal* concept that includes for example the competence to make binding decisions (including enactment of laws), sovereignty as absolute might is a *political* concept, which reduces sovereignty to the power to command without questioning the legal content of such commands.

Internal and external sovereignty

Moreover, one has also to distinguish between the internal and the external sovereignty of a state. A state is sovereign from the external point of view, if it is directly subject to international law. As a subject of international law, the state can deal on a direct and equal footing with other states to conclude treaties, declare war or reach peace agreements, and is also the bearer of duties and obligations under international law. However, the question arises whether, taking into account increasing international interdependency and transnational cooperation, this exclusive concept of external sovereignty is still applicable. When for example the constituent units within a federal state conclude international treaties, should they not also be directly responsible for their international actions and be subject to the jurisdiction of international courts?

In terms of the domestic view of sovereignty, a state is sovereign if it can govern internally without external interference. When the state is considered in relation to its citizens to possess the highest and uncontested authority, the state is internally sovereign.

Sovereignty of a state organ

In relation to internal sovereignty, one is required to ask which organ or which branch of government enjoys the highest and absolute authority with regard to the citizens. Whilst for BODIN the sovereignty of the state was concentrated in the hands of the prince or monarch, in modern democracies ultimate sovereign authority is assigned to the organ that has the power to make decisions on constitutional change. However, in many countries the procedures provided for constitutional amendments are so complex and elaborate that one can regard as sovereign those organs which have the power to make laws (the legislature) and the power decide on the application and interpretation of the constitution (usually the highest court), rather than the body or bodies that have the ostensible power to amend the constitution. In some states (such as France), the head of state has the power to declare a state of emergency. In cases of emergency the head of the state is given the power to invalidate existing laws and thus can effectively exercise unaccountable authority. The state theorist CARL SCHMITT therefore argued that sovereignty belongs to whichever state organ has the power to declare and control a state of emergency (It should be noted that as a scholar CARL SCHMITT supported the political philosophy the NAZI regime, see in this context Izhak Englard, 'Nazi Criticism against the Normativist Theory of Hans Kelsen', *Israel Law Review* 1999).

Relative and absolute sovereignty

Different views can also be found with regard to the content and extent of sovereignty. For some, sovereignty entails original and ultimate authority – a power that is neither subordinate to nor derived from any other power or competence. This understanding of sovereignty also entails exclusiveness: no other state and no international organisation can make decisions on behalf of or instead of the sovereign state. It is clear that this concept of sovereignty, which excludes all other bearers of authority or competence, no longer reflects the reality of an interdependent globalised world order. Others consider sovereignty not as the final and absolute power to make legal decisions, but as a status that contains all the powers that are usually required in order for a state to function effectively. These include defence, police, legislation, judiciary, economy, and internal administration.

6.4.6 *External Sovereignty*

6.4.6.1 Development and Function of External Sovereignty

The law of inter-state relations

The states that entered into communication and relations with each other, exchanged ambassadors, concluded treaties but also waged wars against each other, needed to establish a legal order regulating their mutual rights and obligations. The great Dutch scholar of the 17th Century HUGO GROTIUS developed the basic principles for this new international law, which he deduced from natural law principles. His theories on the just war and on the difference between private law and the law of the state, as well as the famous principle *pacta sunt servanda,* are all based on the assumption that there must exist a legal order which regulates relations between states.

Sovereign states are bound to respect international law, which in principle is only applicable to states and not directly to individual citizens. Under international law states are empowered to conclude treaties with each other, and based on the same law they are obliged to fulfil their treaty obligations. According to GROTIUS, international law also entitles states to declare war on another state or states, to occupy foreign countries as well as to take enemy combatants as prisoners of war. However, all actions taken during war are subject to the international law relating to war (*ius in bello*).

The rights and entitlements enshrined in international law apply only to states as the legal subjects of those laws. This is even the case with regard to internationally guaranteed human rights, which, whilst phrased as individual rights, legally constitute an obligation upon states to implement human rights within their domestic law. Only in exceptional cases do individuals have a direct claim to an international body or court against their state in order to protect their human rights. But even if such individuals succeed in an international legal action, it is ultimately up to the state to fulfil its international obligation to follow the international decision by applying it within the domestic law. According to international law, beyond existing customary international law, only international treaties concluded by states according to the procedures and principles provided by international law can create new legal rights and obligations.

International law added a new dimension to the theory of sovereignty, although this was not explicitly set out by GROTIUS. BODIN too, whilst he mentions explicitly the *ius gentium,* did not speak of international law in the modern sense. He considered the *ius gentium* as encompassing both the domestic laws that all states have in common, as well as the law that applies as between states. Relations between the Christian states at this time were regulated largely by a general consensus, and relations with non-Christian states were forbidden. There was thus no need for formal and abstract laws to regulate inter-state relations (H. QUARITSCH, p. 370).

Equality of states

States could only be empowered in theory and practice to create new international law in the field of inter-state relations, when the principle of equality between states was recognised. Only if the right of states to engage with each other on an equal footing is recognised, is it possible to acknowledge bilateral treaties as binding law. This basic principle of the equality of states was developed by a representative of the small mini-state Neuchâtel, EMER DE VATTEL (1714–1767).

The principle of equality has never been reflected in practice, as there have always been differences in power and influence between states. In recent times this inequality is especially pronounced, as the differences in geographic size and economic and military power between states are to some extent reflected in international organisations. Large and powerful states have gained certain legal privileges in the international arena – such as permanent membership of the UN Security Council, or greater voting weight in the European Union. Nevertheless, whilst the principle of equality is not implemented in practice, the formal recognition of sovereign states as equal subjects of international law has never been formally challenged (see Art. 2 of the Charter of the United Nations: "The Organisation is based on the principle of the sovereign equality of all its members").

The function of external sovereignty

Only sovereign states are legal subjects of international law in the fullest sense. International law does recognise other legal subjects, such as international organisations, the International Committee of the Red Cross, the Vatican and soldiers who are directly bound by the international law of war, however they are only the bearers of rights and obligations under international law in a restricted sense. States on the other hand, are not merely passive bearers of rights and obligations under international law, they can via bilateral or multilateral treaties also actively participate in the creation, amendment and development of the international law.

Strongly connected with the notion of the legal subject of international law is the principle of state equality. States are all on equal footing because they are all legally sovereign. Externally they are all subjects of international law, internally they make autonomous decisions on domestic law and policy.

Sovereignty – direct application of international law and state equality

Nobody, not even BODIN, tied state sovereignty to the prerequisite that the state be recognised as the highest, completely independent and exclusive source of authority. Supreme power (*suprema potestas*) according to BODIN, means only that internally, with regard to his subjects, the prince needs to bear exclusive and supreme power. Such power however is bound by the law of God and by the law that applies between states. When we speak today of external sovereignty, it is more helpful to adopt the concept developed by VATTEL of external independence and external equality with other states. According to this understanding, external sovereignty means that states are the legal subjects of international law and can create international law, that they enjoy legal equality under international law, and that they are responsible to the international community for the application and implementation of international law in their domestic legal systems.

The understanding of external sovereignty as direct subjection to international law corresponds with the prevailing view of this notion in today's theory and practice. The International Court of Justice has however started to make a distinction in this context between political and legal sovereignty. Political sovereignty is the factual independence of the state, which of course varies according to the economic and military power of the state. Legal sovereignty however, means that each state has the equal right to decide on its membership of an international organisation. A state can based on this principle even discontinue its membership of an international organisation, according to international law principles such as *clausula rebus sic stantibus* (things thus standing), even if the organisation makes no specific provision for withdrawal (as is the case with the European Union).

Direct application of international law to federal states

International law still operates on the basis of the old tradition that states are impermeable and unitary monarchies that ultimately can only be legally represented by the head of state. However, since the 17th Century the world and the international legal order have changed radically with the rise of globalisation. The old nation-states have had to dismantle their original monopoly over external affairs, and at least partially decentralise this function to their regions. Today their exists a regional and worldwide network not only of states but also of regions, cities and sub-national federal units. International law has to date not taken proper account of this development. It is still the case that all international law obligations – even those which have been entered into by the semi-autonomous federal units within a nation-state – are legal obligations in respect of which the nation-state is externally responsible for implementation and adherence, even though those obligations have not been explicitly agreed by the nation-state itself. Sub-national federal units which agree to certain international obligations, are not directly accountable to the international community for the fulfilment of such obligations or their imple-implementation in domestic law.

Moreover, whilst federal units of nation-states are not direct subjects of international law, they are often the immediate addressees of international laws and agreements that contain rules relating to matters that fall within the responsibility and competence of the sub-national federal units. These units may therefore be responsible internally for implementing the rules prescribed by an international organisation. However, it is still the nation-states that remain legally responsible to the international organisation. It is only the nation-state that can bring an action or be made party to an action before an international court, and which is legally obliged to adhere to the decision of an international court, even in relation to matters that are in reality within the competence of a sub-national federal unit. To this day, federal units are not empowered by international law either actively or passively to seek direct enforcement of international law.

This can have dramatic consequences. The United States for example refused, in relation to its own federal units, to enforce the decision of the International Court of Justice in the *LaGrand* case (*Germany v. United States*, International Court of Justice, 27 June 2001) in relation to the death penalty. The condemned paid for this legal 'loophole' with his life.

Right to wage war

Direct application of international law to the states has always entailed, even in the times of THOMAS AQUINAS and before GROTIUS, the right of states or of monarchs to wage war, although not private war. Military actions of states according to GROTIUS are required to be 'just', that is, they must comply with the law of war (*ius in bello*). Even this right to wage a just war was reduced by the 1945 Charter of the United Nations to the right of self-defence. Article 2 of the UN Charter prohibits the threat or use of force against another state. Under the Charter, military force is only permitted for self-defence, in the sense of a sanction against states that do not comply with the prohibition on the use of force (Article 51). It is obvious though that such general prohibition of military force and war has not brought about an end to military conflict. The prohibition of military force has merely resulted in attempts by states to justify their wars with often unconvincing arguments of self-defence or of the defence of members of their ethnic group who are perceived to be under threat in a neighbouring state. Some states also seek to invoke the right of self-defence in order to combat and prosecute terrorists in any state where they are assumed to be hiding. Attempts are also made to justify international military intervention based on an expansive interpretation of what constitutes 'aggression' and a 'threat to peace'. At the outset of the war against Iraq, the US sought to justify the war on the basis that Iraq possessed 'weapons of mass destruction'. When it later became evident that there was no such threat, the Bush administration sought to rely on the general violation of human rights by Saddam Hussein as a new and alternative justification for the use of force.

Whilst up until the first half of the 20th Century international relations were dominated by territorial disputes, in the second half of the 20th Century international conflict centred around ideological wars waged by states representing one of the two ideological blocks led by the superpowers. Since the fall of the Berlin Wall, international conflicts have tended to centre around hostilities between different ethnic groups, and often involve international intervention in civil warfare in an attempt to prevent ethnic cleansing.

The growing tensions between North and South, between industrialised states and developing states, result from new battles over the distribution of wealth, resources, and the costs of production as well as trade and consumer prices. States no longer fight to colonise foreign territories. It is only between the former colonies that there are still some territorial disputes, as a result of the arbitrary borders inherited from the former colonial states that have left some peoples and tribes without territory. In order to overcome the problems caused by colonial rule, such states have to find new grounds for sustainable and legitimate polities.

6.4.6.2 The Relationship between International Law and Domestic Law

Dualism

The fact that, with the development of the theory of sovereignty there developed also a new international law that applied to and between sovereign states, led to a dispute over the question of whether and how this new international law should be given effect within the domestic law of the states. Is it for example only states that are bound to respect bilateral treaties of settlement, or can affected citizens derive individual rights from such treaties and seek to enforce them directly against state authorities? In answer to such questions there are two distinct positions. One side is of the view that sovereignty is an impenetrable barrier, which separates the two legal systems from each other – international law and domestic law. International law and domestic law are two completely different systems, in terms of formulation, implementation and enforcement, and it is not possible for them to interconnect. Thus, if international law is to have any validity or effect domestically, it must first be transformed into domestic law by an express legislative act of the domestic parliament. This approach is known as dualism. International treaty law does not vest individuals with rights and obligations, and such law is not binding on nor applied by the national courts unless it has been transformed by the legislature into the domestic law. International customary law does however have automatic application domestically. Most common law countries have traditionally taken the dualist approach (except the United States), and it is for this reason that the European Human Rights Convention was not applicable in the British courts until it was transformed into British domestic law by the *Human Rights Act* of 1998.

Monism

In complete contrast to the dualistic concept is the monistic position, which is based on the principle of the unity of the law. According to this theory, the law is a unified entity that cannot be artificially separated into two distinct systems on the basis of the abstract construct of sovereignty. Accordingly, international law must also be automatically and directly applicable in the domestic context, provided that the international law contains norms that are self-executing and capable of being directly applied and enforced.

The relevance of domestic and international legal institutions

Many modern scholars of international law believe rightly that the dispute between the theories of monism and dualism misses the real issues. According to this view, the main problem of the implementation of international law is caused by the fact that international law is applied and interpreted by different institutions, which according to their status and position within the domestic legal system accord a different weight to domestic and international laws. If international law is applied by an international court, the court will make its decision based exclusively on international law. If however a domestic court applies international law, the court must operate within its domestically determined jurisdiction and apply the international law within the context of the national domestic law. In this respect, it is certainly conceivable, perhaps desirable, that national laws could oblige the courts to directly apply international law and even to give priority to international law over domestic law.

The fact that states are the immediate and primary addressees of international law need not necessarily lead to a dualistic separation of domestic law from international law. International law generally has a different sphere of validity. This difference however, does not require a total separation of the two legal fields.

The dispute is thus much less theoretical than practical. The question is which domestic institution should be given the competence to decide on the application of international law: the legislature or the courts? This question depends again on the internal order of checks and balances with regard to the ratification of treaties. If treaties are ultimately ratified by the same state organ that is responsible for enacting law (the legislature), then there should be no difficulty with automatically according treaties the same internal validity as domestic legislation.

United States

The United States pursued a different concept with regard to the transformation of international law into domestic law. At the time the USA was founded, the former British colony was a weak state dependent on the respect of the rule of law and in particular on respect for international law by the larger powers. This is likely the main reason why the USA departed from the common law tradition by adopting in the Constitution the principle of the direct application of international law. According to Article VI of the Constitution, international treaties are part of the supreme law of the land. Thus, the Constitution adopted in principle the monistic concept. However, whilst in almost all states that have a monistic system it is for the judge to determine whether a norm within an international treaty is clear enough to be self-executing or is non-self-executing and therefore requires express implementation by the national legislature, in the United States this function is performed by the Senate when it decides on the approval of the treaty. Thus the Senate effectively has the power to decide whether or not treaties will have domestic application, and thus to undermine the monistic requirement enshrined in the Constitution.

The monistic theory of KELSEN

Law is not something that can be separated into two distinct substances and thus kept in two different pots. The law is a solid unit and thus valid and binding upon states as well as upon the individual. Justice as the source of the legal system is the same notwithstanding the origin of a particular norm. For this reason the law that flows from this source is all of the same nature. Salt does not turn into sugar when it is poured into a different pot by the states. A murder cannot be justified just because it has been committed for the ends of the state.

KELSEN however, is an advocate of the monistic approach on the basis of different, formal grounds. Similarly to AUSTIN, KELSEN is also of the opinion that the legal order is a system of positive norms or commands. Legal norms seek to regulate behaviour: they command somebody to do or to refrain from doing something. They are concerned with what *ought* to be. All norms are deduced from the supreme or basic norm (*Grundnorm*), which does not need to conform to any particular content, but needs only to command obedience and to be effective. The leads to a formal or pure understanding of the law which is devoid of any substantive content.

How does KELSEN reconcile the notion of sovereignty with this pure theory of law? The legal order understood as a system of norms or 'oughts', is a unified whole, derived from a single *Grundnorm*. This basic norm is largely identical to sovereignty. "Sovereignty in this sense is not of a perceptible or otherwise objectively detectable quality, it is but a prerequisite, that is, the prerequisite of the normative order as the supreme order which can with regard to its validity not be deduced from any other higher order" (H. KELSEN, *Souveränität sowie die "Wiener rechtstheoretische Schule*", p. 272 translated from German by the authors).

KELSEN thus takes a monistic view of the relationship between international and domestic law. Contrary to BODIN, he strips the notion of sovereignty of its political content, and sees it rather as a formal legal notion (as did JELLINEK). In accordance with his monistic approach, he is of the view that two constructions are possible: either international law is sovereign and therefore the domestic law has to be deduced from international law, with international law being supreme; or the domestic law is considered sovereign, and therefore international law must be derived from and subject to domestic law.

KELSEN'S monistic argument on this point is convincing. The dualistic thesis of two separate and independent spheres of law contradicts the fundamental principle that the law according to its basic purpose has to be considered as a uniform whole. However, that aspect of KELSEN'S theory of sovereignty that deprives sovereignty of any political content is ultimately unconvincing. Sovereignty understood as a supreme and irreducible basic norm is an empty formula without any practical or theoretical meaning.

6.5 Sovereignty and Might

6.5.1 Might and Force

6.5.1.1 Defining the Issues

Fear of compulsion

A person who receives an order from the tax office to pay taxes has no alternative but to pay those taxes if he/she wants to avoid being pursued by the state. A person who is held at gunpoint by a criminal demanding money also has no alternative but to give in and hand over his/her money. What distinguishes the payment of taxes from the handing over of money to the criminal?

The usual answer to this question is: taxes must be paid because there is a valid legal obligation to pay tax; whereas the money given to the criminal is given to him because one cannot otherwise escape from the immediate threat of violence and the criminal's momentary power over one's life. This answer is not entirely satisfying, because the taxpayer also fears the execution of his obligation by force. The decisive difference has therefore to be found within the definition of the 'legal obligation'.

Legal obligation

What is a legal obligation? A legal obligation exists if it is an obligation that is derived from a law, for example tax legislation. But how is taxation law to be distinguished from a general rule issued by the mafia that for example, all businesses within a particular area have to hand over 30 per cent of their income to the mafia? The usual answer to this question again would be: The law is *valid,* but the mafia rule has no validity. But what constitutes legal validity?

Laws of nature and laws of mankind

Is a penal law valid in the same manner as a law of nature? If a stone is dropped from one's hand, one knows that according to the law of gravity the stone will fall to the ground. The laws of nature are empirically detected. Because all objects behave the same way, one can conclude that there must be a law which makes them behave the same way. This law was then detected and labelled as the law of gravity, which has its cause in the attractive force of the earth, and which in turn has its deeper cause in the nature of matter.

Based on the normal behaviour of humans one may deduce certain sociological 'laws of behaviour', but not legal norms with legal validity. On the contrary, the law seeks not to reflect but rather to influence human behaviour. The law aims to prohibit, compel or authorise certain types of behaviour. The legal order is based on the general conviction that men recognise their legal obligations and are therefore able to decide whether or not they want to comply with their obligations.

The laws of nature on the other hand do not require or permit any subjective decision-making.

Why are laws valid? Three scientific answers

Let us imagine that an extraterrestrial scientist is charged with the task of finding out why it is that in some parts of the earth cars drive on the left side of the road, whilst in other parts of the planet cars drive on the right. The scientist has three methods by which he can seek to fulfil his task:

> The sociological approach:
>
> The scientist comes to earth and undertakes an empirical examination of the behaviour of car drivers. He observes that in some places the car drivers are driving on the left and in other places they are driving on the right. Why this is so, he will not discover. However based on his empirical findings he is at least able to establish the empirical law that for example in the UK people drive on the left and in Germany people drive on the right.
>
> The positivist approach:
>
> If the scientist follows a different method, he will ask humans why they are driving on the right or on the left side of the road. The earthly beings will point to the traffic rules they are following. Now he knows that the behaviour of human beings is regulated by positive legal norms.
>
> The philosophical approach:
>
> However, it still remains for the scientist to understand why the laws regulate behaviour in one particular way and not in another. In particular, the scientist is yet to answer the question, why in some areas cars are following one law and in other areas they are following another law. If he wants to find an answer to this question, he will have to question the origin of laws, and he will discover the source within the concept of state sovereignty in the sense expounded by AUSTIN.

Legal realism

If he limits himself to the first empirical method, he is following the school of the legal realists. If he proceeds according to the second method, he belongs to the positivist school of KELSEN. If he follows the third method, he is applying the philosophy of HOBBES, AUSTIN and HART. What do we mean, when we assert that a legal norm is enforceable and therefore valid? There are a number of different possible answers to this question. The Uppsala school of legal philosophy (A. ROSS *et al*) proceeds from the hypothesis that only those laws are valid, which have a high probability of being applied. According to this theory, the validity of a law depends therefore on the forecast of the probability of its effective application and enforcement. Such forecasts can however also be made in relation to the dictates of the mafia. It is of course entirely plausible that those whose lives are threatened by the mafia will even be more reliable payers than the tax-payers.

Ultimately, the Uppsala school cannot provide a satisfactory answer to the question of why the judge, at least the judge of final instance, applies the law. For the judge, the prognosis of application of the law cannot be a relevant factor in whether or not the law will be applied, as the judge makes this decision him/herself and thus determines whether the forecast which has been made by the lawyers is correct or not. Could a judge for instance refuse to punish a paedophile, because the case histories in this area of criminal law indicate that the relevant law is very badly enforced and the prognosis for enforcement is therefore poor?

Positivism

For KELSEN on the other hand, the law is valid because it is enacted in accordance with the valid procedure for the enactment of laws and because it is in conformity with the superior law, for example the constitution or international law. This approach then leads to the question: what is the basis for the validity of the supreme law? Why, according to KELSEN, is the constitution to be considered 'valid'? It is valid because the constitution is derived from a fictively assumed basic norm (*Grundnorm*). This basic norm however, is without substance and prescribes only that there are normative obligations, that is, norms that contain an imperative command or prescribe a 'must' or 'ought'. This order of commands prescribing what 'ought' to be exists alongside the order of what 'is'. Each positive law is embedded in this order of the 'ought', just as each concrete fact is part of the abstract category of the order of the 'is'. Since the 'ought' cannot be deduced from the 'is', the content and substance of the 'ought', that is, of norms, cannot be rationally determined. Based on the fact of what a human being is, one cannot logically deduce any obligation to respect the dignity of human beings.

Therefore, if the mafia establishes a procedure for the 'enactment' of directives, those directives are also law, provided they do not compete with or contradict other norms within an existing legal system covering the same territory. In other words, such directives would be valid law in a state ruled by the mafia. In any other state, legal positivism enables us to make a clear distinction between the legal obligation to pay taxes and the compulsion to pay money to the mafia.

AUSTIN'S state philosophy

A third answer to the question of the validity of a legal obligation can be found in the legal philosophy of AUSTIN. According to AUSTIN, legal obligations and laws are valid because they are derived from the sovereignty of the state and thus can be enforced by state power. According to AUSTIN there is a close interconnection between the validity of law and the sovereignty of the state as well as the state's power to enforce the law.

This interconnection between law and the power that enforces the law is obvious. For this reason, we shall now deal with the relationship between sovereignty and power as basic phenomena of the legal order.

Rational legitimacy

The might of the state is only partially dependent on its military and/or police power. A large part of the might of the state depends on rational legitimacy. For this reason we will have to distinguish between the might or force of the state and the power or authority of the state, in order to fully grasp the interconnection between law and power.

The bank teller hands over money to the bank robber because he/she is forced to act by the threat of violence. Taxpayers pay their taxes not only because of the threat of enforcement by the state, but also because they regard themselves as being obliged to act according to their legal obligations. They do not only act because they fear the punishment, but also because they recognise and accept their legal obligation. They acknowledge the legitimacy and rationality of the law which requires them to pay.

Whilst state sovereignty depends not only on the authority and enforcement power of the state but also on its internal legitimacy, there may also be instances in which state power does not enforce justice but injustice. The holocaust or the brutal decimation of the Cambodian population by the Khmer Rouge are but two historic examples of grave crimes and injustices committed by state authorities. But how should people behave in relation to a state of such injustice? Do they have a right or even an obligation to passive or active resistance? This question of the right of resistance is of considerable significance and will be examined at the end of this chapter.

6.5.1.2 Identity of Might and Law

What is the relationship between law and might? Does the right to govern the state belong to whoever has the might, or coercive power, to do so? It is well known that BODIN legitimised the one who was able to assert supreme power within the state with the aura of sovereignty. Was the notion of sovereignty therefore created simply in order to justify factual might?

Obedience creates sovereignty

AUSTIN is the philosopher who has most consistently advocated the logical theory that obedience creates sovereignty: "If a determinate human superior, not in a habit of obedience to a like superior, receives habitual obedience from the bulk of a given society, that determinate superior is sovereign in that society, and the society political and independent" (J. AUSTIN, p. 194).

Sovereignty thus is determined by the loyalty or obedience that the people exhibits towards the government. How such obedience is achieved, whether by incentives and threats or through information and persuasion, is not relevant. What is decisive is the fact that the population is obedient (*Oboedientia facit imperantem*).

But who exactly is sovereign? According to AUSTIN, the sovereign is he who possesses supreme power and who is independent, that is, owes no obedience towards another government. If a government is obliged to observe obedience towards a superior government, this superior government is to be considered sovereign. Another important element of sovereignty is obedience. The majority of the people must demonstrate consistent obedience towards their sovereign. If for example a land is occupied by foreign troops for a short time, sovereignty according to AUSTIN is not therefore transferred to the occupying state. "A given society therefore is not a society political unless the generality of its members be in a habit of obedience to a determinate and common superior" (J. AUSTIN, p. 196).

Legal commands emanate from the sovereign

For AUSTIN, positive written law is derived from sovereignty. Legal obligations are commands. How can a legal command be distinguished from the command of a robber who holds a bank teller at gunpoint and demands money? The decisive distinction is that legal commands can be traced back to the sovereign, whereas the command of the robber cannot. "But every positive law, or every law strictly so called, is a direct or circuitous command of a monarch or sovereign number in the character of political superior: that is to say, a direct or circuitous command of a monarch or sovereign number to a person or persons in a state of subjection to its author. And being a *command* (and therefore flowing from a *determinate* source), every positive law is a law proper, or a law properly so called" (J. AUSTIN, p. 134).

With these remarks (made in 1832), AUSTIN developed and expanded upon the legal positivism introduced by HOBBES. AUSTIN does not contest the existence of the law of God. AUSTIN was in fact a strong moralist and believer in divine or natural law. The natural law of God however, has to be distinguished from the positive law which is derived from the sovereign. Whilst religious or moral norms may sometimes coincide with the positive law, when they differ the moral norms cannot be enforced because they cannot be traced back to the authority of the sovereign.

Secular law is distinct from religious morality

With this theory the secularisation of law was finally complete. In ancient times the law had a divine origin. Since BODIN, law had been derived from the sovereign, albeit a sovereign whose legitimacy stemmed from God and who was bound by divine law. AUSTIN on the other hand, definitively separates positive law from divine law. He derives the positive law only out of the sovereignty of the state; and this sovereignty is not dependent on God but on the obedience of the people, that is, it is dependent on voluntary or enforced recognition by the people.

Acceptance of legal obligation: HART

The modern positivist theories are indebted to and have built upon AUSTIN'S theory of sovereignty and HOBBES' social contract theory. In the 20th Century these theories were developed further from different perspectives. Most closely connected to AUSTIN is undoubtedly the theory of HART. Sovereignty according to HART cannot however be reduced to obedience, habit and commands. The sovereign is also obliged to obey certain rules when it enacts new laws. The sovereign must respect specific rules of procedure. This applies to a democracy in which different organs share in the exercise of state sovereignty. However, it is also true for a state which is ruled by a single dictator. Moreover, all sovereign states are bound to observe international law. The law according to HART cannot be reduced to the concept of commands. Law assumes a binding validity that is not based solely on power or fear of punishment, but relies also on the recognition and conviction that it is just and correct.

6.5.1.3 Might alone is not enough

Bases of the validity of law

With the stipulation that law can only be valid if it has internal validity (that is, if it accords with the rule of recognition), HART opens a new horizon for the theory of law and sovereignty. Robinson can issue certain commands to Friday. Provided he accepts these as law, Friday will obey the commands. If he is convinced that the commands are incorrect or unjust, he will only comply if he is forced to. The internal validity in this case is missing. Sovereign is therefore not whoever has supreme power, but rather whoever within the framework of the prescribed rules enacts legal norms the validity of which is affirmed by the recognition of the people. The more cruel and totalitarian the authority is, the less legitimacy and legality it will have and the less sustainable it will be. Sovereignty therefore does not entail absolute power that enables a sovereign to enact arbitrary laws at whim. Sovereignty permits only the enactment of laws that are recognised by the people as valid. If a dictator wants to issue commands that are regarded by the people as incorrect or unjust, he must resort to enforcing such commands through terror and fear. In other words, he is not superior to the law and therefore cannot change the people's view of what is lawful and unlawful at his discretion. In this sense his might is limited. If he disregards the people's sensibility of justice he will be forced to implement his commands by deploying secret police and state terror.

Limits of legal obligation

A bank robbery does not become a legal expropriation simply because it was ordered by the dictator or committed by the dictator himself. There are some elementary legal principles that have to be observed even by the sovereign. The sovereign cannot alter the nature of human beings and for instance order that people must henceforth fly to their place of employment. Nor can the sovereign force parents to kill their children, or oblige Christians to adopt the Islamic faith or vice-versa.

While the first example (flying to work) is physically impossible, the religious example contradicts the fundamental natural feeling of humans that they should be able based on their human dignity to decide on their relationship to God. Man cannot be compelled to violate natural principles and human rights. The law and thereby the sovereign are bound to observe and to respect the physical possibilities of humans as well as their natural, generally recognised psychological condition. Formal sovereignty does not legitimise every state command.

Limits of sovereignty

From the preceding discussion it does not follow, that the state no longer needs might or the power to enforce law, nor that law which has to be enforced through might is inherently unjust law. Positivism and the secularisation of law which were introduced through BODIN'S theory of sovereignty should however not mislead states to an overestimation of their power and possibilities. Whilst states might be able to enact law within a very broad spectrum, they are also bound to observe certain limits of humanity and of human nature, which cannot be disregarded with impunity.

6.5.1.4 The Sociological Relationship between Law and Might

Civil war

If within a state a minority fights against the might of the state, if it claims sovereignty over the territory it controls, and if moreover it demands the right to unilateral secession, there are always far-reaching and often unforeseeable legal consequences for all people living within the state, quite apart from the terrible damage that any civil war causes to civilians. The minority, based on its right to self-determination, will claim unrestricted sovereignty over the people living within its controlled territory, as well as over its peoples living in the territory controlled by the mother-state. To whom then will citizens have to pay taxes? Who has legitimacy? – The minority which calls for nationalism on the part of its members, or the mother-state which requires acceptance of its legal obligations based on rationality, history and legal security? What kind of consequences might young men be faced with, if they are required to serve in the military for one of the parties to the conflict and possibly have to fight against close relatives in the military of the 'enemy' party? Both parties claim to have sovereign rights over the same territory. The mother-state relies on history and the existing law. The minority claims sovereignty based on the pre-constitutional unity of the people, which gives rise to the right to self-determination and unilateral secession. *De facto* the territory controlled by its forces already belongs to the new state by self-declaration (as in the self-declared Turkish republic of Northern Cyprus), but *de jure* the territory belongs to the former state. (See also the Kosovo conflict, where the Security Council has resolved that the territory belongs to Serbia but Western states are about to recognise the self-declared independence on the basis of the *de facto* separation of Serbia. In the case of eastern Jerusalem, the ICJ has declared that the *de facto* control by Israel is not legal and thus not legitimate).

Legal security

People need to know that the law will be applied and enforced by state authority and even if necessary through state force. If the conviction takes hold that the state is prepared to forego unpaid taxes, nobody will continue to pay taxes, as everybody will assume that his neighbour is no longer paying taxes. If however taxpayers know that all taxes will be collected, forcibly if necessary, they will jealously ensure that every taxpayer fulfils his obligation and that nobody profits from an oversight by the tax authority. Thus, the law requires state force for its implementation. Very often, the mere knowledge that the state will use this force if necessary is sufficient to ensure compliance with the law by the vast majority of the population.

Corruption

On the other hand, the first signs of a corrupt state administration can have catastrophic consequences. Everyone will attempt to bribe civil servants for their own interests, whereby the authority of the state and the law will be undermined and will lose their force and credibility. Once corruption becomes widespread, the law will only be enforced against those who are economically weak, and this marks the beginning of a state ruled by the upper class and a judiciary enslaved to the interests of wealth. Law will serve only the wealthy, whilst the marginalised poor will always be on the wrong side of the law.

Might as the ability to make an impact

What is to be understood by might of the state? A member of parliament has power if she is in a position to convince other members of parliament whose opinions deviate from her own, that their position is wrong and that they should therefore follow the better arguments. If we now try to measure or to define the power of this member of parliament we can observe the following: If one wants to measure the power of this member, one has to know how great the probability or the chance is that the other members of parliament will agree with this member's opinion. ROBERT DAHL (1915) defines power "as the difference between the probability of an event given certain actions by A and the probability of the event given no such action by A" (DAHL, p. 214).

Factors of power

Power is determined by a variety of factors. Power can be based upon the possibility to use coercive force. Power as the chance to influence others however, depends primarily on one's ability to convince others, on trust, as well as on the interests, personality and competence of those who are to be influenced. If the person to be influenced is economically vulnerable, if he is psychologically weak, if he is risk-averse or if he is accustomed to being obedient and being led by others, then it will be easier for the influential opinion leader to gain support for his/her position. If however the person to be influenced is independent, competent, economically and psychologically strong and prepared to take risks, it will be more difficult for the opinion leader to change this person's mind.

Like the power of parliamentarians, the power of the state is also determined by a variety of different factors. Taxpayers pay their taxes because they are to a certain extent afraid of the procedure for the forcible implementation of the law if they default. Thus, they fear the force of the state that stands behind the law. In part however, they also have an inner conviction that they have to pay their taxes because they believe in the correctness of the relevant law. The law was enacted via a just procedure and it contains just prescriptions. The lawmaker has the competence to enact such laws because its authority has been recognised by the people on the basis of tradition, charisma or rationality (M. WEBER).

State force and state authority

The might of the state can therefore be sub-divided into *state-force* and *state-authority*. Let us first examine the *state-force*. Force is the use of coercive physical means to compel certain behaviour. Only organs of the state are entitled to use forceful means to enforce the law and control behaviour. The monopoly on the use of force distinguishes the modern state from states in earlier times. The previous right of the master of the house to beat his servants and slaves has been abolished. Only organs of the state can apply force, and state organs can only use this force in a manner that is reasonable and proportionate in order to implement the law (as a measure of last resort).

Accountable use of force

State force is however relentless. People are permanently exposed to it. Whoever violates law will be punished by the prosecuting authorities. It is therefore necessary to ensure that the authorities that exercise state force are also controlled. State force can only be exercised within the confines of the law. State force must be limited and controlled, and state organs must be accountable to the people for the exercise of state force. Those who can use force without restriction or accountability will become monsters. "Power corrupts and absolute power corrupts absolutely" (LORD ACTON).

In a recent judgment, the Israeli Supreme Court has declared torture to be illegal, despite arguments that it is often the only way to prevent further killing of innocent civilians, with the following reasoning:

> "Deciding these applications weighed heavy on this Court. True, from the legal perspective, the road before us is smooth. We are, however, part of Israeli society. Its problems

> are known to us and we live its history. We are not isolated in an ivory tower. We live the life of this country. We are aware of the harsh reality of terrorism in which we are, at times, immersed. Our apprehension that this decision will hamper the ability to properly deal with terrorists and terrorism, disturbs us. We are, however, judges. Our brethren require us to act according to the law. This is equally the standard that we set for ourselves. When we sit to judge, we are being judged. Therefore, we must act according to our purest conscience when we decide the law" *(Decision of the Supreme Court of Israel as High court of Justice on September 9, 1999).*

The use of force, if it is done in the name of a state authority in accordance with law, may be justified. However when private individuals forcibly detain a person, they are violating the law. The prosecuting authorities of the state on the other hand have the power, based on the judgement of a court, to imprison a convicted person. This power however has to be subject to limits and controls.

The state in any event uses force only in very few instances. Even in totalitarian states, the threat of force is sufficient to ensure obedience to the regime. Everybody fears arbitrary state action and state terror. In liberal states however, the state can gain acceptance and obedience by other means, such as through democratic authority and rational arguments.

Max Weber

What is the basis of state authority? MAX WEBER distinguishes three different types of legitimate authority: Legal authority, traditional authority and charismatic authority (M. WEBER, p. 475). In our opinion, the authority of the state is based on the trust the citizens have in the organs of the state. This trust depends on the rationality of their decisions (M. KRIELE, *Recht und praktische Vernunft*, p. 117), on the decision making process, on tradition and in certain states also on charisma.

Economy

Power always presupposes a relationship between two or more persons. It is based on the strength and superiority of one party to the relationship, and at the same time on the relative dependence and weakness of the other side. A key factor in terms of power relations is therefore economic dependence. In states in which the economy is centralised and nationalised state authorities can, in addition to state force and state authority, also use the economic dependence of the citizens as a means to implement state decisions. Any person within such a state who is in need of employment, housing or admission to study will without coercive force conform to the state order rather than suffer disadvantages. A similar principle applies in liberal states, when individuals are dependent on state grants, scholarships or other state assistance.

It is important that the economic power of the state is subject to the same controls as the application of state force. It has to be applied equally and in the same manner in relation to all people, in accordance with relevant laws and regulations. A student should not be denied a scholarship because she is a member of the 'wrong' party. The old age pension should not be denied to an entitled recipient simply because he once committed a crime. It is therefore an important task of the legislator to ensure that the economic dependence of certain citizens cannot be misused or exploited by the administration.

Law and might

How do coercive force, economic dependence, state authority and law relate to each other? The close connection between these different means of enforcement can most easily be explained using the following image: light will glow, if a functioning lamp is connected to an electric power source. State force and economic power are comparable to the electric power. Electricity can however only generate light through a working lamp. The light (the law) will only be produced if the lamp (state authority) is in working order. In the absence of state legitimacy force can still be exercised, but this will not create law. If the state authority enjoys a high degree of legitimacy it can govern effectively with little force, just as a good economical lamp uses little power. If however, the state authority is weak it will require a lot of power in order to produce light or law. With no state authority, even the greatest force will not generate law.

Trust

Dsi Gung asked his master "what is good governance?" The master answered: "To ensure enough food, enough military force and the trust of the people in its ruler." Dsi Gung continued: "But if one had no choice but to renounce one of those three preconditions, which one should be renounced?" The master answered "The military force". Dsi Gung persisted, asking: "If one had no choice but to renounce one of the two remaining preconditions, which one should be renounced?" The master answered: "The food. All people must die eventually. But when the people has no trust, one cannot establish any government" (CONFUCIUS, p. 123).

This old Chinese wisdom says more about the relationship between law and might than many lengthy and sophisticated theoretical works. The military forces represent the enforcement power of the state, nourishment represents the economic power of the state, and trust corresponds to the legitimacy of the state authority. For the idealistic CONFUCIUS, the legitimacy of authority has absolute priority; for MACHIAVELLI on the other hand, legitimacy has a considerably lower value. Ultimately however, no state authority can be sustained in the absence of internal legitimacy. Sooner or later every ruler must seek internal legitimacy for his/her authority.

The law can only develop and flourish within a state which is militarily and economically strong and which enjoys the trust of its people. Sovereignty cannot be based on force alone. The basis of sovereignty must therefore be the trust of the people in the rational validity of the laws and the legality of government action.

6.5.2 Sovereignty and Legitimacy of the Law

Who gives the state and the law their internal authority? The people? In the sense of *demos* or *ethnos*? The question of who is 'the people' is examined below. For the time being we can simply say that authority increases with recognition by the people. The quality of statehood depends on the condition that only state organs can use force. But every state institution and organ must enjoy the necessary recognition and respect of the people in order to exert authority. The real source of statehood, that is, sovereignty, lies with the people. Without the people, one can exert physical force but one cannot exercise authority. Sovereignty as the basis of the legitimacy of state authority emerges ultimately from the people. How did this shift in the theory of sovereignty come about and what is its significance?

6.5.2.1 From Sovereignty of the Monarch to Popular Sovereignty

Vox populi, vox dei

Ideas on sovereignty have developed considerably since BODIN. For BODIN, the sovereign was the monarch who ruled by the grace of God. The development of democratic theory and in particular the theory of the social contract then declared that sovereignty is in fact borne by the people. ROUSSEAU'S theory transferred sovereignty from the monarch to the people. According to his concept of the social contract, sovereignty is the expression of the general will (*volonté générale*), which is always right and just. The idea of the general will embodies the symbol of the common interest of the people, but at the same time it contains also the danger of an absolutist totalitarian 'democracy' (such as Nazi Germany or the South African apartheid regime), or at least could be interpreted in this way. Nevertheless, one has to concede that ROUSSEAU'S ideal of democracy was based on democracy within a small and manageable group. ROUSSEAU hardly envisaged a large centralised and bureaucratic democracy.

Secularisation and sovereignty

It is also significant that with the shift from the sovereignty of the monarch to the sovereignty of the people, the connection of the monarch to divine law was dissolved. Thus, the rational foundation of secularised popular sovereignty brought an end to the transcendental relation between law and state. This shift led to statements such as: 'The people is always right'. '*Vox populi – vox dei*' – the voice of the people is the voice of God. 'The interests of the people always have priority'; 'the people or the state cannot commit any injustice'. The democratic majority ultimately decides, either through representatives or through a direct democratic process, whether a decision is in the best interests of the state or the nation. Fascist and communist totalitarian regimes have with such statements taken the idea of the absolute and unlimited sovereignty of the people to an absurd extreme.

Who is the people?

The question that still remains unsolved is, who belongs to the people? As the people became the substitute for the transcendental and unlimited legitimacy of God, it has come to be surrounded by a symbolic and almost sacred mystique. Whoever can determine which people within which territory is entitled to claim and exercise popular sovereignty, decides on the economic existence of many people, on the fate of generations and on power relations between peoples. It is therefore hardly surprising that minorities make symbolic claims to sovereignty in order to throw into question the original authority of the state and its majority people. The dispute over the question of who belongs to a people has been a fatal one for many peoples. As there is no clear, just or true answer to this question, we are faced with irresolvable conflicts in which, like in the Greek tragedies, the contradictory convictions of 'justice' on each side ultimately result in cruel injustice for the peoples of both sides.

Abstract notion of the people

There is another basis on which popular sovereignty can hardly be compared with the sovereignty of a monarch. With regard to the sovereignty of a monarch, it is relatively simple to determine who is the bearer of legal and political sovereignty and thus, who is the real power-holder. On the other hand, the people is an abstract mass. Popular sovereignty does not mean that the former powers of the monarch will be distributed equally to each voter or citizen, even though each vote counts equally. The innumerable dependencies of citizens within the modern state, the complex and inscrutable power structures of the state, and the disparate power centres tend rather to result in feelings of uncertainty and powerlessness on the part of citizens. The people often does not see itself as sovereign, but rather as a pawn in a complex and opaque power game.

Pluralism of power

Today, law and power often appear to be divided. Legally, the people has responsibilities in many areas, but in reality it often feels overlooked. The people does not have the feeling that the state is governing in the interest of the people, but rather in the interest of the government itself. The numerous corruption scandals of recent years, even in ostensibly democratic states, have further undermined the credibility of politics and 'good governance'.

Even within the small direct democracies run by the open assembly of the citizens (such as the Swiss *Landsgemeinde*), the sovereignty of the people cannot be compared to the sovereignty of the monarch, as in these small open assemblies majorities and minorities are constantly changing. The same citizens do not exercise long-term control of the majority.

Has the time therefore come to abandon the outdated notion of sovereignty?

'Kompetenzkompetenz'

There is no doubt that sovereignty, in the sense of absolute power, is in the reality of modern democracies dispersed between various national as well as international bodies and in certain cases even private organisations. Such dissection of sovereignty would have been unthinkable for BODIN. None of these organisations however can claim to possess supreme or absolute authority. State powers and functions are rather distributed to different state bodies and local authorities such as municipalities, regions or federal units, as well as to bodies of the international community. This division of sovereignty may lead to the temptation to assign sovereignty to the body that ultimately has the authority to allocate powers and functions to other bodies. According to this approach, the sovereign is whoever holds the so-called '*kompetenzkompetenz*' (*authority-authority*). Thereby however, the discourse on the notion of sovereignty is reduced purely to the legal dimension and separated from the concept of supreme and all-encompassing power.

Indeed, the sovereignty of the modern state is, as we mentioned at the beginning of this chapter, considerably restricted. The economic, political and technical possibilities of the state in the age of globalisation are extremely limited. Even internally, the state cannot simply disregard the history and basic convictions of its people. Moreover, the state has to employ decision making procedures that enable the different power centres to participate and exert their influence. The 'sovereign' is no longer the only master of its decision making process. The constitution, legislation, economy, environment, external relations, tradition and culture impose tight limits on the state's freedom to act. Almost nothing remains of BODIN'S old idea of the unlimited sovereignty of the monarch who reigns supreme over the people.

Legitimacy through democracy

If we again examine the ultimate basis of BODIN'S theory of sovereignty, we will recall that he was primarily concerned to legitimise the authority of the state and the monarch. BODIN sought to justify the sovereignty of the monarch by demonstrating that the monarch has the *legitimacy* to rule over the people. Whoever wields effective power, and who is the supreme and final authority within a country, also has the legal legitimacy to rule. Supreme power entitles the monarch to enact new laws, to abolish customary law and to issue decrees. The power of the monarch gives him legitimacy.

Unlike the monarch, the people does not have to legitimise its authority within a democratic state. The people as sovereign does have to justify itself. The people derives its legitimacy therefore not from its sovereignty but from the principles of democracy and majoritarianism. The majority has the right to make decisions on behalf of the minority, and the majority is entitled to do so not only because it has more power, but also because the majority has more rights than the minority.

From where does the judge derive the power to condemn the guilty person? It is of course from the law that vests him with such authority. From where does the lawmaker derive the right to proscribe certain human behaviour and to empower the judge to decide on the guilt of the defendant? The answer is, from the constitution. But on what basis is the constitution maker entitled to transfer such authority to the lawmaker? The constitution maker derives its legitimacy from the democratic right of self-determination of the people, and not from its sovereignty.

Moreover: The power of legitimate authority is also limited

The great weight that has been attached to the notion of sovereignty and the manner in which the notion of sovereignty has been conceived, have often led states to overestimate the extent of their authority. State rulers have believed that human society can be steered and changed at whim, and that as the bearer of sovereignty it is their task to steer and change society as they see fit. People however can only be steered to a limited extent. It is the task of the state, within the range of available possibilities, to find and steer a just and reasonable course that serves the interests of the people. To this end, the state requires organs that are empowered to enact binding laws of general application, and it also requires state force in order to enable the enforcement of state decisions where necessary. The organs of the state, from the legislature to the judiciary, must always be fully accountable for their actions. The legitimacy of such state activity relies on the people and their constitutionally elected representatives, and not on sovereignty. If the organs of the state do not respect the limits determined by the people, this legitimacy will disappear. At any rate, even the decisions of the majority do not possess unlimited legitimacy. The constitution, which determines the procedures and the powers of parliament, itself requires not only legitimation by the majority of the people but also by the minority. Arbitrary discrimination against minorities and the violation of fundamental human rights by the majority deprive minorities of the possibility to identify with and feel part of the state. Only when the state also seeks legitimacy in the eyes of its minorities can the majority allocate powers to different state bodies.

When seen in this light, legitimation through the people does not lead to a false and totalitarian understanding of the principle of self-determination. Indeed, the people cannot govern itself and take on the day-to-day responsibilities and functions of government. But it can legitimise and limit the government and its daily activities.

6.5.2.2 Sovereign is Whoever can legitimise the Use of Power and Force

Popular sovereignty: Fiction or reality?

Bodin legitimised the exercise of power by the monarch by declaring him to be God's representative in relation to worldly affairs. The complete secularisation of the power of the state occurred finally through Hobbes and the theory of the social contract. With the removal of the moral-religious ties of the power of the state to the might of God, a counterweight to the exertion of power was removed. In consequence, only very few means to defend itself against the misuse of power remained within the hands of the people. The sovereignty of the people remained a fiction, or at best, a symbol. Through the social contract according to HOBBES, the transfer of sovereignty to the *Leviathan* became final and irrevocable.

Secularised legitimacy of power

With the secularisation of state power, the need arose for a new and secular basis on which to legitimise this power. Social contract theory offered such replacement of the basis for legitimacy. With legitimacy based on the social contract however, the content of state power was changed. As long as state power based its legitimacy on God, it was also bound to conform to divine law. Whilst social contract theory justified power in itself, it did not regulate its content. The Leviathan, the totalitarian dictator, the prince by the grace of the people – none of these rulers and power-holders were bound by the social contract to observe any specific principles with regard to their application of the might of the state. According to HOBBES, the exercise of state power was unlimited. According to LOCKE on the other hand, man's inalienable natural rights limited the might of the state, but subject to these limitations there were no prescriptions or restrictions on the content or exercise of state power.

Solidarity and unity of the people

The legitimation of authority based on the social contract brought with it two further significant problems, which to this day have not been resolved but have in fact increased in relevance and severity: namely, the problem of defining 'the people', and the legitimacy of a particular people to rule over another minority people.

How can the people be defined and who belongs to the people? Is the people determined by the territory in which it lives, or is it a unit determined by historical and sociological connection? In our view, all people who form a unit within a particular territory, which unit is characterised on the one hand by the democratic legitimacy of the majority and on the other hand by a certain minimum preparedness for solidarity with the minority/ies in that territory, can be said to belong to the people.

When a people wants to discriminate against or even eliminate a particular community or race, such as the Jews, that people has lost any claim to legitimacy with regard to this community. The 'Aryans' would not have been able to legitimise the Holocaust even based on the unanimous support of the people. If ethnic or other minorities are shown no solidarity at all by the majority, such minorities cannot be regarded as belonging to the people in the proper sense, and so the majority has no claim to legitimacy over the minority. The same is true if a ruling minority terrorises the majority, such as occurred in the apartheid regime in South Africa. It is precisely in multicultural states that discriminatory attitudes can unleash fundamental legitimacy crises, which can eventually lead to the collapse of the state with painful consequences for all people involved.

The state as enemy of the people

With the decline of the Ottoman Empire and the Austro-Hungarian Empire, decolonisation, and the collapse of the Soviet Empire we are faced with a further fundamental challenge. For many peoples exploited under the authority of a colonial state, the state that oppressed them was seen as a symbol of a 'lawless' foreign order. This fundamental opposition to the state and the law enacted by the state has remained even after the decline of colonial and multi-ethnic empires. Thus, the minorities within the newly established nation-states that succeeded the former colonies often see the new nation-state as the successor of the previous colonial oppressor. The rejection of the authority structures of the majority people by minorities is one of the reasons that self-determination has been understood as a claim *against* the state. It is hardly surprising that these peoples, once liberated from the yoke of foreign rule, are searching for a means to establish their own state and political authority, independent of the territorial boundaries of the colonisers and based on features of their own identity such as common tradition, history, culture, language and/or religion.

Does self-determination bestow legitimacy?

Besides the issue of the definition of people and nation, one has to face in connection with the social contract the second question of legitimacy. A ruler who legitimises his/her power based on a transcendental authority superior to mankind does not have to go any further to justify his/her legitimacy: God does not need any legitimation! However, whoever seeks to justify power based on the people, that is, on secular legitimacy, will always have to answer the question, on what basis does the people or the majority people have the right to legitimise legal authority and state power? Ultimately this right can only be based on the right of peoples to self-determination, which right cannot be traced back to any legitimate source other than natural law. The right of self-determination however is itself not without limits. Just as for example the traditional people's sovereignty of the Swiss nation has always been understood as a limited sovereignty that is ultimately also tied to God (see the preamble of the Swiss Constitution as well as of certain cantonal constitutions), so in our view can the right to self-determination not be considered an absolute and unlimited right.

6.5.2.3 The State as Source of the Law

i. The 'Indeterminacy' of the Law

Auctoritas non veritas facit legem

The secularised understanding of sovereignty also led to a different conception of the law: Law became 'indeterminate', that is, something that was not fixed but always able to be made and changed. Whilst the law had originally been understood as something that was predetermined and inherited over generations, according to BODIN law was capable of being repealed, amended or enacted by the sovereign through legislation. According to HOBBES, right and wrong emerge only out of the social contract; and the state is the only source of the law.

With this assumption HOBBES laid the foundation for legal positivism, which in the sense of AUSTIN traces all law back to the sovereign and recognises as legal norms only such norms as are derived from the sovereign. Undoubtedly, AUSTIN is right that only the state is entitled to use state force in order to implement the law. Only the state can forcibly execute the law. But does the state therefore also have the authority to change, repeal and create law in any manner it sees fit? Does law only come into being via the state? Does the state monopoly on the use of force also necessarily mean that the state has a monopoly on the creation and amendment of law?

Law and might are not identical

Legal obligations exist, even if they are not enforced. The offender who escapes the prosecutor and thus avoids the force of the state has still committed a crime even though he is not punished. The law is connected to the might of the state, but not identical with it, and not something that can be arbitrarily changed by the might of the state.

As the law can only be enforced by the state, the state becomes an important but not the only source of the law. It has to shape and to change the law according to the conditions of the time, the needs and character of the people, the geographical conditions, power relations, and the prevailing values in relation to freedom and justice. The state cannot however deal with the law as it pleases. Blatant injustice does not become law even if it is decreed by the state. The coercive force of the state cannot be legitimately applied at large, any time and for the enforcement of any command whatsoever. The state is bound to act within the limits of humanity.

What are the limits of the sovereignty?

There remains still however the question, how can the boundaries of sovereignty – that is, the limits on making and changing law – be ascertained? What are the inviolable norms of humanity?

Legal science, to which one would turn for an answer to this question, has (although it is a discipline of social science) for too long been led by the empirical criteria of the natural sciences, and has therefore recognised as a valid answer only that which can be clearly *proven.* But legal science can only be empirically 'pure' if it relinquishes all prescriptions on the substantive and material content of law and justice.

Rehabilitation of practical reason

In 1979 MARTIN KRIELE called for a rehabilitation of practical reason, the 'prudentia' as opposed to the pure science of the 'scientia' (M. KRIELE, p. 17 ff). If the insights of practical reason were also recognised as scientific findings, jurisprudence would be able to formulate substantive postulates with regard to positive legal orders. One would then at least be able to derive from jurisprudence what is unjust and what would remain unjust even if enacted by a positive state command. Indeed one cannot see how and why systematic genocide, torture, and ethnic cleansing could ever validly be considered as 'legal obligations'. They are rather acts that violate basic human values and ethics that can be deduced from practical reason, and acts that can only be described as crimes against humanity.

Generalisation and discourse

Certainly not every legal norm can be rationally deduced from the nature of man, as was postulated by some natural law theorists of the Enlightenment. On the other hand, state authority has certain limits, which can be recognised through practical reasoning, because crossing those limits would clearly violate the generally recognised basic principles of morality. The methods by which such limits of sovereignty can be determined are those proposed by KANT'S principle of generalisation and discourse. This involves the Socratic, open, unprejudiced exchange of ideas and arguments between equal partners (M. KRIELE, p. 30 ff). Principles that can be generalised, that stand up to public scrutiny and open debate, and which are capable of practical realisation, hold up to the test of practical reason.

The discretion of the state

Practical reason however does not determine each individual decision of the state. Rather, it is on the basis of practical reason that the limits of the freedom of decision of the state can be deduced. Thus, law is created by the state within the frame of the limits recognisable through practical reason. Those limits must leave the state with wide powers of discretion. Because the state's power to enforce the law lends the law a higher degree of binding moral force, the state bears a great responsibility when it makes new law. It has, within the scope of its limited discretionary power, to enact new laws that respect relevant social conditions and popular sentiment, and which are capable of enforcement by the state authorities.

Thus, the state needs to factor a vast array of considerations into the exercise of its lawmaking power.

Principles of international law

In addition to the insights of practical reason, the principles of international law also serve as a source of legal limits on state sovereignty and on the scope for law to be made and changed by the state. If sovereign states are authorised to enact domestic law, then the law which they as sovereign states agree in common to recognise as valid and binding international law must be recognised as being superior to the domestic law.

ii. The Right to Resistance

If we accept that state sovereignty has limits, then the question arises, to what extent are people entitled to resist the force of the state if the state exceeds the limits of sovereignty? With this question of the right of resistance we take up one of the most difficult questions of the theory of state. As with all other similarly difficult questions, here too there is great controversy between the different periods and different exponents of state theory.

Right to resistance in the Middle Ages

The state philosophy of the Middle Ages was influenced by the divine and supernatural authority of the king. The king was obliged to implement and adhere to the divine law of God. But how should subjects behave in relation to a king who violates the laws of God? To this question various theories and traditions of the Middle Ages give different answers. THOMAS AQUINAS rejects the murder of the tyrannical hereditary monarch, on the grounds that the tyrant is likely to be replaced by an even greater tyrant, or that resistance would only provoke the existing tyrant to be even more cruel and unjust. If however the monarch is chosen by the people, he has only a limited and delegated authority (*potestas concessa*), and the right of resistance is valid. If such a monarch misuses his power, the people is entitled to remove him from office (THOMAS AQUINAS, book I, chapter 6, p. 24). In contrast, JOHANNES OF SALISBURY, the supporter of the theory of the two swords, argues in his *Polycratius* that the murder of any tyrant is permissible if the tyrant violates divine law.

Right of resistance and social contract

With the theory of the social contract the point of view changes substantially. Whilst some (such as HOBBES) are of the opinion that the social contract transfers *all* rights to the Leviathan or to the monarch, others (such as LOCKE) endorse the idea of inalienable rights that limit the discretionary power of the state. If, consistently with the HOBBESIAN view, the state is free to determine all rights including the existence and scope of all liberties and human rights, the concept of 'unjust' laws would be unknown, as justice and law are determined exclusively by the state and emanate only from the state. A *right* to resistance must therefore be ruled out. Resistance against the state may at best be a question of morality, but not a legal issue.

Those who hold the view that the social contract vests only limited rights in the state and that man has inalienable rights that even the state (or the tyrant) may not violate, take a different approach to the right to resistance. Logically, LOCKE as founder of the limited social contract calls for a right to resistance, at least in the most extreme necessity. KANT on the other hand, rejects an actual right to resistance.

THOREAU: Passive disobedience

In his 1849 essay 'The Resistance to Civil Government', HENRY DAVID THOREAU (1817–1862) advocated a far-reaching right to resistance against the state. The individual according to his theory is morally obliged to show disobedience towards the state if the state commits injustice. The individual must, based on his conscience and on principles of justice, demonstrate resistance against the state, for example by refusing to pay taxes (H. D. THOREAU, p. 15 ff). This philosophy of non-violent but illegal resistance influenced many political movements of the 20th Century. MAHATMA GANDHI'S (1869–1948) non-violent resistance against British colonial rule in India fed on this philosophy, as did the resistance of American youth against the Vietnam War.

The Catholic and Protestant Churches

In the 19th Century, the prevalence in a number of states of anti-religious ideas inspired by Enlightenment theory led the Catholic Church in particular to endorse a general and comprehensive right to resistance. Pope LEO XIII declared in his Encyclica '*Diuturnum*' of 1881: "The only reason which men have for not obeying is when anything is demanded of them which is openly repugnant to the natural or the divine law, for it is equally unlawful to command to do anything in which the law of nature of the will of God is violated. If, therefore, it should happen to anyone to be compelled to prefer one or the other, viz, to disregard either the commands of God or those of rulers, he must obey Jesus Christ… And yet there is no reason why those who so behave themselves should be accused of refusing obedience; for, if the will of the rulers is opposed to the will and the laws of God, they themselves exceed the bounds of their own power and pervert justice; nor can their authority be valid, which, when there is no justice, is null". Similar statements can be found in the Encyclica '*Redemptor hominis*' (1979) of Pope John Paul II: "[T]he rights of power can only be understood on the basis of respect for the objective and inviolable rights of man. The common good that authority in the state serves is brought to full realisation only when all the citizens are sure of their rights. The lack of this leads to the dissolution of society, opposition by citizens to authority, or a situation of oppression, intimidation, violence, and terrorism, of which many examples have been provided by the totalitarianisms of this century."

The Protestant Church on the other hand, is less inclined to advocate the right of resistance. LUTHER was of the opinion that one must show obedience even towards an unjust state, provided the state permits the free practice of religion.

Right to resistance and international criminal law

The experiences with totalitarian states of the 20th Century and the increasing violation of fundamental human rights through arbitrary detention, torture, and genocide, led to a new assessment of the right to resistance. On the basis of natural law, the judges in the Nurnberg and Tokyo trials passed sentence on the leaders of the Nazi and Fascist regimes. The defendants could not claim in their defence that the orders they had followed and the laws they had executed had been made and enacted in accordance with the correct legal procedure. As no state is entitled to command its subjects and servants to commit crimes, one can and must under such circumstances exert resistance.

With the appointment of the two ad hoc international criminal tribunals for the prosecution of war crimes and crimes against humanity committed in the former Yugoslavia and in Rwanda, as well as the establishment of the International Criminal Court, the theoretical and legal approach to the right to resistance has changed substantially. These courts are based on the conviction that the sovereignty of states is limited. From now on, states can only make and pronounce the law within the bounds of their limited sovereignty. If they violate fundamental principles of humanity, the power-holders and their henchmen will have to reckon with prosecution before an international court. The principle of the universality of human rights has limited state sovereignty, not only theoretically but also practically. He who does not exercise passive resistance against criminal commands of a state will have to reckon with international condemnation. Thus, the right to resistance has to a certain extent found its way into domestic law through the back door of international law.

Principles of practical reason

KRIELE also advocates a right to resistance against any authority that flagrantly violates the principles of practical reason (M. KRIELE, p. 111 ff). As one can deduce out of practical reason directives for positive laws, the positive legal order is justified only if it is in conformity with such directives. If the state authority violates those principles, the individual has – based on the pre-constitutional and pre-positive rights deduced through practical reason – a right to resistance. After the Second World War, the Military Tribunals of Nurnberg passed judgment on the criminals of the Nazi regime. From where did these tribunals derive the right to condemn and punish the criminals of the Nazi regime, whose actions were in accord with the positive laws of the National Socialist legal order of Nazi Germany? Such punishment could only be justified if the positive legal order of Nazi Germany was declared null and void, on the basis that it was in violation of some higher legal order that precedes and trumps the positive law of the state. But this argument alone did not suffice. The judges placed greater emphasis on the principle that the Nazis were obliged, based on the principles of the pre-state or 'natural' law, to exercise passive resistance and refuse to obey the positive legal commands that ordered them to commit criminal acts. Thus, the Nurnberg Tribunals assumed the existence of a right to resistance, even an obligation of resistance, which precedes and overrides the positive law.

Dilemma of the right to resistance

The dilemma that is embedded in the recognition of a comprehensive right to resistance is obvious. It could lead to full-blown anarchy, if citizens refused to obey state authority based on their right to resistance. If every citizen can question and undermine the legitimacy of state authority, the state will become ungovernable. The danger of anarchy however, is not reason enough to relegate the *right* to resistance to the realm of morality, as this would have consequences just as absurd and illogical as the recognition of a general and unlimited legal right to resistance.

Right to resistance and the use of violence

Resistance is certainly only justified against extreme injustice. State authority will always have to prove itself and justify its actions in response to the challenge of critical scrutiny. When the people maintains a critical spirit with regard to state authority, the danger of misuse of power by state authorities is reduced, because the people will be able to respond quickly to such abuse and use peaceful means to defend its rights and interests.

As a general rule, the right to resistance excludes the use of force and violence. If the state uses force to commit injustice, in general resistance with force is not legitimate. Countless examples of recent revolutions reveal that in most cases the old regime of terror will be replaced by new state terror. Only in extreme cases, if it can be assured that through the forceful overthrow of a regime a new legitimate regime with authority recognised by the people can be established without significant bloodshed, can violent resistance be justified.

Contradictions in the right of resistance of ethnic minorities

The increase in ethnic conflicts and bloody civil wars necessitates a new reassessment of the right of resistance. Whilst to date the right to resistance has primarily been invoked against unjust and tyrannical regimes, we are now faced with the claim of the right to resistance of ethnic minorities against democratic majorities. Certainly nobody would seriously question that at the time of the Nazi regime the Jewish population in Germany was legitimately entitled to resist passively and also with violence against the National Socialist state. In its judgment with regard to the dissolution of former Yugoslavia, the Badinter Commission (an EU appointed judicial body) legitimised the resistance of the republics that wanted to separate from the former socialist federation. On what basis however can the resistance of the Corsicans against France, the ETA against Spain, the IRA against Northern Ireland or the resistance of the Palestinians against Israel be legitimised? The international community has recently declared the resistance movement of the Tamil Tigers (LTTE) against Sri Lanka to be a terror organisation.

Why was resistance against Yugoslavia or the resistance of the American settlers against the United Kingdom permissible, but not the resistance of the American south against the liberal north or the resistance of the Corsicans against France? When is an ethnic minority entitled to exercise resistance against the majority?

Gandhi – Mandela

Two resistance movements of the 20th Century may give us at least a partial answer to this burning question: around the middle of the 20th Century, MAHATMA GANDHI successfully employed passive and peaceful resistance against British colonial rule. NELSON MANDELA, as leader of the once prohibited African National Congress, exercised not only passive but also active and violent resistance against the apartheid regime of South Africa. MANDELA has written that violence was justified and necessary as a means of self-defence against an oppressive regime that itself used indiscriminate violence in order to defend its power position. Once the apartheid regime had been weakened, the emphasis of MANDELA'S political strategy shifted to peaceful reconciliation and appeasement of the races that had previously been separated by the cruel policies of apartheid. For his part in South Africa's transition to democracy and the final abolition of apartheid, MANDELA was awarded the Nobel Peace Prize, and in 1994 he was elected President in the first democratic, non-racist presidential election.

From tyrannicide to the international right to self-determination

If the aim of tyrannicide was to replace a bad ruler with a better one, the aim of resistance in the age of revolutions was to change the social order (for example, the French Revolution, Spanish Civil War). Not only was the ruler unacceptable, but also the ideology imposed by the state. The right to resistance was invoked in order to overthrow the entire governmental or social system.

In the secessionist movements of ethnic communities on the other hand, the aim of resistance is not the transformation of the entire state or societal structure, but rather to achieve independent sovereign rule over a certain part of the territory of the respective state. It is not the right to resistance as such, that is, against the entire state, that is being claimed, but only resistance against the authority of the state over a certain part of its territory. Based on the right of self-determination, such movements seek their own statehood over part of the existing state territory. These resistance movements tend to see themselves as forces fighting a war of liberation against an unjust colonial regime in the name of a state that they have founded but which is not yet generally recognised. As soon as the states friendly to these liberation movements start to recognise their forcefully controlled territory as a state, the internationalisation of the conflict is unavoidable. With such recognition by the international community, any intervention by the original state to restore its territory will be considered as an act of aggression, which is prohibited by Article 7 of the United Nations Charter. The UN Security Council would then be empowered to take action to protect the territory that has seceded and is under attack. As this example demonstrates, the international community will be drawn into the conflict as soon as the statehood of the resistance movement is internationally recognised.

Geneva Conventions

This leads to the consequence that such resistance movements always use all possible means to terrorise the population and thereby to internationalise the internal conflict and to transform the civil war into a 'legitimate' international war of self-defence against the aggressive state of their origin. As soon as the domestic conflict has been internationalised, it is subject to international law rather than domestic law. Rebel 'soldiers' cannot be condemned as criminal terrorists but must be treated as prisoners of war protected by the Geneva Conventions. Even in the grey area between an international war and a domestic conflict, some of the prescriptions of the first and Second Additional Protocols of the Geneva Conventions are applicable. The First Additional Protocol effectively assumes the internationalisation of a domestic conflict if the resistance movement is defending its territory against a foreign occupier or against a racist regime. The second additional protocol applies to domestic civil wars that are not covered by the first additional protocol. In the interest of the comprehensive and universal application of humanitarian law, these additional protocols have thereby indirectly internationalised the right of resistance of such movements. Rather than restricting or containing such conflicts, this has had the unintended result that such resistance movements will use all means necessary to internationalise their conflict in an attempt to attract international recognition of their right to resistance, and so to legitimise the conflict. In reality, this increases the brutality of the ethnic resistance and of the state response to suppress the resistance. For their part, the states threatened by resistance movements try their utmost to brand such movements as international terrorist organisations.

Integrative and exclusive nationalism

Are there still some preconditions that would make the violent resistance of a secessionist movement legitimate? Secessionist movements that base their legitimacy on the nationalism of the minority are often a response to the chauvinistic nationalism of the majority that discriminates against its minorities. A nationalism however, which fosters its own values and culture as the foundation of its history and identity will accord equal rights and respect to other nations and cultures, because diversity will be seen as ultimately benefiting the nation and national consciousness. National identity is therefore not negative *per se*. What must be rejected however, is exclusive nationalism, which leads to arbitrary discrimination against 'other' races and ethnicities and which contradicts human rights. Exclusive nationalism can therefore never be a legitimate basis for a secessionist movement. The resistance of the thirteen colonies in North America against the motherland was not based on an exclusive nationalism. The founding fathers of the independence movement legitimised their resistance against the British colonial authority on the basis of their desire to establish a state founded on inalienable pre-state human rights. At the same time they condemned the oppressive colonial rule of the British, and from this injustice derived their right to violent resistance.

International intervention for the protection of minorities

Today's secessionist movements are almost always based on an exclusive nationalism, which reflects the nationalism and discriminatory ethnic policy of the majority nation. Such nationalism cannot give rise to a legitimate right to resistance. Nor can international recognition or international intervention be justified in such cases, in light of the Charter of the United Nations and basic principles of the right to resistance. International intervention in the interest of human rights can only be justified if it is done solely and genuinely in the interest of protecting human rights, and not as a cover for the chauvinistic nationalism of a certain minority which often neglects vital interests of additional minorities living within its territory.

7 Theoretical Aspects of the Organisation of the Modern State

7.1 Theory of State Organisation

7.1.1 Introduction

To empower or to limit the power of the state?

The state embodies political power. In organising the institutions of the state the constitution can concentrate the power of the state in one person, or it can divide state power such that various branches of government provide counterbalancing checks on the exercise of power. The constitution can even go so far as to enable different state authorities to block each other, thus creating a stalemate among the different branches and making government action practically impossible. As we have already seen however, the idea of the state and of supra-familial political power fulfils a basic need of human nature to pursue common security and happiness. If the institutions established by the constitution are not able to effectively administer the power entrusted to the state, society will degenerate into anarchy and the strongest will fill the vacuum of political power. Thus, political power needs to be properly 'constituted', and two different models for doing so have emerged:

According to the American conception, the constitution primarily serves to limit state power. The aim of the Constitution is to restrict the power of the state. According to the continental European view, the constitution has first to create and facilitate political power, and only then to restrain state power in accordance with the constitutional order.

Good Governance

Based on this liberal constitutionalism, there have developed some basic principles to which state organisation should conform. In fact, the international community has effectively made these principles of 'good governance' mandatory for countries in receipt of credit from the World Bank and International Monetary Fund. These principles are namely: democratic legitimacy, transparency, participation, accountability, decentralisation, the rule of law, security of the people, and non-discrimination on the basis of race, religion and gender with regard to resources and welfare. This does not mean that there is only one single model of state organisation that is prescribed for the realisation of these principles. On the other hand, there are certain organisational structures of authoritarian regimes, which would clearly be inconsistent with the aims of a liberal concept of the state and contrary to the principles of 'good governance'.

Democracy determines the rules of the game

Today there is no state that would not declare itself to be democratic. Every state professes to have legitimacy in the eyes of the people and to adhere to the principles of democracy. But what does being a democratic state entail and require? Democracy presupposes people's sovereignty. Popular sovereignty for its part, presupposes a people or a nation which is composed of democratic citizens. A people which aims to dominate other peoples or disregards the rights of minorities can not claim to be a 'demos', that is a people, which has implemented democracy in the true sense of its meaning. Democracy involves a procedural order in which all citizens can participate on equal terms. It is essential that the democratic process is an open process. That means that democracy determines the rules of the game, according to which decisions are to be made. The result of this democratic procedure must be open, which means one cannot foresee the result of the procedure. Of course one can make predictions as to the results of the democratic process, but such predictions can be mistaken. However, if a nation is fragmented by two or more ethnic communities, if an important part of the population (such as foreigners) is excluded from the process, or if parties or powerful institutions can change the rules of the game during the procedure, democracy may degenerate into a tyranny of the majority.

Constituted democracy

Democracy must be constituted, that is, it must be based upon a constitution. Without a constitution, whether written or unwritten, true democracy cannot exist. The constitution determines the basic principles of the rules of the game. It guarantees the opportunity for citizens to participate in the decision making process. The constitution also binds the democratic majority to observe human rights and the rule of law. Only based on the constitution can democratic and open procedures be guaranteed and regulated. The constitution can ensure that no state institution can change or falsify the rules of the game. All institutions that are involved in the decision making process have to adhere to the constitutional order. The results of democratic processes are not foreseeable, but the procedural rules and limits must be known and guaranteed in advance.

Open and informed democracy

Democracy presupposes that the will of the majority of the people can be ascertained. This however is only possible, if the citizens can discern and evaluate the consequences of their decisions or their vote. Citizens must have the possibility to participate in decision making processes and elections, and must be able to make free decisions. They must have the opportunity to freely inform themselves and should not receive one-sided information nor be manipulated with false information. The institutions established by the Constitution must be able to guarantee the rules of the game and enable citizens to inform themselves on all possible alternatives and their consequences, and in particular should ensure that an open discourse of alternatives can be conducted and that a secret ballot is guaranteed. It must be ensured that the result reflects the actual and free will of the people, and that nobody faces any harm or disadvantage as a result of their participation in an election. The equal opportunity of all parties and citizens involved in the democratic political process must be assured.

Citizen participation

What are the basic elements of a democratically constituted political community, that is, a modern political society? A democratically constituted society is a society in which the definitive characteristic of politics is the active status of the citizen (status activus). A democratically constituted political community is a civic society. A civic society can only be fully realised when all people subject to political authority are also accorded the role of active citizen.

The active status transfers to the individual a share of the political power (status of the civic society). Citizens must be able to rely on the fact that they have the opportunity to influence political decisions through the democratic process. The society must be constituted in such way that all social conflicts can be resolved through rational and democratic procedures, rather than by resorting to violence. Democratic decision making must completely displace violence and corruption.

In a representative democracy, the mass of the citizens participates in the democratic process only by exercising the right to vote in elections. However, the open and transparent parliamentary procedure and the possibility to influence the outcome in the next elections gives the people the power to influence the basic policies and direction of the politics of the state.

Civic society

The civic society is the modern form of the political society. It embraces all members of the society in their political capacity as citizens and voters. It presupposes a separation between the public sphere of politics and the state, and the private sphere into which political power may not intrude. In fact, the democratic society assumes the existence of a sphere that is foreign to politics and from which political authority is excluded.

The French Revolution declared the Rights of Man and Citizen as the foundation for an egalitarian political society based on equality, which is not corrupted by any feudal barriers or privileges. The term used to denote this egalitarian civic society of individuals was the ‘Nation’. The active citizen helps to build the democratic consensus that underlies the society. The content of this consensus is decided by means of a pluralistic political process.

Liberal democracy as procedure

Democracy as a state form and as a principle of legitimacy in the liberal sense entails primarily an institutionalised decision making process, the results of which cannot be known in advance. Democracy is understood as a procedure. This understanding of democracy is based purely on the existence of formal 'game' rules and procedures. The procedurally based liberal democracy – which is often also regarded as democracy itself – is an instrument for the taming of political power, and therefore accords with the fundamental goals of constitutionalism. The constitution itself becomes the direct source of the stability of the liberal democratic process (CLAUS OFFE, *Politik und Soziologie der Mehrheitsregel*, Opladen 1984, p. 81–94).

Foundations of the organisation of modern states

The organisation of the modern state has been developed through the interplay of three decisive forces:

- The political, economic, sociological and cultural development of different nations;
- The battle between different state organs over powers and hierarchy, such as for example the dispute between the advisory parliamentary organ and the centralised executive power of the monarch; and
- The grow ing need to justify state power itself and to tie it to the will of the people, as well as to limit and control state power.

7.1.2 Sociological Roots

7.1.2.1 Historical Influences

Economic and social conditions

That the organisation of the state is closely connected to the level of social development is plain to see: as long as people were able, for example as hunter gatherers, to provide for themselves and had little contact with other groups, they did not need to live together in communities and had no need for supra-familial authority structures. Weak forms of oligarchic authority such as councils of elders and even certain democratic forms of authority marked the first phase of the establishment of political communities. As soon as nomads came together as tribes, they needed a tighter order and discipline to bring and hold different people together in order to protect them from external and internal conflicts.

Nomad tribes

Nomadic tribes have a strong sense of belonging and togetherness, based in part on close kinship and in part on the leadership of the group. A charismatic leader (such as Genghis Khan) can lead only if he is clearly superior and can convince people of his abilities. A bureaucratic police state is unthinkable in such a society.

On the other hand, the leader must have comprehensive powers in order to be able to meet the dangers of the environment and of other settled tribes. The monocratic government based on the charismatic authority of the leader, combined with strong group unity and loyalty, is probably the most natural form of government for such nomadic tribes.

Large territories

As soon as tribes began to settle, the conditions of political organisation changed radically. Tribes that settled in large, open areas required large armies in order to defend their territory against external threats (for example China, ancient Egypt). This necessitated strict organisation and leadership, and often also the establishment of a bureaucracy and police.

In principle each family had to provide for itself. However, men who were required to join the army were no longer able to provide for their families. In order to support them the king had to impose taxes on the people. The taxes were not collected by civil servants but by the large land owners, who could keep part of their tax income for their own needs and had to pass the remainder on to the king In return they had to provide protection and assistance to their subjects. Thus the basic elements of the feudal, vertically structured social order were established.

Over time, feudal lords often attempted to misuse their dominion and to exploit their subjects. In doing so they required protection and assistance from the central government, which was able thereby to further increase its centralised power. Thus gradually a bureaucracy and in many cases a tyrannical authority developed, which was able through feudal structures to maintain its power for centuries.

Small territories

Tribes that settled in smaller, geographically fragmented and self-contained areas (such as Greece), were able to protect themselves with less cost and effort, and often developed differently as a result. The smaller societies formed the first state organisations with oligarchic and sometimes even democratic features. These societies did not have to impose high taxes for the defence of the territory. The low risk of foreign invasion facilitated a greater division of labour between families. This division of labour is strongly connected to the idea of *quid pro quo* or the concept of contractual relations, which in turn fostered the principle of equality and the conviction that the state community that binds different tribes and families together can only be ruled by common consensus and with acceptance of the majority.

Taking into account the conditions in which they emerged, it is not surprising that the cultural and intellectual efforts of early democratic and oligarchic societies tended to focus primarily on the realisation of a just political order. On the other hand, states with more extensive and open territory expended great effort on the erection of impressive monuments (such as the pyramids and the Great Wall of China).

Slaves

In later times, the free citizens living in towns were able to afford the time to engage in the public affairs of the state by holding slaves who performed all other work. This is also the reason why in ancient Rome it was possible (at least to a certain extent) for democracy to develop. The right to participate in the political process in early democracies however was not universal, but was restricted to certain chosen citizens. ARISTOTLE wrote: "For the best material of democracy is an agricultural population; there is no difficulty in forming a democracy where the mass of the people live by agriculture or tending of cattle. Being poor, they have no leisure, and therefore do not often attend the assembly, and not having the necessaries of life they are always at work, and do not covet the property of others. Indeed, they find their employment pleasanter than the cares of government or office where no great gains can be made out of them, for the many are more desirous of gain than of honour. A proof is that even the ancient tyrannies were patiently endured by them, as they still endure oligarchies, if they are allowed to work and are not deprived of their property; for some of them grow quickly rich and the others are well enough off. Moreover, they have the power of electing the magistrates and calling them to account; their ambition, if they have any, is thus satisfied; and in some democracies, although they do not all share in the appointment of offices, except through representatives elected in turn out of the whole people, as at Mantinea; yet, if they have the power of deliberating, the many are contented. Even this form of government may be regarded as a democracy, and was such at Mantinea ..... We have thus explained how the first and best form of democracy should be constituted; it is clear that the other or inferior sorts will deviate in a regular order, and the population which is excluded will at each stage be of a lower kind" (ARISTOTLE, book VI, 1319 a).

From the feudal state to the industrial state

What are then the typical organisational models of the modern industrial state? According to BARRINGTON MOORE, the organisation of the modern industrial state can be traced back to three different developments within feudal states. Originally there was a close relationship between feudal lords and peasants. The land that was owned by the feudal lord had to be cultivated by his farmers for the lord's benefit. For this service, the lord had to protect the farmers and to adjudicate over their disputes. The peasant farmers were allowed to cultivate a portion of the land for their own needs. A third part of the land, mostly forest, waterways and pastureland, was used commonly.

After a while the lord forced his subjects to produce more and more, either because he had to pay higher taxes to the king to finance the royal court and the army, or because he sought to profit from the goods he could sell at the town market. Furthermore, if the landlord had the time to take care of his own estate, the farmers became more and more dependent. They were then merely farm workers and effectively became serfs of the landlord (for example, East-Prussia). If, on the other hand, the landlord was serving the court or the army and was therefore frequently or permanently absent from the estate, he had to entrust his farmers with greater responsibilities and afford them more rights over the land (France).

In countries with a predominantly agrarian economy it was possible to maintain this feudal hierarchy for a very long time. In countries with significant industrial and commercial development, the changing social order in the towns also had an impact on the population in the countryside.

Mercantile gentry

Things developed differently in England. In the 15th Century the population was decimated by the plague. The shortage of labourers forced landowners to resort to rearing sheep, as this was an undertaking that was feasible with few workers. The landlords were therefore unable to meet their costs or increase their fortune by taxing farmers, but rather only by selling the wool they had produced. Thus, in England there developed very early a commercially active aristocracy that sought to conduct its business in the towns independently of the Crown, and in particular free from high taxes. In addition, the great amount of wool produced needed to be processed into textile goods, which required factories to be built and led to the industrialisation of textile production.

The commercialisation of agriculture contributed just as much to the development of democracy in England as did the rise of commerce and industrialisation in the towns. In order to fulfil its needs, the nobility was much more concerned with the development of the free market independent from the king than they were with the exploitation of their peasant subjects. They therefore had early on to attempt to create a counterweight to the power of the Crown.

Oppression of peasants and workers

The other major feudal systems resulted in the thorough exploitation of the peasants. The French nobility however, granted farmers some degree of independence and usufructary rights over land, in contrast to for example the gentry in East Prussia. This partial independence helped to enable the early bourgeois revolution in France.

The more the farmers were exploited, the more power the central government needed to protect the interests of its nobility. The nobility thereby lost much of its power and influence. This distribution of power usually hindered the development of a large confident middle class that could have contributed to the achievement of real democracy in the wake of a revolution.

The states in which peasants lived like slaves provided a breeding ground for revolutionary developments. However, often the transition to a new order was so abrupt that it led to a new form of slavery. The centralist and totalitarian authority of the communist parties was therefore primarily able to develop in countries that made the transition from feudal system to modern industrial state without having a sizeable class of independent minded citizens active in commerce or industrial production.

Importance of tradition

However, the transition from feudal society to modern state did not always occur in the manner described. In India for example, after the reign of Genghis Khan the government of the Mogul Kings led to widespread poverty and dependence. The peasant farmers had to finance not only the king and his aristocracy but also the army (B. MOORE, p. 317). Nonetheless it was possible after British colonial rule to build a democratic federation that survives to this day. MOORE attributes this to the highly structured caste system and to the local democratic traditions of India. The caste system prevented communication between the castes and thus impeded the establishment of a revolutionary party that would realise solidarity regardless of caste. On the other hand, MAHATMA GHANDI'S revolution of non-violent resistance against powerful England was successfully able to gain wide currency. This revolution had its roots in the Indian philosophy of life (*Weltanschauung*), which teaches that happiness can only be attained by rising above material desires. The spiritual and independent person cannot easily be seduced by revolutionary ideologies promising material happiness.

In many African states the feudal system also developed differently. The strong internal connectedness within tribes did not allow the establishment of a truly feudal system of authority. Of course, in African societies there were distinctions between nobles, free men and slaves. However, the tight group connection and the consciousness of the tribes was stronger than any sense of class-consciousness that would have been necessary for a class-war along Marxist lines. Magic traditions and charismatic leaders, which embody African identity, tended to favour strong presidential governmental systems.

Four revolutions

Almost all modern states can be traced back to a revolutionary phase that began with the English revolution of the 17th Century, was continued by the American Declaration of Independence and the French Revolution in the 18th Century, and which reached its peak with the various communist revolutions of the 20th Century. Through these revolutionary movements the structures of the feudal state were largely destroyed. The old political structures were replaced by rationally-based and legitimate forms of modern state authority. Indeed, only a rational theory or ideology was able to achieve the break away from the traditional structures of the former feudal state. The predefined traditional social order could only be replaced by a rational political agenda. The different modern ideologies are a consequence of these historical developments. In the 20th Century, these developments led to the establishment of two opposing ideological camps: capitalist and socialist. Within each of these two camps the governmental system, democracy and state organisation were set in accordance with the relevant ideology.

Mobilising the masses

A further decisive step in the development of modern state organisation was made by the rise of mass media: that is, the rousing of populations for the realisation of particular ideological goals. LUTHER'S reformation of Catholic society was only possible with the aid of the first print media, enabled in Europe by GUTENBERG. During the French Revolution, the use of print media made it possible bring together a mass of poor and hungry peasants and workers to storm the Bastille. Since then, totalitarian ideologies have understood the importance of using the mass media to mobilise the masses of unemployed and discontented citizens for revolutionary purposes.

In the modern industrial state with its widespread mass-communication – whether it is manipulated or not – one has to reckon with the fact that in a crisis the discontented masses can easily be mobilised and be induced to carry out an uprising. Thus the branches of government within the state are faced with the constant challenge of integrating and motivating the population, and of legitimating their own policies.

The major modern theoretician and practitioner of mass mobilisation for particular ideological purposes was undoubtedly MAO TSE TUNG: "Our God is none other than the masses of the Chinese People. If they stand up and dig together with us, why can't these two mountains be cleared away?" (MAO TSE TUNG, 'The Foolish Old Man who Removed the Mountains', concluding speech at the Seventh National Congress of the Communist Party of China, 11 June 1945). "[A]ll correct leadership is necessarily "from the masses, to the masses". This means: take the ideas of the masses (scattered and unsystematic ideas) and concentrate them (through study turn them into concentrated and systematic ideas), then go to the masses and propagate and explain these ideas until the masses embrace them as their own, hold fast to them and translate them into action, and test the correctness of these ideas in such action. Then once again concentrate the ideas of the masses and once again go to the masses so that the ideas are persevered in and carried through. And so on, over and over again in an endless spiral, with the ideas becoming more correct, more vital and richer each time. Such is the Marxist theory of knowledge (MAO TSE TUNG, 1 June 1943, *Some Questions Concerning Methods of Leadership*). "Commandism is wrong in any type of work, because in overstepping the level of political consciousness of the masses and violating the principle of voluntary mass action it reflects the disease of impetuosity. Our comrades must not assume that everything they themselves understand is understood by the masses. Whether the masses understand it and are ready to take action can be discovered only by going into their midst and making investigations … [At the same time] our comrades must not assume that the masses have no understanding of what they themselves do not yet understand. It often happens that the masses outstrip us and are eager to advance a step when our comrades are still tailing behind certain backward elements"

(MAO TSE TUNG, 'On Coalition Government', political report to the Seventh National Congress of the Communist Party of China, 24 April 1945).

The 20th Century provided ample demonstration of what the masses are capable of. In the collective mass, emotions can be amplified, the responsibility of the individual evaporates, the mass no longer has a conscience and can destroy in a few moments what has been laboriously built up over centuries. He who understands how to move the masses can thereby subjugate or even destroy entire peoples. Black and white thinking, the loss of any sense of proportion, 'friend' and 'foe' stereotypes, and the search for a 'villain' to blame for everything are dangers from which even democratic states are not immune.

11 September 2001

September 11th and the subsequent war in Afghanistan marked the beginning of a new kind of conflict for the 21st Century. Conflict is no longer focused on disputes between states and regional blocs, but rather on the actions of 'private' organisations and groups that threaten states, democracy and the very legitimacy of state organisation. States are facing an invisible enemy that fundamentally questions and fights against the rational foundation of the state organisation. In place of the invisible enemy, states wage war in the name of self-defence against those states that are assumed to harbour terrorists. Thus we face a new age, in which there are no longer two opposing ideological blocs with fundamentally different state organisational structures, but rather the states on one side, espousing good governance based on constitutional legitimacy, and private terrorist organisations on the other side, questioning the rationality and legitimacy of traditional state power.

7.1.2.2 Foreign Influences in a Globalised Environment

Economy and international cooperation

The modern industrial economy requires extensive organisational capacity. This can lead to economic concentration, which may threaten in particular the autonomy of small states. The state has two options in countering this threat. The economy may be nationalised, in which case the state will possess almost unlimited power. If the government is still willing to afford its citizens some degree of liberty, it has to design its state institutions in such a way that their power is exercised in the interest of the liberty of the citizens.

Alternatively, the state may permit a free market economy, in which case it must ensure that the state can provide an effective counterbalance to the all-powerful economy. If it fails to provide such counterbalance or if it is not possible, the state must at least establish the legal environment for a decentralised economy and fair competition.

The autonomy that states possess in terms of their organisation in the era of globalisation however is considerably reduced. The sovereignty of the nation-state is marginalised. States must therefore attempt to attain more room to move, through international cooperation and networking. The need for greater international cooperation has a marked effect on states' internal institutional organisation. States can only maintain their credibility as partners in international organisations, when they are able to give domestic effect to their international legal obligations. Could one imagine for example, granting membership of the EU to a country which, because it is undemocratic or lacks efficient central institutions or contravenes human rights, is unable to apply and implement the European law within its domestic legislation (which in most European member states encompasses today almost half of all legislation)?

Social partners (employers and employees)

An additional feature of the structure and organisation of modern industrial states is the relationship between employers and employees. The industrial revolution created a need for great numbers of workers, particularly in its early phase. Because individual workers were too weak to defend their interests against the employers, workers formed labour unions in order to strengthen their bargaining power. As a counter-measure, the employers founded employer associations. Subsequently the labour unions enlarged their power by forming branches and divisions that encompassed workers from many workplaces within a particular trade or geographical area. This enabled the unions to have a greater influence over state labour policy and regulation, rates of pay and working conditions.

Majoritarian democracy versus 'contract-democracy' of social partners

Whilst laws regulating labour and social security are determined in parliament, disputes between employers and employees are decided outside parliament and cannot be solved by simple majority decision. If the parties are unable to reach a consensus, they resort to offensive measures such as strikes and lockouts. This demands the creation of labour unions, as only unions have the power to bargain on an equal footing with employers. If they do not succeed in satisfying their interests through negotiation with their 'partners', they may attempt to achieve their aims by lobbying for appropriate legislative action. The consequence is that in democratic states, labour and social security are regulated at two different levels. Legislation is generally confined to establishing the framework required for the order of the free market. The details such as wages, leave entitlements and working hours are usually governed by the terms of collective agreements that are negotiated between unions and employers. The democratic state serves only the function of an arbiter that must help to resolve intractable disputes in accordance with the common interest.

Global market, local labour

However, even the labour unions are today affected by the ever-increasing pressures of the global market. Whilst the market for products and services is largely global, the labour market is still regulated locally. As a result, nation-states have autonomy in relation to domestic labour laws, but must also increasingly take into account the interests and pressures of the global economy. The depletion of state sovereignty also has an effect on the labour unions' room to manoeuvre. To a large extent the parties to labour negotiations, facing international competition and the threat of unemployment, have their hands tied.

The development of the mass media

In addition to far-reaching economic changes, the rise of the mass media certainly contributed substantially to the development of modern state organisation. The invention of the printing press in the 15th Century and the gradual expansion of the press enabled communication of ideas and ideologies on a broad scale. In the 20th Century radio, television, cinema, satellite TV and above all the internet enabled people to get important information on the spot, and gave people possibilities for communication and connection that were previously almost inconceivable. The consciousness of being and belonging together, and the concept of 'public opinion', acquired a new dimension. States are able through the mass media to reach a much wider public than in previous times. The media also serves to convey information in the other direction, helping to inform governments about the issues and sentiments of the people, which should be taken into account in government decision making.

Internet

The internet provides states with new and hitherto barely conceivable possibilities for permanent and interactive communication with the people. In the near future, governments and parliaments will no longer be exclusively reliant upon private firms to conduct public opinion polls. One can imagine, that it will be possible to organise regular online plebiscites of the citizens. This may lead, in the short to medium-term, to a completely new understanding of the principle of representation and thereby to an extension of direct democratic decision making processes, even within large states.

Who watches the watchers?

Between governments and the mass media there is often a special kind of interaction. On one hand, the mass media can be used to serve the interests of the state and may be misused by governments to misinform or manipulate the population. On the other hand, governments in states that guarantee some freedom of the press are under the constant pressure of media scrutiny. One must only observe how seriously most politicians react to negative media coverage to realise that whilst the media may not represent public opinion, it is in command of *published* opinion to which politicians pay a great deal of attention. It is therefore no surprise that from all quarters the question is raised: *who watches the watchers?* That is, the media. So long as the media is not under the control of state officials, it is able to effectively and substantially limit the power of elected executives, members of parliament, and even of judges. If however control of the mass media is placed in the hands of a small number of companies or people, or if holders of high public office are permitted to hold financial stakes in the media and thereby to use their economic power over the media for political purposes (as occurred in Italy under BERLUSCONI), the way is smoothed for an authoritarian regime.

The mass media provides quick and comprehensive information to the people. This does lead to a certain 'levelling out' of information and a degree of superficiality in much of the information provided. On the other hand, what is provided through the mass media leads to a greater demand for more substantial background information and knowledge on the activities of the administration, government, parliament and the economy. This means that those who are in power have to justify their decisions with much more convincing and detailed arguments, and to a much greater public, than in earlier times.

The media in the service of governments

People have always been willing to accept dependence if they receive something valuable in return. The feudal lords of the Middle Ages and the dictators of today's totalitarian states were and are able to simulate such returns (for example, alleged achievements of a socialist state or productivity gains) or exaggerate the significance of actual achievements (such as space travel). They can also intimidate and frighten the population with supposed threats. Publicity is therefore a factor to be taken into political calculations and can sometimes take the form of propaganda. In countries that guarantee freedom of speech on the other hand, the mass media is able to ensure that the performance and 'returns' of the government and administration are scrutinised and discussed. If the population is convinced that there is no return from the government, it can accordingly make its will known through the political process.

The very fact that in countries with free press, governments are held constantly accountable by the mass media for their performance and the benefits and services they provide, has modified the winner-takes-all democracy into a 'contract-democracy' among the political elite. This contractual character of democratic government can only be achieved if a broad spectrum of the population can be comprehensively informed on government performance and public issues, and if institutions are established which are able effectively to hold all power holders accountable.

World Bank and International Monetary Fund

In the age of globalisation, important international credit institutions such as the World Bank and the International Monetary Fund are also able to exercise direct influence over the organisation of states. The principles of 'good governance' developed by these two institutions (transparency, democratic legitimacy, accountability, democratic control, rule of law, human rights and decentralisation) are imposed on those states that rely on international credit and financial assistance. Such states are compelled to demonstrate, at least on the surface, that they meet the standards required by these institutions, for example by enacting a democratic constitution which appears to guarantee the rule of law and government accountability. As the international credit organisations are almost entirely under the control of the developed states, the developed states are able to influence the organisation of developing states without any constraints and with no direct accountability. The United States and the EU, which in their bilateral relationships have also become major credit providers, are also able to exert their influence over the domestic organisation of other states through bilateral cooperation.

Council of Europe

States that want to join the Council of Europe must ratify the European Convention on Human Rights, and must also provide evidence that their domestic legal system meets the minimum standards of the Human Rights Convention. A commission of experts (Venice Commission) that is close to the governments of the member states assesses the internal state organisation of prospective member states, in order to ensure that the democratic preconditions for membership of the Council are fulfilled.

Nongovernmental organisations

The influence of non-governmental organisations (NGOs) on the organisation of weak or vulnerable states that find themselves under the watchful eye of the international community should not be underestimated. NGOs, which are generally privately organised but supported by their home government and/or the international community, may be engaged in vulnerable states for example as expert consultants on governance or conflict management. Such organisations are able through their spending and their expert advice to have a decisive influence over state-building and the organisational structure of a state, without bearing any responsibility for the negative consequences that their advice or influence may have.

Corruption and international terror

In the background of all state organs lurks the cancer of corruption, which threatens to undermine the credibility of all state institutions. Corruption is essentially the misuse of public power for private interests, and includes for example the acceptance by public officials of bribes in exchange for favours. In spite of transparency and mutual checks and balances, almost no government has been able to efficiently counter the evil of corruption.

When one considers that international trafficking in arms and drugs has an annual turnover that far exceeds the annual worldwide production of oil, one has to recognise that there can hardly be any state or organisation that can claim to be immune from this disease. With such vast financial resources at its disposal, organised crime can target almost any public officer in order to avoid criminal charges.

In spite of globalisation, the international community has so far failed to tackle the problem of organised crime at its roots, that is, to really stem the consumption of drugs and the production of arms. The developed countries want the containment of drug production, because they see the drug trade as a threat; the developing countries demand the reduction of arms production, because they are threatened by the constant danger of new civil wars. No state has however been prepared to make the first move and to halt production in their own country.

Venality of politics

If states want to institutionally protect themselves against corruption, they would do well to take heed of the famous wisdom of LORD ACTON: "*power corrupts and absolute power corrupts absolutely.*" Based on experience, it has to be assumed that human beings are in principle venal and that the venality increases the more people are dependent on additional income or the greater the economic advantage they can achieve by selling their public power to private interests. If for example the ordinary income of a judge is hardly sufficient to feed his family, one has to expect that financially powerful parties will 'buy' the judges. In countries in which company executives receive exorbitant salaries, it should come as no surprise that politicians will sell favours to maximise their personal gains.

Human rights after 9/11

The 'war against terror' that has been led by the US since 9/11 is already having a considerable effect on state organisation. The fear of terror has resulted in a major setback to the laborious and lengthy effort to improve human rights protection. Authoritarian police actions and authoritarian regimes will now enjoy support, if they are able to credibly sell their policies as serving the war against terror. Whoever – whether because of their nationality, age, gender, way of life or personal network – falls under suspicion of being involved in terrorist activity, today faces major discrimination and is hardly likely to be afforded appropriate legal protection. Governments hide behind populist claims that special measures are necessary to protect people's 'way of life', and are usually able to convince the majority through the politics of fear.

7.1.3 The Theory of State Forms

The theory of state forms is as old as the theory of state itself. Three questions have to be asked in this context: What should be the criteria to distinguish and categorise the different types of state? Should the theory of state forms be limited to examining only who is or are the power holders? Can one draw any conclusions as to the normative value of the state based solely on the form or type of state – that is, can it be said that for example monarchy, oligarchy or democracy is the best and most valuable form of state?

The typology of ARISTOTLE

"Having determined these points, we have next to consider how many forms of government there are, and what they are; and in the first place what are the true forms, for when they are determined the perversions of them will at once be apparent. The words constitution and government have the same meaning, and the government, which is the supreme authority in states, must be in the hands of one, or of a few, or of the many. The true forms of government, therefore, are those in which the one, or the few, or the many, govern with a view to the common interest; but governments which rule with a view to the private interest, whether of the one or of the few, or of the many, are perversions. For the members of a state, if they are truly citizens, ought to participate in its advantages" (ARISTOTLE, *Politics* Book III, 1279a, translation by Benjamin Jowett).

This statement by ARISTOTLE has for over two thousand years stood at the centre of the theory of types of state. Accordingly, states can be divided into democracies, in which the majority of the people governs in the common interest, and degenerate democracies or mob governments, in which the majority governs only for itself or in which the masses are manipulated by a demagogue; further there are aristocracies, in which the few govern in the common interest of the many, and oligarchies, in which the few govern only in their own interests; in monarchies one person governs for the benefit of all, and in tyrannies the individual ruler governs arbitrarily in his own personal interest.

Whilst for ARISTOTLE it is not primarily the type or form of government that reveals the value or quality of a state, but rather the *way* in which people are governed (whether for example a state governs justly in the common interest), other writers have drawn conclusions about the quality of government on the basis of the form or type of state. For THOMAS AQUINAS for instance, monarchy is the best type of state, because it is consistent with nature that leadership and authority should be vested in one person, whereas democracies and oligarchies lead to disputes in which every person pursues only his personal interest (AQUINAS, *On Kingship*, Book 1, chapter 2).

KELSEN

Seven hundred years later, KELSEN agreed: if "the question of what is socially right, what is good, what is best, could be answered in an absolute and objectively valid manner that was universally and directly binding and obvious to everyone: then democracy as such would be impossible ... However those who know, that human knowledge is amenable only to relative values can only justify the coercive force which may be necessary for their realisation, if he/she has the legitimacy and the acceptance not of all (that would be impossible, and would mean anarchy) but at least of the majority of those to whom such coercive order applies. That is the principle of democracy. It enables the largest possible freedom and seeks the least possible contradiction between the *volonté générale*, that is the content of the state order, and the *volonté de tous*, that is the will of each individual subject to this order" (H. KELSEN, p. 66 ff, translated from the German by the translator/authors).

Is ARISTOTLE'S typology outdated?

Is ARISTOTLE'S typology still adequate to cover the states of the modern world? Today, with only very few exceptions, practically every state claims to be a democracy. At the same time however, states reproach each other for violating the fundamental principles of democracy. China accuses the western democracies of serving the interests of oligarchic economic monopolies, which exploit the socially weak and infringe social rights. Developed western nations for their part indict China for being a totalitarian pseudo-democracy, which violates minority and human rights. Some, such as LENIN and MAO, seek to mobilise the masses for their ideology, whilst others demand rational discourse and solutions based on reflection and choice. Still others regard democracy as a tool to implement and justify the tyranny of the majority. "A majority taken collectively is only an individual, whose opinions, and frequently whose interests, are opposed to those of another individual, who is styled a minority. If it be admitted that a man possessing absolute power may misuse that power by wronging his adversaries, why should not a majority be liable to the same reproach? Men do not change their characters by uniting with one another; nor does their patience in the presence of obstacles increase with their strength" (A. DE TOCQUEVILLE, *On Democracy in America*).

Criteria of the typology of states

For the classification of modern states into different types one can use a diverse range of criteria. We might for example distinguish between states with stable government systems and those with unstable systems of government. Young states often have unstable systems of government, whereas developed industrial nations are proud of the stability of their systems. States could also be distinguished on the basis of whether or not they are liberal. In this case the line is not to be drawn between the industrialised states of the north and the developing states of the south, but rather between authoritarian, patriarchal, totalitarian and parliamentary democratic states. We could also make a distinction between states that accord state institutions a great deal of power, and those states that are based on a fundamental mistrust of power and seek to limit the power of state institutions. Certain states with stable governments give the executive little power (for example Switzerland). In other states, the government has limited power because the government is not yet firmly established, or because conditions are unstable (failed states).

Age and tradition of the constitution

An additional criterion could be the age of a state's constitution. The Japanese imperial family, although it no longer exercises real executive power, can claim more than 2000 years of unbroken succession. Many other states only came into existence relatively recently. States can also be classified according to the extent to which they are able to adapt to a changing environment. There are certain states that are readily able to accommodate new developments and conditions. The Scandinavian states for instance are considered very flexible. Other states, such as Switzerland, require more time to adapt to new situations. States that are linked to a particular religion also tend to be strongly committed to history and tradition and therefore less flexible (for example, Saudi Arabia). Finally, there are democratic states in which a handful of wealthy and powerful families traditionally control political power, in contrast to those that are more open and adaptable.

Geography

One can also distinguish between states with large and established bureaucracies and those that try to contain their bureaucracy as much as possible. For ROUSSEAU and MONTESQUIEU, the size of a state is a critical factor in their categorisation. A state such as China with 1.3 billion inhabitants cannot be governed according to the same principles as a state which has a population more than hundred times smaller, such as Switzerland. Occasionally, distinctions are also made between states on the basis of climate and geographic conditions. Such factors may have an important influence on the way a state is ruled. The simple fact that England and Japan are islands for example, may have a bigger impact on state theory than one might at first glance imagine.

Centralist - federalist

States can also be classified according to their internal structure, such as whether a state is federal or unitary. Today there are 25 states (encompassing 40 per cent of the global population) that have a federal constitutional structure and grant their sub-national units some constitutional autonomy. But within both federal and unitary states, there is a great variety in the degree of centralisation and decentralisation of power.

7.1.4 Criteria of State Organisation

Basic consensus as precondition

Let us return to the island of Robinson and Friday, and imagine that in addition to Robinson and Friday there are three other shipwrecked people stranded on the island. These five people have now to decide how they should organise their community. First they will need to consider what should be decided in common and thus be mandatory for all, and what should be left to the decision of each individual. They will then need to agree on how and by whom common decisions are to be reached – in other words, they will need a procedure for reaching decisions on matters that are to be decided in common.

Our example demonstrates that the question of how a state should be organised only arises if there is preparedness of the people to create a community. The precondition is the basic consensus to manage the future together. This basic agreement gives the community the legitimacy to proceed to establish institutions and procedures. Thus, a state organisation presupposes a basic consensus of those within the state.

Input-oriented criteria

According to what criteria should a new community organise and establish its governmental system? In answering this question, the five inhabitants of the island could begin from two diametrically opposed points of view. They could be of the view that the state must be organised in such a way as to give every individual the freedom to pursue his own interests. According to this view, the state organisation would be optimal if every individual inhabitant was given the broadest possible power to influence the community according to his interest. In this case the value of the state organisation should be assessed not on the results or achievements of the state (output), but rather on the extent to which every individual is able to participate in decision making and have an impact on decisions, for example through universal franchise and the principle of one vote one value.

Output-oriented criteria

The inhabitants may on the other hand be of the view that it is the output of the community that is of greatest importance. If the state organisation is to be assessed according to this criterion, one has to ask the question: how can the state organisation be structured in order to achieve the best results or to serve the interest of the common good? The best state organisation from this point of view is that which best achieves that which is in the common interest. This point of departure was determinative for several theories. PLATO believed that the common good is best implemented when the state is run by philosophers. THOMAS AQUINAS was of the opinion that the common good can only be realised by a king, who is above personal and private interests. And ROUSSEAU argued that only in a small republic would it be possible to give effect to the will of the people in the sense of the *volonté générale*.

Separation of state and society

Apart from these input and output theories, there are others that focus on the protection of individual liberty as the key criterion by which a state should be measured and categorised. The best form of state organisation from this perspective, is the one which guarantees the greatest possible liberty to the individual and which gives as little power as possible to the government.

Conflict management

Another criterion is whether (and to what extent) a state has the institutional and procedural capability to peacefully resolve existing or future social conflicts.

Whether social conflicts are resolved by suppressing the weaker party, through rational discourse, by majority decision or by the wisdom of the rulers may reveal whether we are dealing with an authoritarian state, a democracy or an oligarchy.

Protection of minorities

The important question of how a state deals with its minorities is often overlooked. In the criteria mentioned above, the question of minorities usually receives little attention. The protection of minorities, their rights and autonomy (input), but also their inclusion and their opportunities to participate in the power-sharing of the state (output), should however be a special criterion by which states are assessed.

Ability to learn and adapt

Those theorists who are influenced by cybernetics evaluate state organisation according to a state's ability to learn and to adapt its organisation and procedures on the basis of new information and changing needs. If a state is flexible and can adapt quickly to new societal needs, then it is well organised. If a state proves to be inflexible, difficult to govern and rigid, lacking the capacity to absorb new information and adapt to change, it will according to cybernetic theory have to modify its organisation.

Participation

The assignment of voting rights is also a key factor in the organisation of a state. We must ask not only whether the result or output is just, but also whether the rights of citizens to participate in the political process are assigned on a basis that is equal, just and fair. Is the principle of one person, one vote, one value respected? Does every citizen have the same opportunity to achieve a governmental post? Can foreigners be excluded from the right to vote? These are questions that have to be posed when assessing a governmental system against the criterion of justice.

Minimising human error

Whoever adheres to Lord ACTON's view that "power corrupts and absolute power corrupts absolutely", will prefer such governmental system as is most apt to minimise misguided policies and to mitigate human fallibility. Human beings have the ability to learn, and are therefore able to improve and reform themselves in the exercise of political responsibility, if they are subject to permanent supervision. As soon as they feel independent and uncontrolled however, they tend to misuse their power. For this reason it is necessary to organise state institutions in such a way that there are adequate checks on power and a balance between institutions. Just as there is no perfect or ideal person, so too there is no ideal state. The theory of the types of systems of government therefore should not ask what form of government is ideal, but rather seek to identify which types of state or government organisation are best able to minimise human mistakes and misconduct. CHURCHILL'S remark, that democracy is the worst form of government except for all others, is well known. Obviously he was convinced that democratic states are best able to avoid or minimise human error and wrongdoing, but that this form of state organisation does not guarantee a perfect government.

7.1.5 The Democratic Idea

7.1.5.1 The Foundations of Democratic Theory

Democracy of equals: ARISTOTLE

"Of forms of democracy first comes that which is said to be based strictly on equality. In such a democracy the law says that it is just for the poor to have no more advantage than the rich; and that neither should be masters, but both equal. For if liberty and equality, as is thought by some, are chiefly to be found in democracy, they will be best attained when all persons alike share in the government to the utmost. And since the people are the majority, and the opinion of the majority is decisive, such a government must necessarily be a democracy" (ARISTOTLE book IV, 1291b).

ROUSSEAU

Since ARISTOTLE, there has always been debate over the question of whether democracy is the best form of government. Even the firmest advocate of popular sovereignty, ROUSSEAU, is quite sceptical about democracy. According to ROUSSEAU, democracy is only possible in a small territory in which the people are able to assemble continuously, and furthermore only if the people is made up of gods. "If we take the term in the strict sense, there has never been a real democracy, and there never will be. It is against the natural order for the many to govern and the few to be governed ... Were there a people of gods, their government would be democratic. So perfect a government is not for men" (J.-J. ROUSSEAU, *The Social Contract*, Book III, chapter 4). However, it should be borne in mind that this statement applies only to the executive. ROUSSEAU is more optimistic about democracy as it applies to the legislative branch, and advocates the participation of the people in the legislative process and in making the social contract.

Undisputed democracy

In 1949, UNESCO conducted a survey among scholars from the member states of the United Nations on the issue of democracy. None of the responses gave a negative assessment of democracy. Each respondent supported democracy as the only and the best form of government in this day and age (see S.I. BENN and R. S. PETERS, p. 332). The respondents were however also unanimous in their view that there is a great spectrum of variation in understandings of what democracy is. This has not changed to the present day.

The principle of self-determination

In the foreground of democratic development is undoubtedly the demand for self-determination, that is, the liberty of each member of the community to make autonomous decisions over his/her relationships and obligations. The acceptance of the majority principle probably only developed after people recognised that by granting self-determination to every individual, each person effectively had a veto-right over all others. Such individual veto-right becomes intolerable when for example the majority agrees on a common solution and the minority is able to veto their proposal. In the early beginnings of the local popular assemblies in Switzerland, there was an insistence that the minority had to comply with the will of the majority. This reveals that the right of the majority to impose its decision on the minority only evolved gradually.

Consensus driven democracy

Democracy today, particularly in Switzerland, is dominated by a tendency to seek consensus and unanimity wherever possible. The bigger the majority, the more important is the result of the vote and the more responsive the executive and the parliament will be to such result. Although certain councils in Switzerland can make their decisions on a majority basis, there remains in almost all Swiss representative institutions a preference for reaching decisions by consensus. The federal structure enables extensive citizen participation in small cantons and in the municipalities. But also the proportional system, which is designed to enable as many different sections of the population as possible to be represented in parliament, as well as the requirement of a double majority for constitutional amendments (majority of the people and of the peoples of the cantons), are clear signals that the pure majority principle has been softened in favour of the best possible representation of minorities.

Marsilius of Padua: Majority decision to facilitate the search for truth

Does a majority decision guarantee a more just, truthful, or correct result than would the decision of an individual or a minority? In order to find a democratic majority, rational arguments and persuasiveness are required. The arguments that are then accepted by the majority are generally those that are most convincing. But are they therefore also the best or most correct arguments? "The universal body of the citizens or its prevailing part – which should be taken for the same thing – is more able to perceive what ought to be chosen and what rejected than any of its parts by itself ... For citizens in the plural are neither wicked nor undiscerning, at least in respect of most individuals and most of the time: all or most are of sound mind and reason and of an upright desire for the polity and what is necessary for its survival ... Aristotle affirmed this plainly: ... 'If the multitude be not too base', he says, 'each one of them will be a worse judge than those with knowledge, but all together they will be a better, or at least not a worse'." (MARSILIUS OF PADUA, *The Defender of the Peace*, 1st Discourse, Chapter XIII, § 2, 3, 4, translated and edited by Annabel Brett, Cambridge 2005). If the discourse is carried out on a rational basis the decision will be better and more balanced, because more opinions and views can improve the information and the decision will have to withstand critical examination and be tested by rational arguments.

Emotional democracy?

It must be recognised however, that arguments and debates are often not carried out on a rational basis. Personal political interests and egoistic motives such as pride, envy or prestige can also influence decisions. Ultimately, rational discourse requires as a precondition that there be at least a certain level of solidarity between the participants in the debate. The participants have to be convinced that based on a fair debate they will together achieve a better result. They have also to be prepared to submit to the result and to accept that all interests of the participants have to be considered. If these basic conditions are not fulfilled, the majority will not be able to achieve a decision that is fairer and more just than a decision made by a single individual.

Short-sightedness

Moreover, it is extremely difficult to defend long-term interests in a democratic vote on concrete issues. This makes governance more difficult, particularly in this day and age. On issues connected to energy or environmental protection for example, it is mostly long-term interests that are at stake. It is however more difficult to illustrate for voters the importance of these long-term interests and for voters to visualise the long-term consequences of their decisions, than it is to argue in favour of short-term needs such as building more roads. The petty and short-sighted interests of the middle class continue to dominate the democratic agenda, particularly in the small and parochial Swiss direct democracy.

The majority decision as a means for conflict-resolution

For a long time conflicts between different groups within society were 'resolved' using arms and violence. Those who had stronger weapons, who were prepared to take bigger risks, and/or who used the better strategies and tactics, won the battle. The rule of 'might is right' effectively prevailed. Later, as part of his peace-making role, the king or emperor gradually began to intervene to settle disputes and was able to impose his authority as highest judge. In this capacity the king was able to resolve conflicts using arguments and authority rather than violence. And from this origin, the concept of engaging in a dispute before a court as a rational means of conflict resolution was developed.

But not all conflicts could be settled in this manner. In particular, disputes amongst the nobility were often out of the king's hands. For such controversies there was and is no peaceful means for resolution in a country which is ruled only by one monarch or dictator. Such power-holders can only try to suppress conflicts, remove themselves or allow a part of their territory to secede. In a democracy however, there is much greater capacity to peacefully resolve even serious conflicts. Fundamental social conflicts can be resolved through democratic discourse. This form of conflict-management presupposes however, that the parties are able to participate on an equal footing and with equal opportunity. If one party has unlimited financial means and the other can barely afford a placard and thus cannot convey his/her arguments to the citizens, the latter party is hardly likely to accept the decision of the majority.

The iron law of oligarchy

In any democracy some groups will be more powerful than others. Even in large assemblies, one or more members will be more influential than the other participants, and will be able to capture or shift the mood of the meeting and thereby influence the final decision. In the end, the assembly may either adopt or reject a proposal; the multitude of diverse opinion must ultimately boil down to these two alternatives.

Democracy is thus controlled by the iron law of oligarchy (R. MICHELS). Those who are able to exert a decisive influence on the ballot hold considerable power. Even in the House of Lords, which conducts debates in an unstructured manner, one can find members who are more influential and important than their fellow members or 'backbenchers'. Although it must be noted that the upper chamber of the British Parliament is apparently the only known deliberative council which has been able over centuries to organise political debate without an institutionalised moderator.

Power of experts

It is important for democracy that the various influential groups are known and that their interests are transparent, in order that they can be held accountable by the people. However, it is often unclear which circles belong to the oligarchy and how one can gain admission to this inner circle. If the oligarchy of power holders is restricted to a few economic monopolies, the political autonomy of the state will be seriously compromised. Usually however, the members of the oligarchy represent conflicting interests (such as employers and employees, consumers and producers), and political organs often assume the role of independent moderators or arbiters assessing and balancing competing interests within a very limited space.

There is also an increasing demand for the incorporation of expert advice into the political decision making process (O. HOFFE). Expert committees are often charged with the task of devising long-term plans or projections in fields such as roads and infrastructure, energy or media technology, in order that politicians can draw the 'necessary' conclusions and implement policies accordingly. This 'expertocracy' must however be clearly confined. The expert as a rule bears no personal responsibility for decisions made on the basis of his advice. His view is limited to his specific area of expertise. Of course, the expert can contribute substantially to creating better-informed politicians, but he has, by virtue of his mandate or terms of reference as well as his specific expertise, a limited role. The expert cannot relieve the politician – who should have a broader view and access to all relevant information – of her responsibility for decision-making.

It is extremely important for the democratic structure of a state that the oligarchies are as open as possible. If every person has the possibility to be admitted within the economic, labour, political, media or scientific oligarchy of power on the basis of his/her ability and achievement, then the state is to be classified as a democracy. If the oligarchy is made inaccessible by secret clubs, associations or alliances, then the democracy is in bad shape.

Democracy and legitimacy of state power

The triumph of the democratic state form did not occur until the 20th Century. In the 19th Century there was still serious debate as to whether the kingdom by the grace of God was a preferable form of government to democracy. Today this argument is by all means over. However, the question of how to set up and arrange democracy remains an open issue, and is one that we shall try to examine in more depth. In a democratic state, the people is involved in some way in forming the will of the state. This participation can take a number of different forms. There are some forms of government which see the people only as a basis for legitimising state power; there are those that grant the people the right to vote in elections; and finally there are those systems which provide people with the opportunity to vote directly on concrete issues relating to the constitution, legislation and even expenditure. In the following we shall deal with these different forms of participation.

The principle of popular sovereignty

With the removal of the divine right of monarchical rulers as a basis for legitimacy, a new basis for the legitimacy of state power had to be found. The only possible alternative to legitimation by God was the people. Various social contract theories assume as their starting point that the people originally and literally entered into an agreement with the king to entrust him with the power to govern. For others, the social contract is a mere fiction. RAWLS is of the view that in order to legitimise state power one need not to refer to a factual past, nor does one need recourse to fiction; authority is already legitimised on the basis of a social contract, if one can argue convincingly that it *could have* happened, that the people agreed to a social contract. Many constitutions make express reference to the people as the source of legitimacy for the state. The interaction between the theory of popular sovereignty and these constitutional avowals is obvious. When the French Revolution erased divine royal power, there remained no alternative but to legitimise state power through the people. The self-determination of the people is itself inherent in the idea of popular sovereignty.

Popular sovereignty alone is not sufficient

However, democracy does not gain much by the mere profession of popular sovereignty as the basis for state legitimacy. Robespierre has shown with his interpretation of ROUSSEAU'S concept of popular sovereignty precisely where it can lead: to despotic tyranny. Once the people has elected the government, all government decisions are to be taken as a reflection of the '*volonté générale*' and therefore as being just and correct and made in the common interest of the people. Thus they are no longer open to question. Just as authority legitimised by God, so too authority legitimised by the 'grace of the people' can result in tyranny. The question also remains open whether a simple majority of the voters is sufficient for popular legitimacy or whether a unanimous approval is required. ROUSSEAU for example suggests that "there is only one law, which according to its nature requires unanimity: the Social Contract, because the civic association is the most voluntarily of all acts" (J.-J. ROUSSEAU, *The Social Contract*, book IV, chapter 2).

Limitations of the majority principle

The democratic principle of majority rule cannot be understood as meaning that the same majority always rules and thereby constantly imposes its will on the powerless and permanent minority. Rather, the democratic majority principle presupposes that there will not be one group as a permanent minority, but that majorities and minorities will change and fluctuate. The majority principle does not empower the majority to tyrannise the minority. Obviously, this alternation from minority to majority is only possible if the people is involved in periodic democratic decision-making, such as elections.

The fundamental decision however, that is, the realisation of the right to self-determination by founding a new state, is generally made only once and for all. Can the majority at least in this case disregard the minority? Most constitutions provide that for the most important decisions, such as constitutional amendments, a qualified majority is required. Thus it is acknowledged that in some cases a simple majority is not sufficient, and an attempt is made to come closer to the principle of unanimity. The requirement of absolute unanimity however would be unrealistic, because it would effectively enable one individual member of the community to veto a decision and thereby impose his will on the great majority of the population. This cannot be the sense of democracy. For this reason there exists as a last resort, for those who cannot accept the fundamental decision on which the state is based, the right to emigrate. If one calls into question the very basis of the democracy, the only lawful response is either to accept the majority anyway, or relocate to another state.

A relativisation of the majority principle is also possible through federal solutions to decision making. In a federal country, limits are placed on the majority of the people at the federal level by the autonomy of the federal units. Those units for their part can, within the frame of their autonomy, make and implement their own decisions on particular issues. The division of state power between two or three different levels of government within a federal system provides space for multiple and varying majorities across the respective levels.

7.1.5.2 Semi-direct Democracy

Legitimacy through the people

According to MARSILIUS OF PADUA, the participation of the people in the legislative process is indispensable. In his view only the majority of the citizens can ensure that the law corresponds to the needs and will of the community. If the majority of the people approve their laws and statutes, they also will be prepared to obey them. Only direct approval of laws by the citizens can ensure that the law does not serve special interests. "[T]he primary human authority, simply speaking, to pass or institute human laws belongs to that from which alone the best laws can result. But this is the universal body of the citizens or its prevailing part, which represents the whole of that body ... For because all the citizens must be measured by law in due proportion, and no one willingly harms himself or wants what is unjust for himself, therefore all or most of them want a law that is adapted to the common advantage of the citizens" (MARSILIUS OF PADUA, *The Defender of the Peace*, 1st Discourse, chapter XII, § 5 and 8, translated and edited by Annabel Brett, Cambridge 2001). In addition to the theory of MARSILIUS OF PADUA, in particular the theory of the social contract contributed substantially to the democratisation of the state.

Representation and will of the people

The people is not satisfied merely with being the basis for the legitimacy of the government, it also wants to have an influence on concrete state policies. Without going so far as to support the idea of the identity of government and governed (C. SCHMITT) – even according to ROUSSEAU this is only possible for a people of 'Gods' – still the power of the people to influence the fate of its state can be extended far beyond being the basis for legitimacy. Through the periodic election of its representatives in parliament or the periodic election of the executive, citizens can at least periodically influence political outcomes. Of course, one may well question whether this fulfils the ideal of democracy. ROUSSEAU for example would deny this categorically: "Every law the people has not ratified in person is null and void—is, in fact, not a law. The people of England regards itself as free; but it is grossly mistaken; it is free only during the election of members of parliament. As soon as they are elected, slavery overtakes it, and it is nothing" (J.-J. ROUSSEAU, *The Social Contract*, Book III, chapter 15). This categorical rejection of the principle of representative democracy may have been the reason for the enrichment of representative democracy with different forms of referendum, which enable the people — in particular in Switzerland but also in some of the States of the US and of Germany — to endorse or reject certain parliamentary decisions on legislation. Since the 1970s, other states have begun to provide for referendums in constitutional matters and to some degree even for legislative matters, thereby incorporating more and more elements of direct democracy in the political decision making process.

Direct versus semi-direct democracy

Is ROUSSEAU'S analysis to be rejected as unrealistic because direct democracy cannot be consistently and comprehensively realised in any state? Let us compare the differences between a state with Westminster type democracy (a Parliament that represents the people via two or three major political parties and a cabinet drawn from and responsible to the lower chamber of Parliament) on one hand, and a semi-direct democracy on the other hand. In a representative democracy the people decides by election which political party will be entrusted to govern for a prescribed period. With its majority in parliament the governing party can change the laws in accordance with its program, as well as governing the country and appointing new civil servants to the administration. Based on its legislative activity the party can influence the courts, as judges are required to follow legislation.

In the semi-direct democracy the position of the party is much weaker. It can only propose statutes, which will ultimately have to be approved by the people. It cannot manage the popularity of the executive through legislative activity, as the people can always intervene through a referendum. In the open democratic discourse prior to the referendum, all the weak points of any proposed legislation will be attacked. Thus, a law which caters only to the interests of one party is unlikely to pass the referendum. Only legislation that convincingly promotes the public interest in the sense of the *volonté générale* is likely to receive the final approval of the people. The Swiss experience also shows that the people is well able to distinguish populist proposals that conceal special interests from proposals in the common interest. The very fact that the people have to bear the consequences of their votes requires the controversial parties to make the consequences of any proposed legislation clear and plain.

Even the fact that often only 50 per cent of the citizens or less go to the polls cannot be used as an argument against the right of the citizen to participate in the legislative process or against the legitimacy of the outcome. Any quota requirement or provision for compulsory voting violates the principle of the secret ballot. The right to vote should also include the right to choose not to vote.

Requirement of consensus as a constraint on political parties

In a semi-direct democracy the parties are therefore much more dependent on the approval of the people, and are constrained by the need to seek consensus. This relationship prevents legislative activity being conducted on the basis of a comprehensive party program. New ideas and initiatives are often not introduced via the legislative program of a party, but rather through proposals for specific constitutional amendments. Even though such proposals are often rejected in a referendum, they still have an influence on legislative activity. The power of the parties and even of the executive is relatively limited. The executive does not have to fall into line with a party program, it is rather bound to seek the consensus of the parliament and of the people when it wants to implement new policies or legislation.

The obligation on all influential political groups to constantly search for consensus attracts the criticism that in a consensus-driven democracy the real political debate between interested parties takes place behind the scenes and out of public view. The citizens can no longer identify the real interests behind the negotiated compromise. Thus, the debate between different interests is withheld from the democratic process. In the campaign to win the citizens' support the people cannot decide on real alternatives, but rather it is forced either to accept a predetermined compromise or, as a consequence of a negative vote, to bear responsibility for the shattered remains of the carefully negotiated proposal. Indeed, the permanent search for consensus compels all state authorities, including the executive, to a continuous levelling of their policy. The pressure to respect every party, every language, every religion at all levels of government is great: all authorities endowed with political power are supposed to reflect the diversity of the people. The idea of simple majority rule is thus largely foreign to the semi-direct democracy. With the permanent search for a just and fair compromise, the executive strives to achieve a decision which comes as close as possible to unanimity.

Compromise however is not in itself a negative concept. Often different interests only appear to be contradictory. The political institutions charged with decision making have to try to find the common denominator between ostensibly competing interests, which enables the true needs of the different groups to be substantially met without any major concessions. An effort must be made to avoid a situation whereby powerful economic groups are overrepresented and are given more weight than they would otherwise have in an open public vote. In contrast to the simple majoritarian democracy, the semi-direct consensus driven democracy has given rise to a new political culture in which compromise is regarded as an asset and a strength rather than a weakness.

The value of preliminary legislative procedures

Is democracy better realised, when the citizens are asked to vote once every four years on different party-programs or candidates for presidency, or when all state authorities at all levels are constantly seeking the consensus of the people? Obviously both systems have their advantages and disadvantages. Within the semi-direct democracy, the executive is forced to present legislative proposals that are likely to find a broad consensus amongst the people. In Switzerland it is necessary in the preliminary stages of preparing legislative proposals to ascertain whether it will be possible to achieve a consensus among cantons, parties, economic groups, labour unions, etc. This consultative procedure is often criticised, because it enables interest groups to influence the content of legislation in the early stages prior to parliamentary debate, and thus to assert their particular interests. On the other hand, this preliminary procedure enables the executive and parliament to profit from the experience and practical knowledge of concerned stakeholders, experts and those who will have to implement the legislation. Legislative proposals are often drafted in an ivory tower far from the reality of every day life. They have first to pass the key test of political reality. Teachers can have their say on whether a statute on education really meets the needs of the children, parents and teachers; the civil servants of a local authority may test whether a proposed environmental protection regulation can be effectively implemented in a modern industrial municipality; labour unions and employers' associations can check on the extent to which their interests are safeguarded in a proposed social security law; and consumers can evaluate the effectiveness of proposed consumer protection legislation designed to offer protection against false and misleading advertising.

Balancing competing interests

Certainly, in the preliminary legislative process competing interests collide. Often however, the various interests only appear to contradict each other. In this case the authorities are obliged to analyse the ostensibly competing demands and to reduce them to their essence. In practical law making it is often the case that interested parties overstate their demands, and that the rhetoric of particular interest groups goes beyond what lies at the core of their real concerns. The actual core of a demand can often be reconciled with other seemingly contradictory demands. In some cases, discussion will reveal that certain political demands were based on misunderstandings. Of course, when the requests really are contradictory, it is much more difficult to find the common denominator that enables accommodation of all interests. It is only very seldom however, that the path to compromise necessitates the complete dismissal of the core concerns of any key party.

The need for just solutions

When the executive and the parliament submit a legislative proposal to popular referendum, they have to demonstrate that the proposal accommodates the three essential values: need, liberty and justice. Thus, they have to find solutions which can be defended in light of those values. If a legislative proposal cannot be justified in this way, it has very little chance of being approved. Opposing parties will emphasise the weak points of the proposal and seek to defeat the bill in the referendum. Only proposals that have undergone very thorough preparation will have a real chance of winning the approval of the people.

Plain legal language

The fact that legislative proposals are sometimes subject to popular approval, requires the legislative drafters to use plain and simple language which will be understood by the common citizens. Laws that are drafted in a complicated style, full of legal jargon comprehensible only to lawyers or civil servants, have little or no chance of being accepted by the people. When the very addressees of legislation, the citizens, do not feel that the proposed law addresses them, they will reject the bill.

Protection against minority interests

The lengthy, rational legislative procedure does not however provide for certain minority interests – which may contradict the interests or preferences of the majority but nevertheless be legitimate – to be taken into account. Also demands for social justice often encounter resistance. Thus, in relation to a law that requires popular approval, specific interest groups or parties usually have difficulty achieving their particular aims, and at the same time the executive will also meet heavy resistance if it proposes to protect the legitimate interests of socially disadvantaged classes. The people will generally only approve legislative proposals when the majority is convinced that the legislation coincides with their interests.

Danger of populism

Of course, such voting decisions are not always made on the basis of a rational assessment of interests. In a legislative referendum campaign, irrational and emotional arguments may be more influential than complicated factual explanations of a complex proposal. A balanced proposal may fail because for some it goes too far and for others it does not go far enough. Those adverse to a particular proposal may seek to capitalise on latent divisions within society, such as differences between urban and rural areas or between language or religious regions, to achieve defeat of the proposal. Just as in a public meeting or popular assembly one speaker may be able to stir up hidden emotions and to turn the mood from one moment to the next against a proposal, so too it is easy for television media to sway an audience in a particular direction.

Sparing use of legislation

These difficulties that arise in a semi-direct democracy lead the executive and parliament to think twice before submitting a new proposal to the official legislative process. The protracted legislative process and the reluctance of the people to approve legislation are the principal reasons for the relatively sparing production of legislation in Switzerland. The legislative process is often circumvented, and important issues are instead dealt with by directives or by ordinances or regulations, for which the legislative basis or delegated legal authority is often doubtful.

Legislative programs in a representative democracy

The process is somewhat different in countries with a Westminster system in which the cabinet decides on the legislative program. In these systems, government is formed by whichever party (or coalition) commands a majority in parliament, and the legislation proposed by the government must conform to the party program that was advertised to voters during the parliamentary election campaign. Thus, the parliamentary majority will be less inclined to focus on whether a bill can be sensibly implemented or whether it is appropriately balanced to meet competing demands, and rather more inclined to focus on the extent to which the proposed law will affect the party's chance of retaining a majority at the next election. Obviously in this type of system it is easier for particular special or minority interests to be reflected in legislation, provided such interests are seen to enhance (or at least do no harm to) the governing party's electoral chances.

Conflict resolution through semi-direct democracy

In countries with semi-direct democracy one may get the impression that policies are often haphazard and erratic. In states with a Westminster-style system, the executive can implement its policies according to a pre-determined political vision and strategy. It is not forced continuously to adapt its political agenda to meet new demands, which may be brought into the political arena by parliament or by proposed constitutional amendments. On the other hand, in a semi-direct democracy, any group or political faction which does not fit into a party-program but which represents particular substantive policies or goals, will have much more chance of having their claims seriously considered by the political elite if the elite can be convinced that they may be supported by the majority of the people. There is also no doubt that societal conflicts are more easily resolved in a direct democracy. A popular vote on the concrete issue at the root of the conflict can often (not always) have a purifying effect. When the conflict is resolved by a popular vote and if the voters have made a clear choice, the losing minority will accept the verdict more readily than they would accept that of a parliamentary majority. If the vote is close and the minority only loses by a small margin, it does not have to resort to violence; large minorities can always hope for another chance in a later popular vote.

No tyranny of the majority

Moreover, in Switzerland traditionally the interests of a minority that has lost a popular vote by a small margin are as far as possible taken into account in the resulting legislation. As the complexity of issues may often deter citizens from participating in the vote, it is legitimate after votes with almost even results also to include aspects of the losing minority's position in the legislation.

Gloves off

In a referendum campaign, the nuances and complexities of the issue in question are rarely aired. The adversaries fighting for the support of the voters tend to reduce the issue to simple opposing poles. Either one is for or against tertiary education, centralised zoning, agriculture or public health etc., although the voters are not actually being asked to vote on such basic and fundamental questions. Thus, the battle to win the voters often degenerates into a basic question of trust in the opponents.

Like it or lump it

Sometimes a balanced proposal may be defeated simply because it contains a provision marginal to the entire proposal, which attracts the attention of a strong opposing political group and brings them into the campaign. If this group is able to force a referendum, other opposing groups will want to jump on the bandwagon to prevent the initial group from exerting too much influence in relation to the particular bill in question. The combined effect of lots of small adversaries may thus cause the defeat of important legislative proposals.

Participation in voting

We have already touched on the problem of the growing percentage of absentees at the polls. If the debate on a proposal becomes emotional and if it divides the people into two deeply opposed camps, between 50 to 70 per cent of citizens may be pre-pared to go to the polls. If the proposal is not heavily disputed, not more than 30 to 40 per cent of the citizens will go to the polls. If participation is low, smaller groups may have an easier job of defeating a proposal than when 70 per cent of the voters are prepared to participate. New surveys have shown that active participation in voting depends also on the voters' level of education, social class, age etc. Workers usually are less eager to participate actively in political life than middle class voters. It is more difficult to convince younger citizens to make an effort to vote than it is to convince older people. Some surveys have also shown that a certain percentage of voters do not even understand the question they are asked to decide upon, and therefore they often inadvertently vote against their own interest and conviction.

Voter information

The growing number of ballots makes it difficult to provide voters with comprehensive information on all issues they have to decide, especially when voters are being asked to vote on several federal, cantonal and municipal issues at the same time. A further problem with semi-direct democracy is that the people can only make reactive decisions on things that are being proposed, or at best they can choose between two counterproposals.

Introduction of complex voting procedures

The questions thus will have to be channelled into a few essential opposites. This gives the opponents of any proposed changes different possibilities for defeating a new proposal. They can submit a counterproposal and thus split the majority that is supportive of change into two camps, thereby diminishing the chances of the original proposal succeeding. Several cantons try to overcome this problem by making provision for two different votes on the same issue. First people choose between the two proposed alternatives for change, and once voters have made their choice with regard to their preferred alternative, they vote on whether they would prefer the chosen alternative over the status quo. This complex procedure however often confuses the voters, who would prefer to choose between two clear alternatives in one vote.

Safeguard against bad laws but no guarantee for ideal legislation

Thus we have seen that in a semi-direct democracy such as Switzerland, it is difficult to get a good proposal passed by the majority, but that also a proposal with unjust provisions has little chance of being accepted by the people. Direct democracy thus leads in the sense of ARISTOTLE to greater liberty and less interference by the state. In such a system, it is difficult for the state to be misused for the realisation of special interests, but often it cannot protect the legitimate interests of minorities because the necessary majority cannot be convinced to support them.

7.1.5.3 Representative Democracy

i. Issues of Representation

Where do members of parliament derive the right to make decisions on behalf of the people?

When the executive, such as the president of a municipal council or the president of a cantonal executive, is directly accountable to and stands directly before the people in an open popular assembly, it can often manipulate the people with skilful rhetoric and populist arguments. This plebiscitary character of the semi-direct democracy can be substantially reduced through rational debate within parliament. For countries with semi-direct democracy as well as those with representative democracy, this raises the questions: from where do members of parliament derive the legitimacy to decide for and over the people? What is the relationship between the people and its parliament? And, can members of parliament, although they are supposed to make decisions in the common interest of the whole state, also represent particular private interests?

Which interests of the people are represented by members of parliament?

Does a member of parliament represent the interests of the entire people, or does he/she represent his/her constituency, party, the interests of a specific group or simply the common interest? This is not only a theoretical question, it also has important practical consequences. Thus, one has to ask whether a constitution which obliged members to represent the interests of the entire people would be realistic, and how one would monitor or enforce the rule that members should vote according to their conscience and not pursuant to the dictates of their party.

Relationship between electoral system and principle of representation

The relationship between the people and the members of parliament is strongly influenced by the electoral system. If the member represents the entire people, the entire people should also elect him/her. If he/she represents a specific economic interest group, this group should also elect the member – although this would again lead to a parliament composed along the lines of social class. If on the other hand he/she represents the majority interests of a specific territorial district, he/she should, according to the majority principle, be elected by a small single-member constituency as is done for example in The UK and the US.

If it is supposed that the parliament should mirror the diverse views of the people, members must be elected via a system of proportional representation, as this system alone produces a parliament that truly reflects the diversity of the people and in particular enables minorities to secure appropriate representation. If it is intended that parliament should represent the interests of the majority of the people, then a British-style electoral system based on the majority principle must be adopted. If, in addition to the representation of people's interests, there is also a desire to facilitate the election of outstanding independent personalities, the electoral system would have to combine the majority principle with proportional representation, along the lines of the German model.

Party discipline versus independence of members

If members are obliged to act for the common interest, one has to allow them the freedom to decide according to their conscience. If on the other hand, the parliament is supposed to achieve a compromise between the different conflicting interests of the people, one has to ask whether in this case the members are essentially bound to follow the will of their voters and should only be free as far as they have to interpret their voters' will. Party discipline, that is, the requirement that members vote along their party line, is in the second case more likely.

The question of representation may also have substantial consequences for the self-concept of individual members of parliament and their understanding of their role. Is it permissible for members to lend their support to a proposal which they believe serves the common good, even though they have to assume that their voters would reject it? Are they required to seek contact with the voters in their constituency in order to allow themselves to be influenced by the voters, or do they instead have to take on a leadership role and try to change the political mind of the citizens of their constituency?

One can hardly suppose that these controversial questions, which have been asked since the very beginning of representative systems, will be definitively resolved once and for all. We shall only try to explore these issues somewhat further in the general context of the theory of state.

ii. The Development of the Idea of Representation

The Significance for Democracy of the Development of the British Parliament

The concept of representation

When he first summoned his parliament (which was the successor parliament of the first parliament convoked by SIMON DE MONFORT in 1265), King Edward I declined to choose 'advisors' according to the different estates. The 'advisors' were instead considered as 'representatives' of each of the boroughs. They were asked to represent their territorial district and not a specific estate. This approach was incompatible with the socially stratified and hierarchical feudal system. The basic principle of territorial representation, not limited by feudal structures, facilitated the gradual break up of the feudal state in favour of a government representing the interests of the whole state and its people.

The idea of general representation led also to a substantially different view of what is considered to be the 'public or the state interest.' In the feudal state, the interests of the feudal lord and those of his subjects stood directly opposed to one another. The lord enjoyed privileges and sought to maximise his wealth, but also had to care for his subjects. The subjects on the other hand, were obliged to be loyal to their lord and to provide him with income. The lords and barons in turn were subjects of a higher lord and had to be loyal to their master in order to be protected by him. The king thus had only to care for his direct subjects, but not for the interest of the entire people. The deputies of King Edward I however, were charged with representing the interests of their borough before the King. All of a sudden, the state authority became responsible for the public at large and it had to defend and promote the public good. Thus arose a distinction (and potential conflict) between the public interest and private interests. HEGEL resolved this contrast by making the public interest into an absolute. The contrast between public and private interests prepared the basic precondition for democratic development according to which the people (or at least representatives of the people) decides what is in the public interest.

Parliament as lawmaker

The medieval notion that the law is something predetermined which in essence cannot be changed, meant that the function of parliament was initially limited to assisting the king in his adjudicative role. The parliament had to declare and explain what the existing law was, but was not empowered to create new law. With the creation of ecclesiastical authority in 1529 under Henry VIII, parliament made its first important autonomous political decisions and made itself, together with the King, the highest authority even on religious matters. A lawmaking function in the real sense was first exercised during the 'Long Parliament' (1640–49). Ultimately the King-in-Parliament was recognised as having absolute sovereign power, and henceforth had not only to resolve conflicts but also had the authority to change society – even the moral values of society. So it was that the Long Parliament asserted the authority to pass a special Act abolishing the British monarchy and replacing it with a 'protector'.

Majority rule

The early development of two parties led to an understanding in the consciousness of the British people that democracy always involves a conflict or tension between the majority and the minority. ROUSSEAU'S understanding of democracy based on the '*volonté générale*', which makes no allowance for party interests or minorities, is foreign to the British concept of democracy. The clear separation of majority and minority was the precondition for the exercise of sovereignty by an institution composed of more than 600 members. Periodic elections enabled the majority party to govern the country for a prescribed period. The majority party was always conscious however that it could not represent all interests of the people. Thus, the path to a totalitarian democracy was obstructed. The system of government by the majority party for a limited term makes it necessary for the governing party to include the different interests of the population in its program, if it wants to retain the majority in the next election. The party therefore cannot limit itself to promoting the interests of party members, but must also take account of the interests of the public generally. Both parties are aware of the fact that the interests of the people cannot be reduced to two opposing sets of interests represented by competing parties. The parties may at best represent certain tendencies, and they therefore need to be informed and flexible, and to take account of the real interests of the people during the time they hold the majority.

The Parliament as a collegial council

Parliaments are oligarchic institutions, though they exert no dictatorial power. As collegial organs they are incompatible with totalitarian authority. The history of England is strong evidence for this finding. The Long Parliament made the revolutionary act of sentencing Charles I to death. But it was Oliver Cromwell who exerted real dictatorial power when he dissolved the parliament. As long as parliaments exert effective sovereignty, they will be able to resist totalitarian tendencies. Debate in parliament requires presentation of arguments and counterarguments and thus avoids one-sidedness. Even in the age of the mass media, in which members of parliament often address their arguments on a particular issue directly to the voters rather than engaging in persuasive debate with their opposite number in parliament, one still cannot establish a dictatorship without extinguishing the parliament. Even Hitler, who in 1933 was granted unlimited authority, had first to eliminate the parliament in order to establish an absolute totalitarian dictatorship. The inherent ability of a large collegial council to limit power is so effective, that a one-sided exertion of power is next to impossible. Another question however, is to what extent parliament can be misused by a president or executive government and/or be used as a facade to legitimise a pseudo-democracy.

Self-government of the people?

In a representative democracy the rights of the people are confined to controlling those who govern. The conduct of periodic elections gives voters the opportunity to vote out the ruling majority party and to elect the previous opposition into government. The consequence of this is that the majority party will seek during its time in office to realise a policy program that will again be accepted by the people at the next election. This system of periodic control by the people tends as a rule to prevent extreme measures by government. Majority and minority parties have to try to make their platforms attractive to the voters. The alternation between the two parties is usually only possible when voters situated around the middle of the political spectrum opt to change their voting preference. The people's limited power to control government through periodic elections does not amount to the people governing itself, but it is the means by which the activity of government is legitimised by the people. The continuous consideration of the interests of minorities and majorities as well as the check provided by the opposition, give a certain guarantee that the consent between the majority of voters and the government is not confined to election day, but also exists between elections.

'One vote, one value' as precondition for the changing function of the state

England also contributed significantly to the development of the principle 'one vote, one value' with important changes to the electoral system in 1832 as a consequence of the revolutionary developments in France. From 1832, restrictions on voting franchise were gradually removed. These reforms marked the beginning of the development towards 'one person, one vote, one value', which took almost another century to become fully rooted in the British constitutional system.

Until 1832, 'democracy' was limited to a very small circle of wealthy citizens, who were in addition under the strong influence of the Lords. This small class of commercially active free citizens and nobles had fought since the beginning of parliament for their rights and independence. With the comprehensive extension of the right to vote, which took place in the 19th and 20th Centuries, the ability of the middle class to defend their interests in parliament changed radically. The ever-growing number of Labour Party members in Parliament defended workers' interests. Distribution of wealth through progressive taxation and social security, expansion of the education system, and protection of workers' rights have gradually been realised through the growing power of the representatives of the working class.

Parliament in the Welfare State

Social conflicts become conflicts of the legislature

In contrast to the feudal state, which had to protect and defend the interests of the lords in relation to the lower classes, the state became an instrument to defend the interests of the workers. The shifting nature of the majority caused by the enlargement of the franchise and realisation of the principle 'one man, one vote' necessarily facilitated the emergence of the welfare state. For the first time, the working class had a share in the political power of the state. With these new developments the bourgeois class saw itself fighting anew for liberty from state interference. They considered themselves cheated by the welfare state of the liberty they had managed to wrest from the feudal state. These social conflicts of the 19th and 20th Centuries were only possible because, as a result of the new democratic consciousness, social conditions and structures were no longer regarded as an inevitable fate, but as something to be changed by state legislation. Farm labourers and workers no longer had to accept that their social status was predetermined by destiny. Rather, their lot could be changed by rational political decisions and actions. Thus with the enlargement of the franchise, social conflicts were brought into the democratic political arena.

New state obligations

The sovereign parliament withdrew from its adjudicative function and began through legislation to defend the interests of employees or employers according to its majority. Many social conflicts between workers and employers continued to be resolved between the parties directly, such as issues of wages and tariffs, without the intervention of the legislature. There was however a clear tendency to expand the role of the state, in particular in questions of social welfare, and to restrict the autonomy of negotiation between social partners. It is not just by chance that the legislation regulating labour relations has increased dramatically over the last century. As new functions were transferred to the state, there was of course a concomitant expansion of state bureaucracy. Redistribution of wealth could not be carried out directly by the different social classes. The state was required to collect taxes and to allocate welfare rights to the citizens, and some of these resources had therefore to spent on financing the growing bureaucracy. The growing power and reach of the bureaucracy is therefore an additional phenomenon of modern democracy that we will need to analyse further.

iii. Dogmatic Justification of the Principle of Representation

Only Parliament knows what is good for the people: SIEYÈS' justification of representation

How can one deduce the political authority of a few parliamentary dignitaries from popular sovereignty? EMMANUEL SIEYES (1748–1836) managed to accomplish this feat of reasoning before, during and after the French Revolution. Like ROUSSEAU, SIEYES distinguished between the *volonté générale* (general will) and the *volonté de tous* (will of all). SIEYES was of the opinion that the empirical will of the people could never be consistent with the general will (volonté générale). The people itself could never detect or recognise the common good. Rather, it is the task of the people's representatives, that is, parliament, to identify and protect the common good and to govern for the people. The distinction between the sum of everybody's will (*volonté de tous*) and the general will (*volonté générale*) leads inevitably to the question: who is able to recognise and implement the general will, and by what procedure? If the general will is not identical with the empirical *volonté de tous*, then there must be a body other than people that can determine the content of the general will. Whatever body this is, it derives its legitimacy from a fictive popular sovereignty and can on that basis exercise unlimited and absolute power.

Whilst ROUSSEAU was of the opinion that the general will could never be recognised by the parliamentary representatives of the people, SIEYES took the position that *only* those representing the people in parliament have the political and intellectual competence to put the general will into effect. With the fiction of popular sovereignty it was possible to legitimise the absolute sovereign power of parliament. In order to avoid the possibility that the empirical will of the people (*volonté de tous*) might influence parliamentary activity, all necessary measures were taken to ensure that the parliament remained isolated from the plebiscitary empirical will of the people. The dissolution of the historical provinces in France and the introduction of the system of territorial departments, the centralisation of the state, the prohibition of parties and of the dissolution of parliament were the necessary consequences of such approach. Such measures led ultimately to what ROBESPIERRE described as 'representative despotism'.

EDMUND BURKE

Whilst the states on the European continent were primarily concerned with abolishing the principle of representation of the estates and replacing it with general representation of the people, the concept of general representation had been an essential feature of the English political system since it introduced the representation of territorial boroughs in the model-parliament of 1295. The member did not represent only his estate, but all the people of his constituency. In the 18th Century, EDMUND BURKE (1729–1797) as whip of the Whig Party then suggested that parliamentarians should represent the entire people, not only the people of their constituency. According to BURKE, the member of parliament had not only to be concerned with the mandate from his own constituency, but had also to represent and defend the interests of the entire people, even though he was elected by the people of only one borough. But BURKE was also of the opinion that the member of parliament should not act on the direct instructions of the people, rather he should, as a representative of the people, have the capacity to detect the common good and to contribute towards its implementation. It is this noble task which gives a sovereign parliament its legitimacy.

Empirical will of the people

In 19th Century Germany, the primary task of members of parliament was to limit the power of the king, who derived his legitimacy from God. As the revolutionary notion of people's sovereignty was never mentioned, it was easier to accept the dominion of the parliament as being more democratic than dominion of the king or emperor alone. The people respected the members of parliament as their direct representatives. The parliamentarians' concern was to link the power of the king with the interest of the people. This task however could only be fulfilled, if they were in permanent contact with the people. For this reason the fundamental dilemma or the dialectic between representing the empirical will of the people on one side, and the obligation to realise the general will (*volonté générale*) the other, is much more perceptible in Germany than in other states.

Plebiscitary representation

It is therefore understandable that in particular the left wing political parties of the 19th Century demanded that parliamentarians stay closely connected to the real will of the people, and thus proposed the introduction of plebiscites and direct democracy. In the Eisenach program of 8 August 1869, the social democrats for instance required the introduction of direct legislation by the people. Also in the Gothaer program (1875) and the program of Erfurt (1891), the right of the people to participate directly in the legislative process was demanded (but not effected).

CARL SCHMITT: The Parliament represents a higher embodiment of the people (Höheres Sein)

This direct connection of the parliament to the will of the people stood in opposition to the bourgeois concept of representation, according to which parliament constituted a 'higher being' (C. SCHMITT) than the people itself, and therefore had the power to make decisions independently of the people. "It thus is against the very principle of representation and can only be explained by the already existing decline of representation, when a parliament permits itself in any way to be informed by the people and when it decides accordingly or when the will of the people is allowed to repress the will of the parliament" (C. SCHMITT, *Verfassungslehre*, 5th edition, Berlin 1970, translation from the German by the authors/translator).

Fiction of unity: Hostility of representative democracy to parties

The bourgeoisie of the 19th Century wanted to abolish the principle of representation of the estates and replace it with representation by independent parliamentarians, whose only obligation in parliament was to follow their reason. As identity between the people and its government was impossible, because it would require a permanent assembly of the citizens, it was necessary to create a new body to represent the unity of the people. Originally, the body representing the unity of the people was the monarch. With the democratic constitution of the Weimar Republic, the fiction of the unity of the people was represented by parliament, which served by the grace of the people as a check on the executive power of the President.

This fiction of unity contradicted the reality of the division of parliament by the parties. The parties therefore had to be seen as an alien element in the state and as a threat to the independence of parliamentarians. According to JELLINEK for example, the concept of the 'party' has no place in the state order.

Legitimacy of majority and opposition parties

The more recent disputes on the issue of representation have been influenced by the division of parliament into a governing majority and opposing minority. This split of the parliament into majority and minority seems on one hand to be justified, as both parties in general accept the constitution and thus the integrity of the state. On the other hand, it is recognised that through the acceptance of the party a new democratic plebiscitary element has been introduced into the concept of representation, because each party member is able to influence party policy from the grass-roots level.

Federalist Papers

The founding fathers of the American Constitution took a more pragmatic approach to the question of representation. In the *Federalist Papers* (No. 10), JAMES MADISON (1751–1836) asked himself how the people would decide if it was asked to determine whether local handicrafts should be protected from foreign competition. Farmers and craftsmen would probably be divided in answering this question. But neither farmers nor craftsmen could make a decision which would be acceptable as just and fair for the whole people. When the people makes decisions directly, it will always be split into different interest groups. But neither the majority nor the minority would recognise the general common interest of the people (*volonté générale*). "Under such a regulation, it may well happen that the public voice, pronounced by the representatives of the people, will be more consonant to the public good than if pronounced by the people themselves, convened for the purpose."

Representatives as arbiters between conflicting special interests

Only the people's parliamentary representatives can serve as fair and just arbiters between the different interests of the people and make decisions in the general interest. Whoever wants to be a fair arbiter over the different interests of the people cannot become disconnected or removed from the people, but rather must be familiar with the different interests and opinions of the people. Members of parliament must therefore have a constant connection to their constituencies, otherwise they will be unable to reach decisions in the common interest. Of course, they are not envoys of their district. They should make decisions independently and on the basis of their personal responsibility. The general will is not something predetermined or fixed, which only has to be found by parliament and which may also be found and ordained by a monarch or a president. It is rather the common denominator which includes all different interests and with which all those interests should be able to identify. The task of an independent parliament is to find or to shape this common denominator, that is, the *volonté générale*. Anglo-Saxon utilitarianism, according to which the just solution is that which results in the greatest good for the greatest number, contributed considerably to this understanding of representation.

Decline of the legitimacy of representation through the expansion of direct democracy in Switzerland

The Federal Constitution of 1848 was strongly influenced by the concept of strong and independent representation, hostile to fragmentation by parties. Only by a general initiative to revise the Constitution were people able to participate in the constitution making power. Since 1848 however, new elements of direct democracy have continuously expanded the right of the citizens to decide on concrete constitutional and legislative issues. In 1874 the legislative referendum was introduced, that is, the right of 50,000 voters to require that a legislative proposal adopted by the parliament be submitted to the vote of the people. In 1891, the Constitution was amended by a provision which provided that if a constitutional amendment is proposed by 50,000 voters (now 100,000), it must be submitted to a constitutional referendum of the people (Constitutional Initiative). In 1921 and 1977 rights for popular participation in the procedure to approve international treaties were introduced. Since 1949, the parliament can no longer enact urgent legislation without providing the people the possibility to participate by referendum. On the other hand, male citizens were long reluctant to extend democratic rights to women, and women only relatively recently (1971) gained the right to vote. Provisions for popular initiatives were further extended in 2003. Over the last 130 years the state has become increasingly detached from the fictive *volonté générale*, and increasingly bound to the *volonté de tous*, and this trend appears likely to continue.

Volonté générale and empirical will of the people in semi-direct democracy

Is this bond of the parliament to the empirical will of the people detrimental to justice in the sense of the *volonté générale*? Whoever experiences politics in Switzerland first-hand, will observe that many magistrates and parliamentarians see themselves as servants of the interests of the people. Of course, they do not regard such statements as being merely empty electoral propaganda. They also do not see themselves as being in the service of a *volonté générale* that is to be interpreted by parliamentarians and determined by the authority of the state. They understand the will of the people empirically. Legislative proposals therefore have to accommodate the interest of the people. Parliamentarians and members of the executive have to bow to the will of the people, and to submit proposals that will find the favour of the people (the sovereign). This understanding of representation is however still far-removed from the soviet council system, which gives the people the power to issue mandatory directives to deputies.

Parliament must seek the will of the people

Swiss members of parliament have to pursue and advocate proposals which are not only acceptable within their constituency but which can win the approval of the majority of the entire people. Does this lead to one-sided preferential treatment of certain interest groups? Is MADISON right when he states that justice cannot be realised in this manner? If proposals were to be drawn up directly by a people's assembly, such danger could hardly be avoided. However, given that proposals are debated in the public arena through a more or less rational procedure, and that only the negotiated parliamentary compromise is ultimately presented to the people, the danger of populist legislation is minor. This holds of course only if the entire procedure for drafting and enacting legislation is public and transparent.

Complex network of interests

Moreover, it is actually very seldom that interests can be simply divided into majority and minority interests. Even the example from MADISON, which is based on the contradictory interests of farmers and craftsmen, does not divulge all the interests at play in that scenario. It overlooks for example that both the farmer and the craftsman are also consumers and therefore both have an interest in cheap products of high quality. It also misses the fact that their interests may be intertwined and overlapping, for example as a result of family connections (the son or brother of the farmer could be a craftsman). In rural areas the craftsmen may also be interested in supporting the interests of farmers, while in cities they would be more likely to support consumer interests. Protectionist measures may appear to assist producers, but they also entail greater state intervention and thus more power to the bureaucracy. Even among the different craftsmen the interests may be different. Some branches may profit more and some less from such interventions; moreover, protectionist measures may result in greater market concentration and less competition among different producers. Finally, one cannot overlook that craftsmen even at the beginning of the 18th Century had employees, who might vote against the interests of their employers. This long list of the diversity of interests could go on and on. It merely serves to illustrate, that the more or less theoretically opposing interests are in the reality of every day politics often much more complex and diversely differentiated. Often in the process of drafting a proposal, one cannot foresee which themes will dominate the political debate and determine the outcome of a referendum.

Parliament as the penultimate authority

It is for this reason that parliament is legally and de facto required to make an independent decision; a decision that it can assume however will receive the approval of a majority of the people. Experience proves that a proposal will only have a chance of gaining the approval of the voters, if it satisfies the criteria of justice and if it has been produced according to a fair procedure. The procedure should guarantee a fair debate, in which contrasting arguments are expressed and evaluated. Through such procedure there is a greater likelihood of reaching a just solution that reflects the *volonté générale*, than there would be simply through the majority decision of a parliament controlled by the governing party in a Westminster system, which need only be concerned with re-election and not with approval of proposals via referendum. The dependence on the empirical will of the people does not in fact restrict the independent decision-making of parliamentarians as much as one might believe, because at the time of the parliamentary debate the empirical will of the people has not yet been disclosed, and reveals itself only during the debate on the referendum. The link to the will of the people does on the other hand prevent the misuse of parliamentary power or of the power of a ruling majority party. The representative exercises in this sense the delegated power of the people. The parliament is the penultimate authority, over which the people will finally pronounce its judgment. If the people rejects a proposal, this will not have any personal consequences for representatives who advocated the proposal. Indeed, public opinion would oppose the withdrawal of any representative from office because he/she has lost a referendum. One may ask whether such procedure is not more likely to produce just results in the sense of the *volonté générale*, than the procedure in a representative democracy, in which the governing party introduces measures from the tactical standpoint of trying to win the next election, and in which the minority opposes the initiatives of the government for the same reason.

7.1.6 Separation of Powers

7.1.6.1 Development of the Theory of Separation of Powers

Characteristics of the 'ideal' ruler

Most theorists on government assess the organisation of the state not primarily based on the nature of the institutions, but rather on the character of the leader. PLATO was of the view that leaders of the state should be philosophers. ARISTOTLE tied his classification of 'good' and 'bad' state forms to the character of the ruler: if a ruler governs the state in their personal interest, then the form of the state will degenerate – from monarchy into tyranny, from aristocracy into oligarchy.

This Greek tradition was in the 8th, 9th and 10th Centuries further developed in Arab-Islamic theories of state. In the 9th Century, IBN ABI R-RABI insisted that the leader should be the best and the most powerful personality in the country. He should keep his promises, exercise mercy and protect each person's interest in accordance with law. IBN ABI not only set out the characteristics required of the ruler, he also concerned himself with the qualities required of a good judge: the judge has to be god-fearing, reasonable and familiar with the legal literature. He must be a person of integrity, should not make judgment until all relevant facts are known, and should not delay judgment when all evidence is at hand. He should not fear right or wrong, should not accept gifts or listen to any recommendations, should not have private discussions with any party, should smile seldom and speak little. He should not demand any benefits from the parties and should protect the property of orphans. Similar ideas can be found in the works of FARABI (850–970), who, 800 years before HOBBES and 1000 years before AUSTIN, anticipated the theory of the social contract and of sovereignty (HROON KHAN SHERWANI, *Political Thought and Administration*, 3rd ed, Philadelphia 1963, p. 72). The idealistic tradition was continued by GHAZZALI (1058–1111) and by probably the greatest state theorist of the Arab world, IBN KHALDÛN.

Institutional concepts in Ancient China

Similar reflections on the relationship between the organisation of the state and the personality of the ruler can be found even in the much older tradition of Chinese theories of state. In particular, Confucianism attempts to guarantee good dominion by the requirement that the emperor possess certain characteristics. LAO TSE classifies rulers into the following categories: The best rulers are those who are barely known by their subjects; the second best are leaders, who are praised and applauded by their subjects; the third best are feared by their subjects, and rulers who are hated and despised belong to the lowest category, because they do not believe in their people and cannot command their loyalty. The accomplishments of the best leader the subjects will ascribe to themselves as their own achievements.

HAN FEI

These idealistic concepts were later strongly criticised by HAN FEI (died 234 BC). "Duke Lu asked: 'How can one rule the state well?' CONFUCIUS answered: 'Only with virtuous civil servants'. On another day the Duke of Chi put the same question and CONFUCIUS answered, saying: 'The income and expenditure of the state should be as low as possible'. – What CONFUCIUS said will lead to the ruin of the state" (HAN FEI, Chapter 16, paragraph 38, quoted in GENG WU, p. 12, translated from the German by the authors/translator). HAN FEI takes into account the fact that states are not ruled by superhuman leaders. He therefore tries to develop a theory of state which factors in the fallibility of the average human being, given that princes are usually average people.

In order to avoid the prince being undermined or deceived by his subordinates, HAN FEI proposes a system of mutual checks and balances. If the prince wants to remain in power he must make a precise division and allocation of responsibilities and ensure that his subordinates control each other in their exercise of specific functions. None of them should be given too many functions or responsibilities, as they might otherwise acquire too much power relative to the prince. Because human nature is essentially bad, the prince should not place too much trust in his servants. For the first time, we can observe that HAN FEI seeks to create a state-organisation with institutional precautions such as the division and mutual control of powers. His aim is thereby to serve the prince and to protect him from the misuse of delegated power (GENG WU, p. 82).

ARISTOTLE'S division of state functions

One hundred years before HAN FEI, ARISTOTLE developed in Greece the basic principles of the state theory, which was later to have a great influence on Arab and European philosophy. "All constitutions have three elements, concerning which the good lawgiver has to regard what is expedient for each constitution. When they are well-ordered, the constitution is well-ordered, and as they differ from one another, constitutions differ. There is (1) one element which deliberates about public affairs; secondly (2) that concerned with the magistrates—the question being, what they should be, over what they should exercise authority, and what should be the mode of electing to them; and thirdly (3) that which has judicial power" (ARISTOTLE, *Politics*, Book IV, part XIV).

ARISTOTLE anticipates the later division between legislative (deliberative), executive and judicial power. But his aim is more the achievement of a reasonable division for good and efficient government, than to ensure mutual control as with HAN FEI.

7.1.6.2 Separation of Powers According to LOCKE and MONTESQUIEU

LOCKE

After ARISTOTLE and HAN FEI, more than 1500 years passed until in England for the first time JOHN LOCKE proposed a division of the different powers of the state. He distinguished between the legislative, the executive and the federal (external) power. The reason for this classification by LOCKE is also primarily a division of functions. "But because the laws, that are at once, and in a short time made, have a constant and lasting force, and need a perpetual execution, or an attendance thereunto; therefore it is necessary there should be a power always in being, which should see to the execution of the laws that are made, and remain in force. And thus the legislative and executive power come often to be separated" (J. LOCKE, *Second Treatise*, Chapter XII, sec 144).

MONTESQUIEU

Shortly after LOCKE the French anglophile MONTESQUIEU, in describing the English constitution, espoused the view that the separation powers serves not only as a useful division of functions, but can also serve to guarantee the liberty of the citizens generally. He thus assessed the value of the state, like LOCKE but contrary to many predecessors, not according to the character of the rulers but on the structure of the state institutions.

Not men but institutions guarantee freedom

What are the decisive considerations of MONTESQUIEU? MONTESQUIEU presumes that the system of government alone is not sufficient to guarantee the liberty of citizens. "Democratic and Aristocratic states are not in their own nature free. Political liberty is to be found only in moderate governments; and even in these it is not always found. It is there only when there is no abuse of power. But constant experience shows us that every man invested with power is apt to abuse it, and to carry his authority as far as it will go. Is it not strange, through true, to say that virtue itself has need of limits? To prevent this abuse, it is necessary from the very nature of things that power should be a check to power. A government may be so constituted, as no man shall be compelled to do things which the law does not oblige him, nor forced to abstain from things which the law permits" (MONTESQUIEU, *The Spirit of Laws*, Book XI, chapter 4, translation by Thomas Nugent 1752). At the end of his famous book XI of *The Spirit of Laws*, MONTESQUIEU comes to the conclusion that the liberty of citizens has to be measured according to the separation of powers of the state. The concept of separation of powers in the sense of checks and balances becomes thus a central component of the liberal constitution. Separation of powers is not described merely as a division of functions (ARISTOTLE), nor is it seen as an institutional guarantee to uphold the power of the prince (HAN FEI), but rather for MONTESQUIEU it is the precondition for and the basis of the development of any liberal state and constitution.

7.1.6.3 Separation of Powers in a Constitutional Democracy

Separation of powers as ancient constitutional principle

MONTESQUIEU'S theory did not go unheard. The French Revolution introduced the principle of separation of powers in Art. 16 of the Declaration of the Rights of Man and Citizen, which provided: "A society in which the observance of the law is not assured, nor the separation of powers defined, has no constitution at all." And Article 3 of the Constitution of the unitary Swiss (Helvetic) state of 1800 imposed by Napoleon prescribed: "The legislative, judicial and executive power can never be united."

Checks and Balances: MADISON

The most ardent followers of the ideas of JOHN LOCKE and MONTESQUIEU were the founding fathers of the American Constitution, and in particular the authors of the *Federalist Papers*. MADISON for example in No. 47 of the *Federalist Papers*, contends with the detractors of the new Constitution who criticised it for undermining the principle of the separation of powers. Detractors pointed to the fact that the three functions of the state were not clearly separated from each other and that in particular the executive was given certain legislative powers and the judicial arm could exercise some executive functions. MADISON however, like most proponents of the principle of separation of powers, was convinced that an accumulation of legislative, executive and judicial powers necessarily would lead to tyranny. Thus, whilst the American Constitution might not follow word for word the recipe of MONTESQUIEU, it absolutely fulfils the purpose of the principle of separation of powers, namely, the prevention of the misuse of power and the protection of liberty. These aims of the separation of powers can however only be realised, if the powers are not completely separated from each other. Mutual checks and balances between the powers is only possible, if each of the powers participates also partially in the other powers and each has some capacity to control and influence the others. MADISON was fervently opposed to a dogmatic and rigid understanding of MONTESQUIEU'S theory of separation of powers, that is, he was against the complete isolation of the three different branches of government. Even the British constitution, which served as a model for MONTESQUIEU, does not provide for a total separation between the three powers. It was therefore justifiable that under the US Constitution for example, the executive has a veto-power over legislation, and that the legislature has the power to remove the executive from office through impeachment. Furthermore, the executive has the exclusive power to enter into foreign treaties and to nominate judges. The judges for their part participate in the legislative power through their jurisdiction to provide advisory opinions (*Federalist Papers* No. 47).

Dismantling the rigid theory of separation of powers

MADISON and with him the founding fathers of the American Constitution thus dismantled the dogmatic approach to the separation of powers, which indeed was never understood so rigidly by MONTESQUIEU, and examined the branches of government in terms of both institutions and personnel. The power of the state has to be distributed amongst different persons as well as amongst different institutional bodies. These persons and institutions must exercise mutual control over each other and thus have some share in the powers of the other branches, but each branch must also have the capacity to make independent decisions. Thus the President has the power to nominate the members of his/her cabinet and the highest civil servants, but the Senate has to ratify the nominations. Congress is able through the impeachment procedure to remove the President and the Justices of the Supreme Court from office. On the other hand, the President can impede the legislative process with his/her veto-power, and the Supreme Court can declare statutes enacted by Congress unconstitutional.

Separation of powers and indivisible sovereignty

It was mainly those responsible for the French Revolution who created the rigid approach to the principle of separation of powers. According to this theory, the three powers are all derived from the indivisible sovereignty of the state, which is broken down into three and then delegated to the three branches of government. From this follows that the three powers have to be separated completely and may not have any mutual connection. This dogmatic approach to the principle of separation of powers in fact leads to a loss of the actual sense of the principle, namely to enable mutual control of power in order to guarantee the freedom of the citizens. If each branch of government is totally independent in exerting its powers and therefore cannot be controlled by any other branch, then people will for example be subject to the whim of civil servants, as neither the judiciary nor the parliament would have the authority to intervene in the power of the executive. With very few exceptions, it is today recognised that the three functions and branches of government cannot be entirely isolated from each other, but rather they must control each other mutually according to the principle of checks and balances.

Separation of powers and Westminster government

The exposition of the different systems of government has made it clear that states take different approaches to implementing the idea of separation of powers. The weakest form of separation of powers is found in states with parliamentary responsible government. Although the English cabinet system had already developed by the time at which MONTESQUIEU was in England, he did not recognise the close relationship between the executive and the legislature. A cabinet that depends on the parliamentary majority leads in fact to a merger of the executive and the parliamentary majority. The separation in this case lies not between the executive and the legislature but rather between the government and the parliamentary opposition. Neither the jurisdiction of the courts to review the constitutionality of statutes nor the administrative jurisdiction to protect citizens against arbitrary administrative action were included in the original theory of separation of powers, as neither jurisdiction existed at the time of MONTESQUIEU. At any rate, the civil servants of the British Crown could be held accountable before the common law courts, if they acted *ultra vires* and caused unlawful injury to private citizens. The king however, was not accountable to any judge.

Separation of powers is implemented more strictly, at least in the sense of checks and balances, in the American system of government. As the founding fathers did not have to deal with the issue of how the principle of separation of powers can be reconciled with absolute sovereignty, they were able to vest each of the three arms of government with original and independent powers, which could only be checked by the other branches. None of the three branches is superior or inferior to the others. State sovereignty is rooted concurrently in each branch. As already pointed out, the Americans avoided a complete functional separation of powers, and thus each branch exercises to some extent the executive, judicial and legislative functions.

The major opponents of the principle of separation of powers are the socialist states. It is true of course that socialist constitutions also provide for three branches of government, however they are not independent of each other. As the real sovereign power is exercised by the party, it is party policy which determines how each of the three powers operates. From the Marxist perspective, separation of powers is a bourgeois invention. Protection against the misuse of power is only necessary in a bourgeois state. In the communist state, in which society is emancipated through the proletariat, the leaders of the proletariat are by definition not able to misuse power.

Administration as the fourth branch

In his paper on MONTESQUIEU, FRANZ NEUMANN makes the interesting assertion that: "MONTESQUIEU had changed his conception after a study of English political institutions. He would equally have changed it after a study of a mass democracy in action" (F. NEUMANN, p. 143). Indeed, we might ask to what extent would MONTESQUIEU have changed his views after observing the modern pluralistic mass democracy? NEUMANN is convinced that the focus on the separation of powers as a basic principle of constitutional theory has led to a neglect of the reality of the power of the administration and bureaucracy as a significant element of social change (F. NEUMANN, p. 142). In fact most theories overlook the fact, that alongside the politically accountable governmental branches there can grow an administrative body, which takes on a life of its own and which quietly and gradually reduces the liberty of citizens.

Power of the administration

The growing powers of the administration in the welfare state results in those citizens who are dependent on state welfare being essentially at the mercy of the civil servants who have the power to determine welfare entitlements. The expanding information-base of the administration with the help of modern data collection entangles people in a network of invisible mirrors, from which there is no escape. The citizen feels constantly observed and at the mercy of the bureaucracy. The modern administration is less and less inclined to resort to criminal sanctions for the implementation of public order. It has at its disposal much more sophisticated and effective means to guide people's behaviour. If it wants to create problems in the field of public health, education, taxation, social security pensions, public grants, scholarships, driving tests, employment qualification requirements, housing assistance etc, the administration could ruin the very existence of a person without violating the law and without involvement of a court. If the affected individual attempts to defend himself, he will have a hard time finding a legal cause of action; or if he finds one, he will have to submit to nerve-wracking and costly procedures, with uncertain results.

Is the administration 'evil'?

A former Swiss magistrate once made the statement that 'the administration is evil, but individual civil servants are kind and helpful'. Wherein lies the core of the truth of this sentence? Civil servants, who want to build a successful career in the administration, have to follow the directives of their bosses; they must work efficiently and win the praise of their superiors, in order to be promoted further up the chain. They have to conform to what is expected of a correct, hard-working and honest civil servant, who is loyal to the state and its government. Government employees are seldom assessed or promoted on the basis of what they deliver to the citizens. Who for instance has ever heard of an appraisal which reads: "Does his best to implement the common good", "Shows great care and understanding for the people"; "Has a good sense for fair and just decisions", "Has common sense" etc. Decisive is not the relationship to the outside world, but rather the internal relations within the administration. Bureaucrats often appear to believe they could exist even without the people whom they are supposed to serve.

For the citizens, the administration is anonymous. Citizens do not have contact with a particular person, but rather with an office or authority. They are lucky if during their interaction with the administration they come across a competent professional, who shows some human understanding in dealing with their enquiry. The final decision on their application however is usually not made or signed by the competent professional, but by his/her superior in the hierarchy. As the responsible superior has often had no contact with the affected applicant, they rely on the judgment of their subordinate. But this judgment is not assessed according to the extent to which it shows fairness and human understanding, but according to the efficiency of the machinery of the administration, which should never be hampered by a new precedent or an exception to the rules.

New Public Management

With the ideas of the so-called New Public Management, there is an attempt to break up the anonymous bureaucracy and in particular to introduce the idea that citizens should not be considered as subjects, but as 'clients' of the administration. This concept is intended to bring about a new culture of 'consumer-oriented' administration. With global budgets and performance measurement criteria, the administration should no longer be concerned with how it should fulfil its tasks, but rather with what targets it has to meet. The administration must seek to meet its performance targets as efficiently as possible, with the full support of its clients.

Separation of powers within the administration

The rigid hierarchy, the autonomy of the administration, the technical and inward-looking evaluation criteria, all result in the bureaucracy appearing to be anonymous and dismissive. In states in which the executive is not identical with the parliamentary majority, the extension of parliamentary control of the administration has resulted in greater protection of the citizens. In states with a parliamentary cabinet, the ombudsman has gained importance as an institution to mediate between the administration and the citizens. In some states, the federal division of state power has also led to a decentralisation of administrative activity, which often results in the administration having a more human face. If for example in a small municipality a local committee has to make decisions on construction permits, it will proceed in a different way than would a central bureaucratic body, far-removed from the reality of the municipality and unfamiliar with the concrete problems and conflicts of the members of the community.

The expansion of judicial control of the administration has also undoubtedly contributed to strengthening the protection of citizens. Although the control of administrative activity has developed very differently according to the legal system of the states (common law v. civil law), it is in every state directed toward the same goal: to provide people with better protection against the misuse of power by the administration.

But all these tools do not suffice to ensure just administration in the modern mass democracy. The basic concept of a real separation of powers will probably have to be introduced within the administration itself. The vertical division of powers by delegation to lower bodies leads to a limitation of power, and also enables direct contact with the people to whom the lower body feels directly accountable. It is also important however, that citizens be given more opportunity to have a say in the process of administrative decision making. In Switzerland, citizens have to be consulted when new ordinances are prepared. What would be the consequences if the citizens could also influence decisions relating to the promotion of public employees by providing evaluations of their conduct and service? In the private economy, quantifiable performance such as turnover determines the promotion of employees. In many cases such measures are dependent upon consumers. How much more friendly would public employees become, if their 'clients' could influence their chances of promotion? It would however be essential that the administration be assessed according to different criteria. This does not necessarily have to lead to the system of the ancient Greek Republic, in which state employees were randomly selected by lottery to serve for one year, after which they had to step down and return to being ordinary citizens. However, nor can the idea of professional civil servants employed with lifelong tenure be the salvation of the bureaucracy. The attempt of the parliamentary assembly of the Council of Europe for example to define the rights and obligations of the police in a democratic society can be seen as a positive initiative to improve police activity in the interest of the people. Such initiative should also be extended to other branches of the administration.

From civil servant to employee

The concept of New Public Management has led to a process of rethinking the make-up of the administration. The position of the civil servant can historically be traced back to the professional soldier at the end of the 18th Century. Civil servants were in fact considered as civil soldiers. Over time, the military-influenced hierarchical status of the civil servants gave way to the concept of the civil professional, still accorded a special social status. Today there is a move away from granting special status to civil servants, and a move towards making them simply public employees. Modern statutes in fact provide for the employment of civil servants with similar conditions to the private employee, based on the private employment concept of partnership between the employee and employer.

Does separation of powers weaken the state?

Finally, we have to ask ourselves whether the separation and mutual control of powers does not in fact weaken the state, and expose it to external forces and interests. The federal vertical division of powers enables small groups to corral and exploit weak municipalities or provinces for their own interests. Similarly, powerful economic interests may more readily be able to bring executive or legislative power under their control, if powers are already weakened by separation and mutual control. In particular, the autonomy of small municipalities can be misused by powerful companies for their private interests.

However, it would be erroneous to believe that separation of powers will necessarily make the state more vulnerable to external influence. The contrary is often the case. If for example a private company tries to harness the state for its own commercial interests, it is not sufficient to deal only with one of the governmental branches, rather it will have to win over each of the separate branches of government, and in a federal system also each separate level of government, as each of them has independent and autonomous state powers. This phenomenon, which leads to the splintering of the forces of those who want to bring the state under their control, is well illustrated by the separation of powers within collegiate bodies. Whoever wants for example to influence a collegiate body such as the Swiss Federal Council must win over a majority of its members (in this case at least four of the seven members). If they succeed, they will have in addition to convince the majorities of the two chambers of parliament and ultimately, in the event of a referendum, even the people. The complex network of the divided powers within the state not only splits up state power, it is also difficult for external powers and influences to penetrate.

Of course, one can also see the separation of powers as an obstacle. If for the sake of justice and public welfare it is necessary to take urgent measures for environmental protection or reduction of expenditure for example, the system of separation of powers will necessitate lengthy bureaucratic procedures that may hinder the timely realisation of the common good. This lack of efficiency in public activity ultimately serves to protect the citizens against hasty and ill-considered state interventions in their personal liberty. In fact a system of separation of powers, properly balanced, ultimately strengthens state activity. Authority is based on obedience. This obedience can be enforced by the use of violence by the police. But such police behaviour is not possible in a state with separation of powers. Thus, obedience in a liberal democratic state is based on trust in the state and its institutions, and on the ability of state bodies to convince the public.

Minimalising human error

Finally, we should also recognise that separation of powers is an important instrument with which to avoid or at least minimise the human failures of those public employees who exercise state power. The mutual control of state powers motivates those who work for state authorities to try to do their best. Human weaknesses and errors can thereby best be mitigated and the capacity to learn from mistakes promoted.

7.1.7 Adherence to the Law

7.1.7.1 Development of the Concept of Legislation

Antiquity

The concept of the law has evolved considerably over the centuries. In ancient Greece, the philosophers focused on the content of the laws (*nomoi*). PLATO'S ideal state was governed by wise philosopher-kings, and therefore did not require laws. Only cities, which were not able to establish the ideal state, would need laws. For ARISTOTLE, laws are binding norms which express the will of the legislature, but which at the same time have to correspond to pre-existing morals and custom.

In ancient Rome the emphasis was on procedure. In terms of content, any generalised principle was capable of becoming a law. According to the procedure however one has to distinguish between the '*lex data*', that is the law that has been given by the monarch (e.g. Roman Tabular Law, *Lex duodecim tabulorum*), and the '*lex rogata*', the law agreed with the magistrate. According to GAIUS (117–180 AD), the law is the '*lex*' adopted by the citizenry on a proposal of the magistrate (GAIUS, I, 3). Finally also the decisions made by the plebs (*plebiscitum*) were regarded as law.

German Middle Ages

If one examines the history of German law making, one can find three basic forms of legislation:

- The unwritten law in the form of traditional wisdom;
- The statute agreed by the legal profession; and
- The law commanded by the monarch or the authorities, the legal order.

Looking at these historic concepts helps to explain the tension that is still today inherent in the notion of the law. The wisdom is the tradition of handing down decisions of the courts, which are based on the rules and principles of pre-existing wisdom – the *lex aeterna* or the *lex naturalis* according to THOMAS AQUINAS. The law thus has to correspond to this traditional and pre-existing wisdom. This is a content-specific concept of the law.

MONTESQUIEU

In the course of time, the question arose to what extent the law could ever separate itself from the given and traditional wisdom. MONTESQUIEU for instance, proposed that laws have to correspond to the distinctive characteristics of the people, the climate of the country, the language, history and culture, but that laws must also still be consistent with the predefined reason. "Law in general is human reason, inasmuch as it governs all the inhabitants of the earth: the political and civil laws of each nation ought to be only the particular cases in which human reason is applied" (MONTESQUIEU, *The Spirit of Laws*, Book I, chapter 3, translation by Thomas Nugent 1752).

What for MONTESQUIEU was reason, was for THOMAS AQUINAS the eternal divine order, *lex aeterna*. The predetermined legal order specific to human beings (*lex naturalis* or natural law) is also derived from the divine order. AQUINAS labels the positive law made by the people *lex humana*. These positive laws have to be consistent with the *lex aeterna* as well as with the *lex naturalis* (THOMAS AQUINAS, *Summa Theologica*, Book II, part 1, question 91, Art. 1–5). Finally, we find in the works of THOMAS AQUINAS also the definition of the notion of law: "The law ... is nothing else than an ordinance of reason for the common good, made by him who has care of the community, and promulgated" (THOMAS AQUINAS, *Summa Theologica*, Book II, part 1, question 90, art. 4).

The volitional notion of law

JOHANNES DUNS SCOTUS (1126–1308) and OCCAM (1285–1349) introduced the shift towards positivist theories of law. For them, the law is not the given divine order, but it is a temporal expression of God's will. Laws thus can be willed; their content is not given by the eternal order of being, their content is desired. With this, the preconditions for a volitional view of the law were established.

Law by reason

With the secularisation of the state, MARSILIUS OF PADUA (1270–1442), NIKOLAUS VON CUES (1401–1464) and others developed a new concept of law based on reason and political power. The people must obey the laws which are enacted by the political sovereign. The sovereign has the obligation to enact laws which correspond to the will of God (J. BODIN). The complete detachment of the law from any supernatural tie was effected by HOBBES. For him, the law is the decision of the highest commander of the state: "Civil law is to every subject those rules which the Commonwealth hath commanded him, by word, writing, or other sufficient sign of the will, to make use of for the distinction of right and wrong; that is to say, of what is contrary and what is not contrary to the rule" (THOMAS HOBBES, Part II, Chapter 26). Thereby the final dissolution of ties to natural law was complete. Laws are expressions of will, commands of the sovereign (J. AUSTIN).

7.1.7.2 Positivism – Natural Law Theory – Legal Realism

Decisionism

Since then a relentless battle has been waged between those representing the idea of a predetermined legal order (Natural Law theories) and those proposing a positivist concept of law. The positivists deny that laws depend on a predetermined order, and restrict their examination of law to the positive laws that have been enacted (KELSEN).

A consequence of the decisionist school of the 19th Century is that many laws were drafted without any relationship to reality, as it was believed that the sovereign was truly omnipotent and could make the impossible possible. Unworldly laws, some of which could never realistically be implemented, were enacted. Today it is generally accepted that the lawmaker cannot rely solely on its own will, but that it has to take into account the given realities and context. Social factors, organisational limits, personal, financial and political conditions impose considerable limitations on the legislature. One of the tasks of legal sociology is to detect those general social conditions that have to be considered by the legislature, and to indicate the parameters within which a new law may be enacted that will be realistic and capable of implementation. The practice of lawmaking has led to the realisation that laws cannot be derived from the will of the sovereign alone (decisionism and voluntarism). The arrogance of the decisionism of the 19th Century has given way to a more realistic view of the law.

7.1.7.3 Law and Separation of Powers

Who is the lawmaker?

Apart from the question of the content of the law, one has to ask the more difficult and important political question who has or should have the authority to enact laws: The judge, the government authorities or the people? In fact the notion of law today encompasses all three elements. Undoubtedly first it was the judge, who based on customs and morals had to find or determine the relevant law to be applied in concrete cases. The principles and traditional wisdoms conveyed by the judges gradually acquired a prospective and prescriptive character. Whoever wanted to behave correctly had to act in conformity to the wisdom pronounced by the judges. In time, the state authority that exercised law-making power came to be no longer a judicial authority determining legal disputes but an authority over all subjects that could enact general and prospective laws. From the judge came the legislator, which issued prospective laws according to which legal decisions would be made.

Contract law

Legal obligations were established not only by judgments and the enactment of legal orders by the state authority, they developed also on the basis of contractual agreements. Through contractual agreements between the legal profession and the state authority, new norms were created that were to have the same effect as the laws enacted by the authority. On the European continent, judge-made law was increasingly replaced by legislation and codified law enacted by the state. The reception of the old Roman law certainly also contributed to this development.

Legislation as expression of the volonté générale

There were rigorous disputes between the authorities and the people. In the age of absolutism, the political rights of the people were almost completely denied. The holder of sovereign power had the right to make laws, and would sometimes consult the assemblies of the estates according to his power and according to the tradition of the particular principality. The French Revolution marked an important turning point in the approach to lawmaking power. Article 6 of the French Declaration of the Rights of Man and Citizen (1789) proclaimed: "Law is the expression of the general will. Every citizen has a right to participate personally, or through his representative, in its foundation. It must be the same for all, whether it protects or punishes." However those advocating the political rights of the people were still facing an almost insoluble problem: if they wanted to give to the executive the power to execute the laws, they had to find criteria which would demarcate the execution of laws from the enactment of laws. Whoever has the power to enact laws, needs to know what laws are. Only on the basis of a clear notion of the law is it possible to effect a reasonable division of powers between the legislative and the executing branch. Three different solutions were developed at the time:

General validity

Already contained in the notion of the '*volonté générale*' is the idea of the *general* or *universal*. Laws are therefore such orders as are applied to everybody in the same way and which have general validity (such as 'smoking is prohibited'), as opposed to particular orders, which are addressed to particular person and which prescribe a certain act or omission (such as 'Mr. Smith has to pay 10,000 Euro in tax by 1 October 2008'). KANT introduced with his 'categorical imperative' the idea that orders are reasonable and consistent with general moral principles if they can be generalised and applied to all persons in the same manner. RAWLS represents the modern version of the same idea – according to him, laws should be made in such a way that they will be acceptable to everybody.

Only interventions in liberty and property need a legislative basis

Those democratic assemblies that succeeded in gaining the right to participate in all decisions of general nature (e.g. Kurhessen, Saxony and Prussia after 1815) were thereby able to considerably restrict the power of the executive. However, the powerful princes did not readily permit such far-reaching restriction of their power. They attempted to limit the rights of the assemblies to participating only in relation to such laws as would limit personal liberty or affect people's property rights (e.g. Bavaria). This raised the question, whether aside from laws affecting liberty or property, the prince had the original prerogative power to legislate. This power of the prince or the Crown to legislate was later transformed into the prerogative of the executive to issue ordinances.

Laws should be limited to fundamental principles

KARL SALOMO ZACHARIÄ (1769–1843) proposed a less formal but much more political notion of the law. He suggested that the legislature should regulate the fundamental issues and leave the executive to implement the details. According to ROBERT VON MOHL (1799–1875), the law is the ordering norm which is promulgated by an authorised state authority for the observance of the addressees.

Substantive and formal laws (materielle und formelle Gesetze)

The German constitutionalist LABAND found a way out of this confusion of different notions of the law, by proposing a dualistic concept of the law. He distinguished between the substantive law and the formal law. The notion of the substantive law relates to the content of laws. From this perspective, every general legal norm is a law. The formal notion of law however is determined by the procedure. Formal laws are all decisions which have been enacted according to a formal legislative procedure. Thus, both the legislature and the executive can issue substantive legal norms or orders. However, only the legislature can enact formal laws. With this solution LABAND defused the political dispute between the Crown and the assemblies. At the same time, he left open the question whether, based on the concept of separation of powers, there are certain matters for which the formal legislature is exclusively responsible. So it is that the principle is still observed that any law that limits freedom or property must be enacted by the legislature, whilst other laws in the substantive sense can be promulgated by the executive (G. ANSCHÜTZ, R. THOMA, G. JELLINEK, P. LABAND).

7.1.8 The Organisation of Sovereign Power

Is ARISTOTLE'S classification sufficient?

According to what criteria should the different types of state organisation or governmental systems be categorised? Can we settle for the criterion of the number of people who hold the power of the state? The political reality that ARISTOTLE had in mind was the diversely organised community of Greek city-states. Democratically organised cities stood right alongside cities with tyrannical political orders.

Sovereignty of the individual reason

One of the ways in which modern man differs from his ancient ancestors, is that he does not see himself as an element of nature and the environment subject to a predetermined fate, but rather as a subjective agent with a rational will and the ability to alter his environment and circumstances. Modern man can say "no". The society of the Middle Ages accepted the political power of the state or monarch as a God-given fate. The monarch did not have the function of enacting special laws for the people, but rather his job was to apply the divine law for the people. He was the judge who had to pass sentence on the lawbreaker. Only very few monarchs arrived at the idea of using the law to design or restructure the organisation of the state and society. In most cases, the state and the order of society were seen as something predetermined and handed down.

In the secularised state with complete and unlimited sovereignty, the ruler not only had the power to adjudicate over the subjects, but also to shape the state and the society according to his will. In states ruled by a single individual, state power was effectively unlimited and undivided. The old feudal structure with divided sovereignty was replaced by centralised absolutism.

Sovereignty concentrated in one governmental branch

The concept of unlimited sovereignty was completely foreign to ARISTOTLE at the time at which he wrote his *Politics* and formulated his criteria for the categorisation of state types. For ARISTOTLE, laws were primarily proscriptions of behaviour, that is criminal laws, which had to implement justice. His 'Polis' was based upon a society organised and structured by tribes. The idea of an all-encompassing state power was unknown.

Some modern states entrust one single state body with unlimited and undivided political power. This power may be concentrated in the parliament (parliamentary democracy), in a party (communist states or one-party states) or the army (some Latin American states until recently).

Undivided v. divided sovereignty

There are also states which to this day have not taken the step of concentrating state power in one branch. The United States of America for instance essentially adopted the English constitution of the time of the Glorious Revolution, which means a balance of powers between the President (elected king) and the Congress (parliament). Also in Switzerland, absolute state power has not been realised. Of course, certain cantons have been subject to the despotic dominion of certain cantonal aristocracies. But even in these cantons the people was able to defend its rights in extreme cases. The federally organised confederation of Switzerland thus does not fit into the mould of the modern state with uniform, absolute and indivisible sovereignty.

If we distinguish states according to the way in which they organise their sovereign power, we will find the following: On the one hand, we will have states which have followed absolutist developments and have vested the sovereignty of the state in one branch of government; and on the other hand, we will find states which still structure and divide the sovereignty of the state, entrusting sovereignty to different branches.

Mixed governmental systems

In his thoughts on the democratic constitution, ARISTOTLE expressed the view that the people could in fact govern directly over a small self-sufficient autarchic polis. Indeed, the people at that time did decide many issues directly and autonomously in the assemblies. Moreover there was an attempt at that time, through the random selection of civil servants and their annual turnover, to avoid the development of an oligarchic ruling class. In comparison to the polis of ARISTOTLE however, modern states are much bigger and much more complex. Modern states cannot be governed by open popular assemblies. Rather, ARISTOTLE would classify them as *mixed governmental* systems. The people elects the parliament and/or the executive at regular intervals (democracy), and the parliament enacts the laws (oligarchy).

The executive, which either legally or *de facto* is run by a head of government, tends towards the constitutional design of a monarchy.

However, this assessment does not allow us to gain much insight or make valid judgments in relation to the different forms of democratic government in existence today. Decisive is the original question posed by ARISTOTLE in relation to the *organisation of the highest state authority*. Thus, if we want to analyse today the different types of states, we have to know which governmental body is entrusted with sovereignty and how it is organised.

Sovereignty in one or several organs of state

When we know in respect of any given state how this sovereign body is elected and how it is composed, we shall be able to evaluate the type and the degree of democracy within that state. Viewed from this standpoint, we can categorise states as follows: First we have to distinguish between states which entrust the exercise of sovereignty to one supreme body, and those in which sovereign powers are distributed between several organs of state. The first category includes states with a parliamentary democracy as well as those with a presidential democracy. The United States and some federal states belong to the second category of states, with divided sovereignty being distributed to the different branches and levels of government.

External sovereignty

Another category that should not be overlooked is that of states in which sovereignty is effectively vested in institutions such as a party or a religion, which cannot be considered as being a branch of the state. The communist states as well as states determined by religious traditions belong to this category. In these states, it is not a constitutionally established state institution that holds sovereignty, but rather an institution external to and unaccountable to the state. The constitution of the state is then merely a pretence.

7.2 The Organisation of Modern Democratic States

7.2.1 Sovereignty Centralised in Parliament

7.2.1.1 England

i. Early History of the English Parliament

Lessons from the history of the English Parliament

Many western democracies and also some states of the third world have developed different forms of parliamentary democracy, based on the idea of parliamentary sovereignty (although importantly, in most of these countries the 'sovereignty' of parliament is subject to a written constitution). This parliamentary sovereignty is inextricably linked to the history of the British Parliament. While the United States of America modelled their governmental system on the basis of the English constitution as it was in the 17th Century, the parliamentary democracies of Europe, Australia, Asia and Africa have their roots in the British parliamentary system as it had developed by the 19th and 20th Centuries. For this reason it is indispensable to give a short overview of the interesting and inspiring history of the development of the British Parliament. By understanding these historical developments, one will also gain a better understanding of the very principles of democratic theory.

British parliamentary history is for many different reasons significant to an understanding of the modern theory of state. In contrast to the parliamentary bodies on the European continent, the British Parliament was able over the course of its history to establish itself as an independent decision making body and counterpart of the Crown, and gradually to wind back the powers and prerogatives of the Crown.

Responsible government (Westminster model)

Parallel to the growing empowerment of the Parliament, the system of parliamentary responsible government developed, whereby a cabinet comprising members of Parliament was entrusted with executive powers and was accountable to Parliament for the exercise of those powers. This system of government has since been adopted in many modern constitutions. An understanding of this form of government requires a detailed knowledge of its original development in England.

Early model of representation

The early European parliaments originally represented the estates of the hierarchically structured feudal society. However in the English Parliament, the idea of general representation based on territorial constituencies rather than on estates developed early. Thus, the modern theory of representation is closely tied to the early history of the English Parliament. Initially, the elections of the members of the Commons were largely a farce, at least by modern standards. The idea of free, fair and independent elections based on one person, one vote, one value developed only in the 19th Century. This development was of extraordinary significance not only for uplifting the parliamentary system, but also for the development of political parties and for the extension of democracy.

King in Parliament

In England, sovereignty is vested in the triumvirate of the Crown, the House of Lords and the House of Commons. The sovereign position of these organs has remained unchanged since the Parliament of King Edward I in 1295, but what has changed is the balance of power within the triumvirate. In earlier centuries, the

King could call Parliament when he wished, could decide which questions he wished to consult the Parliament on, and could exercise a veto power over decisions of Parliament. But the balance of powers began to shift in the 17th Century, and sovereignty is now effectively held by the lower house. Today, the Queen can only call Parliament when requested to do so by the Prime Minister or when the government no longer has a parliamentary majority. The Queen must leave all legislative decisions to the Parliament and must give her assent to all legislation passed by Parliament without being able to exercise a power of veto. These shifts in political power however do not change the fact that legally, today as for the last 700 years, sovereignty is vested in the 'King-in-Parliament'. How did this parliamentary tradition emerge?

Assembly of the Wise (Witenagemot)

Even before the Norman invasion, the Anglo-Saxons in accordance with German traditions gave people certain rights to participate in the decision making processes of local barons, especially in relation to questions of war and peace. Superior to these local assemblies was the Witenagemot, an 'assembly of wise men' which was summoned by and answerable to the king. The Witenagemot ratified treaties and gave advice to the king on matters such as administration, security, the granting of noble titles and the grants of crown land. Finally, the Witenagemot had the power to select (and depose) the king. However the Witenagemot did not enact legislation, as there was no legislative power in the sense it is understood today. Nor did it decide on taxes, as the king at this time did not require income from taxes.

But similarly to other original Germanic advisory bodies, the Witenagemot had the power and the obligation to assist the king in the exercise of his judicial function. The king summoned the Witenagemot and decided who should be invited to participate. The people was allowed to follow the debates and to express either their satisfaction or disapproval.

Magna Carta and the first assemblies of the king

With the invasion of the Normans these first democratic institutions were abolished, at least for a time. England was under the yoke of a foreign conqueror, who assumed control over the whole territory of the island and distributed the land amongst his own nobles and bishops. In place of the Witenagemot, the conqueror summoned an assembly of his subjects to provide him with advice. Unlike the Witenagemot, it was no longer a mixed assembly composed of different representatives of the people, but an assembly composed only of directly subordinate nobles – that is, an organ of the feudal state of the Middle Ages.

This feudal body in 1215 produced the Magna Carta, which set out the first basic liberties. However, the Magna Carta had no decisive influence on the development of Parliament. In 1265 the rebel SIMON DE MONTFORT, who led the opposition against Henry I, summoned a national assembly to which he invited not only dukes and other nobles but also representatives from the various districts (boroughs).

SIMON DE MONTFORT thereby initiated the development of the new parliament, which carried on from the earlier tradition of the Witenagemot. Similar assemblies met in 1275 and 1290, until King Edward I summoned the first actual Parliament in 1295. Members of this Parliament were not elected by the people of the boroughs, but were selected by the King to represent the people of their borough. With this prerogative to choose the members of Parliament, the King was able to preserve his influence on the Parliament. The King's influence remained effectively unrestricted until the Bill of Rights at the end of the 17th Century. Nonetheless, the members of this Parliament were responsible for representing the interests of their whole borough, and not merely those of a particular class or estate.

Say in taxation

The decisive authority which Edward I vested in his Parliament, was the power to vote on decisions to levy taxes. "No taxation without representation" has since become the catch-cry of all parliamentarians in the Anglo-Saxon world. This right to have a say in decisions relating to the imposition of taxes later became an important instrument with which to influence the policy of the King. Initially however, this power was a double-edged sword, as the representatives were only asked to assist the King when he wanted to levy new taxes.

Petitions

Apart from the right to participate on decisions to levy taxes, the Parliament had the power to receive and adjudicate over general complaints and petitions. Parliament thereby continued the old tradition of the judicial function of the Witenagemot.

Constitution and expansion of the powers of the Parliament

Under King Edward II in 1322, the powers of Parliament were enshrined in the Statue of York: "[M]atters which are to be determined with regard to the estate of our lord the king and of his heirs, or with regard to the estate of the kingdom and of the people, shall be considered, granted, and established in parliament by our lord the king and with the consent of the prelates, earls, and barons, and of the community of the kingdom, as has been accustomed in times past." Later the Parliament was able to further extend its powers, because King Edward II and his successor Edward III required the support of Parliament for the heavy taxes they sought to levy. Parliament thus acquired the power to participate in the nomination of royal advisors and in the appointment of the new King.

Two chambers

Contrary to developments in Europe and in particular in France, where the King summoned the three estates of the clergy, the gentry and the common citizens, the English Parliament was from the very beginning only composed of the Lords (including the clergy), and the Commons. Exactly when the Lords and the Commons separated into two different chambers is uncertain. Probably the need to have simultaneous but separately located discussions led to the development of two separate chambers. It may also be that the Lords have never debated jointly with the Commons. What was important for the further development of Parliament, was the fact that the major landlords sat together with the other free citizens representing the boroughs, and so a separate class of landlords exploiting the free citizens did not develop.

Comparable developments on the continent

Advisory assemblies, such as were found in England in the 13th and 14th Centuries, were also established in almost all other European kingdoms. In France, the Capetians established the tradition of the 'curia Regis' (the King's Court). In Poland it was the 'Szlachta', which in the Magna Carta of Poland of 1374 reserved the right to participate in decisions on taxation; and in 1493 the 'Sejm' under Piotrkov enacted for the first time statutes for the entire country. In Sweden, King Magnus was forced by the powerful gentry and the free citizens to accept a tentative parliamentary beginning in the form of the first 'Riksdag'. This parliament was composed of representatives of cities and of the clergy as well as nobles. In the Swedish empire, the provincial assemblies (Landtag) acquired a certain political significance. Their members however did not as in England represent all the people of their district, but rather only the members of their own estate. The four estates (Clergy, Lords, Knighthood and the cities (citizenry)) had to deliberate separately. As in most cases they disagreed, the sovereign prince had the important task of mediating, which significantly strengthened his power in relation to the provincial assembly.

In the old Swiss Cantons, the Landammann (Governor) assumed the power which had originally been held by the Vogt (governor on behalf of a colonial or imperial power). He held court and sat in judgment in common with the people. As early as 1294 a common assembly of the people for local decision making (Landsgemeinde) was formed in the Canton of Schwyz.

ii. The Reformation Parliament of Henry VIII

Absolute sovereignty of the Parliament

As in all other European states, the English Parliament was also diminished during the age of absolutism. However in contrast to the French representation of the three estates, the English Parliament was able to regain its power quite early, and even to further extend its powers. What were the reasons for this development? When King Henry VIII entered into conflict with the Pope in Rome, he had to find a new basis to legitimise his authority as king by the grace of God and also as the head of the Church of England. To do this, he had to rely on his Parliament.

The 'Reformation Parliament' in 1529 executed the final separation of England from the Roman Catholic Church, and declared the King the head of the Church of England. Whilst Parliament up to this point (aside from its role in levying taxes) had mainly exercised judicial functions, with the decision to separate from the Roman Church it established itself as the supreme sovereign authority. Without absolute sovereignty, it would not have been able to make such decision.

Parliament bound by divine law

Herewith began in England the great debate over whether Parliament was obliged to observe divine law. CHRISTOPHER SAINT GERMAN (c. 1460–1540) and SIR THOMAS MORE denied that Parliament had full and unlimited sovereignty including the power to violate or contradict divine law. SIR THOMAS MORE, a distinguished jurist who had served as Lord Chancellor, was ultimately convicted of treason for denying the King's supremacy, and sentenced to death.

Constitution making

THOMAS CROMWELL took the final step towards absolute parliamentary sovereignty when he stated the position to Bishop FISHER that Parliament has without any doubt the power to repeal or to amend canon law. In consequence, FRANCIS BACON (1561–1626) was able declare: "For a supreme and absolute power cannot conclude itself, neither can that which is in nature revocable be made fixed; ... " (*Works of Francis Bacon*, VI, by Spedding, Ellis and Heath (1861), pp. 159–160). The theory of secular sovereignty later developed by HOBBES had thus already been anticipated in the practice of the English Parliament. Although with the Reformation the Parliament vested absolute power in the King, at the same time it established itself as the body exercising constituent power, which also marked the real beginning of its legislative function. Parliament was no longer confined to interpreting the law, but could henceforth also prescribe the law. It became, in common with the Crown, the source from which all law could flow. From this point on, law was not something predetermined, but rather it became an instrument in the hands of the legislature with which justice could be achieved and by which society could be moulded and changed.

In light of the historical development of the British Parliament, it is therefore not surprising that, even in the age of European absolutism, the British Kings summoned Parliament quite frequently. During the 37 year reign of King Henry VIII Parliament was in session for 183 weeks, and under Elizabeth I, who ruled for 45 years, Parliament sat for a total of 140 weeks.

iii. Parliament in the 17th Century

King, Lords and Commons

The status and the composition of the Parliament during the 16th and 17th Centuries is important, because the American Constitution later adopted certain essential elements of the British constitution of this period. As we have seen, sovereignty was at this time vested in the triumvirate of King, Lords and Commons. Only these three organs together could execute a sovereign act, such as issuing a statute. As the highest sovereign authority in the land, this triumvirate did not share its sovereign powers with any other authority in the Commonwealth. All other authority or power was delegated by and derived from the sovereign – that is, the King-in-Parliament.

The Lords and the Commons could defend this position, because as a result of the growing commerce and industrialisation, they did not depend like their continental European counterparts on the income from the royal court derived from the exploitation of farmers. The preconditions for the bourgeois development of a commercial and industrial state existed relatively early. Moreover, through colonisation the Crown was able to bring in enough revenue to avoid having to impose taxes on farmers that were as high as elsewhere.

From the Long Parliament to Cromwell

It was no accident, that in 1649 during the 'Long Parliament' it was the high tax burden that led to the Revolution and to the downfall of Charles I. The Commons supported by the people was able to run the country for a limited time. In the 'Act for abolishing the kingly office in England, Ireland and the dominions thereof' of 17 March 1649, Parliament declared that the kingdom and the exercise of power by one man were unnecessary and that these things endangered liberty, security and the common interest of the people. "And whereas by the abolition of the kingly office provided for on this Act a most happy way is made for this nation to return to its just and ancient right of being governed by its own Representatives or National Meetings in Council, from time to time chosen and entrusted for that purpose by the people" (*Act for abolishing the kingly office in England, Ireland and the dominions thereof*, 17 March 1649).

A short time thereafter, the rule that was later to be observed in almost all revolutions – that revolutions eat their own children – became evident. Cromwell abolished the Rump Parliament by military force and appointed himself leader of the country by declaring "[t]hat the supreme legislative authority of the Commonwealth of England ... shall be and reside in one person, and the people assembled in parliament; the style of which person shall be, The Lord Protector of England, Scotland and Ireland". However, he did not want to do away with Parliament entirely. The long parliamentary tradition prevented him from establishing himself as the solitary ruler and completely abolishing Parliament. He therefore attempted during his 'reign' to install a Parliament that would carry out his will. These few years in England's history, the only period that England has been without the legitimacy of the Crown, came to an end shortly after Cromwell's death.

Glorious Revolution: guarantee of 'free' elections

Charles II who then sought to re-establish the old regime, was replaced in 1688 by James II. With the Glorious Revolution and the Bill of Rights (1689), the previous powers of the Parliament were fully recognised and enshrined in a constitutional document. From this point forward, the power of the King and in particular the power of the House of Lords began to decline. In the Bill of Rights, Parliament proclaimed the guarantee that "elections shall be free". However, this did not entail a truly general right of all citizens to vote in free elections in the modern sense. Parliament's insistence on free elections related to the fact that the King had the power to decide on the appointment of the Lords and, through his agents, to influence the election of the Commons. With free elections, Parliament wanted to reserve for itself the power to influence the boroughs in the election of members of the Commons. Thus the issue was not free elections for all citizens. Until the Reform Act of 1832, only 5 per cent of the citizens over the age of 20 had the right to participate in elections.

iv. The Development of Parliamentary Government

From Privy Council to Cabinet

In England during the 15th, 16th and 17th Centuries, the most burning constitutional issue was the achievement and maintenance of a balance between Parliament and the Crown. Towards the end of the 17th Century and in the 18th Century, Parliament began to fight for its superiority over the Crown. The issue at the centre of this battle was the development of a parliamentary system of government. How did this come about?

The King had always had an appointed committee of advisers (usually around 20), which assisted the Crown in its governing responsibilities. This *curia regis* was known as the Privy Council. Originally, the King decided unilaterally whom to appoint as members of the Privy Council. Towards the end of the 17th Century and in the 18th Century however, Parliament acquired the power to influence the selection of the King's advisers. From the Privy Council, 'cabinet' was developed. The cabinet was made up only of members that enjoyed the confidence of the House of Commons. Increasingly, the House of Commons demanded of the King that he include in cabinet advisers who were also members of the House of Commons. Towards the end of the 18th Century, the Commons had gained so much power that it was able to compel the King to remove any Prime Minister and cabinet which had lost the confidence and support of the House of Commons.

Cabinet and Crown

With the support of the Commons, the cabinet thus dramatically increased its power in relation to the King, so that the King was no longer able to make his own decisions on basic policy issues or to govern the country without support of the cabinet.

Parties

Parallel to this development, political parties gained greater importance. Originally the British Parliament was split into two opposing parties: The Tories (conservatives) and the Whigs (liberals). According to the strength of the respective parties in the House of Commons, the cabinet would be composed of either Tories or Whigs. Indeed, the cabinet and the party with a majority in the House of Commons merged to an almost inseparable political unit, so that over time the separation of powers between parliament and executive was replaced by the separation of powers between government and opposition. The Prime Minister was the head of cabinet and also the parliamentary leader of the majority party. Depending on his personality, he could effectively assert power over cabinet and parliament, establish a one-man show and rule the country as the de facto sovereign for a limited term.

General right to vote

The real democratisation of the state did not occur until the 19th and 20th Centuries, and was initiated by the Reform Act of 1832. Up to this time the election of members of the House of Commons was often plagued by corruption and intimidation. The territorial boundaries of some constituencies (boroughs) were designed to guarantee the election of specific representatives (rotten boroughs). In addition, the right to vote was limited to the small circle of wealthy gentry. The Reform Act of 1832 provided for a new repartition of the boroughs, extended the right to vote to men of lower means, and removed the power of the Lords to influence the elections of members of the Commons. This last provision may have been the most decisive reform, as it resulted in the significant decline of the political power of the upper house. Although the Reform Act initiated the development of modern democracy in England, it did not in itself bring about the complete democratisation of the state. Even after the Reform Act, only 7.1 per cent of the adult male population had the right to vote. It took a number of additional reforms up to 1928 until more than 95 per cent of men and women were given the right to go to the polls (1867 16.4 per cent, 1884 28.5 per cent, 1928 96.9 per cent).

Two party system

The stability of the current British system of government is largely attributable to the two-party system. A Westminster-type parliamentary responsible government with several small parties, none of which has a clear majority, would necessarily lead to continuous crises of government. In England the centuries-old tradition of two parties that share in government and opposition, as well as the pragmatic realism of British voters who tend only to vote for a party that has a chance of winning government, have contributed to the long-lasting stability of the system. The majority principle tailored to single-member electorates, which gives victory to the candidate who gains only a relative majority in his/her constituency, has also tended to favour and reinforce the two-party system. However in England since 1906, there has always been a small third party contesting the two major parties. Initially this role of third party fell to the socialists (Labour), who first entered Parliament in 1906 with 50 members. By 1922, Labour had displaced the Whigs to become the second-strongest party in the Commons, and in 1924 and 1929 Labour was asked to form a minority government as the most powerful party among the three competitors. In 1945 Labour won an absolute majority in the House of Commons, and since this date, government alternates between Labour and the Tories.

From the sovereignty of the Crown to the sovereignty of the Commons

To sum up, after this brief and necessarily incomplete overview of the parliamentary history of England one can observe the following: The history of the relationships and the political strength of the different branches within the triumvirate of King, Lords and Commons can be divided into three different periods during which major shifts occurred, in that the power of the Crown was diminished for the sake of the power of either house.

Initially, the members of Parliament are the advisers of the King. They are supposed to assist him to levy the necessary taxes. In accordance with the King's instruction, the members of the Commons have to seek a mandate from their boroughs in order to have the authority to vote on and decide matters in Parliament. Important for the further development of Parliament is the fact that the members of Parliament do not only represent their class or estate, but rather the whole of their boroughs. They must in other words represent the interests of all the inhabitants of their boroughs, even though they have been elected only by a small fraction of the inhabitants.

In the second phase, the former advisers of the King expand their own prerogatives and powers. They participate through the constitutional triumvirate in the sovereignty of the state, and use their sovereign powers to enact laws that no longer have to be justified in accordance with divine law. The state and its parliament become self-confident and begin to take the fate of society and the state in their own hands. This concept of balanced power among the three branches, known as the 'King-in-Parliament' will later become the model for the American Constitution and the position of power of the American President. This model still today has a great influence on all presidential systems.

In the third phase, the House of Commons expands its power relative to the King and the House of Lords to such an extent that the King and the Lords are today almost meaningless. This occurs first through the influence of the Commons on the development of cabinet, which leads to a dissolution of the separation between legislative and executive power. Through the process of democratisation, the influence of the Lords declines and the power of the upper house is steadily reduced, until the Commons effectively stands alone and unchallenged as the real bearer of sovereignty.

Westminster model

This third phase of the system of parliamentary government is often called the 'Westminster-System', and with its pure majority principle or 'winner-takes-all' approach, has become the model for many states of the Commonwealth and for other constitutions in Europe, Africa and Asia. Of course, the English system is always adopted by other states with certain deviations or modifications from the original. In particular, states without a monarch had to replace the king with a president who may be given considerable (e.g. Weimar) or negligible powers (Italy and Israel). Many states adopted the Westminster Model of government but tried to make it work with many small parties (or no parties) rather than a two-party system. This often led to crises and required adjustment of the system, as for example in France, which under De Gaulle in 1958, changed from the Westminster to a special type of presidential model. Indeed, in some former colonial possessions in the South Pacific which have modified versions of the Westminster model, instability and crises resulting in part from a proliferation or an absence of political parties persist today. Some states have combined the Westminster model with federalism (e.g. Australia, Canada), which has the effect of significantly reducing the 'sovereignty' of the central parliament. And, as mentioned, perhaps the most significant modification of the Westminster model as it is applied elsewhere is that parliament (like all other institutions of the state) is subject to the written constitution, and courts generally have the jurisdiction to review legislation and to declare unconstitutional legislation invalid.

7.2.1.2 Germany

i. Differences to British Development

Unitary and federal elements

In contrast to England, the governmental system of the Federal Republic of Germany cannot be traced back to an unbroken history of parliamentary development. The heterogeneous structures within the former empire and the weak powers of the representation of the estates prevented parliament from becoming the central political power of the state as it was in Great Britain. Even today, it does not possess the same sovereign powers as the British Parliament and is restricted by the judicial review jurisdiction of the constitutional court on the one hand, and by the federal division of legislative powers on the other.

In the following pages we shall try, based on the German example, to explain how a system of parliamentary government developed from a very different historical background, and the effects that state (monarchical) mistrust of parliamentary power has at the constitutional level. One may rightly ask whether the Federal Republic of Germany should not be classified as a federal state with divided sovereignty. Certainly, Germany does not belong to those states in which sovereignty is vested entirely in the central organs of the state. However, the unitary and centralised elements of the German system, in particular the power of the German Parliament to change the constitution, are to our mind so strong that it is more accurate to classify Germany as a state with centralised sovereignty rather than divided sovereignty, even though it is a federal state with some powers divided between the *Länder* and the central Government.

Decentralisation of the power of the Empire

A comparison of the development of state institutions in Germany and in England reveals some essential differences. In contrast to the British Island, Germany was always an empire that was vulnerable to attack from almost all sides of its territory and thus had to defend itself constantly from external threats. The early decision of Charles the Great, that the each duke of the empire should provide his own defence for the territory of his duchy, had a significant impact on the history of the German Empire. It led to a strong decentralisation of the power of the Emperor to all the very differently formed dukedoms and free cities. The German Emperor who was elected by the princes hardly had the possibility to build up a powerful central state. He could not levy taxes and did not have his own army.

Decentralised absolutism

The feudal lords, in contrast to those in France or China for example, could not rely on the central power to solve their troubles or to overcome for instance the problems of the Peasants' War precipitated by the Reformation. Little by little the princes and lords established their own realms of absolute authority and thus undermined the general feudal system, which since the comprehensive reception of Roman law had already lost most of its important legal roots. At the end of the Thirty Years War, what had once been a great Empire sank into misery. The authority vested in the *Länder* in the Peace of Westphalia in 1648 to conclude treaties with other powers, provided they were not directed against the Emperor, effectively deprived the Emperor of much of his remaining power. Furthermore, from 1663 the Emperor's remaining powers were bound to the German Reichstag, which had to approve the statutes and the taxes of the Emperor.

Representation of the estates in the Reichstag

In contrast to the members of the British House of Commons, the members of the Reichstag did not represent all inhabitants of territorial constituencies, but rather only the interests of the German estates (*Reichsstände*) with regard to the Emperor. The Reichstag comprised only members directly subject to the Empire (so for example, until the 16th Century even some Swiss estates belonged to the Reichtsag). The knights and the inhabitants of the free towns of the Empire were not represented. The Reichstag was divided into three different collegial councils: The royal electors, the council of the princes and the council of the cities. The right of the cities to vote was however long disputed. The three chambers of the Reichstag deliberated separately. If they disagreed, they had somehow to reach an agreement through difficult negotiations. None of the three chambers could be overruled by the other two. Decisions were enacted in the form of a treaty between the Emperor and the estates of the Empire.

ii. Historical Influences

Weak judiciary

The court of the Empire (*Reichskammergericht*) was given responsibility for maintaining peace within the land (*Landfrieden*), and was independent from the Emperor and his own court (*Hofgericht*). It based its decisions on the 'general', that is, Roman law, as a court of first instance with regard to all self-governing units under the Emperor and, with the permission of the respective prince, it could sit as an appellate court on domestic issues within the *Länder*. The procedure was lengthy and complicated. In 1521 approximately 3000 unresolved cases lay before the court. By 1772, there were 61,233 cases undecided. There were even some proceedings that took more than 100 years to conclude.

1,800 dukedoms and principalities

The Empire itself was fragmented into some 1,800 dukedoms, principalities and free cities. In 1475 dukes ruled over a total of around 500,000 inhabitants in the southwest of Germany. But many dukedoms had no more than 300 inhabitants. The dominion over such small territories corresponded still to the old patriarchal system, and the ruling lords were not represented in the Reichstag. There were also fifty-one free cities that were mostly governed by patrician families, which often ruled their cities for their own interests. Sixty-three *Länder* were under the rule of prince-bishops, who were elected by councils (*Kapitel*) and ruled their Lands – often badly – in common with these councils.

170 to 200 principalities and earldoms were ruled by single families. The earl or the prince knew most of the inhabitants of their small shire personally. He often held an expensive court and ruled the country with an excessive number of advisers and servants, which were funded by burdensome taxes. Only in the southeast of Germany were there large principalities with their own administration and a parliament divided according to the estates. In the bigger *Länder*, the aristocratic landowners were most influential. The estates assumed the right to approve statutes and taxes.

Thirty Years War and French Revolution

After the Thirty Years War, the princes managed to reduce the influence of the estates. The administration of the large *Länder* was markedly better and more efficient than in the small dwarf dukedoms. They had also established a properly functioning judiciary. Thus the preconditions either to secede from the Empire or to assume the leadership through the hegemony of the Empire were set. Timid attempts to liberalise state power were dashed by conservative kings and in particular by the war against Napoleon.

The influence of the General Prussian Land Law of 1794 (*Allgemeines Preussisches Landrecht*) however remained intact. This was the most progressive law at the time. In 1815, under the leadership of Metternich and as a reaction against the liberal endeavours initiated by the French Revolution, a loose federal alliance called '*der Deutsche Bund*' was formed. The assembly of the estates was composed of the plenipotentiaries representing the *Länder*. This assembly was not empowered to make decisions that were directly binding on the citizens but rather, it could only bind the *Länder* as members of the alliance. The assembly was divided into two councils which met in Frankfurt. The plenum was composed of the ambassadors of the 40 member states (which later became 33 member states). Those member states exercised between one and four votes according to their size. The smaller council was a committee of the plenum. In this small council the eleven largest member states each had one vote and the remaining states shared 6 votes together. The chairmanship of both councils belonged to Austria, with its presidential might. The alliance was a confederation which largely left the sovereignty of its member states intact. Decisions of the assembly (*Bundestag*) constituted international law obligations, which were binding on the member states but had no direct application to the people living within these states. The *Deutsche Bund* was a confederation, whose members were already more closely allied to each other than in the old Empire. However, the activity of the alliance was commanded almost entirely by the opposing poles of Prussia and Austria.

Tentative beginnings of liberalisation

Some of the middling and smaller *Länder* such as Baden and Württemberg established a constitutionally based comprehensive system of representation. Attempts at liberalisation however were as far as possible stopped by press-censorship and by infringement of academic freedom at the universities. So for instance in 1815 JOHANN WOLFGANG VON GOETHE (1749–1832), on the question of whether he should ban a publication that criticised the prince, advised his prince CARL AUGUST, Duke of Saxe-Weimar-Eisenach, that the editor should not be punished for his attacks toward the prince, as the editor could misuse the trial procedure and by his sharp pen or his impudent tongue could make the prince look ridiculous, and he continued: "A comprehensive and well thought-out paper has been conveyed to me on the future institution of censorship, which further confirms me in the conviction that I have already precisely expressed. For it highlights, that press-anarchy will be replaced by press-despotism and that a wise and forceful dictatorship has to counter such mischief and to stop it until a legal censorship is reinstalled" (GOETHE, letter to Prince Karl August, Weimar, 5 October 1816, translated from the German by the translator/authors). But in order to take account of the concerns of his master, some lines earlier he proposes: "I return to my aforementioned proposed measure, namely: one should ignore the editor completely, but one has to hold the book printer responsible and to personally and forcefully prohibit him from printing this sheet". The prince did not have to fear any scurrilous backlash from the printer, as the printer was more faithful to the Prince than was the editor.

St. Paul's Church

The July Revolution of 1830 in France, as well as the developments that followed in Switzerland and Belgium, gave the liberal forces in Germany new impetus. In Saxony, Kurhessen, Hanover and New Brunswick liberal constitutions following the model of southern Germany were adopted. Notwithstanding the failed attempt by a parliamentary assembly composed of representatives of the Prussian districts to establish a constitution in 1847, the princes of several small and middling principalities promised the liberals the enactment of a new constitution and installed liberal ministers at the head of their executive government. Following these developments, the conservative Prussian King Frederick Wilhelm consented to the election of a new parliament. On 18 May 1848, the National Assembly convened in St. Paul's Church in Frankfurt and began its discussions. It adopted a liberal constitution for the empire with an extensive catalogue of fundamental rights and liberties, which was in part later included in the current Basic Law of Germany. It elected as a provisional central government a Lord Protector of the empire, however he could never really execute his function. Parliament offered the Prussian King the crown of Emperor, but he refused to be given the dignity of the Emperor by an assembly elected by the people, as he believed an emperor could only derive his sovereign powers by the grace of God.

National unity before liberalisation

In the events that followed, the hope of achieving a democratic state organisation had to be – at least for the time being – abandoned. In a period in which the English Parliament already asserted its absolute sovereignty and was in the process of implementing the general reform of voting rights, Germany was occupied with its struggle for national unity, the abolition of feudal structures, the implementation of liberal fundamental rights and the installation of a real parliament which would be given effective political powers. It was clear that not everything could be realised at once. The achievement of national unity was the first priority. Under the leadership of Bismarck, a new alliance of states under the hegemony of Prussia was created: it was called The Northern German Alliance (*Norddeutscher Bund*). Bismarck reached a compromise with the liberals and managed to convince them for the sake of national unity to give up their claim for a sovereign parliament.

The Constitution of the German Alliance of 1871

On 17 April 1867, the Constitution of the Northern German Alliance was adopted. This Constitution was to be extended to the other *Länder* of the empire four years later. The Constitution provided for general representation of the people in the Reichstag, but it blocked the way for the establishment of an executive government dependent on the parliament until the adoption of the Constitution of Weimar after World War I. The Chancellor of the Empire was not accountable to parliament for his activity, and thus could not be removed by parliament when he lost the confidence of the majority. The parliament itself was composed of a chamber of the alliance (*Bundesrat*) and a national chamber (*Reichstag*). In the chamber of the alliance, the votes of the *Länder* were weighed differently according to their size and importance, with the hegemony of Prussia being constitutionally enshrined. This upper chamber was the highest organ of the empire and had to assent to all statutes. Fourteen votes within the *Bundesrat* could prevent the passage of a constitutional amendment; Prussia had seventeen votes.

Reichstag

Although the Reichstag was elected by the people, the right to vote was still restricted according to the census principle, which prevented the proportional representation of the social democrats. Nevertheless, the Reichstag was able to strengthen its political power and thus to gain a political profile. In 1912 the Social Democrats became the strongest faction in the Reichstag. At the end of World War I on the 28 October 1918, the Constitution was amended with the decisive provision: "...The chancellor of the empire must have the confidence of the Reichstag." With this provision, the last step towards the realisation of a parliamentary constitutional monarchy such as had existed in Britain for centuries, was finally made. However, it did not even last one month. On 9 November the Emperor abdicated the throne.

Executive with two heads in the Weimar Constitution

Thus, a new Constitution had to be prepared, which was adopted in Weimar. But how could a parliamentary system with parliamentary sovereignty be realised without a monarch? The answer was clear: instead of a monarch as head of state, a President of the Empire would have to be elected. This President was given extensive powers. He (not the parliament) appointed the Chancellor of the Empire, concluded treaties with foreign powers, was the commander-in-chief of the army, could submit statutes to the referendum of the people, was given the power to dissolve the Reichstag and was responsible for the guarantee of law and order. He had the power to declare an emergency, and in an emergency could suspend constitutional rights. The President was elected for a term of seven years and could be re-elected. The founding fathers (e.g. Hugo Preuss) wanted to balance the power of the parliament with a powerful double executive composed of the President and the Chancellor. The executive was a collegial organ. Each minister of the Empire managed his department independently. For his activity he was directly accountable to the Reichstag. The Chancellor of the Empire was the *primus inter pares*; he moderated the meetings and was responsible for introducing major policy directives. The large number of parties considerably impaired the power of the Reichstag. No party was able to achieve an absolute majority, which inevitably led to several crises of government, as the Chancellor and his government were dependent on the support and confidence of the Reichstag. In addition to the Reichstag was the Reichsrat (upper chamber), composed of the representatives of the governments of the *Länder*. The primary function of this upper chamber was to advise the government, but it had also to ratify statutes that were adopted by the Reichstag. If the Reichsrat rejected a statute, the Reichstag could overrule the decision with a two-thirds majority.

The minority National-Socialist Party abolishes the Constitution

The constitutional monarchy had been replaced with the double executive of the Weimar Constitution, but in this system the parliament had still not reached full parliamentary sovereignty according to the Westminster model. The sense of identity of a parliamentary democracy along the lines of the British model was still lacking. Parliament was not able to stand up to the increasing power of the President of the Empire, and was so severely weakened by the disputes of the radical parties, that after the death of President Hindenburg the minority National Socialist Party led by Hitler was able to destroy the young parliamentary democracy and establish a totalitarian state.

National Socialism

The new chancellor Hitler, who was appointed by Hindenburg in 1933, had an easy target when he sought to implement his well-known program to abolish parliament. Based on his emergency powers, after the Fire of the Reichstag on 28 February 1933 President Hindenburg promulgated the Presidential Ordinance for the Protection of the People and the State, which allowed the government to prosecute all political opponents. On 24 March 1933 the Reichstag adopted the Law to Remedy the Hardship of the People and the Empire. This enabling act provided in Article 1: "Laws of the empire can … also be adopted by the executive." Art. 2 provided: "The statutes which are adopted by the executive may derogate from the Constitution of the Empire." With this statute the parliament effectively abolished itself.

Reduced powers of the President in the Basic Law

After World War II Germany was divided in two. The German Democratic Republic (DDR) gave itself a communist constitution, whilst the Federal Republic of Germany became a parliamentary democracy in line with the western model. What are the differences between the constitution of this new parliamentary democracy and that of the old Weimar Republic? The principal distinguishing features are the expansion of the sovereignty of Parliament, the corresponding reduction in the powers of the President and the strengthening of the power of the Chancellor. The President is restricted to the largely symbolic function of representing the country as head of state. He is no longer elected by the people but by a special body composed of the Bundestag and delegates of the parliaments of the *Länder*. The dualism of the double-headed executive has been abolished. Many of the former powers of the President have been transferred to the Chancellor. He is the commander-in-chief of the army in times of war or defence of the country, whilst in peacetime the minister of defence is the commander-in-chief. Parliament cannot be dissolved during an emergency (state of defence). If, during a state of defence, obstacles prevent the timely convening of parliament or parliament cannot muster a quorum, a joint parliamentary committee will exercise the authority of the parliament.

Constructive vote of confidence and the power of the parliament

Another new feature is the so-called constructive vote of no confidence. Parliament cannot remove a cabinet with a simple vote of no confidence and thereby cause a crisis of government. The Chancellor can only be removed from office with his cabinet by a constructive vote of no confidence, that is, through a vote to elect a successor as Chancellor. The intention behind this provision is to avoid lengthy governmental crises and vacancies such as those that occurred in the Weimar Republic.

The constitution (das *Grundgesetz*, or 'Basic Law') is based upon the borrowed principles of representative democracy. The parliament, which is periodically elected by the people, wields together with the government almost all sovereign powers. Statutes are not subject to referendum except if they concern a new territorial repartition of the *Länder*. With the election of the Bundestag the voter decides indirectly on the cabinet, as whichever party or coalition of parties has an absolute majority will automatically form government. In elections the voter is also effectively deciding on the political program, and party policies are therefore an important part of any election campaign. Even the reunification with eastern Germany was not ratified by a referendum, but only by the election of the new reunited Bundestag. The fact that usually around 90% of the voters can be mobilised to go to the polls (in Switzerland it is around 50%), demonstrates how seriously elections are taken by the citizens.

Limits of parliamentary power

The constitution also introduced some important provisions limiting the power of parliament. Thus, the parliament has no power to repeal or amend the core provisions of the constitution relating to fundamental rights (Article 19(2) of the Basic Law). In addition, it is one of the very few constitutions that protects the citizens' right to resistance against any person who seeks to abolish the constitutional order (Article 20(4) Basic Law).

Constitutional Court

The most important limit on the sovereign powers of parliament is to be found in the significant expansion of the jurisdiction and powers of the Constitutional Court (*Bundesverfassungsgericht*). In contrast to the limited powers of the United States Supreme Court, the German Constitutional Court can not only quash an existing statute on the grounds of unconstitutionality, but can also review an abstract legal norm under the terms of the constitution and declare it to be unconstitutional. European predecessors of the new German Constitutional Court were the Constitutional Court of Norway of the second half of the 19th Century and in particular the

Austrian Constitutional Court, which was established in the Austrian Constitution drafted by KELSEN after the First World War.

This comprehensive authority to review the constitutionality of abstract legal norms gives the Constitutional Court a political counterweight to the parliament. In particular, the power of the opposition in certain cases to submit a proposed statute to the Constitutional Court places the Court in the difficult position of having not only to determine the issue of constitutionality, but also to serve as arbiter between government and opposition. As with all courts so too the German Constitutional Court will only be able to maintain its legitimacy if it exercises its powers with wise restraint. The experience thus far shows clearly that the court has succeeded in asserting its authority and maintaining legitimacy in relation to the people, parliament and executive.

It is no accident that precisely in Germany – a country in which the legal consciousness is characterised by the long tradition of the judiciary of the Empire – a constitutional court has been charged with the task of limiting parliamentary sovereignty and ensuring that politics can unfold within a constituted order without degenerating into unconstitutional activity. In any case, the Court has contributed considerably to maintaining the internal balance of political powers and has been able to stick to its constitutional function without becoming embroiled in the scrappy disputes of the parties.

Limitation of the sovereignty of the Federation through the Länder

An additional limit upon parliamentary sovereignty is provided by the federal structure of the German Republic. The division of powers between the Federation and the *Länder* and the power of the *Länder* to participate in the upper chamber (*Bundesrat*) place limits on the actions of the Bundestag. This is especially so when the political composition of the Bundesrat differs from the majority of the Bundestag, as it often does. Nevertheless, the federal structure of Germany does not change the fact that the Federal Republic must ultimately still be seen as a unitary federal state, which of course needs to coordinate its activity by cooperation between the Federation and the *Länder*. This federal flexibility is also manifest in article 29 of the Basic Law, which regulates the procedure for the rearrangement of boundaries of the federal units. According to this article, the territory of the Federation can be redistributed taking into account the historical and cultural traditions of the *Länder*, but also taking into consideration their size and competitiveness. In the neighbouring federation of Switzerland, such provision would be inconceivable because of the historically steadfast nature of the Cantons.

Reunification

The German reunification led to some substantial changes to the Basic Law, most of which were connected to the fact that reunification enabled the conclusion of the final peace agreement with the former allies and thereby enabled Germany to reclaim its unlimited sovereignty over the whole, German territory. There was however no fundamental change to the governmental system, although there were repeated requests for the expansion of provisions for direct democracy.

From the point of view of democratic rights, it is significant to note that the reunification did not lead to a complete overhaul of the Basic Law nor to ratification of the reunification by a referendum either in the former DDR or in the new Germany as a whole. The legal basis for the unification was the Unification Treaty and the All-German Election Treaty, which were sanctioned not by referendum but rather by the election of representatives of the former DDR to the new Bundestag. Whilst in almost all other countries in transition the adoption of a new constitution is democratically legitimised through a referendum, the legitimacy of the reunified Germany is based only on the participation of the voters of Eastern Germany in electing their members into the new Parliament, which was interpreted by the authorities as an endorsement of reunification.

Finally, one can note in comparison to England that in Germany as well as in Britain the parliament representing the people is the key institution for the political legitimacy of state power. But the connection of the upper chamber to the *Länder* governments has led to a considerable shift in the political culture, from a winner-takes-all democracy to a much more consensus-driven democracy.

7.2.1.3 France

i. The Revolutionary History

Weak parliament at the time of the monarchy

For almost one thousand years France was a society governed by a monarchy. In contrast to Britain, the role of the ‘parliament’ in this monarchical system was fairly insignificant. It had very little influence and exercised only an advisory function, with no decision making power. Because it was divided into three chambers, representing the aristocracy, the clergy and the common free citizens of the third estate, it was rarely able to reach a consensus. In addition, the King summoned the parliament only very rarely. From 1614 onwards the chambers of the three estates did not meet for 175 years.

From the three chambers to the revolutionary Assemblée Nationale as pouvoir constituant

King Louis XVI decided after almost two centuries to summon the three estates to meet in 1789. On 5 May under the auspices of Louis XVI and Marie Antoinette, the inaugural meeting of the three estates (*Etats Généraux*) took place. With this common meeting in which the three estates were for the first time merged into one chamber, the *Assemblée Nationale* ushered in the new age of the French state. For the first time as many members of the third estate were elected as there were members of the aristocracy and the clergy combined. Although the representatives of the third estate did not have an absolute majority, they were still able to outvote the other two estates, as a liberal minority of the first and second estates supported the ideas of the bourgeois third estate.

On 17 June 1789 the third estate, in light of the fact that it represented 96 per cent of the nation, felt itself called to exert its own power to proclaim a new National Assembly. Although the King tried to resist this initiative and ordered the estates henceforward to meet in different places, he eventually had to submit to the will of the bourgeois estate and ordered the nobles and the clergy to join the bourgeois National Assembly. On 9 July 1789, the National Assembly adopted its own regulations. With this decision the body that had originally been divided into three chambers and had exercised only advisory functions transformed itself into a single-chamber National Assembly with the substantial decision making powers of a *pouvoir constituant*. The new Parliament was no longer prepared to accept the marginal function of advising the King. It gave itself the authority, on the basis of its own legitimacy, to enact laws for the whole nation. The model of the Long Parliament in Britain 150 years earlier served as an historical precedent.

Declaration of the Rights of Man and Citizen

On 26 August 1789, the new National Assembly proclaimed the Declaration of the Rights of Man and Citizen (*Déclaration des Droits de l'Homme et du Citoyen*). This declaration of human rights achieved renewed positive legal validity almost 200 years later with the famous decision of the *Conseil Constitutionnel* of 16 July 1971. As the French Constitution of 1958 does not expressly provide for the protection of fundamental rights, the Constitutional Council had to find another legal basis for the constitutional guarantee of human rights. It decided therefore in a 'revolutionary' decision of July 1971, that the 1789 Declaration of the Rights of Man and Citizen still remains positive and valid law, on the basis that the preamble to the 1958 Constitution refers to the 1946 Constitution, which in turn makes express reference to the Declaration as valid law. With this decision, the Constitutional Council transformed itself from an advisory council into a real constitutional court, able to make authoritative decisions on constitutional issues.

Revolutionary centuries

From the turbulent months of the new National Assembly which led to the French Revolution, up until 1875, France experienced in total:

- 15 different regimes,
- Four revolutions,
- Two coups d'état and
- Three foreign interventions.

With the French Revolution, the moderate Girondists and later the radical Jacobins had created a new social system, but France had not yet found the appropriate system of government for this new society. In fact, the ongoing revolutionary instability continued until the 20th Century. Several reasons can be cited for this volatile situation. In particular, there was disagreement within French society on the following three fundaments of the state: Disagreement on the *basis of the legitimacy* of government, disagreement on the *hierarchy of the branches of government* and disagreement on the relationship between *Church and State*.

For almost one thousand years, France was ruled by a monarch who was believed to have the divine authority to govern the people. He derived his legitimacy from God. With the French Revolution, this divine legitimacy was suddenly replaced by the legitimacy given by the *nation*. The nation constituted by the state (not the pre-constitutional people in the German sense of the concept) claimed to have the sovereign power to decide on the form of the state and society as well as on the government itself.

As a consequence, France oscillated for 75 years between republic and monarchy. In the Constitution of the constitutional monarchy of 1791, which was only in force for six months, the state proclaimed in Chapter III, Article 1: "Sovereignty is one, indivisible, inalienable and imprescriptable. It appertains to the Nation; no section of the people nor any individual may assume the exercise thereof." The power to govern the nation however was still vested in the King. Article 4 provided: "The Government is monarchical; the executive power is delegated to the King, to be exercised, under his authority, by ministers and other responsible agents in the in the manner hereinafter determined."

Long Parliament in France?

A thousand year monarchy is not compatible with limited constitutionally 'vested' powers and functions. On 21–22 September 1792 the National Convention again followed the example of the Long Parliament of England and announced: "The National Convention declares with unanimity, that the Monarchy in France is abolished."

Legitimacy of the monarchy versus legitimacy of dictatorship

From this point on, France shifted constantly between dictatorship and popular rule, up until the fall of Napoleon and the re-establishment of the monarchy in 1814. Who legitimises whom? Does the monarch by the grace of God bestow legitimacy on the Parliament, or does the Parliament by the grace of the people bestow legitimacy on the government? This question alone gave rise to bloody clashes. The Constitution of 18 May 1804 for example declared in Article 1: "The Government of the Republic is vested in an Emperor, who takes the title 'Emperor of the French'. Justice is rendered in his name by the officials he appoints." In consequence, Napoleon was proclaimed as Emperor with the right of hereditary succession. After the fall of Napoleon on 6 April 1814, a new constitutional monarchy was established, which gave the King only the dignity of a King by the *grace of the People*.

The new King however was not satisfied with this formula. Just two months later he abolished the Constitution of 14 June and declared himself in a new constitutional charter to hold legitimacy as King by the Grace of God through the power of divine providence.

Revolution of July 1830

With the Revolution of July 1830 the monarchic principle was somewhat softened. Louis Philippe no longer called himself 'King of France' but rather 'King of the French'. Moreover, the Constitution obliged the King – even in times of emergency – to observe the laws. Aside from these modifications however, the monarchical system remained essentially unchanged.

Revolution of 1848

It was not until the Constitution of the Second Republic in 1848 that the people's sovereignty was again unambiguously proclaimed: "Sovereignty originates from the universal body of the French citizens."

Coup d'état of Napoleon III and 100 years later Pétain

Only three years later however, a new dictatorship was established – this time under Napoleon III. Article 2 of the Constitution of 1852 consequently provided: "The Government of the French Republic shall be vested for 10 years in Prince Louis Napoleon Bonaparte, the current President of the Republic." Almost one hundred years later on 10 July 1940, Marshal Pétain gave himself the same powers. His constitutional law consisted of only one article: "The National Assembly gives full powers to the Government of the Republic, under the authority and the signature of Marshal Pétain, to the effect of promulgating by one or several acts a new Constitution for the French state." Thus, Marshal Pétain claimed to be the holder not only of the constituted power but also of constituent power.

Republican, democratic legitimacy

Is France or are the French under the rule of the National Assembly or of a President as head of state? On the issue of democratic legitimacy one has also to ask who exercises the sovereign powers of the nation: The assembly elected by the people, or the executive which has to ensure the implementation of the *volonté générale*? The dispute over the question of who should have this legitimacy and who should be given superiority – the Parliament, the executive or the head of state – has dominated every assembly which has established itself as the constitution making power.

Republican

Based on the transformation into a constitution making assembly by act of self-rule, the general estates (*Etats Généraux*) effectively elevated themselves to the position of sovereign government. However, as already mentioned the Constitution of 1791 provided for the vesting of executive power exclusively in the King. Following the abolition of the Monarchy on 22 September 1792, the National Convention required that a new constitution be submitted to a referendum of the people. Almost exactly one year later on 24 September 1793, the Constitution was submitted to the people for adoption. Ultimately however, it never came into force.

On 21 September 1792 the National Convention declared it 'year one' of the Republic. But this Republic lasted only until 1799. A short time after the declaration of the First Republic, the Committee of Public Safety (*comitée du Salut Public*) was installed, which upon the admission of Robespierre soon came to exercise dictatorial rule over the National Convention.

Democratic

The Constitution of 24 September 1793, which never entered into force, provided for the real reign of the people in the sense advocated by ROUSSEAU. The legislative assembly was given unlimited powers to legislate, subject to the right of the people to referendum, and was the bearer of sovereignty, superior to all other branches. The members of Parliament were to be elected for one year only. The laws were to be executed by an executive council composed of 24 members. Moreover, the constitution introduced a comprehensive right of the people to submit all statutes to referendum. Although this very democratic constitution had no direct impact on constitutional development in France, decades later it had an influence on the direct democracy elements of the Swiss Constitution.

Separation of powers

The directorial constitution of 22 August 1795 (the first valid and enforced constitution of the First Republic) established for the first time in France a governmental system based on the combination of a collegial executive and a bicameral legislature. This governmental system of the year III of the First Republic also introduced a real separation of powers. On the other hand, the Constitution only gave limited effect to democratic principles, providing for a system of representation by members of parliament elected on the basis of a restricted franchise. It was thought that only by restricting democratic rights would it be possible to put an end to the revolutionary pressure on the street. The two chambers consisted of the Council of the 500 and the Council of Elders. Both chambers had largely similar powers. The Council of the 500 had the power to propose new legislation, but such legislation could only be given effect if the Council of Elders gave its approval.

The Directory (Directoire)

The executive power was vested in a directory of five members. These five members were elected by both chambers on the nomination of the Council of the 500. The constitution required strict observance of the principle of separation of powers. The Directory appointed the ministers but it was not directly accountable to the legislative assembly. On the other hand, it had no power to intervene in the legislative process by exercising a veto over new laws. From the very beginning this new governmental system was under threat from two sides: The royalists wanted to abolish the Directory and replace it with a monarch, whilst the radical Jacobins dreamt of returning to the absolute and indivisible sovereignty of the National Assembly.

Influence of the Directory on Switzerland

The directorial Constitution of 1795 later had an effect on the directorial Helvetian constitution imposed in Switzerland by the French occupiers in 1799, as well as on the Swiss Federal Constitution of 1848. The founding fathers of the Swiss Federal Constitution used the Directory as a model for the federal executive council, which is also composed as a collegial executive. Because in Switzerland the seven members of the federal council are elected and replaced individually on a rotating basis and the council has never been stood down as a whole, in the entire 150 year history of the Swiss confederation there has never been a complete renewal of the federal council. The remaining members have always passed on their knowledge and experience to the new members, so that since 1848 there has been an unbroken continuity in the Swiss executive. In Switzerland, the directorial Constitution has thus led to a system of unique political stability. The model of the collegial directorate has however, apart from a brief period in Uruguay, never been successfully adopted by any other state. Indeed, in a country without popular referendum, a directory has little chance of succeeding. Without referendum, the parliament is the only institution that can counterbalance the power of the executive. Thus, the system would sooner or later evolve into an executive cabinet dependent on the majority of parliament. In Switzerland, the function of the opposition is in fact exercised by the people. It is for this reason that in Switzerland the parliament is interested in ensuring the exe-cutive is composed of members who have the credibility and the political power to convince the people in a referendum.

Monarchic

Even in France where it originated, the directory system lasted for only a short period. In 1799 the Constitution of the Directory was replaced by the dictatorial constitution of Napoleon. This consular Constitution vested all sovereign power in the first consul Napoleon. The two other co-consuls had only an advisory function. The first consul appointed the ministers and civil servants, and had far-reaching powers to enact ordinances. Proposals for new legislation were prepared by the Council of State (the *Conseil d'Etat*, which later became an important administrative tribunal). The 'Tribunal' expressed its approval or disapproval, and the legislative assembly made its decisions by secret ballot without deliberating on the legislation. The Senate reviewed the constitutionality of legislation. There was no council of ministers. The basic ideas for this new constitution came from Sieyès: "Authority must come from above and confidence from below".

Second Republic

After the First Republic ended in 1799, the Second Republic was established in 1848, which also however lasted only a very short time. The Constitution provided for a presidential system with a general right to vote. A unicameral assembly composed of 750 representatives exercised legislative power. The members of Parliament were elected by the people for three-year terms, and the President was elected for four-year terms. If none of the candidates gained an absolute majority of votes, the National Assembly had to elect the President. The President could not dissolve the parliament, and he was not accountable to the parliament.

ii. Dictatorship of Napoleon III

This system, tailored in the interest of strong presidential power, soon led to the dictatorship of Napoleon III (nephew of Napoleon) who had been elected in 1848 as the first President of the Second Republic. Just three years later, by coup d'état he became the second member of the Bonaparte family to impose a dictatorial constitution.

The Paris Commune

On 4 September 1870, after the fall of Sedan in the Franco-Prussian War, the Third Republic was established. In February 1871 the people elected the members of the National Assembly and a new President. With its first election, the National Assembly had elevated the royalist Thiers to the position of provisional Head of State. After a rebellion by the National Guard in which regular forces also participated, on 26 March the socialist Central Committee of the National Guard established the Paris Commune as the ruling government of Paris, in defiance of the pro-monarchist National Assembly. MacMahon quashed this revolutionary movement and the National Assembly was able to resume its activity. Although the royalists were in the majority, they failed to re-establish the monarchy. They were too much at odds with each other, and ultimately had to concede that the time of the monarchy had finally come to an end.

Constitutional Law of 1875

In 1873 a new President was elected and again a royalist, MacMahon, found the favour of the people. On 30 January 1875, the National Assembly adopted a new constitutional law in which the state for the first time was expressly declared to be a Republic. Thus, the President became *de facto* a 'republican monarch'. He was empowered to execute statutes, ratify international treaties, dissolve the National Assembly, and propose new laws, but he was not accountable to either of the two chambers of Parliament. In addition he appointed his own ministers.

The Assembly defies the President

As the left had won the elections for the National Assembly, MacMahon entrusted the role of head of government to Jules Simon as Prime Minister. Simon was a moderate candidate from the centre, but in the eyes of MacMahon he turned out to be too moderate and was thus replaced a short time later by Broglie. The National Assembly condemned the President for this action. In consequence, he dissolved the National Assembly. The new Assembly however was again under a republican majority and thus forced Broglie to resign. With this forced resignation, the National Assembly had in effect wrested from the President his power to dismiss the executive and forced the President to replace it with another cabinet. The Assembly did not relinquish this power until the establishment of the Fifth Republic.

The executive Government appointed by the President was from now on accountable to the Parliament and depended on the confidence of the political majority within Parliament.

Fourth Republic

This power-struggle laid the constitutional foundation for the mutual dependence of state powers in the sense of checks and balances. On the other hand, it also established the superiority of the National Assembly in the hierarchy of powers of the Third Republic, and its role in the appointment and dismissal of executive government. This Republic was able to survive 70 years until Marshal Pétain took over in a coup d'état in 1940. After the Second World War, the Fourth Republic was founded.

Cabinet and multiparty state

The Constitution of the Fourth Republic in many respects closely resembled that of the Third Republic. The powers of the President with regard to the appointment of government however were no longer regulated only by customary law, but were positively expressed and at the same time also limited. The Prime Minister was made more dependent upon the political majority of the National Assembly, as the Assembly not only had to give its consent to the appointment of the Prime Minister but also had to agree to the Prime Minister's nomination of individual Ministers. Moreover, the President lost the power to enact ordinances. Because of the variety of political parties and internal political instability, the National Assembly constantly withdrew its confidence in government. This led to frequent changes of government and great instability, because – unlike England – in France it was not possible to establish a stable two party system.

iii. The Presidential System of the Fifth Republic

Expansion of presidential power

This led in times of crisis or emergency, such as the War in Algeria, to great instability, internal unrest and ultimately to a fundamental constitutional crisis. To salvage the situation, France's former saviour in World War II, General De Gaulle, was called upon to devise a new constitution. For the Fifth Republic, De Gaulle produced a constitution which on the surface appears to strike a balance between the presidential and the parliamentary system, but which in reality conveys to the President the most comprehensive powers that any president of a democratic state at that time possessed. Today however, the might of the Russian president is considerably wider, as he holds the power of the French President (power to appoint the cabinet and the power to enact ordinances) as well as that of the American President (such as veto power with regard to the legislature).

In the Third as well as in the Fourth Republic the constitutional principle of legality, according to which all legislation must be adopted by the legislature, was undisputed. However, during this time governments also engaged in the practice of law making by executive decree. With these decrees the executive could promulgate norms that had the same status and validity as any other formal legislation. It was even possible via such decrees to modify existing legislation. However these decrees became invalid if they did not receive the approval of Parliament within a prescribed period. This practice was enshrined in Article 38 of the new Constitution.

Apart from ordinary statutes, there are at a lower level the so-called organic laws (*loi organiques*, constitutional statutes), which complement the constitution and for this reason are considered to have the same position as ordinary norms of the constitution. These constitutional statutes can only be brought into force by the President, after having been reviewed for constitutionality by the Constitutional Council (Art. 46).

Limited legislative powers of the Parliament

As the Constitution provides Parliament with the power to legislate only on matters expressly listed in Article 34, and provides that all other matters will be regulated by simpler regulations that can be issued by the executive without the approval of Parliament, it thereby diminishes the traditional prerogative of the legislature and strengthens the power of the executive. Head of the executive is not, as the written text of the constitution might suggest, the Prime Minister, but rather the President. Furthermore, as the President has the power to submit certain statutes to referendum (Art. 11), his position in relation to Parliament and also to the Council of Ministers is considerably fortified.

With the limited competence of Parliament under Article 34 to enact statutes only in areas that are expressly permitted, the Constitution establishes a presumption of authority for matters to be regulated by decree. Everything that is not contained in Article 34 as a matter that can only be regulated by legislation, can be regulated by decree. The authority to issue decrees is vested in various organs in the government hierarchy according to their function and authority. An ordinance has the status of Presidential Decree, if it is issued by the President on the basis of advice from the Council of Ministers. It is a decree of the Prime Minister if it is issued by him within his area of responsibility. Finally, there are also decrees issued at the level of Ministers and prefects. But only the President and the Prime Minister have a general power to issue regulations in the form of decrees.

President as holder of the volonté générale

Article 5 of the Constitution provides: "(1) The President of the Republic shall see that the Constitution is observed. He shall ensure, by his arbitration, both the proper functioning of the public authorities and the continuity of the State." Based on this provision, all Presidents since De Gaulle have asserted the right to decide on all major issues concerning the interests of the state. They have interpreted their power to act as umpire or referee as if it were synonymous with broad executive decision-making power. Accordingly, the executive possesses only such power as the President leaves to cabinet, although a literal interpretation of the Constitution would require cabinet and the President to work in harmonious accord with each other.

Since 1962 the President has been popularly elected. The Presidential term was originally seven years, but since 2002 the President is elected for a five-year term. He is not accountable to the Parliament. Moreover, the President is granted emergency powers under Article 16, including the power in times of emergency to suspend the Constitution. The President is thereby really the incarnation of the general will (*volonté genérale*). He decides on emergencies, brings laws into force and has the general power – albeit with the agreement of the Prime Minister – to issue decrees. Finally, he is empowered to submit certain statutes to referendum, to appoint the cabinet and to dissolve the National Assembly.

Prime Minister and Cabinet

Article 21 of the Constitution stipulates: "The Prime Minister shall direct the operation of the government." In fact however, he has to conduct government affairs within the framework of the policy determined by the President, as the Prime Minister as well as the members of his cabinet and the state secretaries are all appointed by the President. According to the practice of the Fifth Republic, a Prime Minister holds office during the pleasure of the President, and so must step down or remain in office in accordance with the orders of the President (with the exception only of Prime Minister Chirac, who resigned of his own volition on 25 August 1976). The President can also force a minister to resign. Accordingly, the President can determine the allocation of government portfolios among the ministers and even reshuffle the cabinet.

Contrary to the principle of parliamentary responsible government, ministers cannot be members of Parliament. This symbol of separation of powers indicates that there was a clear intention to set up a real presidential system, in which the executive is separated from the legislature. On the other hand, the Prime Minister, the Council of Ministers and the Parliament are all able to seek a vote of confidence. If the government does not receive the confidence of the Parliament, it is required under Article 50 to propose its resignation to the President. However, the President decides at his own discretion whether he will accept this offer. Thus, De Gaulle reinstalled Mr. Pompidou as Prime Minister even though he had lost the confidence of Parliament.

In some cases the President has the power to make unilateral decisions, but in other cases he needs the counter-signature of the Prime Minister. The Prime Minister, as the head of government directly subordinate to the President, leads the executive and government business. In this capacity he also makes decisions relating to the army, although the actual Commander-in-Chief is the President, who ultimately has the exclusive power to decide on the use of atomic weapons.

Cohabitation

This special presidential system designed by De Gaulle is shaped for a president who also enjoys the support of the majority in Parliament. Without this majority, he has to govern with a Prime Minister who can use the parliamentary majority to oppose the decisions of the President. If the Prime Minister and the President are not willing to work together cooperatively (‘*Cohabitation*’) they have to manage separately from each other a constitutionally inseparable budget, which will necessarily lead to a permanent and ultimately irresolvable constitutional crisis. The different governments of Cohabitation under Mitterand and Chirac have nevertheless shown that France is prepared to live with confrontation between the President and the Prime Minister.

Parliament

The Parliament is composed of two chambers: the National Assembly (*Assemblée Nationale*) and the Senate. The position, legitimacy and function of the upper chamber were strengthened under the Constitution of the Fifth Republic, after the failure in 1969 of attempts to merge the two chambers. While the people directly elects the members of the National Assembly according to the principle of absolute majority in each district, the senators are elected indirectly through the departments. They are elected for nine years, but have staggered terms, with one third of the Senate facing election every three years on a rotating basis. The President cannot dissolve the Senate. The staggered renewal of the Senate every three years provides continuity of membership of the Senate, and through this continuity the upper chamber contributes to the stability of the country. In particular, the upper chamber is able to protect the individual and fundamental rights of the citizens against an often overzealous lower chamber.

Constitutional and administrative courts

Apart from the President, government and Parliament, the Constitution also provides as additional organs of state the Constitutional Council (*Conseil Constitutionnel*, with the function of a special constitutional court), the State Council (*Conseil d’Etat*, with the function of the highest administrative court) and the Economic and Social Council (*Conseil Economique et Social*).

The State Council is one of the oldest bodies in the constitutional history of France. Today it acts as the highest court for matters of administrative law and also serves as an important advisory body for the administration, in particular with regard to drafting legislation. Like the Council of State, so too the Constitutional Council was originally designed as an advisory body, but it too was able to transform itself into a decision-making body. Since the 1971 decision mentioned above, the Constitutional Council has functioned as a proper constitutional court, which is able to guard against the infringement of fundamental rights by the legislature. It reviews the constitutionality of statutes before they are signed and promulgated by the President. The Economic and Social Council is the advisory body on economic matters, but so far this body does not carry much weight, at least in the eyes of the public.

7.2.1.4 Parliamentary Responsible Government in Other States

Westminster-type parliamentary responsible government spread in the 20th Century first to Europe, in particular to France, Belgium, the Netherlands, the Scandinavian countries, Italy and Greece. But it has also taken root in other parts of the world. Nigeria, Ghana, Israel as well as Japan, India and Australia are just a few examples.

Japan

In many states the Westminster-type system of parliamentary government was seen to be desirable and appropriate because, in addition to a Parliament divided by two or more mutually opposing parties, a symbolic figure (such as a monarch) embodies the national unity. This applies for example to Japan. The Japanese royal family, which has ruled Japan in an unbroken line of succession for 2000 years, was completely stripped of its power after the Second World War but remained as a symbol of national unity and still today plays an important role in integrating the society. In the Constitution of 1890, which was labelled a liberal Constitution (revolution from above), the Emperor declared himself in Articles 4 and 5 as the sovereign power who could exert all rights. The Emperor was given the power to enact statutes, albeit with the consent of the Parliament. Today, Article 1 of the Japanese Constitution of 3 May 1947 proclaims: "The Emperor shall be the symbol of the State and of the unity of the people, deriving his position from the will of the people with whom resides sovereign power." According to the Constitution, the Emperor has no political power at all. He does not have the traditional role of Commander-in-Chief of the armed forces, because Japan's Constitution prohibits the maintenance of any armed forces. Article 9 of the Constitution provides: "(1) Aspiring sincerely to an international peace based on justice and order, the Japanese people forever renounce war as a sovereign right of the nation and the threat or use of force as means of settling international disputes. (2) In order to accomplish the aim of the preceding paragraph, land, sea, and air forces, as well as other war potential, will never be maintained." The Emperor - like the British Queen – must act on the advice of Parliament in the appointment of the Prime Minister and the appointment of the Chief Justice of the highest court. For all his activities the Emperor has to ask Parliament for approval (Article 3).

Like most states with a system of parliamentary responsible government, Japan has a bicameral Parliament: 486 representatives are elected by the voters of 123 electorates by majority according to the principle one person, one vote, one value (two to three members are returned in each electorate). Of the 250 members of the upper chamber, 150 are elected in local districts and 100 by the whole nation. The lower house, the Representatives, has greater powers than the upper house, the Senate. For the approval of a new statute the consensus of both chambers is needed. But if they disagree, the lower chamber can overrule the upper chamber with a two-third majority. In relation to the budget, only if a joint committee is unable to reach a compromise acceptable to both chambers will the budget be approved by the lower chamber alone (Articles 59 and 60). The election of the Prime Minister has to be approved by both chambers. If they disagree, the lower chamber decides.

The strong position of the two major traditional parties, as well as the respect that the old (wise) leaders still enjoy in traditional Japanese society and the strong community feeling, have certainly contributed to the stability of the Japanese governmental system since the end of World War II and to the relatively harmonious development of the old feudal society into a democratic civil society. The Japanese Constitution – which was effectively imposed by the American occupying forces after the War – largely adopts the English system of parliamentary democracy, but in terms of the jurisdiction and authority of the highest court one can recognise the influence of the United States. The court can review the constitutionality of statutes if they violate fundamental rights.

India: Government above the people

Conditions are very different in India. Like England, so too the Japanese Islands were throughout history largely spared from foreign occupation. In stark contrast, there is hardly a people or a land which over the last four thousand years has been looted, massacred and oppressed by foreign peoples and rulers as much as the Indians. The Chinese, the Greeks (Alexander the Great), Arabs and finally the British all left their mark on the country and its people and in particular influenced the centralisation of power by a central colonial government. However, these foreign occupiers effected very little change to the basic nature and structure of Indian society. The caste system and the importance of local communities at the level of the municipalities served also to strengthen an enslaved people against its oppressors. Castes and local communes enabled the strong cohesion necessary to withstand and surmount the injustices suffered. In consequence, the castes cut them selves off from each other and became increasingly self-contained. They established separate jurisdictions and judiciaries for separate castes. These strong structures within a society fragmented by hundreds of different castes meant that, in spite of their cruel reign and in spite of the attempts by Islamic moguls to convert the entire population to Islam, the foreign occupiers controlling the central government remained more or less isolated from the people. They did not govern with the people but rather above the people.

This may also be one of the reasons why India's system of parliamentary government has been maintained since 1949, notwithstanding certain internal and external crises. In contrast to Japan, the Indian Constitution of 1949 could not rely on a traditional institution such as an imperial family. Thus it provides for a President, who, similarly to the President in the Weimar Republic, is vested with considerable powers. The President appoints the Prime Minister, serves as guardian of the Constitution and declares emergencies. However, the long-standing predominance of the Congress Party hindered the President in the exercise of his constitutional powers. The political conditions led in fact to a centralisation of the power of the Prime Minister and Cabinet, even though in this longest constitution in the world (more than 300 articles) only two articles mention the Prime Minister.

The Parliament of the Union of India is composed of the 'house of the people' (Lok Sabha) and the 'council of states' (Rajya Sabha). The Prime Minister is accountable to the Lok Sabha and must have the confidence of this lower chamber. This chamber thereby achieves a privileged position relative to the Rajya Sabha, which applies also to the legislative process. The law-making powers of both chambers are however quite limited due to the federal division of legislative powers between the Union and the States. The Indian Constitution exhaustively enumerates the tasks of the Union and those of the member States.

It is important to note that in addition to the President, the Supreme Court is also mandated to ensure adherence to the Constitution and to guarantee the constitutionality of the law. India did not fully adopt the concept of the absolute sovereignty of the British Parliament. Rather, it has vested its member states as well as the constitutional court with important sovereign powers. The factual weight of the judiciary is related to the strong legal consciousness rooted in Indian society, which was developed through the caste system. The courts in India occupy a similarly important role as the courts enjoy for instance in the United States.

The system of parliamentary responsible government was not as successful in other non-European states as it was in India and Japan. In particular in Africa, where the tribal consciousness of many communities is still linked to the concept of strong and unitary leadership, initial attempts to build parliamentary government systems increasingly gave way to systems of presidential authority in which a charismatic, sometimes totalitarian President had the upper hand. Of course, it must be said that most African states largely emulated the government system of their former colonial masters. Thus, states colonised by France are connected to the French presidential system, whilst the former British colonies tend to be closer to the English Westminster system.

The President and the Parliament

In the Federal Republic of Germany, India and Japan, the sovereignty of Parliament is limited by the power of the constitutional court. In Germany and in India, the power of the people's representatives in the lower chamber is further limited by their obligation to cooperate with the upper chamber and with the states within the federation. We find an even greater circumscription of Parliament's powers however, in states in which the President exercises his own powers and prerogatives in relation to Parliament. In such states, parliament becomes legally (in some Latin-American states) or *de facto* an advisory body of the President, who is able if necessary even to overrule the parliament. This is also the case in certain constitutional systems in which executive power is vested in two heads: President and Prime Minister.

Latin America

MONTESQUIEU recognised that laws and constitutions must correspond to the character, tradition, culture and the local realities and specific needs of a nation (C.-L. MONTESQUIEU, Book I, chapter 3). The development of the presidential systems of Latin American, African and even some Asian states (Indonesia, Pakistan) demonstrates very clearly that constitutions cannot simply be transplanted from one country to another.

Almost all Latin American states were influenced when drafting their constitution by the American presidential system and its concept of separation of powers. Contrary to the United States however, the constitutionally envisaged balance between the three branches of government led in these states to the complete supremacy of the President. Parliament and the courts, cabinet and ministers are largely subordinate to the President. There may be various causes for this development. The Latin American peoples are still accustomed from colonial times to a Viceroy with virtually unlimited authority. When these countries became independent, the Viceroy was replaced with a sovereign *Caudillo*. The *Caudillo* ran a patriarchal regime, with the degree of cruelty varying according to his personality. If the *Caudillo* wanted to present a somewhat more progressive image, he would establish a submissive Parliament with a more or less democratic constitution, which in reality would not be enforced. This tradition of a double legality between formal law and reality dates back to the time of the Spanish colonial rule, in which some idealistic theologians were asked to draft the legislation, which however was implemented by lawyers of the Viceroy.

For some time there have been attempts to make constitutions real and effective fundamental laws and to rid them of their 'alibi' function. The developments in Chile in the 1970s however, indicate clearly that even a constitutional tradition dating back to 1925 with a parliamentary system and limited presidential power had such weak roots that it could be wiped out by General Pinochet with a penstroke. In addition to the colonial history, the economic situation of many Latin American states has a crucial impact on the structure and organisation of the state. As in European feudal times, there is a very small elite that is dependent on state power and which uses this power for its own interests. The bourgeois middle class that was the precondition for democratic development in England of the 16th and 17th Centuries is often completely absent.

While Japan was able to retain its Emperor as a symbol and integrating personality, and was therefore more readily able to manage the transition to modern democracy, the young nations of the post-colonial era had first to find their integrating father figure. It is obvious that such patriarchal systems often give unlimited powers to the president. He must, as 'father' of the nation, fulfil the expectations of the people and must therefore be able to govern directly, without the interference of a cabinet or parliament. He is not accountable to anyone and cannot be removed by Parliament. The impeachment procedure adopted from America – that is, the removal of a President for high treason – has in those places in which it is provided for, remained largely dead letter. Contrary to a hereditary monarchy, the President is (at least once) elected by the people. In the Latin American states the Presidential term of office is almost always limited. At the expiry of the term the President can either not be re-elected at all, or can only be re-elected after a prescribed waiting period.

The system of limiting eligibility for re-election was adopted by the Constitution of Mexico. It was first introduced in the Mexican Constitution of 1917 after the Long Revolution (1910 to 1917). According to this Constitution, the President is elected for six years and is ineligible for re-election after the term of office has expired. This should prevent an unlimited reign of the President. However, this provision is also criticised for being undemocratic because it limits the choice of the voters. If the voters want to re-elect the same President for a second term, they are prevented from doing so by the Constitution. In spite of this criticism, the fear of too great an expansion of presidential power prevented the constitution-makers of many Latin American States from giving up this well proven system.

As in the United States, the President is at the same time also Commander-in-Chief of the army. He declares states of emergency and is able under some constitutions to submit concrete issues to a referendum if his proposals are not approved by the parliament. Moreover, he usually has the power to veto decisions taken by parliament. Of particular significance is the relationship of Latin American Presidents to their armies. The Presidents have the power to appoint the Generals and to determine the size of the army. This creates a relationship of mutual dependence between the President and the army. The President can only implement emergency law with the army. The officers of the army for their part are dependent on the favour of the President. It is therefore no surprise that the Latin American armies have always had a strong influence on the policy of the President and that they have often been misused to overthrow a President if the officers were opposed to him. In fact, the establishment of a professional army linked to a president as Commander-in-Chief is often closely connected to absolutist state developments.

7.2.2 *States with Divided Sovereignty*

Rational basis of state power

Most states of the western world organise the power of their governmental branches on the basis of rational concepts, which enable the comprehensive political participation of the population and which differentiate the various state institutions according to their function. This fact stems from the idea that man must be given the opportunity to arrange and construct his natural and social environment through reason. This Promethean liberation of man from his fate and from his divine destiny brought about, with THOMAS HOBBES' social contract theory, a secular concept of sovereignty and the state. The rational organisation of the state was entrusted to the legislature. "In both its religious and its secular versions, in FILMER as well as in HOBBES, the impact of the new doctrine of sovereignty was the subject's absolute duty of obedience to his king. Both doctrines helped political modernisation by legitimising the concentration of authority and the breakdown of the medieval pluralistic political order" (S. HUNTINGTON, p. 102).

United States and Switzerland

There are two states which did not completely embrace this development towards absolute and secularised sovereignty: The United States and the Swiss Confederation. Whilst in most other states the authority of the monarch and his centralised bureaucracy was destroyed by revolutionary means (In England in the 17th Century, in France in the 18th and 19th Centuries, in Germany in the 19th and 20th Centuries), one can find in the USA and in Switzerland political and social structures which have, since the first settlers in the USA and since the Middle Ages in Switzerland, gradually been developed and modified without being destroyed by a forceful revolution.

USA: JOHN LOCKE

For the American settlers there was no divine right of kings, no absolute sovereignty in the sense of THOMAS HOBBES and also no unlimited parliamentary sovereignty. They considered HOBBES irrelevant, but they followed the ideas of JOHN LOCKE. In the construction of their state order they were therefore wary of entrusting any state organ with supreme sovereign powers. Because for them the sovereignty of the state was limited in any case, they had no difficulty dividing sovereign functions of the state and allocating them to different organs of state as well as dividing them between the federal level and the states. The American settlers thereby designed a modern state without the modern theory of sovereignty. "Americans may be defined, ... as that part of the English-speaking world which instinctively revolted against the doctrine of the sovereignty of the state" (S. HUNTINGTON, p. 105).

Switzerland: Peoples without monarchy

Much the same can be said for the development of the Swiss Confederation. In the history of Switzerland, there has never been an absolute monarch who derived his authority from God (with the exception only of the canton of Neuchâtel which was under a Monarch until 1854). Even the oligarchic forms of government ruling mainly aristocratic cantons ultimately always derived their legitimacy from the people. An oligarchy cannot be God's representative on Earth.

Thus, in Switzerland a modern state developed without absolute sovereignty in the sense of HOBBES. This is seen most clearly in the relationship of the Confederation with its cantons: The Confederation was developed out of the cantons; its sovereignty is limited because the residual power has remained in the cantons, where the people through democratic means exercise their original sovereign rights.

Because of the special development of the state in the USA and Switzerland, it is useful to examine their state organisation from the point of view of limited and divisible sovereignty. We shall first examine the American federation, and then deal with the bases of the Swiss democracy.

7.2.2.1 The United States of America

i. The Influence of the English Constitution of the 17th Century

Separation of powers

As the first English settlers emigrated to America in 1606 during the reign of James I, England still stood under the Tudor constitution characterised by the thought of the Middle Ages. The Parliament had not yet achieved absolute power. The power of the state was still shared between the Crown, the Lords and the Commons. "The government of Tudor England was a government of fused powers (i.e. functions), that is, Parliament, Crown, and other institutions each performed many functions" (S. HUNTINGTON, p. 109).

The Parliament had judicial, legislative and executive functions. Even the Crown was not limited to the executive function, but exercised in common with the Parliament legislative and judicial powers. The separation of powers at that time was not functional but rather personal. Each institution exerted similar functions but it possessed specific power so that the different bodies could control each other.

British constitution of the 17th Century

This British Constitution of the 17th Century became the model not only for the Constitution of the United States of America, but also for the American states, which have followed the model of the first written constitution of the state of Virginia. Whilst in England the different functions were gradually distributed to different branches or organs of the state (legislative, executive and judicial functions) and actual power became increasingly concentrated in the House of Commons, the American concept of the organisation of the governmental system remained at the level of the British Constitution of the 17th Century. "The Constitutional Convention of 1787 is supposed to have created a government of separated powers (i.e. functions). It did nothing of the sort. Rather it created a government of separated institutions sharing powers (i.e. functions)" (R. E. NEUSTADT, *Presidential Power, The Politics of Leadership*, New York (1960) p. 33).

Checks and balances: The judiciary

This may be accurate from a purely Anglo-Saxon point of view. However, if one compares the American concept of separation of powers with the constitutional systems on the European continent, important differences appear. From the point of view of checks and balances, each branch can influence the other branch. The Courts can declare legislation to be unconstitutional, the parliament can remove judges from office via the impeachment procedure and it can regulate the tasks and jurisdiction of the Supreme Court via legislation. The President can appoint judges and the judges can ensure that the President and the administration do not exceed the authority given to them.

Checks and balances: The President

Finally, as mentioned, the President has the power to veto legislation and thus can exert a considerable influence over lawmaking. Except for his annual 'State of the Union' address, the President has no access to the Congress. Only the Vice-President is formally also the President of the Senate. Nevertheless, the President can and does introduce legislative proposals to Congress through the Representatives of his party.

Checks and balances: Congress

The parliament, that is the Congress, has the ability to influence the executive and the administration. The Senate ratifies international treaties and is thereby able to exert important influence on the foreign policy of the President. The Senate also approves the President's appointment of judges and top civil servants. Certainly the most important power of the Congress is its competence to decide on the budget. Through adherence to the Anglo-Saxon democratic principle "no taxation without representation" as well as through the general power to legislate, the Congress exercises a wide-ranging power to control and to influence the activity of the President and his administration. Based on these powers, the Congress can always require activities of the administration and of the President to be controlled by special parliamentary committees, enabling the parliament to determine whether the President has made appropriate use of the expenditures provided in the budget and whether proper effect has been given to legislation imposing specific responsibilities on the executive.

Whereas in Switzerland for example, the administrative control of the executive through parliament has long been limited because it violates the doctrine of separation of powers, there is no doctrine in the USA which would limit the power of the parliament to control all administrative activities of the executive.

Sovereignty of the branches of government

The counterweight to these checks is the doctrine, repeatedly reaffirmed by the Supreme Court, that each governmental branch remains sovereign in the exercise of its own function. This means that for instance only the legislature is ultimately responsible for enacting laws. Only the Court can declare the law that applies to concrete disputes and issue binding decisions according to law to resolve such disputes. For this reason, the court can review the constitutionality of statutes in a specific case, but it cannot repeal or quash laws enacted by the legislature. Only Congress has such authority. The administration for its part – contrary to the Swiss administrative law – has no judicial authority, that is, it cannot issue decisions that are to be executed in the manner of a judicial order. The courts alone are responsible for making binding judgments and orders.

Executive

On the other hand, the President is sovereign with regard to all executive powers. Whatever falls under the executive branch is ultimately the responsibility of the President. The court can review whether the President has acted *ultra vires* and exceeded his executive authority and prerogatives. But when the President acts within the scope of his authority, the court has no power to issue judgment on the exercise of such power. The 'political question doctrine' of the Supreme Court sprang from the doctrine of separation of powers. What is disputed in this context is still the question of whether the War Power Act enacted by Congress during the war in Vietnam – an Act which required the President to consult with Congress before making decisions in relation to war and the deployment of US troops – is a breach of the doctrine of separation of powers, because it intervenes in the exclusive powers of the executive. Since 11 September 2001, Congress has granted the President almost unlimited authority in the 'War on Terror', both internally and externally.

As much as the powers are overlapping, the functions are clearly separated from each other and each function is in this sense exercising sovereign state powers, whilst each branch within the proper scope of its own function is not subject to any other branch. The court makes final decisions on concrete cases and controversies, the President is sovereign with regard to the executive function and the legislature alone exercises sovereign power in the area of legislating.

Limited sovereignty and natural law in the Declaration of Independence

Nowhere is the firm conviction of the American Settlers that all state power must be limited more clearly expressed than in the American Declaration of Independence of July 1776:

"IN CONGRESS, JULY 4, 1776. THE UNANIMOUS DECLARATION OF THE THIRTEEN UNITED STATES OF AMERICA.
WHEN, in the Course of human Events,
it becomes necessary for one People to dissolve the Political Bands, which have connected them with another, and to assume, among the Powers of the Earth, the separate and equal Station to which the Laws of Nature and of Nature's GOD entitle them, a decent Respect to the Opinions of Mankind requires that they should declare the Causes which impel them to the Separation.
We hold these Truths to be self-evident, that all Men are created equal, that they are endowed, by their CREATOR, with certain unalienable Rights, that among these are Life, Liberty, and the Pursuit of Happiness.—
That to secure these Rights, Governments are instituted among Men, deriving their just Powers from the Consent of the Governed, that whenever any Form of Government becomes destructive of these Ends, it is the Right of the People to alter or to abolish it, and to institute new Government, laying its Foundation on such Principles, and organizing its Powers in such Form, as to them shall seem most likely to effect their Safety and Happiness. Prudence, indeed, will dictate, that Governments long established, should not be changed for light and transient Causes; and accordingly all Experience hath shown, that Mankind are more disposed to suffer, while Evils are sufferable, than to right themselves by abolishing the Forms to which they are accustomed. But when a long Train of Abuses and Usurpations, pursuing invariably the same Object, evinces a Design to reduce them under absolute Despotism, it is their Right, it is their Duty, to throw off such Government, and to provide new Guards for their future Security. Such has been the patient Sufferance of these Colonies; and such is now the Necessity which constrains them to alter their former Systems of Government. The History of the present King of Great-Britain is a History of repeated Injuries and Usurpations, all having in direct Object the Establishment of an absolute Tyranny over these States. To prove this, let Facts be submitted to a candid World.
HE has refused his Assent to Laws, the most wholesome and necessary for the public Good.
HE has forbidden his Governors to pass Laws of immediate and pressing Importance, unless suspended in their Operation till his Assent should be obtained; and when so suspended, he has utterly neglected to attend to them.
HE has refused to pass other Laws for the Accommodations of large Districts of People, unless those People would relinquish the Right of Representation in the Legislature, a Right inestimable to them, and formidable to Tyranny only.
HE has called together Legislative Bodies at Places unusual, uncomfortable, and distant from the Depository of their public Records, for the sole Purpose of fatiguing them into Compliance with his Measures.
HE has dissolved Representative Houses repeatedly, for opposing with manly Firmness his Invasions on the Rights of the People.
HE has refused for a long Time, after such Dissolutions, to cause others to be elected; whereby the Legislative Powers, incapable of Annihilation, have returned to the People at large for their exercise; the State remaining, in the mean Time, exposed to all the Dangers of Invasion from without, and Convulsions within.
HE has endeavoured to prevent the Population of these States; for that Purpose obstructing the Laws for Naturalization of Foreigners; refusing to pass others to encourage their Migrations hither, and raising the Conditions of new Appropriations of Lands.
HE has obstructed the Administration of Justice, by refusing his Assent to Laws for establishing Judiciary Powers.
HE has made Judges dependent on his Will alone; for the Tenure of their Offices, and the Amount and Payment of their Salaries.
HE has erected a Multitude of new Offices, and sent hither Swarms of Officers to harass our People, and eat out their Substance.

HE has kept among us, in Times of Peace, Standing Armies, without the Consent of our Legislatures.
HE has affected to render the Military independent of and superior to the Civil Power.
HE has combined with others to subject us to a Jurisdiction foreign to our Constitution, and unacknowledged by our Laws; giving his Assent to their Acts of pretended Legislation:
FOR quartering large Bodies of Armed Troops among us:
FOR protecting them, by a mock Trial, from Punishment for any Murders which they should commit on the Inhabitants of these States:
FOR cutting off our Trade with all Parts of the World:
FOR imposing Taxes on us without our Consent:
FOR depriving us, in many Cases, of the Benefits of Trial by Jury:
FOR transporting us beyond Seas to be tried for pretended Offences:
FOR abolishing the free System of English Laws in a neighbouring Province, establishing therein an arbitrary Government, and enlarging its Boundaries, so as to render it at once an Example and fit Instrument for introducing the same absolute Rule into these Colonies:
FOR taking away our Charters, abolishing our most valuable Laws, and altering fundamentally the Forms of our Governments:
FOR suspending our own Legislatures, and declaring themselves invested with Power to legislate for us in all Cases whatsoever.
HE has abdicated Government here, by declaring us out of his Protection, and waging War against us.
HE has plundered our Seas, ravaged our Coasts, burnt our Towns, and destroyed the Lives of our People.
HE is, at this Time, transporting large Armies of foreign Mercenaries to complete the Works of Death, Desolation, and Tyranny, already begun with Circumstances of Cruelty and Perfidy, scarcely paralleled in the most barbarous Ages, and totally unworthy the Head of a civilized Nation.
HE has constrained our Fellow-Citizens, taken Captive on the high Seas, to bear Arms against their Country, to become the Executioners of their Friends and Brethren, or to fall themselves by their Hands.
HE has excited domestic Insurrection amongst us, and has endeavoured to bring on the Inhabitants of our Frontiers, the merciless Indian Savages, whose known Rule of Warfare, is an undistinguished Destruction, of all Ages, Sexes, and Conditions.
IN every Stage of these Oppressions we have Petitioned for Redress in the most humble Terms: Our repeated Petitions have been answered only by repeated Injury. A Prince, whose Character is thus marked by every Act which may define a Tyrant, is unfit to be the Ruler of a free People.
NOR have we been wanting in Attentions to our British Brethren. We have warned them, from Time to Time, of Attempts by their Legislature to extend an unwarrantable Jurisdiction over us. We have reminded them of the Circumstances of our Emigration and Settlement here. We have appealed to their native Justice and Magnanimity, and we have conjured them by the Ties of our common Kindred to disavow these Usurpations, which would inevitably interrupt our Connexions and Correspondence. They too have been deaf to the Voice of Justice and of Consanguinity. We must, therefore, acquiesce in the Necessity, which denounces our Separation, and hold them, as we hold the Rest of Mankind, Enemies in War, in Peace Friends.
WE, therefore, the Representatives of the UNITED STATES OF AMERICA, in GENERAL CONGRESS Assembled, appealing to the Supreme Judge of the World for the Rectitude of our Intentions, do, in the Name, and by Authority of the good People of these Colonies, solemnly Publish and Declare, That these United Colonies are, and of Right ought to be, FREE AND INDEPENDENT STATES; that they are absolved from all Allegiance to the British Crown, and that all political Connexion between them and the State of Great-Britain, is, and ought to be, totally dissolved; and that as FREE AND INDEPENDENT

STATES, they have full Power to levy War, conclude Peace, contract Alliances, establish Commerce, and to do all other Acts and Things which INDEPENDENT STATES may of Right do. And for the Support of this Declaration, with a firm Reliance on the Protection of DIVINE PROVIDENCE, we mutually pledge to each other our Lives, our Fortunes, and our sacred Honour."

This Declaration, influenced by the ideas of LOCKE amongst others, also built the foundation for the realisation of judicial review jurisdiction; it paved the way for the exceptional position that the Supreme Court would later come to occupy in the course of history of the United States.

Isolated state committed to the rule of law

This impressive history of constitutional development and the rule of law in the United States has, however, had a shadow cast over it by more recent developments. The United States has not only refused to ratify the statute of the International Criminal Court (ICC), but has tried by all means at its disposal to impede the establishment and functioning of the Court. The United States will not permit any international body to review its aggression towards Yugoslavia, Afghanistan and Iraq. The prisoners ('detainees') it has captured in the war in Afghanistan have been excluded from the protection of international humanitarian law and for many years denied the right of *habeas corpus* under US law, until a recent decision of the Supreme Court which granted these prisoners some basic constitutional rights (*Rasul v. Bush* 542 US 466 (2004)).

By invoking its sovereign right to self-defence and emergency powers, the United States seeks to escape any external rule of law control and makes itself completely unaccountable to the international community under international and humanitarian law.

Impeachment

If sovereignty is not absolute, it can readily be apportioned not only between the different branches of government but also between federal and state governments. In contrast to the European concept of the state, which due to the absolutist conception of sovereignty (under the influence of HOBBES) must ultimately ascribe absolute sovereignty to only one state organ, the Americans were able to divide sovereignty. This means that at the federal level, the President, Congress and the Supreme Court are independent and sovereign institutions, each of which performs different functions and is thereby able to hold the others in check.

The power and position of the American President, who is indirectly elected by the people through the Electoral College, is comparable to the position of the English King in the 17th Century. He can veto decisions of the Congress, but this veto can be overruled with a two third majority of both houses. On the other hand, the Parliament cannot withdraw its confidence from the President through a political vote of no confidence. Congress together with the Supreme Court can only remove the President from office through the impeachment procedure (as was done by the Long Parliament in the 17th Century, which impeached two of the King's advisers).

According to ALEXANDER HAMILTON (1757–1804) however, the very possibility of impeachment weakens the power of the President relative to the English King (*Federalist Papers*, No. 70). The impeachment procedure has only been seen through to its conclusion on two occasions: against Andrew Johnson in 1868 and against Bill Clinton in 1999. In both cases the Presidents were acquitted by the Senate. Andrew Johnson narrowly escaped impeachment: his opponents were one vote short of the required two-thirds majority. Bill Clinton was acquitted with 45 votes to 55 for the first and with 50 to 50 for the second charge.

With the Watergate Affair in 1975 there was a change in direction. Richard Nixon escaped the impeachment procedure by voluntarily resigning from office before the procedure could commence. Since this crisis however, the integrity and credibility of the office of President have suffered considerably. Congress now feels even greater responsibility and commitment to hold the President accountable for his activities. The power of the Congress to initiate an impeachment procedure has a preventive effect that should not be underestimated, and contributes substantially to the balance of government powers.

Independence of the President and his Party

Just as the English King in the 17th Century had the power to choose his cabinet, so too the American President chooses his cabinet, subject to the approval of the Senate. The independence of the President in relation to Congress on the other hand, means that also Congress and in particular the party to which the President belongs are largely independent from the President and his government. Whilst in states with parliamentary responsible government, the parliamentarians from the governing party are legally or practically obliged to maintain party loyalty, American parliamentarians enjoy much greater independence from their party because the party vote has no direct implication on the fate of the executive. This has the result that in the two major parties (Democrats and Republicans) the parliamentarians can represent quite diverse political ideas. The parties are not focused on implementing a specific governmental program – this is the responsibility of the President – but on winning the next congressional elections. Thus, the parties are much more centres for the education and promotion of political personalities than they are centres for policy programs in the European sense.

ii. Divided sovereignty between the Federation and the States

Constitutional limitation of federal powers

Through the Constitution of the United States powers were not only divided horizontally among the federal governmental branches but also vertically between the new confederation and its member states. The founding fathers thereby tried for the first time in history to establish a proper balance between the powers of the new federal alliance and the powers of its members. "The powers delegated by the proposed Constitution to the federal government are few and defined. Those which are to remain in the State governments are numerous and indefinite ... The powers reserved to the several States will extend to all the objects which, in the ordinary course of affairs, concern the lives, liberties, and properties of the people, and the internal order, improvement, and prosperity of the State" (MADISON, *The Federalist Papers, No. 45*). This idea of divided sovereignty enabled the founding fathers of the American Constitution to build up a federation which could exercise completely separate constitutionally defined powers independent from its member states.

Implementation of federal law and the administration of the federation

Contrary to the later European concept of federalism, which is based on the idea that federal legislation is administered and implemented by the member states within the federation, the federal government in the US has the power and the duty to administer its own legislation through its own agencies that are accountable to the President and/or to Congress. Thus, the federal system in the US provides for two parallel legal systems with independent administrative and court implementation. The federal laws are implemented by federal agencies and this implementation is controlled by a federal court system. State laws are implemented by state ad-administrative agencies and controlled by the state court system. The powers of the federation and the states are thereby completely separated from each other. This concept of a federal state based on a vertical division of powers, which was realised for the first time in the new American Constitution, has since had a greater influence on the constitutions of the world than has the American system of presidency. However, only very few constitutions have adopted the basic idea contained therein of a true division of sovereignty between the federation and the member states. Many states have erroneously assumed that the idea of absolute and indivisible state sovereignty could be combined with the American federalism concept.

7.2.2.2 The Swiss Confederation (Eidgenossenschaft)

i. Essential Features of the Government System

Democracy and multiculturality as pre-constitutional structures

The Swiss Confederation, which in German is called the Swiss '*Eidgenossenschaft*' meaning co-operative society allied by a common oath, has, apart from its strongly decentralised federal structure, a unique governmental system. This system is determined by Switzerland's democratic history and by the multicultural reality of the country. The federation does not have a monocratic head of state. Rather, it is governed by a collegial executive called the Federal Council, which is elected for a fixed term of four years by the two chambers of parliament combined. Neither the Federal Council as a collegium nor its individual members can be removed from office during their term of office. Moreover, in the 20th Century all members of the Federal Council who stood for re-election at the expiry of their term were re-elected. In practice, as a general rule, the executive is not voted out of office. The body that elects the members of the Federal Council is the united parliamentary assembly of the two chambers of parliament, called the Federal Assembly. Since 1959 the Federal Assembly, pursuant to an unwritten constitutional convention, has elected the members of the Federal Council according to the so-called 'magic formula'. This magic formula prescribes that parties should be proportionally represented in the Federal Council according to their relative strength in the two chambers of parliament. Since 2003, the Federal Council is composed of two radicals (liberal party), two socialists, two members of the Democratic Union (right-wing party) and one Christian Democrat. In choosing the members of the Federal Council, the Federal Assembly has the constitutional obligation to take the interests of the different regions of Switzerland into account. Thus, members of minority language groups (French, Italian and Romansh), the two major religions (Protestant and Catholic), women, employees and employers etc. should be represented according to a reasonable concept of proportionality. As a general rule, the minority language groups, which together make up approximately 20% of the Swiss population, are represented by three members of the Federal Council (over 40%).

In fact, the reality of the semi-direct democracy requires that the executive body takes into account the different cultural traditions and opinions within the country. It must be composed of members who are able to find the necessary compromise, which is likely to win the approval of the people in a referendum. An alternation between opposition and governing majority according to the winner-takes-all principle would not work in Switzerland, as such system would disregard the will of the people.

The executive as 'small council'

The executive has often been called the 'small council' relative to the two chambers of Parliament. As the small council, it acts to some degree as a first instance in relation to legislative proposals, which submits the first drafts for legislation and expenditures to the 'big council', the parliament. The two chambers of parliament will examine the proposals of the executive and (except in relation to the budget) their final decision may be subject to a referendum of the people.

Reflection of the people

An executive identical with the majority party in parliament according to the Westminster system would stand no chance of winning popular approval for its proposals in a referendum. In fact, at the beginning of its existence in the second half of the 19th Century, the Federal Council was composed of only one and later two parties, and the members of Parliament were elected according to a majoritarian system. As a consequence, the sovereign people regularly rejected important legislative endeavours. Thus the system had to be adapted and the electoral system was changed from a majoritarian system to a system of proportional representation, which enabled the composition of parliament to more closely reflect the reality of social diversity. The parliament needed the support of the large majority of the people. Accordingly, the collegial executive as the 'small council' needed also to be adapted to this proportional concept of representation. It had to reflect the existing social diversity and to take into account the different power-centres, cultures and traditions within society. This broad representation allowed the Federal Council to promote policies supported by a consensus of the people, which were conceived more or less independently from the party policies of the parties to which the members of the Federal Council belonged.

The limitation of power imposed by the constitution consisted less of checks and balances between the Parliament and the executive as in the United States, and rather more in the need to find a collegial consensus among the members of the Federal Council in the first executive instance, and in addition among the upper and the lower chamber of parliament in the second, legislative instance. This system is probably more effective at limiting political power than the traditional checks and balances.

The people as opposition

The Swiss governmental system although formally unchanged since 1848, has been considerably influenced by the development of the direct participation of the citizens in the decision making process through referendum and initiative. This new development began 15 years after the commencement of the 1848 Constitution with the first important votes on constitutional amendments, and by the end of the 19th Century and during the 20th Century led to the continuous and gradual expansion of the direct democratic rights of the people. The right of the voters introduced in 1874 to require a referendum on a legislative proposal by the Parliament for instance, enabled certain groups within society, such as employer groups and labour unions, which had the financial and human resources to require a referendum and to finance a referendum campaign, to considerably enlarge their political influence. Those parties on the other hand which lacked the financial resources to finance a referendum campaign, lost substantial influence and thus tended to become organisations that still exerted their influence on the election of candidates for political office, but which largely lost their ability to participate in the policy making process.

Constitution as program

On the other hand, the various referendums and in particular the people's participation in the constitutional amendment process had a substantial influence on the constitutional policy of the Confederation. Although only very few popular initiatives gained the approval of the majority of the people and the cantons in the final vote, every one of them provoked an intensive debate amongst the people, which often led either to a counter-proposal from Parliament or, in the mid- to long-term, to legislative amendments. Often the counterproposals put by Parliament are less extreme than the proposals made through popular initiative, and are ultimately adopted by the people and the cantons. Even when initiatives are rejected by the people, some of the core ideas of the initiative may remain on the agenda and later be taken up successfully by certain parties or sometimes even by the administration, and may thus have an impact on the overall policy of Switzerland. The Swiss Constitution has become an instrument which not only facilitates and simultaneously limits state power, but which also substantially determines the essential policy of the state. The Constitution has thereby taken on an important programmatic character.

We shall now turn to the most important historical developments which led to the development of this system.

ii. History

Common pastoral land in the Middle Ages

The path of development was somewhat different in rural cantons than it was city cantons. In 1291 the three original rural cantons Uri, Schwyz and Unterwalden formed an alliance to defend the free status given to them by the emperor against the governors installed by the Habsburgs. Within the corporations formed by the two valleys of Uri and Schwyz the earl exercised his jurisdiction in an open assembly of all inhabitants of the valley. Public authority thus was already linked to the open assembly of the people. The farmers of Schwyz were free citizens and landowners, united by the corporation of their territory. The peasants of Uri were serfs, but they were united through a pastoral collective, which they formed to make common use of the pastoral land they were allowed to access. The inhabitants of Unterwalden were united in corporations formed by the municipalities. When they acquired by charter the status of being directly subordinate to the empire, the pastoral collectives and the corporations that served as district courts merged together and formed the basis of a common public authority with both public jurisdiction and authority over certain private legal interests (common use of land), under the leadership of a governor of the land or of the valley (*Landamann* or *Talamann*).

Rural and city alliances

Particularly fortunate for the further development of the young confederation of Switzerland was the fact that these corporations began very early to ally themselves with cities such as Zurich, Lucerne and Berne. The cities themselves had also emerged out of municipal corporations (Lucerne) or out of alliances between a group of small areas (Zurich), or had been founded for the purpose of military defence (Bern and Fribourg by the Zähringer Family). The democratic institutions developed differently according to the historical origins and traditions of each specific region or city.

Power of the guilds in the cities

The mercantile and trading towns were given the right to operate market places and conduct trade, and to protect themselves with a proper wall. Originally Zurich was ruled by old families allied with Habsburg dynasty, who exercised their authority through a small oligarchic council. With the first revolution in 1336 led by Rudolf Brun, the old council was replaced by a new council, which apart from the old aristocratic families (*Konstafel*) also included craftsmen. As these reforms did not suit the Habsburg family, Zurich had to look for support to the rural and forest areas in order to defend its independence, which led to an alliance with Uri, Schwyz, Unterwalden and Lucerne. Later, with the so-called Waldmann Constitution (1489), Zurich established its first somewhat democratic constitution. With this Constitution the privilege of the aristocracy (*Konstafel*) was finally revoked and the aristocratic corporation was placed on an equal footing with all other existing guilds. From now on the council was elected by the guilds. The council embodied the highest authority, which authority was exercised by a mayor under the control of the council.

Aristocracy

In contrast to the towns ruled by the guilds, Berne is a city that was founded for military purposes, in which craftsmen and merchants never had a special social and political status as in Zurich or in Lucerne. The town was ruled by a mayor and a small council composed of twelve members, as well as a town assembly, which elected annually the twelve members of the council from amongst the knights and other gentry (J. SCHOLLENBERGER, p. 148–149). In 1294, a new institution called the Institute of Sixteen (die Sechszehner) was created. The members of this institute elected the members of the Grand Council (Grosser Rat) of two hundred. The craftsmen were admitted to the Institute of Sixteen as well as to the Grand Council. But in the Small Council (Kleiner Rat), that is, the executive government, craftsmen were not permitted and in 1373 even the guilds were prohibited. It is one of the important particularities of the town of Bern, that the craftsmen never had any political influence. Until 1798 they were ineligible for any governmental position and thus never participated in any governmental branch of the town. Ruling the town remained a prerogative of the aristocracy and of the old bourgeois families of the town (J. SCHOLLENBERGER, p. 150).

Charter of Stans: First document of compromise

In the rural cantons the government, that is, the headman of the rural state (monocratic), was closely linked to the people because of its election by the periodical people's assembly. The small councils (collegial system) in the towns however had the tendency, in relation to the rural areas that were subordinate to the respective towns, to govern *over* the people. This difference, sometimes still dis cernible today, between urban and rural interests first emerged as a consequence of the Burgundian Wars. The towns banded together into an alliance in order to rule over the population in their surrounding rural areas. This rural population on the other hand, had the support of the rural members of the young Swiss corporation. The conflict was resolved in the so-called Charter of Stans in 1481 (Stanser Verkommnis), in which the towns and regions agreed for the first time to provide each other with mutual assistance in cases of rebellion or insurgency, and the rural cantons agreed to refrain from inciting the rural population to rebellion against their masters. Whilst elsewhere the Lords looked to their kings for help, the Swiss Lords protected themselves by providing mutual assistance to deal with an insubordinate people. This assistance however was only possible to a limited extent. Thus, after the execution of the far-sighted mayor of Zurich, Hans Waldmann, the ambassadors of the rural cantons had to serve as mediators in the conflict between town and countryside.

Essential elements of the early state structure

From the first developments of the Swiss Alliance one can already observe certain fundamental elements of the Swiss understanding of state and political power:

1. The consciousness of forming and being an autonomous political community first emerged out of small, local, collectively organised communities, which in the 13th Century were able to extract from the Emperor their charters of liberty.
2. Every threat to political independence, whether on the part of the empire or on the part of the people, is met not by centralising power, but by strengthening the common alliance and cooperation of the concerned communities in order to maintain local autonomy. The political centre remains with the local, collectively organised communities. These communities protect each other by guaranteeing mutual assistance, as soon as their domestic political order is threatened by external or internal forces (Stanser Verkommnis).
3. The need of the small communities to grant individual freedoms is relatively limited as the individual members of the communities (free farmers or citizens) can exercise great influence on the political decisions of the communities. Liberty is considered to be liberty of the corporation, but not individual liberty.
4. The people's assemblies of the valleys and the towns can be traced back to judicial activities and to the common administration of the use of the land. A separation between state and society in these small communities is not apparent.
5. One cannot however speak of self-government of the people in the sense of ROUSSEAU, as the rural cantons are governed by a governor and the urban cantons are ruled by a small council and a mayor. In cases of conflict though, often the people had to be called upon as the final and highest instance.
6. The separation between worldly and spiritual affairs was carried out by a gradual removal of the spiritual jurisdiction (*Pfaffenbriefe*), whereby the interference of the church in the domestic political affairs of local communities was reduced.

Secession from the Empire

Towards the end of the 15th Century, the confederates had become spiritually and politically separated from the empire to such an extent, that formal secession became only a question of time. Up until the Swabian War (1499) however, as members of the empire they still had to pay taxes to the empire, render military service and submit to the superior jurisdiction of the empire.

When the emperor attempted to reunite the strongly fragmented empire through the Imperial Reform done at Worms in 1495, the confederates were no longer prepared to accept reforms such as the Imperial Court or the taxes of the empire. With the Swabian War and the Peace of Basel that followed on 22 September 1499, the Swiss confederates achieved independence from the empire. This independence however was not formally confirmed until the Peace of Westphalia in 1648 after the Thirty Years War.

Reformation

The secession from the empire occurred shortly before the beginning of the Reformation. The Reformation resulted in a separation between Catholic and Protestant cantons, which lasted several centuries. In contrast to Germany, the Reformation led by ULRICH ZWINGLI (1484–1531) in Zurich and JEAN CALVIN (1509–1564) in Geneva not only resulted in a new conception of the church but also in a new conception of the state, comparable to that which developed in England. The church and state were linked, and either the state was subordinate to the church (Geneva) or the church was subordinated to the political structure of the state (Zurich). This led to the development of democratic (Zurich) or oligarchic (Geneva) political structures within the church, which later found their institutional foundation in the form of the *Landeskirche* (state churches). The new self-confidence and sovereign consciousness of the reformed cantons was however not shared by the Catholic cantons, which were unable to accept the idea of absolute state sovereignty over both worldly and spiritual affairs. This difference in the concept of the state between reformed and Catholic cantons is one that to some extent still persists today.

Absolutist influences in the 18th Century

The Reformation, religious wars between the cantons, the first peasants' revolts and attempts to establish absolutism all brought about fundamental changes in Switzerland. The Reformation had primarily democratic aims, but through the renewed political union between affairs of church and state it led in fact to a concept of an absolute and unaccountable sovereign state power. The influence of absolute monarchies in neighbouring countries on these developments cannot be denied. The neighbouring monarchies were influential in particular because many Swiss legionnaires performed military service for them. The high financial reward from such foreign services enabled some to accumulate substantial fortunes. Other ruling families accumulated wealth from the income from church assets (in return for providing military support to the Pope). Such families used their economic power to establish oligarchic political structures and became increasingly alienated from the people over which they ruled. Political rights were increasingly limited by property and lineage, and the isolation of the guilds and the aristocracy (for example in Berne) excluded more and more inhabitants from exercising democratic rights.

Separation of powers under the sovereign?

Most important is the fact that, unlike in 17th Century England, there was in Switzerland no attempt to develop a concept of separation of powers. Governmental functions and political power were always united in one body, which however did exercise its different powers and functions through various authorities. The people's assembly as the highest authority carried out judicial, legislative and executive functions. It elected the governor (Landamann), who could also be voted out of office. The governor performed his role in the name of the people's assembly, to which he had to submit important issues for final approval. Thus, between the people's assembly and the governor there was no separation of powers, but rather a chain of command. Conflicts that could not be solved by the governor were referred to the people's assembly. So it was that the people's assembly in the canton of Schwyz in 1655 refused to implement legislation issued by the confederation, because it did not recognise any authority higher than itself except God alone. Similar state organisation can be seen in the urban cantons. However, contrary to the monocratic governor in the rural cantons, the urban areas saw the emergence of the first collegial bodies in the form of the small and great councils.

Accountability: The case of a people's assembly in the canton of Schwyz

Whilst up until the Reformation government routinely asked subjects through 'Volksanfragen' for their opinion in relation to important matters, from the Reformation onwards these rights were gradually restricted. Exceptionally however, they remained in some cantons up until the end of the 18th Century.

France and Napoleon

At the end of the 18th Century the strife-torn Swiss Confederation, weakened by the intrigues of foreign powers, was unable to resist the attack of the French revolutionary armies. With the reign of Napoleon a new era of political institutions began, which after much confusion and many disputes in the 19th Century eventually supplemented the traditional political ideas of the cantons with new ideas.

At the end of the 18th Century, the troubled Confederation was overrun by French soldiers and on 12 April 1798 received a new republican constitution, which made out of the very loose and diverse confederation an unmistakably unitary state (Art. 1: "The Helvetic Republic is one and indivisible"). This imposition of uniformity in a Confederation dissected into many semi-autonomous and distinct local units, was bound to run into trouble. Very soon after this first Constitution, new constitutional drafts were proposed until Napoleon in 1803 dictated a new 'Mediation Constitution', which gave greater autonomy and rights to the cantons. With the departure of

Napoleon however, the 'dream' of an integrated and unitary Confederation was over once and for all. On 7 August 1815, the 22 sovereign cantons ratified a new treaty of alliance in order to re-establish the confederation. They swore to provide common defence and protection of their liberty and to defend the rights of the cantons against any external or internal aggressor. Based on this new alliance, the former governing families of certain cantons were able to regain their power and authority.

July Revolution of 1830 and regeneration

Only after the July Revolution of 1830 in France was it possible in Switzerland for the idea of a liberal state with separation of powers to gain acceptance in some cantons (in particular Zurich). The liberal and democratic movements (called 'regeneration') advocated the realisation of liberty and democracy throughout the whole of Switzerland and proposed to put these ideas into effect, even in the conservative cantons, through the power of a unitary state. They achieved these aims only partially in the new Federal Constitution adopted by the people and the cantons in 1848, by which the Swiss federation was established. In this Constitution of 1848 as well as in the later Constitution of 1874, Article 1 begins with the words: "Together, the peoples of the 22 [since 1979, 23 with the Canton of Jura] sovereign Cantons of Switzerland united by the present alliance, to wit: Zurich, Berne, Lucerne, … , form the Swiss Confederation."

Separation of powers at the federal level

Whilst the idea of sovereignty divided between the federal and cantonal levels was carried through, the idea of divided sovereignty among the federal governmental branches could be implemented only partially, contrary to the model constitution of the United States. On the other hand, one can compare the assignment of equal powers to the two chambers of parliament to the American system of power sharing amongst the two houses, a concept which was based on the English Constitution of the 17th and early 18th Century. The national chamber and the chamber of the cantonal representatives have the same functions and powers, and provide mutual limitation and control of each other's powers.

The organisation of federal power was influenced not only by the American but also by the short-lived Helvetian Constitution of 1798. This Constitution adopted the model, influenced by MONTESQUIEU, of a functional separation of powers (see Art. 3 of the draft for a new Helvetian Constitution: "The legislative, judicial and executive powers are never to be united").

According to this model, the three branches are not only to be functionally but also personally separated. Contrary to the parliamentary governmental system, the executive in Switzerland cannot be removed from office by a parliamentary vote of no confidence. The Federal Assembly (the two chambers combined) has only the power to decide at the end of each term of office on the re-election of members of the executive. While in the US the executive power is vested in the President, the Federal Constitution of Switzerland adopted the system of a collegial directorate as seen in the French revolutionary Constitution of 1795–1799. Although this system did not survive in France, in Switzerland it was readily integrated into the traditional system of collegial councils already existing in some urban cantonal governments. The system was also well suited to the political culture and the federal diversity of Switzerland. Attempts to establish a presidential system at the federal level similar to the governmental systems of some rural cantons governed by a single Landamann on the other hand, would have failed precisely because of the multiculturality of Switzerland. The cantons could not permit comprehensive executive power to be vested in one person. They wanted cantonal diversity to be represented not only in the second chamber of parliament but also, albeit in a more restricted sense, in the federal executive. Moreover, there were existing examples of collegial government in the urban cantons with small town councils led by a mayor.

iii. Foreign Influences on the Governmental System

Influence of the French Revolution

Article 132 of the Constitution of the year III (22nd of August 1795) which arose out of the French Revolution provided:

> "The executive power shall be delegated to a directory of five members."

Article 71 of the first Helvetian Constitution imposed on Switzerland by the French revolutionary troops made the identical provision:

> "The executive power shall be delegated to a directory of five members."

Article 174 of the current Swiss Federal Constitution of 1999 reads:

> "The Federal Council is the highest governing authority and the supreme executive authority of the Confederation."

Germany

Article 62 of the Basic Law of on the other hand provides:

> "The Federal Government shall consist of the Federal Chancellor and the Federal Ministers."

And Article 59 provides that the Federal President represents Germany in terms of international law.

France

The French Constitution of 1958 describes the different governmental functions as follows:

Art. 5 regulates the functions of the President as Head of State and stipulates:

> "The President of the Republic shall see that the Constitution is observed. He shall ensure, by his arbitration, the proper functioning of the public authorities and the continuity of the State.

He shall be the guarantor of national independence, territorial integrity and observance of treaties."

Art. 20:

"The Government shall determine and conduct the policy of the nation.
It shall have at its disposal the civic service and the armed forces.
It shall be responsible to Parliament in accordance with the terms and procedures set out in Articles 49 and 50."

Art. 21:

"The Prime Minister shall direct the operation of the government. He shall be responsible for national defence. He shall ensure the implementation of legislation..."

The Federal Council corresponds to the Directory of the first French Republic

The constitutional provisions which define the function of the Directory of the First French Republic and of the Helvetian Constitution, and the constitutional provision which sets out the function of the current Swiss Federal Council are very similar, if not identical, and thus differ considerably from the texts of constitutions which define the position and the function of the executive and the head of state in parliamentary and in presidential systems. The latter systems are based on a completely different concept to the collegial system, as they have to divide executive functions variously between the head of the state, the prime minister, the cabinet and individual ministers, whereas the Directory or collegial council contains all executive functions in one body.

The comparison of the current Swiss Constitution with the French revolutionary Constitution on one side and with other modern constitutions on the other, shows clearly how closely the Swiss governmental system corresponds to the old revolutionary model and how little it has in common with most modern constitutions that provide for a two-headed executive comprising a head of state and a cabinet led by a Prime Minister.

The governmental system of the unitary Helvetian state lasted only a short while. Although the collegial system might have been appropriate, the concept of a unitary state structure did not correspond to the traditional culture or special needs of a Swiss Constitution. Only the liberal cantons, which adopted liberal constitutions during the time of the Regeneration (1830), adopted the model of the directorial system, which corresponded as mentioned to the traditional collegial councils of some cantons.

Directory and Swiss tradition

The people's deeply rooted mistrust of authority and reluctance to entrust any institution or person with too much power, the tradition of federalism and the already tested collegial system in the urban cantons were probably the most decisive historical roots which induced the Swiss founding fathers to provide for a federal government based on the principle of collegiality. It was felt that only a collegial body could be assigned the responsibility of governing this young nation, which had already suffered the strain of various revolutions and civil wars.

In France the directorial Constitution lasted only three years. The Swiss governmental system first established in 1848 however, has remained in place for more than 150 years. It has survived the Franco-Prussian War of the 1870s, the French Revolution of 1870 and the Russian Revolution of 1917, two World Wars, the Third Reich, several economic crises and even the changing world order after 1989 and 9/11, 2001. In France, Napoleon was able to bring down the collegial system. In Switzerland, neither a military General nor any other person or force has been able to dismantle the Federal Council.

Swiss government system as a unique model

The directorial, collegial system of government in Switzerland can be classified as the third model of government of democratic states, which has emerged since the Glorious Revolution of 1689 and has been maintained – albeit in only one country – for almost 200 years. The first model, that is, the American presidential system, is essentially adapted from the British Constitution of the 17th Century. The second model is the system of the parliamentary cabinet based on the British Westminster constitution of the 19th Century, and is the model that is most widespread.

The directorial system is the only governmental system which brings together the functions of the head of state, the prime minister and cabinet in one collegial body and simultaneously decentralises this executive power amongst the seven equal members of the collegial executive body. For this reason, Switzerland is not familiar with some of the problems that other constitutions have to solve, in relation to the division of powers among the head of the state, the prime minister and the cabinet. The problem of dictatorships being established, as has occurred in a number of Latin American states, is also unknown and difficult to imagine in Switzerland. On the contrary, the directorial Constitution enables the parties that make up the parliamentary majority to elect people of various party affiliations to the Federal Council, without granting the parties direct influence over the activity of the executive and without binding the parties to a coalition program.

Incarnation of the volonté générale

Indeed, the various members of the Federal Council do not consider themselves to be primarily representatives of the party, who are supposed to defend their party interests within the Federal Council. For this reason, they are better able to work cooperatively with the other members of the Council to reach common solutions which are closer to the ideal of the *volonté générale* than pure party interests. Members of the Federal Council are not elected because they support a coalition program agreed between the parties. Rather, they are expected to devise independently a government program that reflects the consensus of the members of the Federal Council, and which can be defended before Parliament and the people. As there is no majority party that in common with the executive has to pursue policies that will enable it to win the next elections, there is also no party or coalition majority that considers itself responsible for rushing government-proposed legislation through Parliament. As each Federal Councillor has to seek his/her own majority in Parliament and in the referendum of the people, and as even the largest parties gain no more than one fifth of the votes, no Councillor can rely solely on the support of his/her own party.

No separation between head of state and executive government

In general, almost all original monarchies have adopted the Westminster model of government in one form or another, and have either retained the monarch as Head of State or transferred the functions of Head of State to an elected President. However, only with the American presidential system was it possible to retain the original executive powers of the former British monarch and to replace him/her with an elected President. Those monarchies following the Westminster model had to hand over important executive functions of the monarch to the Prime Minister and cabinet. Only in the United States is the Head of State still identical with the holder of comprehensive executive power.

In principle, all modern governmental systems have thus been influenced either by the American presidential system or by the Westminster model. Only Switzerland has adopted the directorial system of the French Revolution and adapted it to meet Swiss conditions.

Federal Council: Independent adoption of the French model

The Swiss Constitution has however supplemented and amended the French model in some important respects. Contrary to the French Directory, the Swiss Federal Council is composed not of five members but of seven. It was originally planned that the Swiss Federal Council would also comprise five members, but in particular the medium-sized and smaller cantons requested an enlargement of the Council to seven members, as they feared they might otherwise never be represented in the Federal Council.

Lowest instance

The members of the Federal Council are elected for a fixed term of office of four years (previously only three years) by the Federal Assembly (both chambers voting as one assembly). The Federal Assembly elects each member individually. It attempts to accommodate the proportional representation of all regions of the country as well as all major parties. The Federal Council however is not a coalition government which is appointed by agreement between the parties. There are and have been members of the Federal Council who have been elected by the Federal Assembly, even though they were not proposed as candidates by their own party. Because of direct democracy, the power of a majority coalition in Parliament is considerably restricted, as it is the people and not a minority party that serves as opposition to the executive and the Parliament. As a result, there is no unity between the Federal Council and its majority in Parliament. In the legislative procedure the Federal Council is effectively the lowest instance. It makes legislative proposals to Parliament, which in turn will make its decision on such proposals, subject to the power of the highest authority – the people – to make the final decision in case of a referendum.

Stability

In the last 100 years, members of the Federal Council who on the expiry their term of office have run for re-election, have almost all succeeded in being re-elected. The first time a Federal Council candidate for re-election was not re-elected was in 2003, after the representation of the traditional parties in Parliament had shifted substantially in the previous parliamentary election. Moreover, as the Federal Council has never retired as a whole, Parliament has since 1848 effectively only filled individual vacancies as they have arisen. Switzerland may therefore be the only country in the world which has an unbroken continuity in executive government since 1848, since all seven members of the Federal Council have never retired all at once.

Executive and administration

In contrast to the French Directory, which as a replacement of the King assumed only the responsibility of Head of State and which in lieu of a Prime Minister had a General Director who administered government, the Federal Council shares the functions of government and administration amongst its seven members. Each Councillor, in addition to their collegial function in the Council as a whole, also serves as an individual executive officer responsible for heading the administration of their Department or Ministry.

iv. Key Elements of Swiss Popular Sovereignty

Expansion of voting rights and of the proportional system

In the Constitution of 1848 the governmental system was still essentially a representative democracy, but through the cantons gradually more and more elements of direct democracy were introduced at the federal level. In 1874 the legislative facultative referendum was introduced, and in 1891 the right of the voters to initiate amendments to the Constitution was enshrined in the Constitution as an important democratic right. In 1918, the referendum for international treaties (expanded and modified in 1977 and in 2003) was introduced. And finally, most significant was the introduction in 1918 of the proportional system for the elections of members of the national chamber. The basic concept of proportionality of representation was to become the central theme in the political culture of Switzerland. Today the principle is applied to the composition of the executive, the courts, the administration and all authorities and advisory committees. It stands in contradiction to the pure majority-rule system, which imposes decisions on minorities. The proportional representation in all institutions and authorities is designed to ensure that at all levels, compromises can be found which take into account the largest possible range of interests and which enable all of the different elements within society to influence decisions. Thus, the principle of proportionality gives expression to the idea that democracy in Switzerland is not regarded primarily as a tyranny of the majority but rather as a possibility for far-reaching self-determination. Based on this principle, all bodies and authorities seek to reach decisions by a majority that is as close as possible to unanimity.

Not too much democracy

Other attempts to further expand democratisation have been declined by the people, such as for example the direct popular election of the Federal Council, the financial referendum at the federal level, and the popular right to initiate legislation – all of which were rejected by the majority of voters. The continuous trend since 1848 of extending direct democracy has not, in spite of some negative decisions of the people, come to a standstill. The expansion of the treaty referendum and the many new initiatives that seek to resolve major issues through the extension of people's rights (including nuclear power, road infrastructure, etc) are sufficient proof of this.

Checks and balances

What are the key elements of the Swiss governmental system in comparison to other systems? Most significant is the fact that, in contrast to the British parliamentary democracy, the Parliament does not have unlimited sovereignty. Article 148 of the Constitution does provide that Parliament is the highest authority within the federation, but this supremacy is subject to the reservation of the right of the people. Thus, the highest authority and final instance on all important issues are the voters of the nation and of the cantons who have to agree to every modification of the Constitution and who can initiate new amendments for submission to a constitutional referendum.

Right of the executive to participate in the chambers

Contrary to the governmental systems based on the Westminster model, the Parliament and in particular the parties from which the executive is constituted are not involved in activity of the executive government. As the members of the executive cannot be removed during their term of office (neither as a whole nor individually), they are relatively independent from Parliament and from their own parties. Contrary to the President of the United States, the individual Federal Councillors are entitled to propose and defend decisions of the Federal Council directly in the Parliament, and so do not have to depend on a member of Parliament to speak on their behalf.

Thus, the executive can submit and defend in both chambers legislative and budgetary proposals. The members of the Federal Council however do not have any voting rights. Parliament makes its own decisions on the proposals of the executive. Contrary to most other states, legislative proposals are considerably amended in parliamentary committees and in Parliament itself. In Switzerland there is no governing parliamentary majority that imposes party discipline to obtain prior agreement on legislative proposals or to rush them through without amendment once they are introduced.

Highest authority?

The two chambers of Parliament are, according to the Constitution and subject to the reservation of the rights of the people, the highest constitutional authority. Based on this constitutional provision, the Federal Parliament exercises its supervisory rights over the Federal Council and the Federal Court. The executive however, has on the grounds of separation of powers long resisted too much parliamentary control of the executive. In particular, it has constantly defended its constitutional authority against parliamentary investigations. But with the argument that mutual control of powers or checks and balances is an essential aspect of the separation of powers Parliament has succeeded in defending its position. Contrary to the Westminster models however, parliamentary inquiries are not conceived as a minority right of the opposition. The power of Parliament to investigate specific matters is part of the ordinary 'checks and balances' entrusted to the Parliament.

Election of Federal Judges

The united Federal Assembly is also the body that elects judges of the Federal Court. Federal judges are elected for a fixed term of six years. They can be re-elected at the conclusion of each term of office until they reach the age of 70. This re-election is normally a routine matter. However it can occur, that Parliament focuses on particular decisions of certain federal judges, and that members of Parliament may then propose a motion not to re-elect a certain judge. Thus, the independence of the judiciary is not entirely protected from political influence.

Political rights

Another distinguishing feature of the Swiss system aside from the division of executive and legislative power is the political rights of the citizens, which considerably change the balance and the relationship of the three branches of government. Whilst in parliamentary democracies the people vote not only for a person but for the party program the candidate is representing – and government therefore gains its mandate by virtue of being elected on the basis of its stated policies, in the Swiss system Parliament and government gain their mandate less from elections and more from popular votes on constitutional amendments.

The People as highest authority but not as a governmental branch

The Swiss system of government does not correspond to the principle of pure popular rule. The people does not actually govern. However the people is ultimately the highest and final authority. Just as in earlier times the open assembly of the citizens had authority to issue regulations, to approve or reject proposals of the executive on expenditures and to elect members of government, so too today the people is given authority to decide on certain issues according to a procedure regulated by the Constitution and by legislation. All organs participate in governing the country: the people, the Parliament, the Federal Council and the Federal Court. Based on this popular legitimacy the executive can count on broad support from the people when it implements laws. This enhanced legitimacy makes it easier to administer the law and to govern the country.

Constitutional mandate for Parliament and executive

The right of the citizens to participate in the political decision making process has important implications for the position of political parties. Unlike in parliamentary democracies, the parties do not carry a specific mandate to govern the country. Rather, political parties are groups which exercise limited legislative power within the framework of the popular mandate expressed through constitutional referendums. They inform and support the executive to find the necessary majority in a referendum, or as parties not represented in the executive they may point out discontent within the population. The executive thus is not embedded in a coalition of parties or in the parliamentary majority, rather it is responsible for executing its constitutional, legislative and budgetary mandate.

No parliamentary opposition

A division between the governing parliamentary majority coalition and the parliamentary opposition in the sense of a parliamentary democracy would not make sense in Switzerland, since the executive can always take into account proposals and suggestions of the parties not represented in the executive. Thus even the parties not represented in the government contribute to the political acceptance by the population of governmental measures. In addition, the 'opposition' does not have to force new elections; it can achieve its political aims with the instruments of direct democracy – something that is not possible for a minority in the Westminster system. If the majority of the people gives approval to a proposal of the executive however, the opposing parties will have lost the political ground on the relevant issue for the time being. The legitimacy given by the voting citizens is irrevocable for a certain period. Minority parties then have to seek alternative means by which to achieve their ends, as open opposition to the will of the people is not a successful political strategy.

Decline of the power of the parties

The regular use of the instruments of direct democracy leads to a decline in the power of the parties. Contrary to other political systems, the political parties concentrate more on the selection and support of good politicians than on concrete political issues. If citizens wish to influence issues, they do not have to rely on parties. They can rather influence Swiss policies using the instruments of referendum and initiative. Citizens can set up committees for a referendum, or they can try to win the support of business associations or NGOs for their causes and thus gain substantial support for their referendum or initiative.

Separation of powers between people, Parliament and executive

The division of sovereignty between the people, Parliament and the executive accords with the tradition of Swiss constitutional philosophy. On the other hand, it has not been possible in Switzerland to fully implement the classical concept of a horizontal separation of powers between the legislature, the executive and the judiciary. In particular, the people has not been prepared to surrender its right in relation to all matters to have the final word as the highest authority and ultimate source of legitimacy, except with regard to constitutional initiatives which violate international *jus cogens*.

Integrative function of the executive

The broad representation of the different popular political tendencies and thus the broad support for the executive amongst the population gives the executive strong powers of integration. Often the people even have a patriarchal relationship with the executive and in particular with their 'special representatives' within the executive. Both at the cantonal level and the federal level, governments and their individual members are expected to be above party politics. They are supposed to pursue and realise the common good. This special position of the executive is made even more important by the fact that, contrary to most other European states, the legitimacy of the executive in Switzerland has never been derived from the grace of God. The legitimacy of oligarchic dominion was always founded upon the people, which of course was aware of its limited (in Catholic cantons, bound by God) sovereignty. This foundation has enabled the establishment of a sophisticated and structured political power and at the same time has prevented the centralisation of state sovereignty in one branch of government.

Taxation and participation of the people

Today, this people's sovereignty or legitimacy is particularly evident in questions of taxation. At the federal level and in most of the cantons, the imposition of new taxes and in part even increases in existing taxes depend on the approval of the people. Tax decisions, which in other countries are made only by the executive and parliament, are in Switzerland entrusted to the people. As a consequence, the executive and the parliament have to justify their performance in order to win popular support in the referendum. The members of parliament cannot isolate themselves from the people and enact revenue-raising measures to further their own interests. Parliament is subject to the same control as is the executive. The performance and services of the state have to bring a marked or at least recognisable benefit to the citizens, if the government wants to ensure that its tax proposal will be supported by the people in a referendum.

Four-fifths democracy

However, one should not overlook also the deficiency of popular sovereignty in Switzerland. Today around 20 per cent of the population of Switzerland is made up of foreigners. These foreigners are denied political rights (with some exceptions at the cantonal and municipal levels). How in a globalised world can one legitimise a state based on democratic popular sovereignty, when this sovereignty is limited to 80 per cent of the population?

7.2.3 Sovereignty of Powers Beyond the State

The state as façade

In most modern revolutionary states it is difficult to ascertain who is the real bearer of sovereign power. The constitutionally installed government often is not able to make decisions as the final instance, the members of parliament are controlled by powers external to parliament and voters, and the formally independent courts have in reality to serve powers beyond the state. The constitutionally established organs are only façades, to simulate the legitimacy of rational state power. Actual sovereignty is withdrawn from these organs, and is exerted by powers external to the constitution.

In some states, Marxist-Leninist doctrine serves as a theoretical basis for this conception of the state. According to this perspective, the state is a product of class struggle and of the domination of the bourgeois class, and must ultimately be replaced by a classless society. However, such goals can only be achieved by force under the guidance of the Communist Party. During the transitional phase from exploitative bourgeois state to the classless society, the Communist Party has to, make use of an alibi-constitution. This constitution installs the classical constitutional branches of government, so that those organs may provide a façade of legitimacy whilst actually serving the Party, which uses the old instruments of the class-state to transform it into the classless society.

Powers external to the constitution play a central role as bearers of real sovereignty not only in socialist countries, but also in theocratic states. Such states also build a constitutional façade of classic organs of state (executive, parliament, courts), whilst the actual control of these powers is in the hands of external powers that cannot be rationally legitimised and that are unaccountable to the people.

7.2.3.1 Communist Constitutions

Sovereignty of the Party

The communists learned certain lessons from the French Revolution. The young MARX for instance was strongly influenced by the ideas of ROUSSEAU. In particular, the intellectual organiser LENIN saw from the beginning that the Russian revolution could only be achieved by the unconditional realisation of the dictatorship of the proletariat guided by the Communist Party. On the dictatorship of the proletariat, he wrote in 1906: "Dictatorship ... means unlimited power based on force, and not on law" (V. I. LENIN, *Collected Works*, Vol. 10). LENIN was firmly of the opinion that the proletariat could not liberate itself without destroying the state apparatus of the bourgeoisie. The final goal, the withering away of the state, would only be realised after a period of transition. In contrast to the anarchists (e.g. MICHAEL BAKUNIN, 1814–1876), LENIN believed that the transition to a truly democratic society of communist character and persuasion could only be achieved with the help of a powerful state ruled by a dictator.

Dictatorship of the proletariat

In order to suppress the resistance of the exploiters, it is necessary to have a transition period (of unknown duration) of dictatorship of the proletariat, which unlike all previously known state forms will be a dictatorship of the vast majority of society over the remaining propertied classes. Initially, LENIN gave scant consideration to the question of who would lead and represent this ruling majority. Only later he insisted that the proletariat has to be guided by the Party and that the dictatorship of the proletariat has to be a dictatorship of the Party. "But the dictatorship of the proletariat cannot be exercised through an organisation embracing the whole of that class ... It can be exercised only by a vanguard that has absorbed the revolutionary energy of the class" (V. I. LENIN, 'The Trade Unions, the Present situation and Trotsky's Mistakes', 1920, *Collected Works* Vol. 32).

Liberty in the service of the revolution

If the communist ideologists such as MARX, BAKUNIN, PROUDHON, LASSALLE as well as LENIN and LEO TROTSKY (1879–1940) still defended the ideals of the liberal state during the time when they were still a minority – MARX wrote in early times against the German censorship laws – this all changed after the revolution and their assumption of state power. "Earlier on we said that if we took power, we intended to close down the bourgeois newspapers. To tolerate the existence of these papers is to cease being a socialist" (W. I. LENIN, Speech on the Press at a Meeting of the All-Russia Central Executive Committee, 4 November 1917, *Collected Works* vol. 26). "[W]e shall not allow ourselves to be deceived by such high-sounding slogans as freedom, equality and the will of the majority … At the present time, when things have reached the stage of overthrowing the rule of capital all over the world, or at all events in one country... we say that all those who in such a political situation talk about "freedom in general", who in the name of this freedom oppose the dictatorship of the proletariat are doing nothing more nor less than aiding and abetting the exploiters, for unless freedom promotes the emancipation of labour from the yoke of capital, it is a deception" (W. I. LENIN, Speech to the First All-Russia congress on Adult Education, 19 May 1919, *Collected Works* volume 29). Separation of powers also has no place in a communist state. Laws, decrees and judgments are to serve the proletariat. "The courts must not ban terror... but must formulate the motives underlying it, legalise it as a principle, plainly, without any make-believe or embellishment." (W. I. LENIN, letter to D. I. KURSKI, 17 May 1922, *Collected Works* volume 33).

Trotsky

Like LENIN, TROTSKY firmly supported the dictatorship of tyranny, following the principle 'if it has to be war, then war it is'. According to him, the Paris Commune lost its battle in the French Revolution because it was based on a sentimental humanism. "... it can be said with complete justice that the dictatorship of the soviets became possible only by means of the dictatorship of the party" (L. TROTSKY, *Terrorism and Communism* (1920), Chapter 7). "As for us, we were never concerned with the Kantian-priestly and vegetarian-Quaker prattle about the "sacredness of human life". We were revolutionaries in opposition, and have remained revolutionaries in power. To make the individual sacred we must destroy the social order which crucifies him" (L. TROTSKY, *Terrorism and Communism* (1920), chapter 4). Unlike LENIN, TROTSKY had an answer to the unavoidable question of which is the right party to implement the dictatorship: "This idea is dictated by a purely liberal conception of the course of the revolution. In a period in which all antagonisms assume an open character, and the political struggle swiftly passes into a civil war, the ruling party has sufficient material standard by which to test its line of action, without the possible circulation of Menshevik papers. Noske crushes the communists, but they grow. We have suppressed the Mensheviks and the social revolutionaries – and they have disappeared. This criterion is sufficient for us" (TROTSKY, *Terrorism and Communism,* Chapter 7). Next to this hard communist line, one can also find representatives who support a more humane communism.

Transition to anarchy

As a consistent opponent of any state structure, BAKUNIN argues for the withering away of the state and the fulfilment of the end-goal, that is, anarchy, without a period of transition. "A society liberated from the state and from privilege will not only be better: it is also the only society that accords with human nature and the general laws of life, that is spontaneous and creative and suffers no restrictions" (MIKHAIL BAKUNIN, *Die revolutionäre Frage: Föderalismus, Sozialismus,*

Antitheologismus, Münster 2005, p. 62 (translated from the German by the authors/ translator)). Anarchy is not only an ideal; it is also the fulfilment of the natural destiny of human beings.

However, this ideal should not be forcibly imposed on the people. It must already lie dormant in its soul; the people does not need teachers, who create the ideal for it, but revolutionaries, which arouse it from its slumber. According to BAKUNIN, the abolition of the state does not lead to the abolition of all human cooperation and of all other forms of organisation. It will only lead to situation whereby, through small autonomous communes, every decision is made from the bottom up and every person has absolute liberty.

Dictatorship of workers and peasants according to the Chinese Constitution

In the early constitutions of China, the leading position of the party was explicitly prescribed. The President of the central committee of the Communist Party is Commander-in-Chief of the army of the People's Republic of China. Article 16 of the Constitution of 1975, which determined the powers of the National People's Congress, began with the words: "The National People's Congress is the highest organ of state power, under the leadership of the Communist Party of China."

Transition to pluralistic democracy

This explicit subjection of the Parliament to the party has been removed in the new Constitution. Unlike the old Constitution of the USSR, the Communist Party of China has no constitutional claim to propose candidates for elections into the National People's Congress. The members are elected by the people's congresses of the provinces in secret ballots.

Virtue of patriotism

According to Article 1 of the current Constitution, "the People's Republic of China is a socialist state under the people's democratic dictatorship led by the working class and based on the alliance of workers and peasants". Whilst the previous constitution installed the Communist Party as the leading organ of the entire people of China (Art. 2: "The Communist Party of China is the core leadership of the whole Chinese people. The working class exercises leadership over the state through its vanguard, the Communist Party of China"), this leading position of the party can no longer be found in the current Constitution. According to Article 24 however, it remains the responsibility of the state to educate people in communism:

Art. 24 "(2) The state advocates the civic virtues of love of the motherland, of the people, of labour, of science, and of socialism; it educates the people in patriotism, collectivism, internationalism, and communism and in dialectical and historical materialism; it combats capitalist, feudal, and other decadent ideas."

7.2.3.2 The Sovereignty of the Koran

The Koran as legal code

The preamble to the Constitution of Tunisia of June 1959 begins with the words "In the name of God, the Compassionate and Merciful ..." Article 1 declares: "Tunisia is a free State, independent and sovereign; its religion is Islam, its language is Arabic, and its form is the Republic". Also Morocco declares in its preamble its adherence to the principle of an Islamic state. This declared belief in Islam is found in almost all constitutions of states with a Muslim majority. Whether republican, monarchic or socialist, the Muslim state deduces its legitimacy from God, from Islam and more precisely from the Koran. God is considered to be the real law-maker. Just as Moses and Jesus had to proclaim the laws of God, so too Mohammed proclaimed the unalterable and universally binding rules of God. Mohammed was sent not to make new laws, which would apply to certain people or to part of humanity, but in order to confirm the original truth and authenticity of the previous proclamations and at the same time to pronounce for humanity the true universal and definitive law, which has been determined by God for mankind: Islam. This prophetic proclamation is written down in the Koran. This code of laws not only contains prescriptions in relation to the private life of men but also in relation to the regulation of human communities.

Sunnah – Ijma

These rules have been further developed and elaborated by the Sunnah. The Sunnah contains all the rules that can be ascribed to the tradition of the prophet, as every word of the prophet can in some way be attributed to God. Apart from the Sunnah and the Koran there is a third source of Islamic law, the Ijma. The Ijma is the expression of the consensus of the Islamic community, which is formulated by the most capable members of this community. If unforeseen cases arise and have to be resolved, they must be judged by the whole community, that is, by those members of the community who have sufficient knowledge and ability to interpret the holy texts. Does there lie herein a starting point for a democratic understanding of the Muslim community? Could all these knowledgeable personalities be united in an open assembly or must they be elected like members of parliament in a constitutional democracy and make decisions on the basis of majority vote? This problem was recognised in early times, and it was agreed that the Ijma could only be developed by a small group of scholars on the basis of unanimous decisions.

Who appoints the Caliph?

As the prophet was sent by God in order to proclaim the laws and the lessons of God, the people must completely submit to him. The people is obliged to obey the prophet chosen by God. The successor to the prophet is the Caliph. But how is the Caliph to be selected? In the Islamic world there are different answers to this question. According to the orthodox theories, the Caliph has to be chosen by the

Prophet himself and by his family. Others propose hereditary succession. For the Kharijites, there is neither hereditary succession nor family privilege. They are of the opinion that the community has to elect the most worthy and dignified person as Caliph. Another school of thought advocates the selection of the Caliph on the basis of the testament of his predecessor. In practice, the first Caliphs were chosen in a manner similar to the election of clan leaders, by a council of elders. It was thereby a form of gerontocracy. With the later expansion of his power, the Caliph reserved the right to choose his own successor through his testament.

The position of the Caliph

What are the powers and functions of the Caliph? The Caliph has to preserve Islam in its original form. He has to conquer the non-believers, defend the territory against foreign invaders and establish and maintain the necessary armies. One important power or competence however is lacking: The right to enact new laws. He is only empowered to receive, apply and interpret legislation. The only laws he can make are administrative regulations.

Religion and state in Islam

Once the Caliph is in office, he can as the highest sovereign, monarch or despot exercise absolute powers. According to theory, he explains and interprets the Koran, but in practice he exerts uncontrolled and absolute authority. He is not only the highest worldly authority, but also the highest spiritual leader of the people. This relationship between religion and state leadership prevents, contrary to the occident, the gradual secularisation of the state. State and Islam are and remain united. After some time, the Sultan as military leader separated gradually from the Caliph and began to govern the people independently. The Sultan however always derived his legitimacy from the Caliph. As a result, he did not limit his authority to worldly matters but also wanted to participate in decision making on spiritual issues. Thus, the increasingly important institution of the Sultan did not result in any separation between spiritual and worldly matters.

Legitimacy of the Caliphate

The legitimacy of the Caliphate can be found in the Koran. In the chapter of Sad XXXVIII it says: "We have made you a Caliph on earth; judge then between men with truth, and follow not lust." To whatever extent the rule of the Sultan is established, it has to be legitimised by the Caliphate.

States without territory

Apart from the dispute over the question of whether the Caliph should be democratically elected, or selected based on the testament of his predecessor or based on family privileges, the fact that according to the Koran there can only be one Caliph has led to irresolvable conflicts and disputes within the Islamic world. Through its separation from the church the European state found independence. However, in

Islam there was no concept of a territorially based legitimate sovereign state. Within the Islamic world there was and is even today only one basis for the legitimacy of state power: Islam. It is obvious that the division of political power among several states within Islam was necessarily the cause of irresolvable conflicts between several Sultans. Within this context, the establishment of a territorial state in the European sense and the development of a secularised international law binding sovereign states were not possible. Nation- and state-building are thus largely artificial, transitory and not covered by the legal system of the Islamic world. The fact that the various states within the Islamic world belong to different schools of Islamic thought does nothing to solve this problem, but is rather a source of additional tensions. The traditional natural law system marked by the Koran does not permit a legislative system in the modern, rational sense. The Koran and the other customary laws guide men and rulers and show them the way to be followed. The only power left to the state is its competence to interpret the laws, but it cannot modify them. The concepts of democratic legislation, separation of powers and the rule of law are foreign to this world of thought. A state marked by traditional laws need only concern itself with how to implement them and how those who have to apply them should be selected. The guidance of rulers by the people through law, the obligation of rulers to follow binding decisions of the courts – these principles cannot be easily inserted into the Islamic concept of law.

In 1925, ALI ABD AL RAZIK developed a theory that would enable a separation between state power and religion. He tried to prove that the authority of the previous prophets did not depend on their divine mission, but his theory was rejected by orthodox Muslims. However, the idea of a worldly, rational sovereignty legitimising political power seems to slowly be gaining support in the Islamic world, as some modern constitutions in Islamic states demonstrate. The Turkish Constitution marked the first step in this direction. In 1928 under MUSTAFA KEMAL (ATATÜRK), Article 2 of the Constitution, which declared Islam as the state religion, was repealed, and in 1937 a new Article 2 of the Constitution expressly declared Turkey a secular state. Article 2 of the current Constitution of Turkey declares "The Republic of Turkey is a democratic, secular and social state". The decision of Turkey to become a member of the European Union increases the hope for a better understanding between occident and orient. One cannot foresee the future, but these developments may enable the integration of the rule of law in a completely different tradition.

It can hardly be assumed that this secularisation of the state, which in Europe spanned centuries and was linked with bloody religious wars, will in the Islamic world simply occur overnight. Setbacks, controversies and tensions cannot be avoided. It is important however, that a basis for the legitimacy of the state and political power can be found which enables, apart from religion, the establishment of an independent political authority. At the forefront of this secularised theory of state is, as in Europe, the social contract. As some strains of Islam already contain democratic elements such as the election of the Caliph and, as in the early Arab philosophy, the idea of communities controlling political power, it is possible that a new concept of the legitimacy of political power might emerge which is embedded within the roots of the Arab and Islamic philosophical tradition. However, such theories will face the difficult challenge of overcoming the Islamic principle of predestination. Whoever believes in the predestination of human fate will not be able to accept that society may be designed by rational state legislation.

7.2.4 *The States of Central and Eastern Europe in Transition*

7.2.4.1 The Specific Characteristics of Eastern-European States before the Fall of Communism

i. The Fundament of an Authoritarian Political Regime: Autocracy as Governmental System

Unconstituted basis of political authority

All communist states in Central and Eastern Europe were authoritarian political systems. This was a logical consequence of the fact that communism saw the state only as an instrument of the party's monopoly of power and did not permit any constitutional means of limiting or controlling this power. In an authoritarian political regime, one individual person (or a group of persons) can prevent political decisions which would threaten their interests and can promote or even order measures which support their interests. Power is unaccountable and uncontrollable. It is neither constituted nor limited, because the politically powerful person can disregard any limits that are in place. In the case of communist systems, this 'somebody' is the communist party. As however the party is strictly controlled and ruled by a tight leadership, the central committee and within the central committee the general secretary or leader of the party controls the entire potential for despotic tyranny.

Unlimited power of the party leadership

The power of the party to permanently and systematically influence the results of the political process included *ex ante* as well as *ex post* control over the entire society. The party leadership as the actual power-holder was able to determine and control the political process, including the content of the process and its results. The party leadership was always in a position to overturn the result of a political process at its whim.

Goal-oriented democracy as a basis for legitimacy

Whilst the constitutional state of the 19th Century had liberated itself from the divine rule of kings and replaced it with the legitimacy of a constitution based on popular sovereignty, communism re-established the absolute but this time secularised legitimacy of the ruler (communist party) over the people and the state.

The identity of the position of the power-holder as leader of the party and ruler of state and society was clear, as the effective power-holder alone could define the legitimate goals of the society and of state authority. The 'real-socialist' democracy was based on the assumption that the monopoly of the communist party to represent and make decisions for the people would be able to achieve the goals of the society without any further control. And it was these goals which ultimately legitimised the supposedly progressive power-monopoly of the party. The democratic process was permanently perverted, because the process was always subordinated to the socialist goal, which alone had legitimacy.

The fundamental ideological goal of communism is the emancipation of man in the universal sense. The working class is the historical subject of this epochal process of emancipation, and the communist party is its legitimate representative, which alone knows and therefore is able to decide what is good for the working class. Consequently, only the party can determine whether a constitutional system and its political foundation are democratic. Relevant is only whether the results of the state policy accord with the declared goals.

ii. Structural Differences between Communist States and Constitutional Democracies

No demos

In a communist state there is no demos. The nation only has value in so far as it can be used as an instrument to serve the party. If it is used to serve the interests and goals of the party, the nation can contribute to the superficial legitimacy of state structures. In the communist nation-state, all men – of course under the leadership of the party – are united by the universal demand for the emancipation of the working class. The people must pursue this goal. The 'Nation' is integrated into an ideologically exclusive value system, which represents itself as universal.

Sovereignty of the party

For this reason, the communist society is not a community in the modern sense. There is no democratic sovereignty that could serve as the fundament of state institutions. The communist 'state' is therefore not a modern state, as it cannot be constituted as constitutional democracy. The state is a façade in order to feign legitimacy. The real holder of sovereignty is the party. The party wields absolute and completely unaccountable power. The political decision making process is controlled by the party, not by the state. Even the legal system and the judiciary are exclusively in the service of the party. Courts are established and judges appointed at the whim of the party, which can remove them at any time. In all cases which may have a direct or indirect effect on the power-monopoly of the party, the courts interpret and apply the law in the interest of the party. The valid 'law' and the state structure prescribed by the constitution are ultimately marginalised to a shadowy existence.

Law and constitution as facade

Consequently, the law in general and the constitution in particular must in a communist state perform inherently contradictory functions. They have to generate a parallel, fictive, simulated reality, which serves to simultaneously legitimise and conceal the real goals and power structures. The possibility of this parallel and feigned reality creeping into and influencing the actual reality has to be strenuously avoided. The legal system is finally also misused in order to cover up the effective reality of power structures and to protect them from politically 'inadmissible' influences. The law both creates the façade and protects the party leadership that hides behind it.

Mutatis mutandis the constitution should create the legitimacy of the identity between the governing and the governed and feign it through positive law, and on the other hand, it has to make sure that all institutions which transpose this identity into reality and which could empower the governed remain weak and powerless.

The party as the constitution making power (pouvoir constituant)

The actual constitution maker is the party. The party decides in the background on the content of the constitution. The official and publicly visible constitution making organ merely carries out what the party has prescribed: thus the system contains an immanent discrepancy between the constitution-giving and the constitution-passing power.

Political stability is not guaranteed by the constitution, but rather only by the party. The party will continuously modify and adapt the constitution in order to strengthen and expand the scope of its powers. The party is even in the position to preserve its power by permanently violating the constitution. The deficit of constitutional stability is immanent to the system. The constitution is constantly and consciously violated. The *breach of the constitution* is part of the system. Moreover, the system is characterised by permanent *constitutional change. Praeter* and *contra constitutionem* the laws, ordinances, decrees and judgments applying the constitution give way and deviate from the constitution. In summary, one could agree with HANNAH ARENDT, that the *constitution becomes the fundament for lawlessness and injustice.* Absolute power does not exist because of the law, which guarantees legal security, it is rather characterised by a *law in constant change.* The goal of the constitutional policy is the preservation of power within an ever changing environment.

Constitution in constant change

Mutatis mutandis the constitution is in constant motion or in a process of constant modification. Its function is not legally to stabilise the system, but to change and redefine it continuously: what yesterday was constitutional, is today again already unconstitutional. Absolute power of course is not declared as naked arbitrary power, rather, it is given apparent justification because it is in the service of the 'law of history' which realises justice. Thus, the law of history determined by the party becomes the real source of authority!

The constitution is not a basic law in its real sense, which limits state power with legal prescriptions. It is rather a *tool of power in the 'realpolitik' sense,* which serves to retrospectively guarantee legality of political decisions that the party has already made.

Constitutional revision without need for justification

In the former communist states, the party as the effective constitution giver could amend the constitution at whim, because it did not have to justify its decisions as legitimate constitutional modifications. It did not have to argue that the goal of the revision was legitimate; it did not have to demonstrate that the valid procedure for amendment had been observed. It could in fact disregard the amendment procedures. And finally, it did not have to prove whether and to what extent the aim of the constitutional modification could even be realised.

The constitution was therefore merely a positive legal instrument with which to feign for instance the ideologically proclaimed self-governing democracy in Yugoslavia, or to simulate a foundation of legitimacy for the dictatorship of the proletariat in other socialist states of Central and Eastern Europe.

iii. The Communist understanding of Nation

As already mentioned, according to the communist tradition the nation did not represent a political concept. The nation is not a unifying factor; only the communist party is unifying. The nation is only used as the totalitarian variant of an ethnic nation led by the party: as such it becomes a predestined ethnic collective unit that stands above the individual. The nation does not involve the realisation of democratic pluralism in order to further the national interests; it remains rather an additional collective basis for legitimacy of the quasi-state power of the party. In addition to the proletariat, the ethnic-nation must also serve towards the realisation of the totalitarian political goals and the collective interests. The party assumes the role of making authoritarian determinations over any ethno-national conflicts and opposing interests.

Communist federations

For the communist, multiethnic federations, this led to the consequence that the equality of the ethnic nation had absolute priority over any equal rights for individuals. The unequal treatment of individuals should to some extent be equalised and compensated for by the equal treatment of the ethnic-nation – and the equality of the nation necessarily entailed the inequality of individuals. Communism by definition cannot tolerate the citizen. Thus, all communist federations recognised the ethnic-nations and their mother republics as the only other bases for the legitimacy of the federal state aside from the ideological foundation of the socialist system. All constitutional questions and controversies at the federal level thereby inherently contained the potential to intensify into irresolvable inter-ethnic conflict as soon as the tyranny of the party imploded. The common state had no real resources in terms of identity or legitimacy that it could employ to overcome or mitigate such conflicts. Consequently, all former communist federations had to be dissolved after the decline of communism. After the Communist Party lost its claim to authority over all matters within the federation, the exclusionary ethnic nation took over the claim to leadership.

Right to secession

Thus, the constitutions of the socialist 'federations' were the first to provide for an ambiguous understanding of the right to self-determination as a right to ethnic self-determination and ethnic secession.

In the Constitution of the USSR of 1977 for example, the right to self-determination including the unilateral right to secession was explicitly recognised. Although Yugoslavia did not expressly guarantee the right of self-determination in its Constitution of 1974, the so-called 'basic principles' made reference to the right of self-determination of the ethnic nation and its republics as a basis for the legitimacy of the federation.

National consciousness against the state

Historical events have also substantially contributed *to the exploitation of the issue of the Nation*. The national movements in the multi-nation regions in Central and South-eastern Europe developed historically within the framework of the great empires, which they regarded as prisons: the Austro-Hungarian and Ottoman Empires and Tsarist Russia.

In contrast to the German Nation, the national consciousness in Central and Eastern Europe is not developed within and by the state, but rather is characterised by opposition to the existing state. The existing state is the foreign and divisive institution which impedes the development of one's own cultural personality (THEODOR SCHIEDER, *Nationalismus und Nationalstaat*, Göttingen 1991).

Consequently, the modern nation-state can only be constructed by separation and secession. As proclaimed by THOMAS MASARYK, internal democratic freedom can only be achieved through external liberty. Compared to nationalism based on unification, the nationalism based on separation and secession from the 'state prison' of the communist state has much more emotional power.

Federations as communities held together by force without pre-political legitimacy

The new ethno-nations fought vigorously against the straitjacket of the former socialist federations. The ethnically homogeneous socialist states needed to establish the foundations for democratic pluralism, which in the communist system was structurally and inherently impossible. The three socialist federations not only had to fight their way towards democratic, pluralistic – that is, modern – political legitimacy, but they also lacked pre-political ethnic legitimacy. Rather, ethnic identity marked the dominant borderlines along which the political community was split. At the same time, it became the basis for intra-ethnic political mobilisation and homogenisation. In other words: The decline of all socialist federations had structural causes and was ultimately 'pre-programmed'.

Right after the fall of the old regimes, it was clear that a new democratic and multiethnic state could not be established within the original borderlines of the federal state. These societies were torn apart by different ideological camps to the extent that it was impossible to achieve a democratic consensus. The structural tensions between the new liberal claims to achieve legitimacy based on an open and inclusive democratic procedure with guaranteed rules of the game on one side, and the permanent 'ethnification' of political conflicts on the other side, largely explain why all three ex-communist federations (Czechoslovakia, Yugoslavia and the USSR) had to be dissolved.

7.2.4.2 Constitutional Aspects of the Process of Disintegration

i. Introduction

Different roles of the constitution in the transition process

In principle, one has to distinguish between states in which the territory and therefore statehood itself were uncontested, and those states in which – because of their multi-ethnic character – the unity and thereby the very legitimacy and existence of the state itself were fundamentally disputed. If the territory and the state were uncontested, the constitution making process was simultaneously a process to democratise and legitimise the state authority. If the state and the territory were in question however, debates on the constitution became disputes on the legitimacy of the state itself. According to whether the existence of the state as such was legitimate or not legitimate, the constitution had a completely different role and function in the process of transition. Disputes over the constitution could contribute to the consolidation of democracy, or at the other end of the spectrum could lead to the dissolution of the state.

States with undisputed territory

The so-called ethnically homogeneous states were legitimate as states. The territory was not contested and the state community was undisputed as a pre-existing territorially-based unit upon which to base the social contract or popular sovereignty. What was not legitimate was the authoritarian regime. The population had suffered under the arbitrary authoritarian rule of the party. However, as states in the pre-modern sense they were legitimate, because – as for example in Poland and Hungary – they were largely ethnically homogeneous communities. Thus, whilst in these states the regime imploded, the state as such was not destroyed.

Multi-ethnic federations

Multi-ethnic federations on the other hand, suffered from regime crises as well as crises of the state. Both as authoritarian societies and as multi-ethnic communities forced together, they lacked any basic legitimacy. The crisis of the political authority of the regime then triggered a real crisis of the state and its territory, because the state and its territory were identical with the former regime. Thus, for the various ethnic nations the state became the symbol of the enemy.

ii. States with uncontested Statehood

The constitution becomes an instrument of democratic consensus

With the decline of the former social and political order, the constitution and above all the constitution making process acquire a fundamental importance. The new state will be established and designed through the constitution and the constitution making process. The constitution becomes the instrument of the new, emerging democratic consensus and the content of this new consensus will have to be defined by the new constitution.

During communist rule, the party used the constitution making process and constitutional revision to constantly redefine the concept of the state. As a consequence, the most important political conflicts unleashed by the dissolution of communism were fought out in the arena of constitution making. The constitution was expected to find solutions for those disputes. Constitution making was seen to be the way to *achieve a new democratic legitimacy in the modern sense.* In other words, it had to fix the democratic content of the transitional arrangements negotiated and agreed with the old power-holders (at the roundtable).

Roundtables

The '*peaceful transition*' (e.g. Hungary) began without an ideology of its own. People were mainly interested in reconnecting their constitutional culture to the (in no way idealised) West-European tradition. This 'catch up revolution' (HABERMAS) took a constitutional course – and that was essentially the course of the old constitution. Thus, there was no new constitution making assembly established which could have led the transition process. The transition process manifested itself at the constitutional level with repeated amendments of the old constitution, made according to the amendment procedure provided by the former constitution. Constructive majorities were found in the representatives of the people, elected under the old regime.

The content of the proposals however was worked out at the so-called '*round-tables*'. The roundtables that were created in all of these countries in transition did not identify themselves as a 'government emerging from the revolution', but rather as the *representation of unorganised civil society* in relation to the power-holders previously elected by the people. The legitimacy of such roundtables was based on the broad consensus of the population. They had de facto the status and the power of a *pouvoir constituant*.

The central political concept at the heart of the constitutional amendments was aimed at the sustainable legal protection of human rights. Inevitably, such concept brought the constitution into the centre of the transition (ULRICH K. PREUSS, 'Die Rolle des Rechtsstaates in der Transformation postkommunistischer Gesellschaften' in *Rechtstheorie*, 1993, p. 181).

iii. States without Legitimacy

The collective of the ethnic nation becomes new basis for legitimacy

In multi-ethnic states, the crisis of the regime led not only to a new governmental system. The regime crisis was directly followed by the much more serious crisis of the state. The trigger was in most cases the dispute over the new constitution. Such disputes initiated the real process of dissolution.

The different ethnic communities regarded themselves, that is – the collective of the nation rather than individuals – as the real victims of the former communist regime. The state had stood in the service of the regime. The ethnic nations were victims at the mercy of the state. Thus, the state became the true symbol of the enemy of the nation. The nation on the other hand was idealised. Individual interests had to be sacrificed to the interest of the nation. The legitimacy of the state was replaced by the legitimacy of the nation. However, the nation had no democratic decision making process. The members of the nation thus remained subjects with no rights of democratic participation. Democracy was for the time being sacrificed to the right of self-determination of the nation. The nation took over the legitimacy of the state and split away from the mother-state as a still amorphous quasi-state.

Democracy and minorities: Victims of the majority nation

The new state became legitimate solely on the basis of the collective nation. The majority nation not only sacrificed democracy to the nation as the new fundament of legitimacy, but also sacrificed the rights of minorities. The majority nation saw minorities as a potential threat to the new state. As potential enemies, they needed to be excluded and oppressed. Thus, minorities felt even more victimised within the new state than they had under the old regime. The very existence of such minorities was threatened by the majority, which strived for national homogeneity in the interest of collective unity. The majority nation feared that the minorities would also seek to connect state identity with their own nation and thereby claim the legitimacy to secede from the majority nation or to join with other minorities to fight against the majority nation.

Human rights claims become a political pretext for minorities

Thus, minorities could not be satisfied simply with the guarantee of individual human rights or even with minority rights. A state held 'hostage' by the majority nation had no legitimacy to protect human rights. The disputes over human rights ultimately served to de-legitimise the state internationally and to internationalise the conflict. The minority nation considered itself as a collective nation with the right to self-determination and therefore to statehood, that is the right to participate as a state on the basis of the equal rights accorded to all nations.

Ethnification of constitutional conflicts

There was no basis for the establishment of a new federation, as there was no common identity and any foundation for federal loyalty had been lost.

Firstly, the federal structure was contested. Decisions of the federation were blocked. Every constitutional conflict became an ethnic conflict. In the course of constitutional crises and constitutional stalemates, the right to self-determination as an ethnically-based right to secession was claimed. In the process of negotiation no neutral mediator could be identified, because the conflict had led to an absolute friend-or-foe mentality. Any facilitator or mediator was immediately accused of supporting one side or the other. This friend-or-foe schema was even applied to the international community, and served to immediately disqualify neutral facilitators on the grounds of ostensible bias in favour of one of the parties. Within the state nobody could remain neutral because in the face of multi-ethnicity, unlike in ethnically homogeneous states, any sense of community was lost and could not be regained. Without the ideology of consensus, the multi-ethnic state remained nothing more than an *enforced community*.

Referendum on secession

As a consequence, the various nations (for example the republics in former Yugoslavia) organised referendums on the question of unilateral secession. These referendums contained mostly unclear and vague questions. They were based on the pure majority principle and took no account whatsoever of the interests of minorities. If the result of such popular vote was positive, the declaration of independence of the new state followed immediately.

International community

However, it was recognition of their statehood by the international community that enabled these states to become equal sovereign actors within the concert of nations, and to enjoy the protection of the Charter of the United Nations. With the recognition of statehood, attacks against the seceding nation, which would originally have been classified and handled as civil wars, became prohibited military interventions. This enabled the United Nations under Chapter 7 of the UN Charter to intervene in the conflict to protect world peace. Thus, by means of state recognition, the international community exercises great influence over these new developments, without however having any foundation of legitimacy for such role.

The newly created foreigners

With the birth of a new state there emerged completely new internal problems. Citizens of the former federation who now belonged to a minority nation within the new ethnically based state suddenly became foreigners without permission to reside in their homes, to work or to own land. Soldiers, who in the evening had gone to sleep as members of the army of their fatherland, suddenly woke up in enemy territory. Those soldiers who belonged to the new majority nation had out of loyalty to cross over to the new army. For this however, the former army considered them traitors or deserters. New customs borders had to be erected, passports needed to be reissued and diplomatic representation had to be established. What was formerly a minority dialect became a new state language.

7.2.4.3 The Social and Political Environment of Transition and the Problem of Transformability

i. The Goal of Democratic Transition/the Process of Liberalisation versus the Process of Democratisation

Goal: transformation of democracy

The aim of the democratic transition corresponds in principle to the liberal democratic model. According to the concept of the liberal democracy, the constitution establishes the rules of the game for the democratic procedure but makes no prescription in relation to the goals to be achieved. If one proceeds on the basis of this liberal interpretation of democracy, one should begin by making a distinction between liberalisation within an authoritarian system on one hand, and democracy on the other. However, the reality of the transition in Eastern Europe did not proceed in this way.

Liberalisation without multi-party system

The first phase involved liberalisation by granting individuals more liberties. This liberalisation however occurred without democratisation. Democracy as an open process was not permitted in this phase of the transition. The liberalisation was not *a democratic transition.* Indeed, one must still today question whether in the meantime liberalisation has actually led to a true democratic transition. The liberalisation was simply a new strategy, or better: it was a tactic of the power-holders to remain in power. Thus it was restricted to the creation of new political organisations and to the acceptance of pluralistic and contradicting interests, without in any way questioning the power of the party leadership as the final instance of authority. Liberalisation was a party-controlled process of opening up society, which left the essential character of the authoritarian regime intact.

Preconditions for democratic transition

One can only really speak of democratic transition in the true sense when the following preconditions are fulfilled or can be realised:

The old apparatus of the party must be dissolved as the apparatus of might and power. In place of the sovereignty of the party, new structures of authority must be constituted. Such structures need both to achieve democratic legitimacy and to be democratically accountable. Pluralism as a political principle must be translated into a constitutionally established multi-party system of government and thus be democratically recognised. Democracy as an open process must lead to rational and accepted solutions that reflect a political balance of different interests. The power-struggle needs to be fought with rational arguments in the public arena on a footing of equal resources and opportunities. The new democratic order thus has to meet the challenge of ensuring the new constitutional foundation of the state creates the conditions for the integration of its citizens. This makes the search for new constitutional concepts considerably more difficult.

The pre-communist legacy

(PREUSS) As the negative legacy of the pre-communist era, there is a re-emergence of the old conflicts and tensions which had divided the state and the society prior to the establishment of communism. These conflicts existed latently throughout the socialist period. But they were lacking legitimacy in the context of socialism and thus were kept quiet or were subtly suppressed. Now they emerge in new forms. Heritage in this sense is primarily ethnic, religious and cultural conflict.

ii. The 'Dilemma of Simultaneity'

In order for the Western European nation-state to develop into a modern state, three key conditions had to be met (cf CLAUS OFFE, *Der Tunnel am Ende des Lichts*, Frankfurt, 1994):

- The State question needed to be solved for all people living within the state, that is, the borderlines of the state needed to be recognised by everybody as legitimate state borders;
- Democracy had to be installed in place of the old monarchic principle of the divine authority of the King; and
- A social market economy based on private property had to be guaranteed.

Switzerland and Germany as counter-examples

In Switzerland for example, the dispute over democracy was mainly fought at the cantonal level in the 1830s. The territorial question was the subject of the

'Sonderbund' war and was solved in 1848 with the establishment of the new Swiss Confederation. The guarantee of a free market economy at the federal level was only introduced in 1874 by constitutional amendment. In Germany, the national question was at the centre of the war against France of 1870, democracy was introduced after World War I, and the guarantee of property and liberal fundamental rights were introduced in the new Basic Law after the Second World War. All states in Western Europe needed several decades in order to solve these central problems of territory, democracy and market economy.

Market economy, territory and democracy in the states of Eastern Europe

In the process of transition, the Eastern European states were expected simultaneously to solve the question of the state, to introduce democracy and to establish a free market economy. They were, to use the phrase coined by CLAUS OFFE, facing the *dilemma of simultaneity*. These three basic preconditions for any modern political system were realised in other states after revolutionary and often violent conflicts. These elements in other states had led, after a long process, to the development of a political party landscape appropriate to the respective system and tradition. The conflicts that necessarily emerge when such issues need to be solved affect the very existence of the state and the society. For this reason, it is almost impossible to solve all three basic issues of the state at the same time.

The *process of transition* therefore is connected to very high risks. It activates a revolutionary dynamic for the simultaneous alteration of the territory, economy and political system of the state. This historically unprecedented dynamic is initiated as a 'top-down revolution'. For such process there is no historical example, nor any revolutionary theory that could have provided relevant experience or principles to support the change. Instead, the relevant actors attempted to conceal their uncertainty and inexperience with fleeting verbal inventions of vague semantic content such as for example 'Glasnost', 'Perestroika', etc (PREUSS).

iii. What is Socio-politically Specific in the Eastern European Transition to Democracy?

If one compares the Eastern European transition to democracy with the transition processes in other countries after the Second World War, one can distinguish between three different categories of countries:

The democratisation of authoritarian regimes

Immediately after the Second World War, the transition to democracy in the three states of Italy, Japan and Western Germany manifested itself essentially as a process to achieve a modern post-war democracy. In the second group, one can count the Mediterranean democratisation processes of the 1970s in Greece, Spain and Portugal. Finally, in the 1970s and 80s we experienced the collapse of the authoritarian regimes in South America such as Argentina, Brazil, Chile and Paraguay.

In all of these examples, the democratisation of a formerly authoritarian regime was in the foreground. Market economy and territory were largely undisputed and thus not the subject of the state question.

Democracy, territory and economy

The transition that took place in the former socialist or communist countries was in many respects much more radical: in addition to the alteration of the political system, the territorial integrity of the state and the state structure were also in dispute. For this reason, one could not be content with the mere establishment of new governmental systems. The transition could not be reduced only to the issue of democracy. At the same time the economic system required fundamental change. Part of this change involved the difficult politically charged issue of private property, and in addition the issue of privatisation of state enterprises. After socialism came to an end, one could not be satisfied simply with establishing a new political and constitutional basis for a form of government. The relationship between state and society could not be modernised merely by reforming the government system. Without *reform of the economic* system, politics could not be democratised nor liberty re-established. It was imperative that the establishment of the market economy be on the agenda.

In the countries of Eastern and Central Europe one could thus observe a transformation on *three levels*: The establishment and construction of a *new nation-state identity*, the dispute over *constitution making* and constitutional politics generally, and finally the *founding of a new economic* system.

Lack of controllability

All of these countries suffer necessarily from a lack of governability. This lack of governability has to be accepted as a logical consequence of any transition to democracy. In France for example, it took 70 years until a stable democratic system could be established on the basis of the French Revolution. On the other hand, the governability and stability of a country are indispensable preconditions for a democratic transition. Accordingly, these states lack the necessary preconditions for a democratic transformation. Paradoxically they need at the same time to achieve the preconditions as well as the results of the transformation.

For this reason and in contrast to the western European states, which had made a gradual and 'normal' progression through the various stages of the process of state development from the nation-state to capitalism to democracy, the eastern European states facing revolutionary transition were confronted with three challenges simultaneously:

The issue of territory

With the issue of *territory*, the question of the existence of the state itself is raised. As we have seen, only if the three essential preconditions of people, territory and sovereignty are present one can define a polity as a 'state' in the normal sense. If the borders of the state are unclear, one cannot seriously struggle for democracy, as nobody knows which part of the population will participate in the democracy. Certainty of the majority of the population over the territory of the state is therefore the first and most important precondition for state building. Moreover, uncertainty over territory leaves any decision on the internal state structure completely open. Will the state be a federation or a unitary state? Should it be a confederation or a decentralised regional state? Who is part of the people and entitled to participate in the constitution making power? When these most elementary questions remain open, how can the rule of law, minority protection and a free market economy be realised?

The issue of democracy

With the *issue of democracy*, the claim of one party to have a political monopoly within the state is eliminated. At the same time, a constitutional democracy is constructed which has to prove itself immediately as a representative/procedural democracy, and which has to guarantee the rule of law (separation of powers in the sense of checks and balances as well as human rights) including the protection of minorities. The political reform consists of two steps: first individual rights and freedoms have to be guaranteed and protected, then the rights of democratic participation have to be realised. If one installs democracy without the protection of individual liberties, this would in the Eastern European context necessarily lead to a new form of authoritarian populism.

Market economy

With economic reform towards a *free market economy* connected with *private property rights*, not only is the legal system fundamentally changed, but also a new social system is founded. From a constitutional and public law standpoint, privatisation, deregulation and liberalisation including compensation, removal of subsidies and construction of a new social security network as well as fundamental tax reform must be introduced and regulated. In close connection to deregulation is also price reform, that is, the introduction of free, market-oriented prices, as well as the introduction of a banking and monetary system that is investment oriented and can meet the financial needs of the society.

The irreconcilable antagonism

Whilst the guarantee of individual liberties and the reform of the property system are interdependent, there is paradoxically an almost irreconcilable antagonism bet-ween democracy and the reform of property and market prices, because the primary effects of such economic reforms will be labour shortages and inflation. People do not want to wait until the 'blessings' of the market economy have reached all of them, and many will have to face increased disadvantages during the phase of transition. This is the core of the antinomy.

These growing disappointments and frustrations result in demands for a new type of democracy, which is not liberal but populist, and which can lead to the introduction of new authoritarian presidential dictatorships.

As a consequence of the simultaneity of reforms, and in contrast to the previous transition of Western European countries, the process of transition not only involves a huge initial burden of complex decisions (the risk of a strongly dynamic transition process) but it will also suffer from the mutually obstructive effects of contradictory claims. Political procedures and political actors will block each other, and potential solutions to political problems will also be mutually blocked. There is no light at the end of the tunnel, only darkness, and the political economy of patience will be overstrained.

Absence of an economic fundament of civil society

In order to enable the development of a representative democratic system, a minimum of autonomous economic development must be realised. This facilitates the emergence of competing interests from a system of social and political division of labour and builds the foundation for party pluralism. Only then can the constitutional democracy and a rational state authority be legitimised. As long however, as the economic fundament of a true civil society is absent, the massive political mobilisation of the population will only be possible on the basis of an ethnonationalistic or fundamentalist ideology.

Privatisation compared with authoritarian egalitarianism

On the flip side, the countries of Central and Eastern Europe cannot achieve economic liberalisation without democracy. As a result of the way in which it was established, the market economy that has emerged in Eastern Europe manifests itself – unlike its western counterpart – more as political capitalism than as economic capitalism. It is a form of capitalism that has been politically organised and promoted by reform-elites. These elites claim to represent the interests of the society. However, they cannot base such claims on the interests of an existing class of capitalist property owners. For this reason, the reform-elites need a democratic mandate which allows them to carry out privatisation against the political majority culture of authoritarian egalitarianism. However, as long as the new capitalism results predominantly in unemployment and poverty rather than welfare and prosperity, they cannot expect support for their economic policy from the democratic majority.

Freedom from fear

In the face of the somewhat chaotic conditions of the economic transformation crises in these countries, the fledgling liberal democratic political regimes and their constitutional orders can only be stabilised if, in addition to democracy and the market economy, social security is also institutionalised. This however is not possible without reform of the tax system, as only through such reforms will it be possible to generate the required revenue.

Without social security and without trust in the social institutions, the state and its authority will ultimately lack the necessary legitimacy. The people must be 'free from fear' in order to be able to trust that democratic procedures will protect rather than undermine their social well-being. Without such basic trust, the rule of law cannot be established. Only when economic development is accompanied by the general development of the common welfare will the preconditions exist for the consolidation of the democratic transition and the constitutional structures.

Teleological constitutions

Most constitutions of the transition in Eastern and Central Europe contain lists of promises and goals in relation to social rights. Social rights are constitutionally enshrined and guaranteed in many states and should, according to the will of the constitution maker, have priority over other rights. The basic core function of the constitution, namely to simultaneously establish and limit political power, changes: the constitution becomes an instrument for integration.

Whilst the policy of socialism was to provide universal social welfare, under the capitalist democratic system this policy was amended to provide for selective and retrospective welfare. Such welfare however had to be financed by taxes derived mainly from the profits of the market economy. This new logic of welfare policy leads to an immanent conflict between financial viability on one hand, and the goals of the constitution on the other.

Tension between procedural and substantial legitimacy

The transition should achieve the implementation of procedural democracy, as opposed to substantial democracy. The transition process suffers however from a lack of constitutionality, as procedural democracy presupposes that the rules of the game are not thrown into question. *In this transition process however, even the rules of the game have to be negotiated and adapted to the continuously changing requirements.*

Since in the countries of Central and Eastern Europe concepts of collective identity are dominant, there is an almost irresolvable tension between procedural and substantial legitimacy as well as a lack of constitutional stability. As long as the collective of the state-nation as the constituted entity of citizens has greater weight and significance than individual rights, the republican political culture and the constitutional patriotism inspired by this culture cannot be implemented. This ethno-nationalism threatens the rule of law and the democratic transition, and results in constant relapse into authoritarian, military, ethno-nationalist or presidential-populist systems.

Ethnification as political strategy

A thorough analysis of the ethnification of political systems and political conflicts (OFFE) in Eastern and Central Europe is essential if one wants to understand the tensions between the procedural legitimacy to which the constitution aspires and the actual substantial legitimacy of the democracy. Ethnicity is the strategy of many political elites which are embedded within the ethnicity of the nation. Ethnic identity, which is inherently exclusionary in relation to other ethnic groups, becomes the basis of demands for solidarity and obligations. Ethnicity simultaneously provides social integration and homogenisation of the society. The common good is that which is good for *us* (*but not for all*). Such reductionist policy is based on the assumption that ethnic identities are permanent, and also normatively more important and more valid than any other characteristics. Ethnic categories constitute the ultimate source for meaningful social relationships. Those categories ultimately determine rights and obligations, prescribe the content of solidarity to be observed within the community, and are the basis for the readiness of each member of the collective to sacrifice his interests to the interests of the collective.

7.2.4.4 Major Tendencies of the Post-socialist Constitutions

i. The New/Old Pouvoir Constituant

Constitution making as a factor to legitimise revolution

The 'peaceful transition' is not driven by values that could produce or substantiate the unity of the people. Nor is there any claim to the absolute sovereignty of a 'political nation' united by common values in the sense of a *pouvoir constituant*, which could be understood as a nation in the French sense. As the society is pluralistically dispersed and because the people does not consider itself as a unity, there is no intention of the society to impose the sovereign and homogeneous will of the people upon the state nor to use the unlimited constitution making power of the people to design the structure of the state according to a clear political strategy.

Thus, the heteronomous character of the revolution of 1989 (and lack of massive mobilisation of the people, even in Poland) led to the result that constitution making could not be conceived as an objective beyond party-interests. Constitution making did nevertheless substantially contribute to the legitimacy of the 'revolution'. One could even claim *that constitution making was a permanent interaction between a party politicised constitutional policy and a politicially constituted policy* (“*politique constitutionnelle politisée*” *and* “*politique constitutionnelle politisante*”)!

Constitution making thereby became a process of careful readjustment of the old constitutions to the new needs and realities. The constitutional revisions also took into account the various risks associated with a process of transition. Only in countries where the party succeeding the communist party had the political process under control, as in Romania and Yugoslavia (Serbia and Montenegro) and initially also Bulgaria, or in countries such as Croatia, Slovenia, Slovakia and Lithuania in which the new elite coalitions were strong enough to see their constitutional vision implemented, was it possible to undertake a complete revision of the constitution. But even in those cases, the continuity in the institutions of the new constitution was evident.

The new states created through secession had a particular incentive to install a completely new system of state institutions. And these nations made full use of these new possibilities. Within their preambles, some claimed to derive their legitimate statehood from pre-communist societies and polities (e.g. Croatia and Lithuania).

Two different processes of institution building

The construction of new institutions and the establishment of new constitutional orders occurred via two completely different political processes: In Hungary, Poland and Russia the new institutions were negotiated within a genuinely pluralistic process. In many states of the CIS (Community of Independent States) including Lithuania, Yugoslavia, Romania, Croatia, Bulgaria, Slovenia and Slovakia the new ideas were carried out by a single dominant political group. The more democratic and pluralistic the process was, as in Hungary and Poland, the less fundamental were the constitutional reforms. This apparent contradiction with regard to democratic pluralism and necessity to reform the system created by a dictatorial party, reveals that the pluralism of powers within a consensus driven democracy is only in the most exceptional case prepared to take the risk of fundamental reforms.

Participation of the people

The more comprehensive and fundamental the negotiations on the new constitutional order, the less the elites were ready to open the process to the direct participation of the people. During the democratic transition the elites did not allow enough time for a double participation of the people: the people did not participate prior to the process by electing a constitution making assembly, nor were they given the chance to participate at the end of the process via a constitutional referendum. On the other hand, there were cases such as Serbia (1990) and Romania (1992) where a real failure of legitimacy was retrospectively remedied through a referendum. However, mention should also be made of Russia, where a violent power struggle between the President and parliament was decided by a constitutional plebiscite, and where the referendum provided the only way out of the constitutional stalemate and also served as a means of de-legitimising the parliament.

In those systems in which ex-communists played an important role (Romania and Serbia) as well as in ethnically legitimised and homogeneous new states (Croatia), it was possible without great difficulties to make the change to a presidential democracy with a powerful head of state. In most other Eastern European systems, a rational parliamentary system was introduced in an attempt to stabilise the executive. The popular election of the president, the introduction of the constructive vote of no confidence, and the introduction of the collective responsibility of ministers served this goal.

Main goal of constitution making: effective government

The main goal of the constitution makers was to establish new institutions which were efficient and effective, and which had democratic legitimacy. The state organs needed to be embedded within the constitution and the state had to be governable. The main problem of constitution making was therefore to create the institutional preconditions for a new executive government, which was able to implement effective reform and at the same time build a broadly supported democratic consensus. But how could these partially contradictory requirements be realised in a process of transition that necessarily led to a social, political and economic instability? These concentrated and admirable efforts for the development of new constitutional foundations and for the improvement of the governability of the state often led in the end to the pseudo-legitimacy of a benevolent dictator.

Parliamentarism – presidentialism

The dispute between the parliamentary and the presidential system cannot be seen merely as a technical debate between two different constitutional alternatives or options. There are much more fundamental problems and demands at the root of this dispute. In fact, it relates to the actual substance of the 'new democracies'. Constitutions that install a strong head of state have effectively also decided in favour of a nationalist, plebiscitary legitimacy and against a rational, constitutionally democratic governmental system.

Moreover in fact, it is not really the constitutional arguments and motives that are the subject of debate, as:

- The system has often been tailored specifically for certain candidates;
- The powers of the head of the state are 'negotiated' against other political demands; and
- The negotiated compromise is usually based on a miscalculation.

Disputed hierarchy of the governmental branches

With the system of a 'double-headed' executive (head of state and head of government) a new trinity concept was built into the principle of checks and balances: Parliament – Executive – Head of State. The hierarchy of the branches of government was and remains disputed.

Human rights

In the first phase of constitution making, the ideology of negative constitutionalism in the *classical liberal sense* dominated the debate: The most important function of the constitution was to provide a legal basis for the protection of human rights in order to limit state powers. Consequently, the concept of the bill of rights as a catalogue of fundamental rights and the introduction of the constitutional court (as an institutional guarantee of human rights) played a significant role. As human rights stood at the centre of constitution making, and because they were to build the fundament for the legitimacy of the new state, the ideology underlying the constitution making process was focused on the principle of the tyranny of the majority. Other democratic systems were not even taken into consideration. It is for this reason one could even say that there was an 'over-legitimacy' of the constitutional court.

Four models of constitutional transition

Some countries, such as Estonia and Latvia, *re-installed the original constitution* that had been in force prior to the authoritarian regime, in order to be able to demonstrate a modest continuity of the democratic system and thus to brand the soviet period as an illegal and illegitimate act of violence.

A second group (the so called 'negotiated revolutions' – such as Hungary) *amended the previous early-socialist constitutions through partial revisions*, which in their original version still contained strong concessions to the bourgeois state under the rule of law.

A third group followed the route of *total revision*, which of course would in principle be inevitable in the case of a change of system.

When this was not possible, the transition was regulated – as in Poland in October 1992 – by a provisional order, which was labelled the 'small constitution'.

The role of constitutional jurisdiction

Some socialist states had introduced constitutional jurisdiction even before the collapse of communism (Yugoslavia in 1963 and Poland in 1982).

In the newer democracies of the first and second waves of the transition, constitutional jurisdiction exercised a strong stabilising effect. It also was one of the most important contributions to institution building for the transition after 1989 in Eastern and Central Europe.

Constitutional jurisdiction had a distinctive role in resolving disputes between governmental branches and organs. This was the case for example in Hungary, where the constitutional court had to adjudicate between the President and the government including the parliamentary majority. But also in Russia, the constitutional court had often to rule as 'umpire' between the President and the parliament.

Judicial activism

The principle upheld in various constitutional courts of 'judicial restraint' in relation to political questions is one that is only gradually and very slowly internalised. Initially, politicised judicial activism was the favoured approach of many courts.

Some fundamental decisions of the constitutional courts had to deal with the difficult and simultaneously decisive question of the function of the state under the 'rule of law' in the transitional phase from communist to post-communist society. How should the courts retrospectively handle the arbitrary decisions and criminal acts of the earlier regime? Is the court primarily obliged to pursue political justice or the rule of law? In March 1992, the Hungarian Constitutional Court declared as unconstitutional a draft law which sought to provide for the retroactive application of the criminal law to persons who had committed crimes for 'political reasons' in the period from 1945 to 1990, but who had not been punished for those crimes. The main issue here was the massacre after the 1956 revolution.

ii. The Role of the State under the Rule of Law in the Democratic Transformation of Post-Communist Societies

The Dilemma of the State Ruled by Law

The dilemma

The principle of the rule of law contains the same goals with regard to constitution making and legislation for the states in transition as for all other states. However, when it comes to the conception of the constitution, it becomes apparent that there are certain structural paradoxes that can be identified as follows:

- Both the preconditions for the realisation of the rule of law, and the realisation of rule of law itself have to be achieved simultaneously.
- Many people in the Eastern European states placed various expectations in the state ruled by law, which can essentially be summed up by the statement: "We expected justice, and we got the rule of law!" Legitimacy and legality, which in the state under the rule of law should be identical, stand in obvious contradiction to one another.

Core questions

This raises the following core questions:

1. Is it even possible to adhere to the procedures and principles of the rule of law whilst managing the transition from a communist regime with a completely different economic and social order to the political form of a liberal-democratic constitutional state? (PREUSS) The state ruled by law cannot only be envisaged as the goal to be reached at the end of the transition. The process and phase of transition itself should be ruled by the principles of the rule of law.
2. Today the core question to be answered is moreover: *How can the new state which is built upon the principles of the rule of law deal with the injustices of the previous regime without itself violating those basic rule of law principles?*

Discrepancy between legality and legitimacy

In a state committed to constitutionalism and democracy, the principle of rule of law requires that legality and legitimacy correspond. The positive law should be legal but also legitimate. What is legal, that is – in accordance with the positive law, should in principle also have legitimacy. Legality and legitimacy are – so one assumes – ultimately identical. In the Eastern European states on the other hand, legality, that is, those laws enacted by the power-holders, stood against legitimacy. In the phase of transition, in which reforms are introduced from the top down, there remains even today often a certain tension between the 'ordained' legality and legitimacy.

Mastering the past

A discrepancy between legality and legitimacy is – as we shall see – not only apparent with regard to the introduction of the free market economy and the dismantling of welfare rights, but also in relation to the question of how to deal with crimes of the old regime.

When the current generation wants to deal legitimately with its past and with the legal responsibility of members of the previous generation, a clear distinction must be made between legitimate and illegitimate orders, so as to pave the way for the future. However, precisely this condemnation of the illegitimacy of the past finds only limited approval as a legitimate goal amongst the population of many countries in transition.

Attributing legal responsibility for things that have occurred in the past requires finding the truth. However, finding of the truth cannot be reduced to a simple legal procedure, rather, it is always strongly connected to a specific individual.

In the sense of the rule of law, one has also clearly to distinguish between the examination of the past on one hand and claims for redress of past injustice on the other. According to HANNAH ARENDT (*Vita Activa*): "When forgiveness is not possible at all, or is possible but not enough, *punishment* is the only acceptable alternative to revenge!" Undoubtedly punishment must be part of the rule of law. However, it presupposes a fair and just procedure and that justice is not only done but also seen to de done.

Can one require atonement if the need for inner peace demands that the past be forgotten? If past injustices are concealed or overlooked however, how can one justify this to the victims who have still to bear and to suffer from the consequences of the past?

Often even the rule of law itself – namely the prohibition of retroactive legislation – forbids such justice oriented toward the past. The greater the number of people who were involved in carrying out the institutional injustice of the old regime, the less it is likely to be possible to build the new order on the principle of punishment or atonement.

How can a state committed to the rule of law ultimately come to terms with the problem of the illegality of the old regime without undermining the underlying principle of the new state: the rule of law? Virtually all efforts to strengthen the principle of the rule of law can be blocked with the same principle!

The unsatisfactory dilemma of privatisation

When private property ownership is to be re-established, one needs to decide whether and according to what principles the property of the previous communist regime is to be given back to the original owners, or whether privatisation of state property is to be put into the service and interest of a future-oriented economy. Should the available resources be used for the realisation of the future welfare of all and therefore in the service of a dynamic market economy, or should previous rights of former property owners take precedence?

From a purely economic point of view, a past-oriented approach to law and rights will probably not lead to economic prosperity. Does the state committed to the rule of law demand justice for the future, or does it provide protection of historical rights? How can these unsatisfactory alternatives be reconciled? Should unjust but economically successful privatisation be pursued in the name of future-oriented efficiency, or should one decide for the property rights of previous owners and return their property to them? In terms of property ownership, how should one decide between free acquisition capitalism and a socially bound capitalism? Can the individual injustices of the past after so many years and generations really be corrected?

This dilemma tended to dominate the transition in all Eastern and Central European States. The principles of the rule of law alone do not offer clear guidelines for such conflicts. It is ultimately the task of the political legislature to decide whether the state and therefore the current law should be oriented towards the past, or whether politics should decide in favour of future-oriented legal protections. In making such decision, one has also to take into account the interests of persons who were born in the communist system, and who lived and worked there for many years. The rights and expectations of these persons are just as well-earned as the property rights of previous owners. At the very least, their rights are not illegitimate just because they were acquired within a system which today is denied legitimacy.

Rights against market economy: An example

In a concrete case of the Hungarian constitutional court this problem is clearly illustrated:

In a 1995 decision of this court, a statute that sought to abolish certain social welfare rights in order to reduce state expenditure was declared to be unconstitutional. The court had to decide whether social rights acquired under the socialist system were to be protected and were therefore not to be undermined on the basis of the goals of the market economy system.

The court justified its decision on the basis of the argument that the establishment of a market economy is a political goal, whereas welfare is a basic need and therefore a legal claim. This justification of course could lead to judicial activism. The court sees itself as 'the protector and guardian' of the people, and thereby gains in popularity and public authority.

Following the doctrine of the rule of law, the court took the view that security and certainty of the law is an essential part of the rule of law principle. Accordingly, social rights are quasi-property rights, which have been won and acquired over the years.

The Hungarian Constitutional Court thereby ironically based its decision on a concept of substantive justice that stands in conflict with the formal rationality of the rule of law. The achievement of substantive justice can also ultimately weaken the market economy and restrict freedom of contract.

Separation of powers and rule of law

In a system of separation of powers in which the legitimacy of the legislature is weak, the constitutional court judge will take the lead and interpret the rule of law as a principle of justice that entails the legal certainty of the constitution over generations, and as a principle to which all positive law is subject. The contradiction between the protection of constitutionally guaranteed rights and the need for economic modernisation under the specific post-communist conditions thus becomes apparent.

Although one generally assumes that the rule of law accords with the demand for democratisation and the promotion of the market economy, the consistent application of this principle leads in this case to an unexpected result.

Liberty, legal certainty and rule of law

The goal of post-communist societies to establish a political order ruled by law is more difficult to achieve than it may initially appear. Past injustices cannot simply be erased. Nor can the penalty be paid for past injustice through new injustice. An old legal wisdom tells us that no justice can ever come of injustice. This means that past injustice should never be concealed or forgotten. Justice must be found for the victims who have suffered, without creating new injustices. Each generation however is responsible for ensuring that the rule of law is respected and that the laws serve and promote the well-being of current and future generations.

The constitutional guarantees of property, freedom of contract, and freedom of collective bargaining can ultimately only be realised in a system based on solidarity which respects freedom within the state (participatory rights), from the state (negative rights), by the state (social rights) and to the state (minority rights).

Constitutional Jurisdiction

Constitutional jurisdiction enables a court to review statutes enacted by the legislature or ordinances or decisions of the executive in terms of their constitutionality. There are many different models of constitutional jurisdiction. The states of Eastern and Central Europe however have adhered predominantly to the two following models of constitutional jurisdiction:

American model

According to the American model, every ordinary court has the jurisdiction in any concrete case that is before it to review the constitutionality of the statutes upon which the parties are relying. The review of constitutionality occurs along with all other legal assessments in the case. However, such review can only take place in a case where the parties have standing and have a concrete legal dispute to bring before the court. The court can only review the constitutionality of the concrete application of a legislative norm. It has no power to declare a law unconstitutional in an abstract or hypothetical sense. Nor can the court review a statute *prospectively* before it comes into force. Review of constitutionality is therefore limited to retrospective review in concrete cases.

Austrian model

Under the Austrian model, the power to review the constitutionality of legislation is vested in a special constitutional court. These constitutional courts, which exist in most parts of Europe, often also have jurisdiction to assess the constitutionality of abstract norms. That is, they can review the norm itself entirely in the abstract, and if necessary can quash the norm or the statute. Constitutional jurisdiction is centralised within a constitutional court that has original and exclusive jurisdiction over all constitutional matters within the respective country. These courts have the final say as to whether or not a provision is constitutional. There is no appeal against decisions of a constitutional court. These specialised constitutional courts often have the power to review legislation prospectively before it has entered into force. This *ex ante* review generally serves to control the actions of the executive and the legislature and to ensure they stay within the parameters of the constitution.

Constitutional review for the protection of the rule of law

As already mentioned, constitutional jurisdiction serves in many states of Eastern and Central Europe to stabilise politics and society. The constitutional courts provide a final and binding interpretation of the rules of the political game, such as the conduct of elections (e.g. Romania). They contribute substantially to the establishment of the political culture of a country (e.g. Poland). If their decisions and their reasoning are credible and comprehensible, they play a significant role in stabilising the system. From this point of view they can also be seen as an important factor in contributing to democratisation, as they protect democratic rights and provide for their credibility. As an umpire that decides on the rules of the game, they can also enhance and promote the whole democratic constitutional culture.

State and Civil Society

Rule of law in the historical tensions of western states

The liberal constitutional model was developed in a field of political tension within a society that was already stabilised by mechanisms of self-regulation with regard to the challenge of the absolutistic state. All elements of the rule of law that were introduced into the constitutions of the countries in transition are, as we have seen in the fourth and fifth chapters, the result of a lengthy and complex process in which the despotic rule of absolutist governments was gradually broken down. Within this process, the cultural and economic elites of civil society had a decisive function. As promoters of different interest groups they became a source of power that sometimes was even able to exert direct pressure. The elites of civil society certainly played an important role in developing constructive and creative solutions.

Weak society – weak state

In post-communist states such as in South-Eastern Europe however, it was the other way around. According to the communist tradition of those countries, weak societies were faced with a powerful state, that is – an authoritarian regime.

Accordingly, after the collapse of communism these countries were not able to introduce the principle of the rule of law as a fundamental constitutional principle supported by the continuing development of the state. Even if the principle of rule of law was embedded in the constitution as a result of careful constitutional drafting, the state was in any case still not able to implement the rule of law into social and political reality in the manner of the Western European states.

This raises the question: can the rule of law be successfully be implemented in societies,

- Which have no support from a developed political and economic pluralism of interests;
- Which have instead to contend with a variety of NGOs, each of which claims to be acting in the national general interest;
- Which are not based upon fixed legal traditions with corresponding political culture; and
- Which can hardly count on any real economic development?

The state as motor and brake

In South-Eastern Europe the state has to promote and support the growth of society in the spirit of liberalism. This it can only do when it also creates the conditions for a system guided by the rule of law. The state however is only credible if it also itself observes the rule of law, that is – if it constantly limits its own power and authority. The paradox therefore lies in the fact that the state is required simultaneously to promote state activity under the rule of law and to limit the scope of its own authority. The authorities that are to implement the rule of law are at the same time limited by these principles.

The state should establish the constitutional and legal conditions that lead to greater liberation of the society, not only with regard to the economy and business, but also with regard to human rights, decentralised local self-government and the development of a political 'public' articulated through free media.

Odyssey of the rule of law

The first fundamental step in the direction of the rule of law is the enactment and enforcement of a new constitution, which enshrines the principle of legitimacy within the positive law. With this first step however, the Odyssey of the rule of law within these states has only just begun.

After almost 20 years of constitutional practice in many countries in transition, it has become clear that the institutions of constitutional democracy, however carefully and consistently they were conceived and drafted, are facing a weak and already corrupted (privatised) state on one side and an only slowly developing civil society on the other side. These institutions are not embedded within the everyday life of society in a way that corresponds to the constitutional reality of western countries. This problem will certainly have a decisive influence on the constitutional politics of these countries in future, particularly in they how prepare themselves for the next wave of constitutional development (e.g. Bulgaria and Serbia).

iii. The Governmental Systems of the Central and Eastern European Countries between Parliamentarism and Presidentialism

The Concepts

Presidential system

In Eastern and Central Europe one can basically distinguish between two different governmental systems: some countries have opted for a *presidential democracy*, while others have preferred the constitutional set-up of a (*rationalised*) *parliamentary system* as a counter model. In the presidential system of government, the president is directly elected by the people and functions as the head of state and executive. The president is not directly politically accountable to the parliament. On the other hand, he/she often has the power to control the parliament and if necessary to call new elections and to declare an emergency.

Parliamentary governmental system

Within a parliamentary governmental system, the executive depends on the parliamentary majority and thus on the confidence of the parliament. The role of the president is reduced almost exclusively to symbolic and ceremonial matters. He/she has to be content to remain within the shadow of power. However, within these systems the president's symbolic role as a representative of national unity who stands above party politics is still significant. If for example parliament tries to solve conflicts that appear to be irresolvable, the president as national mediator can maintain or restore the unity of the country. Thus for instance, the Hungarian president was able successfully to resolve the conflict between anti-communists and the anti-anti-communists.

The Socio-Political Environment affecting the choice of Governmental System, or: What Kind of President is desired, and what Consequences can this have for the Consolidation of Democracy?

The choice between a presidential or parliamentary system was much more far-reaching than any other open issue of constitution making, as it was influenced by the aim to simultaneously achieve legitimacy and governability of the institutional system. When it was difficult to achieve a democratic consensus and when society was strongly fragmented, there was an attempt through the usually already existing personal charisma of a strong president to connect the charismatic legitimacy with the efficiency of a powerful presidential office.

Strengthening the head of state

Accordingly, the strengthening of the position and function of the head of state had at first *positive aspects*:

The '*pouvoir constituant*' tended to opt for a presidential system primarily in situations where it was feared that with general free elections it would not be possible to establish a coherent parliament with enough strength to install and control a politically homogeneous executive that could take on the responsibility of managing the transition and could govern efficiently and effectively.

One opted for the flexibility and effectiveness of semi-presidential governmental systems with a bipolar executive, that is – a head of state who also heads the executive government, because with this institutional mechanism one can always guarantee that the executive is capable of acting and that it can push ahead with the reform process, keep it on track, and react to the specific problems of transition. A president elected for a fixed term of office represents, relative to constantly changing cabinets, the degree of continuity that is required to guarantee the progress of the reform process.

Risks

Governmental systems which strengthen the office of the head of state contain however also the following *negative aspects*:

States that still face the burden of disputed territory and an open 'state question' and which therefore base their legitimacy on ethno-nationalism, such as for instance Serbia or Croatia, can with a strong president who symbolises the ethnic nation in fact establish a mock democracy. With a powerful head of state, one can feign a rational constitutional democratic legitimacy in order in fact to legitimise a nationalistic, plebiscitary democracy.

When the president is directly elected by the people, he/she can be tempted to impose his/her power in the name of the people against the parliament, and thereby to effectively eliminate the parliament through his/her populist charisma. By addressing him/herself directly to the people, he/she can marginalise the legislature because the ethno-nation sees its unity symbolised by the president and endangered by the fragmentation of the parties.

The conflict between the two organs democratically elected by the people, namely the parliament on one side and the president on the other side, is almost inevitable in presidential systems. The structure of parallel legitimacy of the two executive organs involves the immanent risk of an almost irresolvable constitutional conflict. The paradox is that this system does not provide a democratic institutional tool to solve this conflict, which leads necessarily to an authoritarian-populist appeal to the plebiscite. There remains always a constitutionally unsolved ambivalence between the president elected directly by the people and the prime minister linked to the confidence of parliament.

The Different Governmental Systems

The five different forms of government

Between the pure presidential system and the pure parliamentary system one can distinguish five different mixed systems. Each of these systems aims to achieve the sustainable political stability of the state and society.

The rationalised parliamentary system provides in the interest of stability for the popular election of the head of the state as an essential additional element.

In order to provide for further stabilisation of the executive, votes of no confidence can be limited to the so-called constructive vote of no confidence.

But the constitution can also provide that cabinet ministers are collectively responsible to parliament.

Such mixed forms of a semi-presidential governmental system can, according to the political environment, be categorised as tending more towards a parliamentary or towards a presidential system, without exhibiting all the characteristics of one or the other system.

The following five different forms of government can be distinguished:

- The pure presidential (Ukraine) or super-presidential governmental system (Russia, Belarus).
- The premier-presidential governmental system (Romania).
- The presidential-parliamentary governmental system (Croatia, Serbia).
- The parliamentary governmental system with a directly elected president (Bulgaria, Macedonia, Poland and Slovenia).
- The pure parliamentary governmental system (Hungary, Chechnya, Slovakia, Albania, Lithuania).

8 The Multicultural State: The Challenge of the Future

8.1 Challenges of the Multicultural State

8.1.1 Introduction

Multiculturality: The challenge of our time

Today ninety-five per cent of the world population lives in multicultural states. In these states, society is fragmented into different ethnic groups, cultures, languages and religions. Around forty per cent of the world population lives in federal states and 60 per cent in so-called unitary states. In many states the diversity of cultures has led to an almost intolerable fragmentation. Since the fall of the Berlin Wall multiculturality has become a fundamental challenge, with increasingly brutal intra-state conflicts posing a threat to the stability of states and the international community.

How can states capitalise on their diversity? How can different societies and cultures be brought back towards unity in diversity? All states that have to cope with globalisation of the world order on one hand, and need to meet the challenges of their local social order and local diversity on the other hand, are confronted with internal conflicts. These conflicts were effectively frozen until 1989 because of the bipolar division between the capitalist and communist blocs.

Who should govern whom?

Up to now the problems of states have essentially been reduced to the issue of how states and state authority should be organised in order to achieve broad support and legitimacy. Good governance was at the centre of traditional state theory. How should state authority be arranged? How should states be structured in order to meet the need for justice and rule of law? Today, we are confronted with much more difficult and controversial questions, namely:

1. Who should govern whom?
2. Which majority should have authority over which minorities?
3. To whom should political power be assigned?
4. And above all: Who should decide and by what procedure should they decide who is to be the bearer of political power, and what should the nature and extent of such political power be?

Federalism: A state organisation that can hold diversity together?

For a long time the federal state structure was analysed only from the perspective of the vertical separation of powers. In federal states, federalism enables in addition to the horizontal separation of powers also a vertical separation between the powers of the federation and those of its federal units. Thus, federalism was seen merely as an additional tool to limit the governing power of the state. In this context the vertical separation of powers has also been criticised, as it leads to inefficient state activity and is detrimental to the equal protection of rights.

We understand federalism as being the state concept which provides for (and realises) a constitutionally guaranteed balance between self-determination in the sense of the autonomy of the federal units (*self-rule*) and the participation of the federal units in the decision making process of the central government (*shared-rule*). In this sense, federalism can be an additional response to the burning question: what in terms of state authority can be done in order to keep or bring diverse ethnicities, cultures and/or religions together in one state? Federalism not only answers the question, *how* one should govern multicultural societies, but also, *who should govern over whom*. Federalism is thus a constitutional system which in its very nature aims at the prevention and peaceful management of conflicts within multicultural states. But whoever analyses the smouldering intra-state conflicts resulting from multiculturality, will find many controversial answers to the following questions:

1. Why does multiculturality inherently contain the potential for conflict?
2. Can federalism and/or decentralisation contribute to bringing or holding multicultural societies together? Can federalism and/or decentralisation provide special tools and procedures to prevent or solve intra-state conflicts in fragmented societies?
3. The undisputed governmental system of the modern state is democracy. To what extent can a democratic society that is made up of several cultures regard itself as a *single* civil society, which legitimises and controls state power? Can a fragmented civil society only be united with additional political and legal instruments and procedures?

8.1.2 Multiculturality and the Modern State Concept

Equality of Homo sapiens

The political and theoretical foundations of modern constitutionalism are based on the idea of the secularised state, which recognises only popular sovereignty and the social contract as the source of legitimate state authority. Political authority thus has its roots in the idea of the 'Homo sapiens'. The man of modernity can say "no", because he is capable of judging what is true, just and correct. Modern secularised democracy therefore presupposes that all people are in principle *equal* as:

- egocentric beings (HOBBES);
- bearers of inalienable rights (LOCKE);
- reasonable citizens (in the sense of ROUSSEAU'S 'citoyen');
- exploiters or exploited (MARX);

- political beings ('homo politicus' of ARISTOTLE and THOMAS AQUINAS);
- cost-benefit oriented beings ('homo oeconomicus' of ADAM SMITH, JOHN RAWLS).

The democratic and liberal constitutional state of modernity is rooted in the idea that ultimately all people, as members of the species Homo sapiens, are substantially equal. All people have the capacity to use their reason to acquire knowledge, to make rational judgments based on their knowledge and insight, and to act accordingly. The nature of man, who has the capacity to say "no" or "yes", is what led to the new legitimacy of the secular state based on the social contract. Without insight into basic human equality there would not be a secularised democratic state. However, it is precisely this equality that impeded the ability of the state to take into account those 'inequalities' and identities of human beings, which are caused by their culture, tradition, language and religion. Whoever considers only the equality of human beings, overlooks the fact that people identify with their particular community on the basis of their special or distinctive features, and want to distinguish themselves from the other members of their species.

Does inequality legitimise the building of special political communities?

If we thus accept that all individuals as representatives of their species are equal, then we have to ask, what are the reasons for which some individuals are inclined to attach themselves to particular groups and what would legitimise such exclusiveness? Why and on what basis do they feel a sense of belonging to a certain community ('we' or 'us'), whilst other groups are viewed only as partners, opponents or even enemies ('others' or 'them')? Why do groups exclude specific individuals and why do they allow certain others to join the group? Are the reasons purely private, or is there some political motivation underlying this behaviour? Can groups or communities stake their own claim to sovereignty and establish their own polity?

In this context one has to question the legitimacy of a (cultural, religious or linguistic) community which, by virtue of its perennial majority and the democratic majority principle, has authority over minority groups and regularly outvotes them. What are the criteria by which certain communities are included within the state identity and others are excluded? Why are Austrians and German-speaking Swiss not regarded as Germans, since East Germans and resettled Germans in the East are considered to be of German ethnicity? Why does the Italian-speaking majority of the canton of Tessin prefer to identify with Switzerland than with Italy, and why do Italian-speakers in the region of Istria (Slovenia and Croatia) feel differently?

In other words: why did the international community in the Peace of St. Germain after the First World War prohibit the reunification of Germany and Austria, and why did it then celebrate the reunification of East and West Germany after the fall of the Berlin Wall and applaud the famous remark of former Chancellor Willi Brandt "what belongs together must come together"?

The nation ignores diversity

The nation, which is created by the state and its constitution, is composed of equal individuals enjoying equal rights. The constitution serves as a rational political instrument to bring people of different cultures and ethnicities together. The conception of man that is based on the principles of equality of all human beings and their universal reason (in the sense of Homo sapiens), excludes by its very definition cultural, traditional, historical and linguistic differences.

The political diversity that would result from political recognition of these different cultural communities has to be ignored by the state and its constitution. Man is thereby however reduced to a rational political being (*citoyen*), whose emotional connections to an ethnic community are dissolved by the social contract and the establishment of the rational state community.

The people excludes diversity

In the reverse sense too, a state dependent on the culture of its *people,* that is, a state developed out of a predestined community (*Schicksalsgemeinschaft*), excludes diversity. Such states are marked by the congruence of the identity of the existing pre-constitutional ethnic community and the polity created out of this community. The political recognition of other ethnic groups and granting such groups equal rights and the right to participate in the constitution-making process would therefore threaten the original unity of the state and the 'monocultural' people's sovereignty.

Demos

Through the social contract, people have agreed to join together as a political unit, a *demos*. Based on their reason and their will the members of this unit become political beings, that is, citizens. They have created this political unit by their own reflection and choice and want to sustain their polity in the future. But what values underlie the willful act of establishing a polity or uniting with another demos? When Napoleon presented the confederates of Switzerland with the choice either to remain a small and marginal federal state or to unite with the 'great nation', they opted for the former. Why? Was it the shared history, religion or certain common political values such as democracy and federalism, which generated for them a greater feeling of community with each other than with the 'Grande Nation'?

Pre-constitutional unity of the people

Finally, there are states which build their concept of the nation on the culture of the majority people. The people which legitimises the sovereignty of these states is culturally homogeneous. Each citizen of the state has the same cultural identity. Whoever does not belong to the culture of the people will be regarded as a second-class citizen and unable to fully identify with the state. These nations are in fact not built upon common values and are not held together by reflection and choice. It is not the will and rational choice of the people, but rather nature that has forged the people into a common unit. Their identity and communality is pre-political, pre-state and pre-constitutional. The state unity is based on the natural and given cultural identity of the people. Such states cannot admit other cultures. In the best case scenario, they can tolerate foreigners as guests; in the worst case, they require total integration or assimilation of foreigners and expect them to renounce their cultural identity in order to acquire citizenship and equal rights. Whoever wants to change nationality, must also change their cultural identity. Although most of these states acknowledge universal values in their constitutions, their ethnic foundation is often evident in their laws on citizenship. On the one hand, these states privilege members of their own culture who live in another state, whilst on the other hand, in the case of naturalisation they require citizens of other states to renounce their previous citizenship and completely surrender their cultural identity. They exclude dual citizenship and thus also multiple loyalty. Moreover, these states consider it their duty to defend the interests of members of their cultural nation who live in and are subject to the sovereignty of neighbouring states, even if these people are citizens of the neighbouring state (see Art. 116 of the Basic Law of Germany).

States that are held together by a common pre-political culture must, if they want to survive as a unified entity, exclude other cultures. The guiding culture (*Leitkultur*) is regarded as the only identity- and community-building engine of the nation. Multiculturality has no place within such an *exclusive* concept. Cultural diversity is rather seen as threat to the very existence of the state and its nation.

If the polity defines itself as a community of common culture, language, religion or history, particular values such as language, religion, race or ethnicity will become decisive factors in politics. Peoples whose identity is determined by these values should grow closer together. In consequence, the multiculturality or fragmentation of a community caused by traditional minorities, immigrants or foreign workers will be feared as a threat that splits the natural unity of the nation.

Collective ethnic nationalism as dominant ideology: The example of Eastern Europe

The ethno-nationalism of several newly established states in Eastern Europe has ethnic, that is – pre-political, cultural roots and causes. The centrality of ethnic codes has a direct impact on ethnic minorities in a number of ways:

- First, it produces a tendency wherever possible to draw territorial borderlines in such a way as to maximise the ethnic homogeneity of the population.
- In addition, civil rights and socio-economic status are determined according to the ethnic group to which a person belongs.
- And politics, in particular constitutional politics and the party system, is directed towards promoting the interest and well-being of the dominant ethnic community.

Accordingly, issues and conflicts relating to ethnicity (including religious, cultural and linguistic issues) will take precedence over political issues relating to class and the just distribution of resources.

Nation state and constitutional nationalism

Within such a socio-political environment two different situations can arise: the population of the given state in terms of its ethnic composition is either internally heterogeneous (e.g. Bulgaria, Serbia-Montenegro, Romania) or externally heterogeneous (e.g. Hungary or Albania).

In summary, one can classify the aforementioned tendencies as ethno-radicalism: this includes all political endeavour that bases the distinction between friend and foe on ethnic characteristics and pursues its aims accordingly, even by violent means.

Citoyen-states

If a people or a nation identifies with the polity and not with the dominant cultural community, the political people (*demos*) will embrace all persons within the territorial authority of the polity. This inclusive political value however presupposes that individuals internalise the political values of the polity and that they forego recognition as a special cultural-political entity. The common interests of the polity must be given priority over all private interests and allegiances. Multiculturality and diversity will tend to be ignored primarily because, as structure-building factors they could become the basis of decentralisation and could thus threaten the unity of the nation. For this reason states such as France or Turkey, which are held together by political values, reject any cultural pluralism and derive their legitimacy from the political values that create a homogeneous unity. Culture has to be excluded from any rational political decision making process, as it puts the very existence of the state in question. Without rationality there is no nation.

Nations that negate culture as political value are built upon the rationality of their citizens and exclude the cultural dimension of man. Cultural identity in these states cannot be an acceptable political identity. Turkey for example prohibits the official use of the Kurdish language, because it would endanger the republican unity of the state. France has refused to ratify the Council of Europe's Framework Convention for the Protection of National Minorities. In Switzerland, the canton of Geneva has prohibited schoolteachers from wearing a veil or chador, as it puts into question the secular status of government schools and the principle of the secular state. As rational human beings all citizens are equal. Cultural differences must remain politically irrelevant and should not even be visible in the political sphere.

Immigration countries

When people choose a specific territory as the geographical basis and unit for their polity (as was the case in the classical immigration countries) they must necessarily relinquish their culture and history as unifying factors, as they come from different cultural backgrounds. The preamble of the Constitution of the United States, "We the People of the United States...", expresses the fact that all persons living in the United States belong to the people because they live within the same territory (*jus soli* principle). Culture and history are regarded neither as relevant nor harmful to nation building. This cultural blindness is compensated by the guarantee of '*universal equality for every human being*'. The USA however has not always consistently upheld equal rights. Slavery and the later discrimination of the Afro-American people were gross violations of the principle of universal equality.

Constitutional patriotism as pretext

In addition to their cultural roots, culture-states (*Kulturstaaten*) also refer to the values contained in their constitutions, which are supposed to supplant the nationalistic and exclusive character of the state (constitutional patriotism according to J. HABERMAS) and which reflect a universalistic affiliation to the polity. Each person can, as a rational being with equal rights, decide whether he/she can identify with the universal principles and procedures of the Constitution. Indeed, with constitutional patriotism, states that were initially based upon the pre-political ethnic unity of their people can proclaim universal values. However, it remains to be seen whether they can really break free from the Procrustean bed of the dominant ethnic culture. Even though constitutionally proclaimed values may effect external changes, the subconscious mind of the people clings to the identity of the pre-state cultural community. The fact that today almost all constitutions proclaim universal values that should be based on a purely political nation, does not disguise the fact that the real identity of the people is to be found in their common culture, language or religion.

This may in a certain sense apply to the French Nation, which through the French Revolution laid the foundation for the a-cultural citizen-state. The first constitutional draft of 1791 provided that all persons who lived for at least one year within the state territory would automatically be granted French citizenship. In relation to anti-foreigner trends that exist in France today, it is apparent that the French people sees itself as a nation that is deeply rooted in the French history of the catholic Kingdom and the later revolutions. Although France very credibly confesses republican values and although it promotes the French language as 'universal' and open for all cultures, the idea of cultural unity as a state-building and state-sustaining factor still shines through.

Universal v. particular values

Almost all of the constitutions of modern constitutionalism are, at least from outward appearance, shaped for the universal citizen. Today it seems that universal values alone give legitimacy to the state authority within a particular geographical territory. Whilst the polity proclaims universal values, it is *particular* values that determine whether a person belongs to a certain group or community. Peoples have to create a 'we', by which they can distinguish themselves from the 'others' and which can serve as an external barrier. The state must be based on values that are universal and '*good for all*', yet at the same time the constitution has to be rooted in particular values which reflect the identity of the relevant entity (*good for us*). In both cases, the constituted values exclude cultural fragmentation or diversity.

Diversity as a political value?

In writing a constitution for a culturally heterogeneous nation that aims at unity in spite of diversity, one must ask what values would foster a conception of the nation that can be distinguished from other states or polities and that can at the same time enable each of the different communities to identify with the common nation? How can a political identity be established for several cultures, which does not erase those cultures nor exclude them from the common political identity? Are there certain political values, which are not universal but which are compatible with a culturally diverse state, and which can create a 'we' and a common denominator for different cultures? These questions of multiculturality pose the greatest challenges to the constitutional concepts of modernity. In the face of the potential for internal conflicts within multicultural states, it is essential to create political units, which in relation to ethnic minorities do not practice discrimination, segregation, apartheid or ethnic cleansing and which do not perpetrate human rights abuse.

Constitutionalism and cultural diversity

The basic state philosophy that has developed out of modern constitutionalism ignores the reality of today's multicultural society. The political recognition of cultural diversity as a requirement of collectives within the state would shake the very foundations of the state concept. As long as the unity of the state is identical with the majority culture or is defined by the culture of the majority, minorities living within the state will at best be second-class citizens. In no case will multiculturality be recognised as a relevant basis for state building.

States tend to ignore multiculturality (settler countries such as the United States), reject it (France, Turkey), or suppress it (Germany with its preamble to the Basic Law: "*the German People have adopted, by virtue of their constituent power, this Constitution*").

Challenges of multiculturality

These different concepts of the nation are not only inherently contradictory, they are also one of the causes of the various ethnic conflicts of the last few decades. Moreover, these different state concepts are not able to meet the challenges of the reality of 'transnational citizenship' caused by modern migration. The traditional concepts of state and nation do not equip states to manage their ethnic conflicts (see for example the Basque region, Northern Ireland, Corsica), nor do they provide a solid political answer on how to integrate the growing number of transnational citizens into their own political system.

A state concept that sought to integrate diverse cultures within the state and which granted each cultural group a certain political autonomy, such as responsibility for education, judiciary, police and so on, could perhaps resolve some of these conflicts. Such concept would not question the political unity of the state – and thus could be acceptable to the majority – nor would it relegate minorities to the status of mere guests of the state. In the absence of such concept however, states cannot afford political fragmentation caused by multiculturality.

8.1.3 *What are the Causes of Conflicts within Multicultural States?*

Various causes

If one wishes to search for new state concepts that could prevent ethnic conflicts or at least manage them peacefully, one needs to know the real causes of such conflicts. However, the views and theories as to the causes are as diverse as the conflicts themselves.

Possible causes include:

- economy (social injustice),
- history (retaliation for historical injustice, denial of self-determination, historical discrimination),
- Interference in intrastate conflicts by neighbour-states that support their ethnic communities living in foreign neighbouring territory,
- religious fundamentalism,
- power-hungry warlords,
- lack of legitimacy of the state or of the nation with regard to its minorities,
- fear and mistrust as consequence of terrorism of minorities and terrorism of the state.

Ethnic chauvinism as cause

What is uncontested however, is that all of these causes are in some way related to the issue of ethnic identity and the attendant self-awareness. The ethnic dispute is marked by a friend-foe mentality, which can be manipulated and radicalised by various private interests. Ethnic differences can be emotionalised in order to pursue economic, political, cultural or mere power interests, or to divert attention from other internal problems.

Symptom or cause?

Within the scientific community, there is no doubt that one of the main reasons for the remarkable development of medical science is the fact that at the end of the 19th Century doctors began to investigate the causes of illness, rather than analysing and treating only the symptoms. In the social sciences one can discuss the symptoms of social pathology, however the real causes are hardly investigated. There are those who see the causes in the hearts and minds of men, and who think that all conflicts are subjective and can be solved by 'group-therapy'. Others in turn discern within the linguistic and religious differences qualitative human differences, which ultimately do not allow for the integration of different peoples into a single political order. What is required therefore is a thorough analysis of the causes of such conflicts, as only when there is agreement as to the causes can there be sensible discussion of solutions. The question however, as to the real causes of a conflict, is often as controversial as the conflict itself.

Can globalisation contribute to solutions?

It is commonly believed that through globalisation the sovereignty of the nation-state will gradually be absorbed into the global market. The private market will undermine the need for political and social concepts and solutions at the local level. This will change the arena in which opponents and advocates of ethnic demands operate, from the local nation-state to the global market. Conflicts over the explosive questions, who should govern whom, how should one govern over multiculturality, and who should exercise constituent power, will become largely redundant as the effective political power of the nation-state and its ability to implement solutions will gradually disappear. As governments of nation-states lose some of their scope for action it may no longer be possible to hold them responsible for the problems of intra-state conflicts. The need for national government will lose its significance because the state will effectively be privatised.

Globalisation versus localisation

In fact we are currently confronted with contradictory tendencies. On the one hand, one can observe a strong trend towards globalisation. On the other hand, there are equally strong tendencies towards ghettoisation and localisation. Indeed, the needs of people who want to survive in the uncertainty of today's world are contradictory:

- Consumers favour the global market in order to achieve optimal benefits at optimal costs;
- Citizens and voters demand the universality of human rights;
- Individuals in their emotional dimension wish to withdraw into the security of their 'home'; they find their refuge and their identity within the local community;
- There is a global market for products, services and finance. The labour market however is still local and requires local solutions for local social problems;
- Workers therefore seek primarily local security.

Legitimacy of the 'globaliser' and the 'universaliser'

These contradictory human needs obviously pull in different directions. People demand globalisation and seek refuge in universality on one hand, and flee to the local homeland on the other. Decision making power over the global market however, is just as unevenly distributed as the power to decide on the content of the universality of human rights. Though the market is global and human rights are universal, decisions over content are made by the 'global universaliser'. That is, control over globalisation belongs to the only super-power. Its decision makers are elected through the local democratic procedure according to local interests. The global power thinks locally and acts globally.

Localisation

The greater global needs become, the greater the expectations citizens have of local governments. Local authorities are asked to find local solutions for problems caused by globalisation. It would therefore be fatal if one were to analyse the question of the state purely from the perspective of globalisation and the gradual erosion of sovereignty. One must also take into account the tendencies towards localisation.

What effects does this have for multicultural states? It is obvious that globalisation will strengthen the need for localisation as well as the need for local identity and local security. These needs however, in contrast to the global market, cannot be privatised. They can only be reasonably and realistically addressed by political decisions. Only local political structures are ultimately able to deal with human needs and fears. These local solutions must find their roots in the local community, as only there, where the people have their roots, can one provide people with greater security and alleviate their fears.

Homo oeconomicus versus homo politicus

The more relentless globalisation becomes, the more it will lack humanity, and the greater will be the need to compensate for global injustices with local justice. For this reason, local conflicts will not gradually subside. On the contrary, they will expand and become more radical if no preventative political, economic and social solutions can be offered. The cost-benefit oriented *homo oeconomicus* seeks his profit in the global market, whilst the *homo politicus* expects local compensation for injustices caused by globalisation. Thus, the challenges and the need for solutions with regard to multiculturality will in future grow and not disappear, particularly given that globalisation will increase global migration.

8.1.4 What Tools and Procedures are available to States in order to meet the growing Challenges of Multiculturality?

What is good for all, what is good for us?

Tendencies towards globalisation and localisation will become stronger. This will lead to greater fragmentation of multicultural states. We must take into account that multicultural states will rarely be able to overcome the increasing problems of multiculturality peacefully. The gaps between communities will become wider and the danger of increasingly violent conflicts will become greater. States will not be able to withstand these conflicts, if they cannot gain legitimacy for their governmental system in the eyes of the vast majority of the population, that is, the majority of individuals and communities. If states want to bring or keep their multicultural society together, they will need to be able to find a legitimate answer not only to the question what is good for all, but also what is good for us and what is good for our communities. This answer must be one with which the vast majority of the population can identify. States have to create a 'we' that encompasses the diversity within the state and does not exclude, but admits and fosters, the smaller 'we' of the various communities. Multiple loyalties should become the general rule. States that suppress multiple loyalties will radicalise their ethnic conflicts.

Who should govern whom?

When seeking tools for the rationalisation of emotional conflicts, the classical instruments of so-called 'good governance' will not suffice. In particular, states with multicultural societies will have to find legitimate solutions to the following problems: Who should govern over whom? In what instances can minorities make autonomous decisions? When and how should they participate in the decision making process of the majority? In what manner and by whom should it be decided, how the power of the state is distributed, and how decision making processes should be arranged (*pouvoir constituant*)?

To date, states have developed various instruments in order to meet the demands of multiculturality. Whoever wants to find or develop such instruments needs to know which conditions have to be realised in order to peacefully hold or bring a multicultural society together.

8.1.4.1 Politics of Tolerance

Guarantee of human dignity as minimal standard

States can try to win legitimacy for the authority of the ethnic majority over minorities through constitutional tools of tolerance, and to bring various communities together using the means of tolerance. However, one must be aware that those who are merely (but nonetheless) tolerated will never feel fully integrated into the community. On the other hand, tolerance provides a minimum standard that members of minority communities may rightly claim from the majority as a basic protection of their human dignity. Mutual respect is a minimum requirement, without which peaceful coexistence within a state is not possible. He who is tolerated can at least live in a community as a respected individual without suffering discrimination. However, as members of ethnic, religious or linguistic communities that are merely tolerated, people will still feel that they are second-class citizens.

So far as tolerance is integrated into the legal system of a state, it guarantees individual human rights on an equal basis for all individuals regardless of race, religion or language. Tolerance requires a comprehensive guarantee of human rights on the basis of the equality of all human beings living in the respective state.

Whoever belongs to a minority cannot be discriminated against because of his/her race, language, religion or gender.

Tolerated guests

However, those who are only tolerated will never feel part of the 'we' that forms the fundamental basis for the political legitimacy of the state. It will therefore hardly be possible to demand solidarity from the tolerated minority. Tolerated minorities consider themselves guests of a more or less generous host-state. They cannot influence the political strategy of the country. Diversity has to be respected, but it is not seen as an integral part of the state and is viewed more as a burden than an asset. Minority protection has to be guaranteed as it is part of the universal human rights that must be proclaimed and protected in every constitution. Diversity however cannot be internalised, if the state is not prepared to move beyond tolerance and protection of minorities to the protection of *collective autonomy* for minorities.

Affirmative action

In order to guarantee tolerance as a minimum standard, every state must protect the fundamental right to human dignity as a universal value and as the starting point for all human rights guarantees. States however can achieve protection of minorities not only by strengthening the protection of individual rights. They can improve the social and economic opportunities of minorities by providing for quotas and affirmative action. If states offer support to minorities that have been discriminated against for decades, through positive measures for advancement such as quotas for admission to higher education or to public service positions, some members of those minorities may be able to work their way out of disadvantage. Members of minorities might then actually be able to compete on an equal footing with members of the majority. This 'positive discrimination' may lead to discrimination against certain members of the majority. However, the majority will simply have to accept such discrimination, if it really wants to achieve equal social and economic opportunities for all people notwithstanding their race, religion or language.

8.1.4.2 Politics of Reconciliation

Peace as constitutional goal

The preamble to the new South African Constitution contains the following meaningful wording: "... adopt this Constitution as the supreme law of the Republic so as to ... heal the divisions of the past and establish a society based on democratic values, social justice and fundamental human rights." Article 70(2) and (3) of the Swiss Constitution provides: "(2) The Cantons shall decide on their official languages. In order to preserve harmony between linguistic communities, the cantons shall respect the traditional territorial distribution of languages, and shall take indigenous linguistic minorities into account. (3) The Confederation and the Cantons shall encourage *understanding and exchange* between the linguistic communities" (emphasis added).

Strategy of compromise

Peace and harmony as constitutional mandates are indispensable for any state that, because of its cultural diversity, is threatened by a considerable potential for conflict. Any effort to bring different cultural communities peacefully together cannot be restricted simply to the guarantee of individual rights. It is also necessary to provide tools and procedures for reconciliation, restoration of harmony and peaceful and rational conflict resolution. Compromise seen as a virtue and not as weakness needs to be given priority in politics. Multicultural states need to develop a strategy of compromise and procedures to find compromise, as well as a philosophy of balance and justice among the different ethnic communities, in order to stem the potential for conflict.

Self-determination of the nation versus self-determination of ethnic communities

In addition, states need procedures for the stemming and resolution of conflicts. Article 235 of the South African Constitution for example, requires a balance between the claim for self-determination of ethnic communities that are held together by common language, culture or historical heritage on one side, and the right of self-determination of the entire South African nation on the other.

Constitution making as process for reconciliation

The South African constitution making process clearly demonstrates how important the process of drafting and adopting a constitution can be for the building of a new civil society. The entire process effectively served as a process of healing and reconciliation between ethnicities split by deep hatred. Mistrust could be dismantled, trust restored, fears eased and hope fostered. The two-part process contributed greatly to this result. First, an interim constitution was negotiated between all key parties involved in the peace process. This constitution was then formally approved by the existing legally constituted (but exclusively white) parliament. On the basis of this interim constitution, which already contained fundamental principles to be included in the final constitution including rights protections, a constitutional assembly was elected on the basis of a general and equal right to vote. This assembly drafted the final constitution, which had to adhere to the fundamental principles contained in the interim constitution (the principles could be altered by a 2/3 majority). The assembly was subject to the supervision of a constitutional court that was charged with ensuring that the constitution complied with the agreed principles. The long time period from the first negotiations to the election of a government under the final constitution, during which new solutions were transparently negotiated and realised by all parties under the watchful eye of the people, had a healing effect on the building of a new nation.

Direct democracy

Semi-direct democracy is another means towards peaceful conflict resolution. At first glance, direct democracy appears to be majority-driven and thus may seem ill–suited to the protection of minorities or even to gaining legitimacy in the eyes of minorities. However direct democracy, at least in Switzerland, has turned out to be an essential factor in the peaceful coexistence of different cultures and communities. The primary reason for this is that voters tend to reject proposals from parliament or government unless they are supported by the vast majority of the political elite. This restraint on the part of the people forces the political elite to reach compromises that are acceptable to most parties. Consensus and compromise have thus become a fundamental element of the political culture. The people, in its role as 'opposition', compels the government by direct democracy to find and accept compromises. Moreover, an analysis of various referenda results will reveal that it is not always the same minority opposed to the same majority. Different contrasting factors such as urban versus rural areas, mountain regions versus lowland, language, religion etc, means that almost every person in Switzerland belongs at the same time to a majority as well as to a minority. Direct democracy also has an educative effect. If for example, a minority is dependent on special economic or social support, it will win the approval of a majority only if it gains the support of other minorities. The other minorities will only grant their approval if they are confident that they can rely on similar support when they need it. Thus, the procedures of direct democracy in Switzerland have indirectly contributed to the rationalisation and resolution of disputes. Direct democracy has become an instrument of reconciliation and peaceful settlement of emotional conflicts.

8.1.4.3 Equality of Peoples and Minorities

Equality of peoples as constitutional goal

Democracy is based upon the majority principle. Majorities however should not misuse their power. The majority should not degenerate into a tyranny over minorities. If states want to hold different ethnicities together, the majority will have to grant minorities the right to be recognised as ethnic units or communities on equal footing with other ethnicities including the ethnic majority. It is not enough that people as individuals are treated equally. It is essential that members of minorities can see themselves as belonging to an ethnic unit or group, which as a collective entity is on an equal footing with all other communities within the state. Equality cannot be reduced simply to equality of individual rights. The principle of equality is only realised if every human being is treated equally both as an individual as well as a member of an ethnic community or collective.

For this reason, minorities also claim the right to be treated as a collective unit equally to the majority unit. Individuals who belong to a minority are not content to be treated equally only as individuals. They also want as part of their community to enjoy equal rights in relation to other groups and communities. The goal therefore must not only be to accord equal rights to every individual but also to provide people as members of an ethnic community with equal rights as a collective.

In 2001, an expert commission for a new Serbian constitution presented a sensational proposal, which was acclaimed by the Venice Commission of the Council of Europe as a model for many other states. This draft constitution proposed for example, that the preamble should include the following:

> "Conscious of the state tradition of the Serbian people and determined to establish the equality of all peoples living in Serbia…"

Peace and liberty: The balance between individual and collective rights

How does the aforementioned Serbian constitutional draft seek to implement the principle of equality of ethnic communities? The answer can be found in Chapter III of the draft: "*Persons belonging to a national minority shall have special rights, which they exercise individually or in community with others.*" When states with fragmented societies want to pursue the constitutional goal of equality of peoples, they have to grant collective rights to those communities in order to reach such goal. Collective rights can however also limit individual rights. Thus, the collective right of a fundamentalist sect to religious freedom might empower the religious community to infringe the religious liberty of its individual members. To what extent may such collective rights restrict individual rights? In Switzerland, the Federal Court has consistently decided that individual linguistic freedom may be restricted for the sake of the principle of territoriality, that is – collective linguistic rights, if the existence of a linguistic minority is threatened. For the protection of an endangered minority language for example, it may be prohibited within the territory of the minority language to post public advertisements in other official languages. Therefore, if states with multicultural societies want to hold themselves together, they cannot – as HANNAH ARENDT suggests – restrict themselves to the pursuit of freedom as the highest political goal. In addition to freedom, peace between ethnic communities must be an equally important state goal.

A state that wants to realise these principles will have to translate the principle of equality of peoples into concrete constitutional law, that is, into enforceable collective rights. So for example in article 232 of the Constitution of Brazil one finds the right of Indians to defend their rights before the court not only as individuals, but also as a collective ethnic community.

However, minorities cannot use collective rights to infringe the core of individual rights or the human dignity of individuals. The core of individual rights, which according to international treaties must remain inviolable even in cases of war or emergency, may not be undermined by the recognition of collective rights.

8.1.4.4 Fostering Diversity

Minorities too must be able to identify with their state

The multicultural state can set itself the goal of holding society together by regarding diversity not as a burden but as an asset, and by fostering diversity as something that enriches society rather than merely 'tolerating' diversity. Article 2 of the new Swiss Constitution provides for example: "*[the Confederation] shall promote ... the common welfare, the sustainable development, the internal cohesion and the cultural diversity of the country*".

Autonomy

How can cultural diversity be fostered? The only known means to foster diversity is to not only grant rights and liberties to the various communities, but to also equip them with the necessary autonomy to develop themselves according to their own values. It is necessary to construct the constitutional framework in such a way that the vast majority of the population can identify with the multicultural state and can see it as 'their' own state ('we'). People within such a state should be able to find a common answer to the questions: What is good for us as a multicultural community and what is good for us as a collective community?

If one can find legitimate answers to these essential questions, then logically one should also be able to find answers to the questions: Who should govern over whom? And which majorities and which minorities under which conditions should be entitled to exercise governmental powers or majority rights?

Indeed, decentralisation is an excellent instrument with which to grant local communities limited autonomy and thus to enable them to exercise a limited right of self-determination. Decentralisation alone however, leaves communities with no possibility to participate in decision making at the centre. Moreover, the degree of decentralisation and the borders of sub-units can be changed by simple majority. Minorities will therefore remain at the mercy of the majority, as they do not enjoy any special constitutional protection.

Shared rule

For this very reason, only a balanced distribution of powers between the centre and the decentralised units and a decision making mechanism by which various minorities are able to contribute to decisions at the central level, will result in solutions that are legitimate and acceptable for minorities. Such balanced regulation of autonomy and power sharing can ultimately only be realised by federal constitutions. A federal constitution protects the minority against the tyranny of the majority by providing a balance between self-rule and shared rule and vesting constitutional jurisdiction in an appropriate court.

8.1.4.5 Conclusion

These instruments and procedures that enable states to bring and to hold communities together and thus to overcome fragmentation, are only possible if states are prepared to radically adjust their political vision. They must be prepared to take diversity seriously in a political sense. They should neither ignore it nor should they exclude or eliminate cultural diversity from their political institutions. If they wish to take diversity seriously, states and their constitution making bodies cannot settle merely for creating constitutions that proclaim universal values. They must also address the much more difficult questions: what is good for them and their communities? What can be done within the state without violating universal values? Who should govern over whom and by what procedure should this question be decided?

Federalism

Federalism can be understood as a constitutional model which does not merely tolerate diversity, but rather consciously fosters it as a special value for which the multicultural state stands. Viewed from this perspective, federalism is to be seen not only as an instrument to further limit governmental power, but also as a means of enabling different communities to have a share in governmental power and of giving them the opportunity, within the limits of the overall common interest, to govern themselves according to their own values and priorities. States should not manifest their openness to universal values by ignoring cultural diversity. Rather, states ought to adopt cultural diversity as a value in itself and enable all inhabitants and all cultural groups within society to share governmental power and to participate in the common endeavour to realise peace, justice and liberty.

Federalism in this sense can serve as the guarantor of the multicultural state which not only preserves diversity, but rather fosters it. Federalism thus becomes the constitutional instrument that gives effect to the principle of unity in diversity. The various cultural communities within the state deserve to be fostered. If governments concentrate on fostering diversity, they can at the local level satisfy the needs and emotions of their inhabitants. The values of the state are values that are good for its people and also good for its diverse cultural communities. Different ethnicities within a state are almost always linked to the corresponding kin ethnicities of neighbouring states. If the multicultural state does not achieve full integration of its ethnic minorities, and if the state is not accepted as father- or motherland by these minorities, it will always encounter difficulties with its neighbour states. Only if diverse communities are integrated will the multicultural state be fully embedded within the international community of states and enjoy harmonious relationships with neighbour states, which themselves harbour corresponding cultural communities.

8.2 Towards a Theory of Federalism: Typology of Federations and Models of Decentralisation

8.2.1 Federalism: Self-Rule and Shared Rule

What is federalism?

Federalism can be defined as a state form in which the autonomy of sub-national units and their participation in government at the centre are constitutionally guaranteed. In other words, federalism describes a state in which the constitution prescribes a balance of self-rule and shared rule. Federalism is a system of political organisation, in which various political units are united under a superior political entity, and whereby the powers of the centre and of the sub-units are divided and allocated in such a way as to ensure the viability, authority and legitimacy of the whole system as well as of the sub-units.

The powers and functions of the state and its sub-units have to be defined and determined by the constitution, and in distributing powers between the federation and its units a certain balance must be observed. The balance between the federation and the federal units is the institutional basis for the vertical separation of powers. This vertical separation of powers enables the different levels of the state to exercise mutual control over each other in the concrete exercise of powers (checks and balances), and the vertical balance also serves to underpin the political system itself.

The main goal of a federal state structure may be to provide an additional restriction and control of state power in the interest of better national integration. This is undoubtedly the case for the United States and many other federal states, the legitimacy of which is based on a homogeneous nation. The goal of federalism can however also be to legitimise the federation and at the same time to provide for the conditions to enable the federal units to establish their own powers based on their own legitimacy. The presupposes a common state, which is constructed upon multiple loyalties and which does not seek to integrate diverse groups into the national unit, but rather to preserve and to foster the existing diversity.

Differences between decentralisation and federalism

Federalism is the *constitutionally* guaranteed autonomy *and* participation of the federal units at the federal level. Decentralisation on the other hand, is autonomy that is only provided for by ordinary legislation. In addition, decentralisation generally does not provide for shared rule by the sub-units at the central level. In a federal state, every structural modification between the federation and the federal units must be regulated by the constitution. Since the federal units participate in the procedure for constitutional amendment, the distribution of powers among the federation and federal units receives a higher overall legitimacy from both the nation as a whole and the peoples of the sub-units. In the case of decentralisation on the other hand, such decisions are made by the central legislature alone. Thus, because ordinary decentralisation lacks constitutional protection, minorities are entirely dependent on the majority, and their autonomy can be modified, amended or even abolished by simple majority of the legislature.

The dynamics of the different forms of government

Every state finds itself in constant flux between the poles of centralisation and decentralisation. Influenced by economic, social and political developments as well as by the international environment, governments will have either to centralise or decentralise responsibilities. Increasing globalisation poses a further fundamental challenge for states and will result in greater tensions between the centre and the periphery. According to the prescriptions of the World Bank and the IMF, decentralisation has become a key element of 'good governance'. States that are reliant upon credit from international financial institutions must therefore demonstrate that they are decentralising their state powers. Globalisation limits the margins of independent governmental decisions considerably. States have to hand sovereign powers over to international organisations and are forced in the interests of international cooperation to implement international standards through their central domestic institutions.

Today it is not only traditional nation-states that have a federal structure. The international community, and in particular regional organisations such as the European Union, often have a federal outlook or some federal and/or confederal characteristics. Federalism is no longer a monopoly of the nation-state. One then has to ask, whether a state structure with four vertical levels from local government, to provincial or state government, federal government and finally a fourth, supranational level of government such as the European Union, is conceivable. If sovereignty is understood as the basis for the legitimacy of the exercise of governmental power at each of the various levels, then such structure is perfectly conceivable. According to such model, each of the governmental levels has its own original source of legitimacy for the exercise of its delegated powers.

What is the engine that drives states either to centralise or to decentralise? What are the causes of this dynamic? On one side, the dynamic is influenced by the human need for security, identity, self-determination and integration into one's own culture, language and religion. On the other side, foreign and external influences lead states to decentralise or centralise certain functions. Areas affected by such external influence include social security, mobility, division of labour, environment, globalisation and the need for equality.

But what are the fundamental political ideas and principles that underlie the concept of federalism?

8.2.2 *Philosophical and Historical Foundations*

The great philosophers of the 16th, 17th and 18th Centuries

In the 16th, 17th and 18th Centuries, the issues of secularisation of the state, its separation from the Pope, and the establishment of popular sovereignty which finds its expression in the Nation, were at the centre of political philosophy. These revolutionary changes, which led to the dissolution of the feudal state of the Middle Ages, were only possible through the establishment of a strong and independent central government. The theoretical foundations for these developments can be attributed to the great philosophers BODIN, HOBBES, LOCKE and ROUSSEAU.

BODIN justified the legitimacy of the king by the grace of God: "*Car qui méprise son Prince souverain, il méprise Dieu, duquel il est l'image en terre*" (Since those who disregard their prince sovereign, disregard God, of whom he is the image on the earth). This absolute and uncontested position of the monarch does not permit any division of sovereignty, let alone any minority rights. The power of the state has to remain central, undivided and absolute.

The final step towards absolute but secularised sovereignty was made by THOMAS HOBBES. According to HOBBES, the people replaces the authority of God by means of the social contract. The people, without any claim to exercise control or hold the state accountable, legitimises the absolute authority of the state as the sovereign Leviathan. HOBBES however leaves open the most burning question of today: who belongs to the sovereign people? For him, the people is merely an abstract notion. All human beings in this world belong to 'the people'. These people now want to exercise political power. But within which territorial borders can or should human beings establish the association necessary to constitute a 'people' for the purposes of a social contract that will lay the foundation for state sovereignty? Is it all Spaniards, the Basques, or the Catalans? Is it the English including Northern Ireland, or is it the people of the whole Irish island or all the inhabitants of the United Kingdom?

The mandate of the ruler: ALTHUSIUS

ALTHUSIUS was born in 1557, that is, after BODIN but before HOBBES. He was influenced by the concept of alliance theology as developed by ZWINGLI and CALVIN. Both reformers refer back to the Old Testament and hold the view that God never conveyed absolute power to a King of the people of Israel. Rather, the people of Israel through its alliance with God was entrusted with political power, and the people of Israel conveyed this power to the King. According to ALTHUSIUS, sovereignty does not find its basis in a King with divine authority, but in the alliance concluded between God and the people. However, the people does not possess unlimited and absolute sovereignty, as sovereignty is not based on a secular social contract concluded only by the people, but rather is rooted in an agreement between God and the people. Thus, the alliance only conveys to the people a limited mandate to govern the respective territory for the benefit of the people. If this mandate is violated, the people has the right to resistance.

Mandate – not sovereignty

As the mandate is limited and does not convey unaccountable powers but only specified authority, the powers encompassed by the mandate can also be divided and thus distributed to different bodies. Accordingly, aspects of the mandate can be allocated to local government authorities. Thus ALTHUSIUS develops a concept according to which municipalities, provinces and also the empire are given separate and distinct mandates to govern and administer their respective territories for the benefit of the people. The empire is a federally structured empire, in which there is no absolute power and in which power and sovereignty can therefore be distributed amongst central and local authorities. This concept of ALTHUSIUS is, in comparison to the social contract, more flexible and takes better account of the dynamics and 'glocalisation' of today's world. Moreover, it contains in itself a dynamic model of legitimacy, as it enables the foundation of a state structured by vertical distribution of powers, beginning from local or municipal government, up to provinces and to the national/federal and even supranational level.

Ultimately the theoretical concept of the mandate developed from alliance theology is also democratic, as it entrusts the mandate to the people and not to a monarchical ruler. ALTHUSIUS builds upon the right of the people, as only the people can convey the mandate to be governed. Finally, it is not nationalistic, as the right to govern requires those who hold and exercise the mandate to treat equally all people within the respective territory. The legitimacy to rule is not derived from the ethnic nation, but rather from a limited and assigned mandate. Since the people can never achieve absolute sovereignty, the imaginary unity of the people or an ethnic community cannot have an interest in acquiring a monopoly on sovereignty, nor in exercising an unlimited sovereign right to self-determination in order to create a new state, as this state would not have the legitimacy to exclude 'other' communities.

The influence of the American and French Revolutions

The two democratic revolutions at the end of the 18th Century led to two different systems of government: The founding fathers of the United States established with their Constitution a new Union with a federal structure. The goal of the new governmental system was to strengthen the existing democratic and republican elements of civil society and to secede from the colonial ruler. On the other hand, the French Revolution overthrew a hierarchical, aristocratic, feudal system and replaced it with a centralistic, unitary, republican-democratic state, committed to a declaration of Human Rights that promised liberty, equality and fraternity for all.

The French Revolution installed the *Assemblée Nationale* as the supreme legislature with absolute and centralised powers. This new absolutism finds expression for example in Article 6 of the Constitution of 1795: "*La loi est la volonté générale, exprimée par la majorité ou des citoyens ou de leurs représentants*" (the law is the general will, expressed by the majority of the citizens or their representatives).

The French Revolution thus abolished the former bases for the validity of the law and laid the foundation for the legitimacy of the absolute decision making power of the legislature. Such absolutism can only be asserted, if the state denies any claim to local autonomy and decentralisation, centralises all political authority, and thereby permits neither an external nor an internal division of sovereignty. The National Assembly is the only source of the unified and recognised law.

In contrast to the French Revolution, the American Revolution was not intended, in addition to assuming control over government, also to change the society. The new state with its republican government was rather conceived to serve the existing social system. It is for this reason that the founding fathers were primarily concerned to establish a state with carefully limited powers. Consequently, they sought to divide government powers not only horizontally but also vertically through a federal system. Such limited constitutional government was within their direct revolutionary interest.

8.2.3 Federalism and Decentralisation as a Modern Concept for Democratic Governance

Globalisation

The decentralisation of federal as well as unitary states has become an expedient tool of modern governance, as it enables many problems of today's globalised world to be solved in a more simple and efficient way.

However, it must be acknowledged that decentralisation does not always lead to greater democracy and greater autonomy for local bodies. Decentralisation can privilege local power holders and clans. If such rulers or clans can rule without transparency and accountability, decentralisation will actually undermine the idea of democratisation. On the other hand, a state with strong decentralisation can respond more quickly to changing circumstances, as decentralised units are generally much more flexible than the central government. In addition, the central government can adapt in response to successful innovations of the decentralised units, and through constitutional amendment can take over responsibilities from its dec-entralised units.

The complex networks of today's structured global world enable decentralised units in addition to connect with other sub-national units through international cooperation. Federal and/or decentralised units are thus able to substantially increase their autonomy through transnational and regional cooperation.

Claims of minorities

Linguistic, religious and cultural minorities claim in specific domains such as education, cultural activities and religion, a certain autonomy and the right to administer their own affairs, even if it is only a limited form of organisational autonomy within their own territory. They demand that their problems be handled by representatives who belong to their community. Some minorities claim economic support for their region. They want to be able to cooperate with their kin cultures in other states and to have friendly neighbouring relations with those states in order to maintain cultural exchanges. Above all, minorities demand that within a state dominated by a majority culture, they be allowed to foster and develop their own identity, to live according to their way of life, and to maintain and develop their culture. For this reason they claim institutional and legal guarantees that allow them to influence the decision making processes of the legislature, the executive and the judiciary.

Often minorities are settled within clearly defined territorial borders. In these cases, the state can to a great extent take their demands into account by way of territorial federalism. However there will always be areas, especially cities, which are inhabited by various cultures and minorities. This is the case for example in Brussels, where both the French-speaking Walloons and the Dutch-speaking Flemish have settled. In such cases the claims of cultural communities cannot be addressed by territorial decentralisation. It is however possible in such cases to accord autonomy and rights to certain groups of people independent of territory. The Lebanese Constitution for example establishes a state that is federally organised according to personal criteria, and in which religious communities rather than territories are represented in the legislature.

Personal federalism

European states have tended to be wary of adopting such constitutional solutions based on personal federalism. In the Middle East however, such models have a long tradition, which can be traced to the millet system of the Ottoman Empire. This system has its roots in the Koran, which requires that the autonomy of different religious communities should be respected. According to the millet system, the different communities could foster their own culture and religion autonomously, whilst being subject to the territorial authority of the Sultan. In the face of increasing minority conflicts in areas in which different minorities and ethnicities live together, this form of personal federalism is likely to be of growing interest in the future as a means of conflict management and prevention.

8.2.4 An answer to the Problems of the Former Communist Countries

Federalism as pretext

After the fall of the former socialist federations (Soviet Union, Yugoslavia and Czechoslovakia) in Eastern Europe, it may sound daring to speak in favour of federalism and to suggest that these societies will ultimately only be able to solve their interethnic conflicts and brutal nationalism on the basis of federal cooperation. These countries were, as we have seen, pseudo-states under the authority of the Communist Party, and not states in the sense of constitutionalism. The peoples and their states were ruled by one party, which pretended that its despotism would serve the interests of the *volonté générale*.

Federal states serving the interests of the party

The problems connected with transition to a new constitutional state, including constitution making and the establishment of a modern state, were particularly difficult for peoples living in former communist federations. Once the people had been freed from the yoke of communism, the minority communities in particular rejected not only communism but also the legitimacy of the successor state whose federal boundaries had been drawn by the previous communist regime. They therefore wanted and needed to fill the resulting vacuum of political authority with a new tradition that accorded with the people, their territory and their history, tradition and culture, and which lent a new legitimacy to the historical Nation.

Every nation has the right to its own state

Initially, the communist rule of multiethnic societies was legitimised by the principle of the equality of nations. In terms of content, this claim to equality either meant the right of each nation to have its own state, or the right of each nation to equal membership within a 'just federation'. Although equality was proclaimed in the constitution, legally it could not be implemented. The realisation of the principle of equality remained within the powers of the ruling party, which had to resolve conflicts arising from contradictory interests between the different nations. The nation did not see itself – as in democratic societies – as a unity in the political sense, which could achieve independence, equality and democratic pluralism. The nation saw itself rather as a totalitarian collectivistic unit, superimposed on the individual and held together by the three principles of one people, one state, one ruler. For this reason, nobody ever really questioned the existing political inequality of single individuals. Nationalism in these countries is therefore nothing more than the last collectivist phase of communism.

Nationalism replaces the legitimacy of the party

Once the legitimacy of the communist party had collapsed, the power-holders of the party sought a new legitimacy in order to justify their totalitarian authority, and found it in the universally recognised value of the 'national interest'. In order to remain in power, they capitalised on ethnic conflicts and manipulated existing 'friend/foe' attitudes to their own advantage. Without the substructure of a civil society they gave the state an outwardly democratic appearance. From now on they pursued a strategy based solely on ethnic interests and ethnic symbols: the value of ethnic identity was misused in order to conceal the true interests at play, namely, the maintenance and consolidation of the power of the ruler.

One has to assume that as long as these federations were ruled by the communist party, they were never federations in the real sense, as federalism can only be realised within a democratic, rule of law-based society with a legitimate constitution.

8.2.5 *Peaceful Conflict Resolution*

Federalism fosters international cooperation

In the long term a 'European House' will only be established by a democratic and federal system. Democracy however can only be developed in a pluralistic society, in which political, economic and social forces are diversified and are institutionally distributed across different cultural, linguistic and religious communities. Only then can citizens effectively participate in the decision making process.

The concept of the federal state rests upon an understanding of popular sovereignty, which allows the distribution and division of sovereignty between different levels of government. Understood in this way, sovereignty can be entrusted to internal bodies as well as to external bodies. Federalism is the state structure, which does not throw its own existence or integrity into question when it entrusts part of its sovereignty either to internal sub-units or to supranational bodies or organisations.

Internally, federations have a much more flexible structure than unitary states, which readily allows – or even promotes – international and regional cooperation. Federal units also often possess specific external powers and can therefore effectively generate and foster regional and international cooperation.

Intrastate conflicts

In the event of the outbreak of intrastate conflict, federal states have at their disposal various procedures and options for conflict resolution, including the capacity to adapt their structures to the conflict. Federal states can for example found new federal units and thus re-establish the federal balance (the Tamil State in India, the Canton of Jura in Switzerland). They can also increase the autonomy of federal units by strengthening decentralization, or even provide asymmetric autonomy to certain units in order to neutralise the conflict (Russian Federation). In a federal state, this dynamic is possible because the decentralised structure is already in place and need only be adapted to the new situation. As the federal units have already gained original legitimacy in relation to their *demos*, they are also able to build their own political structures. The constitutions of the federal units can also provide for the separation of powers between the three arms of government at the sub-national level.

If a conflict cannot be solved democratically, federations should be able to find a compromise based on negotiation. The tradition and the political culture of federal systems are particularly well-suited to negotiations which lead to compromise solutions, because compromise is an essential feature of federal politics. Compromise is legitimised through the federal state, which in itself is already the result of a compromise.

The federation is based upon the principle of self-determination of its people as well as of the peoples of the federal units. The clear political will of a federal unit or of its people has to be respected and thus taken into account, if it is expressed through a fair and democratic procedure. Federal states are not satisfied with according minorities the minimal standard of human rights protection. They also enable minorities to arrange themselves into territorial units, to participate in the decision making process at the federal level, and to maintain and foster their own cultural identity. People belonging to minorities are therefore not only protected by individual rights, but also by their collective autonomy.

8.2.6 Growth of Administrative Efficiency

Parallelism of power and responsibility

The current structures of public administration have developed into a threatening complex of clumsy, opaque, inefficient, inflexible and anonymous bodies. This impersonal administrative structure shows decidedly centralistic tendencies. The central bureaucracy is not prepared to inform itself over the real needs and problems of the decentralised units and their peoples. Those who exercise power in the central bureaucracy usually do not bear the corresponding responsibility, as the decisions made by the bureaucrat have an effect on persons for whom he/she has no direct responsibility and by whom he/she cannot be held directly accountable. Often the central bureaucracy does not have to bear the consequences of its own inappropriate or impractical decisions, but rather these consequences are borne by the decentralised units.

Easy flow of information

Federal and decentralised systems make the flow of information at the level of the local decentralised unit easier. Local bodies are closer to the people. If the citizens of local units decide on the election, income and expenditure of their local authorities, they have a direct impact on their behaviour. Thus, local authorities are able to make informed decisions and at the same time they are directly accountable to the people. Problems will be recognised and solved more quickly. The authorities elected by the local population and answerable to local councils or local parliaments will have to react rapidly and effectively to demands and complaints of their voters. Within the sphere of their autonomy, they do not have to take into account the diverging interests of other regions, but rather can decide on the basis of their own local public interest. Local authorities are therefore able to be responsive to local needs and to efficiently make decisions that will be accepted by the local population.

Competition

If decentralised units also possess financial autonomy that enables them to raise the revenue necessary to finance the development of the local unit within the local interest, competition will produce incentives between the different local units.

Such incentives will enhance the efficiency and cost-effectiveness of the federal units. However, such competition will only have a positive effect on the state as a whole, if it is supplemented by solidarity between the decentralised units (which is indispensable for the state).

Creativity

Federal government systems work more effectively and efficiently than centralised unitary states. Because decisions are likely to be based on consensus and accepted by the people, and because of the social and ethnic peace brought about by federalism, federal states need not waste unnecessary energy on a difficult implementation process. Policies can be easily implemented and realised, because they are accepted by the people. Federal states are also more flexible, because decisions at the lower levels can be made autonomously. They are more innovative, because it is easier to experiment on a small scale in a local area. Local areas can learn from neighbouring regions and, based on their experiences, can develop new models for the solution of their own problems. If experiments prove unsuccessful, the damage can be more quickly contained and remedied than would be the case at the central level, where one would have to mobilise an enormous bureaucracy to correct its procedures and decisions.

Globalisation

In the face of increasing international insecurity and the limited possibilities available for nation-states to eliminate the negative effects of globalisation, peoples' need to retreat into the security and identity of their local homeland is continuously growing. It may well be that nation-states will deem it necessary to resort to authoritarian means of government, in order to contain the social unrest caused by globalisation. In the wake of 9/11, states have already imposed substantial restrictions on individual liberty in order to fight against terrorism. In federal states, decentralised structures may to a certain degree impede the development of authoritarian systems, thanks to the vertical division of powers and the local democratic responsibility of the authorities, and may thereby contribute to internal peace and harmony.

8.3 Federalism and Decentralisation in Comparison

8.3.1 What is Federalism?

Decentralisation, devolution, federalism

There is no centralised unitary state that does not delegate certain tasks to decentralised units. Every state is composed of local units, which have certain public responsibilities. What distinguishes the decentralisation or devolution of unitary states from federal systems? In fact, a distinction can be made between three levels of decentralisation: '*déconcentration*', devolution or decentralisation in a limited sense, and federalism with strong local autonomy.

The French word *déconcentration* denotes a delegation of tasks by central authorities to lower authorities, without transferring full responsibility. The exercise of the delegated tasks or functions by the lower authority remains under the legal direction and control of the central authority. Such delegation can be revoked at any time by the central authority. The responsibility for implementation remains with the centre, and the lower authorities are only mandated to execute and to follow the directives of the higher authority. If the mandate is not fulfilled according to the directives, the lower authorities may be subject to disciplinary action.

Decentralisation is the legally regulated delegation of legislative and executive powers and responsibilities to local territorial units. Decentralisation or devolution is the technique of the unitary state to provide either asymmetric or general autonomy to its regions. The central authority does not retain responsibility for decentralised powers. It must merely ensure that the lower authorities adhere to the law and to the terms of their autonomy. The decision over decentralisation is not made by the administration, but rather by the legislature. However, even a state with strong decentralisation remains a unitary state, because the scope of decentralisation is always determined by simple parliamentary majority. Moreover, financial responsibility usually remains with the central government, with the lower authorities relying largely on grants or transfers from the centre to fulfil their functions. On the other hand, decentralised units are directly politically responsible to their citizens for the exercise of the powers within the scope of their autonomy. The fulfilment of this responsibility is for decentralised units of the utmost importance. The more transparently the authorities embrace democratic accountability within their units, the more effective decentralisation will be, and the more it will be possible to avoid the danger of undemocratic elitism. However, simple decentralisation has no constitutional quality. The performance of decentralised functions amounts merely to the exercise of responsibility delegated by the central legislature.

In federal states there is no delegation of tasks to the federal units. The federal state is only responsible for executing its own tasks as determined by the constitution. All other powers which are not assigned by the constitution exclusively to the federal state are to be taken care of by the federal units. They decide autonomously within the scope of their authority on their own tasks and priorities. Apart from these independent powers, the federal units in certain states – in particular the federal states with civil law systems – are often obliged to execute some or most of the federal functions. This delegated responsibility for implementation empowers the federal units with greater autonomy than is the case with delegation in a unitary state, as the federal units are usually free to determine the mode of implementation and they usually bear full political and financial responsibility for the execution of the delegated task. In the case of the legal directives of the European Union, member states bear the financial burden of execution and are also politically responsible to their own parliaments for the domestic implementation of 'federal' EU responsibilities.

Autonomy

Federal units in federal systems command their own original autonomy, which is not vested only by statutes but rather is enshrined in the constitution. A modification of the distribution of powers within the federation cannot be effected by the simple majority of the legislature, but only by constitutional amendment. As constitutional amendments at the federal level generally require a higher consensus than legislative decisions, the autonomy of minorities is better protected than in systems where decentralisation is provided for only in ordinary legislation. In federal systems, autonomy in fact attains the quality of partial sovereignty, implemented by the three branches of the federal units: the executive, legislative and judicial branches. The federal units determine autonomously their own institutional organisation on the basis of their own constitutions, and implement their own laws within their sphere of authority. Local authorities are accountable for their activity not to the federation but to their own federal unit. Unlike authorities within decentralised units, they are subject neither to disciplinary nor legal accountability to the central authorities. They are legitmised by the *demos* within the federal unit, to which they owe full political accountability.

Participation

In addition to their constitutionally protected autonomy, the federal units also participate in the decision making process of the federation. The federal units participate in forming the consensus or the '*volonté générale*' of the federation. This participation is not based on simple majoritarian democracy. The smaller federal units, regardless of the size of their territory or population, are usually accorded a proportionately greater voting power than the larger federal units. The principle of the equality of federal units in terms of participation is either applied unconditionally to all units (USA, Australia, Switzerland) or the smaller units are at least proportionately privileged (Germany and Austria).

Residual power

Federalism is the constitutionally guaranteed balance of self-rule and shared rule between federal units and the governmental branches of the centre. If a federation is founded through decentralisation from the top down, as in Belgium, the central state does not delegate powers to the lower units, but rather abstains from claiming unlimited sovereign power and authority, and leaves it to the federal units to deal with certain constitutionally specified areas. The federal units thereby receive through constitutional decentralisation some new residual powers. If however the federation was established from the bottom up through agreed centralisation, residual power simply remains with the partially sovereign federal units.

Scope of autonomy

Whoever seeks to ascertain the scope of decentralisation within a particular federal state, will need to know how many powers have been left to the decentralised units, who makes decisions on decentralisation and by what procedure, and finally what is the nature or 'quality' of the autonomy granted to the federal units. Do the federal units have to rely on the central government to provide revenue for the fulfilment of their tasks, or are they obliged or able to finance their own activity? To what extent can the authorities of federal units be made accountable by representatives at the level of the federal unit, and what (if any) powers of supervision and oversight do the central authorities have? Whoever can provide clear answers to these questions, will know the scope and quality of the autonomy accorded to the federal units in the respective federation.

Financial powers

The degree of decentralisation cannot be measured only by the distribution of legislative powers. It does not suffice for example to impose upon local authorities the responsibility for the health care of their population. In order to be able to fulfil this responsibility, the local authority will have to decide by law, which aspects of health care are to be private and which are to be public. In addition, it must also possess the necessary human and financial resources to implement and apply the law. It will have to be able to build and manage hospitals, to educate and train medical personnel and regulate the medical profession, and must also be able to take preventive measures.

Distribution of powers among the branches of central government

It is self-evident that the assessment of the quality of decentralisation is also dependent on the distribution of powers at the centre. If the balance and control of the three central powers is guaranteed by checks and balances, the autonomy of local units will enjoy greater protection than in a system in which for example a powerful head of state is able to exercise executive power unchecked and therefore able to misuse his/her power in relation to the federal units.

Legal culture

Decentralisation is finally also dependent on the legal culture and legal history of the state in which it is implemented. Decentralisation in states with a common law tradition has to be assessed differently from decentralisation in states that recognise a clear separation between public and private law. In civil law systems, almost everything is regulated by legislation. The distribution of legislative powers between the centre and the federal units is thus the decisive indicator for the assessment of the autonomy of the federal units. In common law federations however, the decentralisation of the judicature and the jurisdiction of the courts are of much greater significance. In the USA for example, much of the criminal law as well as the traditional contract law and other fields of 'private' law have remained within the authority of the traditional common law courts rather than being exhaustively regulated by legislation. As the courts of the states are the direct successors of the common law courts of the former British colonial power, they have retained much of the traditional jurisdiction of their colonial predecessors. In accordance with common law tradition, the state courts decide criminal and civil matters on the basis of precedents from their own courts as well as from the British courts prior to American Independence.

The legal pyramid in continental European civil law tradition

According to the positivist, continental concept of law, the legal system represents a single and internally coherent unit. Contradictions are avoided by a principle of hierarchy and priority of certain law. Thus, the legal order is based on the idea of a pyramid, in which—in order to maintain the unity of the system – laws passed by a higher level within the legal hierarchy will always be superior to laws passed at a lower level. As a logical consequence, federations with a continental civil law system will be much more inclined towards a system of federalism that provides for the implementation and execution of federal laws by the federal units. This of course does not prevent the federal units from exercising certain original legislative powers. In such federal systems, federal legislation must also be applied by the local courts within the federal units, and the higher federal courts ensure the unity and conformity of the lower court decisions.

Municipalities in common law and continental European civil law

The common law is a legal system developed by a range of different courts, each with different jurisdiction, whereby each court makes decisions according to its own precedents and develops its own concept of law. Local authorities may also exercise powers that have not been formally legislatively delegated to them, such as for example certain tasks originally given to the police, because they are considered as prerogative powers (whereas in continental legal systems all powers must be expressly determined by the constitution or the legislature).

The system of municipalities on the continent on the other hand, is regulated quite differently. Napoleon came up with the idea of making the local private corporations of farmers into 'agents' of the central state, which could exercise certain public powers delegated to them by the central state. Thus, insofar as the communes or municipalities in the French state performed public functions, they did so on the basis of a mandate from the central state. It is for this reason that a distinction must be made between decentralisation in common law states and decentralisation in unitary states with a French, that is, continental European legal tradition.

Enforcement of the law

The enforcement of the law in decentralised units is guaranteed in the French tradition by the power of the central authorities to issue directives and to take disciplinary measures against any local authorities that violate those directives. In the British legal system, the writ of mandamus was introduced early on, in order that the central authorities could summon the local authorities to court and thus compel local authorities to adhere to central laws. Whilst it is now the case in France that the central government can call local authorities to account only by court decisions and no longer by disciplinary measures, the old French law still applies in many former colonial states.

According to the old British tradition, it is also possible by a decision of the Parliament at Westminster to empower local authorities to issue so-called local 'bylaws'. Local units do not have any original power to legislate. However, Parliament has long been in the practice of delegating to those units important powers to issue bylaws, which powers it can at any time revoke.

Competition between federal units and the federation

The distribution of powers between the federation and the federal units can vary enormously from one federation to the next. In the American federation, the power and sovereignty of the state is divided not only vertically but also horizontally among the branches of government at the federal level and also at the level of the federal units. The federation implements federal legislation through its own federal agencies and for the resolution of disputes in federal matters it has federal courts. Federal units on the other side are responsible for the execution of federal laws as well as for the implementation and enforcement of their own state legislation. The consequence of this dual legal system of course, is that there are conflicts of power and functions between authorities, for example between the federal law enforcement agency (FBI) and state police forces. Citizens constantly find themselves facing agencies of both the federal and state governments. It may be difficult for the average citizen to appreciate that federal servants will act according to federal law and state agents according to state law.

8.3.2 Decision Making Power and Government Authorities

8.3.2.1 Constituent Power (pouvoir constituant) and the Constituted Representative Authority (pouvoir constitué)

In relation to constitution making power, one has to distinguish between the actual *pouvoir constituant* on the one hand – that is, the authority which originally made the constitution and created the state – and the *pouvoir constitué* on the other – that is, the constituted power, or the authority that has been installed by the constitution to amend and modify the constitution. The theory of the *pouvoir constituant* developed by SIEYÈS is ultimately based on the idea that the highest revolutionary authority, based on its factual political power, is the absolute sovereign and can command and enforce absolute obedience. The constitution of the state flows out of the *pouvoir constituant*, and it is then the constitution which determines how and by whom the already adopted constitution can be amended. The *pouvoir constituant* generally exercises an unlimited charismatic power, acquired as a result of revolution or violent coup d'etat. Through the act of constitution making, the *pouvoir constituant* develops its rational and legal legitimacy, and is transformed into the *pouvoir constitué*.

Pouvoir constituant

It is evident that the theory of the *pouvoir constituant* contradicts the fundamental idea of federalism. Federalism entails a division of powers and sovereignty among different state units. If one accepts the theory of the *pouvoir constituant*, one would have logically to assume that each federation was originally established by a revolutionary act and that the federal units ultimately derive their sovereignty from this centralised revolution. This however does not correspond to reality. The Australian federation for example was formed by the agreement of the Australian colonies to unite in a federal state, and the *Commonwealth of Australia Constitution Act* (1901) was passed by the British Parliament at Westminster, as well as being adopted by the people of the Australian colonies in a series of referenda. There was no revolutionary violence at any stage of the process, but rather several years of planning and negotiation. The formation of the Australian federation was not a revolutionary act, because Australia did not secede from the British empire and assert itself as an independent republic, but rather, having formed a united federation, acquired sovereignty and independence gradually over the ensuing decades. To this day, the British monarch is formally the Australian Head of State. At any rate in terms of constituent power, the federal Constitution of Australia, which has survived for over a century thus far, was made by the agreement of a group of representatives of separate self-governing colonies (which became federal units), by the colonial power, and by the peoples of the separate colonies.

Today, Europe is faced with the unresolved question of how to establish a federal constitution by and for the member states of the European Union. According to the theory of the *pouvoir constituant*, the establishment of a European constitution would require as a precondition the existence of a *demos*, which can provide the legitimacy for the constitution making power. In reality, notwithstanding the concept of a European citizenry, Europe is composed of different peoples of the various member states. Is one to draw from this the conclusion, that one must first create a European *demos* and that only then would it be possible to adopt a European Constitution? The history of federal states teaches us that the gradual construction of a federation based on transition from the sovereignty of the member states to a confederation and then to a federation is entirely conceivable and appropriate. The constitution making power in federal states is itself composed of different peoples. Thus, the Constitution of the United States that had been approved by the Convention could only enter into force after it had been ratified by the member states of the confederation, and was from then on open to any other states that wanted to join the union.

Apart from the European Constitution, we are also contemporary witnesses of the exercise of constitution making powers in other federal states. The Constitution of Bosnia was drafted at the American military bases in Dayton through the cooperation of the warring parties, and was then signed in Paris with the participation of the international community. The United Nations has been mediating for years between the Greek and the Turkish Cypriots, in an attempt to establish a new Constitution for Cyprus. A constitutional proposal called the 'Anan Plan' has been rejected by an overwhelming majority of Greek Cypriots and approved by a large majority of Turkish Cypriots. One of the reasons for this important gap between the two societies may be the constitution making process itself and the fact that the diplomatic negotiations have not paid sufficient attention to the need for nation building. If the process ever does result in an agreed constitution, it will be a constitution agreed through compromise, which lays the foundation for the government of a *demos* that is yet to be developed.

If on the other hand, a federal system is created by decentralisation within a unitary state, as in the case of Belgium and perhaps soon in the United Kingdom, the original *demos* as the legitimate constitution making power is uncontested. The new federal constitution itself creates, in addition to the unitary *demos*, additional peoples or '*demoi*' of the new federal units, which will be asked in future to share the constitution making power at the federal level.

Pouvoir constitué

Once the federation is established, the question of the procedure and power for constitutional amendment will arise. Which institution should have the power to amend the constitution, and by what procedure? To what extent should the federal units participate in the decision making process? Should the majority of the federal units or the majority of the people be given greater weight in decisions to amend the constitution? Should each of the federal units be given an equal say regardless of the size of their population and/or territory? Should the procedure for constitutional amendments be more difficult than the legislative process, or should it be possible to adapt the constitution quickly and easily to changing conditions? What should be the relationship between the constitutional court, which can effectively modify the constitution through interpretation, and the democratic majority of the people, which is empowered to amend the constitution by political decision? In the USA for example, it is very difficult to amend the Constitution through the formal amendment procedure. This formal rigidity of the Constitution means that the constitution making power is effectively exercised by the Supreme Court through constitutional interpretation. Although the text of the United States Constitution has barely changed over the last two hundred years, the interpretation of the text has changed considerably, and one can only understand the content of the US Constitution today in connection with a thorough analysis of the constitutional cases of the Supreme Court. In a similar fashion, the meaning and content of certain European treaties have altered as a result of interpretation by the European Court of Justice.

Since international treaties can only be changed and adapted by the unanimous agreement of the member states, the courts empowered to interpret those treaties are entrusted with considerable power and responsibility to adapt the treaty to new needs. Thus, the European Court of Justice has become the actual motor of development of the European Union.

8.3.2.2 Parliaments

Electoral system and parliament

In a unitary state, the people's chamber of parliament represents the entire population of the country and thus also the so-called '*volonté générale*' of the nation. For this reason, the national chamber also has the legitimacy to amend the constitution. The electoral system by which representatives are elected is therefore of great importance. Which electoral system can produce fair and accurate representation of the people and on the other hand produce efficient majorities to ensure stability? The UK and the USA elect their members of parliament from single-member constituencies on the principle of simple majority. It is also conceivable for an entire country to form one constituency, which as a whole elects all members of parliament on the basis of either a proportional or a majoritarian system (Israel). Many European countries have developed proportional systems or a mixture of proportional voting for parties and majoritarian voting for personalities (Germany). Such proportional systems have multi-member constituencies that are generally larger than single-member constituencies but smaller than the whole country. In federal states, electoral boundaries often coincide with the territory of the federal units. If within those constituencies representatives are elected according to the proportional system, the parties of the federation usually have a strong influence on the selection of candidates and the election of members. Depending on the influence of the parties and on the electoral system, candidates may be elected who are committed to more autonomy for the decentralised units or to greater centralisation.

Thus, the electoral system may have a considerable influence on the centralisation or decentralisation of a particular state. If the constituencies are identical with the decentralised units and if the choice of the candidates is made by local parties, the elected representatives are more likely at the national level to represent the interests of their local region than if the choice of candidates is made by a central party.

Local politics plays a particularly prominent role in the second chamber. In federal states, the second chamber is usually designed to represent the federal units in order to defend local interests. Even in unitary states, local entities can often exercise direct influence on the election of candidates to the second chamber. Thus, within the French Senate for example, local interests are better served than within the lower chamber.

Governmental system and parliament

The governmental system itself also has a decisive influence on decentralisation or centralisation of the state. In a purely parliamentary system of government such as that developed at Westminster, the two parties fighting for the majority have a strong interest in a strict and centralised party discipline. Thus the majority party, the leader of which becomes prime minister, both forms the executive and dominates the parliament. Only with a tight leadership can the party retain its dominance at the next election. In such a system it is difficult for local units to make their voices heard in the political debate. If on the other hand, the fate of the executive does not depend on the result of the parliamentary elections, as in Switzerland for example, local interests are more likely to be taken into account at the national level.

Legislative power

Whoever has the power to make the laws is also the principal decision maker in relation to the structure of the state. In a unitary state, only central bodies are entitled to make laws. Without express delegation, decentralised units have no legislative power. In the UK for example, local units need to be expressly and specifically empowered to make by-laws. In a federal state on the other hand, the power to make laws is divided between the federation and the federal units. Within the framework of the constitution therefore, the law-making power of the federation is limited to matters of federal power.

In France, as now also in several Eastern European states, the fact that the executive together with the President can exercise extensive law-making authority has an important centralising effect.

The budget

The power over the budget is one of the most important and most traditional powers of the Parliament. The budgetary power enables parliament to control government finance and gives the majority far-reaching possibilities to influence day-to-day politics. By deciding on the budget, parliament also decides on the financial means to be granted to decentralised units. Parliament can thereby decide on the concrete extent of decentralisation during the budget period. If parliament is generous in its provision of revenue, the decentralised units may have a better chance to prove themselves within regional politics, to fulfil their functions and to meet the expectations of local citizens. If the revenue granted by parliament is inadequate, the decentralised units will inevitably encounter the criticism of the population for unsatisfactory fulfilment of their role, and will lose power and credibility.

Indirectly, parliament can also influence decentralisation via the tax system. If it grants local authorities the power to levy local taxes, it ties the local units to the local democracies, since local authorities will only be able to levy taxes if they can convince local representatives of the importance of the tax and of the purposes for which the revenue is to be used. At the same time, the local representatives will have an interest in controlling the expenditure of revenue collected from the local taxpayer. Without sufficient control and local accountability, the danger of corruption is increased. Lack of transparency and lack of democratic accountability will lead to mismanagement of the finances available to local authorities.

8.3.2.3 Relationship between Parliament and Executive

Parliamentary government versus presidential system

In a Westminster-type parliamentary system, the fact that the same political party controls both the executive and the parliament can have a strong centralising effect on the state. The majority party has an interest in remaining in power. Access to this power is only possible by gaining the electoral support of the majority of the people. In such a system, minorities or small decentralised units are hardly able to make their voices heard at the central level. The influence of the party leadership on party politics is much greater in Germany for instance than in the USA or Switzerland where the executive does not depend on the majority of parliament. In Germany, the parliamentary elections of a federal unit (*Landtag*) may in effect turn into a vote of approval or disapproval of the federal Chancellor, and local interests will therefore hardly be represented even within the local parliament. In Switzerland on the other hand, national elections often reflect local and cantonal interests more than national ones.

Head of state

For national Governments, the position of the head of state is an important factor in relation to centralisation or decentralisation. While in many countries the head of state is essentially only a symbolic figure, the Russian President for example possesses far-reaching powers. There the constitution has entrusted the head of state with the powers of the American President (who is Commander-in-Chief and also controls the administration) as well as those of the French President (who has certain legislative powers, the power to declare a state of emergency and to dissolve the parliament). Thus, for the duration of his fixed term the Russian President has constitutionally almost unlimited powers.

In federal countries following the Anglo-Saxon system, the head of state often competes with the governors of the federal units. In Australia for instance, the governors of the federal units still represent the Crown within the federal unit. In the USA each of the states has a governmental system similar to the federal system. The governors compete as heads of the local state power with the President. This gives the federal units at least a certain symbolic equality to the federation. The President on the other hand has important influence on federal unit policies, because he decides largely independently on the award of federal grants and can influence economic development in addition through federal contracts e.g. for military purposes.

In many states the head of state is also Commander-in-Chief of the army. The army is in almost all states highly centralised. With the power to control the army, the head of state can usually also decide on the use of emergency powers and other exceptional measures. These powers avail the Commander-in-Chief of a means of centralisation that should not be underestimated. It is no accident that, unlike the United States, Switzerland has always resisted the idea of a single powerful head of state who is also Commander-in-Chief of the army. The diverse communities in a multicultural state such as Switzerland would hardly have been able to identify with the symbol of one president. It is for this reason that in Switzerland there is no actual Commander-in-Chief of the army. Only in case of defence (the case of armed neutrality) is the army to be mobilised. In this event it is parliament and not the executive that elects a General to serve as Commander-in-Chief. The mandate to defend the country however is given to the General by the executive, the Federal Council.

Executive

In a unitary state the executive represents the interests of the nation. The '*volonté générale*' is symbolised within the executive. The executive also decides what administrative tasks should be undertaken by the local authorities and what means should be made available to them. The national governing authority can ensure that these delegated functions are properly fulfilled by issuing directives, controlling the finances and, if necessary, by taking disciplinary measures. The functions delegated by deconcentration can at any time be revoked or expanded. However, the central executive can never delegate to local authorities its own actual responsibilities. Only the legislature has such authority by way of decentralisation.

Judicature

Unitary states, but also some federal states, have a centralised judicature. The central organisation of the judicature regulates the structure, jurisdiction and procedure of the different courts. The unified law should be applied at all levels of the unitary, unified and hierarchically structured court system. Decisions of the lower courts can be appealed to a court higher in the hierarchy, right up to the highest court at the national level. Judges often are appointed by the head of state, on the advice of a special centralised body that proposes new judges. In the UK, the Lord Chancellor appoints the members of the higher courts, which again demonstrates how much the different powers of government are intermingled in Great Britain, particularly in the office of the Lord Chancellor. In Israel, judges are appointed by a special committee, which is composed of members of the parliament, the executive and the judiciary.

In assessing the judicature one has however to take into account that – in terms of the rule of law and the judicial protection of legal rights – the centralisation or decentralisation of the court system is not of great significance. The most important factors are the independence of the judiciary and general access to justice. The decentralised judiciary in some federal states is significant primarily for enhancing the credibility and legitimacy of the courts within a federal system.

8.3.2.4 Distinctive Features of Federal States

i. Diversity of Federal Forms of Organisation

Twenty-five federations around the world

If we survey the world map today, there are twenty-five states that may be categorised as states with a federal system. In each of these states, the Constitution guarantees some kind of autonomy to the local federal units and also makes some constitutional provision for participation of the federal units in shared rule at the federal level: On the American continent – Canada, the USA, St. Kitts and Nevis, Mexico, Venezuela, Brazil and Argentina have federal systems. In Eurasia we will find Australia, Federated States of Micronesia, Malaysia, Pakistan (Constitution for the time being suspended) and India. On the African continent: South Africa, Nigeria, the Comoro Islands and Ethiopia are federal. In the Middle East, the United Arab Emirates are federal and in Europe: Belgium, Spain, Germany, Austria, Switzerland, Serbia and Montenegro, Bosnia-Herzegovina and Russia have federal or strongly decentralised constitutions. In addition, the European Union is undoubtedly also on the way to becoming a federation. The constitutional draft speaks of a 'Constitution for Europe' and labels the new 'state' a 'Union' as is the case in India. If one compares the inner structure of the constitutional draft for Europe with the constitution of Serbia and Montenegro for example, this new Union provides for much stronger internal state coherence than is the case for Serbia and Montenegro. Thus, it is not the label given by the constitution that is decisive, but rather the internal structure of the state. Switzerland for example still refers to itself as a confederation ('*Schweizerische Eidgenossenschaft*' in German), although it is undisputedly a state with a federal structure. South Africa and Spain seek to avoid the term 'federal' wherever possible, because it is seen in South Africa as a symbol of apartheid and in Spain as a symbol of anarchy or secession. The federalist founding fathers of the American Constitution were called into disrepute for being centralists, which is one of the reasons the UK is opposed to reference being made to the EU as a federal state. Whoever promotes federalism as a solution for the European Union is regarded in the UK as an advocate of centralism in the same way that defenders of American federalism were labelled as centralists in their time.

States that in recent years have become strongly decentralised are, on the European continent: Italy (with limited constitutionally shared rule of the regions at the central level), the UK, and recently even France with its constitutional amendment of 2003 making constitutional provision for regionalisation.

Special mention should also be made of those states which are still governed as unitary states, but which in the sense of an asymmetrical federalism provide extensive autonomy to certain regions, such as China (Hong Kong), Finland (the Åland

Islands), Italy (South-Tyrol), Philippines (Mindanao), Tanzania (Zanzibar) and Denmark (Greenland, which although Danish is not under the jurisdiction of the European Union from which it seceded in 1985).

Meaning and purpose of the federal state

In the United States and in Germany, federalism is clearly aimed at limiting the power of the state by implementing not only horizontal but also vertical separation of powers, in order that the effect of institutional checks and balances is strengthened. The purpose of these multiple checks and balances is to increase the protection of liberty and to avoid the misuse of government power. In Switzerland on the other hand, federalism is unthinkable without the multicultural background. Multicultural Switzerland can exist only through federalism. The purpose of federalism therefore is not simply the vertical separation of powers, but rather *to bring and to hold multicultural Switzerland together*. The Swiss federal order is designed to strengthen the federal units in order to protect and enhance diversity. In this sense Switzerland has designed its own and specific type of federalism. In the USA and Germany, federalism is ultimately also designed to strengthen national unity, and not so much to preserve and foster national diversity.

Status and size

As we have seen, federalism can be broadly defined as a state composed of various federal units, in which the balance of shared rule and autonomous self-rule of the units is constitutionally guaranteed. This definition of federalism is open and permits many variations in the structure and design of different federal states. Today around 40 per cent of the world's population lives within the 25 federations, which differ substantially in size, population, tradition and structure. From the small islands St. Kitts and Nevis, to the United Arab Emirates, to the most populous federation: India, and from the United States of America, to the federations of Latin America, to the Russian Federation and Nigeria we find the most diverse array of federal organisation. Even within Western Europe, the differences in federal structures between Belgium, Germany, Austria and Switzerland are enormous. It is still disputed whether one can already classify the European Union as a federation and whether strongly and asymmetrically decentralised countries such as Spain and Italy can be properly labelled as federations.

Federal states include countries with continental European civil law legal systems as well as some that follow the common law tradition. There are federations that have developed through the decentralisation of a once unitary and centralised system, such as Belgium and Canada, and those that have been constructed bottom-up out of confederations such as the United States, Switzerland and arguably the European Union.

Autonomy

The autonomy of federal units is also differently arranged from one federation to the next. Whilst in Austria for example, universities are overseen by the federal government in Vienna, in Germany and Switzerland universities are regulated by the federal units. Powers over income and expenditure are also differently allocated in each federal system. In some federations the taxing power is essentially entrusted to the federation, whilst in others the federal units raise much of their own revenue by imposing their own taxes. In Switzerland for example, the parliaments of the cantons and the local municipalities decide over two thirds of the total public income and expenditure, while in many other federations most income is generated by the centre. The federation of Serbia and Montenegro, designed according to a proposal of the EU, has even allowed each of the two federal units to have its own currency and to print its own money. Often disputed is the allocation of powers in the areas of police and military. In Switzerland, the police agencies are decentralised to the cantonal level. In the US and in Germany, a special federal police (FBI, National Guard, *Bundesgrenzschutz*) is responsible for law and order at the federal level, whilst the state police forces deal with law and order within their respective states.

The Arab Emirates have formed a federation without taxes, as the sheikh distributes income from oil production to the federal units on an annual basis. This federal state is essentially ruled by sheikhs, who continue to govern according to the traditional patriarchy.

In addition to the true federal states, as mentioned several unitary states provide for a specified part of their territory to enjoy extensive autonomy. Such arrangements result in an asymmetrical distribution of power and autonomy amongst different parts of the territory within the state. The Åland Islands of Finland for example enjoy autonomous status, which is fixed and prescribed by both the parliament of the unitary state and the parliament of the autonomous islands, and can be altered only on the basis of a consensus of the majority of both parliaments. Greenland is part of Denmark, but it is not part of the territory of the EU. South Tyrol has a special status in Italy. And within the UK, which considers itself to be one the most traditional unitary states, Scotland is accorded a certain autonomy which may in future lead to greater decentralisation or even to federalism. Zanzibar is an autonomous island of Tanzania, and various republics within Russia enjoy a special autonomous status relative to other federal units within the country. Regionalisation in Spain is also asymmetric, with Catalonia, the Basque country and Galicia being accorded special status.

Second chamber

There is also great diversity in the way in which second chambers in bicameral parliaments are constituted. There are second chambers which are designed for the purpose of representing directly the interests of federal units, such as the German *Bundesrat* and to a certain extent also the Council of Ministers in the EU. In other states, the upper house has the same status and powers as the lower house. Often in such cases however, the upper chamber is composed of members representing their federal units on an equal footing, each unit having the same number of elected representatives notwithstanding its size (such as USA, Switzerland and

Australia). Other second chambers are composed according very different principles. In Canada for instance, the members of the upper chamber are appointed by the Governor (representing the Crown). Finally, there are even federations which do not have a second chamber, such a St. Kitts and Nevis and the Federated States of Micronesia (although in both cases this is due to the small size of the federation, and provision is made for representation of the federal units in the single chamber parliament).

Equality of the federal units

The position of the federal units with regard to the federation also differs between the various federal systems. Both the USA and Switzerland generally adhere to the principle of legal and sovereign equality of the federal units, although in Switzerland for historical reasons some cantons have the status of 'half canton' and Switzerland therefore is not as consistent as the USA in its application of the equality principle. Although the USA and Brazil do not provide for legal or constitutional inequalities, the factual inequality in terms of economic development and other factors among the different federal units is considerable and ultimately also has constitutional consequences for the federation. Far-reaching legal asymmetry is provided for in Spain and Italy. But probably the greatest differences between federal units exist in the Russian Federation. Russia not only makes constitutional provision for the federal units to be treated differently, in some cases certain powers of particular federal units are regulated by additional treaties between the Federation and the respective federal unit/s. Moreover, the Constitution of Russia applies a range of different labels to its federal units according to the differences in status and autonomy: the units are labelled variously as republics, territories, regions, autonomous regions, autonomous territories and finally the two cities Moscow and St. Petersburg (Art. 65 of the Constitution).

Foreign policy

For a long time foreign policy was regarded as a matter within the exclusive purview of the central state. Even in strongly decentralised federations such as Switzerland, the principle of 'internal diversity, external unity' was upheld, even though the Constitution of 1848 provided for the cantons to exercise limited external powers. The principle that ultimately only the head of state can enter into international treaties and thereby impose binding international obligations on the state, stems from monarchical tradition. In substance, all external or foreign policy decisions were beyond the authority of federal units. According to international law, states are the only recognised subjects of the law of nations. Only states can be the bearers of rights and obligations under international law and only states can proactively participate in international decision making processes.

However, in the era of globalised networks, the need for greater international cooperation has shifted from the centre of the state to all levels including local or municipal government. As a consequence, federal constitutions tend no longer to vest exclusive power over external affairs in the federation, but rather tend increasingly to empower the federal units with certain external powers. This development should also lead to the recognition in international law that today's international community no longer lives according to the monarchical tradition whereby states are represented externally by one person. Thus, at least with regard to international court proceedings, federal units should also be recognised as subjects of international law. In our interdependent world, states cannot be seen as impenetrable and isolated islands of sovereignty in the sea of the international community. Borders have become permeable and people have cross-border commonalities. They constitute communities independent of territory and state policies. These new realities should be recognised by modern international law.

The development of new external affairs functions and powers for federal units will become increasingly important. And it is precisely here that the advantages of the internal and international flexibility of federal states will become evident. Without losing prestige, federations can devolve powers and can considerably broaden the authority of federal units to act internationally. International law and in particular the law of international organisations will have to take such internal adjustments of states into consideration, and accord recognition to federal units of federations as valid actors on the international stage.

ii. Right to Self-Determination

Right to unilateral secession?

For centuries legal and political philosophers were in disagreement on the question of whether, on the basis of the natural law right of self-determination, a people could exercise a right to unilateral secession. Against such unilateral right one can evoke the argument that unilateral secession affects not only the rights of the people claiming self-determination but also the rights of the 'mother-state'. For this reason the existing state, based on its own right to self-determination, should be granted the right to participate in the decision on secession with the community seeking to secede. The right to unilateral secession is most often invoked by minorities. As in the territorial area of the minority that is seeking to secede there will usually be further minorities, the principle of self-determination of minorities could ultimately lead to the complete dissolution of the state and to anarchy. If the principle of self-determination is followed through to its logical conclusion, it could also lead to the consequence that once each of the minorities has established its own polity, they will forcibly expel the other minorities remaining in their territory in order to avoid any aspiration for self-determination on the part of those smaller communities. Ethnic cleansing has historically often been the consequence of secession.

On the other hand, those in favour of a right to secession often point to the example of the secession of the United States from the colonial authority of Britain. In the Declaration of Independence, the colonies justified their secession as a reaction against the exploitative policies of the colonial power, as well as on the basis of the inalienable rights of the people to establish a new state that would guarantee the protection of those rights. Accordingly, throughout history there has been much greater acceptance of the right of colonies to self-determination against their colonial masters than there has been of a general right to self-determination of minorities in other states.

One can derive a right for a federal unit to enter into negotiations for secession out of the preamble of a constitution, if a federation has been constructed from the bottom up by the free will of the member states and the member states profess in the preamble their free agreement to form a federation on the basis of their own sovereign will. In this case the federal unit with a clear will to secede must try to convince the rest of the federation to agree to the secession. A unilateral decision can only be valid if the right and the procedure are clearly determined in the constitution, as for example in Art. 39 of the Ethiopian Constitution.

The legal claim to a right to unilateral secession however cannot be based upon a positivistic interpretation of international law or (in most cases) of constitutional law. There are situations which are of such an unusual nature that they cannot be satisfactorily resolved by the application of general legal rules and principles. It would for example make little sense to maintain the integrity of a federation at any cost, if a large number of the federal units were longer prepared to play a role in the federation and strongly wished to secede.

Rebus sic stantibus

For federal units in which a clear majority of the citizens want at all costs to leave the federation, it is likely that the preconditions according to which they first entered the federation have in the meantime radically changed. In a certain sense the principle of *rebus sic stantibus*, which requires a new assessment of the situation, is applicable here. Since the conditions have changed in a way that was unforeseeable, and as it is no longer reasonable for the population to remain in the federation, one has to search for solutions that will accommodate and satisfy all parts of the population of the 'mother-state' and of the secessionist federal unit. In so doing, not only the right to self-determination of the people that is desirous of leaving the federation, but also the right of the population that will remain in the federation has to be taken into account. In this sense, Article 53 of the new Swiss Federal Constitution, which provides for internal secession and foundation of new cantons, could arguably be used in the event of a major crisis also for external secession.

No homogeneity

Furthermore, it must be recognised that today there is scarcely any territory that contains an ethnically homogeneous population. In every region there are native-born people as well as immigrants. In relation to the right to self-determination, even the rights of immigrant minorities consequently have to be considered.

Whoever claims the right of self-determination will thus have to recognise such right for all communities living under the same constitution that will all also be affected by the majority decision of the population claiming its right of secession. This means in other words, that secession can only occur peacefully if all parties concerned are prepared through compromise to find the necessary consensus.

Constitutional provision for secession

Aside from the constitutions of Ethiopia and of St. Kitts and Nevis, and in a certain sense Article 53 of the Swiss Constitution, federal constitutions do not expressly regulate the right of federal units to secede. In St. Kitts and Nevis, the federal unit Nevis recently held a referendum on the question of secession, however the secessionists did not attain the required majority. Without any explicit constitutional right, Quebec has also held several referenda on secession, without achieving the desired outcome. In the former Yugoslavia, Montenegro threatened to conduct a referendum on the question of secession, and it was this threat that led to the redesign of the federation along confederal lines. Not even the European Union recognises the right of a member-state to leave the union unilaterally. Nevertheless, the draft EU constitution prepared by the European Convention provides that each member state may unilaterally declare its decision to leave the Union (Part I Article 59).

Historical secessions

Perhaps the most widely known historical attempt to secede is that of the southern states of the US in the latter half of the 19th Century. This claim was rejected by the federation and the southern states were defeated in the bloody civil war that ensued. The secession of Panama from Colombia and the secession of Norway from Sweden at the end of the 19th Century are also well known historical examples. In Switzerland in 1847, the catholic cantons established a special alliance (*Sonderbund*) with the intention of seceding from the rest of the confederation. This attempt at unilateral secession was defeated in the civil war, which led to the establishment of the Swiss federal state out of what had been a loose confederation. The USSR and Czechoslovakia were dissolved peacefully, while in Yugoslavia the secession of Slovenia and in particular of Croatia and Bosnia triggered a brutal and bloody civil war.

The right to self-determination as collective right of the nation

The right to self-determination is a product of the idea of popular sovereignty. The US Declaration of Independence of 4th July 1776 not only proclaimed the idea of limited governmental powers in the sense *that men should be governed by law and not by men*, but also proclaimed the recognised natural law principle of self-determination of peoples. This concept is based on liberal, natural law theory influenced by the philosophy of JOHN LOCKE. The right of self-determination is also recognised in the Charter of the United Nations (Article 1, paragraph 2). In addition, both United Nations Conventions on human rights provide in Article 1 the right of all peoples to self-determination (ICCPR Article 1, paragraph 1; ICESCR Article 1, paragraph 1).

In spite of the clear and express recognition of the principle of self-determination, there is much that remains unclear when it comes to the interpretation of the principle and to determining who are the bearers of such right.

Self-determination as a principle and a right was historically the basis for the legitimacy of the process of decolonisation (UN Declaration on the Granting of Independence to Colonial Countries and Peoples, General Assembly Resolution 1514 (XV), 14 December 1960).

The notion of the *external* right of self-determination includes however the right of a state not to tolerate any external interference in its internal affairs by any foreign state. Such interference would have to be regarded as an infringement of state sovereignty. Accordingly it should not be possible, in the case of secession of one part of the state, to realise this demand without the consent of the concerned state.

If one were to deduce from the international law principle of self-determination the right to unilateral secession, this would result in the permanent questioning of state borders. International peace and order would then be permanently and fundamentally threatened.

According to *our understanding*, the right to self-determination must be understood as an intra-state right and not as international right. Such understanding enables a progressive interpretation of self-determination on the basis of Article 1, paragraph 1 of the UN Covenants of 1966. This provision provides according to its content for an intra-state right to self-determination. Thus, the right to self-determination means the right of all individuals to democratic participation in the political process, as well as the right of every ethnic community or people to be given autonomy within the state.

Such interpretation entails a comprehensive guarantee of democratic participation rights, according to which universal and equal suffrage is granted to all individuals and individuals have the right to vote freely in periodic elections by secret ballot (Article 21 of the Universal Declaration of Human Rights). From this, one can deduce the right of the people to government for and by the people. The right to self-determination recognises that the people as a *demos* is an essential democratic element of the state.

Who are/is the people?

But who is the bearer of the right to self-determination? In what manner is such right to be realised and by whom can it be invoked?

1. The federal units within a federation?
2. The people or the peoples?
3. Minorities?
4. Only those minorities which are recognised as having the status of an ethnic community – and if this is so, by whom is such status to be recognised or conferred?
5. The *demos* (the nation in its political sense)?
6. The *ethnos* (the nation in its pre-political cultural sense)?

Can one in the face of such divergent possible interpretations identify the nation or the people as the bearer of the right to self-determination? What can be done if minorities see themselves as nations and demand on the basis of their entitlement to self-determination the right to found their own states?

The right of self-determination of peoples in relation to their 'mother-state' will be claimed, when their loyalty to the existing mother state is lacking. A feeling amongst the citizens of belonging and togetherness is thus an essential precondition for the very existence and maintenance of the state. The consequences of the different and usually externally influenced interpretations of the 'nation', the 'people' or the 'peoples' could however become politically and historically fatal for a society and nation composed of different peoples.

On the other hand, to ignore the right to self-determination may lead to the aggravation of potential and existing conflicts between ethnic groups. Thus, the Canadian Supreme Court decided in a case on Quebec's right of secession, that Canada would have to take account of the will of the Quebec nation expressed by a clear majority of the people of Quebec in a referendum that posed a clear question. But with regard to the legal effect of such decision, it also clearly warned that such obligation to take account of and respect the result does not amount to a unilateral legal right to secession. It rather required the search for a consensus solution that included the whole people of Canada, which should recognise the rights of minorities, the principles of democracy, and the rule of law (Decision of 20 August 1998). Here it is also relevant to note that the French inhabitants of Quebec regard themselves as a nation. Would they, if Quebec were to become an independent nation-state, accord the English speaking population within their territory the right, in relation to the newly independent French-speaking state, to assert themselves as an independent nation with the right to self-determination?

A completely different approach with regard to this type of conflict was taken by the Arbitration Commission composed of the presidents of the constitutional courts of the European Union under the presidency of Frenchman Professor Badinter. This Commission was asked to consider the legality of the secession of the various republics of former Yugoslavia. According to the Badinter Commission, a federal state is much less stable and sustainable than a unitary state. Federations are in a sense, in terms of their durability, second-class states relative to unitary states. If federal units within a federation find themselves in major conflict with the institutions of the central government, it must be assumed that the federal state legally no longer exists! The federation would be in a process of dissolution. Therefore the federal units would have the right, of their own accord, to found their own state. This would be an expression of the right to self-determination, but not secession, as legally there is no longer an original state from which to secede. This unrealistic and impractical decision, which effectively relegates all federal states to second-class status, provided (retrospective) justification for the unilateral secession of the Yugoslavian republics which led to one of the most brutal civil wars of the 20th Century (Decision of 20 November 1999).

8.3.2.5 Statehood of Federal Units

i. Sovereignty

Division of sovereignty

The classical theory of sovereignty cannot be applied to federations. According to this theory, the supreme power of the state is exclusive and absolute, and therefore cannot be divided. The supreme power is either held by the federation, in which case the federal units are not states; or the absolute and exclusive power resides at the level of the units, in which case the federation is not a state but at best an alliance of states or a confederation. The state is something unitary and indivisible, because sovereignty is indivisible. Thus, when the Swiss Federal Constitution speaks in Article 3 of the sovereignty of the cantons, the advocates of the prevailing Swiss theory of the absolutism of sovereignty (not shared by the authors of this book) claim the meaning of 'sovereign' in this article is not to be understood in the classical sense, but rather relates to delegated powers. Sovereignty is vested in the Swiss federation, which has the authority to change the constitution and to allocate powers. The cantons possess only such powers and functions as have been delegated or left to them by the federation. Therefore it is legally inaccurate when cantons label themselves as 'free states' or 'republics' within their cantonal constitutions, as they are not states in the true sense.

Sovereignty of the 'super-state'

HANS NAWIASKY (1880–1961) developed a special theory with regard to this question of federal sovereignty: As sovereignty is indivisible, but as the federal units still exert original powers, he constructed a theoretical 'super-state', which as a legal personality encompasses both the federation and the cantons and allocates powers amongst them. Thus, neither the federation nor the federal units are sovereign, but only the fictive super-state, which embraces both levels. The basic problem with this construction however, is that there is no institution that can act on behalf of the 'super-state' and actually exercise sovereignty, because this extra 'level' of authority is purely fictive. Of interest in this context is the relatively recent creation in Switzerland of a University Conference. This Conference comprises representatives of the cantons and of the federation and makes decisions on the coordination of cantonal and federal tertiary education institutions. It derives its powers and functions from a federal statute as well as from treaties between the cantons and the federation. In so far as this Conference can make decisions that are binding on the cantons as well as the federation, it corresponds to the NAWIASKY'S notion of a 'super-state' institution.

Legitimacy of the local democracy

If a driver in the canton of Vaud (Vaud is a French-speaking canton in Switzerland in which the population is markedly federalist) was to be stopped on the streets of

Vaud by a federal police officer, the driver would regard this as a serious threat to his/her identity. For this driver it is unthinkable that the federation, merely because it has sovereignty or the power to allocate functions, can exercise sovereign powers within the territory of Vaud. He or she would instead take the view that the federal police officer has no powers whilst on Vaud soil, because the people of the canton have not granted the federal police any such authority or jurisdiction. On the streets of Vaud only the cantonal police with cantonal authority can exercise state powers. For the Vaud driver, only the Vaud police have the legitimacy to exert control. The cantonal police force does not derive its authority from federal legislation but from cantonal statutes and from the cantonal constitution.

The legitimacy of the cantonal constitution is derived from the people of the canton, which has approved the constitution in a referendum. A citizen of Vaud would never entertain the idea that the cantonal decision has to be or is justified, because the Federal Constitution entrusts the cantons with the power to organise its own police force. For him/her, the idea that sovereignty has been delegated to the canton is completely foreign. Rather, he/she searches for the legitimacy of state power within his/her own canton, that is, in the democratic decision of the people.

On the other hand, he/she would only recognise the right of the federal government to exercise state powers, to the extent that the Federal Constitution expressly grants such powers. In other words: he/she finds the basis for the legitimacy of the power of the canton or the federation within the democratic decision of its people. The legitimacy of cantonal decisions does not require any further justification or approval by a decision of the federal state. In terms of federal matters, as every conferral of new powers on the federation can only occur by constitutional amendment, such conferral of authority is legitimised by the democratic approval of the people and the cantons in the requisite referendum.

This example shows that the legitimacy of state power in the federation is, according to the perception of the citizens, divided between the two levels of government. The justification of the jurisdiction and authority of the federal unit within the federation is given by the people of the federal unit; it is not derived from the authority of the federal state. The preamble of the constitution of the new canton of Jura (before 1980 a region of the canton of Berne) expresses this consciousness very clearly:

> "The people of the Jura, conscious of its responsibility towards God and to the people, with the intention to restore its sovereignty and to establish a united community, gives itself the following constitution: ... based on these principles the Republic and the Canton of Jura, founded by the act of free self-determination of 23 June..."

As disputed as this preamble was, it gives clear expression to the federal consciousness that is still dominant in Switzerland.

Original and divided sovereignty

If we see sovereignty not as the supreme and ultimate state power which is not derived from any higher authority, but rather assume that sovereignty resides in any people, which is able to confer legitimacy on the power of the state within its respective territory, we can of course also accept that sovereignty can be divided between the federation and its federal units. Such understanding however presupposes that the people's sovereignty within a federal unit is original and that it is not derived from the federal state. In the Swiss federation precisely this is the case, as the federation was constructed from the bottom up out of the cantons, and cantons have retained some of their original sovereignty (residual powers).

These explanations also demonstrate that real federalism is only possible on the basis of popular sovereignty. Hierarchical authorities legitimised by the 'grace of God' cannot be designed on the basis of federalism in its true sense, just as totalitarian regimes, which do not tolerate any disobedience on the part of their 'autonomous' communities, can never be truly federal.

Partnership, not social contract

Whoever accepts the phenomena of genuine federalism will therefore also find it difficult to recognise the social contract as the basis for the legitimacy of state authority. The theory of the social contract presupposes a united people which agrees to entrust state power to a central state. Precisely this however is not possible within a federal system. The federation in fact has taken over some structural divisions from the times of feudal hierarchy, and adapted them to the needs of a modern, rational democratic state.

"I do not know exactly what is meant by federalism. For me it is the relationship and the cooperation between the different governments of the member states between each other and with the government of the centre or the whole". These and similar definitions of federalism can be found in the writings of practitioners as well as scholars. They show how difficult it is to get a clear grasp of the diverse and dynamic phenomena of federalism. This difficulty is particularly evident when it comes to examining the question of sovereignty within federalism. Cooperation and competition among the different state units is one of the key elements of federalism. Partnership is the real core of federalism. It implies distribution of powers among different power-centres, which have to negotiate with each other in order to achieve common goals. If one seeks to put the basic idea of federal democracy into practice, one cannot take as a starting point the classical concept of BODIN'S absolute and indivisible sovereignty, which is concentrated within one state body. Federations and their federal units have different bases of legitimacy. The sovereignty behind this legitimacy rests upon different nations and thus also different popular sovereignties, that is the people's sovereignty of the federation and of each of the federal units.

Sovereignty has therefore to be understood as being divided between the federation and the federal units, as proposed by MADISON and HAMILTON in the *Federalist Papers*. Sovereignty can quite simply not provide the basis of legitimacy for unlimited power of the centre nor for the absolute power of the federal units.

Summary: Constitutive elements of a federation

The constitutive elements of sovereignty of a federation can be summarised as follows:

1. State character of federal units (self-determination of the federal units with regard to their constitutions);
2. Autonomy including fiscal autonomy;
3. Decentralisation of state powers;
4. Shared rule: participation of federal units in the design of the federal system and federal responsibilities, and in ongoing decision making at the federal level;
5. Common overall responsibility of the federal units with regard to the federation, and of the federation with regard to the federal units.

ii. The Nation

Diversity and multiculturality

There is almost no state in which the state borders correspond exactly to the borders of a homogenous linguistic, religious or cultural group. In the Federal Republic of Germany, there are people who follow different Christian religions as well as Jewish people. In terms of language groups, in addition to the German-speaking majority, Germany is home to native Danish-speaking minorities in Schleswig-Holstein and to a Slavic minority (Sorbs) in the eastern part of Germany. In Italy, there are French-, German-, Slovenian-, Croatian- and Greek-speaking minorities. France is the homeland of Corsicans, Catalans, Basques, Bretons and Alsatians. In Great Britain there have lived for centuries the Welsh, Celts (Jersey and Guernsey) and Scots. Slovenians and Croatians also live in parts of Austria. The Eskimos of Greenland belong to the territory of Denmark, to mention just one example of Scandinavian minorities. Many other native minorities in Eastern Europe, Africa, Asia and in the Middle East as well as the indigenous inhabitants of North and South America, Australia and New Zealand have in recent decades acquired a tragic sort of fame. In addition, there are minorities that are not attached to any particular territory, such as the Sinti and Roma, the Tuareg and the Bedouins. And finally, above all in wealthy countries of the North, there are minorities that have resulted from modern migration.

Jurisdiction over territory and nation

Within federations such as Switzerland for example, the territorial borders of the federal units are usually not identical with the borderlines of linguistic, cultural or religious communities. The conflict between the French-speaking minority and the German-speaking majority within the canton of Berne ultimately led to the formation of the new canton of Jura. Whilst within this new canton, the religious borderlines are identical with the new cantonal borders (the canton of Jura is predominantly Catholic), the linguistic borderlines are not, because a small French-speaking minority preferred to remain within the German-speaking but predominantly Protestant canton of Berne. Finally, Belgium provides a clear illustration of the problems that can arise if one seeks to set linguistic borders in stone on the basis of political decisions of the majority. The problems of cultural diversity cannot be resolved by simple concepts such as federalism, minority protection and the like. Inter-ethnic conflicts require a permanent and continuous process of conflict management, which is sensitive to the particularities of the specific conflict.

Legitimisation by minorities

By making the constitutional protection of minorities through institutions, procedures and territories a constitutive element of the state order, the federal state in a multicultural society obtains its basis for legitimacy. This legitimacy however can only be realised if certain indispensable preconditions are met:

1. A federal state has to be built upon a democratic consensus, which at each of the different institutional levels provides for different democratic procedures according to their impact and influence on cultural diversity. These include for example procedures for reaching a consensus and for managing conflicts, the creation of a compromise-oriented political culture, and institutional solutions that soften the pure majority principle of democracy such as a proportional electoral system.
2. The values of civil society must become the fundament of the state and a political culture must be able to develop which presupposes a pluralistic society but extends beyond ethno-nationalist thinking and excludes a feeling of dominance by the majority. If the fundamental values of civil society are threatened by nationalistic values and emotions, the state will be torn apart by 'us v. them' animosities and will dissolve into anarchy. The ethnic principle will become the basis of politics, and within the majoritarian democracy the minority people will become a second-class nation, which rejects the state as an oppressive instrument of the majority nation. This is how formally recognised minority nations come into being; but the peoples of these minorities will feel fundamentally discriminated against, or at best will feel as though they are merely tolerated as guests within the country. As a logical consequence, such minorities will claim their political rights as absolute rights including the right to self-determination and secession.
3. The majority nation of a particular state must refrain from invoking an exclusive right to identify the unity of its nation with the sovereignty of the people. It must rather, in order to overcome antagonistic interests, direct itself towards finding institutions and procedures that can produce a credible compromise between all peoples. At the same time, minorities will have to relinquish their claims for absolute autonomy, which call the existence of the state into question. Furthermore, they should not provoke situations that will lead to conflicts in which violence will be considered by both parties as a legitimate means to enforce their interests.

8.3.2.6 Internal Organisation of Federal Units (Autonomous Constitution Making of Federal Units)

Separate constitution

The position of the federal units is guaranteed in the federal constitution, which essentially determines the basic structure of the federation. Besides the federation however, the federal units are also territorial bodies equipped with their own state authority and jurisdiction. In most federal systems, the federal units have their own constitutions providing for a horizontal and sometimes also vertical division of powers between the institutions of the federal units and local or municipal government. They provide procedures for revising and amending their autonomous constitution. By giving themselves their own constitution, the federal units acquire the necessary and autonomous legitimacy for their state authority, and give expression to the fact that the source of their constitution making power is the original sovereignty of their people or 'nation'.

Territory

Federal units within a federation should have authority over their own territory, the integrity of which is guaranteed by the federal constitution. According to the classical theory of federalism, federations are divided according to territorial borderlines and not by personal differences such as language or religion. The territorial divisions therefore acquire a central significance. In particular, federal units would not be able to exercise the classical state powers of police protection without clear territorial separation.

Several states make provision within their federal constitution for the manner in which the borders of federal units can be altered, including the procedure by which new units may be established or existing units merged or abolished. Article 29 of the German Constitution for example, regulates the procedure for the adjustment of the borders of the *Länder*. According to Article 79 of the Constitution however, the basic principle of federalism cannot be repealed or undermined by constitutional amendments.

Personal federalism

Personal federalism has its historic roots in the millet-system of the Ottoman Empire and the Austro-Hungarian Empire (KARL RENNER). This form of 'federalism', which was adopted from the feudal structure of the Middle Ages, was practised in Estonia before the Second World War and was also part of the Polish governmental structure in the 17th Century. Today, personal federalism is most closely realised in Lebanon. The Belgian Constitution accords the status of state units to both territorial regions as well as communities based on personal characteristics. In Switzerland and in Germany there are certain personal federalist structures in the area of religion. The German *Länder* and most Swiss cantons recognise the concept of state-church community, according to which persons belonging to a certain church are bound to a community held together by state law and supported with some state authority. In so far as personal federalism is restricted to the cultural functions of the state such as education, religion and family law, it may in certain cases be quite appropriate. It is not however appropriate for the exercise of other state powers such as policing. For such tasks it is necessary to overcome personal fragmentation through power-sharing models applied throughout the state. But as the case of Lebanon shows, these possibilities are very limited.

Countries that adopt systems of personal federalism connect self-rule and shared rule not to territory but to communities. Accordingly, communities such as religious or language communities may have special autonomy with regard to their own educational system or with regard to some specific rights given to religious communities such as the right to levy taxes (as in most Swiss cantons). In Lebanon there are certain institutional tools designed to grant shared rule to different religious communities. The constituencies for the national chamber are communities not territories. Although the constitution provides that the gradual abolition of confessionalism is a basic national goal, in the meantime the Christian and Muslim communities are still represented in the national chamber according to the principle of equality.

In the old constitution of Cyprus, even the presidency was divided with a president representing the constituency of the Greek Cypriotes and the vice-president representing the Turkish-Cypriots.

Bearers of the three classical state powers

As bearers of the three classical state powers, the federal units exercise legislative, executive and judicial functions. The federal units in their own constitutions autonomously regulate the organisation and functions of three governmental branches and the checks and balances between them. Unlike decentralised units in a unitary state where authorities are principally accountable to the centre, the authorities of federal units are directly accountable to the people of the respective federal unit. The federation has no power to hold specific agencies of the federal unit directly accountable to the federation. The federal units are only accountable *as a unit* to the federation, which has to ensure that the federal units abide by the limits of their autonomous powers and that they do not violate federal law.

Foreign policy

In many federations the federal units are empowered, within the framework of the federal law, to pursue their own foreign policy. Thus they can conclude international treaties of cooperation. These powers over external affairs are a product of the 'statehood' of the federal units. Foreign policy belongs to the traditional function of every state, and the federal units are also part of the international legal personality of the state. Internationally, only the federation is recognised as a sovereign subject of international law. The federation however has divided and distributed its international sovereignty internally, thus the federal units must also within the bounds of their sovereignty have their own external powers. They share the external relations power with the federation, but they still have their own specific responsibilities.

Constitutional guarantee of autonomy

The autonomy of the federal units, which is the basis of their 'statehood', is of course not unlimited. Legal acts of the federal units are only valid if they comply with the federal constitution. Federal units are subject to the supremacy of federal law and have to abide by the international treaties ratified by the federation.

It is for precisely this reason that the judicial control of the constitution is of such central importance in a federal state. Every action at both the federal level and the level of the federal unit raises the question, whether the action was within the constitutionally prescribed powers of the respective authority.

In interpreting the federal constitution, the judiciary plays a very important role as umpire between the federal units and federation. During the 'New Deal' period, the American Supreme Court by its dynamic interpretation of the commerce clause essentially expanded the powers of the central government. The Constitutional Court in Germany however cannot influence federalism in the same way, as the German Constitution (Basic Law) is much more precise and can be more easily amended than the American Constitution. On the other hand, the European Court of Justice has, in the course of interpreting European treaties, modified the division of powers between Brussels and the member states by significantly expanding the powers of the European Union. In particular, the new clause of subsidiarity in Article 3 of the treaties could end up being interpreted in a manner contrary to the purpose for which it was introduced. The Spanish Constitutional Court also plays an important role as the custodian of regionalism, as it is responsible for interpreting the division of powers between the centre and the autonomous regions under the Spanish Constitution.

Distribution of powers

Many federations – and in particular those that have been built from the bottom up by centralisation – expressly list in the constitution all the powers of the federation, and assume that all powers not expressly allocated to the federation are left to the federal units. In some federations, the constitution provides for a clear distribution of powers and lists all the powers entrusted to the federation as well as expressly enumerating those entrusted to the federal units. Finally, there are constitutions which enumerate only the powers of the federal units and leave all residual powers to the federal level (federalism by decentralisation: Canada).

Fiscal provisions of the constitution

Through constitutional provisions on fiscal arrangements federal states have to decide:

1. Which taxpayers will have to pay taxes at which level of the state to finance which public goods?;
2. At which level of the state will public revenue be made available for expenditure on which public services?; and
3. How injustices and imbalances that may be caused by decentralisation of fiscal powers can be equalised (fiscal equalisation).

The decentralisation of fiscal powers is based on four different assumptions: There are certain local goods and services which have to be financed by those who use and benefit from them; The mobility of the taxpayer should neither be hindered by the fiscal system nor steered in a particular direction; Federal or decentralised units should neither suffer nor profit from external effects ('spillover'); The fiscal system should respect the historically developed, legitimate structures and should aim for a just distribution of public services that is transparent and can be accounted for to the citizens and taxpayers.

In order to counter corruption within the decentralised units, there must be effective instruments available at the central level as well as at the level of the local democracy, which can prevent and if necessary combat corruption. In order that such goals can be achieved, political, cultural and economic wisdom must be brought together into a comprehensive whole that reflects the public interest. Such consolidation has been lacking to date, as economics, politics and constitutional law have each developed their own concepts and ideals, without taking the interrelationship of other scientific disciplines into account.

Decentralisation of taxation powers

In confederations as well as in supranational organisations such as the European Union, the member states decide on the finances to be granted to the confederation or supranational organisation. Neither the confederation nor the supranational organisation can autonomously raise its own revenue. The budget is dependent on the unanimous or majority decision of the member states.

In contrast, the regions within unitary states usually have no financial autonomy. Taxes are raised at the central level. The regions either receive grants to finance specific tasks, or they receive a global budget allocation and can set their own priorities for expenditure. In addition, the budgetary policies of the regions are controlled by the central government.

Between these two extremes there is a wide array of different possibilities and solutions. With regard to taxes, the federal units within a federation may for example be empowered to levy specific taxes. Based on their projected tax revenue the federal units can then determine their own budget and decide how the tasks for which they are responsible are to be financed (USA, Switzerland). If the federal units have far-reaching tax autonomy they can use this autonomy to develop their own (albeit restricted) economic policy and even provide economic incentives to attract investment within their region.

Another possibility is that every person within the federation is taxed according to the same principles, and that each federal unit according to its specific tasks and demographics receives a global contribution from the federation (Germany). This however invariably leads to considerable tensions among the different units, which accuse each other of wasting federal funds or reproach the federation for assigning them an excessive burden of tasks.

Decentralisation of spending powers

The next step to financial autonomy consists of granting the regions or federal units limited or unlimited autonomy with regard to expenditure. In this case the regions have their own budget and can decide autonomously on their own political priorities. This means that the federal government limits its control over the budgets of the federal units to monitoring the transparency of expenditure in order to ensure legitimacy.

Equality, justice and solidarity

Does the principle of equality before the law require that all inhabitants of a federation, regardless of the federal unit in which they reside, should be subject according to their income and assets to an equal tax burden (Germany and Spain)? If so, then logically one must also ask whether the federation should be obliged to ensure that the inhabitants of all federal units, regardless of the economic wealth of the federal unit, have access to the same standard of public services. Federal states must therefore decide on the principle according to which financial burdens will be distributed.

Hotly contested is the question of how to fund expensive services (such as hospitals or universities) or infrastructure (such as roads) which yield benefits for the people of the federal unit in which they are located but which are also in the overall interest of the population of the federation. Which level or levels of government should foot the bill and in what proportion?

If the federal balance is to be maintained, it is essential that the federal units have sufficient financial resources to fulfil their original and delegated functions. Federal grants should only be used for fiscal equalisation, but should not be relied upon for the fulfilment of general functions. Only when federal units make their own decisions on income and expenditure do they bear the necessary political responsibility with regard to the taxpayers, citizens and consumers. And only then are they really able to properly balance competing interests for the common good.

Efficiency

The distribution of fiscal powers must also be assessed from another point of view: which level of the federation can fulfil specific tasks most efficiently, economically, effectively and also legitimately? According to the answer to this question, one will have to consider how powers and tasks are to be divided between the federation and the federal units, and how the finance of each level is to be regulated.

Mobility

The distribution of powers and the degree of fiscal autonomy will also have effects on the mobility of the population and on investment and other economic activity. Federal units will attempt to implement a fiscal policy that is attractive to investors, in order to obtain more income. However, federal units that are geographically, historically and possibly even culturally disadvantaged, will turn to the federation for equalisation payments based on the principle of solidarity.

In multiethnic states, such equalisation may cause far-reaching conflicts. The majority ethnic community may for example be convinced that the minority ethnic community is profiting from the strong economic performance of the majority but is not prepared to work hard to improve its own efficiency and performance. On the other hand, the minority may be convinced that because it suffers from discrimination it does not stand a chance of succeeding in free competition and thus will never be able to overcome its economic disadvantage.

All of these reflections clearly show that the financial aspects of decentralisation or fiscal federalism are not merely of a technical nature, but rather are highly political.

8.3.2.7 Decentralisation of the Three Arms of Government

Legislature

Through the delegation of legislative powers to the federal units, the first and probably most important step towards the establishment of a federation is accomplished. Whoever acquires legislative sovereignty has achieved the status of statehood, as – at least according to the continental European understanding of law – it is through the exercise of the legislative function that the state manifests its sovereignty and statehood.

Legislative power includes the power to pass the budget, which in most countries is submitted in the form of a statute for parliamentary approval. It is through this 'power of the purse' that parliament is able to control the executive and the administration. Through the budget it determines political priorities. When dealing with the budget, parliament must also decide on how the projected expenditures are to be financed, and may therefore have to make decisions relating to taxation. If the budget cannot be wholly financed by taxes or by federal grants, either expenditures will have to be reduced or parliament will have to increase taxes or take public loans (debts to be paid back by future generations) in order to cover the deficit. These budgetary powers are part of the power of the legislative branch, which must lie in the hands of the parliaments of the federal units. It is crucial that the central power does not intervene in these budgetary powers, for example by determining the budget of a federal unit in lieu of the parliament of the federal unit, or by seeking to dictate policy priorities to the federal units. Such interventions are possible in decentralised units, but not in a real federation.

Before 1988, the establishment of regions and language communities in Belgium had not made the Belgian state a federation. It was not until the constitutional amendment of 1988/89 that Belgium became a proper federation, as by this amendment the communities and the regions were for the first time assigned comprehensive legislative powers. In addition, they were given important shared power in a collegial executive (parliamentary cabinet) and the language communities were able to represent minority interests in the first chamber. Since 1993 Belgium has expressly identified itself as a federation in the Belgian Constitution. This example shows the significance of legislative powers of the federal units as a principal attribute of federalism. This is especially true for countries with a continental European civil law system, as in these countries legislative power is seen as the most important element of sovereignty and statehood.

Even in France, there are today serious efforts to assign greater powers to the regions. But even if, as suggested, regionalism is to be added to the principle of a unitary and indivisible France in Article 1 of the Constitution, this will not make France a federal state, as the regions would not have statehood and would not enjoy shared rule of the central state.

Executive

Federal units must necessarily also have their own executive powers and therefore their own executive branch, which is accountable to the federal unit. This executive government of the federal unit should not be dependent on or answerable to the central government. The central authorities should not be able to issue directives to the government of the federal unit, nor to enforce directives with disciplinary measures. The governmental branch of the federal unit, which is accountable to the parliament and/or the people of the federal unit, must of course have its own administration through which it can execute the laws of the federal unit and the federation.

Judicature

An additional essential element of the power of the federal unit is its authority to establish its own judicature. In contrast to unitary states in which there is a unitary court system, in federal states the federal units regulate their own judiciary. The courts of federal units may be structured as a system that is separate and parallel to the judiciary of the federation, whereby courts of federal units apply the law of federal units and federal law is applied by federal courts (USA), or they may have jurisdiction over both federal and federal unit law within the territorial jurisdiction of the federal unit. In civil law systems that practice 'executive federalism' (*Vollzugsföderalismus*), often the courts of the federal units are also asked to apply federal law, whilst the unity of the law is ensured by the right of appeal to a federal court of final instance.

8.3.3 Shared Rule by the Federal Units at the Federal Level

Shared rule as a basis for the legitimacy of the federation

The right of federal units to participate within the decision making process of the different levels of the federation is a key factor that distinguishes federal states from decentralised states. The main argument for participation or shared rule by the federal units lies in the legitimisation of the federation. The federation can only achieve legitimacy if it accords proper recognition to the federal units and includes them in its decision making process, as the federal units must also gain legitimacy with respect to their people. The federal units exist on the basis of their own popular sovereignty. If they were to be integrated within a federation which paid no respect to the popular sovereignty of the federal units, the federation would lose its credibility and its legitimacy.

PAUL LABAND (1838–1918), one of Germany's most influential constitutional scholars, considers the shared power principle as the only decisive element that distinguishes federal states from unitary states. The federal units are brought into the federal decision making process, because the federation is bound by the participation of the federal units in its exercise of sovereignty. French scholar GEORGES BURDEAU also considers the shared power principle as decisive for federalism.

These considerations have led certain federal states to attach great importance to the participation of the federal units at the federal level. The most far-reaching solution is contained in the German Basic Law, under which the federal units (*Länder*) participate directly in the decision making process at the federal level, through membership of the second parliamentary chamber (*Bundesrat*). Members of the *Bundesrat* are not elected senators representing the people of their respective federal unit as is the case in the USA, Australia and Switzerland, but rather are delegates of the executive governments of the federal units which participate directly in the decision making of this chamber. The *Bundesrat* can be likened to a council of ministers in a confederation or international alliance, as the ministers voting in this chamber vote on behalf of their respective governments. Votes are weighted according to the population of the *Länder*, although such weighting is not entirely proportional. By comparison, in the USA, Australia and Switzerland every state or canton elects an equal number of representatives to the upper chamber, regardless of size or population.

The *Bundesrat* participates in all legislative decisions of the federation, which then have to be implemented by the *Länder*. It is because the *Länder* are responsible for implementing and administering federal legislation that the executive governments of the *Länder* are directly involved in the federal legislative process. The Ministers sitting in the *Bundesrat* represent the opinions of their governments, which is not the case in almost all other second chambers, where the governments of the federal units have no direct influence on the decisions of the members of the second chamber.

Privileging minorities

The main arguments against shared rule by federal units at the federal level are based on efficiency (involvement of the federal units may hamper the federal decision making process) and discrimination (equal representation of the federal units at the federal level effectively discriminates against the larger federal units). At the time of the formation of the new Swiss Federation in 1848, in debates over whether the federation should have a second chamber of parliament, the large cantons argued against the equal voting rights of the smaller cantons on the grounds that it would create an unjustified legal inequality and would unfairly disadvantage citizens of large cantons. They were also concerned that equal voting rights would effectively give the small cantons the power to block important legislation and to thwart the development of the federation. The positive experience of the American Senate, which, as history at the time showed, did not impede the progress of the American federation but rather tended to enhance the legitimacy of federal decisions, was the decisive factor in the establishment of a second chamber with equal representation for all cantons based on the American model.

In Switzerland today, this equality of cantonal representation is again in dispute, as it excessively privileges the small federal units. The small cantons claim however that the quality of sovereignty transferred to the federal units is the same notwithstanding the size of the canton. A solution between these positions can only be found on the basis of the principle of diversity. If the value of diversity is as important as the value of majoritarianism, then it should be possible to find a balance between inequality to protect diversity and equality to protect the majority. This balance is arguably struck in those federal systems that provide for equal representation on the basis of population in the lower chamber, and equal representation for all federal units (therefore unequal representation on a per capita basis) in the second chamber.

Shared rule in systems with two ethnicities

The realisation of shared rule or comprehensive participation of federal units at the federal level may lead to problems such as deadlocks, particularly in federal states with only two ethnicities and two federal units. In relation to Cyprus, Serbia-Montenegro, and Sri Lanka, opponents of a federal solution have consistently evoked this deadlock argument. Indeed, the problem of a stalemate between two groups is the principal reason why the long-running conflict in Cyprus has yet to be resolved. The deadlock problem is also the reason why Yugoslavia (albeit under pressure from the EU) decided to transform the two-unit federation with Serbia and Montenegro into an alliance, which, like the EU, resembles a confederation in terms of institutions, but which has a legal system with federal characteristics.

Overcoming the veto problem

Deadlocks between the two chambers, and in particular between majorities and minorities, can be overcome with special procedures which are usually based upon the majority principle but which, where key interests of small federal units are affected, provide special protection for minorities.

A particularly interesting example is the solution of the so-called 'alarm clock' procedure in Belgium, according to which the parliamentarians of a particular language group can declare that a proposed law that has been presented to Parliament affects the special interests of the language group. The proposed law must then be put to cabinet for a decision. The Constitution prescribes that the Belgian cabinet is comprised of an equal number of members from each of the two language groups. It can therefore find the necessary compromise that will be accepted by both sides as a just solution.

Participation in constitutional decisions

In a confederation, all decisions that intervene in the sovereign rights of the member states and which change the allocation of powers to the confederation, must be reached by the unanimous agreement of the member states. This applies at least partially also to the European Union. However, the treaties of the EU contain a number of provisions that could lead to a *de facto* expansion of the powers of the EU, but which do not require the unanimous ratification of all member states. Furthermore, it should be recalled that the European Court of Justice, through its interpretation of the European treaties, can substantially expand the powers of the Union in much the same way as the United States Supreme Court has expanded the powers of the federation by means of constitutional interpretation.

The requirement of unanimity for the amendment of the distribution of powers is not compatible with a federal state. Federal states must be able, at least by qualified majority, to adapt to changing circumstances and if necessary to change the allocation of functions between the federal units and the federation. It would be inconsistent with the principle of solidarity between the federal units, if a single federal unit was able through its veto power to bring the federation to a standstill. The principle of unanimity cannot however be replaced by the opposite extreme, namely, the simple majority principle. Constitutional amendments in a federal state must not only be legitimised by a simple majority of the nation; in addition, the federal units as bearers of sovereignty must also be taken into account. For this reason, a majority principle must be found that takes account of both the people of the state as a whole and the federal units, that is, a double majority of the people and of the federal units.

Participation at the legislative level

In addition to constitution making, the federal units also participate in the exercise of legislative power at the federal level. Federal units are not restricted to implementing laws at the level of the federal unit, they also influence the content of federal laws and share responsibility for the passage of federal laws. However, the manner in which the federal units participate in this exercise of legislative power varies enormously. As we have seen, there are federal states in which the governments of federal units participate directly in the federal legislative process (Germany). Then there are those federal states that seek to give effect to the 'double public interest', that is, the *volonté générale* as the general interest on the one hand, represented in the first chamber, and the *volonté générale* of all federal units on the other hand, represented in the second chamber. This leads to two chambers in which, on the one hand, the people is represented on the basis of the equality of all citizens and on the other hand, the federal units are represented on the basis of the equality of all peoples. The public interest of the federal state cannot be reduced only to the welfare of the nation; the welfare of the whole of the peoples of the federal units is also an element of the welfare of the federal state.

Participation at the executive level

Belgium provides an example of the direct representation of the federal units at the level of the federal executive. Article 86 of the Constitution provides that Cabinet must have an equal number of Ministers from each of the two language groups. The Prime Minister cannot be seen to represent either of the two language groups. Thus, when the two language groups within Cabinet are evenly divided on a question, the Prime Minister decides with his casting vote. This principle means that Ministers have an interest in finding a consensus and compromise within Cabinet, and in reaching a decision that can be accepted by the majority of all members.

Under Swiss constitutional law, the various regions of Switzerland must be fairly represented in the Federal Executive Council. This provision is an attempt to ensure that all regions (cities and countryside), languages and the main religions are represented in the seven-member collegial executive body.

8.3.4 Federal Supervision of the Federal Units

The challenges

Federal supervision and control over federal units is one of the most difficult challenges faced by federal states. How can federal states ensure that federal units implement federal statutes correctly? How can they enforce federal laws and decisions against a federal unit that puts up clear resistance or opposition? This problem occurs particularly in relation to the international relations and international obligations of the federal state. Does Switzerland for example possess the appropriate tools to enforce international obligations and in particular the obligations under the bilateral treaties with the EU? How should a federal constitution for Cyprus be designed, in order that this country can become a full member of the EU, and can maintain control of the implementation of directives and ordinances of the EU and the decisions of the European Court by the federal units?

With regard to human rights obligations, Switzerland was confronted with the problem of how to compel the cantons to adhere to the decisions of the European

Court of Human Rights. Article 6 of the European Convention on Human Rights entitles every person, in relation to the determination of his/her civil rights and obligations, to a fair hearing before an independent and impartial tribunal. For a long time the administrative law of the cantons limited citizens' access to the federal courts in relation challenging administrative decisions. There was no procedure or instrument available to the federal government to interfere in the legislative autonomy of the cantons, in order to enforce the necessary legislative implementation at the cantonal level of Switzerland's international legal obligations under the ECHR. Finally, the cantons themselves changed their legislation on their own initiative because they were aware that their legislation would not have withstood challenges at the European level. The new Swiss Constitution now provides in Article 29a for a human right guaranteeing access to justice in all those cases.

Different instruments for the implementation of federal law

The Swiss Constitution provides the federation with the authority to intervene in cantonal affairs, only when the constitutional order of the canton is disturbed. According to the German Basic Law the federation can, subject to the approval of the *Bundesrat*, forcibly enforce the federal obligations of rebellious *Länder*. In such cases, the federal cabinet has the power to issue enforceable directives to the authorities of the *Länder*. Federal states with common law systems may seek to enforce the legal obligations of the federal units or their officials by means of injunction. Failure to abide by injunctions or other orders can be pursued by a charge of contempt of court.

Of particular interest in this context is the *Francovich* decision of the European Court of Justice. In this case, Italy was held liable for failing to enact the necessary social insurance laws required by a directive of the European Commission. Italy was required to pay compensation to Francovich, who did not receive the social payments required by the European directives. This decision has far-reaching consequences, as it makes member states financially liable before the European Court of Justice for failure to enact the legislation required by European directives, and means that legislatures can indirectly be compelled to take the measures necessary to implement federal law.

Parallel administration in the USA

Another distinctive feature of federalism in the USA is the parallel administration of federal institutions and state (federal unit) institutions. Federal laws are implemented and enforced within the states by federal agencies, state laws are implemented by state agencies. Thus, within the states two parallel administrations act side by side. Accordingly, there are two parallel judiciaries to enforce federal statutes and state statutes respectively.

8.3.5 *Can Fragmented Multicultural Societies be Peacefully Held together by Ethnic Federalism?*

8.3.5.1 Mapping the Issues

Connection between multiculturality and federalism

Federalism provides instruments for the resolution of interethnic and intercommunal conflicts. At the same time however, federalism as well as multiculturality and multi-ethnicity as political movements based on identity, may throw the essential universality of the state into question. Thereby federalism takes account of both fundamental challenges of multicultural societies with regard to the traditional liberal state, which is based on the guarantee of inalienable individual freedom on one hand, and on pure majoritarian democracy on the other.

Concept of ethnic federalism

Under the term 'ethnic federalism' we are referring in the following not to all federal solutions in multiethnic societies, but in particular only to those federal solutions that involve the territorial organisation of multiethnic communities and which at the same time aim to bring and to hold ethnic diversity together. Ethnic federalism developed out of the nation-state principle, as the nation-state is directly confronted with different ethnicities. Most states however are either based on the concept of the dominant culture of the majority people (*Leitkultur*) and thus tolerate minorities at best, or they are built upon the principle of the a-cultural nation, which by definition ignores the political existence of minorities.

Federalism as a political principle of partnership

From a purely legal perspective, federalism can be seen as a territorially fragmented state structure. One can however also define federalism as an organisational principle which holds different political units together within an overarching political system.

From whichever of the two different perspectives one proceeds, federalism is characterised by a constitutionally prescribed balance between autonomy of the lower political units (self-rule) and participation of those units in the decision making processes of the higher political level (shared rule). This structural balance leads to a vertical separation of powers and in particular to mutual checks and balances between the different levels of the state, and also between the various 'democracies' and institutions within the state. If this constitutional principle is applied at the political level, federalism requires institutions which supplement the majority principle with the principle of negotiation and the principle of partnership.

Nation-state versus ethnic state (Volksstaat)

The modern nation-state requires within its specific, clearly defined territory unlimited universality. The link between universality and territorial delimitation is made by the principle of citizenship. The principle of citizenship can as a bond only hold a state together, if it builds upon an identity that creates an accepted homogeneity of the citizens, and thereby builds the foundation for the legitimacy of the state through the consensus of the majority of the people. This homogeneity of the state community (nationality) is either based on common political values or on a common language, culture or religion ('nation' state versus ethnic state). Identity and homogeneity are therefore the two indispensable preconditions of a modern democracy. Modern societies however require a policy that accommodates a variety of different identities and not only one single and exclusive identity.

Special challenges of countries in transition

An additional distinction is imperative: Whilst in the western democratic states federalism and multiculturality are merely permanent challenges of modern statehood, in other states – namely, Eastern European countries in transition – federalism and multiculturality have become explosive issues, which, since the fall of communism, have led to state collapse or to permanent conflict. This has even been the case with regard to states that emerged from pre-existing federal structures. Federalism and multiculturality still remain immanent obstacles to the establishment of stable political democratic conditions within those societies.

Balance of unity and diversity?

This raises the question, whether federalism is able to achieve a balance between unity and diversity. Another closely related question is that of the relationship between federalism and democracy. Why? Simply because federalism as an instrument of conflict management for multiethnic societies can only be successful if it is able to find an institutional and political answer to the question of how multicultural contradictions can be resolved that is both democratic and also able to establish the necessary loyalty to the overall state.

The *demos*, as the foundation of sovereignty as well as of the state and the governmental system, provides democracy with the procedures to ensure that the people can exert permanent and sustained control over the political decision making process. By its nature, each political power position ultimately depends directly or indirectly on the acceptance of those who are prepared to submit to its authority. This preparedness is based upon the citizens' assumption or belief that the decisions of the political authority and their obedience to that authority are ultimately in their best interest.

8.3.5.2 The Structural Challenges

i. Federalism and Democracy

Equality and diversity

In order to understand the relationship between federalism and democracy, we begin from the following premise: from a basic constitutional perspective, both federalism and democracy can be seen as instruments and procedures for the control of power. However, they are based upon different values and political preconditions: Federalism is based on diversity; democracy presupposes equality.

Separation of powers and group rights

Federalism and federal structures emerged out of the social demand for collective or group rights. Ethnic federalism as a normative concept presupposes that regional diversity based on different ethnic communities is recognised as legitimate. Ethnic federalism must therefore set itself the goal of preserving this legitimate diversity, or even of fostering and promoting it. Such goal however stands in contradiction to the basic principles of modern democracy, which include individual political liberty and the guarantee of the absolute equality of all individuals and citizens. Federalism is built in part upon the concept of separation of powers – a basic principle of the modern state – but at the same time it is based upon the principles of group rights and inequality, which contradict the principles of the modern state. Federalism thereby poses a permanent challenge to the republican understanding of democracy and popular sovereignty.

Federalism and popular sovereignty

Federalism has thrown permanently into question both pillars of the modern liberal state, namely: democratic sovereignty and legitimisation through the political process. Federalism denies the entitlement of the majority of the nation to be the only legitimate basis of popular sovereignty. As already mentioned, the federal state replaces absolute sovereignty with a diffuse distribution of sovereign powers between the federation, the federal units and sometimes also municipalities. In other words: By recognising collective liberty, federalism changes the nature of democratic sovereignty as the basis of legitimacy as well as the supreme power.

Public status of minorities

Federalism also substantiates the legitimacy provided by the political process in all those cases in which the structure of the federation aims at accommodating minorities by giving them a public political status, e.g. as a federal unit within the multi-ethnic and multicultural society. In this case, democracy not only guarantees a specific political process, but it also guarantees the result, in that the openness of the result is limited by the constitution making procedure, because the outcome cannot be one that would endanger the special claims of minorities.

Different types of federalism

Federalism and democracy both serve to limit the power of the state through specific institutions and procedures, and do so at the ground level of the establishment of the state and constitution making. If one puts the two principles side by side, one can speak of the democratic control of federal power on one hand,

and of the federal control of democracy on the other. However, in terms of the relationship between federalism and democracy there exist wide variations amongst the existing federal models. Different types of federations express an inherent ambivalence. On the one hand, the federal state has to legitimise its system according to the modern principle of legitimacy; and this principle of legitimacy is largely based on democratic procedures. On the other hand, the federation has to take into account the structural challenges with which it is confronted as a result of its ethnic diversity. Ethnic diversity based on the principle of equality of all ethnicities independent of the size of population, and the democratic majority principle, cannot easily be reconciled.

Complement of democracy: MADISONIAN-federalism

For the federation that is based on the principles of federalism developed by MADISON – who together with JOHN LOCKE recognises individual freedom as the only legitimate goal of the state and for whom democracy is organised solely on the majority principle (USA and to a certain extent also Canada) – democracy is the foundation of the state, which is supplemented by federalism and corrected by the additional vertical separation of powers. In so far as accountability to the people is mainly realised by the control of state powers, the federal vertical separation of powers complements the horizontal checks and balances. In this sense it fulfils MADISON'S prescription in *Federalist Papers No. 51*, that great caution must be exercised in establishing new state powers. The major problem with which federations are confronted however, consists in the fact that they have to build a federal balance based upon the principles of partnership and negotiation into a system based on pure majoritarian democracy. In addition, they have to be able to bring together into one national unit different communities with different loyalties.

According to MADISON, the Constitution of the United States must be labelled as federal with regard to its historical roots, but also as national in so far as the constituted branches of government are concerned which have to serve the common interests of the United States (*Federalist Papers No. 39*). The American federation can therefore be classified as democratic federation in the sense that it is committed to the values of majoritarian democracy, and at the same time has to overcome the structural tensions between the majority principle and federalism.

Universal versus particular diversity

For liberal democracies, the challenge of multiculturality is existentially immanent to the state, as these democracies are based on the individualistic majority principle. These states are essentially oriented towards the equal representation of all individuals; and equality of individual representation is a procedural arrangement that ultimately results in the political exclusion of diversity. Authentic liberalism cannot accept differences between groups as a basic foundation for state building. Pure liberalism is therefore structurally incapable of meeting the demands and claims of a multicultural society and of incorporating the value of diversity into the political system. It excludes the recognition of collective rights. Indeed, the liberal state is on the defensive when it is confronted with the argument of multiculturality: that individual equality is in reality no guarantee of real equality, as long as the individual equality of human beings is not complemented by their equality as members of a group. Liberal democracy recognises diversity only from a universalist but not a particularist perspective.

Federalised democracy

European federalism however, which is influenced by the philosophy of ALTHUSIUS, is more open to collective values. Switzerland can be taken as a paradigm for the type of federalism that is open with regard to the collective values of communities. Switzerland is founded principally upon strong cantonal identities and upon a democratic integration, which, in terms of constitution making as well as with regard to the decentralisation of state powers to cantons and municipalities, recognises and fosters linguistic and religious diversity as well as cantonal and local loyalties. Swiss federalism therefore lacks almost all of the institutions and procedures found in other federal systems, which are aimed at integrating and uniting the society at the federal level. Unlike Madisonian-federalism, the exercise of state powers is federal, not national. In Switzerland, federalism is neither a correction nor a complement to democracy, but much rather a structural foundation for a consensus-oriented democracy.

Reconciliation of democracy and federalism

Based on the communal character of the Swiss democracy, which is aimed at serving the principle of communal liberty, state policy does not set itself the goal of reconciling federalism and democracy. Rather, the state regards and applies participatory democracy as a federal element, to better articulate and protect the interests of structural minorities in a multicultural society. Since federalism is integrated as a structural element into a consensus-oriented democracy, one can categorise Switzerland as a federalised democracy. More precisely, one can say that the Swiss form of substantial legitimacy not only reconciles federalism and democracy, but it builds upon the view that these two elements are and should be integrally related.

Particular Swiss conception of the 'citoyen'

In addition to the two different concepts of 'nation' or 'people' that underlie the recognition of citizenship in western democracies, namely, citizenship without or in spite of ethnicity (USA, France), and citizenship based on ethnicity (Germany), Switzerland has developed a third 'combination' model: citizenship which builds upon various democratically integrated ethnicities.

ii. Can Ethnic and Political Pluralism be reconciled with Democracy?

Ethnic conflicts are territorial conflicts

Ethnic disputes, which develop into irreversible conflicts, are inherently territorial conflicts. That is, the close connection between territory and ethnic identity emotionalises the conflict. Territory thereby becomes a strategic symbol.

In terms of the territorial character of the modern nation-state, it can often be difficult to separate the ethnic connection to territory from the actual source of national identity. This is so notwithstanding the fact that connection to nation and connection to territory are historically rooted in two different systems of citizenship: namely the *jus soli* (patriotism) and the *jus sanguinis* (ethno-nationalism), and that in most cases the ethnic community is not identical with the state territory. This is one of the main reasons why ethnic conflicts can only very rarely be resolved by a human rights strategy, and why the problem in most cases is suited to federal solutions in the sense of conflict management rather than conflict resolution.

Integration through state creation

Indeed, in so far as federalism can give diversity a territorial dimension, it is understandable that federalism is often seen as a state model for conflict resolution. However, federalism can only live up to this expectation if there is also a democratic consensus on the solution! In other words: ethnic conflict cannot be solved simply by the imposition of federal institutional structures. The resolution of a conflict is only possible if the different communities within the multiethnic society are included in the process of state-building and are democratically integrated in the process of constitution making.

How can the 'ethnification' of constitutional conflicts be avoided?

The main paradox of federalism as an instrument of conflict management for multicultural societies is to be found in the hidden potential for conflict within the relationship between territory and the ethnically-oriented constitutional solutions of a multiethnic federation (because federalism is territorial and ethnicity is personal). It must be recognised that because constitution making and the decision making process at the federal level form the basis of ethnic federalism, constitutional conflicts can quickly and easily be misinterpreted as being disputes over ethnicity, and may very quickly degenerate into ethnic conflicts. Probably the greatest challenge confronting ethnic federalism is to find solutions that enable the federation to prevent constitutional conflicts from descending into ethnic conflicts.

Overlap or identity between territory and ethnic community

It is sometimes claimed that ethnic federalism can only contribute to internal harmony or to the building up of a citizens' democracy, if the respective ethnic communities are each concentrated in their own specific territories and thus can be territorially separated from each other. The Swiss example shows however, that this need not necessarily be so. In Switzerland the various ethnic communities overlap and cut across the territory of the cantons. Furthermore, the ethnic communities are not organised into one cantonal territory each, which can serve as the home or the symbol of their ethnic identity. There is no 'mother canton' for the German- or French-speaking Swiss. Even the Italian-speaking Swiss are concentrated in two cantons and not only one.

Radicalisation of ethno-regionalism

On the other hand, the example of the former Yugoslavia has shown paradigmatically that federalism can become radicalised into ethno-regionalism when the dominant ethnic community seeks to capitalise on the diffuse territorial overlap of ethnicities by imposing institutional and constitutional solutions that entrench its dominant position. The expectations placed upon federalism, namely that pluralism can be sustained, led the parties to renegotiate the federal alliance from scratch. In the process of doing so, each and every slight controversy became emotionally charged and descended into a conflict to be fought along ethnic rather than ideological lines. Accordingly, the success of ethnic federalism depends on whether a federation that was founded in order to accommodate ethnic diversity is able to foster double or multiple identities and loyalties. If on the other hand, ethnic conflicts are radicalised, in that the ethnic communities systematically exclude the democratic identity and legitimacy required for a common state, ethnic federalism cannot succeed.

It is however much easier to postulate the requirements for successful ethnic federalism than it is to implement it in reality. Some recent conflicts in which an attempt has been made to give a new legitimacy to ethnicity through federal solutions, have shown dramatically how difficult it is to create new ethnic foundations for a political community. In Ethiopia for example, it is not the Constitution but rather the leading coalition of ethnic parties which holds ethnic federalism together. It remains to be seen, whether the Constitution will still be able to hold diversity together when the leading coalition has to hand over power to a pluralistic multi-party system. On the basis of an ethno-territorial political structure, neither multi-ethnic nor ideological parties representing 'universal' values are likely to have a real chance in the future.

iii. The function of the constitution in the dissolution of former communist states

Constitutional conflicts as instruments of disintegration

Constitutions can neither establish nor destroy federations. But as the foundation of the state they reflect the structural deficiencies of the constitutional order. In the case of the former multiethnic communist federations, the basic principles of the federal order made it apparent that in fact a real federal alliance as the basis of the federation did not exist. For this reason once the communist regime had fallen, every constitutional dispute also raised questions about the actual basis of the federation.

Thanks to the structural deficiencies of all three dissolved ex-communist federations (Czechoslovakia, Soviet Union and Yugoslavia), the constitution was considered to be the most appropriate tool with which to dissolve the common state. In all three federations the process of disintegration was triggered by constitutional disputes over the new federal structure that was to be designed for the common state.

Construction of federalism by the ethnic perception of the nation

It is no coincidence that in all multiethnic communist federations the decline of the political domination of the party occurred parallel to the collapse of the common state. The manner in which this collapse occurred however, differed in each case. The different historical circumstances under which the communist federations were established led to different types of conflict. However, the structural and constitutional causes that led to the breakdown of the state were the same in all three communist federations. The crucial factor was that the communist constitutions were founded upon an ethnic perception of the nation, which led to a construction of the federation that was rather different from other federations.

Principle of equality of the nation

As already explained, the communist parties of multiethnic states used the principle of equality of the nation as a further basis for the legitimacy of their political power. This had the following effect: first it presupposed the right of each ethnic-nation to its own state; and second, it meant that every ethnic-nation had the legitimate claim to be a member of a 'just federation'. Of course, the principle of equality of the nation was not proclaimed expressly in the constitution. But it enabled the Party, in addition to or outside the constitution, to establish a para-constitutional order through which it could further expand its authoritarian power by manipulation and by the constant redefinition of the interethnic balance and of interethnic relationships.

The constitutional crisis was a crisis of the state

In a federation constructed only upon an alliance of the nations and their relationship to each other, every constitutional dispute had necessarily to degenerate into an ethnic conflict. In the long run, this has probably been the most devastating effect of the authoritarian exploitation of interethnic relationships. The goal of this exploitation was not to transform the diffuse power of the ethnic nation into an accountable power of the citizenry; the aim was rather to completely deprive the federal state of its legitimacy by inflaming conflicting loyalties through the continuous confrontation between different ethnicities.

Friend-foe perceptions

Legitimacy was based on the differences between ethnic groups and not on the common values between them. Thus, a negative-legitimacy was established, on the basis of which political relationships were characterised by black and white perceptions of 'friend' and 'foe' (or 'us' and 'them') in the sense described by CARL SCHMITT. For this reason, the constitutional crises should have signalled the alarm that not only the constitution and the governmental system were at stake, but rather the common state and its territorial structure and borders were also in question.

Federations without federal loyalty

Thus, it is clear that the three multiethnic federations at the time of the fall of communist rule were not only 'illegitimate' pre-modern societies that were looking for an appropriate constitutional foundation for a new state in which citizens became actual partners of and participants in the state and thus received a new *status activus*. They also were illegitimate pre-modern communities because they regarded the state, which compelled them to enter into the federation, as an artificial and forcibly imposed community. Thus it was not only the regime but also the state as such which lacked legitimacy. A tension existed between the normative demand of liberal democracy for legitimacy through constitutionally guaranteed procedures, and the pre-modern socio-political background (outcome- and ethnicity-oriented democracy) which effectively precluded the establishment of a new state entity. As soon as the multiparty system was introduced, the dissolution of the state became the only realistic and desirable political goal. A federation without federal loyalty stood no chance with the ethnic nation, as the only acceptable political legitimacy was in fact the legitimacy of the nation.

The phases of dissolution of the federations

Constitutionally, the dissolution of the federation in all three states followed the same model:

First, the constitutional crises led to constitutional stalemates and dead ends, because there was not a single proposal for constitutional revision that was aimed at the common interest of the federation. Rather, the goal of every proposal was the consolidation of the exclusive political position of a particular group or region. Then, the process of decentralisation forged ahead, to the point where it developed into a process of secession. Finally came the various declarations of independence, legitimised by popular referenda.

Human rights declarations as a façade of constitutional democracy

The technology of the constitution explains better than anything else the two other important factors:

1. The dissolution of the state in connection with the collapse of the regime had structural causes. It cannot be explained simply by pointing to power-hungry political leaders. They were a result rather than the cause of the whole process.
2. Ethno-nationalism always tries to give the outward appearance of being a 'decent and respectable state' by making constant reference to democracy and human

rights. This is why the political leaders were able to conceal the facts, to portray the dissolution as a highly cultivated process, and to give the new ethnic state the façade of a real constitutional democracy.

As in the previous communist states no constitutional rights could be individually enforced and as all rights were considered to be collective rights, there were no socially recognised individual rights, but only collective rights and values. Thus, it was only normal that the collective rights of the previous communist party were transferred to the new collective, the nation.

Just as earlier the dissidents and opponents of the communist ideology had been cast out of society as traitors of the national interest and declared outlaws, it was now the members of other nations who were considered at least as potential traitors and in any case as outcasts, unless they swore and professed their absolute loyalty to the new state in the prescribed manner.

Federal façade

Thus it is easy to understand that the constitution, in this historical and sociological environment at the time of the collapse of the party, had a completely different function than in other communist states with a more or less ethnically homogeneous population. The constitution became the most appropriate instrument to carry out the dissolution of the common state, as the federation was not a constituted federation but a federal façade, which had been held together by the force of the Communist Party. The party was the real and sustained power structure, which had used the constitution simply as a pretext for its authority. Therefore, the constitution could only function as long as the decision making process of the party was sufficiently centralised to ensure the survival of the federation of 'sovereign' ethnic nations without a common democratic policy.

Ethno-nationalism

Finally, the notion of constitutionally based ethno-nationalism needs additional explanation. It is no coincidence that the phenomenon of ethno-nationalism is typical of almost all multi-ethnic states in transition, because it is only through ethno-nationalism that a strategy of the ethnification of politics can be carried out. This can be observed in all Central and Eastern European states in transition. In a multiethnic society, citizenship can only be implemented based on the ethnicity of the majority nation. The constitution making power lies in the hands of the majority nation. It is the majority nation which, with the goal of establishing an ethnic state, invokes a claim to 'universality' in order to legitimise the new political order.

Constitutional text and constitutional reality

However, one should not forget that ethno-nationalism leaves barely a perceptible trace in the text of the constitution. If a nationalist regime does not want to be pushed into complete isolation, it will always have to seek allies in order to maintain the appearance of a real democracy with the guarantee of human rights.

Nationalism can be recognised on the basis of facts and actions, and not by the words of the constitutional text. And when it comes to the application of the law, nationalism will not be seen within the positive text of the statutes, but in the manner and the climate in which the law is applied and which give it its character.

Hints of ethno-nationalism in the constitutions

Nevertheless, in those constitutions that were proclaimed as acts of a sovereign ethnic nation in the sense of the *pouvoir constituant*, one can find certain hints of the fundamental message that the constitution is that of an ethnic nation-state. The dominant ethnic nation perceives itself as the real source or *cause* of the state and as the *owner* of the new statehood and of the territory. Logically, the 'others' will be treated as foreigners, who should behave as loyal state citizens. They belong to the tolerated minority. The constitution makers of all these states have used a similar drafting technique. The ethnic foundation of statehood is found in the preamble of the constitution, while the normative part of the constitution speaks only of the *demos* as the exclusive basis of state democracy! In fact, in all these cases the constitution serves the function of fostering the further ethnic homogenisation of the state. But this function is permanently questioned by the underlying controversy: in a multiethnic society, in which ethnicity is misused as an instrument of political mobilisation and homogenisation, ethnic divisions will necessarily lead to fundamental ethnic conflicts.

8.3.5.3 Conclusion: Why is ethnic federalism largely dysfunctional?

Causes of democratic unity of the multicultural state

There have on a number of occasions been attempts to bring federalism and multiculturality into harmony, by searching for the basis of a common identity that would be able to hold the multicultural state together. From our point of view however, multiculturality structurally questions the existence of the liberal state when it seeks to bring and hold ethnic diversity together through federal instruments. In this sense, one has to ask principally why ethnic federalism is scarcely functional. Yet there is still no satisfactory answer to the fundamental question: what are the real causes of and reasons for democratic unity within a multiethnic state? Ethnic communities that claim group equality and respect for difference are still waiting for new constitutional principles for a democratic state which can achieve the democratic integration of a multicultural society, and at the same time establish new types of corporations that can establish the structural preconditions for a real human rights policy.

How can ethnic claims be transformed into political principles?

Federalism has developed into an instrument for the management of inter-ethnic conflicts. This development however has only been possible for federations which are based on principles that are foreign to liberalism. In many cases however, ethnic federalism has radicalised the problems that it was supposed to solve. Why has liberalism not been able to de-ethnicise the conflicts? Because it has not taken ethnic claims seriously and has thus been unable to solve ethnic problems. *Ethnic demands should be converted into political principles and structures.* Liberalism however is structurally ill-equipped to provide political solutions for such demands.

8.3.6 Concluding Theses for a Theory of Federalism

1st Thesis: legitimacy

How can peoples or cultural, religious or language communities be brought or held together in a state? The answer can only be: If the state is able to achieve legitimacy in relation to all of these communities, it will also be able to bring and hold these communities together. But how can the state build up such a widely supported legitimacy with regard to these communities? Two elements are necessary: Firstly, the state has to be able to embody common values, which are for each of the communities preferable to complete independence. Secondly, it has to be inclusive of all communities and to include them in the process of state building and decision making in such a way that all communities can identify with the state. This however is only possible, if instead of a purely majority-based democracy, a consensus-oriented democracy with a political culture of negotiation and compromise can be established.

This goal can only be attained if the state is simultaneously built upon various bases of legitimacy: Legitimacy of the municipality, legitimacy of the federal unit and legitimacy of the federation. In turn, such structured legitimacy can only be realised, if at each level decisions that affect the specific interests of a particular community can be made autonomously. A uniform legitimacy would destroy the federation.

In any case, fragmented states need to create a foundation that enables all people within the state, regardless of the cultural community to which they belong, to identify with the state. This is probably the most difficult and still inadequately addressed challenge of our time.

2nd Thesis: divisible sovereignty

In the era of globalisation, sovereignty as the idea of the 'Big Bang' to which the state owes its existence and from which all state authority flows has outlived its usefulness. There is however still no state that is prepared to dispense with sovereignty as a symbol of the state. In the future, it will not be possible to invoke absolute and exclusive sovereignty as the basis of state power, rather only divisible sovereignty.

State power and sovereignty must now be open, divisible and participatory. The state, however it is constructed, can therefore only claim to hold a part of sovereignty. If sovereignty is divisible, then it can be divided internally and can even be transferred externally.

This presupposes a new concept of sovereignty. Sovereignty is not simply power or authority, but rather the foundation of the *legitimacy* of the state. Today, sovereign is whoever legitimises local, national or international power. In a federal state, legitimacy is divided: the federal unit derives its legitimacy from the people of the federal unit, and the federation derives its legitimacy from the people of the whole federation.

The concept of divisible sovereignty is only conceivable in a state that is open, not only internally with regard to its citizens, but also externally. The federal state is open to division in its internal structure, but also open to international integration. The division of functions and powers according to the principle of subsidiarity, but also legitimacy and democratic decision making, are the foundations of genuine federalism. International or regional integration is a natural and organic progression for a polity which has developed bottom-up from the municipality to the federal unit up to the federation and which is open and adaptable to further development.

Globalisation fosters federal structures, because federal structures are best suited to the developments of transnational and international networking. If the symbol of the Middle Ages was the hierarchical pyramid, and the symbol of industrialisation and Enlightenment was the interlocking cogwheels of machinery, the symbol of globalisation is the network. Within this network, those 'interfaces' or 'points of intersection' that have a high degree of legitimacy and flexibility have the greatest chance of success. Unitary states have only one interface within this network. The federation however, can utilise the interfaces of its federal units, the municipalities and of course of the federation.

Traditional nation-states developed in the 19th Century into isolated 'islands of sovereignty', which controlled important colonial territories. Federalism has no colonial tradition. Many federal states have in fact been created out of former colonies. Federalism as state concept is open and flexible, both internally and externally. Internal openness means the ability to constantly adapt the internal organisation of the state to changing circumstances and conditions. And in terms of external openness, only those states that are open to the outside world will be properly equipped to deal with ever-expanding and more internationalised state functions.

The nation-state with its impenetrable shield of sovereignty must be re-examined, if it wants to be able to respond flexibly to the increasingly diverse range of demands and responsibilities through internal decentralisation and externally through internationalisation. In France, every debate on further integration within the EU as well as on internal decentralisation triggers a discourse on the existence or the survival of the republic. In contrast, federal systems can only develop with a political culture that is open to internal and external developments, and in which disputes on greater centralisation or decentralisation form part of daily political life without triggering a discussion on the very existence of the state as such. This fosters a culture of negotiation and compromise, which is necessary to manage conflicts.

3rd Thesis: power and responsibility

Only in federal systems can powers and functions be assigned to territorial units, which are also able to bear the corresponding responsibility. A basic principle of modern organisation requires every organisational unit be assigned only such powers and functions as it is able to properly manage and account for.

Modern multinational companies have long recognised that the secret to flexible and efficient leadership lies in the decentralisation of power and responsibility. In most states, it is still the central legislature that decides on the organisational form of the regions and municipalities and on the nature and scope of the citizens' democratic rights at those levels. Can the central legislature or the central state also bear the responsibility for ensuring that these organisational forms take proper account of the historical and cultural particularities of the regions, or that the democracy of the regions is maintained?

Corporations, which for instance have to decide on the planning of hospitals or general health care, must have the necessary means at their disposal and also be able to influence the selection and training of personnel, as well as being able to guarantee that the planning corresponds to the concrete needs of the people.

Too many modern conflicts are directly attributable to the fact that governments have decided over the fate of regions and peoples far-removed from the centre because they have the formal power to do so, but have not been exposed to the consequences of their decisions (positive or negative) and have therefore borne no direct responsibility! An appropriate balance of power and responsibility can ultimately only be realised in decentralised units. Modern public and private institutions should be designed in such a way that every person who has to make decisions on behalf of other people, also immediately feels the effects of his or her wrong decisions.

When municipalities decide over the construction of a new school building, they should have only such powers and financial means as the voters, taxpayers and prospective users of the school building have entrusted to them. The central government should not decide on such issues because it is too far removed from the effects of the decision. If the central government is empowered to decide on the language and curriculum of schools in a certain region, it is likely that neither the ministers nor the civil servants nor their children will be directly affected. It is therefore likely that such decisions will not be considered or made with the necessary care.

Only in a polity which accords real autonomy to regions and municipalities is government close enough to the people to be able to directly perceive the effects of their actions and decisions, and thus able to respond appropriately. Only when the population can react directly to flawed decisions, will the authorities have the necessary flexibility to amend and improve their policies.

4th Thesis: capacity to adjust

Only through federal decentralisation can democracy be developed in such a way that citizens can quickly and flexibly initiate changes to meet their needs, and can also react promptly to measures that they regard as unjust or inappropriate. Competition between the various democratic bodies produces the motivation to experiment and to find the optimal solutions that serve the common interest of the people in the respective federal unit.

5th Thesis: diversity

Diversity is wealth; diversity destroys uniform identity, equality and loyalty. The opinions on diversity could not be more contradictory. There is no doubt that federalism is built upon the conviction that diversity contributes to the cultural, spiritual and even economic enrichment of a country. Diversity is a value which must be continually fostered. Through federalism the liberty of the individual can be brought into harmony with the freedom of linguistic, cultural and religious communities. Humans need multidimensional loyalties. Loyalty to a cultural and/or religious community on the one side, and loyalty to a local community and to the federal unit on the other side, can all sit perfectly well with the simultaneous political loyalty to the federation.

The unitary state embodies either a uniform culture, which then becomes standardised as the dominant culture of the state, or it bases its democracy upon the rational political '*citoyen*', thereby making culture a private matter. Both solutions are unsuitable as conflict resolution models in new states.

Horizontal separation of powers was for LOCKE and MONTESQUIEU and remains today the precondition for individual liberty. Vertical separation of powers on the other hand, is the precondition for securing the autonomy and self-development of linguistic, religious and cultural communities within an overarching common polity.

Modern history teaches us that the atomisation of society into millions of isolated individuals can have dangerous effects. Man is free as an individual only when he also has freedom within his collective unit, that is, the family, and the local and cultural community. Therefore, in addition to the liberty guaranteed to the single individual, religious, linguistic and cultural communities must also be guaranteed independence and autonomy. In a federal polity, such limited group autonomy and liberty can be realised without endangering the indispensable solidarity with the common polity. In contrast, a centralised unitary nation-state may see demands for group autonomy as threatening the existence of the state.

The federal state is much more flexible. It can pragmatically accord greater autonomy or call for more solidarity without surrendering its basic structure. For the federal state, the autonomy of territorial units secures its wealth of cultural diversity and is just as important as the liberty of the individual. For this reason, besides fundamental individual rights, the group rights of cultural communities should also be recognised. Diversity is not seen as burden or as an impediment to national unity, but rather as the engine that ensures constant dialogue and debate and therefore fosters vitality, innovation and creativity within the federation. However, the federal state should not confine itself to its traditional and classical understanding of cultural diversity. In this age of increasing international migration, the federal state must also be able to accommodate and integrate the diverse immigrant populations.

6th Thesis: social balance

Federalism permits the necessary equalisation between the various regional economies and is thereby able to achieve greater social balance. Social justice in today's state is realised not only between social classes but also between the wealthy, developed industrial centres and the economically marginalised regions.

The modern state has achieved the conditions for a reasonable social and economic balance between employers and employees. The centrally-oriented market economy however has also induced the uncontrolled growth of large urban centres that harm the environment and result in the depopulation of the economically weak regions at the margin of the state. Globalisation will only increase this distortion.

Federalism enhances the balance between social groups and strives to achieve a just distribution of economic wealth between the underdeveloped marginal regions and the large economic hubs, because in a federation all federal units are in equal partnership with each other. Some units may be economically weak and sparsely populated, but constitutionally they have the same political rights and powers as their stronger neighbours. Moreover, through fiscal equalisation they can participate in the economic prosperity of the common polity much more efficiently than marginalised regions of a unitary state. Such equalisation however is only possible, if the federal state is able to generate enough solidarity among its population. Such solidarity requires the existence of common values, with which all cultures can identify and for which they are prepared to pay the price of solidarity in the interests of maintaining a harmonious common polity.

7th Thesis: liberty and peace

The goal of the modern state is individual liberty. If the state recognises and protects only individual liberty, culture becomes politically invisible and the traditional cultural communities will fade into private obscurity. Individual liberty is of little help to minorities who want to cultivate their language. The majority, through its exercise of individual rights, will displace the minority culture. If one wants to protect and foster the culture of minorities one has to recognise the right of communities to assert and develop their own group values. Minorities that feel threatened or assailed by the majority will not recognise the state as legitimate and will initiate secessionist procedures. For the sake of peace, the state will therefore in some instances have to give group rights priority over individual rights.

A precondition of every federal concept of the state is the recognition of human rights – that is – the guarantee of human dignity. Human dignity protects human beings in their rational capacity as well as in their emotional dimension. It protects the *homo oeconomicus* as well as the *homo politicus*. Federal diversity takes the complexity and multidimensionality of human beings into account. In a federal state, every human being should be able to find a niche in which he/she feels secure and protected.

The balance between individual liberty and collective rights is to be found in man's need for peace and harmony. When peace is at stake, the dignity of a community as well as the dignity of the individual have to be weighed against each other. If peace and harmony are gravely threatened, the dignity of the community must be protected, provided that this does not destroy the core of personal human dignity.

8th Thesis: self-determination and democracy

The centralistic majority principle can be opened up through the federal separation of powers and complemented by an appropriate model of modern partnership and peaceful conflict resolution. Indeed, the majority principle alone no longer suffices as the only model for resolving conflicts within the modern state. It has to be accompanied by the recognition of autonomous group rights and the opportunity for groups to participate as units in the decision making process of the state.

The pure majority principle of modern democracy often leads, as TOCQUEVILLE pointed out, to the tyranny of the majority. When the fate of the community is at stake, the majority should not be weighed only by a head count of individuals. Each single territorially-based cultural community should as a unit, independent of its size, have equal rights to participate in the decision making process of the state. The equality of votes should reflect the equal value of all cultural and/or territorial communities. Fundamental conflicts cannot be solved by a simple majority vote, but only based on partnership-oriented solidarity, recognition of the equality of groups, and negotiation towards compromise and consensus.

A pure majoritarian democracy destroys the federal balance. Federalism cannot be reconciled with a winner-takes-all democracy. The majoritarian democracy legitimises majority decisions on the resolution of differences of a *distributory* character (for example on issues such as welfare, taxation, employment relations, etc). But *categorical* conflicts over religion, language, territory and symbols of sovereignty or culture cannot be dealt with by simple majority. Moreover, it is generally not possible through purely majoritarian democracy to convert categorical conflicts into distributory issues and thereby defuse the issues.

Conclusion

The American founding fathers were led by the principle: "Let us be guided by experience, because reason might mislead us". Based on their experience, and for the protection of their local democracies, the Americans created an overarching democracy, that is, a federal state with divided sovereignty in which the smaller democracies were able to develop freely within the larger democracy.

This idea that it is possible to maintain and develop a democracy within a democracy was at the time quite revolutionary. By realising this new state concept, the Americans had effectively reinvented the 'constitutional wheel' and found a counterbalance to the centralism of the French Revolution and the European continent.

The experience of the US demonstrated that democracy in a federal state can only be developed if it is built upon existing smaller democracies and if it fosters rather than destroys these local democracies.

Switzerland adds to this experience with new federal concepts. It has succeeded through federalism and direct democracy in maintaining and developing a complex multicultural society in the middle of a continent rife with conflict. Switzerland had to enhance American federalism with new concepts of democracy, legitimacy and political culture. It has thereby given federalism a new identity, namely the identity of a state-concept that through the permanent conflict management of direct consensus-oriented democracy is able to bring and hold diverse cultural, religious and language communities together.

8.4 Theory of Swiss Federalism

8.4.1 Multiculturality and Swiss Federalism

Unity in diversity

The seemingly paradoxical formula '*unity in diversity*' encapsulates the federal principle of Switzerland. It expresses not only the importance of the contribution of the language and cultural communities to the common will of the nation, but also the dialectical tension between self-rule, shared-rule and solidarity. Federalism as the organising political concept of the federal state is based upon the constitutional balance between the autonomy of the federal units (self-rule) and their rights to participate at the centre (shared rule). The assignment of responsibilities to the different levels of the federation usually involves functional differentiation and simultaneous interconnection of the different levels through multifaceted rights of participation. In contrast to the USA and Germany however, Swiss federalism is not only an instrument or an institution to guarantee vertical separation of powers. Rather, the multiculturality and diversity of the country provide the 'pre-constitutional' basis for a deeply rooted federalism, which, as one of the key structural principles of the Constitution, is essential for the legitimacy and survival of the Swiss nation.

Peace and liberty

The primary goal of the modern state is to protect and promote individual freedom. A multicultural state such as Switzerland with an inherent potential for internal conflicts must, in addition to protecting individual liberty, also endeavour to ensure harmonious relations between different cultures. The goal of Swiss federalism is therefore, besides guaranteeing individual liberty, to maintain the cultural diversity of the society and to provide politically legitimate institutions and procedures to facilitate peaceful coexistence. Not only liberty, but also peace among the different cultural communities is the declared goal of the Constitution. Individual liberty must therefore often be subordinated to *collective rights* in the interests of maintaining the peace among cultural and linguistic communities.

Federal responsibilities of the federation

Diversity and autonomy were previously guaranteed only by the limited powers assigned to the federation. Direct democracy, the constitutional guarantee of cantonal autonomy, and a political climate in which any political decision was only enforceable if it was justified under federalist criteria – these were until recently the factual guarantees of multiculturality in Switzerland. These instruments served to regulate conflicts and to protect minorities. However, the new Constitution now imposes clear responsibilities on the federation to maintain federalism, to foster diversity and to build solidarity and the common national consciousness. The Federal Council must foster languages, strive for a better mutual understanding between the different language communities, and support poor regions as well as mountain areas and urban centres.

According to Article 46(2) of the Constitution, the federation must in the course of all federal legislative and administrative activity take the cantonal particularities into account, and must provide for the greatest possible autonomy of the cantons. It must respect cantonal independence as well as the right of self-determination. At the same time however, the federation must determine under which circumstances and conditions it is necessary to make federal regulations in the interest of national uniformity.

Each of the three federal governmental branches must therefore assume new functions and responsibilities. When they propose decisions or plan new measures, they have to evaluate whether such decisions or measures are necessary and beneficial to the interests of federalism and what effects the decisions or plans are likely to have on federalism. Thus, in future, the federation will decide what is good for federalism and what could damage the federal balance.

8.4.1.1 Cultural and National Differences in 'Multiethnic' Switzerland

Swiss diversity

Switzerland, with a mere 42,000 sq km of territory, undoubtedly has the greatest linguistic and religious diversity of all the western European countries: Three equally recognised official languages, four national languages and four religious communities recognised by cantonal public law. Even greater diversity is present in many states in other parts of the world, including parts of Eastern Europe such the Balkans and the Caucasus, albeit with certain essential differences in comparison to Switzerland.

Swiss federalism (in Latin *foedus*: alliance, treaty) developed out of a multitude of quite different, independent polities, some of which were organised democratically and some of which were more oligarchic. Whilst their larger neighbours went through a lengthy process of developing into nation-states, these small corporations managed to dissociate themselves from the large neighbouring states in order to maintain their independence. Thus, at the edge of the three large linguistic regions of western Europe, twenty-six small polities grouped themselves together within a diverse alliance, in order to defend their political and cultural independence against their powerful neighbours. Each of these polities was able to develop its own legal system, its own political and religious culture and historical identity, and at the same to remain connected to the culture and language of its neighbour state. The citizens in each of these twenty-six polities, partly influenced by modern constitutionalism and also based on their rural, democratic, cooperative or aristocratic tradition, developed their own state consciousness and identity.

From religious conflict to language conflict

Until the end of the 19th Century it was primarily the tensions between the two main religious groups, the Catholics and the Protestants, which necessitated federal institutions for maintaining the peace. However, since the beginning of the 20th Century it has mainly been the tensions between language and cultural groups that have required new federal solutions. Thus, it is no coincidence that the new Federal Constitution accords special weight to the four equal national languages (Article 4) in terms of freedom of language (Article 18), the diversity of languages (Article 69(3)), and the harmony between language communities (Article 70(3)).

The municipality as the smallest homogeneous territorial body

Switzerland is historically embedded within the political culture of the western nation-states, which is based upon the principle of territoriality and tends to assume relative homogeneity within the nation-state in terms of language and religion (based on the homogeneity of most western nation-states in the 18th and 19th Centuries). Accordingly, the concept of personally-based group autonomy independent of territory – such as the old 'millet system' of the Ottoman Empire or the concept of autonomy of nationalities within the Austro-Hungarian Empire – is foreign to Switzerland. Even in the culturally diverse canton of Grison, the language groups (German, Romansh and Italian) and regionally overlapping religious communities (Catholics and Protestants) are territorially divided into relatively homogeneous municipalities. For a long time, even the Jewish population was assigned its own specific local territory in order to establish its own small ethnically homogenous municipalities.

No melting pot

In contrast to the United States, which has provided a 'melting pot' for immigrants from Europe, Asia and Africa based on exclusively individual rights of freedom and equality, in Switzerland as in the rest of Europe one finds territorially determined linguistic and religious borders that have been recognised and immovable for centuries.

Stability of ethnic borders

In contrast to many Eastern European peoples, the Swiss population has never been forcibly displaced *en masse* by war or foreign occupation. The religious wars of the 17th Century did lead to a certain territorial separation of religious communities based on the principle *cujus regio ejus religio*. But, apart from the separation of the canton of Appenzell into two half-cantons, there were no major resettlements of religious communities. On the contrary, the territorial borderlines between language and religious groups have remained remarkably stable to this day.

No concept of the 'motherland'

The Eastern European concept of the 'motherland' or 'mother-state' is completely unknown in Switzerland. If one were to transplant Switzerland into an area of Eastern Europe, the German, French and Italian speaking populations would have their corresponding motherland or mother-state in Germany, France or Italy. According to this concept, only the smallest minority, the Romansh-speaking population (0.5 percent of the Swiss population), would have the legitimate claim to build its own mother-state. Such ideas are however unfamiliar to the Swiss. Whilst the various language communities in Switzerland feel culturally connected to the respective neighbour-state with whom they share a language, there is not the slightest reason for any of those Swiss communities to lean on their kin-nation politically.

Nor is this need felt by the neighbour-states or their nationals. Whilst for instance Italians feel a close political connection to and some sense of responsibility towards the Italian-speaking population of Istria (in Croatia and Slovenia), they feel only a *cultural* connection with the Italian-speaking population of the Swiss canton of Tessin. In any case, it is unlikely that any Italian would seriously contend that either territory is or should be *politically* connected to Italy.

Nation without minorities

This independence of the language communities can be attributed to the way in which these communities were structured historically: the German-, French- and to a lesser extent the Italian-speaking Swiss have for centuries been divided into separate, politically independent cantonal territories. For the language groups within these units there is generally no feeling of being a minority, as in most cases the territory of the canton is either homogenous or shared with only one other language group.

8.4.1.2 Swiss Procedures and Institutions for Dealing with Ethnic Conflicts

No tyranny of the majority

In most modern democracies the only foundation of legitimacy is the majority rule of parliament as the representative of the people. Multiethnic or multicultural states however cannot simply entrust the entire governmental responsibility to a majority party or majority coalition, as in such states this authority can easily degenerate into a tyranny of the majority over the minority. Thus, in order to build a state composed of multiple ethnicities, there are certain important principles other than the pure majority principle that have to be applied and observed.

Basic principles

Such principles may be summarised as follows:

- Concept of a state without nation: 'a-national' state;
- Power and responsibility: power should be vested in authorities that feel responsible and accountable, because they themselves will bear the consequences of their decisions;
- Limits on state power: not only horizontal but also vertical separation of powers;
- Authority and responsiveness: flexible democracy, which can react quickly in order to correct failures and improve policies according to the needs of the population;
- Internationally open state and open society: a multicultural state with important links to neighbour-states needs to pursue an international policy of neutrality;
- Diversity should be fostered and promoted as a common value;
- Social balance: solidarity, fiscal equalisation;
- Humanity: Guarantee of human dignity and local governmental and administrative activity close to the citizens;
- Self-determination: autonomy.

8.4.1.3 'A-national' State

Principle of domicile for political voting rights

Throughout Switzerland, democracy is organised according to the principle of domicile. As citizenship in Switzerland is threefold (municipal, cantonal and Swiss citizenship), the Constitution guarantees that after a short period those who have Swiss citizenship but not the citizenship of the canton and the municipality have the full right to vote at the municipal, cantonal and federal levels. This means every citizen is entitled to exercise his/her political rights in whichever place he/she lives. All citizens are to be treated equally in the exercise of their political rights. Political rights are tied to Swiss citizenship. Swiss citizenship is difficult to obtain for those born outside Switzerland, but it is not tied to a specific nation and does not afford any special privileges to members of any particular national origin (as Germany does, see Article 116 German Basic Law).

No cantonal ethnicities

Also internally, that is, in the relationship among the different cantons, the concept of 'nations' of people is unfamiliar to the Swiss tradition. Most cantonal constitutions which refer in their preamble to the 'people', are referring to the citizens living within the canton. Only in exceptional cases do they speak of, for example, the 'Jurassian people'. Even in the previous Federal Constitution, Article 1 contained no ethnic or national concept of the peoples of the cantons: "Together, the peoples of the 23 sovereign Cantons of Switzerland united by the present alliance, to wit: Zurich, Berne, Lucerne, ... Geneva and Jura, form the Swiss Confederation." It does not refer to the 'Genevans', the 'Zurichians' and 'Jurassians', etc. Similarly, the wording of the preamble of the United States Constitution makes no reference to ethnicity: "We the people of the United States", whereas the preamble of the Bosnian Constitution on the other hand refers to the 'Bosnians', the 'Croats' and the 'Serbs'.

Citizenship

The idea of a state of the 'German People', of the 'Georgians', 'Croats' or 'Serbs' is foreign to the Swiss Constitution. According to Article 14 of the Swiss citizenship law, Swiss citizenship can be granted to any person who:

a) Is integrated within the Swiss society;
b) Is familiar with the Swiss way of life, customs and values;
c) Respects and follows the Swiss legal order; and
d) Does not endanger the internal or external security of Switzerland.

Although this provision has led to some peculiar and partly even humiliating practices in the process of naturalisation, one cannot deduce from this provision a national or ethnic perception of 'Swissness', especially since such a perception would vary substantially according to language, culture and cantonal tradition.

The Jurassian people

The only canton which at least during the phase of its establishment had a certain ethnic perception of the nation was the canton of Jura. In the process of making arrangements as to who would have the political right to vote on the self-determination of the Jurassian part of the canton of Berne, certain Jurassians demanded that only old-established inhabitants who had lived in Jura for at least seven generations or who had parents of Jurassian origin should be entitled to vote. Even persons living outside the canton but belonging to this concept of the Jurassian 'nation' should be entitled to vote. However, this demand was rejected on the grounds that in Switzerland the right to vote is defined by the principle of domicile.

No national minorities

Switzerland is by definition an 'a-national' state. It is neither based upon a cultural or linguistic nation determined by blood and descent, nor upon any other concept of a pre-existing natural Swiss nation. The preamble to the Constitution only mentions the Swiss People and the cantons. It avoids however the use of the term 'nation'.

As there is no naturally predetermined original nation, there can also be no *national* minorities. Since the federation is not legitimised by the nation and since Switzerland through its Constitution has not established a new national state, all persons who have acquired Swiss citizenship either by birth or by naturalisation have equal rights and are able, independent of any previous nationality, to identify with the state in the same way.

Whoever speaks one of the four Swiss languages belongs on this basis to a language community, but not to a nation. French-speaking Swiss are *not* 'Swiss French' in the way that the Serbs living in Bosnia are called the 'Bosnian Serbs'. All citizens see themselves primarily as belonging to their canton and to the federation and only in a secondary sense as members of a specific language or religious community. This is the main reason why the term 'ethnicity' is fundamentally unfamiliar to the Swiss political culture.

No territory for nationalities

If the traditional concept of the nation was recognised in Switzerland, the cantons would long since have formed alliances along national lines and would have created three or four 'national' or linguistic regions within Switzerland. A division of the country along linguistic lines would cause great problems in the canton of Grison, which contains three language groups. Such a division would ultimately result in the complete dissolution of Switzerland, as by drawing national borderlines Switzerland would lose its historical roots, which are primarily cantonal and not regional or linguistic. Fortunately, most of the cantons in Switzerland established their unity, identity and territorial borders not at the time of nation-state building in Europe of the 18th and 19th Centuries, but already in the early Middle Ages.

Switzerland could not survive as a traditional 'nation' state

If Switzerland were to be converted into a traditional 'nation' state, in the sense of the Spanish state for example, one would have to decide which should be the national language. As a nation can only have one national language, it would be necessary, as in Spain, to declare the majority language the national language – which in the case of Switzerland would be Swiss German. This would inevitably lead to discrimination against minorities. A people with three or four equally recognised languages cannot be a uniform nation. As however Switzerland is located amongst several neighbouring 'nation' states, it had to develop its own conception of the nation as a *political nation* with which most Swiss people of the various language groups can identify.

Secularisation of the federation

As the Swiss population is composed in almost equal parts of Protestants and Catholics, the federation had practically no choice but to secularise the state and to guarantee religious freedom. Switzerland cannot allow itself to privilege one religious community over the other – this is one of the reasons why for a long time Switzerland had no representative at the Vatican. Religious conflicts led the federation to withdraw its Vatican representation in order to eliminate any possible mistrust by the Protestant community with regard to the religious neutrality of the federation.

8.4.1.4 Legitimacy and Democracy

Legitimacy of Switzerland as a polity

The only basis of the legitimacy of the state and of the common Swiss identity that transcends and holds together the different cantonal, language and religious identities is the broad recognition of *political Switzerland,* that is, of federalism, democracy, liberty and independence. This political identity is the reason why for example the French-speaking Swiss citizen does not see him/herself as a member of the French nation. Those who live in a municipality within Swiss territory know very well that they can decide on their own, whether and when they want to build a new school for example. Those living on the other side of the border in neighbouring states would first have to seek permission from Paris, Rome, Vienna, or Berlin.

However, this fragmented Swiss federation built at the end of the 19th Century will have to continuously struggle to maintain its legitimacy. The overall legitimacy of the state can ultimately only be earned through the provision of far-reaching cantonal autonomy and by the participation of all cultures in the federal consensus.

The unique challenge of the Swiss federation lies in its *multiculturality* and thereby also in maintaining the *legitimacy* of a political nation held together by the common will of the people which has no pre-constitutional homogeneity. This challenge is particularly great in an era marked by the contradictory tendencies of economic globalisation on one side and nationalistic, emotional 'localisation' on the other side. Will the French-, Italian-, and Romansh-speaking Swiss also in future be able to identify with Switzerland as their political 'homeland' in the same way as the German-speaking Swiss?

Legitimacy and diversity

The legitimacy of Switzerland is based on the one hand on the peoples of the cantons, and on the other hand on the diversity of a fragmented and 'composed' Swiss nation. This nation in turn is split up into the political units of the cantons, as well as into the various cultures that cut across cantonal borderlines. The homogeneity of the state is to be found within an internalised common understanding of the 'political'. This historically developed reality determines the character of the federal order of the state. Thus, the Constitution declares in the preamble that Switzerland lives according to the principle of unity in diversity, and in Article 2(2) charges the federation with the task of fostering diversity. This acknowledgement and this res-ponsibility on the part of the federation and the cantons establish the legitimacy of the authority of the federation.

What are ultimately the reasons that induce the different communities to refrain from violence and to participate in a peaceful and rational democratic decision making process? The decisive reason is probably the legitimacy within the unity of the composite nation. Unity in diversity can only be realised, when all sides are prepared to compromise. At the same time, for many it is clear that it is only through this diversity that they can survive as Swiss people. An ethnically homogeneous Switzerland would be no Switzerland! Switzerland exists only by its diversity.

Political nation

However culturally diverse Switzerland is, it is homogeneous in the declared belief in the basic political values of the state and democracy, and in particular the local corporate democracy, federalism and liberty. The unity of the nation has been built upon these basic political values, to which everyone can adhere regardless of their culture or religion. These political values have been 'internalised'. Provocatively, one could even say the Swiss nation has by virtue of its common political values become one homogeneous 'ethnicity'.

Switzerland is one of the very few states which do not base their legitimacy and identity on the self-concept of a linguistic, cultural or religious nation, but on the belief of the vast majority of the society in the basic values of the state. In so far as it is possible to regard Switzerland as a unified entity, this unity is based on historical and political factors but not on culture, religion or language.

Only because Switzerland is based upon generally recognised and accepted political values is it able to grant the four languages equal rights and to avoid handling the numerous smaller language and religious groups as legally inferior minorities. The 70 per cent of the Swiss population that is German-speaking effectively has a dominant position, but it does not have a legally privileged position.

Since the language and religious borderlines only coincide with the territorial borderlines of the cantons in exceptional cases, the historically developed political tradition, local autonomy and the political culture of the canton have a greater significance for the identity and unity of the people of the canton than common language or religion. This common political identity of the canton is an essential feature of the 'civil society'. The emotional identification with the canton has become stronger than the feeling of belonging to a language or religious community.

Consensus-oriented (concordance) or majoritarian democracy

The legitimacy of important decisions cannot be established only by simple democratic majority decisions. Legitimacy for fundamental political and social decisions requires the acceptance of the principal communities, groups and decision makers within the state. This search for consensus and harmony corresponds to the old tradition of political culture in Switzerland. A small majority of only 50.01 per cent is generally regarded as the worst-case scenario. Whenever possible, an attempt is made to generate a higher consensus for democratic decisions. If the majority only slightly exceeds 50 per cent, it will have to try through concessions and compromise to take into account the arguments of the substantial minority. The idea of the domination of one majority party over a large minority, as frequently occurs in the 'Westminster' system, is completely foreign. Such coalitions with the support of 50 per cent of the parliament would later stand no chance of winning a popular referendum. A government only has good prospects of succeeding in a referendum if it has obtained the consensus of all major parties.

The procedure of direct democracy has substantially contributed to the maintenance and development of this political culture, as based on experience the political elite of the country can only win a referendum if its proposal is supported by a general consensus of all major parties. Furthermore, any party that attempts to abuse the process, for example by seeing to block the consensus by veto, is unlikely to win much support in a referendum, as the people does not usually reward obstructive political behaviour.

Equality of the cantons

The idea of concordance also finds expression in the principle of the equal rights of the cantons. This equality can be seen in the manner in which the cantons are represented in the upper chamber: every canton (except the 'half-cantons') has two representatives, irrespective of the canton's size, population or economic strength. It can also be seen in constitutional referenda, as any constitutional amendment requires, in addition to the approval of the majority of the Swiss people, also the approval of majority of the cantons. The cantons (including the 'half-cantons') also have equal status as limited sovereign units in relation to the federation and in relation to each other.

Proportional system

Furthermore, the proportional system that applies to almost all elections also facilitates concordance. As a result of proportionality, all the important minorities are represented at the federal, cantonal and municipal levels in parliaments and even in the executive and the courts. There is in Switzerland almost no committee, authority, court or other institution, which is not composed proportionally.

Double and multiple loyalties

Switzerland is not composed of 26 'national' cantons, but rather of 26 different peoples of the cantons (Article 1 of the Constitution of 1874). In these cantons it is not membership of a nation, but *citizenship* that is important. One can acquire citizenship through a formal naturalisation process, based on duration of domicile and basic knowledge of the political system. Eligibility for naturalisation is in no way affected by language, religion, kinship or blood. Through naturalisation the Swiss citizen professes loyalty to Switzerland in a political sense, but not towards a specific cultural nation. Their loyalty towards the culture of their previous homeland remains and cannot be lost by the acquisition of the Swiss nationality.

According to the Swiss understanding, it is to be assumed that the Swiss citizen will have various loyalties: to their canton and to Switzerland, towards the culture of their neighbour-state, perhaps to a previous homeland and also to their religious community. Citizenship does not involve absolute and undivided loyalty to the state. Citizenship bestows political rights and forms the basis of the obligation to perform military service. In all other respects however, Swiss citizens and foreigners residing in Switzerland enjoy more or less the same rights.

Multiple nationality

This may be one of the reasons that citizenship no longer has the same meaning as it once did. Many people in Switzerland for example have more than one cantonal 'citizenship'. For decades, cantons have accepted the idea of double or multiple cantonal citizenship.

As double and multiple citizenship at the cantonal level had long been undisputed, it was possible to extend the idea of multiple loyalties to the level of national citizenship without any great controversy. Thus, today it is possible to acquire Swiss nationality without, as required by other states, having to renounce one's original nationality. The citizenship laws thereby recognise the reality of migration caused by globalisation, which must lead to transnational citizenship. The state can no longer demand absolute and undivided loyalty from its citizens. This openness of citizenship is a rejection of the traditional exclusionist nation-state.

Political alliances of the cantons

In the 19th Century, Switzerland was internally very unstable and under constant threat from the neighbouring monarchies. This threat to the internal balance was the primary reason why the Constitution of 1874 explicitly forbade the cantons from forming any political alliances among themselves or with other countries. The new Constitution no longer contains such prohibition, as Switzerland is no longer threatened by conservative monarchies. This however may also be a sign that the democratic and federal procedures have laid the foundation for real nation-building and that therefore the internal balance of the political nation has been achieved by the nation itself. Democracy and federalism have over time provided the basis for the undisputed legitimacy of a state, which in the 19th Century was still extremely frail and unstable.

Peace as a constitutional goal

Every multi-ethnic situation has its own particular characteristics. The specific problems of a multinational or multicultural identity can almost never be transposed from one state to the next. For this reason, institutions and procedures which in certain countries such as the USA, Switzerland, Spain or Italy have led to peaceful resolution of ethnic tensions, cannot simply be transplanted and applied in other countries.

In other words, constitutional instruments cannot be transferred indiscriminately from one state to another. However, constitutional experiences and procedures that can be successfully developed and tested in a free and democratic environment can give instructive hints as to what may be supportable for the population of a multiethnic country, what may be feasible and appropriate, and which well-intentioned proposals are likely to be hopeless, counterproductive or inflammatory.

Freedom of religion and religious harmony

For a long time, the Federal Court has recognised not only the fundamental individual constitutional right of freedom of religion (Article 15 of the Constitution), but also the overall interest in maintaining peace among the different religious communities and thereby indirectly a collective right of religious communities. This concern for harmony between religious groups is no longer at the forefront of the Federal Court's jurisprudence. Still, Article 72(2) of the Constitution contains a provision that expressly empowers the federation and the cantons to provide for measures to maintain public peace among the different religious communities.

Freedom of language and principle of territoriality

Throughout the world, in addition to religious conflicts, conflicts between different linguistic communities have been increasing in recent decades. In Switzerland too, the tensions between the different linguistic communities have grown. For this reason special emphasis is placed on the constitutional obligation of the federation and the cantons to seek and promote communication and mutual understanding between the different language communities (Art. 70 of the Swiss Constitution). In addition, the inherent contradiction between the fundamental individual right of freedom of language (Art. 18) and the collective right to territorial integrity of minority language groups (Art. 70(2)) is likely in future to cause headaches for the Federal Court.

Constitutional procedures for the resolution of territorial conflicts

The Constitutions of 1848 and 1874 were drafted under unstable conditions at a time when, in the wake of the civil war, the fragile peace was threatened by internal instability and by neighbouring monarchic regimes. The new Constitution refrains from repeating those provisions that prohibit cantons from concluding political treaties. Internal peace was however still under threat, because there remained certain hidden conflicts between various cantons over the issue of territory. The peaceful resolution of the conflict in Jura undoubtedly contributed to the fact that the new Constitution is no longer silent on the issue of adjusting cantonal borderlines and territories, but rather provides for a special democratic and federal procedure that takes account of all relevant majority and minority interests (Art. 53 of the Constitution).

Neutrality and relationship towards the neighbour states

The Swiss policy of neutrality is not based upon Switzerland's foreign policy interests, and is only to a limited extent the result of the desire to maintain external independence. The traditional Swiss policy of neutrality is rather a consequence of the internal religious conflicts of the 17th Century. The Thirty Years War wrought havoc not only in Germany but also in Switzerland. The religious conflict divided the Swiss into two opposing religious camps. In order however not to perish in the hostilities of the neighbour-states, the Catholic and Protestant states of the Swiss Confederation banded together under the 'Wiler Defensionale' in order to defend Swiss territory against any invasions of foreign troops. This alliance is the origin of the long-standing policy of neutrality.

In the 20th Century, neutrality was the indispensable precondition for the maintenance of internal peace between language groups. In particular during World War I, the enemy parties Germany and France could have destroyed the peace among the language communities in Switzerland by concluding alliances with the German- and French-speaking communities and thereby expanding the conflict to Swiss territory, if the Federal Executive Council had not observed (in spite of distinct German-friendly tendencies) a strict policy of neutrality. The example of Swiss neutrality demonstrates that multiethnic states with cultural links to the nations in the neighbouring countries can only survive as states, if they treat all neighbour countries equally. Such equal treatment is only possible through a permanent and strict policy of neutrality.

Of course, one should not overlook the fact that Swiss neutrality has had certain negative effects. In particular, it has contributed to a sense of isolation. A 'head-in-the-sand' mentality, self-satisfaction and even arrogance, are the price to be paid for such an isolationist policy. Integration – together with the preservation of identity and plurality – are today the greatest and most difficult and challenges which the small state of Switzerland has to meet in the new international and European environment.

Example: Secession and foundation of the new canton of Jura

An impressive example which substantiates the culture of compromise and concordance, is the procedure by which the new canton of Jura was established. For over one hundred years, the so-called 'new' part of the canton of Berne, known as Jura, fought for its right to self-determination, and thereby for secession from the canton of Berne. In the 1970s, the Canton of Berne changed its constitution in order to grant the right of self-determination to the people of Jura. Two different issues had to be decided. First, the question was posed whether the majority of the population even wanted to found a new canton, and then the borderlines of the new canton had to be democratically determined.

In order to enable the population of the region of Jura within the canton of Berne to exert its right of self-determination, it was necessary to amend the Constitution of Berne. This amendment required the democratic approval of the voters of the entire canton. The overwhelming majority of the voters of the canton approved the amendment and thereby introduced into their constitution the following procedure with four different phases of democratic votes:

1. In the first vote, the population of the region of Jura had to decide whether it approved of the foundation of a new canton of Jura.
2. After the majority of the region had voted in favour of exercising its right of self-determination, the districts in which the majority had voted against the

establishment of a new canton were entitled to decide in a second vote whether they wished to be part of the new canton or to remain within the canton of Berne.
3. After the determination of the new district borders, the peoples of the municipalities along the new borderlines were given the opportunity to decide under which of the two neighbouring cantonal jurisdictions they would prefer to live.
4. Following the approval of a new Constitution for the canton of Jura by the constitutional convention and by the voters within the new borderlines, the voters of the Swiss Federation and of the cantons had to approve an amendment to the Federal Constitution in order to insert the new canton of Jura in the list of cantons in Article 1. Jura thereby became the 23rd full canton in the Swiss federation (26 including the half cantons).

This lengthy and complicated process was designed to facilitate the building of a consensus, not just of a small majority, but the consensus of the majority of all affected communities right down to the municipal level.

The pragmatic and somewhat cumbersome procedure of secession of the region of Jura from the canton of Berne was based on the following constitutional and political values and principles:

1. All parties agreed by consensus to submit to a procedure, the outcome of which was open, but which was accepted as legitimate by all parties.
2. The idea of unilateral secession from Switzerland was realistically never on the table.
3. The final decision over the establishment of a new canton first required an amendment of the Constitution of Berne, which was approved by popular referendum. Then the voters within the region of Jura had to make their own decision regarding their future fate. First the majority of the region decided, then the various districts that were not in agreement with the regional majority could separate themselves from the region, and finally the municipalities along the new borderline were able to have their say as to which side of the border they would prefer to belong to.
4. Once the borderlines of the new Canton had been settled, a constitutional convention had to be elected in order to draft a new cantonal constitution. This required, like all cantonal constitutions, the approval of the Federal Parliament. Finally, the people of Switzerland and the peoples of the cantons had to approve the necessary amendment to the Federal Constitution, and thereby to decide whether they agreed with the foundation of a new canton of Jura.

Democratic decisions were not dependent on the simple majority principle in the sense of a 'winner-takes-all' democracy. Districts and even municipalities, which did not want to join the seceding majority, were entitled to decide to which canton they wanted to belong. The questions of secession and the establishment of a new federal unit were not left to the simple democratic majority. Even the interests of the smallest municipalities on the borderline were taken seriously in the determination of these questions.

8.4.1.5 Local Autonomy and Decentralisation

The Swiss Federation is in reality not a two-tiered federation, but rather a *three-tiered federation*. Autonomy is granted at the level of the municipality, the canton and also the federation. This autonomy is exercised not only by institutions, but rather above all by the citizens through the democratic bodies and at the ground level through the citizens' assembly in the municipality.

Municipalities

The municipality enjoys a constitutional right to local autonomy. Municipalities grant at the lowest level of the federation the citizenship of the municipality. They enact their own municipal regulations (which have legislative validity), decide on the income tax to be paid by the inhabitants of the municipality, and decide on expenditures for the fulfilment of local functions such as primary schools, police, social welfare, health, culture, sport, waste disposal, planning and zoning.

The municipalities can tailor measures that correspond to their particular local needs. Towns will place a high priority on issues of housing and drug abuse, mountain areas will focus on protection from natural disasters and provide facilities to promote tourism. Industrial centres will pay most attention to matters such as childcare, environmental protection and unemployment, whilst suburban municipalities will give priority to sport, relaxation and culture.

Proximity to the citizens

As it is easy to contact members of municipal authorities personally, the citizens prefer to make direct contact with their local authorities and to turn to their local authorities for assistance, than to make contact with cantonal or federal authorities. The citizens' needs, wishes, and problems can thereby be more effectively handled at the local level than they would be if all matters had to be directed in writing to anonymous civil servants in the central or cantonal bureaucracy.

Deficits of decentralisation

It would however be wrong to idealise the small communal democracy. Often, local municipalities are too small and overwhelmed to properly fulfil their functions. Powerful business interests or important taxpayers can easily misuse the municipalities for private interests. Municipalities often lack the human and financial resources they need to perform their role effectively. Corruption is easier to get away with at the level of the small inefficient local government than at the more transparent level of the canton or the federation. And egoism and local provincialism are often mobilised against solidarity and the common interest, and can hinder progress at the higher levels.

Public spirit at the local level

The Swiss are simultaneously citizens of the municipality, the canton and the federation. Citizens are also taxpayers at each of the three levels of government.

In return, the municipalities provide their inhabitants with the services that are essential for their day to day life: energy, water, transport and waste disposal are as much part of the traditional tasks of local government as schools, social security, planning and the environment. The municipalities provide for the daily needs of their citizens in accordance with the rules and plans determined through direct democracy.

School of democracy

The exercise of political rights through direct democracy enables the citizens to control the income and expenditure of their municipal authorities. Citizens elect their representatives to local parliament and the municipal executive. It is at the local level that young politicians have to prove themselves. Municipalities often serve as an experimental field for many political initiatives. It is the arena in which citizens can develop their social and political competence. It is for this reason that the local level is regarded as an important part of the Swiss federal structure, as it builds the democratic federal state through local democracy.

Constitutional guarantee of local autonomy

The Constitution (Art. 50) dedicates an entire section to the municipalities. It guarantees municipal autonomy – albeit according to the provisions of the respective cantonal law – and requires the federation to assess all measures for their possible effect on municipalities. Federal law has to be palatable for municipalities.

Pressure of globalisation on local communities

The rapid pace of economic development and in particular the effects of globalisation (loss of jobs in small municipalities), as well as the complexity of welfare, planning, and environment in the modern state have all become too much for the many small local communities with less than 500 inhabitants. Up to now, Switzerland has refrained from adapting its local government structures to the new requirements of streamlined administration as has been done in Germany and in the Scandinavian states. Like France, Switzerland has left unaltered the municipal structures that date back to the time of Napoleon, and has left it to the cantons to make provisions in their constitutions and regulations that will enable the municipalities to fulfil the complex functions of the modern state efficiently.

The cantons are able to meet this challenge with regard to local structures only partially. Thus, they have made legislative provision for the merger of small municipalities and facilitated cooperation between municipalities through new procedures. However, the calls for efficiency and tax-reduction often go unheeded by the citizens who are deeply rooted in their local democratic identity. They feel emotionally bound to the local community by their ancestors, and are not prepared to give up their municipal identity even if they have to pay a high price for it. In the short term this may cripple efficiency, but in the longer term it will enable internal peace and social harmony to be maintained, without which even the most efficient administration would be powerless. Since however the local expenditures prescribed by the federation and the cantons are quite comprehensive, there remains very little room for self-determined local policy. All the aforementioned benefits of local autonomy and proximity to the people are therefore only illusory if local governments are not given the space to freely exercise their autonomy.

Homogeneous municipalities

As the Swiss system of local government is structured into very small territorial municipalities, it is still possible in the cantons with different ethnic communities such as the trilingual canton of Grison, to maintain ethnically more or less homogeneous municipalities. Thus, one can find within this canton small Romansh-speaking Catholic and Romansh-speaking Protestant municipalities and German-speaking Protestant as well as Catholic municipalities side by side within a small area. They do not fall into conflicts, because each municipality can still decide independently on issues of education, security and public order, social welfare, and culture, and through the tax revenue that it receives the municipality has the financial means to fulfil these functions for the benefit of their inhabitants.

Cantons as small states

The Canton gives itself its own Constitution, organises the three branches of cantonal government and the checks and balances between them, regulates the political rights of the citizens including referendum and initiative of the people, collects the necessary taxes and determines for which cantonal functions the tax revenue is to be spent. Approximately one third of the total public revenue in Switzerland is raised and spent by the cantons, a further one third by the municipalities and the remaining third by the federation. The canton also determines its own internal structure, grants and regulates municipal autonomy and organises its own territorial divisions.

The cantons organise their own courts and until now their own civil procedure (this power has been substantially diminished by the European Convention on Human Rights and will be further diminished by the proposed centralisation of procedural law). Cantonal law has developed in accordance with the civil law tradition of the French *Code Napoléon*, and with that of the German and Italian civil law. The political culture of the cantons is influenced by Italy, France or Germany respectively. In the schoolbooks of Protestant cantons, the history of CALVIN and the reformation period is presented differently to the way in which it is taught in Catholic cantons. The Catholic cantons in turn regulate their relationship to the church differently to those cantons with a Protestant tradition or those with different religious communities.

No asymmetrical federalism

In contrast to Spain (e.g. the Basque and Catalonian regions), Canada (Quebec) and Italy (South-Tyrol and Aosta Valley), in Switzerland neither the cantons nor the municipalities have requested a special status or a special autonomy because of their language or religious situation. The autonomy of all territorial federal or cantonal units has always been based on the idea of equality. The principle of sovereign equality has dominated all federal constitutional regulations. Since cantonal and municipal autonomy is so extensive, there is no need for any special autonomy or status to be extended to particular territorial units. If in Switzerland special minorities had to be granted additional autonomous rights, such autonomy would necessarily also have to be extended to all other territorial units. Undoubtedly the demands for autonomy of the various small minorities together with direct democracy has largely contributed to the fact that the three-tiered federation is so strongly decentralised.

Two branches of government on all levels

At all three levels of the federation the respective polities have their own *legislative* and *executive* powers and institutions. The federation and the cantons also have their own *constitutions* and their own *courts* and jurisdiction, whereby the federal courts –in contrast to the United States – serve almost exclusively as courts of appeal against decisions of cantonal courts. Even in relation to public and administrative law – in contrast to the Queen's Bench in the UK or the Supreme Court in Israel – they exercise original jurisdiction only rarely.

i. Direct Democracy

Educational laboratory of the nation

Many foreign observers of Swiss democracy attest that Swiss citizens have a certain maturity and simultaneously use this assessment as an argument to prove that in their own country direct democracy would be inefficient and would lead to emotional and populist decisions, because their own citizens are not sufficiently mature. Actually the contrary is the case: Switzerland, as a society with a high potential for conflicts, is dependent on institutions which enforce equality and balance, and which demand reason. Democracy does not function because the country is mature, the immature country can only function because of its democratic institutions. In fact, direct democracy is primarily a school for the whole society; an educational laboratory in which citizens are educated to think in principled and universal dimensions. Citizens are educated to see the advocates and opponents of certain proposals not merely as party-strategists, but as people who follow particular political goals and endeavour through rational arguments to motivate other people to come to the same conclusions. Direct democracy compels the citizens to engage with political issues and to make their own decisions.

Influence of direct democracy on the political system

Whoever wants to understand the political system of Switzerland must be conscious that direct or semi-direct democracy influences the political system at every level. From the system of the collegial executive to the concept of the people's civil servant down to the system of decentralisation, there is no institution and no procedure, which is not influenced by the system of direct democracy. The Swiss people's mistrust of a legal system that vests too much power in the judiciary is ultimately rooted in the concept of direct democracy. Moreover, the Swiss syndrome of proportionality of parties, languages, religions, sexes, and generations as well as the basic mentality of concordance and compromise are influenced by the tradition of direct democracy.

ROUSSEAU'S mistrust of parties

The basic view of ROUSSEAU that in a direct democratic assembly parties would only fragment the decision and hamper the common interest and should therefore have only a limited influence, finds support in the reality of the Swiss direct democracy. When the people decide in a municipal citizens' assembly or through voting at the ballot box on the construction of a school building or an important municipal road, or even when they are asked to decide on the abolition of the army, party-proposals and recommendations have only a very limited influence on their decisions. Decisive are the more concrete factors such as cost, tax implications, personal advantages and disadvantages. In political debates, the strategy of political parties is of little importance to the citizens. Rather, the costs and benefits for the affected people are always the decisive arguments that can convince people to vote 'yes' or 'no'.

Separation between political personalities and political issues

As the most important issues within a polity are decided by the voters at the ballot box, political parties in Switzerland have less influence and less significance than in political systems with a Westminster-type parliamentary democracy. When the party is empowered by its victory to form government and is able through its parliamentary majority to implement a comprehensive legislative programme, the voters do not only elect the person of the Prime Minister but with him/her the entire party programme. The choice of politicians and the political issues are inextricably intertwined. If no party succeeds in winning an outright majority, the coalition partners that form government must not only decide on which persons to include in cabinet, but also on the content of the common governmental political programme which they will push through parliament with their majority coalition. Within direct democracy on the other hand, the citizens decide at the election only on the people who will represent them in parliament or in government. On all issues of importance they will make their own decisions through popular referenda. Thus, the choice of political representatives and decisions on political issues are separated from each other.

Parties and interest groups within direct democracy

The parties for their part are hardly interested in direct-democratic decisions. They have much greater influence on the members of parliament than they have with the people directly. Therefore it tends rather to be the interest groups representing economic interests, civil society interests (such as environment, consumer protection etc.) labour unions and minorities which use the instruments of direct democracy such as initiative and referendum in order to increase their general influence and to achieve their political goals. The consequence of this is that the parties have less political influence than parties in states with parliamentary democracy, as it is seldom the parties that are the moving force behind new initiatives or popular referenda. In addition, when the voters want to oblige the state to introduce certain laws or prevent the introduction of particular laws they need not appeal to the parties, as they have available the instruments of direct democracy which are much more effective than exerting pressure on any political party. The opportunities for parties to influence political decision making are therefore greatly restricted.

No ethnically-based parties

This is the reason why in Switzerland there are virtually no parties that have been built along ethnic lines. Parties distinguish themselves from each other based on political concepts and not ethnic allegiance. The only important exception in this context may have been the Catholic-Conservative Party, which had as one of its political aims the removal of the constitutional prohibitions of the Jesuit order and of the reopening or establishment of monasteries. As soon as this goal had been achieved (1973), the party had some difficulty trying to find a new party concept, which no longer relied on the battle against the religious discrimination of the Catholics.

Direct democracy and civil society

Through direct democracy, voters are educated not to assess political adversaries from the perspective of a particular party ideology, but rather from the perspective of a rational cost-benefit analysis. This helps to make the politics of direct democracy more objective, which in turn enhances the development of a civil society that is not fragmented into party camps.

This approach also prevents the construction of stereotyped concepts of the enemy between different language and religious communities. In a political debate that requires a personal decision from every voter (even those who choose not participate in the poll are making a decision), citizens cannot allow themselves to be influenced merely by the interests of a language or religious community. What is decisive for them is the question of what benefit they can personally gain from a decision. From this perspective, they will also assess the views of representatives of the other language and religious communities. Those participating in the decision see themselves first as people and not as party representatives. In this sense direct democracy educates citizens directly in the building of a civil society.

Federalism and decentralisation

Direct democracy is also critical to the strongly decentralised structure of the Swiss polity. The fact that two thirds of all public revenue is raised and expended by the cantons and the municipalities is evidence of the vigour and vigilance with which local, direct democratic decisions defend the preservation of their autonomous and democratic rights.

Influence on small democratic assemblies

The smaller the polity, the greater is the influence of the individual citizen in direct democratic decisions. If a municipal initiative requires the support of only 500 voters in order to be approved, the possibility of each individual voter to influence politics within the municipality is much greater than in polities where an initiative requires the agreement of 100,000 voters in order to be approved. The authorities of municipalities and towns cannot afford in the long term to be blind to the needs, desires and demands of the people.

Democracy and local autonomy

The impact of direct democracy is certainly one of the essential reasons, why the autonomy of the cantons and the municipalities has been preserved to such an important extent, and why the small democratic polities still are expected to assume such important tasks and responsibilities. Citizens are generally reluctant to transfer powers and functions to the federation, because with any centralisation they lose influence, power and responsiveness. Arguments of efficiency, subsidiarity, equality, or profitability will not be sufficient to convince citizens to hand power and responsibility to the federation. For the voter, it is a question of legitimacy and influence.

Even the higher costs of a decentralised administration will have little influence on the voters, so long as they have the feeling that at the local level they will be able to fulfil the functions of government more economically than the monolithic federal bureaucracy. This may also be the reason why the financially weak cantons and municipalities are often even stronger advocates of greater autonomy than financially strong cantons, even though the financially weak cantons often lack the human and financial resources to fulfil their functions effectively.

Equalisation and harmony through direct democracy

If local municipalities or cantons are composed of diverse religious and/or language communities, they must in the direct-democratic process always seek a political balance that will facilitate the peaceful coexistence of the communities. Of course, majority language communities are interested in preserving the dominance of their language. However, they will be very careful not to take measures which would force minorities to change municipality, as the majority depends on the tax dollars of all inhabitants and is therefore also interested in maintaining harmony amongst the citizens. All citizens, including the minorities, contribute for example to the success of a football or hockey team, they all participate in industrial development, are all engaged in social associations and all want to protect employment.

Minorities and the majority principle

When it comes to a decision affecting the core interests of a linguistic or religious minority, it is likely that all the members of that community will participate in the vote. This is rarely the case for members of the respective majority community, as for them the 'core interests' of the minority, such as the maintenance of a minority school, are not of such great significance. A united minority of 20 to 30 per cent of the population may have realistic chances of winning against a majority fragmented by political parties, as on average not more than 40 per cent of all voters go to the polls.

At the local level, direct democratic structures are more adept than traditional party hierarchies at facilitating the rational and civil management of conflicts among different religious or language communities.

Open procedure for consensus building

In a direct democratic debate, it is impossible to predict the outcome on the basis of predetermined majorities and/or minorities. Generally it will only be possible to reach a positive outcome by building a consensus among various communities. Only by seeking concordance among the most important groups can decisions be prepared, which will ultimately also be accepted by the sovereign people. In this sense, direct democracy educates people to practise tolerance and a civic sense of responsibility for the polity.

Flexibility and accountability of the municipal democracy

Not only the citizens but also the political authorities of the municipalities have to decide on rules and measures, which directly or indirectly affect themselves. Those who lend their support for a new school building may do so because their own children attend the respective school, because the teachers of the school have persuaded them or because as neighbours they have an interest in a more attractive building. These decision makers will also have to take into account, that because of this new building a dangerous intersection may not be improved, that garbage disposal will remain highly problematic and that the police of the village will continue to be under-resourced.

On the small scale of the municipality, policy experiments are easier to conduct than at the higher level of the canton or the federation. Parents can be better integrated in the management of the schools. School experiments can be carried out without the risk that a failure will have a negative effect on thousands of people. The municipality is adaptable and can draw lessons from bad decisions and experiences. The strong integration of local authorities within the direct democracy of the municipality will ensure that they respect the interests of the citizens as clients to be served by the administration, if they want to maintain the support and goodwill of the citizens. On the other hand, conservative forces may often impede new policies and developments with emotional arguments. By invoking tradition and loyalty to history, such forces can hamper flexibility. Still, it is an advantage if such conflicts are dealt with at the local municipal level, because it is there that the decision makers will be best able to gauge the likely consequences of their decisions and to directly experience the effects of their decisions.

Chances for minorities

With their democratic voting rights minorities can, as paradoxical as it may sound, make themselves heard by the majority in a manner that would be unthinkable in a parliamentary system. In a parliamentary democracy, minorities have to find the support of a specific party. Their ability to find this support will depend on whether a particular party believes that supporting the minority will pay off in terms of additional votes at the next election. However, supporting minority causes is seldom electorally popular. Which party would be ready to fight for the better integration of foreigners? Such causes can only be pursued through a popular initiative. Although such cause may not find the necessary majority of the voters, at the very least the democratic discourse that precedes the vote will have a certain educative effect.

ii. Cantons as Partners of the Federation

Network of solidarity

A federation can only survive, if the partners of the alliance or federation maintain solidarity. Partnership is not only indispensable between the federal units, it has also to be fostered vertically between the federation and the cantons from the top down, and between the cantons and the federation from the bottom up. Without such elementary solidarity, the Swiss federation could not survive. This is the philosophy that underpins Article 44 of the new Swiss Constitution:

> "(1) The Confederation and the Cantons shall support each other in the fulfilment of their tasks and shall collaborate generally.
> (2) They owe each other respect and support. They shall mutually grant each other administrative and judicial assistance.
> (3) Disputes between the Cantons, or between Cantons and the Confederation, shall, as far as is possible, be resolved through negotiation or mediation."

In fact, federalism in a country as small as Switzerland can only survive if the vertical separation of powers is supplemented by a network of informal cooperation at all levels of the government, including economic partners. Such network is often non-transparent because it is largely informal. But such network strengthens commonalities and the sense of community which contribute to the nation building process.

The explicit obligation of solidarity is to be found in Article 44(2), with the requirement that the federation and the cantons owe each other respect and support. This obligation goes further than the simple federal loyalty required by the German Basic Law. It requires not only loyalty but also proactive support, that is, initiatives and measures to assist other cantons in case of need. Thus, this provision involves a commitment to solidarity, which cannot be integrated into a hierarchical system, but is fundamentally conceived as a partnership. If those partners, in particular those which represent majorities, are not ready to make compromises for the benefit the community, multicultural diversity will suffer.

Balance between shared rule and self-rule

The challenge of the European Union will certainly lead to further centralisation in ways that are not yet foreseeable. This may have been the main reason why the new Swiss Constitution is less concerned with the protection of cantonal autonomy, than with the greater participation of the cantons in the decision making process at the federal level. In this regard the influence of German federalism on Swiss federalism appears to be increasing.

In terms of the new emphasis on shared rule, there are three important factors that have to be taken into account: The first two are obvious: rights of the federal units to shared rule with regard to foreign policy, and their participation in the legislative process of the state. In addition, one should not underestimate the provision that grants the cantons wide-reaching power to conclude treaties for inter-cantonal and international cooperation. This chance to establish new partnerships with the federation, with neighbouring cantons and with foreign countries provides the cantons with important new opportunities. If they can make the most of them, they may breathe new life into Swiss federalism.

Shared rule and executive federalism

The new Federal Constitution has reduced the autonomy of the cantons, but has expanded their participation in shared rule at the federal level. The increased cantonal participation in the federal decision making process however has not been effected, as one might expect, by enlarging the powers of the second chamber, but rather by strengthening the participation of the cantonal governments. Although the cantons had the constitutional possibility (theoretically) to have the members of the second chamber elected not by the people nor by the parliament but by the cantonal executive, which would enable them to effectively turn the second chamber into a chamber of cantonal ministers, to date nobody has made such a proposal. Such a change would at any rate stand no chance of being endorsed by the voters, because it would place too great a restriction on the democratic rights of the people.

The new Constitution establishes executive federalism by providing for the constitutionally guaranteed inclusion of the cantonal governments in the legislative decision making process of the second chamber of federal parliament. Their participation will be effected through the Conference of Cantonal Governments, a body that has existed for some years. The Constitution does not prescribe the principles or procedures to be followed by the Conference. In contrast to the second chamber, which comprises an equal number of democratically elected representatives for each canton, the large cantons will have considerable weight in the decision making process of the Conference of Cantonal Governments (similar to the large *Länder* of the German Federal Council). Here we can observe, probably as a consequence of the increasing significance of the administration, a *shift from legislative federalism to executive federalism.* The new Constitution is based on the idea that in future, the fate of the cantons is not to be left to the second chamber of parliament alone.

Governmental system

The Swiss system of executive government, with a Federal Council of seven equal collegial members individually elected by parliament for a fixed term and not removable during their term of office, is not replicated anywhere else in the world. This executive council decides as a collegial body by consensus, and if necessary by majority, on executive ordinances and legislative proposals. As the seven members of the Federal Council also serve the functions of the head of state, Prime Minister, cabinet and the final instance for complaints against the administration, and as this body is composed proportionally with regard to parties, religion, languages and gender, the most important cultural and political communities consider themselves to be directly represented in the federal government, and are therefore able to identify with the state.

Balance of the mass media

The mass media, and in particular television, has substantially changed the existing language diversity of Switzerland. Regional thinking at the level of the language regions has in many areas replaced the focus on the cantons. The German-speaking Swiss television viewers have a different political conception of themselves than the French-speaking audience. They are familiar with the German-speaking members of the Federal Council and of parliament, while the French-speaking audience is much more familiar with their French-speaking counterparts, because they tend to be the focus of the French-speaking media.

The way in which radio and television are arranged and formulated is therefore of great significance for the future development of the country. For historical reasons, Switzerland has only one radio and television institution that is licensed to broadcast public and official programs throughout Switzerland. This organisation however is fragmented into regional sub-divisions, each of which has substantial autonomy with regard to program design.

A financial equalisation concept favouring the smaller language regions guarantees that the four language communities have access to an equivalent range and standard of programs. The Constitution obliges the public broadcaster to provide equal services to all language groups and to promote respect and mutual understanding between the different language regions.

Solidarity and fiscal equalisation

A federal alliance (*foedus*) is based on solidarity and partnership. It presupposes essentially a partnership among the federation and its federal units. These units owe each other mutual solidarity. Without such solidarity, the federation cannot exist. In this sense, Article 44 of the Swiss Constitution requires the federation and the cantons to cooperate in the implementation of their tasks. In fact however, within the territorially small Swiss federation, state tasks can only be fulfilled with the help of informal and non-transparent networks of authorities, civil servants and social partners at the federal, cantonal and municipal levels. This is expressed laconically in Article 44(1) of the Swiss Constitution. However, when paragraph (2) obliges the federation and cantons to exhibit mutual respect, assistance and support, such provision is nothing more than the express requirement to show solidarity, without which the partnership between federation and cantons would fall apart.

A multicultural federation with a fragmented society depends not only on solidarity between single individuals, but also above all on solidarity among the different cultural, linguistic and religious communities. Solidarity is the glue that can hold the potentially conflict-laden society in Switzerland together. For this reason the aim of the state cannot be limited to providing equal rights and opportunities for individuals. The various peoples and communities must also be given the opportunity to compete on an equal footing with each other. Equality of these communities may even have priority over equality of individuals. For this reason, the Constitution contains provisions which require an equal standard of public services for the entire population.

The right to individual equality and the right to equality as a member of a minority group have to be seen on the same level, since a multicultural state requires a double equality. On the one hand, equality of individuals has to be ensured, and at the same time the different communities require equal treatment, as only then can the individuals of those communities feel that they are equal to members of other communities. If for instance, persons belonging to the Romansh-speaking minority language group are only granted individual equality, they will always feel as though they are second-class citizens because their cultural identity is not treated on an equal footing with other cultural groups. If on the other hand, their cultural community is treated on an equal footing as all other cultural communities, they will feel secure in and be able to participate in a society that respects all cultures and communities equally. Clearly the Swiss federation seeks to find the balance between equal individual rights and the right of all persons belonging to a particular cultural community to be valued and treated equally.

The extent to which equality is truly recognised within a federal state is expressed through the reality of fiscal policy. In Switzerland, people are subject to varying tax burdens according to the canton, and within the canton according to the municipality. Respecting the federal principle of cantonal autonomy, the Federal Constitution limits the taxing powers of the federation in order to leave the cantons and the municipalities a sufficient tax base. The federation however has the authority to harmonise the tax system including tax procedures within the cantons, but not the rate of taxes to be levied. Accordingly, the taxpayers pay taxes to the canton and to the municipality in which they reside, at rates that vary enormously throughout the country.

This however leads to inequalities with regard to taxes, which from the perspective of justice and solidarity cannot be justified. Cantons in mountainous regions for example do not have equal taxation opportunities as cantons with large and prosperous towns. In addition, they have to spend enormous sums on the construction and maintenance of roads, while town cantons are burdened by the growing traffic of the urban centres. Certain cantons have to assume federal responsibilities which are in the interest of the entire country or of a whole region, but for which other cantons only bear a small part of the cost and responsibility if any, such as major cultural events. The cantons have to fulfil important federal functions, but the burdens that the cantons have to bear for the fulfilment of these functions are varied. Often they are determined by the different starting conditions of the respective cantons. Equalisation with regard to the burdens borne by the cantons is therefore indispensable. Finally, the cantons enjoy certain location-specific advantages (airports), which can be used for the benefit of their economic development. These are all arguments which should lead to a just fiscal equalisation. However, one should not overlook the fact that for every argument there is usually a corresponding counter-argument. Strong economic development often leads to higher pollution, which affects rural areas less than towns. Without a real preparedness for solidarity, which focuses on the interests of the entire country and its fragmented society, any long-term and sustainable fiscal equalisation solutions will be difficult to achieve.

Supremacy of federal law

Not all federations include within their constitution clear and plain provisions which guarantee the supremacy of federal law over the law of the federal units. From the outset of the federation, the Swiss Constitution has followed the model of the American Constitution which clearly enshrines the supremacy of federal law. One must also take into account that the Swiss federation is integrated into the continental European civil law system. Therefore all statutes and court decisions must form a coherent and unified body of law. Definitive is not the law expressed through court decisions, but the legislation enacted by the 'sovereign' parliament. Accordingly, the legal system has to be conceived as a hierarchical pyramid, in the manner described in the legal philosophy of HANS KELSEN. The highest level in the hierarchy is occupied by the Federal Constitution, with all other federal law immediately below. The cantonal law and the laws of the municipalities are at the bottom of the hierarchy, and have to be in conformity with the higher law. This supremacy of higher law is also provided in the German Basic Law and has been applied at the European level by the European Court of Justice. The courts of the member states do not contest the European application of this principle. Legal certainty and equality before the law can only be guaranteed if the lower laws are consistent with the higher laws.

Constitutional jurisdiction and the rule of law principle

Switzerland is one of the very few states, which in the 19th Century already provided jurisdiction for judicial review, albeit limited to the judicial review of cantonal legislation. Accordingly, the constitutionality of cantonal decisions and legislation could be challenged in the Federal Court. The rationale behind this constitutional review jurisdiction has federal roots. The Federal Constitution could only achieve legitimacy and credibility in the eyes of the citizens of the cantons if the citizens were given the right to seek redress for breaches of the Constitution. The protection of the Constitution by the highest court has been understood as a democratic right, aimed at protecting the people against the arbitrary exercise of cantonal authority. To date, citizens have been vigilant in ensuring that this protection against the improper exercise of cantonal power is maintained.

On the other hand, it must be noted that in spite of several initiatives for constitutional amendment, Switzerland has not yet been able to introduce comprehensive constitutional review in relation to federal statutes. The parliament has ultimately blocked all proposals which would finally have given the court the jurisdiction to review the constitutionality of statutes adopted by the federal parliament and submitted to a facultative referendum of the people. The majority of the people is still influenced by the concept of the absolute and unquestionable '*volonté générale*', which is manifested in laws passed by the legislature and embodies absolute justice, and which therefore cannot be called into question by any court. In the view of the Parliament, it is Parliament (subject to the people) that is the highest authority in the land, and its decisions therefore cannot be reviewed by a small body of judges. Politicians have played off the spectre of the 'judicial state' against democracy, and naturally democracy has won. The argument that judicial review would in fact strengthen the credibility of democracy was politically unsuccessful. The strongest argument against the introduction of judicial review of the constitutionality of federal legislation is undoubtedly the fact, that at every opportunity for such change the people themselves have either refrained from referenda, or tacitly or explicitly approved laws that disallow such jurisdiction.

As a result, there is no judicial authority that would have the legitimacy to overturn a law because of its unconstitutionality, when it has been explicitly or tacitly accepted by the people. Even today the majority supports this argument, although the European Court of Human Rights now has jurisdiction to review federal legislation for compliance with mandatory human rights standards. Accordingly, the cantons have no ability to defend their autonomy before the courts (not even before the European Court of Human Rights), when federal law infringes their constitutionally guaranteed autonomy. Thus, federalism in Switzerland has remained a matter of politics, which as mentioned however, is oriented towards consensus and thereby accords a certain protection to the interests of minorities and provides indirect means of defending their constitutional autonomy.

iii. Pluralism in Cantonal Constitutions

Overlapping cantonal, linguistic and religious borders

The fact that neither linguistic nor religious borders are identical with cantonal political borderlines has a significant beneficial effect on the peaceful coexistence of the various ethnic and cultural communities. By this mere fact, many cantons are forced to introduce institutions and other solutions which enable the different communities within the cantonal territory to feel that they are a part of the cantonal unit on the one hand, and to develop and maintain their own cultural identity on the other hand.

Goal: civil society

The goal of every constitutional and political rule and regulation at the cantonal level must ultimately be to create a foundation for the realisation of a civil society. That is, to ensure that the people living within the canton regard themselves first as human beings and only secondarily as German-speaking, Jewish, Protestants, foreigners, Catholics or Romansh-speaking.

Equality of individuals and collective equality of territorial units

A basic precondition for achieving this is the guaranteed provision of equal political rights for every citizen based on the principle of domicile. Swiss citizens are able according to their domicile to exercise their political rights at all three levels: municipality, canton and federation. They are equal members of the municipal assemblies with the right to elect and to be elected to any position within the municipality. Thus, in relation to political rights, membership of a language or religious group carries no special significance.

The federation and most cantons and municipalities however do discriminate against foreigners, by denying political rights to all non-Swiss citizens. Only the cantons of Neuchâtel and Jura provide limited political rights for foreigners with permanent domicile in the respective canton. In other cantons, the Swiss citizens have refused to extend political rights to foreigners. This denial has serious implications, as non-citizens account for approximately 20 per cent of the population of Switzerland. Although foreigners residing in Switzerland are expected to pay taxes and to contribute to the economic wealth of the country, they are denied the right to participate as equal members of the Swiss civil society.

iv. Religious Diversity

Peace through equal treatment of religions

The policy of maintaining the balance between the different religions and confessions was the starting point of securing peace amongst the religious communities and thereby maintaining multicultural diversity. In the 19th Century, a request by the Italian district of Valtellina to become part of the canton of Grison was rejected by the citizens of Grison on the grounds of religious balance. Such change would have led to the domination of the Catholics within the canton.

At the beginning of the 19th Century, the canton of Aargau provided for the equal representation of Catholics and Protestants in the cantonal parliament in order to uphold the balance between religions, even though amongst the population of the canton the Protestants outnumbered the Catholics. Until the 1970s in the canton of Fribourg, in addition to the religious schools of the municipalities (Catholic or Protestant), there were also free public schools that were open to children who did not belong to the majority religion of their municipality. The Constitution of Fribourg at this time imposed an explicit obligation on the canton to meet the costs of education for those children who did not belong to the principal religion of their municipality if the municipal public school had a religious orientation. In the canton of St. Gall, the municipalities usually ran both a Catholic and a Protestant school.

This 'policy of balance' was readily implemented within cantons that were more or less clearly divided into a religious majority and minority. Cantons with a definite and sizeable religious majority such as the cantons of Valais, Uri and Tessin, were for a long while reluctant to grant to their religious minorities full religious liberty with regard to primary education, and often used resource constraints as an excuse. In this context it must also be noted that in Switzerland, unlike many other countries, schools are run by municipalities and most children (95 per cent) attend public schools.

If one analyses the decisions of the Federal Court of Switzerland with regard to freedom of religion, it becomes apparent that the Court has never dealt only with the individual side of religious freedom, but has always also taken the issue of peace among different religious communities into account. The primary goal of the Court in this regard has always been the preservation of religious peace. The Court has on the other hand never expressly recognised a collective right of the religious communities. Its argumentation on the maintenance of religious peace, combined with its preparedness to limit individual rights in favour of this higher goal, can only be justified if one weighs the collective rights of religious communities as an equal right against the religious freedom of the individual. Today, freedom of religion has lost much of its significance with regard to the traditional religions of Switzerland. New religions such as scientology or other modern religious beliefs and the religions of the immigrant populations (Islam, Buddhism, Hinduism etc.) are at the forefront of most European human rights decisions. Whilst the nature of religious diversity in Switzerland has changed somewhat in recent decades, Article 72(2) of the Constitution still requires federal and cantonal authorities to undertake the necessary measures to ensure that religious freedom can be exercised and that religious peace is maintained.

Conflict management through secularisation

Some progressive cantons have adapted to this shift in religious diversity by secularising public education and introducing a clear separation between church and state, such as Neuchâtel and to a certain extent also Zurich.

Based on the constitutional guarantees of freedom of religion and freedom of conscience, the cantons felt increasingly compelled to recognise the religious freedom of their minorities. However, as soon as they were required to protect multicultural diversity beyond the traditional Christian confessions, the cantons were more reluctant to extend comprehensive religious liberty. This was already the case in the 19th Century with regard to the Jewish religion, and has become even more pronounced with regard to Islam.

Even at the federal level, freedom of religion was originally only granted in respect of Christian religions. The constitutional amendment of 1866 improved the legal protection of citizens of non-Christian confessions. But it was not until the new Constitution of 1874 that a comprehensive general guarantee of religious freedom was introduced. Even then, the protection of this human right was primarily aimed at maintaining peace among the religious communities. Its function as an individual right that could be defended in the courts was only secondary.

Protection of multicultural diversity through territorial autonomy

The cantonal borders serve as an instrument to maintain and promote multicultural diversity through territorial autonomy. The Federal Constitution provides for the relationship between church and state to be determined and regulated by the cantons. For this reason, the cantons are able to reflect their traditional views on the relationship between church and state in their cantonal constitutions and can regulate this relationship autonomously. Accordingly, Catholic cantons have a different relationship to the church than do Protestant cantons. Cantons with a religious mix in turn have to find pragmatic solutions, which accommodate the traditions of both Christian confessions.

Personal autonomy: The politically recognised religious communities

An additional means that has been adopted by the cantons to preserve multiculturality is the legal assignment of public status to the church community and the granting of autonomy to the church. When a church has recognised public legal status, it can levy taxes from its members by a bill enforced through the state tax system. In this case the church community is subject to limited financial control by the state, but otherwise has extensive autonomy with regard to expenditure, provided such expenditure is applied for church purposes. Recently the Protestant and also Catholic cantons have begun to accord such special public status also to the religious minorities.

In cantons with a majority of Protestants, the Catholic Church has been able to achieve its public recognition through the cantonal synod. Catholic cantons, which delegated church issues mostly to local parishes, have had greater difficulty finding a concept that would facilitate public recognition of the Protestant community through a cantonal synod-like structure.

It is obvious that for the large religious minorities such public recognition plays an important role. For small religious communities or for those communities that do not yet have a socially recognised status, the granting of privileged status to other religious communities has a discriminatory effect.

v. Language Communities within the Cantonal Legal Order

Problems of language diversity

An almost irresolvable problem is the protection of multiculturality with regard to language. The foremost issues in this context are:

- Which is the official language or the language of public authorities?
- Which language is or can be used in parliament?
- Which language is spoken and written in court proceedings? and,
- Which language is used in schools?

Romansh

In relation to linguistic diversity, a distinction has to be made between the three main languages on the one hand (German, French and Italian), and the Romansh language spoken only by a small minority in the canton of Grison on the other hand. While the three main languages are able to retain an entirely self-contained and independent character in their respective schools, courts and also in the political arena, Romansh can only maintain itself within a predominantly German-speaking environment. Every person speaking Romansh will thus necessarily also have to speak at least one of the main languages. On the other hand, a person whose mother tongue is Italian can easily survive without a second language, as can the German- or French-speaking Swiss.

Multiculturality through decentralisation

The most important protection of multiculturality with regard to language is implemented through territorial decentralisation. Cantonal autonomy in relation to education and culture is in itself a substantial element of this decentralisation. The French-, Italian- and German-speaking cantons can organise and design their education system, their curricula and their cultural affairs in accordance with their linguistic tradition.

Within those cantons that have two (Fribourg, Valais, Berne) or three languages (Grison), the protection of multicultural diversity occurs through a far-reaching delegation of responsibility for educational and cultural matters to the municipalities. The municipalities are the providers of primary school education, and the canton provides secondary and tertiary education and vocational training in the languages of the canton. In Fribourg for example, the canton provides bilingual tertiary education through the University of Fribourg.

As the judiciary cannot be decentralised to the municipal level, the language of court proceedings is usually determined according to district. If the district is bilingual, the courts must also be bilingual. This is for instance the case in the Lake District of the canton of Fribourg, but not in the bilingual city of Fribourg, as the city no longer forms its own district but has been incorporated into the French-speaking district of Sarine (Saane).

Multiculturality by the principle of territoriality

The principle of territoriality as the basis for the protection of language or religious communities is of essential importance on the European continent. The principle of territoriality is in two respects an instrument that protects multicultural diversity. Genuine decentralisation can only be achieved on the basis of territorially defined units, such as municipalities and cantons. It is consistent with the principle of territoriality that, analogous to the principle *cujus region ejus religio* (subjects have to follow the religion of the ruler), territory is also determinative of language. In this sense for instance, the principle of territoriality is strictly applied in the canton of Grison for the sake of the protection of the endangered Romansh language. Thus for example, municipal building regulations can prohibit advertising and signage in any language other than the official language of the municipality.

When the language territory is not under threat, the principle of territoriality serves to maintain peace among different language communities. This means that linguistic borders should not be changed at whim to the advantage of one group or the detriment of another. In this sense for instance the cantonal constitution of Berne identifies the French-speaking, German-speaking and bilingual districts. In spite of this constitutional determination of the territorial division of language groups, the Federal Court has held that a municipality within the German-speaking district was allowed on the grounds of municipal autonomy to provide for children of the French-speaking minority to attend a school in the bilingual neighbour town of Bienne.

The Constitution of the canton of Fribourg has recently been expanded by a special provision with regard to language. This article provides that within the canton of Fribourg, the French and German languages are on an equal footing (The German-speaking minority comprises about one third of the total population of the canton). At the same time, the article provides for the respect of the principle of territoriality and declares that the official language used by the authorities is to be determined according to the principle of territoriality. In addition, cantonal authorities are obliged to promote harmony among the different language communities.

Protection of multicultural diversity through bi- or multilingualism

The protection of cultural diversity by promotion of bi- or multilingualism has been realised primarily within the canton of Grison. In order to protect the different language communities, the municipalities decide the language to be used for public school education. As the German language plays a very important social role, the law provides that in Romansh- or Italian-speaking schools, German must be taught as a second language. In order to promote bilingualism in German-speaking schools, the law provides the municipalities that conduct primary education in German with the option of making education in Romansh or Italian mandatory.

The Italian-speaking canton of Tessin is faced with a growing German-speaking minority. Traditionally the small mountain commune of Bosco/Gurin was the only German-speaking enclave within an Italian-speaking environment. Even in this municipality, the official educational language is Italian. However, children whose mother tongue is German are given an additional teacher for German lessons by virtue of a special decree of the cantonal government.

vi. Political Protection of Multiculturality

The ability of the cantons to accord political privileges to different language com-munities is considerably restricted by the principle of equality. Thus, cantons cannot make constitutional provision for special representation of ethnic, linguistic or religious minorities or foreigners within the cantonal parliament. The principle of universality dictates against such tendencies. Cantons are also unable to provide cultural communities with a special position in popular votes, for example by requiring a double majority of district and individual votes, which *is* possible at the federal level. At the cantonal level such 'federalism' is prohibited, because the Federal Constitution requires that cantonal constitutions can be changed by the majority of the people. This principle would be violated if, in addition, the acceptance of a certain minority was also required.

Guarantee of specific territorial representation within cantonal authorities

Whilst the principle of equality has up to now prevented the specific personal representation of minorities within the authorities, a certain territorially based representation is still possible. Thus for instance the Constitution of the canton of Berne requires that one member of the seven-member cantonal executive should come from the Jura region of Berne. However, it is not the citizens of the region of Jura alone who elect this 'Jurassian executive councillor'. Rather, he/she must have the support of the majority of the citizens of the whole canton. Thus, the minority on its own cannot determine by whom it is to be represented.

A somewhat different solution can be found in the bilingual canton of Valais. Of the five-member cantonal government, three members are to be elected out of three regions composed of several districts. Two members are elected by the voters of the whole canton. The constitution provides however, that there can be no more than one member from any one district. Only in this manner can the representation of the German-speaking minority by one member of the government be ensured.

The constituencies for the election of members of parliament are in almost all cantons based along district lines. The influence on cantonal politics that this system gives to the districts should not be underestimated. The members of parliament must seek legitimacy within their district. In parliament they will therefore seek to defend and promote the special interests of their district. As the district borders usually correspond to the dividing lines of historical, cultural and linguistic tradition, a certain protection of multicultural diversity is also afforded by this electoral system.

Proportional election and political culture

The proportional electoral system also contributes significantly to the protection of multiculturality. Through proportional election the smaller parties have a chance of being represented in parliament. Parliament is thus able to reflect the diverse range of opinions and cultures within the society.

As no canton requires a minimum quota of electoral support for a party to be entitled to representation in parliament, it is possible for even very small parties to be represented. The governmental system effectively prohibits a system of enforced party discipline. For this reason it is possible for a single member of parliament to have considerable political influence by virtue of persuasive argumentation, even if he/she does not belong to a major party.

The proportional system that was introduced at the beginning of the 20th Century has had a major impact on the political culture and the political thinking at both the federal and cantonal levels. Every Swiss authority, every court and all committees and commissions must include at least one representative of each of the major parties, a sufficiently large representation of the different language communities and representatives of both main Christian confessions. This newly developed political culture has led to an over-proportionate representation of the numerically smaller language communities in the various decision making bodies of the federation and the cantons, without such representation being constitutionally prescribed. Thus for instance, in the canton of Valais, a customary practice has developed whereby the two cantonal representatives in the second federal chamber must come from the two different language groups, even though the German-speaking population is a minority. This practice has been maintained for some time by the approval of the voters.

Furthermore, the two major established parties from the German-speaking region within the canton of Valais have agreed that the German-speaking representative of the canton in the federal upper chamber will be selected from one and then the other of the two parties on a rotating basis. This means that the German-speaking representative voluntarily steps aside after one legislative term to enable the representative of the other party to take their turn.

In the canton of Fribourg, the cantonal representatives in the second federal chamber were formerly elected by the cantonal parliament and not by the people, in order to ensure that both the French-speaking and German-speaking populations would be represented. Since the shift to popular election, the German-speaking minority has continued to be represented in the federal upper chamber. In fact, in the legislative term from 1987–91 *both* representatives were German speakers.

These examples show that in addition to constitutional and legislative measures, it is also necessary to have a political culture that fosters and promotes multiculturality. The effect of such culture is that rights may be extended to the numerically smaller cultural communities that will sometimes result in these minorities being over-privileged. But only through this political culture can the conditions required for harmonious relations between the majority and minorities be established.

vii. Conclusion

Democracy is not only a procedure to appoint legitimate governments. Democracy is also a procedure for the peaceful settlement of conflicts, including the 'categorical' conflicts of a fragmented multicultural state. Within the democratic discourse, parties have to search for rational arguments with which they can convince undecided citizens. Whoever is forced to translate their emotions into rational arguments will also be prepared to agree to a pragmatic compromise that can be rationally justified according to principles of justice.

The actual motor for such a consensus-driven policy is, in Switzerland, direct democracy. When a party or an executive body is seeking new solutions, they will have to search for a consensus among the political elite if they do not wish to risk likely rejection of their proposal in the democratic referendum. The essentially majority-oriented democracy thus has the indirect effect of inducing the political elite to accept compromises and to adopt a consensus-oriented approach.

This consensus-oriented democracy has become a major and fundamental pillar of the Swiss governmental system. It gives minorities a real chance even in democratic procedures. In the Westminster system, an ethnic minority would be condemned to be the perennial loser. In the Swiss system, which always seeks the approval of the greatest possible majority, democratic procedures also take minorities seriously. They are not condemned to folklore. Their legitimate interests have to be taken seriously by the majority, if it wants to win the support of the people in a democratic referendum. The foundations for the broad-based legitimacy of a multicultural state and nation are thereby laid within a consensus-oriented democracy.

Permanent losers will never be able to identify with a state in which they have no chance to make themselves heard. They will constantly feel like second-class citizens. A multicultural state can only survive in the long term, if it sets itself the goal of searching for a consensus amongst all minorities and of motivating all minorities to participate in decision making processes. This however can only succeed, if these minorities can see that they will have a real chance to successfully represent their point of view.

In a multicultural state in which the cultural communities strive to be able to maintain and develop their own identities, they should not be mutually assimilated into one cultural melting pot. In order to avoid this kind of assimilation and destruction of cultural diversity, it is necessary to ensure that decisions of the federation which affect the interests and the survival of cultural minorities are made on the basis of a broad consensus. The majority of these different communities must share in such decisions.

8.4.2 *Minorities and their Legitimisation of the Federation*

8.4.2.1 What Gives Compromise Legitimacy?

Switzerland: 'Sonderfall' or model case?

The Swiss federal system has long been regarded as a special case (*Sonderfall*) that cannot be replicated elsewhere. It is often argued by Swiss scholars that the Swiss system cannot be seen as one of many models of government that can simply be selected for export or transplantation. At the same time, it has remained the subject of considerable academic interest among scholars outside Switzerland. No doubt, an outsider analyses the Swiss model from a different perspective, as they will see its institutions and principles in a different light, and certain matters that an insider would take for granted may not be self-evident. Thus for example, the draft of the United Nations for a constitutional solution for Cyprus of February 2003 makes direct reference to the Swiss model as an inspiration:

> "The status and relationship of the United Cyprus Republic, its federal government, and its constituent states, is modelled on the status and relationship of Switzerland, its federal government, and its cantons."

With a somewhat ironic undertone, the Swiss writer FRIEDRICH DÜRRENMATT writes in his novel, *Justice*: "Either the world will be drowned or it will become swissified" (*verschweizern*). The German constitutional scholar HANS PETER SCHNEIDER analysed this remark in a seminal academic paper, and came to the following conclusions:

> "The Swiss model can, as has been pointed out by Dürrenmatt, be quite helpful ....Why then should the experiences in relation to all of what are described in Switzerland as being the characteristic elements of the Swiss Confederation, namely size without expansion, people without nation, democracy without parties, government without opposition, alliance without bond, a country without power, public spirit without altruism and finally tradition without nostalgia, not be exported to every country in the world and there be held up as the standard for good governance and orderly statehood?" *(In P. Hanni (ed), Mensch und Staat: Festschrift für THOMAS FLEINER, Freiburg 2003, p. 201ff).*

The following exposition is aimed at examining, from the perspective of political theory, the basic principles upon which the Swiss federal model is built.

Inclusion of minorities in nation and state-building

What lessons can be drawn from the Swiss *Sonderfall*? To what extent is the system, divorced from its historical context, still influential or instructive?

We will seek to address these questions by exploring the constitutive principles of the Swiss federal system, and examining their relevance for handling minority issues at the fundamental level of constituting and legitimising a multi-ethnic federal state. Many multi-ethnic states, including Yugoslavia and other countries in transition and newly constituted multi-ethnic federations, are faced with a radicalised minority problem that has plunged them into a permanent legitimacy crisis, or threatens to collapse into such. Therefore, if one seeks democratic and constitutional stability, there remains little choice but to deal with minority demands at the crucial level, namely constituting and legitimising the state.

Legitimising function of compromise

It is precisely here that the Swiss federal system can be particularly instructive. The lesson to be drawn from the Swiss model can be simply formulated, but can only be understood, without being simplified, if one has knowledge of all the decisive institutional and political factors: *What gives compromise a crucial legitimising function?* Is it just a case of a peculiar, 'unexportable' and non-transparent network of history and institutional design? Or is it likewise a phenomenon of the political socialisation of 'power elites', a process of social learning, undertaken with a full awareness of the fact that a society with ethnic, religious, linguistic and other diversities that are often territorially cross-cutting, simply cannot afford the luxury of having winners and losers? Compromise is in other words not – as elsewhere – merely a necessary evil of daily politics and tactics, but rather a fundamentally accepted *political value in itself*, which has its roots in the long-term political strategy of democratic integration of multicultural diversity right at the constitutive level of the *Confoederatio Helvetica.*

8.4.2.2 Core Elements of the Swiss Polity

i. Communal Civism

Taking multiculturality seriously

The paradigm of the *Willensnation* is regarded by most Swiss scholars as one of the obvious key factors that explain the successful nation-building process in 19th Century Switzerland. Political unity lives off the cultural diversity from which it emerged and which it supports and fosters. Such a diverse political alliance was possible due to the fact that the people of Switzerland *share the same basic notions about political society, which differ from those found abroad*, and the fact that they *take diversity seriously*. The Swiss Constitution was created out of pragmatic political experience and is therefore not a construct that was crafted from reason and scientific logic. The motto of the founding fathers of the American Constitution: "Let us be guided by experience, because reason might mislead us", has been the inspiration behind the Swiss Constitution since the founding of the federation.

Where does Swiss modernity come from?

The basis of Switzerland, namely the phenomenon of the Swiss political nation, is amazingly enough generally regarded as a matter of course that warrants no further examination. The outside academic observer cannot help but be a bit surprised by the fact that Swiss scholars have largely taken for granted the basis of the phenomenon of the Swiss political nation. The very fact that scholars of political and social science have not been moved to reflect more fully upon this concept and its related problems, can from an epistemological standpoint also be interpreted as a part of the Swiss *Sonderfall*. The phenomenon of the *Willensnation* reveals not only the extent to which reason and choice led to this historical experience; it also leads us to the very core elements of the Swiss polity, usually denoted as 'communal democracy' or 'communal liberty'.

But where does Swiss modernity come from, where does it end and what constitutes its particular, historically determined content? To give a more basic form to the question: What specifically makes a Swiss citizen (in the sense of the '*citoyen*') today; *what are the immanent, basic tenets of contemporary Swiss civism?*

German Volk – French Nation – Swiss 'Willensnation'

The Swiss nation is a political entity based upon commonly shared political values that have been defined through a nation-building process over a period of centuries. One may indeed argue that Swiss citizenship accords with the French political concept of nationhood without ethnicity, and runs counter to the German concept of nation as ethnic community (*Volksgemeinschaft*) based on pre-political, premodern, cultural common features such as ethnicity, religion, language, race and the like (*Schicksalsgemeinschaft*). Given that the French concept is political and voluntary, it is also unitary and universal in its essentially political understanding of nationhood as a 'daily plebiscite'. The nation is composed of individual citizens (*citoyens*) united in a voluntary political association and endowed with inalienable natural rights. Whoever enjoys such universally valid rights within a given polity is by definition a *citoyen*. Consequently, citizenship is eminently an inclusive, assimilationist concept, which sees the nation as a result of a culturally heterogeneous collection of peoples joining together to live within one unified state.

Does Switzerland not serve as a model example that corresponds exactly to these characteristics? We will argue on the contrary that the two models are quite different.

Distinguishing the Swiss 'Willensnation' from the French Nation

The '*Willensnation*' is based on a political understanding of the nation, but is nevertheless distinctly different from the French concept and is therefore to be understood in a fundamentally different way. What the Swiss *Willensnation* has in common with the French concept of citizenship is the very fact *that* they have created the political citizen; but the Swiss approach to political citizenship, that is – the nature and content of political citizenship – is substantially different from the French concept.

The character of political citizenship in Switzerland is of a particular and unusual nature. Behind the Swiss concept of *Willensnation*, there is no social contract theory and no natural rights doctrine. The Swiss citizen is indeed a *citoyen* in the sense of sharing in a common set of political values, but he does not *become* the citizen by enjoying – as an *individual member* – his inalienable rights within the polity. No such liberal universality underlies the Swiss political tradition. On the contrary, the Swiss polity is based *a priori* on the local community, on the strength of which the confederation is built. It is thus primarily *collective rights*, that is, the rights of local political entities, such as those of the *Gemeinde* (municipalities), which as pre-positive and extra-constitutional rights, constitute the foundations of Swiss communal democracy. Individual liberty has always had its place, but only within the political community, never apart from it.

German Staatsbürgerschaft (citizenship)

In this specific sense it could be argued that the Swiss concept of political citizenship does in fact have something in common with the German concept of citizenship. It entails exclusiveness and uniformity in a sense akin to the German *Volksgemeinschaft*, and certainly lacks the openness of the French idea of 'nation'. The political values that underlie the Swiss concept stem from a particular, both traditional and modern, somewhat radical democratic understanding. The 'old Swiss freedom', implying the *outward independence of the collective*, has persisted as a permanent collectivist underpinning of modern individual liberty.

Exclusive concreteness of the old Swiss tradition

The ideas of Enlightenment and those of the American and French Revolutions were not alone in effecting the 'decisive paradigm shift' in the evolution of Swiss political thinking. *Almost all important ideas of the modern Swiss state system – individual liberty and equality, popular sovereignty, rights and freedoms, division of powers, rational legitimacy of the political system* – are imbued with the values of the 'old Swiss tradition'. One can indeed speak of the *exclusive concreteness of the Swiss Willensnation*: the underlying basic principles do not have a general and universal application, since they can hardly be internalised as self-evidently valid by any random person who does not share in the Swiss history and tradition.

Swiss modernity ends at the cantonal level

However, this concreteness and exclusivity cannot be anything but politically based, because the local entities, whose rights are at stake and whose membership free individuals enjoy, are already *political* communities. Switzerland is today probably the only country in the world that still recognises a special municipal citizenship. Further, the fact should also be taken into consideration that in Switzerland civic identity is based upon a voluntary political fact. It can thereby be distinguished from pre-political qualities such as ethnicity, language, and religion. And yet, as already pointed out, Swiss civic identity refrains from basing its political status upon general values that are universally valid for all persons.

Swiss political status is instead inherently connected to and integrated within the locality of the municipalities and/or the cantons. The process of modernisation, which elsewhere in Europe resulted in the centralisation of conflicting religious loyalties at the nation-state level, served to reinforce cantonal loyalties in Switzerland. Swiss modernity ends at the cantonal level. It is local peculiarities – and not universality – that have become part of the political and civic identity as well as part of the political culture.

The most relevant consequences of this communal understanding of political citizenship – from our point of view – are as follows:

Integration through common values

Given that the Swiss democratic polity has been *organised around common interests and integration rather than (as in such homogeneous states as France and the United Kingdom) sectional conflict, the combat of interests, and clashing power*, it has found a legitimate way to unite the existing diversity into a politically homogenous unit on the basis of generally accepted political values. Compromise has thereby retained its legitimising function for the establishment of political and civic identity.

Because citizenship serves as the 'common ground' of adversaries and forms the basis of the search for agreement, with decisions made through different pluralities, the notions of 'majority' and 'minority' do not have as much significance in Switzerland as they do in democracies that are controlled by the pure majority principle.

In contrast to states in which political tradition is determined by liberal, democratic principles, Switzerland has never been guided by the paradigm of 'the individual versus the state'. Common and active citizenship has of itself excluded the idea of state as a potential intruder upon the inalienable rights of man and citizen.

Communal Civism

In other words, local communal civism has profoundly affected the Swiss polity in the following respects:

a) the particular understanding of the state and the constitution;
b) the reinterpretation of rational legitimacy based on the majority principle;
c) the peculiar tension in the relationship of federalism to democracy.

We will deal with each of these aspects in turn.

ii. The particular understanding of the state and the constitution

Unity of people and society

The liberal state is based on the principle of the separation of state and society. Accordingly, there is an immanent opposition between the needs of society (private) and those of the state (public). We start from the assumption that this principle is completely foreign to the democratic constitution of Switzerland. If one accepts this thesis, then the crucial question must be formulated as follows: To what extent can Switzerland even be classified as a constitutional democracy, that is, as a democracy founded and limited by a constitution?

Undoubtedly the Swiss concept of constitutionalism does not correspond to the Anglo-American understanding of constitutionalism, which assumes that the rights of the sovereign, both in the exercise of constituent power as well constituted power, are inherently limited by individual human rights regardless of the way in which the sovereign is democratically constituted. It is precisely here that the Swiss understanding of democracy differs, as according to Swiss constitutionalism, the people is the bearer of unlimited sovereign power, whose democratically articulated will is the common source of validity both for governmental power and positive law. The *demos* is the supreme und uncontrollable *pouvoir constituant*.

Accordingly, Swiss constitutional democracy does not constitute the will of the people bound by the basic principle of natural law, but rather constitutes a constitutionally regulated process of permanent and substantively unlimited democratic decision making.

The Swiss conception of the state largely corresponds with the idea of a 'politicised community'. It is a 'citizen-state,' based on the radical democratic idea that the *citoyen's* primary virtue is to transcend his private will and to freely identify himself with the community within which he actively participates. The understanding of the state as a natural extension of the common will is inherent in common citizenship.

How 'Rousseauist' is Switzerland?

This inevitably leads us to the question: How 'Rousseauist' are the Swiss? The Swiss polity is undoubtedly Rousseauist in so far as it identifies with the idea of the state as a 'political society'. However, when one gives sovereignty and primacy to the 'political', this does not necessarily imply that the institutions of the community must be designed in such a way that political power is exercised from only one centre or from one supreme authority. In other words, the potentially authoritarian or even totalitarian consequences of ROUSSEAU'S General Will have not been realised in the Swiss context. In the heterogeneous polity of Switzerland, the *volonté générale* could never be understood as *a consummation of democracy, but as something to be held at bay*. The Swiss understanding of political 'civism' in the sense of federal and participatory democracy is essentially based upon 'decentralised loyalty', and therefore stands in stark opposition to any centralist state design which institutionalises authoritarian populism. As G. IONESCU rightly noted, *Confoederatio Helvetica* seems to be "a *society* with a multiplicity of centres of equal powers working in *association*".

On the other hand, the Swiss conception of democracy, in which participation is more important than representation, has much in common with ROUSSEAU'S teaching that a genuinely democratic government can only be built on the basis of the unlimited and direct exercise of sovereignty. Switzerland has put into practice the legislative procedure that ROUSSEAU suggested was the only correct procedure to ensure that the laws correspond to the *volonté générale*, and not the *volonté de tous*. According to ROUSSEAU, the only way to articulate a legitimate common will is to provide a common basis by which as many individual opinions as possible can be brought together into a common decision.

Whilst Switzerland may not have adopted 'self-government of the people' in the sense of ROUSSEAU, the principle of 'the people as the highest authority' in Switzerland has been nonetheless accommodated through powerful instruments of participatory democracy. The significance of the initiative and referendum is not simply that they permit public participation in national legislative and constitutional issues, but most of all that they change the public's attitude towards government and the state.

According to the Swiss understanding, democracy cannot be reduced simply to elections, and elections are in fact not seen as being of primary importance. People do not control their representatives through elections, but rather through the much more effective process of initiative and referendum. With these instruments of direct democracy the people can have a direct influence on concrete constitutional and legislative decisions. In other words, the representative principle, so crucial in preserving accountability in systems where there is otherwise little participation, is relatively less important in a system where considerable power is devolved to the cantons and municipalities, and what remains at the federal level is subject to constant public review through the legislative and constitutional referenda, and the initiative process.

Anti-Locke?

The Swiss population does not conceive of political power in the LOCKEAN sense, namely negatively, as something to be controlled. On the contrary, political power is viewed as something in which people should participate as extensively as possible. On the basis of this understanding of power and government, democracy and the Constitution stand on an equal footing as complementary instruments. The function of a constitution is merely to outline in positive legal form, how, on what matters and through what procedure the will of the people is to be discerned and carried out. The act of constitution making is thus an expression of the exercise of supreme authority, not because the governmental system is thereby laid out in positive law, but because it concretises and makes operational the idea of the *demos* as the supreme, uncontrollable political power. The Constitution gives positive legal status to the common will, but it does not control its content.

The Constitution reflects how Switzerland is governed

This necessarily leads to a more or less instrumentalist, technical perception of the Constitution. The Swiss Constitution contains in large part provisions that cannot be regarded as constitutional norms in a material sense. As STEINBERG puts it, "the Swiss use their constitution not to control the abuses of human nature but to regulate the relationships among the elements of government. It is a kind of protocol of decisions taken and compromises agreed. ... Unlike the United States, then, Switzerland is not governed by its constitution; *its constitution reflects how it is governed*" (JONATHAN STEINBERG, *Why Switzerland?*, Cambridge 1996, p. 56).

Now and then critics also warn that the voting population as the supreme constituent authority does not always possess the necessary political maturity. They find particular fault with the excessive flexibility of the Swiss Constitution. Some German scholars have even suggested that the constant revision of the Swiss Constitution could ultimately lead to a "constitutional infarction". Some critics assert that Switzerland has the most unstable constitution in the world and carries out plebiscites on a scale and with a frequency not seen anywhere else in the world. This certainly stands true, at least as far as the procedure for constitutional revision is concerned. Some argue that Switzerland is therefore structurally incapable of meeting "the European challenge".

However, in a more substantive sense, it can be nevertheless argued that the Swiss people understand the fundamental constitutional principles *stricto sensu*, as reflecting the core essence of the state and by no means as capable of being easily revised. That is, those provisions that set out the fundamental rights and constitutional principles and that outline the basic institutional design of the Swiss federal democracy.

Finally, republicanism has always been closely linked to communal and participatory democracy. Not only does Swiss civism show a strong inclination for non-personalised government. The implementation of the republican element is almost a structural precondition for communal democracy and in particular for its efforts to realise far-reaching self-determination, as self-determination can only be realised in a republican form of representative democracy. The republican elements of popular participation can be introduced at all levels of the governing process.

iii. Reinterpretation of Rational Legitimacy

New content of the rational legitimacy of the state

As already pointed out, the Swiss idea of the state is also based upon modern rational legitimacy. Beginning with HOBBES and LOCKE and continuing with ROUSSEAU, the modern theory of natural law developed a substantially new conception of legitimacy. In contrast to the previously dominant metaphysical postulates, the new legitimacy principle was based neither on God nor on nature. It was, rather, imbued with the idea of *consensus*, deductible from *ratio* (reason). Now the original legitimating *ratio* governs nothing other than the procedures and preconditions that have to be fulfilled in order that the people can arrive at decisions of general application and validity that are determined by the public interest.

This theory of rational legitimacy that emphasises procedural rationality, acquires, when applied to Switzerland, both a specific character and a fairly novel content, as the idea of the social contract is largely foreign to Switzerland. Switzerland has remained instead deeply rooted in the tradition of Swiss federalism, which is characterised by the use of covenants as devices to promote federal political integration.

Given that, according to the basic idea of rational legitimacy, the validity of a given political order is entirely dependant upon whether it has fulfilled the necessary procedural preconditions for arriving at a consensus, the idea of rational legitimacy must assume that only the majority is entitled to represent the public interest. Such an understanding of consensus indeed underlies liberal representative democracy. But this understanding of rational legitimacy cannot be justified within the Swiss communal democratic tradition. In Switzerland, a federal alliance based on communal civism, it was necessary to rethink rational legitimacy and to meet the challenge of modernity with its own particular concept of decentralised legitimacy in order to accommodate conflicting religious loyalties.

Procedural as well as substantive democracy

Swiss rational legitimacy is based upon both procedural and substantive principles, which provide a rational justification for the validity of the state and government. In order for the state to be just and for government power to be properly exercised, it is not sufficient merely to enable *individuals* to participate in decisions that affect them (the issue of 'representativeness' of political representation). It is also necessary to provide the institutional structures that ensure collective political rights are given proper consideration in the decision making process. Only on the basis of such a concept is it possible to provide for the democratic integration of minorities at the constitutive level.

Power-Sharing of structural minorities

Power-sharing among different linguistic and religious groups emerged as the basic principle of Swiss federal design. In functional terms, the Swiss concordance democracy could be interpreted as structural model for a highly integrated decision making process that satisfies the needs of a relatively heterogeneous, fragmented society. Switzerland was thus able, as a relatively heterogeneous society, to achieve legitimacy on the basis of common political values that create sufficient homogeneity to integrate linguistic and religious diversity. *Rational legitimacy incorporated as self-evident these cultural diversities and gave them a constitutive political relevance.* Ethnic-cultural divisions are not taken as 'pre-existing' in the sense of 'pre-political'. On the contrary, *structural minorities* as such constitute a *substantive* value of democracy.

This is why the rational legitimacy principle upon which the modern Swiss state is built does not oblige the state to recognise the simple majority decision making procedure as being valid in itself. More precisely, it frees both the majority and the minority of the burden of permanent confrontation, and of permanently opposing each other as life-long 'winner' and 'loser'. This particular concept of legitimacy focuses instead on autonomy, understood as the *freedom of political self-determination and the relinquishment of domination by the majority.*

It is this autonomy of structural minorities within a democratic decision making process which governed the emergence of modern Switzerland as a politically coherent society. The federal governmental structure thereby obtained both its democratic legitimacy and its identity. This legitimacy was based neither upon differences ('negative legitimacy'), nor upon isolating from decision making processes the structures that stem from 'pre-political' ethno-cultural diversities. Rather, these structures were integrated into the state as a whole through the guarantee of autonomy for minority groups, without endangering the collective identity of minorities as subjects of their own political rights. The principles and institutions that guarantee such status for minorities run through the whole Swiss constitutional system. They include amongst others, the federal structure of the state, the principle of cantonal independence within a federal structure, municipal autonomy, cantonal authority over language and the freedom of language, as well as the cantonal authority over the public status of churches combined with religious freedom and provisions for religious peace.

iv. Mingling of minorities and majorities as a product not a precondition of the Swiss federation

Overlapping minorities

Many scholars point to the phenomenon of overlapping and cross-cutting minorities as the crucial factor in explaining the more or less successful political integration of cultural diversities in contemporary Switzerland: Almost every Swiss person is in some way simultaneously a member of a minority and a member of a majority.

In contrast, one could argue from the opposite perspective that this phenomenon of overlapping minorities – taken from a *constitutive* point of view – is simply an outcome and not a prerequisite of the Swiss model. Minorities participate in legitimacy not at the pre-political level, but at the political level. It has never been proposed, beyond the constitutional principles of the federation and canton, to erect structures that would guarantee the equality of different ethnic segments of the community. Thus, the idea of giving ethnic communities their own 'mother cantons' and accordingly drawing cantonal borders along prevailing ethnic lines is completely foreign to the Swiss.

On the contrary: Switzerland has created institutions and procedures at the federal, cantonal and municipal levels that enable all politically interested 'entities' to enjoy and develop their diversity. This helps to explain another important peculiarity of the Swiss federal system: cantonal borders are ignored when it comes to integrating cultural diversity into procedural structures and decision making processes of the federation. LEHMBRUCH claims that, contrary to what one might assume from preconceived ideas, the cantons themselves, as institutionalised corporate actors, essentially have no great influence on federal policy making. The important political actors on the periphery have, in the past, been successfully co-opted and integrated into the federal centre.

In accordance with the historical logic that underlies the democratic integration of minorities, Switzerland considers only certain collective political entities as minorities. Integration was and has remained restrictive from a socio-economic point of view. What has been described as the specific Swiss culture of institutional democracy should rather be qualified as a *democracy of institutionalised cultural (linguistic and religious) diversity*, within which there is not much room left for socio-economic cleavages.

Democratic pluralism has since 1874 been seen as the *modus vivendi* for religious and linguistic/ethnic groups. The 'magic formula' that provides for proportional representation even at the level of the Federal Council, went hand in hand with the minority position of labour in politics and industrial relations. The political left was denied what Catholics and farmers had long since achieved: recognition, political influence and participation in the Federal Council. This shows that the Swiss system was able to accommodate different cultures but was less successful accommodating political pluralism.

Switzerland has accommodated its diverse minorities primarily in order to counter outside pressures, and not so much to offset social and economic inequalities. The Swiss democratic pluralist system has remained inherently 'immune' to social and economic conflicts, which have been addressed through social-state mechanisms. Due to the pre-modern understanding of Swiss participatory democracy, its populism has never been inspired by egalitarian ideology.

A systematic and entrenched economic and social inequality of major language and religious groups would however shake the very foundations of the Swiss power-sharing system developed through participatory democracy. The same is, however, certainly not true of those socio-economic cleavages that have developed within and around existing cultural diversities. This shows, generally speaking, how important cultural background is in relation to those minorities that have been integrated into the political system, which should be borne in mind when one seeks to understand why the integration of new immigrant minorities is so problematic.

v. The Secession and Foundation of the canton of Jura as an example of disintegration on an integrative basis

The secession of three northern Catholic and French-speaking districts of the canton of Berne, and the creation of the new canton of Jura in 1978, can be cited as *the* exceptional example in modern Swiss history in which integration failed. The region of Jura belongs to the few areas in which socio-economic, linguistic and religious differences coincide.

The fact that language and religious difference within the canton of Berne coincided with socio-economic inequalities ('cumulative disadvantages'), meant that the power-sharing system at the cantonal level lacked legitimacy for the three districts in northern Jura, and generated a radical separatist movement already at the beginning of the 20th Century. With the secession of one part of the region and the establishment of the new canton of Jura, the French-speaking region of Jura was in fact split up into a Protestant part and a Catholic part. Thus, the separatists or 'autonomists' made their opposition known and continue to struggle for the independence of the entire French-speaking region of Jura.

The debate over the secession of Jura lasted decades, and tore open deep divisions that led to polarisations all over Switzerland. If one takes account of the conformity of structural conditions throughout the federal order, the process can nonetheless be interpreted as paradigmatic for the Swiss model, as it shows how minorities even at the constitutive level of the state are democratically integrated. The cascade of popular votes within the Jura region, from the highest level of the whole region, to the districts and right down to the municipalities, is a clear demonstration of the basis of legitimacy upon which the validity of the Swiss federation is built: *Cultural minorities cannot be overruled on constitutive issues, because these affect state legitimacy itself.*

If the authorities of Berne had stuck strictly to the principles of procedural legitimacy, the separation process would have been valid if the authorities of Berne had been content simply to make constitutional provision for a procedure by which the majority could have arrived at a consensus. However, the people of Berne proceeded differently. The people did not vote on the secession procedure merely to make secession procedurally legitimate, that is, valid for the majority. Rather, the procedure accorded the various majorities and minorities constitutional rights to self-determination.

The procedure took into consideration the founding tenet of the Swiss federalist political culture: that of decentralised loyalty. The minority problem was addressed at the level of political integration, where in other conflicts it is so often ignored; that is, it was recognised that minorities have to be taken into account and integrated in the phase of constituting the state.

By being given the possibility to decide against the majority, *the minority also democratically legitimised the creation of the new canton.* The Protestant French-speaking population, which wanted to remain within the canton of Berne, was vested with the same right to territorial self-determination as the separatist majority.

However, the Jura problem was thereby not completely settled. The authorities of Berne and Jura as well as the federation subsequently took steps to find a solution to the ongoing conflicts between the two cantons that have an impact on the cantonal structure of the Swiss federation. The Agreement on Political Settlement of the Jura Conflict was signed on 25 March 1994 by the governments of Berne and Jura and by the Federal Council. This demonstrates once again the fundamentally important role of compromise in Swiss politics.

The parties to the Agreement committed themselves to "a real inter-Jurassian dialogue," as the only way to arrive at a political solution of the Jura problem, since a community of interests connects the two parts of the region of Jura to each other. However, the Agreement is faced with two diametrically opposing positions. On the one hand, neither the separatist minority in Berne nor the canton of Jura itself has given up on the idea of '*d'un Jura uni*' (united Jura). On the other hand, the authorities of Berne refer to "the existence of the canton of Berne in its territorial integrity", which includes Jura as a "regional authority", in the new Constitution of the canton Berne. The real cause of the conflict thereby remains open and unresolved. What has been agreed is 'merely' a peaceful conflict-resolution procedure – that is, the parties have agreed to a dialogue within an inter-Jura Assembly (*interjurassischen Versammlung*).

The Agreement once again demonstrates how procedural democracy can be reformed, through the uncontested acceptance of the position that the implementation of a pure majority decision would in this case be undemocratic, as such confrontations hinder the identification of the real problem: "*Si le but est fixé d'avance, le dialogue risque d'être denature*". This is why, if one takes fundamental democratic values seriously, political goals can only be pursued and realised by means of convincing the opposing side: "*Si l'on veut respecter la volonté démocratique, il s'agit de parvenir à l'objectif en gagnant des convictions*".

This approach was clearly explained in governmental statements to the people, and was not merely the subject of secret political negotiations. It proves that for the Swiss, compromise is a legitimate political strategy and not merely a '*realpolitik*' tactic. One can even speak of the ideological function of the 'Helvetian compromise'.

The very fact that the procedure of dialogue in itself formed the basis for the legitimacy of the Agreement, reveals the Swiss belief in the value of "the conscious choice of self-restraint", which DEUTSCH has identified as a precondition for successful political integration (K.W. DEUTSCH, *Die Schweiz als ein paradigmatischer Fall politischer Integration*, Bern 1976).

vi. Tension between Federalism and Democracy

Democratic control of federalised power – federal control of democracy

It has become commonplace to describe the relationship that exists between federalism and democracy, in Switzerland as well as more generally, as one of tension ('*Spannungsverhältnis*'). If one assumes that democracy is based on the majority principle according to one-man-one-vote, and if one compares this to the principle of equality between (unequal) cantons, one must accept that both federalism and democracy are implemented only in 'limited doses'.

From another perspective, federalism and democracy can also be seen as *the constitutive foundation for the control of power within a given political community*. It is important to note in this regard that *federalism and democracy are based upon fundamentally different values, namely, on diversity and equality respectively*. Consequently, their relationship within a given political order implies much more than a compromise between the equality of citizens as voters and the equality of cantons as units of the federation. Rather, it involves the *democratic control of federalised power and the federal control of democracy*.

Federalism as a supplement to democracy

For a federal state that is designed according to the principles of liberal democracy, like Canada and the United States, federalism serves to bring different groups together, and to transcend particularistic loyalties. Consequently, democracy is a means for finding a consensus according to the majority principle, and federalism supplements or corrects democracy through the principle of the control of power, that is, the vertical separation of powers (vertical checks and balances). The essential problem that these federations have to resolve is how to maintain equilibrium between the federal alliance and majoritarian democracy.

Federalism as a structural principle of democracy

In contrast, the Swiss federation is based on strong cantonal identity on the one hand and democratic integration on the other, by maintaining linguistic and religious diversities and decentralised, communal and cantonal loyalty. This is why Switzerland lacks the institutional instruments of state unification that are usually found in federal systems. In Switzerland, *federalism* has been introduced as a *structural principle of democracy*.

The formula for the substantive legitimacy of the Swiss federal system not only reconciles federalism and democracy, but rather, understands them as *intrinsically* linked to each other. Due to the local and communal character of the Swiss polity, democracy cannot be reduced merely to the principles of majority rule and political equality of individual voting rights. Communal civism has embraced *participatory democracy as a federalist element* to protect inherent minority interests. The abstract principle of popular sovereignty has been put into operation through the traditional instruments of Swiss democratic decentralisation (*Landsgemeinde*, referendum). The outcome is a complex federal system with a basic consensus about the fundamentals of social and economic rights, high enough to make the institutional set-up work effectively.

It could be even argued that the Swiss have functionalised participatory democracy as a means of protecting their decentralised loyalty. '*Volksrechte*' are also justified on the basis that they safeguard other fundamental collective rights of structural minorities. Collective rights are constitutive elements of the federation and cannot be reduced to an instrument of popular sovereignty for the limitation and control of government power. Through the 'federalisation' of participatory democracy, which has tempered federal power through referendum and initiative, federalism has also acquired the key function of ensuring competition in the Swiss political arena.

Democratisation of the federalist principle

On the other hand, the federalist principle of minority protection has been democratised through popular initiative. The popular initiative accommodates minorities by providing them with a chance to introduce new ideas and proposals into the political debate, thereby also giving them the chance to eventually win over the majority of the people and the cantons – as has often occurred – in spite of the opposition of government and parliament.

Shifting majorities and minorities

One should not overlook the fact that the various groups that oppose each other in the process of democratic negotiation vary according to the subject in dispute. This constant shift in majorities and minorities is precisely what makes Swiss concordance democracy able to function. As RHINOW puts it, "the principle of concordance entails a constant *search for inclusive and 'workable' majority solutions*, guarantees *different and changing minorities* opportunities for effective influence and collaboration, and thereby also makes easier the acceptance and enforceability of majority decisions" (RHINOW, 'Grundprobleme der Schweizerischen Demokratie', *Zeitschrift fuer Schweizerisches Recht*, 1984, p. 254).

The decision making procedures in which compromise-oriented bargaining and negotiation take place are based on strongly decentralised structures. Concordance democracy could thus be defined as a principle that tends to recognise the majority, as the procedure for arriving at a consensus usually ends in a majority decision. Swiss democracy is not anti-majoritarian. It is, rather *minority-friendly in the sense that minorities can be overruled only by a broadly supported consensus* (qualified majority). This may serve to clarify the function of compromise in concordance democracy.

Individual political rights are also integrated into the Swiss federal democracy. It is only through the common political community that individual liberty in the sense of individual self-determination can be protected. The federal structure allows a wide-ranging participation of the citizens at the level of the cantons and the municipalities. Switzerland provides the citizen with comprehensive rights of participation at all levels and moderates the pure majority principle through the strong representation of minorities.

Democratic deficits

Recent trends towards legal and administrative centralisation and closer relations between the authorities of all three levels of government have changed Swiss federalism. The emergence of a non-transparent network of various forms of cooperation and coordination between governments and administrative units at the three levels has been described as a sign of a 'dramatic' change. However, what began in the mid-1970s as a reform to support the federal order, has ended up resulting in 'weak decentralisation'. Thereby the territorial dimension of politics has gained new impetus from functional and economic inputs.

The growth in socio-economic inequalities appears to be increasingly displacing territorial differences, and leading the Swiss democracy to decision making problems that do not accord with its tradition. In other words, the very 'representativeness' of participatory democracy has come under question. This representative deficit is not purely quantitative, but also qualitative. The low participation in the polls has often been referred to as a sign of a deep crisis of Swiss participatory democracy. However, it must be taken into account that:

a) The number of polls on constitutional matters has increased by 100 per cent approximately every twenty years since 1930; and
b) The impression that the percentage of those who participate is steadily decreasing is a false one. Over an extended period, 80 percent of the electorate has at some point turned out to vote, if not all on the same occasion then at least when voters want to participate in a vote that interests or affects them.

On the other hand, it is a qualitative deficit in representation that has become a matter of concern. LINDER correctly points out that "the most important restriction on the democratic norm of equal and general participation therefore lies in the unequal representation of the social classes. And it is this increasing inequality of representation that makes low overall participation problematic" (LINDER, *Swiss Democracy, Possible Solutions to Conflict in Multi-cultural Societies*, London 1994). One could indeed speak of 'elitism' in Swiss semi-direct democracy.

8.4.3 Inherent limits of the Swiss Federal Democracy and its Lessons

Alternative model of the nation

The Swiss model of nation building under conditions of multi-ethnic and religious diversity has created an alternative to classic liberal democracy. It is an empirically developed, historically verified counter-argument to the underlying axiom of individualist democracy, which does not reject the category of collective rights as such, but cautions against structuring social and political relationships through collective rights. In the light of Swiss communal democracy, 'modernity' acquires a somewhat new meaning. The democratic institutionalisation of cultural diversities has politicised ethnic, religious and linguistic principles in a positive sense. This was only possible because the diversities were integrated at the founding constitutive level of the polity. This observation marks a starting point from which to understand the inherent limits of the Swiss federal democracy, and from which to draw possible lessons for newly established multi-ethnic federations in Eastern Europe.

Exclusion of foreigners

The inherent limits of Swiss federal democracy stem from the communal civic identity. As already pointed out, the basic political values of the '*Willensnation*' cannot be readily internalised by an individual who has not shared in the Swiss history and tradition. The system emerged and persists as the one model that is able to integrate cultural diversities. However, *it excludes any minority that is not structurally a part of the system.*

This is why the problem of immigrant workers, who have now reached almost 20 per cent of the population in Switzerland, can never be solved through the traditionally given assumptions of Swiss federal democracy. The only institutional means to provide naturalised immigrants with a chance to break into the system would be to introduce majoritarian democracy. This would give the new political minorities a structural relevance. On the other hand, this would delegitimise the system for all those who perceive their Swiss citizenship as participation in the Swiss '*Willensnation*' through various communal bodies. This is why, in the long run, the only feasible and viable solution for the immigrant minority is their *voluntary assimilation* into the system.

Decentralised minority-friendly democracy as a solution for multicultural states

On the other hand, Swiss federal democracy can offer a number of highly relevant lessons to new multi-ethnic federations.

Individualist liberal democracy with its associated institutional order of constitutional government cannot cope with the problem of the *ethnification of politics*, with which all Eastern European countries in transition are faced. This is the political reality that one must live with. The basic principles of the Swiss model of decentralised, minority-friendly democracy can, as we have tried to demonstrate, certainly pave the way for the positive politicisation of ethnicity, if it cannot provide an answer.

The examination of the Swiss federal experience shows that in terms of legitimacy, a multi-ethnic federal state cannot afford to overlook minorities. In other words, minorities cannot be outvoted at the level of constituting the polity. This is the only strategy to build a democratic federal order with sufficient internal coherence to hold off secessionist movements. Once the federal order has been given a broad, genuinely representative democratic legitimacy, the necessary decision making powers of the central government will not be perceived by minorities as a threat to their various collective identities. This is how the defensive nationalism of minorities, which has been and will always be politically exploited, can be avoided.

It accords with the inherent logic of participatory democracy that the minorities also give legitimacy to the modern Swiss federation. Thus, the minority issue cannot become a state issue. The minority question has been democratised, without putting minorities at the mercy of the majority through the pure majority principle. Rather, minorities have been politically integrated through the system of proportional democracy. Because minorities do not question the legitimacy of the state, there is more room for constitutional and legislative accommodation of minority rights.

The vertical and horizontal inter-ethnic tensions within Russia and Yugoslavia reveal that these new multi-ethnic federations seem not to have yet learned the lesson that political communities which lack their own democratic legitimacy and identity are destined to disintegrate. They still refuse to articulate the essentials of a founding democratic consensus. The first challenge they have to overcome is to decide on what principles the *demos* for the common state is to be constituted. What constitutes a basis for legitimacy that creates sufficient homogeneity to integrate the diversities of a multi-ethnic structure into a united political entity? The Swiss model of constitutive democratic integration of minorities cannot, as such, provide them with a ready-made solution. However, it can certainly demonstrate how to articulate the minority issue as a basic legitimacy issue at the constitutive level. Above all, it provides a warning to all those who, in brutal ongoing inter-ethnic conflicts, stubbornly persist in making others lose what they 'self-evidently' have the right to win.

If there is any message to be taken from the Swiss case, it is the following: Multi-ethnic societies can only survive if *all* groups within the society can feel like 'winners'.

8.4.4 *Conclusion: 14 Constitutional Principles for a Multicultural State*

8.4.4.1 Legitimacy

1st Principle: Take cultural diversity seriously

Modern constitutionalism is based on the concept that human beings are universally equal as *Homo sapiens*. Factors such as cultural particularities are either denied or ignored as politically irrelevant. At most, culture may be considered as a nation-building factor for homogeneous nations. Thus, modern constitutionalism makes no allowance for the reality that 95 per cent of the world population lives in multicultural societies, and ignores the fact that many citizens are not satisfied to be politically respected only as rational citizens without cultural roots. They require political recognition as cultural human beings, equal as human beings with reason and understanding, but significantly different with regard to their language, religion and historical roots.

Constitutions of multicultural states that deny or ignore culture as a political factor need to change the basic concept of their national legitimacy and to make the reality of multicultural diversity the basis of their constitutional and political system. That is, they must recognise culture as an essential political value, and thereby adopt the promotion of cultural diversity as a constitutional goal. States based on the pre-cultural homogeneity of the people will have to recognise not only the culture of the majority, but also the cultures of all communities living under their jurisdiction, as forming the political basis of the state. This means that cultural communities must be given the political recognition that guarantees them the autonomy to maintain and develop their own cultural identity and to participate in the decision making process of the common state.

2nd Principle: Homeland for minorities

If a state wants to take the diversity of languages and cultures seriously, it cannot treat minorities only as tolerated guests; rather, it must give each of the various language and cultural communities a constitutionally recognised status and acknowledge the cultural communities as being an essential part of the state. Cultural communities will only be able to recognise the state in which they live as being their Homeland, if they are able to contribute to shaping the state and to identify with 'their' state.

3rd Principle: Composite nation

A political system that builds upon the cultural diversity of its people requires a new foundation for legitimacy, namely, a legitimacy based upon the concept of a composite nation. Up to now, the concept of the nation united by the social contract has been based upon an '*us*' versus '*them*' mentality. The '*us*' is united on the basis of commonly recognised political and cultural values (what is good for us) or on the basis of universal values that can hold the people within a particular territory together. A composite nation needs a social contract that can unite diverse cultural communities through commonly recognised values. At the same time, this social contract must recognise the cultural values and independence of each of the particular communities. The common values establish that which is good for a given cultural community (good for us) and also good for the various communities living within the state (good for the others), but not necessarily good for all human beings in the sense of universality.

4th Principle: Double and multiple loyalties

Most states demand absolute loyalty of their citizens to the basic values of the nation, and therefore prohibit dual- or multiple-citizenship. On the other hand, states that recognise the political value of their different cultural communities have to accept at least internally that citizens will have double loyalty: loyalty to their cultural community on one hand, and loyalty to the state on the other. At the same time citizens must be able to exhibit loyalty in relation to their cultural community based in another state. The recognition of such double or multiple loyalties must find its expression in a concept of citizenship which accepts dual- or multiple-citizenship. The common citizenship of the European Union may mark the first step towards such recognition of multiple-citizenship.

8.4.4.2 Rule of Law

5th Principle: Individual and collective equality

The prevailing concept of equal rights is based on the assumption that all human beings are equal and should be treated equally, and that all individuals should have equal opportunities within the political community. However, in multicultural states people want to have equal opportunities within their cultural community.

They also want their community to be treated equally to other cultural communities, for example in terms of equal language rights. In terms of their cultural particularity, people want their difference to be recognised. Members of minority cultures want to be respected as citizens on an equal basis to members of the majority culture, and to be seen as representing an equally valuable and valued cultural tradition, irrespective of their numerical inequality. The cultural particularity of minorities has to be recognised in the sense that difference is considered to be a value and not a burden.

6th Principle: Collective rights

Individuals belonging to different cultural communities therefore want not only to be treated equally as individuals. They also expect their cultural community and themselves as members of that community to be treated equally to members of other communities. If a minority culture is not recognised as having equal cultural value to the majority culture, the members of the minority culture will feel discriminated against. Harmony between the different cultural communities is primarily based on the equal cultural and political recognition of the collective value of the different communities. The collective value of culture has to be equally recognised for all cultural communities regardless of numbers or statistics. The multicultural state must find a balance between the freedom of the individual and the collective autonomy of the community.

7th Principle: Liberty and peace

The aim of the liberal state is to protect, maintain and promote individual liberty. A state composed of different cultural communities must additionally aim to maintain peace among the different communities. The constitution will have to perform a difficult balancing act between individual liberty on one side and peace among the different communities on the other side. For the sake of peace, it might be necessary for example to restrict individual language rights in order to uphold the collective rights of a minority that fears for the survival of its culture. Peace will also be fostered by the recognition of collective rights to cultural autonomy and limited territorial autonomy for different communities, such as that which is accorded to the cantons and municipalities in Switzerland.

8.4.4.3 Shared Rule

8th Principle: Participation of minority cultural groups in constitution making

Constitution making in multicultural states can only succeed in justifying, establishing or limiting the power of the state if the constitutional principles are perceived by all cultural communities as being legitimate. This legitimacy can only be achieved if the various cultural communities are given the right to participate on an equal footing in the constitution making process, and are therefore able to identify with the state and its constitution.

9th Principle: Power sharing of cultural communities

In multicultural states, a system of government based on the pure majoritarian principle of 'winner-takes-all' will not be able to achieve lasting legitimacy in the eyes of minority communities. Under such a system minorities will feel permanently marginalised. The pure majority principle, according to which a democratic winner with 51 per cent of the votes can acquire 100 per cent of the state power, has to be modified in order for the principle of democracy to be acceptable to minority cultural groups. Such moderation can be achieved by introducing elements of power sharing, thereby enabling minorities that would otherwise be permanently excluded from participation in the political decision making process to have their say and to actively contribute to the common welfare of the state.

8.4.4.4 Self Rule

10th Principle: Autonomy

Cultural and language communities must be able, through territorial autonomy or group autonomy, to independently and autonomously regulate matters relating to their own cultural development and cultural heritage. Moreover, they must be empowered to implement, within their own cultural community, decisions made at the higher level on the basis of the principle of shared rule. This entails autonomy over matters such as education, court jurisdiction, administration and police.

11th Principle: Fostering diversity

A multicultural state can only establish lasting legitimacy if it does not just tolerate diversity, but actually promotes and fosters diversity and accords it a value that can bring all cultural communities together into a common polity. This aim will only be fulfilled if each cultural community is convinced that its own internal values will be better realised within the existing common state than in its own state established through secession and self-determination. The development of polyphonic music has long been regarded as a sign of high culture and civilisation. In the field of politics and democracy however, many states and peoples still prefer monotony to polyphony. Federal states on the other hand are examples for the development of more complex forms of political order. Analogous to polyphony in music, they can be considered as an expression of the complexity of human reality. Federal states do not suffocate diversity with monotony, but promote diversity as a value of a 'polyphonic' state.

8.4.4.5 Democracy

12th Principle: Self-determination of individuals as a democratic aim

Democracy should not be reduced to a state principle, the sole purpose of which is to produce an efficient majority. Rather, democracy should be seen as serving liberty and as establishing through public discourse the legitimacy of procedures and institutions for political consensus building (LINCOLN: With the people, by the people and for the people). A consensus oriented democratic process in which decisions are made from the bottom up, is based on the conviction that each decision of the polity should provide for the single individual as much self-determination as possible: whether this be through individual liberty or through optimal participation in the community. The smaller the community in which decisions are made, the less individual self-determination is limited. Within the small group, the single individual has the greatest chance contribute to the design of the polity and to exercise freedom within the group. The federal division of democracy into two or three levels of democratic units, which can even be extended to the international level, provides for an optimal balance of self- and co-determination. It guarantees that the broadest possible consensus will be sought for the decisions at each respective level in order to guarantee the greatest possible self-determination.

13th Principle: Value of compromise as an alternative to the 'winner takes all' democracy

Most democracies enable a party or coalition to assume 100 per cent of the state power on the basis of support from 51 per cent of the voters. In a multicultural state, this system needs to be adapted to accommodate the reality of cultural diversity. Pure majoritarianism suppresses diversity. Diversity can only flourish in a culture oriented towards consensus and compromise. The political decision making process and the political institutions have to be guided by the idea that a compromise which produces broad agreement has a higher value than a small majority. This of course presupposes a political culture that regards compromise as a value and a strength rather than a weakness, because compromise enables the achievement of a higher consensus and thus a more comprehensive majority. In a multicultural democracy therefore, the small minority of only 51 per cent must through compromise seek the consensus of a much larger majority. Decision making procedures and political institutions must be guided by the value of compromise as an instrument for conflict management.

14th Principle: Conflict management

Democratic procedures should not serve only to produce efficient and legitimate decisions. They must also be conceived as tools for managing conflict between different communities. This requires that the procedures are designed in such a way as to facilitate the resolution of disputes through rational discourse. This means that categorical conflicts need to be minimised through appropriate state structures and procedures, so that conflicting groups will feel sufficiently secure that they will opt to engage in discourse rather than resorting to violence.

9 Outlook: The Constitutional State at the Threshold of a New Millennium

9.1 Introduction

Diverse constitutional origins

When the Pacific island nation of Vanuatu applied for membership of the United Nations, it received an application form from the UN bureaucracy that required applicants, amongst other things, to attach a copy of their constitution.

Behind the attachment to the application form could be a constitution born out of bloody revolution as in France, or an agreement to form a civil body politic such as the Mayflower Compact. It could be a constitution imposed on a military basis by NATO such as in the Republic of Bosnia-Herzegovina, or a constitution forced by Parliament upon a weakened monarch such as the Magna Carta of 1215.

From these examples of some of the varied methods of constitution making, the diverse functions that constitutions can serve and some of the reasons for their varied content become apparent.

Commonalities of constitutional documents

What do these numerous constitutional documents have in common? Can we find a common thread that runs from the Magna Carta to the Bill of Rights (1679) through to the South African Constitution (1996) that was built upon an interim constitution and had to be certified by a constitutional court? The constitutions of various Eastern European states have been drafted in roundtable discussions, whilst others were drafted by the old constitutional organs or were imposed by a powerful post-communist executive.

In other cases, constitutions have formed new territorial units through alliances, such as the United States of America, Switzerland and the European Union. Constitutions have also served to justify revolutions and secessions and to legitimise the new secular and democratic governmental systems that flowed from them. In these cases constitutions did not constitute a new state, but a new government. In the process of transferring political power from the king by the grace of God to the president by the grace of the people, such constitutions shifted the hierarchy of power from the Head of State to the executive, to parliament and finally to the people. In communist regimes, however, constitutions were mere façades, created to disguise the uncontrolled and unaccountable power of the communist party leadership.

Enlightenment

During the Enlightenment period, the constitution was accorded the task of limiting governmental power and implementing the rule of law. The French

Revolution utilised the constitution as the formal method of conferring power on the nation, the state and the parliament. The constitution was charged with transforming a feudal society of subjects into a liberal civil society of equal citizens. In Switzerland, the constitution enabled the enforcement of the democratic decisions of the people on government policy and legislation. The Israel and New Zealand do not have a comprehensive written constitutional UK, document, but they are nonetheless constitutional states.

Since the end of the Second World War, a total of 113 new states have been recognised by the international community (*Der Fischer Atlas, globale Trends auf einen Blick*, Frankfurt a.M. 1996, p. 152 (with updated figures)). This trend is likely to continue because the international community is currently faced with potential state-breaking and state-making conflicts in South and North Korea, Cyprus, Northern Ireland, Basque country, Congo, Canada, Indonesia, Georgia (Abchasia), Russia (Chechnya), China, Sudan, Somalia, Serbia-Montenegro and Kosovo, Indonesia, Philippines, India – Pakistan (Kashmir), Sri Lanka and Macedonia.

There is no doubt that we are living through a crucial period for the future development of constitutionalism. The developments immediately before and after the turn of the millennium will be decisive for the course that constitution making will take in the future. Time will tell whether the liberal constitutionalism born of the British Enlightenment will have to give way to new constitutional theories shaped by the universality of human rights, multiculturality, globalisation and consensus-oriented democracy. Will the people remain the fictive bearer of constituent power or will the people become the real constitution maker? Will states in the era of globalisation and migration continue to exclude people and isolate their own ethnicity? What meaning will be attached to sovereignty, which is increasingly becoming a symbolic fiction? Will states stray from the path of reason down which the Enlightenment has led them and allow the citizens to lead them down the uncertain path of emotion? These are the questions with which we must grapple at the end of this theory of constitutional democracy and at the start of the new millennium.

9.2 'We are the People' versus 'We are One People'

'We are the people'

Before the fall of the Berlin Wall, several thousand East German citizens prayed for freedom at huge gatherings at the Church of Saint Nicholas in Leipzig. The justification for their peaceful protest and resistance against the government was their fundamental belief that the Communist Party and its leadership no longer represented the people, and that the people should represent itself.

The slogan 'we are the people' legitimised not only the democratic movement of 1989/90. From the 'Glorious Revolution' to the events in Leipzig, many tyrants have been overthrown with this slogan, and in each case both the revolutionary organ claiming popular sovereignty and the post-revolutionary civil government have differed significantly. Whilst in England the more or less anarchic meeting of the Long Parliament of 1640 was replaced by Oliver Cromwell; the symbolic Assemblée Nationale of 1789 in revolutionary France relinquished its sovereignty to the 'Committee for Public Safety' (*comité du salut publique*); and the elected 1848 German National Assembly convened in St. Paul's Cathedral, Frankfurt, offered the crown to the King of Prussia (which he declined).

It was not until the end of the 19th Century that the struggle over who should occupy the highest position in the hierarchy of government – Head of State, executive or parliament – produced a real variety of constitutional models. Usually after fierce and sometimes violent struggles between various political groups, the constitution making powers opted either for a strong Westminster-type parliament or for a presidential system along the lines of the French or American models. The constitutional systems tried to find a balance between the legitimacy of state authority and the need for efficient government, and the necessary protection against misuse of power.

The secularisation of state authority marked the real beginning of modern constitutionalism. With the shift from authority by divine right to popular sovereignty, constitutional principles emerged to govern and limit the exercise of power by representative institutions. However, there was no clear or uniform answer to the question of who could most legitimately represent the people: an elected president, a parliament, or an executive composed of members of the majority parliamentary party? The Communist Party answered this question with a claim to absolute power. Only the party could legitimately determine the true interests of the people, and only the party could represent the popular will. The democratic movement of Leipzig however provides a recent and symbolic reminder that nobody, neither the Communist Party nor its leader, can act for or in place of the people, but only through the people.

'We are one people'

After the collapse of the illegitimate government of the DDR and the fall of the Berlin Wall in late 1989, the movement for democratisation became a movement for German reunification. The slogan 'we are the people' shifted to 'we are one people'. The main argument of this movement was that the German people are a pre-state historical entity, with a natural right to be unified; thus reunification was not legitimised by popular ratification through a referendum, but by reference to the former historic unity of the German people. A common election procedure gave sufficient legitimacy to unite two formerly independent states and peoples into the Federal German Republic. In other words, it was recognised that one people which is by nature a common unit has a fundamental right to self-determination as a single political entity.

This concept reflects an important shift in constitutional thinking. The secularisation of sovereignty to the 'people' did not include the transfer of their historical or religious heritage. In fact, it intentionally made the 'citizen', as the unit of the people, a culturally barren construct. As a result, modern constitutionalism has ignored the natural unity as well as the diversity of different peoples. The validation of the cry 'we are one people' in Germany has the potential to give cultural content back to ethnic groups, and with it concomitant political rights. For example, if a people is part of another state as a minority nation, it could demand unilateral secession based on the argument that historically it has always been a separate nation and thus has a right to self-determination. The questions will be what constitutes a natural right to self-determination and what historical period should be considered decisive. These issues are currently being faced in the Middle East, where Palestinians and Israelis have fought for over 4000 years; in the Balkans, where ethnic groups have been in conflict for almost one millennium; and in many settler countries, where the indigenous people are claiming the historical rights of their native nations. One of the major constitutional problems facing us today is the resolution of issues over self-determination and, as a logical consequence of territorial claims based on historical disputes, the foundations of nations and peoples.

The modern constitutional state has secularised political power and declared the 'people' sovereign without taking into account the cultural, historical or religious roots of the people. The 'citizen' as the unit of the people is devoid of culture. Historical unity, sense of identity and feelings of belonging of cultural and ethnic groups have generally been ignored in modern constitution making. But today it is precisely these factors of multicultural diversity that have become the bone of contention in numerous constitutional battles. As a result of the territorial claims of ethnic minorities, democracy is being exploited for ethnic interests rather than for the '*volonté générale*' or the common good. Self-determination is seen as a natural right to unilateral secession and thereby to the group's own sovereign state. This 'state' would give rebels, terrorists or liberators (depending on one's perspective) the status and rights of statehood, before the ethnic community has even formed itself into a coherent political entity.

9.3 Inclusive States versus Exclusive Ethnicities

From universality in theory to universality in practice

The first modern constitutions proclaimed universality and inclusiveness as part of the inalienable natural rights of all human beings. The French Constitution of 1791 was based on the idea that all individuals living within the constitutional territory would automatically become French citizens after one year of permanent residence. Hence, citizenship was not based on cultural or historical background, but was accorded on the basis of an individual's acceptance of the liberal constitution and willingness to reside in the country. This inclusive concept of citizenship reflected the liberal idea of the political citizen (*citoyen*), who is part of the social contract as a political human being. Every person is also the bearer of inalienable natural rights, guaranteed by the constitution. These constitutions, which were based upon the principles of liberty, democracy and the rule of law, thereby created a 'homeland' for every person, regardless of their origin or descent.

But although the early constitutions avoided direct references to ethnicity and apparently proclaimed universality and inclusiveness, in reality they also had significant exclusive elements. The French language, for instance, was regarded as having universal cultural value and as therefore being open to everyone. Similarly, the Declaration of Independence, which proclaimed the natural rights of every human being, excluded native Americans and African Americans.

The European constitutions of the second half of the 20th Century lay claim to openness and universality, yet at the same time they cannot come to terms with modern migration. Of the Swiss population of 7 million inhabitants, approximately 20 per cent are foreigners. These people are effectively treated as second-class citizens with almost no voting rights. Switzerland has thus become an 80 per cent rather than a 100 per cent democracy. The German Basic Law refers to universal constitutional patriotism, but under Article 116 expressly privileges foreigners with ethnic German origin in the acquisition of German citizenship.

Most constitutions do not directly and openly refer to ethnic origin. They proclaim universality and inclusiveness but in reality they exclude foreign populations.

Up to now, territory and people have been regarded as natural elements of the state. The social contract was originally defined by the people within a particular territory. In today's age of globalisation however, territory is beginning to lose its importance. What remains are 'transnational citizens' with more or less stable residence. In future, constitution making will have to deal with the issue of transnational citizenship and its consequences for 'the people' and democracy, as well as with the diminishing relevance of people and territory.

From homogeneity to diversity

Liberal values such as democracy and individual legal equality can be best implemented in a unitary state. In a unitary system freedom and equality have the same content throughout the country. In particular, within a unitary democracy parliament can represent the whole population without discriminating against or privileging particular territorial units.

On the basis of the innumerable ethnic conflicts, demands for autonomy and secessionist movements that marked the 20th Century, it is apparent that the classic nation-state model has reached its limits. The classical constitutional systems have tended to regard diversity as irrelevant (US), to ignore it (France) or to suppress it by assimilation (Germany). Switzerland takes a somewhat different constitutional approach to diversity. The revised Constitution of 1999 not only recognises and protects diversity as an enrichment of society, it also promises the active promotion and support of diversity.

In multicultural states the pure majority principle often leads to a tyranny of the majority over minorities. But in order to achieve true legitimacy the state must be seen as legitimate also in the eyes of its minorities. In future, constitutions will no longer be able to ignore cultural, religious and historical realities. They will have to recognise that people are not only rational human beings but that their emotional dimensions are also relevant. The need of every human being for identity and community must be politically recognised and cannot be relegated to the private sphere. Constitutions will be faced with the task of developing criteria to identify which elements of diversity is to be politically promoted and supported, and which elements of diversity is to be merely tolerated or even excluded.

From majoritarian to consensus driven democracy

To properly recognise diversity as a social value, the constitutions of tomorrow will have to accord autonomy to local communities and ensure their participation in the decision making process. In order that all communities can identify with the state, they must not only be integrated at the constitutional level, but must also be included as part of the *pouvoir constituant* in the constitution making process itself. Only on the basis of such state-building consensus amongst communities can a new constitution gain the required acceptance of all relevant political communities and thereby acquire legitimacy.

The 'winner takes all' democracy can have disastrous effects in a multicultural state. Majoritarian democracy can only achieve stability and ensure protection against the misuse of power so long as political questions are not radicalised, and political parties succeed through argumentation in changing majorities and minorities. However, in ethnic conflicts political opponents become political enemies. Disputes degenerate into conflicts in which demands are polarised and compromise is therefore unreachable. Majoritarian democracy establishes the ethnic majority as the permanent winner and renders the ethnic minority a perennial loser. In this configuration the decision of the majority cannot be taken as a legitimate expression of the popular will. The goal of the constitution can no longer be to produce efficient majorities and to guarantee individual rights. Instead, the constitution must promote willingness to compromise and the achievement of unity through fostering diversity.

Liberal democracy is essentially procedural democracy. It determines the rules of the game and leaves the outcome open. The result is not significant, rather what is important is that the popular will can be formed and expressed on the basis of equality of arms and transparency. The liberal constitution therefore provides procedures which enable the building of efficient majorities based on a democratic discourse. The result that is produced will be legitimate, whatever it is. Communist democracy was arranged quite differently. Its aim was to 'democratise' the society without respecting procedural rules. It was the result rather than the procedure by which it was produced that was most important. The results of the liberal democratic decision-making process on the other hand are unforeseeable and are also not questioned, provided they do not infringe upon protected inalienable rights. Democracy tends to focus on producing a majority to decide between opposing interests, rather than on producing lasting compromise solutions.

In future, the constitutions of multicultural states will have to find an innovative democratic concept which extends beyond the procedural facilitation of majority decisions and which conceives of legitimacy as something more than majority approval. By searching for consensus amongst all groups within the state, enemies incapable of compromise should become opponents ready to compromise. The democracy of the future should not serve only as an instrument to legitimise efficient government. As an instrument for the strengthening of self-determination and the guarantee of liberty, the constitution should provide people with the opportunity to contribute to shaping their society through the political process. The decentralisation of democracy to local units and the provision of autonomy increase the potential of the individual to have an influence in the political process and produces new political identities. The increased participation and the closeness of local government to the people strengthen the integration of communities within the state and institutionalise the peaceful settlement of conflicts.

Equal rights – right to be equal

The feudal system, which liberal constitutionalism sought to eradicate, was based upon the extended family. The head of the family, as the owner of real estate and other family property, was the bearer of constitutional rights. It was not until the 19th Century that workers and those without land or fortune gained voting rights. The 20th Century finally was marked by the struggle for women's suffrage and for the emancipation of women in all areas of society.

The focus of political debate has since shifted from voting rights to the realisation of legal equality in the sense of equal opportunities. Every person should have the same opportunity and the same starting position to achieve any position within society, whether it is through access to education and employment, through the right to marriage or the right to social security. Minorities such as the handicapped, the elderly and formerly discriminated groups such as homosexuals are claming and gaining equal rights. The guarantee of equal rights increasingly involves the recognition and protection of every form of lifestyle as equal.

Members of ethnic minorities demand equal respect and political recognition not just as individuals but collectively as members of a linguistic, cultural or religious community. They claim not just individual legal equality and freedom from discrimination, but also the right to equality in their diversity as a group. Affirmative action is regarded as an appropriate means to eradicate historical injustice and discrimination. However, more recent developments suggest that the sovereignty of the global market will slowly replace affirmative action with a culture-blind guarantee of individual equal opportunities (not equal results), and on the other hand at the same time the growing need for local collective identity will strengthen the importance of collective rights. These trends will make the conflicting constitutional positions of individual versus collective rights even harder to reconcile.

9.4 From Real Sovereignty to Symbolic Sovereignty

Sovereignty as 'Big Bang'

Sovereignty was the determinative factor of statehood in the 19th and 20th Centuries. It was the symbol of the nation-state and the basis of state legitimacy. Sovereignty was a magic formula that guaranteed individual freedom and enabled the achievement of social justice through the state. Just as Prometheus stole fire from the gods and thereby transferred 'cultural sovereignty' to the individual, so HOBBES and the philosophers of the Enlightenment stole sovereignty from God in order to secularise the state. From this point sovereignty was no longer derived from God, but from the people, which transferred its sovereignty to the Leviathan through the social contract. This political body represented the will of those who had installed it. Since HOBBES, sovereignty has been considered the essential foundation of every state and every legal order. It is the 'Big Bang' from which the authority of the state originates. It serves to justify the isolation of the state from the outside world and the right of the state to make its own decisions over war and peace.

The international community as 'pouvoir constituant'

This concept of sovereignty no longer has a place in today's globalised world. International conflicts and wars are regarded by the international community as a threat to global peace and the international community, based on the prohibition of aggression under the United Nations Charter, claims the right to intervene. As a result of the increasing internationalisation of human rights, states can no longer hide the treatment of their own citizens behind the veil of sovereignty and claim that it is an internal matter. Human rights are considered universal values and fall under the overall supervision of the international community. Thus states no longer have sovereign constitution making power concerning the guarantee and implementation of fundamental human rights. The international human rights charters have effectively become an integral part of modern constitutions.

Even international organisations without democratic accountability such as the World Bank and the IMF decide on good governance and examine whether the governments of member states are respecting and implementing basic and universal constitutional principles such as the rule of law, democratic accountability of government, separation of powers, human rights and decentralisation. Within this new spirit of universal values and international supervision, sovereignty has for most states effectively been reduced to a symbol. Sovereignty was once crucial for any constitution making power, but today it merely serves to implement international constitutional law within the state.

Sovereignty of the global market

Nowadays when formulating constitutions, states seek to create a legal and political order that will be recognised by international and regional organisations, that will attract international investors, and that will satisfy the conditions of the World Bank and the IMF. Constitutions should enable good government and sustainable development in the common interest; they should protect minorities and demonstrate openness to the real sovereignty of the global market. Through these demands, constitutions have effectively become interchangeable documents, which no longer embody or emphasise national pride in the sense of MONTESQUIEU: "It is the business of the legislature to follow the spirit of the nation, when it is not contrary to the principles of government; for we do nothing so well as when we act with freedom, and follow the bent of our natural genius" (MONTESQUIEU, *The Spirit of Laws*, Book XIX, section 5). It is no longer a goal of constitution making power to produce a constitution which reflects the origin and spirit of a nation. At a time in which diversity is becoming increasingly important, it is not considered advantageous to produce diversity in relation to constitution making.

The sovereignty of the global market is gradually gaining the upper hand over national sovereignty. The global market is regulated by the 'invisible hand' and by the only remaining superpower. The sovereignty of the free market guarantees the free flow of goods, capital and services. The free flow of labour and people on the other hand still falls within the control of national sovereignty. It remains to be seen whether the division of the market into a global flow of capital and products on one hand and the local regulation of labour on the other hand can be maintained over the longer term. Social unrest caused by migration and internal identity crises may well be the consequence if the constitutions of the future are unable to resolve this tension.

9.5 From Reason to Emotion

Reason – religion – ideology

According to philosopher AGNES HELLER, modernity began when man learned to say 'no'. Affirmation and negation are the result of reflective evaluations of what is good and bad, right and wrong, just and unjust. Human beings distinguish themselves precisely by being the only known living beings that are able to arrange their lives on the basis of their own reflection and choice. The ability, through reason and experience to distinguish good from bad, just from unjust, sensible from foolish, belongs to the core of human dignity.

The sovereignty of the individual lies in the human intellect. Reason enables the individual, independent of authorities or other people, to form his/her own judgments and to make independent decisions. This view of man underlies modern constitutionalism. The sovereignty of the state and the legitimacy of the constitution arise not from theology or from the grace of God, but from the reason of the individual.

With the secularisation of the state, various concepts of the relationship between church and state have found their expression in constitutions. The only common feature is the guarantee of freedom of religion. The French considered secularisation essential in order to prevent the Catholic Church from intervening in state affairs. The American Constitution guaranteed freedom of religion in order to maintain the diversity of different religions. Germany granted freedom of religion but bestowed special privileges upon certain Christian communities, and England maintained the connection between church and state but protected the freedom of religion of other religious communities. In spite of these rules, the relationship between church and state remained a subject of conflict and required ongoing compromise.

Today, many ethnic conflicts are rooted in religion. In contrast to the Islamic culture of the Middle Ages, which was much more tolerant towards other religions than was Christianity, many Islamic states today deny the right to freedom of religion that is embodied in the International Covenant on Civil and Political Rights. Religion has been the trigger for numerous ongoing conflicts as, for example those in Ireland, the Middle East, former Yugoslavia, India, Pakistan, Sri Lanka, Chechnya, Tibet and Indonesia. Religious communities in these states reject a fully secularised society and demand that their constitution should at least foster the majority religion if not establish the majority religion as the official state religion. They demand collective rights and political recognition, which includes the use of political powers to limit the individual rights of their members. This revival of theological claims to constitutional control may considerably change our basic constitutional concepts. With regard to religion, the individual will lose his/her freedom to make independent decisions and to say 'no'; the individual's only options will be to join the sate religion or to change citizenship.

For discriminated minorities, such privileging of religion will mean even greater potential for conflict. Many religions go so far as to demand control of the state, law and justice. They influence criminal law and education systems, and impose the morality of religion on the family system and thereby on the whole society. Such tendencies contradict the principle of secularisation of modern constitutionalism. Exclusive particularities will gradually displace inclusive universality.

Parliament and the internet

The invention of the printing press was an essential precondition for the development of modern constitutionalism. MARTIN LUTHER'S theses of Reformation could only be distributed thanks to GUTENBERG and his invention. GUTENBERG'S printing press enabled the French philosophers of the Enlightenment to pave the way for the French Revolution. Because the constitution could be distributed as a printed document, citizens had a clear and direct means by which to inform themselves on the limits of governmental power. The constitution as a written document was able to enhance democratic accountability by transparently setting out the powers and responsibilities of government. Modern democracy was only possible with the help of modern means of communication.

However citizens' limited ability to influence governmental affairs only through their parliament and the election of representatives is also partially attributable to the limited communications possibilities of the print media and later the mass media. The new communications possibilities offered by the internet and mobile telecommunications have created a whole new communication society. Constant contact between voters and government and the practice of government by consent are no longer utopian dreams. It may well be that in future the traditional concepts of representative democracy will change and will be at least partially replaced by the direct democratic influence of the citizens through the internet.

From civil society to consumer society

The image of the 'citizen', who as a rational and reasonable being is prepared to put the public interest of the state ahead of his own private interests, and who is integrated by a social contract into a nation committed to freedom, human rights and the rule of law, is the fundament of the state according to ROUSSEAU. "To all general purposes we have uniformly been one people – each individual citizen everywhere enjoying the same national rights, privileges, and protection" (J. JAY, *Federalist Papers* No. 2). This image of man, as a public 'civil soldier' and a private consumer, changed radically towards the end of the 20th Century. Society shifted from the national sovereignty of a public-spirited universal civil society towards a private society ruled by the sovereignty of the global market. The political citizens committed to liberty and interested in public issues have made way for a fragmented, pleasure-seeking society in which the main aim is to fulfil private needs. Self-realisation is reduced to lifestyle choices. This could lead to a further division of society (as in Brazilian society) between the marginalised and powerless fringe groups (foreigners, minorities etc.) who cannot afford to choose, and the integrated individuals, who use the state for their interests, that is, for the benefit of their private lifestyle.

The dividing line between 'public' and 'private' is becoming increasingly blurred. Private terrorists wage wars against all of humanity, and the attacks of 11 September 2001 struck a great blow to western society. The balancing act of the liberal state between security and freedom was severely disturbed. Will liberal institutions fall victim to the new maxim 'less freedom, more security?' The rampant growth of corruption is another alarm bell for the private misuse of public power. The manipulation of the public interest through the private economy and privately owned media is the political order of the day. Public functions such as police, security, prisons etc. are in some states fulfilled by private companies. Public agencies no longer make any effort to convince citizens of the public interest; instead they 'sell' public products and services through advertising agencies and influence the choices of the consumer-citizens through marketing policies.

The formerly uncontested authority of the executive and even of the legislature is increasingly being questioned. The result of this is that consensus democracy will gain greater significance. The judicature on the other hand appears not only to have retained its authority, but in fact to have strengthened its credibility and its political role within civil society. Accordingly, new power holders make radical attempts to bind the judicature into their own network of control (Italy).

9.6 Conclusions

If one were to assign a geometric symbol to each of the various historical periods, the Middle Ages could be graphically portrayed as the hierarchical pyramid. The Age of Industrialisation would be depicted as a wheel in which every cog fits neatly into the other and all wheels are turned by an invisible hand. The current age on the other hand is wrapped up in a multidimensional network. Networks are complex and non-transparent. Each intersecting point has its own function and contains the potential to influence the network and to foresee and avert dangers in other parts of the network. But each intersection can also easily be marginalised and isolated.

Constitutions have grown older and have entered into a 'mature' age. Nations and states will not disappear, but they will take on different functions and will transfer some of their existing functions to the network of international, transnational, regional and private cooperation. Future constitutions will have to create the foundation and the environment to enable state authorities to make the best use of this network. The network for its part will increase in density and complexity.

In concluding we will formulate some final theses, which we argue should be taken into account by the constitutional states of tomorrow, without abandoning the core achievements of modern constitutionalism.

1. The aim of a multicultural constitutional state should not be merely the protection and promotion of individual liberty and basic rights, but also the mainten-ance of peace within the multicultural society. The constitution must therefore provide for politically legitimate institutions and procedures that facilitate peaceful coexistence. The task of the state is to determine how it will deal with the diverse identities and multiple loyalties of its communities. It has to assess which diversities should be relevant and which it should therefore promote.
2. The current discourse on human rights should shift its main focus from the issue of universality to the question: up to what point can particular cultural peculiarities be universally accepted and guaranteed through particular group rights? The golden rule 'do not unto others that which you do want done unto you', which is reflected in almost all religions, should be the fundamental criteria for the recognition of such particularities.
3. The goal of democracy is not only to produce an efficient and legitimate government; democracy has rather become an essential tool for the peaceful management of conflict and is therefore closely tied to individual and collective rights. Democracy should guarantee the highest possible degree of self-determination within the state. Decentralisation to local authorities does not contradict the principles of democracy but is rather a core element of democratic governance.
4. A constitution that is geared towards meeting the challenges of today should also reconsider the principle of representation in light of the modern global communication society.

5. Universalisation and globalisation require constitutionalists to broaden their horizons beyond the borders of the nation-state. The discourse on democratic legitimacy, the rule of law and democratic accountability should also encompass the regional and international communities and their institutions. The constitutionalist's primary concern in this respect must be to bring the national constitution making procedure into harmony with the constitutional principles of the international community and in particular with the principles of democratic governance. At the same time, constitutionalists should attempt to bring the institutions and principles of the international community into harmony with the concepts of democracy and representation that are applied at the national level, to the extent possible, thereby enhancing the democratic legitimacy of international institutions and their activities.
6. The reality of multiculturality, which leads to the local emotionalisation of politics, can shake the very foundations of the modern state if it is not able to integrate the local needs of collective groups into the transnational, global and universal network.

In general, modern constitutionalism should take into account a multi-dimensional view of human nature. Human beings are not simply profit oriented, security oriented, egocentric, exploited or rational citizens. Human nature is much more complex. Any constitutional theory should recognise this complexity and accord with the multidimensional nature of human beings.

Index

The Index is designed as a complementary tool to a very detailed Table of Contents. This is why the key concepts underlying this book cannot be found singled out in the index, notably: democracy, federalism, legitimacy, multiculturalism, nation and nationalism, rule of law and sovereighnty.

A

Absolutism
  enlightened, 237
  European, 418
  French, 55, 298
  of authority, 133
  of Hobbes, 289
  of Louis XIV, 5
  royal, 226
  state, 95
  the age of, 409, 417
Althusius, 91, 531–532, 580
Antiquity
  the understanding of the state in, 110
Aquinas, 90, 152, 172, 322, 345, 368, 371, 407, 408, 513
Aristocracy
  double, 309
  feudal, 298
  French, 292
  of public offices, 56
Aristotle, 38, 46, 87, 90, 109, 131, 211, 222, 288, 358, 368–369, 373, 398, 407, 411–413, 513
Asian values, 134, 161, 165
Augustine, 87, 91, 172
Austin, 95, 317, 325, 328–330, 343, 398, 408
Australia
  Commonwealth of Australia
    Constitution Act, 544
Austria
  constitution, 146, 189, 431
Autonomy
  Charter for the Protection of Local Autonomy, 198
  collective, 523, 537, 590, 595, 638, 648
  cultural, 648
  local, 9, 70, 461, 533, 539, 601, 608, 609, 613
  of minorities, 540, 638
  of nationalities, 595
  of territorial units, 379, 512, 541, 566, 576, 590, 594, 610, 613, 616
  of the family, 37, 54, 59
  of the state, 271, 279, 308
  political, 70, 376, 518
  territorial, 623, 648, 649

B

Bacon, 226, 418
Bakunin, 475
Bentham, 229
Berlin
  Congress, 6, 7
  Wall, 8, 9, 19, 72, 189, 282, 294, 322, 511, 513, 652
Bill of Rights, 136, 138, 148, 173, 202, 225, 232, 416, 419, 651
Bismarck, 25, 286, 427
Bluntschli, 113
Bodin, 311
Braudel, 49
Burke, 392

C

Calvin, 91, 462
Carolingian Partition, 3
Charles the Great, 296, 424
Charter
  for Regional and Minority Languages, 198
  for the Protection of Local Autonomy, 198
  Magna Carta of Poland (1374), 417
  of Fundamental Rights of the European Union, 198
  of Stans, 460
  of the European Union, 280
  of the United Nations, 17, 68, 78, 281, 291, 305, 320, 322, 350, 489, 556, 658
  The Great Charter of Liberties (Magna Carta), 135, 148, 222–225, 311, 415, 651
China, Chinese
  Communist Party, 362, 477
  constitution, 187, 477
  National People's Congress, 477
  People's Republic, 123, 187
  philosophy, 131, 133
  state theory, 35–36

Christian
  Enlightenment, 134
  philosophy, 129
  tradition, 133, 154, 166
Christopher Saint German, 418
Cicero, 55, 110, 172
Citizen, citizens
  active, 355, 633
  citizen-state, 119, 517, 634
  contemporary Swiss civism, 631
  equality, 62, 95, 516, 641, 652
  European, 10, 69
  free, 358, 390, 417, 432, 459
  French, 287, 435, 517, 654
  historical association of, 40
  liberty, 62, 202, 362, 399, 403
  national, 115, 290, 518, 603, 655
  participation, 355, 374, 458, 643
  political (citoyen), 118, 654
  political citizenship in Switzerland, 405, 597, 621, 631, 632, 645
  rational, 41, 646, 663
  rights, 252, 276, 290, 355, 372, 380, 395, 420, 433, 442, 472, 609, 633
  Rights of Man and Citizen, 355, 433
  second-class, 285, 291, 514, 518, 522, 618, 628, 655
  trans-national, 290, 518, 655
  universal, 517
Conflict, conflicts
  between Church and State, 298, 308–311
  constitutional, 225–227, 489, 509, 582
  cultural, 138, 491
  emotional, 22, 522, 525
  ethnic, 8, 9, 75, 129, 348, 485, 489, 515, 518, 522, 534, 558, 563, 581, 583, 586, 596, 646, 655, 660
  ethnification, 486, 496
  in multi-cultural societies, 519, 644
  internal, 4, 50, 68, 122, 195, 292, 350, 356, 511, 518, 536, 593
  international, 293, 304, 322, 444, 658
  Jura, 598, 639–641
  Kosovo, 333
  language conflict in Switzerland, 595
  management, 292, 366, 371, 376, 512, 534, 563, 577, 581, 588, 593, 614, 623, 650
  minority, 292, 293, 534
  religious, 138, 491, 595, 599, 604
  resolution, 243, 375, 384, 524, 536–537, 581, 590, 592, 641
  territorial, 295, 306, 322, 581, 604
Confucius, Confucianism, 54, 131, 134, 165, 336, 398
Congress
  Berlin, 6, 7
  National Congress of the Communist Party of China, 361
  Vienna, 6
Constituent power, 544–546
Constitution
  Austria, 146, 189, 431
  Berne, 605, 625, 641
  Bosnia, 545
  Brazil, 526
  China, 187, 477
  Cyprus, 565
  England, 136, 231, 399, 412, 418, 449, 464
  Ethiopia, 193, 555
  European Union, 280
  France, 109, 189, 433, 465, 654
  Fribourg, 622, 625
  Germany, 143, 183, 201, 239, 564, 566, 571, 575, 597, 615, 619, 629, 655
  Hungary, 193
  India, 445
  Japan, 443–444
  Jura, 560
  Mexico, 447
  Norway, 146
  Republic of Ireland, 282
  Russia, 553
  Serbia and Montenegro, 550
  South Africa, 129, 523, 524, 651
  Switzerland, 174, 188, 201–202, 342, 395, 400, 437, 459, 463–469, 523, 527, 555, 559–560, 575, 595, 597–598, 604–606, 615–620, 623, 626, 630–633
  Tunisia, 478
  Turkey, 480
  USA, 146–148, 161, 401, 449, 455, 516, 545, 579
  USSR, 477, 485
  Virginia, 144, 449
  Weimar Republic, 393, 427
Constitutionalism
  American, 233–234
  British, 137, 155
  European, 36
  French, 135
  liberal, 12, 151, 155, 154–157, 230, 353, 652, 657

modern, 5, 20, 74, 86, 92, 135, 268–270, 512, 517, 595, 646, 653, 659–662
values of, 268
western, 72, 135
Convention
European Convention for the Protection of Human Rights and Fundamental Freedoms, 76, 78, 130, 143, 190, 195, 197, 199–200, 202, 264, 323, 366, 574, 609
Framework Convention for the Protection of National Minorities, 161, 186, 198, 516
Geneva, 79, 149, 293, 305, 350
National, 434
Council
Constitutional, 189, 433, 440, 442, 443
Human Rights, 130
of Europe, 129, 186, 198, 366, 405, 516, 526
of Ministers, 198, 440, 552
of State, 142, 189, 190–191, 251, 254, 257, 261, 442
Cromwell, 92, 136, 137–138, 174, 389, 653

D

Darwin, Darwinism, 181, 182, 213
De Gaulle, 423, 440–442
Declaration
American Declaration of Independence, 1, 32, 145, 156, 232, 294, 360, 451, 556
French Declaration of the Rights of Man and Citizen, 140, 158, 232, 235, 400, 410, 433
of Human Responsibilities, 187
of universal values, 287
Swiss Declaration of Independence, 136
UN Declaration on the Granting of Independence to Colonial Countries and Peoples, 557
Universal Declaration of Human Rights, 287, 433, 532
Defoe, 45, 48
Duns Scotus, 408

E

Empire
Austro-Hungarian, 7, 75, 282, 285, 342, 564, 595
British, 544
German, 52, 60, 191, 298, 424
Middle, 3, 55–56
of Charles the Great, 2–3
of laws, 228
of the Incas, 48
Ottoman, 7, 13, 20, 53, 55–56, 75, 282, 285, 299, 342, 485, 534, 564, 595
Roman, 1, 8, 55, 58, 281, 296, 309–310
Soviet, 342
Swedish, 417
Engels, 103
England
colonial power of, 145
Common Law, 25, 222, 243, 247
Commonwealth, 94, 222, 408, 419, 422, 544
constitutionalism, 137, 155
development of human rights, 188
English law, 57, 140, 453
House of Lords, 271, 376, 414, 420, 422
parliament of, 137, 175, 225–228, 413–417, 427, 434
upper house, 421, 444, 552
Whigs and Tories, 138, 420–422

F

Federalist Papers, 394, 400, 456, 561, 579, 661
Fichte, 157, 174

G

Gaius, 407
Gandhi, 349
Goethe, 426

H

Habeas Corpus, 136–137
Hamilton, 455
Han Fei Tzu, 24, 398
Hegel, 24, 113, 116, 174, 205, 207, 317, 388
Hindenburg, 429
Hitler, 7, 389, 429
Hobbes, 16, 34, 37, 72, 95, 99, 103, 121, 138, 155–156, 178, 188, 229, 289, 303, 308, 312, 316, 327, 340, 343, 345, 398, 408, 418, 454, 512, 531, 636, 658
Holocaust, 7, 72, 145, 329, 341
Hume, 212, 219
Hungary
constitution of, 193

Golden Bull of 1222, 136
Revolution 1956, 501

I

Ibn Khaldûn, 24, 36–39, 56, 288, 296, 309, 398
Imboden, 259
India
constitution, 445
philosophy, 165, 360
International Monetary Found (IMF), 9, 134, 530, 658
Islam, Islamic
Arab-Islamic theories of state, 397
culture of the Middle Ages, 660
fundamentalists, 129
law, 478, 480
philosophical tradition, 481
state, 129, 478–481, 660
Sunnah, 478
world, 478

J

Jeanne d'Arc, 107
Jefferson, 32–33, 145–146, 294
Jellinek, 86, 110, 292, 293, 325, 394, 411
Jesus, 89, 129, 346, 478
Jewish
Holocaust, 84
minority, 53
religion, 14, 53, 174, 623
the chosen people, 309
John of Paris, 296
Jus
cogens, 131, 473
sanguinis, 581
soli, 516, 581

K

Kant, 16, 86, 97, 102, 157, 165, 174, 237, 303, 346, 410
Kautzky, 105
Kelsen, 25, 34, 95, 146, 189, 317, 327, 368, 408, 431, 619
Kropotkin, 213

L

Laband, 411, 571
Lactantius, Firmianus, 172
Lao Tse, 35, 398
Lassalle, 475
Legal Realism, 327
Lenin, 19, 105, 369, 475–476
Liberal state
modern, 219, 578
pillars of, 278
Switzerland, 464
theory, 102, 268, 576, 633, 648
Liberty
Anglo-Saxon perception of, 166
definition, 204–209
economic, 177, 183
European philosophy of, 165
formal, 207, 208
fundamental, 201
individual, 118, 156, 161, 164, 166, 183, 185, 204, 222, 237, 268, 279, 371, 461, 538, 591, 593, 632, 643, 648, 650, 662
of cult and worship, 174
of the church, 135
of the citizens, 62, 135, 202, 362, 399, 403
of the other, 208, 217
personal, 176, 223, 261, 406, 410
political, 207, 399, 578
spiritual, 170
Lincoln, 650
Locke, 12, 16, 24, 34, 73, 95, 100, 112, 138, 155–156, 177–178, 188, 201, 207, 229–230, 234, 242, 289, 303, 316, 341, 345, 399, 400, 448, 454, 512, 531, 556, 579, 590, 635
Long Parliament, 5, 92, 138, 388–389, 419, 434, 653
Luther, 88, 91, 347
Luxembourg, Rosa, 105

M

Machiavelli, 24, 35, 281, 336
Madison
James, 394–396, 400–402, 456, 561, 579
Marbury v Madison, 146, 188
Magna Carta, 135, 148, 222–225, 311, 415, 651
Mandela, 349
Mao Tse Tung, 361
Marsilius from Padua, 35, 215, 374, 375, 379, 408
Marx, 16, 35, 106, 512
young Marx, 475
Marxism, 8, 36, 102, 105, 158, 182, 360, 402, 474
neo-Marxism, 24

Mill, J. St., 176, 205
Milton, 157, 174
Minority
  Afro-American, 146
  collective rights, 161
  concept of, 186–187
  discrimination of, 171, 202, 340, 599
  ethnic, 130, 187, 282, 285, 348–350, 515, 518, 528, 628, 654, 656
  Minorities Charter of the Council of Europe, 161
  protection, 133, 186–187, 196, 198, 202, 351, 372, 493–494, 523, 525, 563, 594, 642, 659
  religious, 161, 614, 621–624, 626
  self-determination, 291–292
Miranda rule, 148
Mohl, R. von, 237, 410
Montesquieu, 253, 370, 402–403, 407, 446, 590, 659
  separation of powers, 190, 231, 399–400

N

NATO, 129, 651

O

Ombudsman, 62, 193, 404
Organisation
  for Security and Cooperation in Europe (OSCE), 130, 195–196
  International Labour (ILO), 71
  of African Unity (OAU), 293
  World Trade Organisation (WTO), 19, 68, 183, 274, 299, 301–302

P

Peace
  as constitutional goal, 523, 603
  of Basel, 297, 462
  of St. Germain, 282, 513
  of Westphalia, 5–6, 272, 298, 424, 462
Petition of Rights, 136, 224

R

Rawls, 102, 212, 216–218, 219, 377, 410, 513
Rechtsstaat, concept of, 236–239
Religion
  Baptist, 173
  Catholic, 5, 7, 55, 89, 172, 346, 361, 417, 462, 473, 517, 556, 562, 595, 599, 605, 609, 612, 621, 623, 639, 660
  Christian
    philosophy, 86
    theology, 86
  freedom of, 5, 129, 172–174, 199, 203, 217, 526, 599, 604, 621–623, 638, 659
  Hinduism, 134, 622
  Islam, 13, 53, 55, 479, 622
  Judaism, 14, 53, 174, 623
  liberty of cult and worship, 174
  Mormon, 203
  Protestant, 5, 7, 172, 346, 457, 462, 563, 595, 599, 605, 609, 621, 623, 640
  Shintoism, 14, 54, 241
Renaissance, 56, 132, 153–154
Revolution
  American, 63, 533
  French, 12, 63, 95, 109, 138, 140, 151, 174, 232, 234–236, 247, 252, 292, 349, 355, 361, 377, 391, 400, 409, 425, 433, 465, 467, 475, 493, 517, 532, 592, 632, 651, 660
  Glorious, 63, 136–138, 225, 237, 242, 412, 419, 467, 652
  Industrial, 363
  October, 105, 106
  Russian, 64, 467, 475
Right
  Bill of Rights, 136, 138, 148, 173, 202, 225, 232, 416, 419, 651
  collective, 7, 21, 40, 73, 107, 161, 186, 270, 526, 580, 585, 592, 593, 622, 632, 642, 644, 648, 657, 660, 662
  Declaration of the Rights of Man and Citizen, 232, 235, 355, 400, 410, 433, 633
  natural, 156, 229, 232, 234, 341, 631, 653
  of the citizens, 252, 276, 290, 372, 380, 395, 420, 442, 609
  Petition of Rights, 136, 224
  to resistance, 99, 101, 133, 145, 151, 311, 345–351, 430, 531
Rousseau, Rousseauist, 24, 34, 39, 106, 219, 236, 258, 337, 370, 531
  citoyen, 16, 115, 118, 157
  concept of state, 110, 118, 661

democracy, 116, 269, 373, 436, 611
general will, 64, 113, 157, 205, 212, 214, 378, 392
self-government, 461
Switzerland, 634
vision of liberalism, 157
welfare state, 215–216

S

Secession
right to, 282, 291, 485, 489, 554, 558
unilateral, 74, 332, 489, 554–558, 606, 654
Self Rule, 649
Shared Rule, 648
Slavery, 52, 88, 115, 130, 200, 359, 379, 517
State
colonial, 8, 322, 342, 543
constitutional, 42, 103, 133, 219, 481, 501, 513, 535, 652, 662
Islamic, 129, 309, 478–481, 660
legitimacy of, 132, 603
modern nation-state, 135, 267, 271, 485, 576, 581
pluralistic, 174
welfare, 12, 69, 180, 210, 224, 239, 250, 270, 272, 278–280, 391
world state, 274
Switzerland
concordance democracy, 637, 643, 645
constitution, 174, 188, 201–202, 342, 395, 437, 459, 463–469, 523, 527, 555, 559–560, 575, 595, 597–598, 604–606, 615–620, 623, 626, 630–633
democracy and federalism, 580
democracy limits, 644–646
democratic deficits, 643
direct democracy, 395, 449, 525, 610
federal administrative law of, 168
Federal Court, 188
four-fifths democracy, 474
law of, 143, 299
Swiss Declaration of Independence, 136

T

Terrorism
and Communism (Trotsky), 476
and state of emergency, 68, 200–201
attacks of 9/11, 80
war against, 18, 78, 200, 203, 451, 538
Tolerance
politics of, 522–523
principle of, 173
Treaty, treaties
All-German Election, 432
European, 287, 545, 566, 573
German Unification, 432
International treaty law, 323
on state borders, 306
Tyranny
of the majority, 108, 133, 164, 234, 268, 354, 369, 384, 470, 500, 527, 592, 596, 655
over minorities, 525

U

United Nations
Anan Plan, 629
Charter, 17, 68, 78, 281, 291, 305, 320, 322, 350, 489, 556, 658
Covenant on Civil and Political Rights, 76, 195, 556, 660
Covenant on Economic, Social and Cultural Rights, 76, 195, 556
Declaration on the Rights of Indigenous Peoples, 198
democratic deficit, 277
economic sanctions, 277
Geneva Conventions, 79, 293, 305, 350
Human Rights Council, 76, 130, 196
International Covenant on Civil and Political Rights, 76, 195, 660
Mission in Kosovo (UNMIK), 277
protectorates, 77
Security Council, 17, 19, 68, 71, 78, 274, 350
Universal Declaration of Human Rights, 187, 195, 197, 557

W

War
against terrorism, 162, 200, 203, 451
Cold, 65, 76, 162
first world, 7, 68, 72, 146, 189, 236, 239, 249, 285, 427, 429, 440, 492, 513, 605
right to wage war, 322
second world, 68, 72, 146, 166, 191, 239, 249, 259, 347, 429, 439, 443, 492, 564, 652
World Bank, 9, 71, 78, 134, 277, 353, 365, 530, 658
World Trade Organisation (WTO), 19, 68, 71, 183, 274, 299, 301–302

Printed in the United Kingdom
by Lightning Source UK Ltd.
136516UK00001B/22-66/P

9 783540 764113